ROUTLEDGE LIBRARY EDITIONS: INFLATION

Volume 8

# INFLATION AND UNEMPLOYMENT

# INFLATION AND UNEMPLOYMENT

## Theory, Experience and Policy-Making

Edited by
V. E. ARGY AND J. W. NEVILE

Routledge
Taylor & Francis Group
LONDON AND NEW YORK

First published in 1985 by George Allen & Unwin (Publishers) Ltd

This edition first published in 2016
by Routledge
2 Park Square, Milton Park, Abingdon, Oxon OX14 4RN

and by Routledge
711 Third Avenue, New York, NY 10017

*Routledge is an imprint of the Taylor & Francis Group, an informa business*



*British Library Cataloguing in Publication Data*
A catalogue record for this book is available from the British Library

ISBN: 978-1-138-65251-4 (Set)
ISBN: 978-1-315-62042-8 (Set) (ebk)
ISBN: 978-1-138-65916-2 (Volume 8) (hbk)
ISBN: 978-1-315-62038-1 (Volume 8) (ebk)

**Publisher's Note**
The publisher has gone to great lengths to ensure the quality of this reprint but points out that some imperfections in the original copies may be apparent.

**Disclaimer**
The publisher has made every effort to trace copyright holders and would welcome correspondence from those they have been unable to trace.

# Inflation and Unemployment

## Theory, Experience and Policy-Making

Edited by

**V. E. Argy and J. W. Nevile**

London
GEORGE ALLEN & UNWIN
Boston Sydney

**George Allen & Unwin (Publishers) Ltd,**
**40 Museum Street, London WC1A 1LU, UK**

George Allen & Unwin (Publishers) Ltd,
Park Lane, Hemel Hempstead, Herts HP2 4TE, UK

Allen & Unwin, Inc.,
Fifty Cross Street, Winchester, Mass. 01890, USA

George Allen & Unwin Australia Pty Ltd,
8 Napier Street, North Sydney, NSW 2060, Australia

First published in 1985

**British Library Cataloguing in Publication Data.**

Inflation and unemployment: theory, experience and policy-making.
1. Inflation (Finance) and unemployment
I. Argy, Victor II. Nevile, J. W.
332.4'1 HD5709
ISBN 0-04-339036-6

**Library of Congress Cataloging in Publication Data.**

Main entry under title:
Inflation and unemployment.
1. Unemployment—Effect of inflation on—Addresses, essays, lectures. 2. Inflation (Finance)—Addresses, essays, lectures. 3. Wage-price policy—Addresses, essays, lectures. I. Argy, Victor. II. Nevile, J. W.
HD5710.I53 1985 331.13'72 85-6200
ISBN 0-04-339036-6

Set in 10 on 11 point Times by Pintail Studios, Ringwood, Hampshire and printed in Great Britain by Mackays of Chatham

# Contents

# 1 Introduction

*V. ARGY and J. W. NEVILE*

## I BACKGROUND

The papers collected in this volume were originally presented at a conference sponsored by the Centre for Applied Economic Research of the University of New South Wales and the Centre for Studies in Money, Banking and Finance of Macquarie University. The conference was held in September 1983 and those who attended are listed on p. 386. The papers fall into two groups. The first group are predominantly theoretical, dealing with some aspect of policy design and with the costs and benefits of an anti-inflationary policy. The papers by Buiter and Miller (Chapter 1) and Fischer (Chapter 2) are both concerned with the determinants of the costs of disinflation and with potential policies to alleviate these costs. Argy's paper (Chapter 3) summarizes the views of monetarists and supply-side economists on how monetary and fiscal policies ought to be designed in both the short run and the long run. Carmichael, Fahrer and Hawkins (Chapter 4) survey the theoretical literature on the macro-stabilization implications of wage indexation. In Valentine (Chapter 16) there is some theoretical discussion of financial indexation.

The second group of papers review country experiences. There are four individual studies of large developed economies (Chapters 7–10): West Germany (by Willms and Karsten), Japan (by Hamada), the UK (by Artis and Lewis) and the USA (by Clark). There are five papers dealing with different aspects of the Australian experience: those by Jonson and Stevens; Hewson and Nevile; Gregory and Smith; Challen; and Valentine (Chapters 12–16). McClam and Andersen (Chapter 11) review the experience of four other small developed economies: Austria, Belgium, Canada and Sweden. Chouraqui and Price (Chapter 5) survey the monetary and fiscal policy experience of OECD countries during the 1970s and early 1980s. Braun (Chapter 6) tries to draw some general lessons from incomes policy experience, focusing particularly on the Netherlands, the UK, Norway and Austria. Carmichael, Fahrer and Hawkins also include a brief section at the end of their paper on the international experience with wage indexation.

This introduction will centre on three issues raised by the conference. First, we try briefly to review the underlying causes of the stagflation of the last ten–twelve years. Second, we summarize the kinds of macro-policies that were adopted to deal with the stagflation. Third, we indicate some lessons that can be extracted from recent experience and identify the unresolved issues.

## II THE UNDERLYING CAUSES OF INFLATION AND UNEMPLOYMENT

While it is not difficult, from this vantage point, to identify the causes of the upsurge in inflation during the 1970s, there remains considerable controversy over the causes underlying the upsurge in unemployment.

For the industrial countries as a whole, we can now explain in retrospect the broad trends in inflation in the last decade or so in terms of the combined effects of money growth and the price of oil. Aggregate figures are given in Table 1.1. There were two oil-price shocks, the first in 1973/4 and the second in 1979/80; since 1981 the price of oil has fallen significantly. The two oil-price shocks would have directly added some two percentage points to the inflation rate, while the subsequent wage–price spiral would have added several additional points. Each of the oil-price shocks came in the wake of easier monetary policies, which served to compound the inflationary problem. The fall in inflation after 1975 was partly due to the decline over time of the effects of the first oil-price shock and to the tight monetary policies in the mid-1970s. Finally, the recent easing of oil prices has come in the wake of tighter monetary policies, which are now serving to reinforce the disinflation.

For individual countries, a more eclectic approach is needed to explain the inflationary experience. In some, the relationship between money growth and inflation is fairly close (e.g. the USA, Canada, Belgium); in others it is weak (France, Sweden, Austria, UK). The relationship turns out to be more complicated than simple monetarism would postulate. In some, money as an indicator has been significantly distorted by recent financial innovations (UK, USA, Canada). In others, the trend in inflation is dominated by non-monetary shocks, including oil prices but also indirect taxes, public utility prices, wage shocks, other commodity prices, exchange rate developments and real trends (such as fiscal policies and real developments in the rest of the world).

Turning now to unemployment, there was a major upsurge in unemployment in nearly all developed economies from 1974/5, some slight easing in 1978/9 and a new upsurge beginning in 1980. Figures for OECD countries are given in Table 1.1. In trying to explain these trends there is still some division of opinion between those who would emphasize aggregate demand influences and those who would emphasize the role of classical real wage considerations.[1] A more recent sharp division has emerged between those who emphasize the impacts of inflation itself on the 'natural' unemployment rate and those, by contrast, who emphasize the impacts of disinflation itself on the 'natural' rate. There is also some support for the view that demographic considerations as well as the levels of real unemployment benefits have served to raise the natural unemployment rate, at least in some countries.

We would want to adopt an eclectic explanation of the trends in unemployment that draws on all of these views. To begin with, there is little doubt that demand influences in the last decade or so have been predominantly negative. Real money growth has been held low, fiscal policies, particularly from 1976, were tight and the two oil-price shocks injected a sharp deflationary impact. All these factors led to a downward trend in economic activity that became self-reinforcing, both over time and between countries. We would, however, not

**Table 1.1** *Summary statistics: industrial countries*

| Year | Money growth | Broad money growth | Fiscal policy – 7 largest[a] | Rate of inflation | Unemployment rate (OECD countries) | Real money growth: Money | Real money growth: Broad money | Price of oil[b] |
|---|---|---|---|---|---|---|---|---|
| 1971 | 11.2 | 13.9 | −0.6 | 5.2 | 3.8 | 6.0 | 8.7 | – |
| 1972 | 11.9 | 14.4 | −0.3 | 4.7 | 3.8 | 7.2 | 9.7 | 2.45 |
| 1973 | 10.6 | 14.7 | −0.2 | 7.7 | 3.5 | 2.9 | 7.0 | 3.37 |
| 1974 | 7.6 | 12.5 | +0.4 | 13.3 | 3.9 | −5.7 | −0.8 | 11.25 |
| 1975 | 9.1 | 10.6 | −1.8 | 11.1 | 5.4 | −2.0 | −0.5 | 11.02 |
| 1976 | 10.2 | 11.6 | +0.7 | 8.3 | 5.6 | 1.9 | 3.3 | 11.89 |
| 1977 | 8.8 | 10.9 | +0.4 | 8.4 | 5.5 | 0.4 | 2.5 | 12.95 |
| 1978 | 10.9 | 11.7 | −0.7 | 7.2 | 5.4 | 3.7 | 4.5 | 12.98 |
| 1979 | 9.6 | 11.3 | +0.5 | 9.2 | 5.4 | 0.4 | 2.1 | 19.0 |
| 1980 | 6.5 | 9.6 | +0.2 | 11.9 | 6.1 | −5.4 | −2.3 | 31.51 |
| 1981 | 6.0 | 9.2 | +0.7 | 10.0 | 7.0 | −4.0 | −0.8 | 35.01 |
| 1982 | 6.7 | 10.4 | −0.1 | 7.5 | 8.5 | −0.8 | 2.9 | 33.41 |

*Notes:* a positive = *restriction*.
b US dollars per barrel.

*Sources:* 'Money growth and rate of inflation', in *International Financial Statistics Year Book and Supplement on Money*, 1983.
'Unemployment rates', in *OECD Historical Statistics 1960–1981*.
'Price of oil', in *OECD Economic Outlook*, July 1983, p. 75.
'Fiscal policy – 7 largest OECD countries', in R. W. R. Price and J. C. Chouraqui, *Public Sector Deficits: Problems and Policy Implications*, *OECD Economic Outlook*, *Occasional Studies*, June 1983.

want to deny that, in many OECD countries, real wage cost considerations have made some contribution to unemployment. In some countries, too, some role would have to be assigned to demographic and real benefit considerations in raising the 'natural' unemployment rate. Finally, inflation itself and the disinflation process can both add to unemployment.

## III POLICY

Policies were adopted on five fronts: monetary, fiscal, wages–incomes, specific employment-creating measures (public employment, employment subsidies) and exchange rates.

On the monetary front, beginning in the mid-1970s, all the large developed economies adopted the practice of announcing money growth targets. Although the details have varied widely (in respect of the choice of aggregate and the band, if any, allowed), the underlying objectives have been very similar. In all cases, targeting was intended to act as a discipline on governments, to create a more stable and predictable financial environment and to influence expectations about inflation. In most cases, the intention was gradually to reduce money growth with an eye on reducing inflation (e.g. in Canada, Australia, the UK, from 1979, France).

In retrospect it is possible to say that these policies have met with only mixed success, with difficulties surfacing that had not originally been anticipated. First, as already noted, inflation was subject to influences other than money growth. Second, in some cases money demand shifts and financial innovations weakened the relationship between money growth and inflation. Third, it has proved difficult in some cases to control money growth. Fourth, many governments allowed themselves to be diverted by other objectives: notably to stabilize exchange rates and/or interest rates. In many cases this led to some overshooting of money growth (e.g. West Germany and the UK in 1978).

It is perhaps significant that none of the large developed economies succeeded in gradually reducing money growth after 1975. Moreover, by 1981/2 some had begun to have serious doubts about money growth targeting and were developing a more eclectic approach (e.g. the UK and the USA).

In sharp contrast to the large developed economies, very few of the smaller economies announced money growth targets. In part this was due to some scepticism about the stability of money demand (Belgium and Sweden), in part it was due to the adoption of a hard currency policy (which implies that, at least over the longer term, one is importing the money growth targets of the dominant economy, e.g. West Germany). The two important exceptions are Canada and Australia. Canada met with some success in meeting its money growth targets and reducing its money growth. By 1982, however, rapid financial innovation made money targeting impractical and targeting was (temporarily) abandoned in late 1982. In Australia there was less success. Between 1978/9 and 1980/1 there were three successive years of overshooting (again because of interest rate and exchange rate objectives).

On the fiscal front the experiences have been mixed. In the large developed economies, faced with an upsurge in unemployment in 1974/5, fiscal policy eased. In 1976/7, these policies were reversed and, although 1978 saw some relaxation of fiscal policy, after 1979 many governments, concerned over the budget deficits and the new upsurge in inflation, adopted consistently tight fiscal policies. The USA stands out in 1981/2 in its attempt to implement easy supply-side policies. France, too, briefly went against the trend in 1981/2. In the small economies, policies have been divergent. Australia (from 1976) and Canada (from 1979) have implemented relatively tight fiscal policies. In contrast, both Austria and Sweden, attaching considerable importance to maintaining low levels of unemployment, have used fiscal policy to fine tune the economy.

Many of the developed economies attempted, some time between 1976 and 1983, to implement some form of incomes policy. Unfortunately these policies are extremely hard to evaluate. Many also adopted specific employment-creating policies.

All the developed economies have managed their currencies. The two principal motives here have been to stabilize the exchange rate and to avoid the importation of inflation. This last has been strongly in evidence since 1979 when the US dollar began its pronounced upswing.

## IV LESSONS AND UNRESOLVED ISSUES

It is easy to point to failures of macroeconomic policy in the last ten years or so. At the same time it needs to be recognized that policy has had to operate in an environment that has had certain unique features, which, combined, have created new dilemmas and difficulties for policy. The more important new features were: flexible exchange rates, acute stagflation, a recurrence of major supply shocks, large budget deficits, huge shifts in current account positions and, in some cases (notably the Netherlands, the UK, Australia, Norway), an attack of the so-called 'Dutch disease' brought on by oil, gas or mineral discoveries.

We begin by summarizing what appear to be the principal 'lessons' to be learned from the experience of the last decade or so.

(1) The belief propounded by rational expectations theorists that a credible restrictive monetary policy can bring inflation down with minimal costs is now known to be overly optimistic. There are difficulties on two fronts here: first, how to make the policy credible; second, credibility in itself is not nearly sufficient for success – conditions in labour markets, particularly the degree of stickiness in wage adjustments, are at least as important. As an illustration, the anti-inflationary strategy adopted in the USA at the end of 1979 was credible but the associated costs remained broadly similar to previous similar policies.[2]

(2) Monetarist convictions that money growth can be easily controlled, that it provides the overriding explanation for inflation and that money demand is stable have all been shaken in recent years. More attention needs to focus on potential weaknesses in money stock control; a more eclectic view is also now needed of the causes of inflation; finally, potential shifts in money demand

need to be more carefully monitored and, if possible, allowed for; this may require attention to be given to more than one money aggregate.

(3) Short-run policy objectives may sometimes collide with longer-term objectives. As an illustration, in West Germany, the UK in 1978 and Australia in 1980/1, foreign exchange market intervention to counter strong upward pressures on the currency led to substantial overshooting of monetary growth and subsequently to some acceleration in inflation.

(4) The early belief that flexible rates would shelter countries from policies and developments abroad has not been borne out by recent experience. Countries remain almost as closely integrated in a flexible-rate world as in a fixed-rate world. In 1969–72, when exchange rates were fixed, Europe felt acutely the effects of US monetary policy swings; these policies then came under severe criticism. The abandonment of Bretton Woods was, partly at least, motivated by a wish to enjoy an independent monetary policy. In 1979–82, however, with flexible rates, Europe continued to feel the impacts of US monetary policies and criticism of US policies was equally fierce.

(5) In the face of a very large disturbance such as an oil-price shock, several arms of policy need to be invoked: monetary, fiscal, wages and exchange rate policies all have a role to play. Austria provides a good example of careful management in this regard.

(6) A most important lesson is the key importance of a flexible wages policy to minimize the costs of adjustment to a disturbance. There is little doubt that the most successful economies have been those that have performed best on this front. Institutional differences across countries in labour markets are at the heart of differences in adjustment performances. Unfortunately, while there would be general agreement on this, there is no agreement on how to implement a more flexible wages policy. Successful policies in individual countries are not easily replicated elsewhere.

(7) At a time when inflation is already high and an incomes policy is not in operation or is unlikely to be successful, governments should try to avoid policies that add directly to inflation. A conspicuous example of the effects of unconcern about this is Thatcher's decision in 1979 to switch from income to indirect taxes.

We now turn to continuing unresolved issues.

(1) A major unresolved issue is the appropriate monetary–fiscal mix in a strategy of disinflation. On the one hand are those who argue for complementary deflationary policies (as in the UK and Australia). On the other, those (e.g. supply-side economists) who argue that fiscal policy might be used to ease the cost of monetary disinflation (US, 1981/2). Others argue a case for a cut in indirect taxes to ease the cost of disinflation.

(2) There was considerable disagreement at the conference on the question of whether or not a disinflationary policy (starting, say, with an inflation rate of the order of 10–15 per cent) is worth the cost. This also reflected the considerable theoretical uncertainties about the costs and benefits of disinflation. Some felt that living with inflation by widespread indexation remains a viable alternative.

(3) There was also disagreement over the appropriate stance of policy in the current economic environment with unemployment still very high. The difficulties here centred on two issues: first, how much of the present unemployment was structural; second, to the extent that it is 'Keynesian', how was it possible to reduce it by expansionary financial policies, while minimizing the inflationary effects, for example by an incomes policy, some reduction in indirect taxes or an employment subsidy.

(4) Although there would be general agreement that, in the longer run, money growth needs to be contained to control inflation, there is a wide divergence of opinion on how monetary policy should be conducted in the short run. Many large countries announce a band in money growth targets, but it is still unclear what use should be made of the band.

(5) There is still wide disagreement over the importance that should attach to large budget deficits, with argument about whether attention should be focused on the actual deficit or on the structural deficit, about whether government borrowing for capital purposes should be distinguished from government borrowing for consumption, and about the extent to which the 'inflation tax' on the holders of government bonds should be offset against the deficit.

## NOTES

1 For a recent review of these issues and application to a number of developed economies, see Sachs (1983), Symons and Layard (1983) and Artus (1984).

2 See on this Perry (1983).

## BIBLIOGRAPHY

Artus, J. R. (1984), 'An empirical evaluation of the disequilibrium real wage rate hypothesis', unpublished manuscript, April.

Perry, G. L. (1983), 'What have we learned about inflation?', *Brookings Papers on Economic Activity*, 2, 587–602.

Sachs, J. D. (1983), 'Real wages and unemployment in the OECD countries', *Brookings Papers on Economic Activity*, 1, 255–289.

Symons, J. and Layard, R. (1983), 'Neo-classical demand for labour functions for six major economies', Centre for Labour Economics, *London School of Economics Discussion Paper*, No. 166, October.

PART I

# Theory and General Issues

# 2 Costs and Benefits of an Anti-Inflationary Policy: Questions and Issues

*WILLEM H. BUITER and MARCUS H. MILLER**

## I INTRODUCTION

Unlike many contributions to this subject, this chapter has the virtue that at any rate its title (which was chosen by the organizers of the conference) makes sense. As Hall (1981, p. 432) states, 'Inflation is an outcome of economic processes, not an exogenous causal influence'. At the level of the economy as a whole, it is therefore a nonsense to refer, as is often done, to the costs of inflation or to the benefits from lower inflation. Since inflation is endogenous, the benefits or costs of lower inflation can be discussed sensibly only by specifying the changes in exogenous variables and parameters (policy actions or rules, external events, etc.) that bring about and sustain the lower rate of inflation. Partial equilibrium or single-structural-equation 'costs of inflation' analyses are void of policy implications.

As regards the benefits from policies to achieve a sustained reduction in the rate of inflation, we shall be brief, because we have nothing much to add to the received wisdom on the topic.[1] First consider a non-stochastic economy. We shall assume that a permanent reduction in the proportional rate of growth of the nominal stock of money is a necessary condition for a permanent reduction in the rate of inflation. Unless debt neutrality prevails or government interest-bearing debt is index linked, the reduction in the growth rate of the nominal money stock will have to be matched by an equal reduction in the growth rate of the stock of government bonds in order to achieve sustained reduction in the rate of inflation.

It is important to appreciate that it is the same institutional feature of the economy that causes costs to be associated both with policies that cause inflation and with policies to reduce inflation. That feature is the existence of nominal contracts that are not perfectly price-level contingent or inflation contingent. The reasons for the existence of such contracts have to do with the advantages of using money in the first place – the benefits from using a common numeraire, standard of deferred payment, medium of exchange and means of payment. They are either too obvious or too deep to be considered in this paper. Bringing down inflation is costly because of the existence of non-contingent money wage and price contracts. In a deterministic setting, imperfect and incomplete indexation of prices and rates of return is the main reason

* We wish to acknowledge financial support from the Social Science Research Council.

for welfare costs to be associated with policies that cause inflation. The only other cost is the 'relabeling cost', i.e. the cost of changing prices more frequently, which can be generalized to the cost of the disruption of well-established methods of transacting business (Carlton, 1982, p. 139).

The best-known cost of non-indexation is the loss of consumer surplus suffered when the demand for real money balances declines as (and to the extent that) the nominal interest rate rises in response to an increase in the (expected) rate of inflation. With the nominal rate of return on money balances assumed fixed (typically at zero), the nominal interest rate represents the opportunity cost of holding money. Partial equilibrium approaches take the real interest rate as given and have the nominal interest rate rising one for one with an increase in the (expected) inflation rate. This represents a tax on the holding of money balances. If the demand for money is interest sensitive and money is produced costlessly, this will impose a dead-weight loss of consumer surplus given by the trapezoidal area under the (compensated) money demand function between the low inflation and high inflation quantities of money demanded.[2] General equilibrium approaches treat the real interest rate as endogenous and not necessarily invariant to the policy changes that cause the higher rate of inflation. In a multi-period setting, the entire sequence of discounted instantaneous (or single-period) trapezoidal utility losses must be considered (Feldstein, 1979).

Non-indexation or incomplete indexation extend in practice well beyond the rate of return on high-powered money balances, and affect private contracts as well as tax laws and regulations. Extensive work on the subject has been done by Fischer and Modigliani (1978), and Fischer (1981b).

When comparing a situation of low inflation with one of high inflation, the lower level of welfare (presumably) enjoyed in the latter can be attributed either to the policy that brings about the higher inflation (i.e. higher monetary growth) or to the failure to implement policies that permit a partial or complete adaptation to the higher inflation. If indexation is cheap, let alone costless, dead-weight losses, incurred because of a combination of inflation and incomplete indexation, can be attributed with as much justice to the failure to implement policies to adapt to inflation as to the policies that cause the inflation. This holds for any undesired distributional consequences of policies that cause inflation as much as for the inefficiencies that they entail.

Turning to a stochastic world, a vast literature has sprouted in recent years on the costs of variable or uncertain inflation and on the links between expected inflation and the variability or uncertainty of the price level, the rate of inflation or relative prices.[3] Even in deterministic models it is possible, if not all prices can be adjusted costlessly and continuously, to establish a causal link between the (anticipated) mean inflation rate and the (anticipated) variability of relative prices. The costs of such anticipated variability can be evaluated using conventional deterministic welfare economic tools. In what follows only unanticipated or currently unperceived variability, i.e. inflation or relative price uncertainty, will be considered. Causal chains have been proposed that run from high (expected) inflation rates through to relative price uncertainty, suggesting that inflation may raise the noise-to-signal ratio for relative price movements, thus impairing the allocative efficiency of the price mechanism.

Since the expected rate of inflation, its variance and the variance of relative prices are all jointly endogenous in any reasonable macroeconomic model, it is very hard to understand what the 'costs of inflation uncertainty' literature is trying to say. It is certainly interesting to study the time series behavior of mean inflation, of inflation variability and uncertainty and of relative price variability and uncertainty (see e.g. Fischer, 1981a). By regressing any one of these on any subset of the remaining ones, one cannot hope to extract a structurally invariant relationship. The statement 'high expected inflation causes highly uncertain inflation' makes no sense. The statement 'certain policies or events that cause the first moment of the distribution function of inflation to increase also tend to raise its second moment' does make sense. For example, if higher mean monetary growth is associated with increasingly unpredictable monetary growth, both the higher mean inflation and the increasing unpredictability of inflation can be attributed to monetary policy.

Perhaps the argument is that there is a structurally invariant relationship between mean monetary growth and the unpredictability of monetary growth for a monetary aggregate with the following two properties. First, it is the relevant causal one in the inflation process and, second, the parameters of its distribution function can be chosen by the authorities only subject to some constraints, e.g. the authorities cannot control monetary growth exactly, but they can choose the first two moments of its distribution function, subject to the contraint that mean and variance are positively related. Since it is likely to be welfare-reducing for the authorities to throw more extraneous noise into the system, a further argument for lower mean money growth exists if the variance of the innovation in the money stock process is an increasing function of the expected rate of monetary growth. Unless this is the case, finding a positive pattern of covariation between mean inflation and relative price uncertainty carries no implications for monetary policy.

Note that none of this provides an argument for maximizing the predictability of future monetary growth rates but only for minimizing the variance of the innovation in the money stock process. Consider, for example, the monetary growth rule $m_{t+1} - m_t = \alpha_t + u^m_{t+1}$, where $m_t$ is the logarithm of the nominal money stock, $u^m_t$ is the random, unpredictable, component in the money growth process, i.e. $E_t u^m_{t+1} = 0$, while $\alpha_t$ is the predictable component, i.e. $E_t\alpha_t = \alpha_t$. Let $\sigma^2_{m,t} \equiv E_t(u^m_{t+1})^2$; the inflation uncertainty hypothesis can be represented by

$$\frac{\partial \sigma^2_{m,t}}{\partial |\alpha_t|} > 0.$$

$\alpha_t$ itself could be a non-stochastic known function of current and past realizations of random variables, i.e. it could be governed by a non-stochastic feedback rule. While such rules tend to make $m_{t+2} - m_{t+1}$, say, less predictable, in period $t$ and earlier, than a non-stochastic open loop path for money growth, such feedback rules may well help diminish the uncertainty that matters. Examples are changes in the information content of observed market prices induced by monetary feedback rules (Turnovsky, 1980; Weiss, 1980; Buiter, 1980, 1981).

From the proposition that governments should not throw extraneous random noise into the economic system by randomizing their monetary policy rules, it also does not follow that minimizing uncertainty about future inflation or future relative prices is sensible policy. For example, by freezing all relative prices through legislative fiat, their predictability is maximized but any shocks to demand or supply will have to be absorbed through rationing and other disequilibrium mechanisms. Random shocks to the system will, in general, be absorbed by unexpected changes in prices and in quantities produced, sold and consumed and by unexpected changes in the values of policy instruments such as the money supply, which are set according to some contingent or conditional rule. By removing the elements of conditionality in the monetary rule to enhance the predictability of the future money stock path, shocks will have to be absorbed in some other way. Only detailed analysis of fully specified models can determine what kind of monetary rule maximizes expected utility.

A final argument for policies consistent with low or zero inflation is that price-level stability (zero inflation) is the only stable equilibrium. Positive inflation inevitably entails rising rates of inflation. (The symmetric argument for negative inflation rates is not made; there have been hyper-inflations but no hyper-deflations.)

The political economy of inflationary monetary growth creating pressures for higher and more inflationary rates of monetary growth has never been spelled out satisfactorily. The historical experience of most OECD countries would seem to contradict it. If any inflation carried in itself the seeds of a hyperinflation (with some non-negligible probability), the case for striving for price-level constancy would of course be strengthened considerably.

## II THE COST OF POLICIES TO ACHIEVE A PERMANENT REDUCTION IN INFLATION

In this section we shall consider the familiar Okun-style output costs of securing a lasting reduction in the rate of inflation. There are well-known objections to taking the cumulative net output loss (perhaps discounted) associated with an anti-inflationary policy as a measure of its cost. It ignores the benefits of additional output produced at home by the unemployed and not recorded in GNP, as well as the marginal valuation of their leisure and search time. We shall proceed regardless for two reasons. First, it has been argued (see e.g. Gordon, 1973) that if one attempts a conventional triangle approach grounded in applied welfare economics, the answers do not come out all that differently from the crude Okun's gap measure. Second, it is hard to take seriously an approach that cannot differentiate between an employed worker taking a vacation and a worker becoming unemployed. Conventional microeconomic analysis models utility as increasing in leisure (i.e. leisure is a 'good thing') and thereby confines labour to the category of 'bads'. Overwhelming empirical evidence on the importance of work (i.e. of being employed, of having a job) for most people's well-being, happiness and even sanity has not made much of a dent in the 'extended holiday' approach to unemployment.

Formally, it is quite easy to combine the 'leisure as a good thing' and 'work as a good thing' approaches. Consider the state-dependent utility function $v(\cdot\ \cdot)$ given below, where $c$ is a vector of goods and services other than leisure, $L$ is the endowment of time and $l$ is hours spent working. $\theta$ is an indicator variable that takes on values $\theta = 1$ if employed and $\theta = 0$ if unemployed.

$$U = v(c, L - l, \theta).$$

The utility function is well-behaved in consumption and leisure (strictly increasing and quasi-concave). The benefit from being employed is represented by the assumption that, for any given $c = \bar{c}$ and $l = \bar{l}$ we have

$$v(\bar{c}, L - \bar{l}, 1) > v(\bar{c}, L - \bar{l}, 0).^4$$

Depending on what further properties one attributes to the utility function[5] and on the budget constraints when employed and unemployed, one could still have people choosing voluntary unemployment.

In this chapter, only conventional output gap costs will be considered. Even if they have no clear welfare significance, it would still be worthwhile from a positive economics viewpoint to know their magnitude.

### BRINGING DOWN INFLATION WITH A POLICY-INVARIANT NATURAL RATE

In this subsection we consider models that have the long-run natural rate property: the same level of real output (rate of unemployment) is consistent with any steady-state and fully anticipated rate of inflation. While output and unemployment can differ from their natural levels outside the steady state, these natural levels themselves are taken to be constant. For this class of models we shall show that *price-level inertia* is not sufficient to generate output costs of policies to bring down inflation. For there to be such costs, inertia should attach to the *rate of change* of the price level. A number of 'Keynesian' models – e.g. Buiter and Miller's (1981, 1982) variant of Dornbusch's (1976) overshooting model, Calvo's (1982a,b,c) continuous-time version of Taylor's (1980) staggered overlapping money wage contract model,[6] Mussa's (1981) sticky price model and Obstfeld and Rogoff's (1982) version of a price adjustment rule of Barro and Grossman (1976) – all have the property that, in principle, inflation can be reduced or eliminated costlessly. Well-designed and credible monetary and fiscal policy can make these economic systems mimic the real behavior of a completely flexible money wage and price economy.

After considering these models, we analyze the cost of bringing down inflation in models with sluggish core inflation. These costs, and the properties of desirable anti-inflationary policies, turn out to depend crucially on the relative importance of backward-looking ('long-term contracts') versus forward-looking ('expectations') determinants of current inflation.

### CLOSED ECONOMY MODELS

This subsection deals with closed economy models. Much of the analysis requires consideration only of the wage–price block. Where a complete, if rudimentary, macroeconomic model is required, the following standard log-linear *IS–LM* model will be used.

$$m - p = -\lambda r + ky \qquad \lambda \geqslant 0; k \geqslant 0 \tag{1}$$

$$y(t) = -\gamma[r(t) - \dot{p}(t, t)] + \varepsilon[m(t) - p(t)] + \eta f(t) \qquad \gamma > 0; \varepsilon \geqslant 0; \eta \geqslant 0. \tag{2}$$

where $m$ is the nominal stock of money balances, $p$ the general price level, $r$ the short nominal interest rate, $y$ real output and $f$ a measure of fiscal impact on aggregate demand. All variables except $r$ are measured in logarithms. For any variable $x$, $\dot{x}(t)$ denotes its time derivative, i.e.

$$\dot{x}(t) \equiv \lim_{h \to 0}\left(\frac{x(t + h) - x(t)}{h}\right)$$

$x(s, t)$ denotes the value of $x$ expected, at time $t$, to prevail at time $s$. We assume $x(s, t) = x(s), x \leqslant t$. The expected instantaneous rate of change of $x$ is denoted

$$\dot{x}(t,t) \equiv \lim_{\substack{h \to 0 \\ h > 0}}\left(\frac{x(t + h,t) - x(t,t)}{h}\right).$$

The unexpected change in $x$ is denoted by

$$\frac{\partial}{\partial t} x(s,t) = \lim_{\substack{h \to 0 \\ h > 0}}\left(\frac{x(s,t) - x(s,t - h)}{h}\right).$$

## COSTLESS DISINFLATION WITH PRICE FLEXIBILITY

Let capacity output or the natural level of output be denoted $\bar{y}$. This is treated as exogenous and constant. The benchmark case for costless disinflation is represented by the flexible price-level model, which complements (1) and (2) with the assumption of continuous full-capacity utilization:

$$y = \bar{y}. \tag{3}$$

For simplicity, it is assumed here and in what follows that the initial position of the economy is one of full stationary equilibrium with a high constant rate of monetary growth $\bar{\mu}$. All models considered will have the classical property that the steady-state rate of inflation equals the steady-state rate of growth of money.[7]

It is easily checked that, regardless of what the initial rate of inflation happens to be, an unanticipated, immediately implemented and permanent fixing of the rate of monetary growth $\dot{m}(t) \equiv \mu(t)$ at $\bar{\bar{\mu}}$ will immediately and permanently set the rate of inflation at $\bar{\bar{\mu}}$ if expectations are rational. If the *IS* curve is vertical ($\gamma = 0$) and there is a real balance effect ($\varepsilon \neq 0$), this follows trivially from the stronger proposition that real money balances are determined uniquely by $\bar{y}$ and $f$. If neither $\gamma$ nor $\lambda$ equals zero, the behavior of expected real money balances is governed by

$$\dot{l}(t,\, t) = (\lambda^{-1} + \gamma^{-1})l(t) + \mu(t) - (\gamma^{-1} + \lambda^{-1}k)\bar{y} + \gamma^{-1}\eta f(t)$$

where

$$l(t) \equiv m(t) - p(t).$$

Since $\lambda^{-1} + \lambda^{-1}\varepsilon$ is positive, there is, for a given information set, a unique continuous convergent solution given by

$$l(t) = \left(\frac{\lambda + k\gamma}{\gamma + \lambda\varepsilon}\right)\bar{y} - \int_t^{\infty} e^{(\lambda^{-1}+\gamma^{-1}\varepsilon)(t-s)}[\gamma^{-1}\eta f(s,t) + \mu(s,t)]\, ds.$$

When both $f$ and $\mu$ are expected to remain constant at $\bar{f}$ and $\bar{\bar{\mu}}$ respectively for all future time, this simplifies to

$$l(t) = \left(\frac{\lambda + k\gamma}{\gamma + \lambda\varepsilon}\right)\bar{y} - \frac{\eta\lambda}{\gamma + \lambda\varepsilon}\bar{f} - \frac{\gamma\lambda}{\gamma + \lambda\varepsilon}\bar{\bar{\mu}} \tag{4}$$

Thus, while the level of the real stock of money balances will, in general, be a function of the rate of monetary growth (even across steady states) through the effect of anticipated money growth on the expected rate of inflation and thus on the nominal interest rate, the adjustment of the real stock of money balances to a new rate of growth of the nominal money stock will be instantaneous. The price level will jump discontinuously if required to satisfy (4). After that, the rate of inflation equals the new constant rate of money growth.

The general solution for the expected rate of inflation for constant $\bar{y}$ and $\bar{f}$ is:

$$\begin{aligned} \dot{p}(t,t) &= (\lambda^{-1} + \gamma^{-1}\varepsilon)\int_t^{\infty} e^{(\lambda^{-1}+\gamma^{-1}\varepsilon)(t-s)}\,\mu(s,t)\, ds. \\ &= \bar{\bar{\mu}} \quad \text{if} \quad \mu(s,t) = \bar{\bar{\mu}} \quad \text{for } s \geqslant t. \end{aligned} \tag{5}$$

The actual rate of inflation – the sum of anticipated and unanticipated inflation – is given by

$$\dot{p}(t) = \int_t^{\infty} e^{(\lambda^{-1}+\gamma^{-1}\varepsilon)(t-s)}\left[(\lambda^{-1} + \gamma^{-1}\varepsilon)\mu(s,t) + \frac{\partial}{\partial t}\mu(s,t)\right] ds.^{8} \tag{6}$$

Note that in this model the *credibility* of current announcements of future policy is both necessary and sufficient for a sustained reduction in inflation to any level. Although, by construction, there never are any output costs of bringing down inflation, a desired reduction in inflation may not be achievable, regardless of the actual past and current path of monetary growth, simply because expectations concerning future monetary growth are sufficiently pessimistic. Inflation, and policies to combat inflation, are exclusively forward-looking. We shall return to this credibility issue when we discuss the fiscal preconditions for a sustained deceleration of monetary growth below.

## COSTLESS DISINFLATION WITH PRICE-LEVEL INERTIA

The following four sluggish price-adjustment mechanisms permit, in principle, costless and instantaneous sustained reductions in the rate of inflation:

$$\dot{p}(t) = \Psi[y(t) - \bar{y}] + \mu^{+}(t) \qquad \Psi > 0 \text{ (Dornbusch)} \tag{7}$$

$$\dot{p}(t) = \Psi[y(t) - \bar{y}] + \dot{\bar{p}}(t) \qquad \text{(Barro–Grossman)} \tag{8}$$

$$\dot{p}(t) = \Psi[y(t) - \bar{y}] + \dot{\bar{p}}(t) \qquad \text{(Mussa)} \tag{9}$$

$$\dot{p}(t) = \delta[v(t) - p(t)] \qquad \delta > 0 \text{ (Calvo)} \tag{10a}$$

$$\dot{v}(t, t) = \delta\{v(t) - p(t) - \Psi[y(t) - \bar{y}]\}. \tag{10b}$$

In all four cases the price level, $p$, is treated as predetermined: it cannot move discontinuously in response to current changes in expectations about the future. Also in all four cases, the rate of change of the price level is an increasing function of excess demand pressure, measured as the excess of the level of current output (which is viewed as demand-determined) over the natural level of output. In equations (7), (8) and (9) it is only current excess demand that, given 'core' inflation, affects current inflation. In Calvo's model both current and anticipated future excess demand affect current inflation. Equations (7), (8) and (9) differ only in the augmentation term, or core inflation – the rate of inflation when there is no excess demand or supply. In equation (7), core inflation is identified with the right-hand-side derivative of the money stock path:

$$\mu^{+}(t) \equiv \lim_{\substack{h \to 0 \\ h > 0}} \frac{m(t + h) - m(t)}{h}.$$

In equation (8), core inflation is given by $\dot{\bar{p}}$, which is the right-hand-side derivative of the equilibrium price path that would be generated if the price level were fully flexible. This is, of course, the rate of inflation calculated in equation (5). Mussa's equation (9), as developed by Obstfeld and Rogoff (1982), specifies core inflation as the right-hand-side derivative of the price path $\bar{p}(t)$ that would clear the output market (set $y(t) = \bar{y}$) given the actual (and in general non-Walrasian equilibrium) values of the other endogenous variables, $p(t)$, $\dot{p}(t, t)$ and $r(t)$. $\bar{p}(t)$ is therefore defined by:

$$\bar{y} = -\gamma[r(t) - \dot{p}(t, t)] + \varepsilon[m(t) - \bar{p}(t)] + \eta f(t).$$

In the spirit of Taylor, Calvo specifies the current contract price, $v(t)$, as a forward-looking moving average with exponentially declining weights of the future expected general price level $p(t)$ and future expected excess demand:

$$v(t) = \delta \int_t^{\infty} \{p(s,t) + \psi[y(s,t) - \bar{y}]\}e^{-\delta(s-t)}\,ds + e^{\delta t} \lim_{\tau \to \infty}[e^{-\delta\tau}v(\tau,t)]. \tag{11a}$$

Note that the current contract price $v(t)$ is non-predetermined. The general price level, which is predetermined, is a backward-looking, exponentially declining moving average of past contract prices:

$$p(t) = \delta \int_{t_0}^{t} v(s)e^{-\delta(t-s)}\,ds + e^{-\delta(t-t_0)}p(t_0). \tag{11b}$$

In a full employment, stationary equilibrium $\dot{v}(t, t) = \dot{v}(t) = \dot{p}(t)$. A positive (zero, negative) steady-state rate of inflation requires a current contract price, $v(t)$, above (equal to, below) the current general price level, $p(t)$.

It will be apparent that all four mechanisms in equations (7)–(10) have flexible core inflation. It would appear that simply reducing monetary growth to $\bar{\mu}$, say, and keeping it there would be sufficient to reduce inflation in (7) without output costs. In equations (8), (9) and (10a,b), the further proviso of credibility of current announcements of future reductions in monetary growth has to be added.

The reason that this is not quite correct is that a *ceteris paribus* reduction in money growth would in general affect the money market and output market. To effect a permanent reduction in inflation at full employment other policy parameters will have to be changed when monetary growth is reduced. Steady-state output $y = \bar{y}$ is, from (4), sustained by monetary and fiscal policy as follows:

$$y(t) = \bar{y} = \frac{\eta\lambda}{\lambda + k\gamma}\bar{f} + \frac{\gamma\lambda}{\lambda + k\gamma}\bar{\bar{\mu}} + \left(\frac{\gamma + \lambda\varepsilon}{\lambda + k\gamma}\right)[m(t) - p(t)].$$

The long-run effect of a reduction in money growth is to reduce inflation one-for-one, reduce the nominal interest rate (but less than one-for-one if there is a real balance effect[9]) and thus raise the demand for real money balances. In the classical flex-price model, the real money balances required to effect an instantaneous transition to low inflation at full employment comes about through a discontinuous jump down in the price level. With a predetermined price level, the required increase in real money balances can instead be achieved by a discrete, discontinuous increase in the level of the nominal money stock at the same time, $t$, that its rate of change is reduced permanently. The required money jump is given by:

$$dm(t) = \frac{-\gamma\lambda}{\gamma + \lambda\varepsilon}\,d\bar{\bar{\mu}}.^{10} \tag{12a}$$

Alternatively, expansionary fiscal policy could accompany the reduction in money growth in such a way as to leave the nominal interest rate unchanged. The required fiscal expansion is given by

$$d\bar{f} = \frac{-\gamma}{\eta} d\bar{\bar{\mu}}. \tag{12b}$$

This fiscal action relies on the direct aggregate demand effect of increased public spending or lower taxes. We shall show below how cost- and price-reducing indirect tax cuts could be used as a substitute for an increase in the nominal money stock as a means for achieving an increase in real money balances at a given before-tax price level.

It can be checked easily that, provided the money stock is raised according to (12a) or a fiscal stimulus is provided according to (12b) when monetary growth is lowered to $\bar{\bar{\mu}}$, the rate of inflation will settle immediately and permanently at $\bar{\bar{\mu}}$ while output remains equal to $\bar{y}$ throughout.[11]

For Calvo's model the existence of costless disinflation policies may not be quite as transparent as for the other three. First note that, treating $y - \bar{y}$ as exogenous, both roots of the dynamic system (10a,b) are zero. Following Buiter (1983c), the convergent solutions for $v$ and $p$ are given by:

$$p(t) = p(t_0) + \delta \int_{t_0}^{t} K(s)\mathrm{d}s + \delta^2\psi \int_{t_0}^{t} \int_{s}^{\infty} [y(\tau,s) - \bar{y}]\mathrm{d}\tau\mathrm{d}s \tag{13a}$$

$$v(t) = p(t) + K(t) + \psi\delta \int_{t}^{\infty} [y(\tau,t) - \bar{y}]\mathrm{d}\tau. \tag{13b}$$

$K$ is a parameter to be determined from the terminal boundary condition. A natural transversatility condition to determine $K$ (and one consistent with (11a)) is

$$K(t) = \lim_{\tau\to\infty}[v(\tau,t) - p(\tau,t)] = \lim_{\tau\to\infty} \frac{\dot{v}(\tau,t)}{\delta} = \lim_{\tau\to\infty} \frac{\dot{p}(\tau,t)}{\delta}. \tag{13c}$$

It is easily seen from equations (1) and (2) that, along any (anticipated) full employment path ($y(\tau, t) = \bar{y}$) with a constant expected rate of money growth $\bar{\mu}$ and a constant expected value of $f$, it must be true that $K(t) = \bar{\mu}/\delta$. Thus, as $\bar{\mu}$ is lowered from $\bar{\mu}$ to $\bar{\bar{\mu}}$ and $m$ is increased once and for all to maintain full employment, $v$ will drop discontinuously by $(\bar{\mu} - \bar{\bar{\mu}})/\delta$ and inflation is reduced costlessly and permanently. The dependence of the current price level on a 'two-sided' moving average of output expectations will re-emerge in a slightly modified form when inflation inertia is added to prive-level inertia.

If monetary or fiscal policy actions to maintain full employment when the monetary growth rate is reduced are ruled out, the increased demand for real money balances resulting from a successful anti-inflationary policy can be satisfied only by a lowering of the price-level path relative to the nominal money stock path. This will involve unemployment and excess capacity in all four sticky price-level models. For example, in the Dornbusch variant,

$$\int_{t_0}^{t} (y(s) - \bar{y})\mathrm{d}s = \psi^{-1}[l(t_0) - l(t)].$$

By the time the economy settles down to a new stationary equilibrium and a new, higher, stationary stock of real money balances after a reduction in $\mu$, the undiscounted cumulative net output loss will be

$$\int_{t_0}^{\infty} [y(s) - \bar{y}]\mathrm{d}s = \psi^{-1} \frac{\gamma\lambda}{\gamma + \lambda\varepsilon} (\bar{\mu} - \bar{\mu}).$$

The net output cost of reducing steady-state inflation decreases as the short-run Phillips curve steepens and the interest sensitivity of money demand decreases.

These costs of bringing down the price *level* will be different for the four price-adjustment mechanisms considered in this subsection. They are not considered any further here because of space constraints. The methods of the next subsection, which deals with inflation inertia, can be brought to bear on the problem of price-level inertia with obvious modifications.

### INFLATION INERTIA

The simplest way of introducing inflation inertia is by postulating a backward-looking adaptive process for core inflation, $\pi$, as in (14a,b).

$$\dot{p} = \Psi(y - \bar{y}) + \pi \tag{14a}$$

$$\dot{\pi} = \xi(\dot{p} - \pi) \qquad \xi > 0. \tag{14b}$$

Both the price level, $p$, and core inflation, $\pi$, are predetermined. It is now no longer possible to avoid paying the output or unemployment cost of bringing down inflation merely by manipulating aggregate demand as in the previous subsection. In the model of equations (14a,b), a sustained reduction in inflation requires a reduction in core inflation. Since

$$\pi(t) = \pi(t_0) + \xi\psi \int_{t_0}^{t} [y(s) - y]\mathrm{d}s,$$

the undiscounted cumulative net output cost of bringing down inflation permanently is given by

$$\int_{t_0}^{\infty} (y(s) - \bar{y})\mathrm{d}s = \frac{\pi(\infty) - \pi(t_0)}{\xi\psi}. \tag{15}$$

It is a decreasing function of the slope of the short-run Phillips curve and an increasing function of the mean lag of the backward-looking core inflation process $1/\xi$. This loss measure cannot be altered by changing the timing or the intensity of the anti-inflationary package. Given $\xi$, $\phi$ and the desired reduction in steady-state inflation, the net output cost is a constant. (See e.g. Miller, 1979; Buiter and Miller, 1982, 1983.)

Clearly, with discounting, policy makers will not be indifferent between different trajectories with the same net output cost. We shall not address these issues as they are both well understood (see e.g. Phelps, 1972, and Hall, 1976) and comparatively unimportant: characterizing efficient policies (and inefficient policies!) would seem to be more useful than searching for an optimal policy.

The major drawback of the model of core inflation in equation (14b) is the complete irrelevance for current core inflation of current and/or past anticipations of future economic events. To remedy this (14b) is replaced by (15a,b). Core inflation, $\pi$, is a backward-looking exponentially declining moving average of past 'contract inflation', $q$, while $q$ is a forward-looking moving average of future expected inflation.

$$\pi(t) = \pi(t_0)e^{-\xi_1(t-t_0)} + \xi_1 \int_{t_0}^{t} q(s)e^{-\xi_1(t-s)}ds \qquad \xi_1 > 0 \tag{15a}$$

$$q(t) = \xi_2 \int_{t}^{\infty} \dot{p}(\tau,t)e^{-\xi_2(\tau-t)}d\tau.^{12} \tag{15b}$$

By differentiating (15a,b) and using (14a) we obtain the two-equation system:

$$\dot{\pi}(t) = -\xi_1[\pi(t) - q(t)] \tag{16a}$$

$$\dot{q}(t, t) = -\xi_2[\pi(t) - q(t)] - \xi_2\Psi[y(t) - \bar{y}]. \tag{16b}$$

Comparing this with Calvo's model in equation (10a,b), two differences stand out. First, equations (16a,b) have 'slipped a derivative' compared to (10a,b). Inertia now attaches both to the level and to the first derivative of the price-level path. Second, the mean lags of the backward-looking core inflation process, $\xi_1^{-1}$, and of the forward-looking contract inflation process, $\xi_2^{-1}$, are permitted to be different from each other.

Treating the output gap $y - \bar{y}$ as exogeneous, the convergent solutions for $\pi(t)$ and $q(t)$ are found to be:[13]

$$\pi(t) = \pi(t_0) + \xi_1\xi_2\,\psi \int_{t_0}^{t}\int_{s}^{\infty} e^{(\xi_2-\xi_1)(s-\tau)}[y(\tau,s) - \bar{y}]\,d\tau\,ds \tag{17a}$$

$$q(t) = \pi(t) + \xi_2\,\psi \int_{t}^{\infty} e^{(\xi_2-\xi_1)(t-s)}[y(s,t) - \bar{y}]\,ds. \tag{17b}$$

For convergence it is assumed that $\xi_2 \geqslant \xi_1$: current contract inflation adjusts more quickly than core inflation, or the mean lag of the contract inflation process is no longer than that of the core inflation process.

Equation (17b) shows that 'current contract inflation', $q(t)$, can be brought down discontinuously by announcing, at $t$, a credible path of future recession. Core inflation, $\pi(t)$, is a function of the expectations, formed at each instant in the past, of the entire future path of the output gap. It can come down (gradually) only in response to credible announcements that policies to generate a recession will be pursued in the future.

To get a better appreciation of the cost of bringing down inflation in this model, we now consider an example of a specific path for expected output. The initial position at $t_0$ is one of current and expected future full employment with actual, core and current contract inflation all equal to each other. At $t_0$, output is unexpectedly lowered to $y(t_0) < \bar{y}$. The output gap is then expected to decay exponentially at a rate $\gamma$ so that

$$y(\tau, t) - \bar{y} = [y(t_0) - \bar{y}]\, e^{-\gamma(\tau - t_0)} \qquad \tau \geqslant t_0 \cdot \gamma > 0. \tag{18}$$

Substituting (18) into (17a,b) yields

$$\pi(t) = \pi(t_0) + \frac{\xi_1 \xi_2 \Psi}{(\gamma + \xi_2 - \xi_1)\gamma} [y(t_0) - \bar{y}][1 - e^{-\gamma(t - t_0)}] \tag{19a}$$

$$q(t) = \pi(t) + \frac{\xi_2 \Psi}{\gamma + \xi_2 - \xi_1} [y(t_0) - \bar{y}]\, e^{-\gamma(t - t_0)}. \tag{19b}$$

The long-run effect on core inflation of this policy is, from (19a),

$$\pi(\infty) - \pi(t_0) = \frac{\xi_1 \xi_2 \Psi}{\gamma + \xi_2 - \xi_1} [y(t_0) - \bar{y}] = \dot{p}(\infty) - \dot{p}(t_0^-) = q(\infty) - q(t_0^-).^{14} \tag{20a}$$

The undiscounted cumulative net output loss incurred for this reduction in inflation is

$$\int_{t_0}^{\infty} (y(t) - \bar{y})\, \mathrm{d}t = \frac{y(t_0) - \bar{y}}{\gamma}. \tag{20b}$$

Consider the special case where $\gamma = \xi_1$ (the mean lag of the output process equals the mean lag of the core inflation process). In this case the impact of the current and expected future recession is to reduce actual inflation and current contract inflation immediately to their new long-run equilibrium levels:

$$\dot{p}(t) = q(t) = \pi(t_0) + \Psi[y(t_0) - \bar{y}], \qquad t \geqslant t_0.$$

Core inflation only approaches its long-run equilibrium value gradually according to

$$\pi(t) = \pi(t_0) + \Psi[y(t_0) - \bar{y}][1 - e^{-\gamma(t-t_0)}].$$

In this case, actual inflation and current contract inflation have been eliminated immediately and permanently, but the output cost is still to come. This would be obvious to an observer who can measure core inflation, which has yet to be brought down. It will be shown below that there are policies that reduce both actual and core inflation to any desired level before any of the output costs have actually been incurred. This raises the problem of time inconsistency and credibility of policy.

### 'GRADUALISM' VERSUS 'COLD-TURKEY'

It can be seen from (19b) and (20a) that if, $\gamma$ is larger (smaller) than $\xi_1$, current contract inflation will on impact fall below (stay above) its new long-run equilibrium level. This might suggest that a short sharp recession would, by changing current contract inflation promptly, be a more effective means of bringing down core inflation than a longer and milder recession. In fact, the opposite is the case. From (20a,b) it follows that, holding constant the cumulative net output loss $[y(t_0) - \bar{y}]/\gamma$, a deeper initial recession (a smaller value of $y(t_0)$) followed by a faster recovery (a larger value of $\gamma$) would produce a smaller reduction in steady-state inflation. The reason is, from (17a), that later expected output gaps, although discounted as regards their effect on $\pi(t)$, are also counted again and again (in fact continuously) on the interval $t_0 - t$.

In the presence of inflation inertia that is due to contractual or other institutional arrangements rather than to sluggish expectation adjustments, there are 'diminishing returns' to cold turkey deflation and gradualism is preferable. Only if a short, sharp shock can break down the nominal inertia, i.e. if the adjustment equations (15a,b) or (16a,b) are not structurally invariant to certain dramatic changes in the policy regime, is there a case for anti-inflationary heroics.

### TIME INCONSISTENCY AND THE TIMING OF ANTI-INFLATIONARY BENEFITS AND OUTPUT COSTS

It has already been shown that it is possible, through credible policy announcements, to bring down actual and current contract inflation immediately – before the output losses (whose expectation generated this reduction in inflation) have been incurred. It will be apparent from equations (17a,b) that it is also possible, if policy announcements are credible, to bring down core inflation gradually (i.e. over any finite time interval) to any desired level before any of the output costs have been incurred. Consider, for example, a policy that, starting at $t_0$, keeps output at its capacity level $\bar{y}$ until $\bar{t} > t_0$, at $\bar{\bar{y}}$ from $\bar{t}$ till $\bar{\bar{t}} > \bar{t}$ and again at $\bar{y}$ after $\bar{\bar{t}}$.

$$y(\tau, s) = \begin{cases} \bar{y}; \ t_0 < \tau \leqslant \bar{t} \\ \bar{\bar{y}}; \ \bar{t} < \tau \leqslant \bar{\bar{t}} \\ \bar{y}; \ \tau > \bar{\bar{t}}. \end{cases} \tag{21}$$

It follows that

$$\pi(\bar{t}) = \pi(t_0) + \frac{\xi_1 \xi_2 \Psi}{(\xi_2 - \xi_1)^2}[1 - e^{-(\xi_2-\xi_1)(\bar{t}-t_0)} - e^{-(\xi_2-\xi_1)(\bar{\bar{t}}-\bar{t})} + e^{-(\xi_2-\xi_1)(\bar{\bar{t}}-\bar{t}_0)}](\bar{\bar{y}} - \bar{y}).$$

A recession strategy announced (and made credible) at $t = t_0$ that permits a reduction in core inflation at $t = \bar{t}$ *to* $\bar{\pi}(\bar{t})$, say, is therefore given by (21) with $\bar{\bar{y}}$ defined by

$$\bar{\bar{y}} - \bar{y} = \frac{[\bar{\pi}(\bar{t}) - \pi(t_0)](\xi_2 - \xi_1)^2}{\xi_1 \xi_2 \Psi[1 - e^{-(\xi_2-\xi_1)(\bar{t}-t_0)} - e^{-(\xi_2-\xi_1)(\bar{\bar{t}}-\bar{t})} + e^{-(\xi_2-\xi_1)(\bar{\bar{t}}-t_0)}]} \qquad (22)$$

As expected, the announced future recession is deeper the larger the reduction in core inflation, $\bar{\pi}(\bar{t}) - \pi(t_0)$, that is required.

Having achieved the desired reduction in core inflation at $t = \bar{t}$ without actually having suffered any output costs as yet, the temptation to renege on the earlier commitment to create a recession between $\bar{t}$ and $\bar{\bar{t}}$ would be hard to resist.

The argument that the recession must take place in order to validate and confirm the expectations held between $t = t_0$ and $t = \bar{t}$ and thus to preserve or invest in credibility for future policy announcements is unlikely to prove a political winner. Why have a recession when core inflation has already subsided? A policy maker treating bygones as bygones will, at $t = \bar{t}$ and beyond, keep output at its capacity level.

What this suggests is that any optimal policy will be time-inconsistent (Kydland and Prescott, 1977; Buiter, 1981, 1983b) if it has the property that some output costs still have to be incurred (if previous expectations are to be validated) after the inflation objectives have been achieved. Unless credible precommitment is possible, such policy announcements will not be believed by the private sector.

Time-consistent policies must be characterized by a better matching of the time profiles of costs and benefits: if a credible strategy cannot have the costs following the benefits, the recession will have to be brought forward in time. If a speedy reduction in inflation is sought, a deep, short recession will be the only credible strategy. It has already been shown that 'short, sharp shocks' of this kind are likely to be inefficient.

The model under consideration has implications not only for policy design but also for policy evaluation. Consider again the general expressions (17a,b). Conventional cost measures focus on output or unemployment costs incurred up to the time that a given reduction in core inflation has been achieved. When forward-looking expectations and inflation inertia play a role (as they do in this model), some, most or all of the costs attributable to the reduction in core inflation may be incurred after the anti-inflationary objective has been achieved.

## HIGHER-ORDER INERTIA

It is not difficult to visualize economic systems in which not only the price level and the core rate of inflation but also the rate of change of core inflation adjusts sluggishly. Attributing inertia to higher derivatives of the price and wage process is the continuous-time analogue to increasing the number of periods for which nominal contracts hold in discrete time models. For example, by slipping another derivative in the model of equations (14a and 16a,b) we obtain:

$$\ddot{\pi}(t) = \xi_1[\dot{q}(t) - \dot{\pi}(t)]$$

$$\ddot{q}(t, t) = \xi_2[\dot{q}(t) - \dot{\pi}(t) - \Psi[y(t) - \bar{y})]$$

$$\ddot{p}(t) = \Psi[y(t) - \bar{y}] + \dot{\pi}(t).$$

With nominal inertia in the price level, core inflation and the rate of change of core inflation, the output costs of bringing down steady-state inflation will be high indeed.[15]

## SOME OPEN-ECONOMY CONSIDERATIONS AND THE SENSIBLE USE OF FISCAL POLICY IN A DISINFLATIONARY PROGRAM

In an open economy, appreciation of the exchange rate might seem to offer a mechanism for bringing down inflation more rapidly or at less cost than in a closed economy or an economy on a fixed exchange rate.

This will be considered in an open-economy extension of the model with backward-looking core inflation given in (14a,b). Possible direct cost and price effects of direct and indirect taxes are also introduced here. They can be applied to all closed-economy models in an obvious way. The economy is a price taker in the world market for its imports, whose world price is $p^*$, and in international financial markets. The country has some market power in the market for its exportable. Perfect capital mobility and international asset substitutability are assumed. The model is given in equations (23–29), where $r^*$ is the foreign nominal interest rate, $w$ denotes domestic costs, i.e. labor costs per unit of output or even the GDP deflator at factor cost; $p$ is the consumer price index; $e$ is the price of foreign exchange, $g$ is exhaustive public spending; $\tau_i$ is the rate of indirect taxation; and $\tau_d$ is the income tax rate. All coefficients are positive.

$$\frac{d}{dt}[w(t) - \beta\tau_d(t)] = \psi(y - \bar{y}) + \pi(t) \qquad 0 \leq \beta \leq 1 \tag{23}$$

$$p(t) = \tau_i(t) + \alpha w(t) + (1 - \alpha)[p^*(t) + e(t)] \qquad 0 < \alpha < 1 \tag{24}$$

$$\dot{\pi} = \xi[\dot{p} - \pi(t)] \tag{25}$$

$$y(t) = -\gamma[r(t) - \dot{p}(t, t)] + \delta[e(t) + p^*(t) - p(t)] + \varepsilon[m(t) - p(t)] + \eta_1 g(t) - \eta_2[\tau_i(t) + \tau_d(t)] \tag{26}$$

$$m(t) - p(t) = ky(t) - \lambda r(t) \tag{27}$$

$$\dot{e}(t, t) = r(t) - r^*(t) \tag{28}$$

$$c \equiv e + p^* - w \tag{29a}$$

$$l \equiv m - w. \tag{29b}$$

The model is similar to the one considered in Buiter and Miller (1982, 1983). Note that taxes have both aggregate demand effects (equation 26) and direct cost effects (equations (23) and (24)). Only a fraction $\beta$ of an increase in income tax rates is translated into higher wage settlements (equation (23)). One interpretation of (23) is that it is the (adjusted) after-tax money wage, $w - \beta\tau_d$, that is predetermined or sticky rather than the before-tax wage, $w$. Note that the consumer price index (CPI) can move discontinuously, even if $w$ is predetermined, through changes in indirect tax rates and in the exchange rate. The latter influences the CPI through the share of imports in final consumption $1 - \alpha$.

From equations (23)–(25) and (29b) it follows that

$$\pi(t) - \pi(t_0) = \xi\psi \int_{t_0}^{t} [y(s) - \bar{y}]\, ds + \xi(1 - \alpha)[c(t) - c(t_0)] + \xi[\tau_i(t) - \tau_i(t_0)] + \xi\beta[\tau_d(t) - \tau_d(t_0)] \tag{30a}$$

or

$$\int_{t_0}^{t} [y(s) - \bar{y}]\, ds = \frac{\pi(t) - \pi(t_0)}{\xi\psi} - \frac{(1 - \alpha)}{\psi}[c(t) - c(t_0)] - \left[\frac{[\tau_i(t) - \tau_i(t_0)] + \beta(\tau_d(t) - \tau_d(t_0))}{\psi}\right]. \tag{30b}$$

The familiar closed-economy output costs given in equation (15) are found back as the first term on the right-hand side of (30b). They can be reduced by an appreciation of the real exchange rate, $c$, by a cut in indirect taxes and, if $\beta \neq 0$, by a cut in direct taxes.

A balanced budget cut in indirect taxes matched by an increase in direct taxes helps reduce the output cost of disinflation only if direct tax increases do not raise before-tax wage settlements one-for-one.

Consider the steady state of the model:

$$l = \tau_i + (1 - \alpha)c - \lambda(r^* - \dot{p}^* + \mu) + k\bar{y} \tag{31}$$

$$\bar{y} = -\gamma(r^* - \dot{p}^*) + (\delta\alpha - \varepsilon(1 - \alpha))c + \varepsilon l - \varepsilon\tau_i + \eta_1 g - \eta_2(\tau_i + \tau_d) \tag{32}$$

$$\dot{p} = \pi = \mu = \dot{p}^* + \dot{e} \tag{33}$$

$$r = r^* - \dot{p}^* + \mu. \tag{34}$$

Across steady states, a reduction in monetary growth lowers actual and core inflation one-for-one. It will have no effect on competitiveness if there is no real balance effect ($\varepsilon = 0$). If there is a real balance effect, the increased stock of real balances associated with a lower rate of monetary growth will require a loss of competitiveness to maintain equilibrium in the output market if $(\delta + \varepsilon)\alpha > \varepsilon$. Assuming that there is no long-run effect on competitiveness from a reduction in the rate of inflation, any favorable short-run or impact effects on the price level, the rate of inflation and the core rate of inflation from an initial appreciation of the exchange rate will not lower the undiscounted cumulative net output cost of securing a sustained reduction in core inflation. Buiter and Miller (1982, 1983) show that, on impact, a reduction in monetary growth will be associated with a discrete, jump appreciation of the nominal exchange rate (a step down in $e$ and $c$). If $e$ jumps down, so, from (24), does $p$ and so, from (25), does $\pi$. Core inflation jumps on impact but the apparent reduction in output cost that entails is nullified by the net depreciation of the real exchange rate that will be required during the remainder of the adjustment process to restore competitiveness. Only if the short, sharp shock of a sudden revaluation breaks down the inertia captured in (23) and (25) will it help reduce the output cost of bringing down inflation.

In principle, by using indirect and, if $\beta \neq 0$, direct tax cuts to melt core inflation instantaneously, a costless and immediate transition to a sustained lower rate of inflation is possible. The higher stock of real money balances demanded in a low-inflation equilibrium can be provided either by engineering a step increase in the level of the nominal money stock at the same time that its growth rate is reduced or by cutting taxes. Indirect tax cuts will do the job and so will direct tax cuts, if $\beta \neq 0$ and if it is the after-tax money wage rather than the before-tax money wage that is predetermined. If step adjustments in $m$ are ruled out, immediate attainment of the new long-run equilibrium values of $m - p$ and $\pi$ while maintaining full employment will, in general, require use of all three fiscal instruments, $g$, $\tau_i$ and $\tau_d$.

Finally, in the context of this model, incomes policy can be seen as the ability to 'override' the core inflation adjustment equation (25). An extreme version would permit the authorities to pick a new starting value for $\pi$. The model clearly is not rich enough to suggest reasons why such policies have a habit of breaking down.

## HYSTERESIS[16] IN THE NATURAL RATE

One of the most striking macroeconomic coincidences of the last fifteen years has been the way in which estimates of the natural rate of unemployment have moved up, along with the actual rate of unemployment. In this subsection we consider the implications of the hypothesis that this co-movement represents a causal influence running from current and past actual unemployment to the current natural unemployment rate. Letting $-y$ stand for the actual unemployment rate and $-\bar{y}$ for the natural rate, we postulate that

$$\bar{y}(t) = \bar{y}(t_0)\, e^{-\theta_2(t-t_0)} + \theta_2 \int_{t_0}^{t} y(s)\, e^{-\theta_2(t-s)}\, ds + \theta_1 \int_{t_0}^{t} e^{-\theta_2(t-s)} \dot{R}(s)\, ds \quad (35)$$

or

$$\dot{\bar{y}}(t) = \theta_2[y(t) - \bar{y}(t)] + \theta_1 \dot{R}(t), \qquad \theta_2 \geqslant 0. \quad (35')$$

$R(t)$ stands for whatever structural factors or policies may affect the natural rate (union power, unemployment benefits, minimum wage, etc.). The second term on the right-hand side of (35) and the first term on the right-hand side of (35′) represent the hypothesis that unemployment destroys human capital by having a negative effect both on attitudes towards working and on the aptitude for work. The idea is an old one. Recent formalizations can be found in Buiter and Gersovitz (1981), Hargreaves Heap (1980), Gregory (1982, 1983) and Gregory and Smith (1983). Clearly, as written in (35) the hypothesis is too strong, since no bounds are set on the natural rate in the long run: by selecting an appropriate path for unemployment, the natural rate can be steered to any level. Such global hysteresis is implausible. Over some finite range of unemployment rates, the hypothesis may, however, have merit. Equation (35) should be viewed as the log-linear approximation in the relevant range of unemployment rates to a model with local hysteresis. While the long-run or stationary Phillips curve is vertical, it can be made vertical at any point within that range.

To keep the exposition brief, the simple sluggish core inflation model of equations (14a,b) is added to (35). It is, of course, still true that

$$\pi(t) = \pi(t_0) + \xi\psi \int_{t_0}^{t} [y(s) - \bar{y}(s)]\, ds.$$

Since the natural rate no longer is invariant under the disinflation process, deviations from the natural rate cease to be a useful measure of cost. In the absence of tax cuts or incomes policy, core inflation can only be lowered by raising the actual unemployment rate above the natural rate. This, however, will, by (35′), begin to raise the natural rate, thus reducing gradually the disinflationary effect of any given increase in the actual rate. Formally, since

$$\bar{y}(t) = \bar{y}(t_0) + \theta_1[R(t) - R(t_0)] + \theta_2 \int_{t_0}^{t} [y(s) - \bar{y}(s)]\, ds,$$

it follows, using (35), that, if structural factors affecting the actual rate remain unchanged (i.e. if $\dot{R}(t) = 0$),

$$\int_{t_0}^{t} [y(s) - \bar{y}(s)]\, ds = \int_{t_0}^{t} [y(s) - \bar{y}(t_0)]\, e^{-\theta_2(t-s)} ds.$$

The disinflationary effect of any given increase in unemployment above its initial value will decay exponentially over time as the natural rate catches up with the actual rate.

In the hysteresis model a *permanent* increase in the rate of unemployment $-\Delta y$ will buy only a finite long-run reduction in the rate of inflation $-\Delta\pi = (\xi\psi/\theta_2)(-\Delta y)$. With an exogenous natural rate, that same steady-state reduction in inflation can be achieved by having the same constant increase in unemployment for only a finite period of time.

The simple hysteresis model outlined here has much the same implications for the inflation–unemployment process as does entering the rate of change of output (unemployment) rather than its level as an argument in the Phillips curve. The simplest version of this model is

$$\dot{p} = \phi\dot{y} + \pi \tag{36}$$

$$\dot{\pi} = \xi(\dot{p} - \pi). \tag{14b}$$

The solution for core inflation is:

$$\pi(t) = \pi(t_0) + \xi\phi[y(t) - y(t_0)], \tag{37a}$$

while current inflation is given by

$$\dot{p}(t) = \phi\dot{y}(t) + \phi\xi[y(t) - y(t_0)] + \pi(t_0). \tag{37b}$$

The striking implication of this model is that all anti-inflationary gains from a contractionary policy are completely reversed if the economy is permitted to recover. As Tobin (1980, p. 61) says,

> It is possible that there is no NAIRU, no natural rate, except one that floats with actual history. It is just possible that the direction the economy is moving in is at least as important for acceleration and deceleration as its level. These possibilities should give policy makers pause as they embark on yet another application of the orthodox demand management cure for inflation.

Note that equation (37b) is consistent with some of the early work on Phillips curves, which argued that both the level and the rate of change of unemployment could be significant in inflation equations but ignored endogenous core inflation (e.g. Phillips, 1958, and Lipsey, 1960).

This similarity between the hysteresis model and the model of equations (36) and (14b) is especially striking when we consider the effect, in the hysteresis model, of a constant path $y(s) = \bar{\bar{y}}$ for $t_0 < s \leq t$. This yields the following expression for core inflation:

$$\pi(t) = \pi(t_0) + \frac{\xi\phi}{\theta_2}[\bar{\bar{y}} - \bar{y}(t_0)][1 - e^{-\theta_2(t-t_0)}].$$

As $t$ goes to infinity, this approaches

$$\lim_{t\to\infty} \pi(t) = \pi(t_0) + \frac{\xi\phi}{\theta_2}[\bar{\bar{y}} - \bar{y}(t_0)].$$

Asymptotically, the hysteresis model too has complete reversibility of inflationary gains achieved through contractionary policy.

Although the economic mechanisms involved are very different, the output, or unemployment, costs of achieving a permanent reduction in inflation are similar for the hysteresis model and the 'unaugmented', pre-Phelps and Friedman, Phillips curve. With the $\dot{p} = \phi(y - \bar{y}) + \pi$ specification, an exogenous natural rate $\bar{y}$ and no adjustment, however gradual, of core inflation $\pi$ towards actual inflation, the 'sacrifice ratio' – the cumulative, undiscounted net output or unemployment cost (expressed as a percentage) divided by the steady-state reduction in the inflation rate – is infinite. The same specification with an exogenous natural rate but gradual convergence of core inflation to actual inflation yields a positive but finite sacrifice ratio, whose exact magnitude depends on the details of the core inflation adjustment mechanism. The assumption of instantaneous adjustment of core inflation through rational perception and anticipation of credible policy actions produces a sacrifice ratio of zero. The hysteresis model with gradually adjusting core inflation again yields an infinite sacrifice ratio. Not because, as with the old Phillips curve, core inflation never adjusts but because the natural rate adjusts gradually towards the actual unemployment rate. The case for any policy action(s) that can 'override' the core inflation adjustment equations is therefore even stronger if the hysteresis hypothesis has anything to recommend it.

## CREDIBILITY AND THE CONSISTENCY OF MONETARY AND FISCAL POLICY

All models considered in this chapter have the property that a sustained reduction in the rate of inflation requires a long-run reduction in the rate of monetary growth. While the exact nature of the relevant monetary aggregate is not apparent from these models, it seems reasonable to assume that a long-run sustained reduction in the rate of growth of any monetary aggregate presupposes corresponding reduction in the growth rate of the monetary base. If this is the case, a necessary condition for the credibility of a policy to reduce steady-state inflation is the consistency of the long-run monetary objectives with the government's fiscal program.

We can get some sense of the 'eventual monetization' implied by the government's fiscal program by considering the government's comprehensive balance sheet (see Buiter, 1983c, given in (38)).

$$N(t) \equiv p_k(t)K(t) + p_R(t)R(t) + T(t) + \pi(t) - \frac{M(t)}{p(t)} - \frac{B(t)}{p(t)} - \frac{p_c(t)C(t)}{p(t)}, \tag{38}$$

where $N$ is real government net worth, $K$ the public sector capital stock, $p_K$ the present value of the future returns to a unit of public sector capital, $R$ the number of shares of public sector natural resource property rights, $p_R$ the price of a share in these property rights, $T$ the present value of future taxes net of transfers, $\Pi$ the capital value of the government's note issue monopoly, $M$ the nominal stock of high-powered money, $B$ the stock of nominally denominated short bonds, $C$ the number of consols paying a coupon of £1, $p_c$ the price of a consol, and $p$ the general price level.

Let $\delta_K$ be the capital rental rate, $\delta_R$ the return on a share of public sector natural resource property rights, $g$ government consumption, $\tau$ current taxes net of transfers, $i$ the short nominal interest rate and $r$ the short real rate. Then, assuming that $r(t) = i(t) - [\dot{p}(t, t)/p(t)]$,

$$p_K(t) = \int_t^{\infty} \delta_K(s,t) \exp[-\textstyle\int_t^s r(u,s)\, du]\, ds \tag{39a}$$

$$p_R(t) = \int_t^{\infty} \delta_R(s,t) \exp[-\textstyle\int_t^s r(u,s)\, du]\, ds. \tag{39b}$$

$$T(t) = \int_t^{\infty} \tau(s,t) \exp[-\textstyle\int_t^s r(u,s)\, du] \tag{39c}$$

$$\pi(t) = \frac{1}{p(t)} \int_t^{\infty} i(s,t)\, M(s,t) \exp[-\textstyle\int_t^s i(u,s)\, du]$$

$$ds = \int_t^{\infty} r(s,t) \frac{M(s,t)}{p(s,t)} \exp[-\textstyle\int_t^s r(u,t)\, du]\, ds \tag{39d}$$

$$p_c(t) = \int_t^{\infty} \exp[-\textstyle\int_t^s i(u,s)\, du]\, ds. \tag{39e}$$

Note that the capital value of the note issue monopoly, $\Pi$, is given by the discounted future income derived from the assets that are (and will be) held to 'back' the note circulation. Equalization of expected rates of return is assumed.

Since the present value of future planned public consumption cannot exceed public sector net worth (a constraint we shall assume to hold with strict equality), we have

$$G(t) = N(t), \tag{40}$$

where

$$G(t) = \int_t^{\infty} g(s,t) \exp[-\textstyle\int_t^s r(u,t)\, du]\, ds. \tag{40'}$$

Let

$$S(T) \equiv \pi(t) - \frac{M(t)}{p(t)}.$$

Integrating by parts, it is found that $S(t)$ is the present value of future seigniorage, i.e.

$$S(t) \equiv \frac{1}{p(t)} \int_t^{\infty} \dot{M}(s,t) \exp[-\textstyle\int_t^s i(u,t)\, du]$$

$$ds \equiv \int_t^{\infty} \frac{\dot{M}(s,t)}{M(s,t)} \frac{M(s,t)}{p(s,t)} \exp[-\textstyle\int_t^s r(u,t)\, du]\, ds. \tag{41}$$

Treating $S(t)$ as the residual item, (40) and (38) tell us the amount of revenue to be raised through seigniorage (in present-value terms), given the present value of the government's consumption program and the government's tangible and intangible non-monetary assets and liabilities, i.e.

$$S(t) = G(t) - \left[p_K(t)K(t) + p_R(t)R(t) + T(t) - \left(\frac{B(t) + p_c(t)C(t)}{p(t)}\right)\right]. \tag{42}$$

Let $y$ denote trend output and $n$ its rate of growth. A real (index-linked) consol will have a coupon yield $\bar{R}$ if the instantaneous real rate of return is $r - n$, where $\bar{R}$ is given by

$$\bar{R}(t) = \left\{\int_t^{\infty} e^{-\int_t^s [r(u,t)-n]du} ds\right\}^{-1}$$

We can solve (42) for a constant proportional rate of monetary growth $\dot{M}/M$ and a constant trend income velocity of circulation $V \equiv py/M$ to yield

$$\frac{\dot{M}}{M} = V\bar{R}(t)\left[\frac{G(t) - T(t)}{y(t)} - \frac{p_K(t)K(t) + p_R(t)R(t)}{y(t)} + \frac{B(t) + p_c(t)C(t)}{p(t)y(t)}\right] \tag{43}$$

If (and only if) the public sector consumption and tax programs together with its other non-monetary assets and liabilities, imply a high value of $\dot{M}/M$, then a fiscal correction is a necessary condition for achieving credibility for an anti-inflationary policy. Note that in full steady-state equilibrium, (43) becomes the familiar expression

$$\frac{\dot{M}}{M} = V\left[\frac{g-\tau}{y} - (r-n)\left(\frac{p_{\mathrm{K}}K + p_{\mathrm{R}}R}{y} - \frac{B + p_{\mathrm{c}}C}{py}\right)\right].$$

Eventual monetary growth is governed in steady state by the trend public sector current account (or consumption account) deficit, with debt service evaluated at the real interest rate net of the natural rate of growth. This deficit measure can differ dramatically from the conventionally measured public sector financial deficit (PSBR), which is often and erroneously taken as a guide to eventual monetization.

## III CONCLUSION

One conclusion that emerges strongly from this chapter is the importance of fiscal policy in securing a lasting reduction in inflation at least cost. First, the long-run reduction in monetary growth that is necessary for a sustained reduction in inflation is credible only if it is consistent with the government's spending and tax programs and its outstanding non-monetary assets and liabilities. Second, indirect tax cuts (and, under certain conditions, direct tax cuts) can be used in ways first suggested by Okun (1978) to secure a painless melting away of core inflation. Tax cuts or a once-and-for-all increase in the level of the nominal money stock path must also be used in order to provide the higher stock of real money balances demanded when the inflation rate is lower at a given price level rather than through a further downward shift in the price-level path.

A final comment suggested by the analysis of the chapter relates to the apparent contrast between the findings of R. J. Gordon, who has documented many historical episodes during which bringing down inflation appears to have been costly (Gordon, 1982), and T. S. Sargent, who finds that the ends of four hyper-inflations in the post-World War I era were achieved without dramatic output losses (Sargent, 1982). These findings can be reconciled by arguing that, during hyper-inflations, inflation inertia (if not price-level inertia) disappears. All the advantages of longer-term non-contingent nominal contracts are overriden by the need to revise prices almost continuously. During hyper-inflations (at any rate in their final phases) the inflation process is characterized by models like the ones in equations (8), (9) and (10a,b) or even by the purely classical flexible price model.

If there is no inflation inertia but still some price-level inertia, optimal anti-inflationary policy has the following features. First, a credible announcement of current and future reductions in monetary growth. This was provided by fiscal reform and currency reform plus the general realization that something had to be done and was going to be done to stop the hyper-inflations. Second, a once-and-for-all increase in the level of the nominal money stock to raise the stock of real money balances without any need to lower the price-level path. The real world counterpart to this was the very large increases in the nominal money stocks in the periods following the sudden ending of the hyper-inflations (Sargent, 1982). Such money stock jumps make no sense in a flexible price model[17] but may be called for in models with price-level inertia.

Gordon (1982) considered episodes of moderate inflation. Long-term non-contingent nominal contracts are adopted because they permit economic agents to economize on frequent, costly renegotiations, on the search and information costs of first identifying all possible relevant contingencies and then monitoring them and on the costs of enforcing complicated conditional contract clauses. Continuously variable and perfectly flexible prices or fully contingent contracts are costly and undesirable when the benefits from changing prices frequently outweigh the costs. In moderate inflations, long-term nominal contracts are still viewed as viable and desirable by private agents. Such changes in the length of these contracts and in other relevant characteristics as one would expect to occur when the trend rate of inflation changes are likely to be second-order for the range of inflation rates experienced in most OECD countries since World War II. With the unconditional long-term nominal contract structure intact, even fully credible announcements of future reductions in monetary growth will not remove the need for a period of (expected) output losses and unemployment if inflation is to be brought down.

## NOTES

1 An elegant statement and extension of the traditional theory of the welfare costs of inflation is Fischer (1981b).

2 This assumes that lump-sum taxes are available to the government. If higher monetary growth and the associated higher inflation increase the real value of new money issues (if the elasticity of demand for real money balances with respect to the interest rate is less than unity), the same real public spending program can be financed with lower explicit taxes. If these taxes are distortionary, the usual welfare loss measure overstates the true cost.

3 The most careful and informative work in this area has been done by Fischer (1981a,b; 1982). See also Taylor (1981).

4 $v(\bar{c}, L - l, 1) > v(\bar{c}, L, 0)$ for any $l$ $(0 \leq l \leq L)$ would mean that, even without any pecuniary advantage of employment over unemployment, people would choose to be employed. It is a much stronger condition than the one given in the text.

5 Separability, i.e. $v(c, L - l, \theta) = v[u(c, L - l), \theta]$, would be convenient analytically.

6 See also Buiter and Jewitt (1981).

7 The natural rate of growth is assumed equal to zero.

8 Actual and expected $\bar{y}$ and $\bar{f}$ are again held constant.

9 In the long run,

$$r = \left(\frac{-1 + \lambda^{-1}k\lambda\varepsilon}{\gamma + \lambda\varepsilon}\right)\bar{y} + \frac{\eta}{\gamma + \lambda\varepsilon}\bar{f} + \frac{\gamma}{\gamma + \lambda\varepsilon}\bar{\bar{\mu}}.$$

10 When both $\gamma$ and $\varepsilon$ are equal to zero, a reduction in monetary growth and inflation leaves the nominal interest rate unaffected and costless disinflation is automatic.

11 Note that, since $m$ and $f$ are manipulated to keep output at its full employment level, the Barro–Grossman equation (8) and the Mussa equation (9) coincide.

12 It is assumed that there is no long-run trend in the rate of inflation.

13 Note that the characteristic roots of the homogeneous system (16a,b) are 0 and $\xi_2 - \xi_1$.

14 For any variable $x$, let $x(\bar{t}) \equiv \lim_{\substack{h \to 0 \\ h > 0}} x(t - h)$.

15 This is very similar in spirit to John Flemming's suggestion in Flemming (1976).

16 Hysteresis is the property of dynamic systems that the stationary equilibrium is a function of the initial conditions and/or the transition trajectory towards the steady state. In systems of linear differential equations with constant coefficients such as $Dx = Ax + Bz$, hysteresis is present when $A$ has one or more zero eigenvalues.

17 Except for government revenue reasons. We owe this point to Bob Flood.

## BIBLIOGRAPHY


Barro, R. J. and Grossman, H. I. (1976), *Money, Employment and Inflation*, Cambridge, Cambridge University Press.

Buiter, W. H. (1980), 'Monetary, financial and fiscal policy under rational expectations', *IMF Staff Papers*, 27, December, 758–813.

Buiter, W. H. (1981), 'The superiority of contingent rules over fixed rules in models with rational expectations', *Economic Journal*, 91, September, 647–670.

Buiter, W. H. (1983a), 'The measurement of public sector deficits and its implications for policy evaluation and design', *IMF Staff Papers*, 30(2), June, 306, 349.

Buiter, W. H. (1983b), 'Optimal and time-consistent policies in continuous time rational expectations models', LSE Econometrics Program, *Discussion Paper No. A 39*, June.

Buiter, W. H. (1983c), 'Saddlepoint problems in continuous time rational expectations models: a general method and some macroeconomic examples', revised, March. Published in *Econometrica*, 52(3), May 1984, 665–680.

Buiter, W. H. and Gersovitz, M. (1981), 'Issues in controllability and the theory of economic policy', *Journal of Public Economics*, 15, February, 33–43.

Buiter, W. H. and Jewitt, Ian (1981), 'Staggered wage setting with real wage relativities: variations of a theme of Taylor', *Manchester School of Economic and Social Studies*, 49(3), September, 211–228.

Buiter, W. H. and Miller, Marcus (1981), Monetary policy and international competitiveness', *Oxford Economic Papers*, 33, July, Supplement, 143–174.

Buiter, W. H. and Miller, Marcus (1982), 'Real exchange rate overshooting and the output cost of bringing down inflation', *European Economic Review*, 18, May/June, 85–123.

Buiter, W. H. and Miller, Marcus (1983), 'Real exchange rate overshooting and the output cost of bringing down inflation; some further results', in J. Frenkel (ed.), *Exchange Rates and International Macroeconomics*, Chicago, Ill., University of Chicago Press.

Calvo, G. A. (1982a), 'Staggered contracts and exchange rate policy', *Discussion Paper Series No. 129*, New York, Columbia University.

Calvo, G. A. (1982b), 'Staggered contracts in a utility-maximizing framework', *Discussion Paper Series No. 130*, New York, Columbia University.

Calvo, G. A. (1982c), 'Real exchange rate dynamics with fixed nominal parities: on the economics of overshooting and interest-rate management with rational price setting', *Discussion Paper Series No. 162*, New York, Columbia University.

Carlton, Dennis W. (1982), 'The disruptive effect of inflation on the organization of markets', in Robert E. Hall (ed.), *Inflation: Causes and Effects*, Chicago, Ill., University of Chicago Press, 139–152.

Dornbusch, R. (1976), 'Expectations and exchange rate dynamics', *Journal of Political Economy*, 84, December, 1161–1176.

Feldstein, Martin S. (1979), 'The welfare cost of permanent inflation and optimal short-run economic policy', *Journal of Political Economy*, 87(4), August, 749–768.

Fischer, Stanley (1981a), 'Relative shocks, relative price variability and inflation', *Brookings Papers on Economic Activity*, 2, 381–431.

Fischer, Stanley (1981b), 'Towards an understanding of the costs of inflation: II', in K. Brunner and A. H. Meltzer (eds), *The Costs and Consequences of Inflation*, Carnegie–Rochester Conference Series on Public Policy, 15, Amsterdam, North-Holland, 5–42.

Fischer, Stanley (1982), 'Relative price variability and inflation in the United States and Germany', *European Economic Review*, 18, May/June, 171–196.

Fischer, Stanley and Modigliani, Franco (1978), 'Towards an understanding of the real effects and costs of inflation', *Weltwirtschaftliches Archiv*, 114, 810–833.

Flemming, John (1976), *Inflation*, London, Oxford University Press.

Gordon, Robert J. (1973), 'The welfare costs of higher unemployment', *Brookings Papers on Economic Activity*, 1, 133–205.

Gordon, Robert J. (1982), 'Why stopping inflation may be costly: evidence for fourteen historical episodes', in R. E. Hall (ed.), *Inflation, Causes and Effects*, Chicago, Ill., University of Chicago Press, 11–40.

Gregory, R. G. (1982), 'Work and welfare in the years ahead', *Australian Economic Papers*, 21, December, 219–243.

Gregory, R. G. (1983), 'The slide into mass unemployment; labour market theories, facts and policies', *Annual Lectures*, The Academy of the Social Sciences, Australia.

Gregory, R. G. and Smith, R. E. (1983), 'Unemployment, inflation and job creation policies in Australia', unpublished.

Hall, Robert E. (1976), 'The Phillips curve and macroeconomic policy', in K. Brunner and A. H. Meltzer (eds), *The Phillips Curve and Labor Markets*, Carnegie–Rochester Conference Series on Public Policy, 1, Amsterdam, North-Holland, 127–148.

Hall, R. E. (1981), 'Comment' on S. Fischer 'Relative shocks, relative price variability, and inflation', *Brookings Papers on Economic Activity*, 2, 432–434.

Hargreaves Heap, S. P. (1980), 'Choosing the wrong "natural" rate: accelerating inflation or decelerating employment and growth', *Economic Journal*, 90, September, 611–620.

Kydland, F. and Prescott, E. (1977), 'Rules rather than discretion: the time-inconsistency of optimal plans', *Journal of Political Economy*, 85(3), June, 473–491.

Lipsey, R. G. (1960), 'The relationship between unemployment and the rate of change of money wages in the United Kingdom, 1862–1957: A further analysis', *Economica*, 27(105), February, 1–31.

Miller, Marcus (1979), 'The unemployment cost of changing steady state inflation', mimeo, University of Warwick.

Mussa, M. (1981), 'Sticky prices and disequilibrium adjustment in a rational model of the inflationary process', *American Economic Review*, 71, December, 1020–1027.

Obstfeld, M. and Rogoff, K. (1982), 'Exchange rate dynamics with sluggish prices under alternative price-adjustment rules', unpublished, May.

Okun, A. (1978), 'Efficient disinflationary policies', *American Economic Review*, 68, May, 348–352.

Phelps, E. S. (1972), *Inflation Policy and Unemployment Theory: The Cost Benefits Approach to Monetary Planning*, New York, Norton.

Phillips, A. W. (1958), 'The relation between unemployment and the rate of change of money wage rates in the United Kingdom, 1861–1957', *Economica*, 25(100), November, 283–299.

Sargan, J. D. (1980), 'A model of wage–price inflation', *Review of Economic Studies*, 47, January, 97–112.

Sargent, Thomas S. (1982), 'The ends of four big inflations', in R. E. Hall (ed.), *Inflation, Causes and Effects*, Chicago, Ill., University of Chicago Press, 41–97.

Taylor, J. B. (1980), 'Aggregate dynamics and staggered contracts', *Journal of Political Economy*, 88(1), February, 1–23.

Taylor, John B. (1981), 'On the relation between the variability of inflation and the average inflation rate', in K. Brunner and A. H. Meltzer (eds.), *The Costs and Consequences of Inflation*, Carnegie–Rochester Conference Series on Public Policy, 15, Amsterdam, North-Holland, 57–68.

Tobin, J. (1980), 'Stabilization policy ten years after', *Brookings Paper on Economic Activity*, 1, 19–71.

Turnovsky, S. J. (1980), 'The choice of monetary instruments under alternative forms of price expectations', *Manchester School of Economic and Social Studies*, 48(1), March, 39–62.

Weiss, L. (1980), 'The role for active monetary policy in a rational expectations model', *Journal of Political Economy*, 88(2), April, 221–233.

# 3 Contracts, Credibility and Disinflation

*STANLEY FISCHER**

Predictions of the costs of disinflation made in the few years preceding the recent recession and disinflation ranged from the pessimism of Arthur Okun's (1978) summary of six Brookings papers relating to the United States that 'the cost of a 1 point reduction in the basic inflation rate is 10 percent of a year's GNP, with a range of 6 per cent to 18 per cent' (p. 348) to the carefully hedged optimism of Thomas Sargent (1981) that 'under the proper hypothetical conditions, a government could eliminate inflation very rapidly and with virtually no "Phillips curve" costs in terms of forgone real output or increased unemployment' (p. 4).

The difference between the two forecasts reflects Sargent's emphasis on the credibility of policy as the key determinant of the flexibility of wages and prices, and the lesser emphasis placed on expectations by the researchers quoted by Okun.[1] Once long-term nominal contracts are taken into account, however, credibility of policy is not enough for rapid disinflation. John Taylor (1983) concludes that, given the structure of labor contracts in the United States, it would take four years to disinflate from a rate of wage increase of 10 per cent per year to 3 per cent without creating unemployment, even if there were no doubts about the continuance of disinflationary policy.

In this chapter I first describe the contracting approach to the problem of disinflation and discuss criticisms of the approach and characteristics of contracts that affect the possible speed of disinflation. In Section II, I calculate the sacrifice ratio – the percentage points of GNP lost per 1 per cent reduction in the inflation rate – for alternative policies and parameter values. Section III examines the problem of the credibility of policy intentions, and the effects of a lack of belief that a policy will be maintained; Section IV briefly describes alternative policies for disinflation. In Section V, I compare the costs of disinflation in the United States from 1979 to 1986 with predictions of those costs.

## I A CONTRACTING MODEL

In this section I set out a simple model, which combines elements of the Taylor (1980) and Fischer (1977a) approaches to the modeling of labor contracts in

* I am indebted to Katherine Abraham, Otto Eckstein and James Medoff for useful discussions; Oliver Blanchard, Rudi Dornbusch, Mervyn King, Julio Rotemberg and Jeff Sachs for comments; David Wilcox for research assistance; and the National Science Foundation for financial support.

macroeconomic models. The model attributes the existence of wage and price stickiness, and thus the difficulties of disinflation, to the existence of long-term contracts. Labor contracts, agreed upon at different dates in the past, specify the nominal wage to be paid in period $t$ to workers under each contract. The price level increases with the average nominal wage. The level of output is determined by aggregate demand.

The aggregate demand function is:

$$y_t = m_t - p_t + v_t. \tag{1}$$

Here $y$ is the level of output, $m$ the nominal money stock, $p$ the price level, and $v$ a disturbance term, for instance a shift of the demand for money function. Lower case letters denote logarithms. From the viewpoint of the analysis of disinflation, the major simplifications in this equation are, first, the omission of interest rates, and thus expectations of inflation, as determinants of aggregate demand, and, second, the omission of fiscal variables and the exchange rate. [2] The price level is related to the average wage:

$$p_t = \bar{w}_t + u_t. \tag{2}$$

Here $\bar{w}_t$ is the average wage and $u$ is the percentage excess of the price level over the wage. The formulation is sufficiently general that $u$ can be thought of as a supply shock, or could be systematically related to the behavior of any of the other variables in the model, such as the level of output. The price equation is that used by Taylor (1980).[3]

In any period, the proportion $\theta_j$ ($j = 1, \ldots, J$) of the work force is being paid a wage that was agreed upon $j$ periods back. Thus the average wage is

$$\bar{w}_t = \sum_1^J \theta_{j\,t-j}w_t, \tag{3}$$

where ${}_{t-j}w_t$ is the wage that was agreed to for period $t$ in period $(t-j)$. It is assumed that the wage specified for period $t$ in period $(t-j)$ is the same for all contracts, of whatever duration.[4]

The relationship between the proportion of contracts of length $k$, defined as $\eta_k$, and the weights $\theta_j$ in the expression for the average wage is:

$$\theta_j = \sum_{k=j}^J \frac{\eta_k}{k} \tag{4}$$

where it is assumed that the distribution of signing dates of contracts of a given length is uniform.

The wage set in period $(t-j)$ for period $t$ is assumed to be:

$${}_{t-j}w_t = (1-\mu)[\lambda_{t-j}p_t + (1-\lambda)_{t-1}p_t + h_{t-j}y_t + q_{t-j}u_t] + \mu_{t-j}\bar{w}_t. \tag{5}$$

The notation ${}_{t-j}p_t$ means the expectation formed at time $(t-j)$ of $p_t$, and similarly for other variables except $w_t$. The wage-setting equation assumes that the real wage responds to the expected level of output, with coefficient $h$ representing the sensitivity of the real wage to output; the real wage is also permitted to respond to expectations of the variable $u_t$, with $q$ representing the sensitivity of the real wage to a supply shock, thereby providing an interpretation of equation (5) as asserting that the (logarithm of the) expected real wage is set equal to its expected equilibrium value.

The coefficient $\mu$ represents the extent to which contracts are based on the relative wage rather than on the real wage. The larger is $\mu$, the less the weight of the fundamental factors – the price level, the level of output and $u$ – in determining the nominal wage, and the greater the weight of the average wage. The notion that workers are concerned with the relative wage does not necessarily reflect irrationality or envy, but may result rather from a sophisticated understanding of a labor market in which there are costs to mobility: if the wage diverges far from the average, there are incentives for one side or the other in the labor contract to initiate a separation.

The coefficient $\lambda$ is a measure of the extent of price indexation of contracts. When $\lambda$ is equal to unity, there is no price indexation, and contracts are fully nominal. When $\lambda$ is equal to zero, the nominal wage to be paid in period $t$ is determined at the end of period $(t - 1)$, on all contracts of whatever length. It is important to note that wage indexation here adjusts the nominal wage to the *expected* price level rather than for past changes in prices. Indexation in practice tends rather to adjust nominal wages for past inflation. The nominal wage is indexed only for changes in the expected price level that have occurred since the signing of the contract – there is no adjustment for other unforeseen contingencies that have taken place since period $(t - j)$.

## CRITICISMS OF THE CONTRACTING APPROACH

Before using this model to examine disinflation, I briefly discuss criticisms of the labor-contracting model (e.g. Barro, 1977). The basic criticism is that labor contracts that specify a wage rate without also specifying a rule for the efficient determination of output are incomplete. In this context, an efficient level of output is one at which the marginal value product of labor is equal to the shadow marginal value of leisure (Hall and Lilien, 1979). Taking this argument further, it is sometimes asserted that the wage need play no allocative role in contracting models, serving merely to determine the transfer payments made by firms to their workers (Hall, 1980).

There is no question that the type of labor contracts assumed in this paper leads to inefficient allocations of resources in the face of disturbances not taken into account when the contracts were entered into. Such inefficient allocations are precisely the central problem of macroeconomics; they have alternatively been explained as resulting from incomplete information. I have little to add to my (1977c) response to Barro on the issue. The essential point is that a careful examination of actual labor contracts in the United States suggests that they are of the form assumed in this chapter: the contracts specify the wage and leave output to be determined by the firm. The omission of explicit conditions for output determination is not a casual matter that can be glossed over by reference to implicit contracts, for a remarkable feature of labor contracts is their very detailed specifications about many aspects of the job, including for instance the order of layoffs by seniority. It is reasonable to embody relevant characteristics of the wage-setting process of the economy in models used to study price and output determination – and indeed it seems to be essential to understanding the process of disinflation.

At the same time, the Barro critique does point to the need for a theory to explain the existing form of labor contracts. There has been significant microeconomic research in this area (for summaries of the literature, see Azariadis and Stiglitz, 1983, and Hart, 1983) examining the effects of differential risk aversion and differential information between firms and workers on the optimal form of contract. In some of these contracts, it is optimal for the firm to determine the level of output. The research to date has not examined reasons for specification of wages in nominal rather than real terms, and thus omits the most important link between contracting and price behavior. It is likely that the costs of complexity in contracts, and differences in price indexes relevant to different economic agents, will play a key role in the explanation of nominal contracting.

A second criticism of the contracting approach as applied to the United States is that it exaggerates the role of unions and formal contracts in the labor market.[5] It is argued that it is misleading to base a theory on long-term labor contracts when less than 25 per cent of the labor force is unionized, and when some of the unionized labor force works on one-year contracts.[6]

If one includes professional associations, or white-collar unions, about 28 per cent, rather than less than 25 per cent, of the labor force is unionized. More significantly, about 50 per cent of the labor force works in establishments in which some workers belong to unions.[7] Presumably the wages received by the unionized workers in such establishments influence the wages received by the remaining workers. Further, there are large firms that are entirely non-unionized and whose devotion to remaining that way leads them to provide wage and benefit packages that on balance match those obtained by unionized workers. The *a priori* case for building a theory on the characteristics of observed labor contracts is stronger if we assume that more than 50 per cent of the labor force, rather than less than 25 per cent, is closely affected by the terms of union contracts.

Empirical research on the relationship between union and non-union wages in the United States, much of it surveyed by Mitchell (1982), has been inconclusive. Early findings by Flanagan (1976) and Johnson (1977) that non-union wages cause (in the Granger sense) union wages have been shown by Mitchell (1980a) and Vroman (1980) to be sensitive to the data samples used.

A third criticism of the labor-contracting model notes that labor contracts typically include reopening clauses, and therefore argues that changes in policy can potentially operate much more rapidly than the contracting model implies. It is indeed correct that contracts can be, and sometimes are, reopened. Mitchell (1982) examines concessions in union contracts during the recent recession, including twenty-six renegotiations of existing contracts (mostly in industries affected by international competition or deregulation). Less than 2 million workers were covered by the contracts on which there were concessions, as defined by Mitchell, and most contracts were not reopened. The infrequency of renegotiation confirms the suggestion from the existing form of US labor contracts that there are major costs to the negotiating process.

A related criticism of the contracting approach notes that the form of contracts responds to changes in economic policy regimes.[8] This is undoubtedly true and probably provides a good test for detecting a change in policy regime. There is no general way of handling the problem of the potential endogeneity of elements that are taken as structural, beyond examining the reasons for and the likely effects on the conclusions reached of induced changes in the model.

There is no denying the logic of the criticisms of the labor-contracting model discussed above. They point to potential theoretical and empirical problems with using the model. The significance of those problems for the particular conclusions reached using the contracting model has to be evaluated in each case, and, at the extremes, could produce results that are equivalent to those that would obtain if wages were continually readjusted as in a spot market. But there is no reason to think that the extreme versions apply in fact, and therefore the criticisms do not imply that the contracting approach should be abandoned.

## SOLVING THE MODEL

We return now to the model. Expectations are assumed to be rational, in the sense that expectations of prices and output are based on the structure of the model.[9] A solution for the price level and output is obtained for arbitrary paths of the money stock and disturbances.[10]

Substituting (5) into (3) and (2), and using (1) to substitute for $y_t$, we obtain the price-level equation:

$$p_t = \sum_{j=1}^{J} \theta_j \{[1-\mu)(\lambda - h) + \mu]_{t-j}p_t + (1-\mu)(1-\lambda)_{t-1}p_t$$

$$+ (1-\mu)h_{t-j}[m_t + v_t] + [(1-\mu)q - \mu]_{t-j}u_t\} + u_t. \tag{6}$$

Since the velocity shock, $v_t$, always enters additively with $m_t$, it will be dropped and $m_t$ should henceforth be understood to represent the sum $(m_t + v_t)$.

The rational expectations solution for the price level is:

$$p_t = {}_{t-J}m_t + (1 + q - h)\frac{{}_{t-J}u_t}{h} + \sum_{i=1}^{J-1} c_i x_i + \sum_{i=1}^{J-1} \gamma_i z_i + u_t$$

$$= {}_{t-J}m_t + (1 + q)\frac{{}_{t-J}u_t}{h} + \sum_{1}^{J-1} c_i x_i + \sum_{1}^{J-1} \gamma_i z_i + (u_t - {}_{t-J}u_t) \tag{7}$$

where

$$x_i = {}_{t-J+i}m_t - {}_{t-J+i-1}m_t$$

$$z_i = {}_{t-J+i}u_t - {}_{t-J+i-1}u_t$$

$$c_i = \frac{h(1-\mu)b_{J-i}}{D_i}$$

$$\gamma_i = \frac{[q(1-\mu)-\mu]b_{J-i}}{D_i}$$

$$b_{J-i} = \sum_{j=1}^{J-i} \theta_j$$

$$D_i = b_{J-i}(1-\mu)h + (1-b_{J-i})[(1-\mu)\lambda + \mu].$$

The level of output can be deduced from the aggregate demand equation (1).

The solution for the price level is based on expectations of the money stock and of $u$ formed at time $(t-J)$, and updated by innovations in expectations of $m_t$ and $u_t$ occurring in subsequent periods.[11]

To understand the solution for the price level, I first consider the equilibrium levels of output and prices when there are no surprises. In that case, the innovations $x_i$ and $z_i$ in (7) are zero, and

$$p_t = m_t + \frac{(1+q)u_t}{h}. \tag{8}$$

From (5), noting that $\Sigma_1^J \theta_j = 1$, we have

$$\bar{w}_t - p_t = hy_t + qu_t, \tag{9}$$

so that the real wage is determined solely by the level of output and the supply shock ($q$ may be negative). Substituting (9) into (2), we obtain

$$y_t = \frac{-(1+q)u_t}{h}. \tag{10}$$

The (logarithm of the) level of output is zero when the supply shock is zero. The supply shock reduces the level of output, to an extent that depends on $q$, the sensitivity of the real wage to the shock, and $h$, the sensitivity of the wage to output. Returning to equation (8), we see that the price level is proportional to the money stock, with a factor of proportionality $[(1+q)u_t]/h$ that depends on the supply shock.[12]

Any fully believed change in the money stock, expected at least $J$ periods before it occurs, has *no* effect on output and has its full effects on the price level. Thus an implication of the structure of contracts in this model is that a monetary change announced and believed far enough in advance will be fully neutral.[13]

The coefficients $c_i$ in (7) determine the dynamics of prices and output during a disinflation. Before examining the properties of the $c_i$, I indicate the way the $c_i$ should behave. First, the longer the time a change in the money stock has been expected, the larger the effect of that change on the price level and the smaller the effect on output. Accordingly we should have

$$c_i > c_{i+1}.$$

We also expect that price indexation should increase the responsiveness of the price level to monetary changes, that a concern over relative wages will lessen that responsiveness, and that the response of prices to monetary shocks will be larger the steeper the Phillips curve (the larger $h$). Thus we should find

$$\frac{\partial c_i}{\partial \lambda} > 0, \quad \frac{\partial c_i}{\partial \mu} < 0, \quad \frac{\partial c_i}{\partial h} > 0.$$

Since $b_{J-i}$ is decreasing in $i$, we can discover whether $c_i > c_{i+1}$ by checking whether $\partial c_i/\partial b$ is positive. Writing

$$c_i = \frac{1}{\{1 + (1 - b_{J-i})[(1-\mu)\lambda + \mu]/h(1-\mu)b_{J-i}\}} \tag{11}$$

it is clear that $c_i > c_{i+1}$. It is similarly clear from inspection of (11) that increases in both $\lambda$ and $h$ increases the sensitivity of the price level to monetary innovations and therefore reduce the sensitivity of output to innovations. Rewriting $(1-\mu)\lambda + \mu$ as $\mu(1-\lambda) + \lambda$, it can also be confirmed that $\partial c_i/\partial \mu < 0$. Thus a concern over relative, rather than real, wages reduces the responsiveness of the price level to monetary shocks.

In the extreme case in which indexation is complete ($\lambda = 0$) and there is no concern over relative wages ($\mu = 0$), we find

$$c_i \equiv 1. \tag{12}$$

In this case, monetary innovations are completely reflected in prices and not at all in output. This is obviously because the contract terms are able to adjust fully to purely nominal disturbances so long as they occur in any period before $t$. From the viewpoint of the response to nominal disturbances, indexation is completely equivalent to the use of one-period contracts. However, this result disappears if $\mu \neq 0$, that is, if wages are based in part on the average wage. In this case it is assumed in (5) that the nominal wage is partly predetermined, based on the expectation ${}_{t-j}\bar{w}_t$.

Figure 3.1 presents a smoothed version of the typical responses of output and

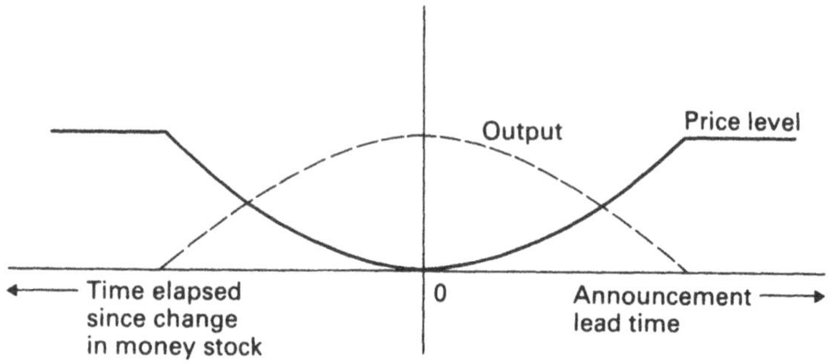


**Figure 3.1** Price-level and output responses to a permanent change in the money stock

prices to changes in the money stock. The right-hand side of the diagram shows the responses of prices and output in the period the money stock changes to a preannounced change in the money stock as a function of the announcement lead time. The left-hand side shows the responses of prices and output to an unanticipated change in the money stock, as a function of the length of time since the change occurred.

EXAMPLES

To provide some intuition for the implied price- and output-level responses, I present several examples.

(a) Assume that all contracts last three periods (years). In this case $\theta_1 = \theta_2 = \theta_3 = 1/3$. Assume further that $\mu = 0$, $\lambda = 1$ (no indexing), and $h = .2$. Then:

$$c_1 = 2/7 = .29$$

$$c_2 = 1/11 = .09.$$

With this set of parameters, changes in the money supply have very little effect on prices until all contracts have been renegotiated. The main reason is that only the one-third of the contracts come up for renewal each year. In addition, until all contracts have been renegotiated, it is the coefficient $h$ that primarily determines the response of prices to the monetary stock.

(b) Suppose that we have the same parameters except that $h = .5$. This means that a 1 per cent shortfall in real output reduces the real wage by $\frac{1}{2}$ per cent. Then:

$$c_1 = .50$$

$$c_2 = .20.$$

Thus, within the period during which existing contracts remain outstanding, the slope of the Phillips curve ($h$) has a substantial impact on price and output responses to monetary disturbances.

(c) We now allow for the role of relative wages in contracts, by setting $\mu = \frac{1}{2}$. We maintain $h = .5$.

$$c_1 = .33$$

$$c_2 = .11.$$

Relative wage concerns in contracts thus slow down the response of prices to monetary policy.

(d) Indexation speeds up responses. Setting $\mu$ back to zero and with $h = .5$ (so that (b) is the baseline case); and assuming $\lambda = .5$ (instead of 1):

$$c_1 = .67$$

$$c_2 = .33.$$

(e) Next consider the effects of assuming that one-third of all contracts are for one year, one-third for two years, and one-third for three years. Thus:

$$\theta_1 = 11/18 \qquad \theta_2 = 5/18 \qquad \theta_3 = 1/9.$$

With such a structure of contracts, the economy should react much faster to monetary changes. Assuming $\lambda = 1$, $h = .5$, $\mu = 0$, we obtain:

$$c_1 = .80$$

$$c_2 = .44.$$

The responses are much more rapid in this case. Nearly half the response is completed in the first period (since 61 per cent of the labor force signs new contracts each year, this is not surprising) and 80 per cent within two years.

## II DISINFLATION

Suppose now that the government wishes to disinflate. The money stock and thus the price level have been growing at the rate $g$, implying that $m$ and $p$ have each been increasing by amount $g$ from period to period. The new target rate of inflation is $(g - .01)$. The government will announce and implement a growth rate of the money stock equal to $(g - .01)$. In this section I assume that the announcement is completely and immediately believed by private agents.

As noted earlier, if the change in monetary policy is announced at least $J$ periods (for example, three years) ahead, it will have no real effects. By the same token, however, it will also have no nominal effects until it goes into operation.[14] Thus, in this model, adjustment to a disinflation program that is announced sufficiently far ahead is abrupt. There is no effect on inflation until the date monetary policy actually changes; on that date the rate of inflation adjusts completely to the change in policy, and there is no effect on output.

It might thus seem that a disinflation program would have no real costs if only it were announced long enough in advance. However, the delay in implementation means that the existing inflation rate is maintained until policy is changed. If there were no costs to the high rate of inflation, there would be no call for the disinflation program. Accordingly, the strategy of delaying a change in monetary policy should be recognized as involving the trade-off of continued inflation at the original rate for $J$ periods for the avoidance of unemployment. Alternative strategies that incur the costs of unemployment can result in more rapid disinflation.

At the opposite pole from the policy announced $J$ periods in advance is a monetary policy change implemented without warning. Assume that the growth rate of money is reduced in the current period by 1 per cent, and that the lower growth rate is maintained in perpetuity. Assume also that expectations of policy adjust simultaneously with the policy change. With policy changing in period $t$, the effects on the inflation rate and output in subsequent periods are given by:

$$\Delta(p_{t+i} - p_{t+i-1}) = c_{J-i} + i(c_{J-i} - c_{J-i-1}) \qquad i = 1, \ldots, J;\ c_J \equiv 0. \qquad (12)$$

$$\Delta y_{t+i} = \Delta m_{t+i} - \Delta p_{t+i}. \qquad (13)$$

The adjustment is complete after $J$ periods.

## EXAMPLES

Suppose that all contracts last for three years, but wages are readjusted every six months. Then $\theta_i = 1/6, i = 1, \ldots, 6$. Table 3.1 shows, in examples A–C, the effects on inflation (at an annual rate, period over period) and on output of a reduction in the growth rate of money by 1 per cent per year ($\frac{1}{2}$ per cent per period), under alternative assumptions about indexation and the role of the relative wage in wage determination.

The basic pattern is the same in cases A–C. There is very little effect on the inflation rate to begin with, and there is at the end of the adjustment period a very low rate of inflation. The rate of inflation falls throughout the adjustment period. This characteristic is, however, a result of the assumption that all contracts are for three years. Example D in Table 3.1 shows the disinflation path when one-third of the contracts are for one, two and three years, respectively, with the wage being adjusted every six months. In this case the disinflation is much more rapid and the inflation rate does not behave monotonically. It remains true in example D that the largest reduction in the inflation rate occurs in period $J$, but that too is a result of the structure of contracts.

The last column of Table 3.1 shows the sacrifice ratio implied by this model to reduce the inflation rate by 1 per cent, through the policy of reducing the growth rate of the money stock immediately to its new steady state level. The

**Table 3.1** *Disinflationary effects of a reduction in the growth rate of money*

| $\theta_i = 1/6, i = 1, \ldots, 6, h = 0.5$ | | *Period* | | | | | | | | *Sacrifice ratio* |
|---|---|---|---|---|---|---|---|---|---|---|
| (A) | | 0 | 1 | 2 | 3 | 4 | 5 | 6 | 7 | |
| $\mu = 0$ | Inflation rate (% p.a.) | 0 | −0.18 | −0.42 | −0.73 | −1.17 | −1.78 | −2.72 | −1.00 | — |
| $\lambda = 1$ | Output | −0.05 | −0.91 | −1.2 | −1.33 | −1.25 | −0.86 | 0 | 0 | 3.03 |
| (B) | | | | | | | | | | |
| $\mu = 0.5$ | Inflation rate | 0 | −0.10 | −0.24 | −0.47 | −0.86 | −1.67 | −3.67 | −1.00 | — |
| $\lambda = 1$ | Output | −0.05 | −0.95 | −1.33 | −1.60 | −1.67 | −1.33 | 0 | 0 | 3.65 |
| (C) | | | | | | | | | | |
| $\mu = 0$ | Inflation rate | 0 | −0.33 | −0.67 | −1.00 | −1.33 | −1.67 | −2.0 | −1.00 | — |
| $\lambda = 0.5$ | Output | −0.05 | −0.83 | −1.00 | −1.00 | −0.83 | −0.50 | 0 | 0 | 2.32 |
| $\theta_1 = \frac{11}{36}$ $\theta_2 = \frac{11}{36}$ $\theta_3 = \frac{5}{36}$ | | | | | | | | | | |
| $\theta_4 = \frac{5}{36}$ $\theta_5 = \frac{1}{18}$ $\theta_6 = \frac{1}{18}$ | | | | | | | | | | |
| (D) | | | | | | | | | | |
| $\mu = 0$ | Inflation rate | 0 | −0.36 | −0.97 | −1.07 | −1.60 | −1.37 | −1.69 | −1.00 | — |
| $\lambda = 1$ | Output | −0.5 | −0.82 | −0.83 | −0.80 | −0.50 | −0.32 | 0 | 0 | 1.89 |

sacrifice ratio is the ratio of the cumulated percentage loss of output (at an annual rate) to the reduction in the inflation rate. These sacrifice ratios are substantially below the range of 6–18 quoted by Okun.[15] Thus the model implies faster disinflation than the standard econometric estimates. The model also implies that the sacrifice ratio could be reduced to zero by announcing a policy change sufficiently far in advance.[16]

## ALTERNATIVE MONETARY POLICIES

Alternative paths of the money stock imply different paths of inflation and output. I examine here the path of the money stock that is needed to reduce the inflation rate immediately to its new steady-state level, assuming for simplicity that the change in monetary policy is announced one period ahead. With $\Delta\pi$ as the desired change in the inflation rate, equation (7) implies that the change in the money stock needed to achieve the new price path is given by:

$$\Delta m_{t+i} = \frac{i\Delta\pi}{c_{J-i}} . \tag{14}$$

It is understood that the reduction in the money stock in (14) is relative to the path that was previously expected.

When all contracts are of the same duration, the monetary policy implied by (14) consists of a sharp first-period reduction in the money stock, followed later by a higher rate of increase than the new steady-state inflation rate. After $J$ periods the money stock is back at the level it would have reached had the money growth rate been reduced immediately in period 1 to its new steady-state level. This path of the money stock of course induces a large recession in the first period, and produces a much larger sacrifice ratio than the examples in Table 3.1.

The general point to be made about the sacrifice ratio for alternative policies is clear from the fact that a policy change delayed $J$ periods has no output cost, whereas policies that attempt to reduce the inflation rate rapidly have high output costs. This is because, in the short run, policy can drive the inflation rate down only by forcing reductions in the wage rates negotiated in contracts that come up for renewal in those periods.[17]

## MODEL SPECIFICATION AND THE SPEED OF RESPONSE

The dynamic patterns shown in Table 3.1, particularly in example D, appear to suggest that the inflation rate would respond very quickly to changes in monetary policy, with small output costs. For instance, in example D[18] the inflation rate is down by nearly 1 per cent (per annum) within eighteen months of a reduction of 1 per cent in the growth rate of money. In this subsection, I briefly examine characteristics of the model that produce this rapid response of inflation to monetary policy.[19]

A major factor responsible for the rapid response in this model is the synchronization of adjustments to wages. Every contract specifies a potentially different wage rate for each period. Examining equation (5), we see that all the expectations that affect the wage set for period *t* relate to variables in period *t*. Thus the contracts aim to obtain the 'correct' wage in every period. It is well known that non-synchronized adjustments create the possibility of slower adjustment. For example, Taylor (1980) produces long adjustment lags in a model with two-period labor contracts in which the same wage applies in both periods of the contract.[20] When wage adjustments are not synchronized, wages for any given future period are based not only on expectations of conditions in that period, but also on expectations of conditions in other periods. Adjustment lags may be very long even with short contracts, in particular when wage determination reflects concern about relative wages.

Non-synchronization of wage adjustments in the United States takes the form of wages being held constant within each year of a contract, although not for its entire life. Results by Taylor (1983) suggest that non-synchronization in this context does not substantially change the speed of disinflation. But it is clear that non-synchronization is potentially important in explaining, for instance, the difficulties of disinflating in Britain as compared with the relative ease of doing so in Japan.[21]

The adjustment patterns in this model are simplified too by basing all the dynamics on wage contracting. Independent lags in price adjustment – for instance by including a lagged price term in equation (2) that results from modeling a cost of price change (Rotemberg, 1982) – would slow the response. It would also result in the adjustment to a change in the growth rate of money being spread over the entire future, rather than being complete within $J$ periods. Backward-looking elements in wage setting – for instance, attempts by labor to catch up for the effects of past inflation – would also slow and smooth the responses of wages and prices to monetary policy changes.

Similarly, the inclusion of the expected rate of inflation in the aggregate demand equation would affect the time profile of adjustment to monetary changes. A major change in the conclusions of the analysis of disinflation in that case would be that even long preannounced changes in monetary policy would have real effects. Any announcement of a future change in monetary policy would trigger a rise in wages, and thus in prices, and result in the short run in changes in output. These changes would be smaller the longer in advance the change in policy is announced, and would be completed by the time the change in policy took place.

A third reason that adjustment of inflation to policy changes is relatively rapid in the examples studied earlier is that all policy announcements are immediately believed and incorporated in wages being negotiated for the future. Adjustment is much less rapid when policy intentions are not believed.

## III CREDIBILITY

In the present model the credibility of policy affects prices and output entirely by its effects on expectations of future money stocks. We can thus use the model to examine output and price effects of monetary policy changes under alternative assumptions about expectations of policy.

I consider two examples in this section. In the first, the growth rate of money is reduced by 1 per cent per annum, starting in period *t*. The reduction may be announced in advance, but is simply not believed by private agents, who continue to expect that money growth will proceed at its former rate. The policy change thus has no effects on wages before it goes into effect. After the policy change, economic agents do not believe there has been a change in the growth rate of money. Each reduction in the money stock relative to expectations is treated as a permanent, but one-time, shock. Wages do adjust to the unanticipated changes in the money stock, because such changes are believed to be permanent and reduce estimates of the *level* but not of the growth rate of future money stocks.

The price and output effects that follow from this set of assumptions are shown in example A in Table 3.2. The inflation rate does fall by 1 per cent as a result of the new policy and a new steady state is reached, but the expected inflation rate is by assumption not equal to the actual inflation rate. Correspondingly, the level of output is permanently below the full employment level. This extreme example indicates the effects of a lack of credibility of monetary policy in this model in which wages are set entirely on the basis of expectations of future events.

Example B in Table 3.2 allows expectations of policy to adjust to experience. All observed changes in the level of the money stock, resulting from unanticipated policy actions, are believed to be permanent. Now, however, there are adaptive expectations about the growth rate of the money stock. In each period (half year), the expected rate of increase of the money stock is increased by one-quarter of the excess of the actual growth rate of money over the expected rate. Eventually the economy will converge to full employment with a 1 per cent reduction in the inflation rate, although Table 3.2 shows that the adjustment is lengthy. After six periods, output remains more than 1 per cent below the full employment level. At that stage the expected growth rate of money is over 80 per cent of the way to converging to the new rate. The sacrifice ratio in this latter case – summed over the entire adjustment period – is 6.0.

It is clear from these examples that a lack of credibility of policy can substantially prolong the adjustment of output and the inflation rate to disinflationary policy.[22] Credibility is unfortunately very difficult to obtain, however. This is partly because the private sector knows that the government (usually) is not prepared to go to any lengths to reduce inflation. In the model of this chapter, the monetary authority can monitor the effects of its announcements on wages by examining contract terms in newly negotiated contracts. A long preannounced policy will have small output effects when implemented only if contract terms have adjusted appropriately. But what is the monetary authority to do with its preannounced policy if it observes that contract terms have not changed? It is then in precisely the position it was in when it announced its future policy change some periods back. Namely, it knows that putting the policy change into effect immediately will cause unemployment. That is why it chose in the first place to announce a future policy change, rather than to implement it immediately.

Proposals for enhancing the credibility of policy changes typically rely on some form of precommitment of policy. There are two difficulties with precommitment, however. First, intelligent policy makers cannot be sufficiently certain of their understanding of the dynamics of the response to

**Table 3.2** *Disinflation under alternative expectations of policy*

| $\theta_i = 1/6, \quad i = 1, \ldots, 6$<br>$h = 0.5, \quad \mu = 0, \quad \lambda = 1$ | | 0 | 1 | 2 | *Period*<br>3 | 4 | 5 | 6 | *Sacrifice ratio* |
|---|---|---|---|---|---|---|---|---|---|
| (A) Policy change not believed | Inflation rate | 0 | −0.09 | −0.20 | −0.33 | −0.50 | −0.71 | −1.0 | — |
| | Output | −0.5 | −0.95 | −1.35 | −1.69 | −1.94 | −2.08 | −2.08 | — |
| (B) Adaptive expectations about money growth | Inflation rate | 0 | −0.12 | −0.26 | −0.50 | −0.78 | −1.18 | −1.80 | — |
| | Output | −0.5 | −0.94 | −1.31 | −1.56 | −1.67 | −1.58 | −1.18 | 6.0 |

disinflationary policy to be sure that precommitment to a rigorous policy will succeed in bringing the inflation rate down at low cost. It may at some point be necessary to change policy. Second, in democracies it is difficult to devise methods of committing future governments to policies – particularly potentially costly and controversial policies – being undertaken at present. The credibility of policy, while obviously important, may be one of the stickiest of the elements that determine the response of the economy to attempts to change the inflation rate.

## IV ALTERNATIVE POLICIES

I shall not discuss other policies to speed disinflation in any detail. The variable $u_t$ in equation (2) above can be taken to represent supply-side factors that can affect the price level. Changes in $u$, for instance in payroll taxation, could be a useful adjunct to the start of a disinflation program. One difficulty of using such supply-side policy instruments is that it is rarely obvious when payroll taxes should be increased for stabilization reasons. A one-time reduction may be desirable if a major effort is being made to institute a change in policy, and if quick success is needed to persuade economic agents that the policy will be successful.

Ingenious tax incentive plans (TIPs) to reduce the inflation rate have received considerable attention. Such plans are discussed in detail in Okun and Perry (1978); at least in the United States, their implementation looks administratively too complicated for success. Layard (1982) suggests a tax on wage increases above a certain norm and begins to discuss the 'nuts-and-bolts issues of tax design' (p. 229) in the British context.

Any approach to the problem of disinflation that emphasizes the role of expectations is bound to consider the possibility of using incomes policies or wage and price controls. The argument for wage and price controls at the macro level is that they can be used to force prices and wages to follow the paths they would follow if all contracts were immediately renegotiable. Controls have the further advantage that they enhance the credibility of any restrictive policy measures undertaken at the same time. Wage and price controls not accompanied by restrictive policies are a waste of time. Unfortunately, it appears that controls are frequently used instead of, rather than along with, restrictive monetary and fiscal policies.

Because the distortions produced by controls increase the longer the controls are in place, they cannot be used for long. However, there is no reason to shrink totally from the use of controls because some distortions are bound to be created: the unemployment that results from the implementation of disinflationary policies is also a distortion.

## V UNITED STATES DISINFLATION, 1979–86

In October 1979, with the inflation rate for the previous twelve months at over 12 per cent, the Federal Reserve announced a new monetary policy designed to reduce the inflation rate. Four years and two recessions later the twelve-month inflation rate (CPI, October over October) was down to 2.9 per cent. What lessons about disinflation can be learned from this episode?[23] The main lesson is that there is no cheap way out of an entrenched inflation. The cure for inflation during this period used the old-time medicine of recession.

Figure 3.2 shows the unemployment rate and the GNP deflator inflation rate (quarter over the same quarter a year earlier) for the USA over the period 1950–83. Vertical lines mark off recessions. The rate of increase of the deflator in the last quarter of 1983 was somewhat below the lowest level it reached in the 1970s, but it took a prolonged period of high unemployment to achieve that low inflation. Further, the inflation rate is now cyclically low.

The general outlines of the disinflation were as expected. Quantitatively, though, the disinflation may have been slightly faster than predicted. I have calculated the sacrifice ratio for this disinflation making the following assumptions: the Okun's law coefficient is 2.5; the stabilization period begins in early 1980; unemployment will move smoothly from the current (last quarter of 1983) 8.4 per cent to 6.5 per cent at the end of 1985; and the inflation rate will by 1985 have fallen from 10 per cent to 5 per cent.

Assuming the natural rate of unemployment is 6.5 per cent, the cumulative output loss is 23.6 per cent; with a 6 per cent natural rate, the output loss would be 29.8 per cent. These estimates give a sacrifice ratio around 5 or 6, at the lower end of the range quoted by Okun. This estimate is, however, very sensitive to the assumption that the fall in the inflation rate is 5 per cent: with a 4 per cent decline, the sacrifice ratio would be 6–7.5, closer to the mean Okun

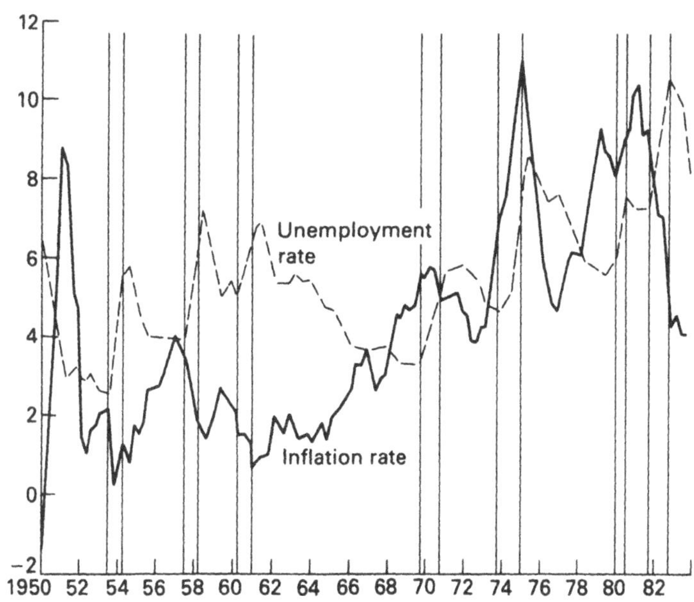


**Figure 3.2** Unemployment and inflation (GNP deflator) in the United States, 1950Q1–1983Q3

estimate; with a 6 per cent drop in the inflation rate the ratio would be 4 or 5, below the Okun range. All these estimates are below the median sacrifice ratio suggested by Okun.

The calculated value of the sacrifice ratio of 5–6 thus suggests that disinflation this time was somewhat less costly than in past episodes.[24] Examination of some earlier estimates of the output costs of reducing inflation gives the same impression. Perhaps the most famous of these is by Tobin (1980). In a model that is a 'stylized version of the consensus view' (p. 67), he examines effects of a policy that reduces the rate of increase of nominal GNP with the aim of reducing the inflation rate to zero. The path he illustrates, described as a cautionary tale, starts in 1980 and shows the unemployment rate hitting 10 per cent and an inflation rate of 2.5 per cent in 1987. The USA succeeded in reaching this point in less than half the predicted time. However, Tobin notes that the inflation rate might well come down more rapidly than his diagram suggests.

Among the reasons he offers is the possibility that actual and prospective bankruptcies and plant closings could lead to more rapid changes in wage and price patterns than had been experienced in the post-World War II period. There were such concessions in the recent recessions, in industries and plants that were threatened with bankruptcy or closing. Similar concessions have taken place in earlier recessions (Mitchell, 1982) but were later taken back. The depth of the recession, and the high real interest rates that made bankruptcies more likely, both probably contributed them to greater flexibility of wages than would be predicted by a simple contract model.[25] However, the general outlines of the disinflation path taken in the United States since 1979 are consistent with the contracting model, with appropriate allowance being made for the slowness with which expectations of future policy adjust to actual policy.

## NOTES

1 The quotation from Sargent continues 'The "measure" that would accomplish this would be a once-for-all, widely understood, and widely agreed upon change in the monetary or fiscal policy *regime*. Here a *regime* is taken to be a function or *rule* for repeatedly selecting the economic policy variable in question as a function of the state of the economy'.

2 The aggregate demand function derived from an *IS–LM* model includes the expected rate of inflation as a determinant of aggregate demand. The inclusion of the expected rate of inflation would complicate the solution of the model, because it makes the current price level a function of all future money stocks. A solution for a related model, which explicitly uses the *IS–LM* framework, is presented in Fischer (1977b).

3 Fischer (1977a) includes an aggregate supply function that makes the level of output an increasing function of the real wage. This formulation is frequently criticized on the empirical grounds that it implies that the real wage is countercyclical. However, the behavior of the real wage resulting from such a (Keynesian) supply function differs depending on whether output is changing because of a supply or a demand shock. In response to a supply shock, the real wage in such models moves procyclically; in response to demand shocks, the real wage moves countercyclically. Although (2) above can be made consistent with the earlier supply function by allowing $u$ to be correlated with $y$, I use the present formulation to avoid taking a stand on the inessential (from the viewpoint of this chapter) issue of the response of the real wage to demand shocks. Factors omitted from this model, such as capacity utilization, certainly affect the response of the real wage to disturbances.

4 This, too, is a substantial simplification. In particular, it will be assumed below that the extent of indexing in contracts is independent of the length of the contract. In practice, longer-term contracts are more likely to be indexed.

5 I have benefited from discussions on this point with James Medoff.

6 Most union contracts involving more than 1,000 workers are for three years: over the period 1978–80, 88 per cent of workers whose contracts were recorded in *Current Wage Developments* were on three-year contracts, 9 per cent on two-year contracts, and less than 3 per cent on one -year contracts. The total number of workers recorded as being involved in a three-year settlement involving at least 1,000 workers during that three-year period was 7.5 million, less than 10 per cent of the labor force. (Calculations are based on data presented in Taylor, 1983.)

7 This statistic is developed in Freeman and Medoff (1984).

8 It is surprising that Stigler's (1977) 'Conference Handbook' does not include among its list of comments 'Of course, it is not appropriate to treat that feature of the model as exogenous'.

9 The rational expectations assumption is not an innocent one, because adjustment in the model to preannounced policy changes will be much slower if expectations are formed adaptively than if they are formed rationally. In Section III below, I examine a situation in which expectations about future *policy* adjust adaptively; this produces reaction patterns that are similar to those obtained when expectations of inflation are adaptive.

10 It is more usual in rational expectations models to specify a feedback rule for monetary policy. The form of the solution presented below is more convenient for discussing the implications of private sector beliefs about future policy.

11 The variable $u$ will henceforth be referred to as supply shock, although it should be understood from the earlier discussion that it has other potential interpretations.

12 Note, incidently, that if (1) were generalized slightly to

$$y_t = \alpha(m_t - p_t) + v_t \qquad (1)'$$

the coefficient $h$ would be replaced everywhere by $\alpha h$. Thus the dynamics of the price level are affected by the product of the strength of the effects of changes in the money stock on aggregate demand and the effect of aggregate demand on the real wage.

13 Alternative contract structures, to be discussed below, do not have this implication.

14 The sensitivity of this result to model structure is examined below.

15 The Okun sacrifice ratios, calculated in 1978, assumed a 3 to 1 Okun coefficient translating unemployment into GNP; with a 2.5 to 1 ratio, the sacrifice ratios would range from 5 to 15 rather than 6 to 18. (I am indebted to Ben Friedman for this point.)

16 Recent estimates by Gordon (1982) imply a sacrifice ratio of less than 5, well below his earlier estimates. The change reflects the inclusion of an exchange rate channel in the inflation process: tight money causes an appreciation that reduces the price of imports.

17 The contracting model used in this chapter implies that workers with different contract renewal dates work at different wage rates. Accordingly, further development of the model would imply that relative price dispersion increases when there are unanticipated changes in the inflation rate.

18 Although the maturity structure of contracts in example D is much shorter than that discussed above for US union contracts, it is an open question how non-union workers should be treated in the contract model – and thus example D may be relevant to United States behavior.

19 Despite the emphasis on factors that might make the response of prices and output less rather than more rapid than implied in the model described above, it should also be recalled that the reopening of contracts would make for more rapid responses. Further, if the existence of long-term contracts is a result of large negotiating costs, a very large change in monetary policy would be more likely than a more gradual change in policy to lead to reopening of contracts and thus to a rapid response of the inflation rate to policy.

20 Blanchard (1983) shows how non-synchronization of price changes can lead to long lags in the adjustment of prices to monetary policy changes.

21 I plan to extend the model of this section in a subsequent paper to include non-synchronization.

22 See DiTata (1983) for an interesting analysis of credibility in a related context.

23 Eckstein (1983) and Friedman (1983) examine this episode, concluding that the disinflation is consistent with earlier estimates of the Phillips relationship.

24 The favorable oil-price shock has received some of the credit for the relatively rapid disinflation. However, low demand during the recession contributed substantially to creating this 'shock'. The exchange rate channel – attributable to the fiscal monetary policy mix – is appropriately credited with speeding the disinflation.

25 This suggests that the monetary–fiscal mix, which produced high real interest rates and thus a greater risk of bankruptcy, was partially responsible for the speed of the disinflation.

## REFERENCES


Azariadis, Costas and Stiglitz, Joseph (1983), 'Implicit contracts and fixed price equilibria', *Quarterly Journal of Economics*, 98 (Supplement), 1–22.

Barro, Robert J. (1977), 'Long-term contracting, sticky prices, and monetary policy', *Journal of Monetary Economics*, 3, July, 305–316.

Blanchard, Olivier J. (1983), 'Price desynchronization and price stickiness', unpublished manuscript, Department of Economics, Massachusetts Institute of Technology.

DiTata, Juan Carlos (1983), 'Credibility gaps and persistent disequilibria: some intriguing ideas', Central Bank of Argentina, Discussion Paper No. 13, June.

Eckstein, Otto (1983), 'Disinflation', Data Resources Inc., Economic Studies Series, No. 114, October.

Fischer, Stanley (1977a), 'Long term contracts, rational expectations, and the optimal money supply rule', *Journal of Political Economy*, 85, April, 191–206.

Fischer, Stanley (1977b), 'Wage indexation and macroeconomic stability', in K. Brunner and A. H. Meltzer (eds), *Stabilization of the Domestic and International Economy*, Carnegie–Rochester Series on Public Policy, 5, Amsterdam, North Holland, 107–147.

Fischer, Stanley (1977c), '"Long-term contracting, sticky prices, and monetary policy": a comment', *Journal of Monetary Economics*, 3, July, 317–324.

Flanagan, Robert J. (1976), 'Wage interdependence in unionized labor markets', *Brookings Papers on Economic Activity*, 3, 635–673.

Freeman, Richard and Medoff, James (1984), *What Do Unions Do*?, New York, Basic Books.

Friedman, Benjamin M. (1983), 'Recent perspective in and on macroeconomics', National Bureau of Economic Research, Working Paper No. 1208, September.

Gordon, Robert J. (1982) 'Inflation, flexible exchange rates, and the natural rate of unemployment', in Martin N. Baily (ed.), *Workers, Jobs, and Inflation*, Washington, DC, Brookings Institution, 89–152.

Hall, Robert E. (1980), 'Employment fluctuations and wage rigidity', *Brookings Papers on Economic Activity*, 1, 91–133.

Hall, Robert E. and Lilien, David (1979), 'Efficient wage bargains under uncertain supply and demand', *American Economic Review*, 69, December, 868–879.

Hart, Oliver D. (1983), 'Optimal labour contracts under asymmetric information: an introduction', *Review of Economic Studies*, 50, January, 3–36.

Johnson, George E. (1977), 'The determination of wages in the union and non-union sectors', *British Journal of Industrial Relations*, 15, July, 211–225.

Layard, Richard (1982), 'Is incomes policy the answer to unemployment?', *Economica*, 49, August, 219–239.

Mitchell, Daniel J. B. (1980a), 'Union/non-union wage spillovers: a note', *British Journal of Industrial Relations*, 18, November, 372–375.

Mitchell, Daniel J. B. (1980b), *Unions, Wages, and Inflation*, Washington, DC, Brookings Institution.

Mitchell, Daniel J. B. (1982), 'Recent union contract concessions', *Brookings Papers on Economic Activity*, 1, 165–201.
Modigliani, Franco and Papademos, Lucas (1978), 'Optimal demand policies against stagflation', *Weltwirtschafliches Archiv*, 114, December, 736–782.
Okun, Arthur M. (1978), 'Efficient disinflationary policies', *American Economic Review, Papers and Proceedings*, 68, May, 348–352.
Okun, Arthur M. and Perry, George L. (1978) (eds), *Brookings Papers on Economic Activity*, 2, Special Issue.
Phelps, Edmund S. (1978), 'Disinflation without recession: adaptive guideposts and monetary policy', *Weltwirtschaftliches Archiv*, 114, December, 783–809.
Rotemberg, Julio J. (1982), 'Sticky prices in the United States', *Journal of Political Economy*, 90, December, 1187–1211.
Sargent, Thomas J. (1981), 'Stopping moderate inflations: the methods of Poincaré and Thatcher', unpublished manuscript, University of Minnesota.
Stigler, George (1977), 'Conference handbook', *Journal of Political Economy*, 85, April, 441–443.
Taylor, John B. (1980), 'Aggregate dynamics and staggered contracts', *Journal of Political Economy*, 88 (1), February, 1–23.
Taylor, John B. (1983), 'Union wage settlements during a disinflation', *American Economic Review*, 73(5), December, 981–993.
Tobin, James (1980), 'Stabilization policy ten years after', *Brookings Papers on Economic Activity*, 1, 19–71.
Vroman, Susan (1980), 'Research note. Union/non-union spillovers', *British Journal of Industrial Relations*, 18, November, 369–372.

# 4 The Design of Monetary and Fiscal Policy: Monetarism and Supply-Side Economics

*VICTOR ARGY*

## I INTRODUCTION

This chapter focuses on the contributions made by both monetarism and supply-side economics to the debate over the way in which monetary and fiscal policy ought to be designed.

These two schools have exercised considerable influence over macroeconomic policy in recent years. Monetarist thinking has had a major impact on several conservative governments, notably in the UK under Thatcher, in Australia under Fraser and in the USA under Reagan. Supply-side policies have been espoused in a weak form by Thatcher, at least in 1979, and in a stronger form by Reagan in 1981 and 1982 (Argy, 1983b).

In more general terms, a switch in many industrial countries towards money stock control and money targeting owes a great deal to monetarist thinking. In addition, spurred by supply-side contributions, there has more recently been some rethinking about the role of, and general burden of, taxes, notably in the context of incentives to save, work and invest. Again, spurred by these schools, there has been a re-examination of the role and size of the public sector in general and of the appropriateness of government involvement, intervention and regulation of the economy.

In this chapter I am going to concentrate essentially on three schools of thought. The first and most important is Friedman's brand of monetarism (hereafter monetarism I).[1] The second is the neo-classical school (hereafter monetarism II).[2] The third is supply-side economics (hereafter SSE).[3]

## II COMMON GROUND AND DIFFERENCES BETWEEN THE THREE SCHOOLS

On the general design of policy all three schools agree (a) on the crucial importance of reducing inflation to modest, very low levels by, ultimately, containing the growth of money, (b) that the size and role of government should be drastically reduced, (c) that the budget should be balanced, at least in the medium run, and that governments should follow simple long-run fiscal rules, (d) that governments should forgo 'fine-tuning' stabilization.

SSE differs from monetarism I in several important respects. First, supply-side economists attach tremendous importance, in the design of policy, to correcting 'supply-side' weaknesses: improving incentives to work, save, invest, innovate and assume risk. With this aim in mind their stress has been on cutting income taxes and regulations. Second, the 'strong version' of SSE also believes that most Western economies are located on the right-hand side of the 'Laffer Curve', implying that a cut in income taxes will have such powerful 'supply-side' effects that revenue will actually increase. Third, some supply-siders, at least, believe that the best way for any single country (for example, the USA) to contain money growth in the long run and at the same time maintain a credible stance on inflation is to adopt a domestic 'gold standard'. Monetarism I, on the other hand, thinks it is sufficient to maintain a tight control over the growth of a reserve asset. Fourth, SSE would prefer to see a return to fixed exchange rates by restoring a worldwide gold standard (Wanniski, 1978; Laffer, 1980). Monetarism I rejects this, believing instead that unmanaged exchange rates would serve the world economy better. Fifth, supply-siders appears to be less concerned about budget deficits over a span of, say, two years or so than monetarism I. In particular, they recognize that a policy of cutting taxes to stimulate the supply side may take some time to restore revenue (Gilder, 1981, p. 267). Sixth, SSE sees the size and role of the public sector, and more particularly the level of taxes and regulations, as lying at the heart of the inflation problem. To attack inflation by demand policies alone (as proposed by monetarism I) is inadequate; such policies need to be complemented by supply-side policies. This emphasis on tax-push in the generation of inflation is reminiscent of earlier work by Clark (1945) and Bacon and Eltis (1979).

While the differences between SSE and monetarism I are easy to identify, it is perhaps a little less clear how monetarism II differs from monetarism I. There are two crucial ideas shared by monetarism II. The first is the belief in rational behaviour and in rationally formed expectations. The latter requires that there be no 'biased errors' in expectations formation. In practice, this is translated into an assumption that the particular model manipulated also provides the basis for the formation of expectations. The second is the belief in continuous market clearing (spot auction equilibrium markets). This is assumed to apply not only to markets that are widely acknowledged to have this characteristic (e.g. certain commodities, exchange rates, interest rates) but also to goods and labour markets.

Consider a typical two-equation system widely used to represent monetarism II. The aggregate supply equation takes the form: [4]

$$U_t - UN = \alpha_1(p_t - p_e) + \alpha_2 U_{t-1} + v_t. \qquad (1)$$

The aggregate demand equation is:

$$U_t = a_{0t} + \alpha_3(m_t - p_t) + n_t. \qquad (2)$$

In these equations $U$ = unemployment rate, $UN$ = the natural unemployment rate, $p$ = the log of the price level, $p_e$ = the log of the expected price level, $a_0$ = other influences on real demand (assumed here to be fiscal policy), $m$ = the log of the money stock, $v$ and $n$ are assumed to be random error terms with a mean value of zero.

It is easily shown that, assuming rationally based expectations:

$$p_e = \frac{1}{\alpha_3} a_{0et} + m_{et} + \frac{1}{\alpha_3} n_{et} - \frac{1}{\alpha_3} UN - \frac{\alpha_2}{\alpha_3} U_{t-1} - \frac{1}{\alpha_3} v_{et} \,. \tag{3}$$

The subscript 'e' in equation (3) is used to represent expected values. Since the means of $n$ and $v$ are zero, their expected values must also be zero.

Using these three equations,

$$p_t - p_e = \frac{1}{\alpha_1 + \alpha_3}(a_{0t} - a_{0et}) + \frac{\alpha_3}{\alpha_1 + \alpha_3}(m_t - m_{et}) + \frac{1}{\alpha_1 + \alpha_3} n_t - \frac{1}{\alpha_1 + \alpha_3} v_t. \tag{4}$$

Substituting this solution in equation (1) we have:

$$U_t - UN = \frac{\alpha_1}{\alpha_1 + \alpha_3}(a_{0t} - a_{0et}) + \frac{\alpha_1\alpha_3}{\alpha_1 + \alpha_3}(m_t - m_{et}) + \frac{\alpha_1}{\alpha_1 + \alpha_3} n_t + \frac{\alpha_3}{\alpha_1 + \alpha_3} v_t + \alpha_2 U_{t-1} \tag{5}$$

and finally

$$p_t = \frac{1}{\alpha_1 + \alpha_3} a_{0t} + \frac{\alpha_1}{\alpha_3(\alpha_1 + \alpha_3)} a_{0et} + \frac{\alpha_3}{\alpha_1 + \alpha_3} m_t + \frac{\alpha_1}{\alpha_1 + \alpha_3} m_{et} + \frac{1}{\alpha_1 + \alpha_3} n_t - \frac{1}{\alpha_1 + \alpha_3} v_t - \frac{1}{\alpha_3} UN - \frac{\alpha_2}{\alpha_3} U_{t-1}, \tag{6}$$

Where $a_{0t} - a_{0et}$ and $m_t - m_{et}$ represent, respectively, unanticipated fiscal and monetary policies.

These solutions carry important implications for policy. Fully anticipated monetary and fiscal policies ($a_{0t} = a_{0et}$ and $m_t = m_{et}$) can have no real (and only price) effects. Hence, credible restrictive monetary policies (however sharply applied) can secure rapid reductions in inflation without substantial, if any, real costs. A consistent policy of fine-tuning (stabilization) will also fail ultimately because it will become anticipated (errors in forecasting policy will be random). It follows that only unanticipated policies can have real effects, but these may persist for a while because of adjustment costs on the supply side ($\alpha_2$).

Monetarism I shies away from these policy implications. The disagreement has to be grounded on a rejection either of rational expectations as defined by the neo-classical school or of the assumption of continuous market clearing or of both. Since Friedman's own early modelling did assume continuous market clearing (Friedman, 1968; McCallum, 1980) and, as well, adaptive expectations, a reasonable conclusion is that monetarism I rejects the assumption of rational expectations. This is surprising because Friedman himself and his followers have always had strong convictions about the efficiency of markets, at least in all other areas.

The strong conclusions about macro policy advanced by monetarism II can be criticized by attacking each or both of the key assumptions underlying their analysis. The existence of diverse expectations itself poses problems for rational expectations. In addition, while it may be true that rational agents will try and eliminate systematic expectational errors, this still leaves open the question of the time horizon over which this happens and, moreover, how or why this somehow allows these agents to stumble implicitly upon the correct model of the economy, whatever that is. Even if one accepted rational expectations (perhaps because every alternative appears inferior), the assumption of market clearing is in conflict with observed facts. If rational expectations were combined with an assumption of some stickiness in the adjustment of labour and goods markets, the strong conclusions no longer follow (see Begg, 1982, Ch. 6). There is now indeed evidence to support the view that even fully anticipated monetary and fiscal policies may be effective (Gordon, 1982; Mishkin, 1982).

Monetarism II is also committed in terms of its theoretical underpinnings to explaining a long-term increase in the unemployment rate in terms of an increase in the natural rate of unemployment (NRU). Consider equation 1 above. If $p - p_e$ is itself a random term, it follows that the actual unemployment rate is determined by the NRU, the lagged unemployment rate and a random error term. Since the lagged unemployment term is hardly likely to account for a persistent upward trend in $U$, given an unanticipated shock, it follows that nearly all of such a trend must be accountable in terms of the NRU (Hall, 1975). It also follows that a long-term unemployment problem has to be attacked by policies designed to reduce the NRU.

Monetarism I again appears to shy away from such extreme implications. Indeed, if adaptive expectations are used, it no longer follows that $p - p_e$ is a random term.

## III ELEMENTS OF POLICY AND THEIR RATIONALE

### THE DESIGN OF LONG-RUN MONETARY POLICY

Monetarists tend to think in terms of a 'target' (alternatively called 'optimal' or 'efficient') rate of inflation at which policy should aim. If the current rate of inflation exceeds this target, money growth should be slowed down (at what pace is something we look at shortly) until the desired rate of inflation is reached. At this point money will be allowed to grow at a rate determined by the target of inflation, plus capacity growth, less the long-run percentage increase in velocity. As these last two change, so will (strictly) the optimal money growth rate.

What is this target rate of inflation? It is convenient to begin by making certain initial assumptions:

- changes in money growth have neutral effects on the real economy;
- there are no distortionary taxes on goods;
- the dynamics of adjustment (notably unemployment costs) are disregarded;
- there is widespread indexation of wages, taxes and financial instruments (except money).

Friedman (1969) made an important early contribution to this debate by developing his 'full liquidity rule'. This rule rests on two propositions. First, the real return on money and capital is equalized at the margin.
That is:

$$r_d + k - P = r_k - P, \tag{7}$$

where $k$ represents the liquidity services enjoyed by money, $P$ is the rate of inflation, $r_d$ is the interest on money and $r_k$ is the return on capital. Second, the marginal cost of money creation equals the marginal benefits from holding money. The marginal cost is equal to the interest paid on money plus the production cost of money creation; the marginal benefit is the interest rate earned plus the liquidity services. If the production cost of money creation is zero it follows that $k$ should also be zero.
Setting $k = 0$ yields the optimal rate of inflation ($P_o$):

$$P_o = r_d - (r_k - P). \tag{8}$$

This simply says that the optimal rate of inflation is determined by the interest rate paid on money and the negative of the real return on capital. If $r_d = 0$ we have the familiar result that, so long as the real return on capital is positive, the optimal rate of inflation has to be negative. At the same time, the nominal return to capital is zero (since $r_d = r_k$). Friedman himself actually preferred to have interest paid on money rather than to aim for a negative rate of inflation. A positive interest rate on money allows an optimal rate of inflation that is zero or positive. In what follows we continue to suppose that interest is not paid on money ($r_d = 0$).

Now consider what happens when the first assumption is dropped. Suppose that inflation has positive effects on savings and capital intensity (through its effects on real money balances) and suppose, moreover, that the rate of savings is below optimal. Then, to optimize savings, some positive rate of inflation may be needed, which in itself conflicts with the 'full liquidity rule' (concerned with minimizing the deadweight loss from economizing on cash balances) (Summers, 1981; Drazen, 1979).

Consider now what happens when the second assumption is relaxed. Inflation imposes a tax on money balances; this is distortionary. However, taxes are also imposed on other goods. Hence, the optimal rate of inflation is one that equalizes at the margin the excess burden of the different taxes. There is now no reason why this optimal rate of inflation should not be positive (Gordon, 1976).

So far, then, we have shown that, staying within the confines of comparative statics, full employment and efficiency gains, it is no longer evident what the optimal rate of inflation is. If interest is paid on money, if there is a shortage of savings, if resources are misallocated in the first place, the optimal rate of inflation may be positive (but nonetheless unknown).

Suppose now that the third assumption is relaxed. Consider this in the context of an assumed natural rate of unemployment (NRU) at which a given rate of inflation is stable. Suppose that the optimal rate of inflation (however arrived at) is *B* and the economy is resting at *A* where, say, the mean rate of inflation is now fully anticipated and there is, as assumed, widespread indexation (Figure 4.1). Bringing down money growth to secure *B* will entail some transitional unemployment costs. So we now have to trade the ultimate 'efficiency' gains (which last forever) against the transitional loss of output. In principle, at any rate, it is no longer true that having reached *A* it is necessarily beneficial to move to *B*. Feldstein's (1979) analytical results are relevant in this context. He shows that in a growing economy the benefits of reducing inflation must exceed the costs if the growth rate is equal to or exceeds the discount rate[5]

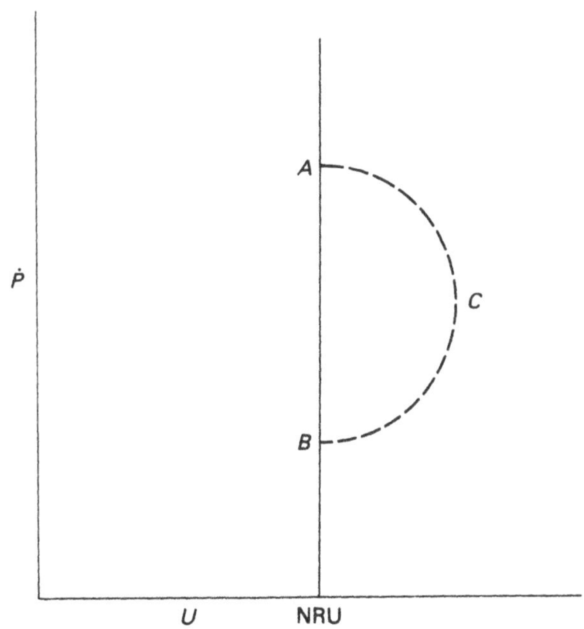


**Figure 4.1** The costs of a disinflationary monetary policy

(because the present benefits will then approach infinity). The existence of an NRU serves, then, to reduce the long-run costs of an anti-inflationary policy.

Finally, if we drop the assumption of full indexation but continue to assume that the high mean rate of inflation at *A* is anticipated, the issues become much more complex (Fischer and Modigliani, 1978). With indexation incomplete and irregular (notably with respect to taxes and public expenditure), distortions will surface that may well have real effects on investment and equilibrium unemployment. Moreover, higher inflation may be associated with greater uncertainty about inflation and this additional uncertainty at higher rates of inflation may, again, raise the NRU.

These last considerations (still relatively underdeveloped but, in any event, outside the scope of this chapter) led Friedman (1977) to suggest in his Nobel Prize lecture that, over the medium term, the relationship between inflation and unemployment may be positive (Mullineaux, 1980; Fischer, 1981). This is the rationale underlying the view that the rate of inflation needs to be brought down in order to reduce, ultimately, the rate of unemployment. The movement from *A* to *B* will now actually lower the unemployment rate. Equally plausibly, however, one could argue that the descent from *A* will also raise the NRU in the medium term (e.g. by reducing the capital stock and/or by reducing the efficiency, the capacity for work and ultimate employability of the unemployed) (Phelps, 1972; Gregory, 1982; Buiter and Miller, Chapter 2 above).

A key consideration then in any cost–benefit analysis of an anti-inflationary policy is the question of how much additional unemployment will need to be created to achieve the ultimate result. It is here that monetarism I differs from monetarism II.

As already demonstrated, monetarism II argues that, if the restrictive money growth policy is announced, anticipated and made convincing, inflation may be brought down with little or no unemployment. (In other words, the economy will move almost directly from *A* to *B* in Figure 4.1.) This is because, in a world where wages are flexible and determined by expectations of inflation that, in turn, are determined by money growth, wages and prices will adjust quickly downwards.

What does monetarism I have to say about this? In reply to a question put to him by the UK House of Commons Select Committee in 1980 about the unemployment costs of an anti-inflationary policy, Friedman (1980, p.61) said:

> The best evidence is from the prior experience in the U.K. and other countries. As I read that experience . . . I conclude that (a) only *a modest reduction in output and employment will be a side effect of reducing inflation to single figures by 1982 and* (b) *the effect on investment and the potential for future growth will be highly favourable.* [Emphasis added].

Whatever these costs (and there is some uncertainty about how severe Friedman thinks these costs might be), Friedman has, however, indicated in numerous places (Friedman and Friedman, 1980; Friedman, 1974b) that the costs would be substantially reduced by the adoption of widespread indexation of wages, taxes and financial contracts, at the same time as money growth is reduced. Friedman favours indexation, to begin with, because it makes inflation less attractive to governments and so reduces political resistance to the adoption of an anti-inflation strategy. Inflation would be less attractive because indexation reduces gains to governments on two fronts: it reduces the windfall tax yields (bracket creep) and it reduces the gains from the fall in the real value of outstanding debt. At the same time Friedman contends that widespread indexation will reduce the associated unemployment costs of an anti-inflationary policy.

There is a difference, too, between monetarism I and monetarism II in their attitude towards the pace at which money growth should be slowed. Assuming full indexation is not feasible, Friedman has argued in favour of a gradualist policy to mitigate the side effects of disinflation. Monetarism II, however, tends to favour the shock treatment, understandably since the sharper reduction in money growth will not itself aggravate the unemployment costs (Minford and Peel, 1981).

Supply-side economists differ again, importantly, from the other two schools of thought by contending that, if a restrictive money growth policy is to be convincing as a permanent solution to the problem of inflation, it must be associated at the least with a restored gold standard (Bordo, 1981; Commission on the Role of Gold, 1982). To quote the advocates of the restored gold standard:

> The monetarists share our view that the Federal Reserve's discretionary policy of the last several decades has been the cause of our inflation . . . . Both monetarists and gold standard advocates want to stop the present inflation. Monetarism claims that a gradual reduction in the rate of money growth can get us to where we want to be. Gradualism does not ensure credibility. Restoring convertibility and defining the dollar as a precise weight of gold is the only way the psychology of inflation can be broken . . . (Commission on the Role of Gold, 1982, Minority Report, ch. 1).

Laffer has also contended that 'returning to a gold standard will dramatically change inflationary expectations and bring about a sharp drop in interest rates' (*Business Week*, 1981, p. 61).

To summarize, there is clearly no consensus about what the 'target' rate of inflation is. Monetarists and supply-side economists are, however, agreed that whilst it may be positive it will not be much above zero. In their judgement, then, the case for reducing inflation from rates, over say, 3 per cent remains strong on grounds already reviewed. These views notwithstanding, the issues continue to be highly contentious (see Meyer and Raasche, 1980; Gordon and King, 1982; Fischer, 1981; and Fischer and Modigliani, 1978). There is also no consensus over the pace at which money growth should be reduced. Finally, there is disagreement, notably between monetarism and supply-siders, over the methods by which monetary growth should be reduced.

## THE DESIGN OF SHORT-RUN MONETARY POLICY

I address two issues here: first, the money aggregate to be selected as the intermediate target for policy; second, the amount of discretion in money growth that will be allowed on a year-to-year basis. Monetarists have strong views about these issues. I concentrate first on monetarism I and II, then briefly review the ideas of SSE.

*The selection of a money aggregate*

There are two approaches to this: empirical and analytical. In principle, both ought to yield the same outcome.

The empirical approach, favoured by monetarists, is to select the aggregate that explains best, by use of a single (reduced-form) equation regression, the movement of nominal income or inflation (Friedman and Meiselman, 1963). Monetarists also believe that this relationship is a relatively stable one.

The analytical approach to the selection of an intermediate target derives from Poole's seminal work on the choice of a money instrument (Poole, 1970; see also Argy, 1983a). Suppose the authorities have to choose between a money aggregate and base money. Suppose, too, that the authorities aim to minimize the variance of output. The model is represented by four equations:

$$Y = -\alpha_1 r_d + a_1 \tag{9}$$

$$M_d = -\alpha_2 r_d + \alpha_3 Y + a_2 \tag{10}$$

$$M_s = \alpha_4 r_d + \alpha_5 B - \alpha_6 Y + a_3 \tag{11}$$

$$M_d = M_s \tag{12}$$

where $Y$ is income, $r_d$ is the domestic interest rate, $M$ is money, and $B$ is base money. Equation (9) is a very simple goods market equation with a disturbance term $a_1$. Equation (10) is a money demand equation with a disturbance term $a_2$. Equation (11) is a money supply equation again with a disturbance term $a_3$.[6]

If money were the target (fixed), the solution for income is

$$Y = -\frac{\alpha_1}{\alpha_2 + \alpha_1\alpha_3} a_2 + \frac{\alpha_2}{\alpha_2 + \alpha_1\alpha_3} a_1 \tag{13}$$

and for the variance of income (disregarding covariances)

$$Y_{var} = \left(\frac{\alpha_1}{\alpha_2 + \alpha_1\alpha_3}\right)^2 a_{2_{var}} + \left(\frac{\alpha_2}{\alpha_2 + \alpha_1\alpha_3}\right)^2 a_{1_{var}}. \tag{14}$$

If base money were the target, the solution for income is now

$$Y = -\frac{\alpha_1}{k} a_2 + \frac{\alpha_1}{k} a_3 + \left(\frac{\alpha_2 + \alpha_4}{k}\right) a_1, \tag{15}$$

where $k = \alpha_2 + \alpha_4 + \alpha_1 (\alpha_3 + \alpha_6)$, and for the variance of income:

$$Y_{var} = \left(\frac{\alpha_1}{k}\right)^2 a_{2_{var}} + \left(\frac{\alpha_1}{k}\right)^2 a_{3_{var}} + \left(\frac{\alpha_2 \ \alpha_4}{k}\right)^2 a_{1_{var}}. \tag{16}$$

Consider now the effects on income of each of the three disturbances. For $a_2$ (a money demand shift) base money is the better (but not perfect) stabilizer ($\alpha_1/\alpha_2 + \alpha_1\alpha_3 > \alpha_1/k$). The reason is that an autonomous increase in the demand for money lowers income and raises interest rates. With a base money target, the fall in income and the rise in interest rate both serve to raise the money supply above its mean, which in this case is stabilizing.

For $a_3$ (a money supply shift) a money target is the better (now perfect) stabilizer. The reason is that, with a base money target, money supply will be allowed to change and this destabilizes income.

Finally, for $a_1$ (a real disturbance) the outcomes are ambiguous. Base money is the better stabilizer if $\alpha_2\alpha_6 > \alpha_3\alpha_4$, while money is the better stabilizer if $\alpha_3\alpha_4 > \alpha_2\alpha_6$. The rationale underlying this is as follows. A real upward disturbance increases income and the interest rate. With base money as the target, the volume of money will rise or fall depending on whether the income or the interest rate effect is dominant. The rise in income lowers the volume of money (by increasing the demand for cash); the rise in interest rate increases the volume of money (by reducing the demand for bank cash). If money supply decreases (increases), base money (money) is the better stabilizer.

It is evident from the above, then, that for some disturbances base money is preferred while for others money is preferred.

We have so far briefly reviewed two approaches to the selection of a money aggregate. In the end neither approach turns out to be very helpful at the practical level of policy making. On the first (empirical) approach, the outcomes are highly sensitive to the form in which the equation is estimated (e.g. the variables that appear on the RHS) and the time period selected. On the second approach, one needs to form a (difficult) judgement about the relative importance of different disturbances. Moreover, even if these studies pointed unambiguously to a particular money aggregate as the appropriate one, there is still the problem that restricting its supply might itself induce financial innovations that will have the effect in due course of discrediting that aggregate.

*The use of discretion in the conduct of short-term monetary policy*

Monetarists favour the announcement, in advance, of money growth targets. Friedman (1982) would allow 'a constant band (of say 1%) around the targeted level' (of the money supply), but the band is to accommodate potential errors in controlling the money stock not to allow the exercise of discretion. Thus, after the optimal long-run money growth is reached the authorities will (effectively) follow a constant money growth rule (CMGR).

The theoretical rationale underlying the advocacy of a CMCR is different for monetarists I and II. Monetarists I accept that monetary changes (be they anticipated or random) may have short-run real effects. So, in principle at any rate, such policy shifts could offset shocks to the economy or at least speed up the adjustment back to the NRU. They, however, contend:

(a) that, with relatively stable monetary and fiscal rules in place, the private sector will also be relatively stable in the short run. Monetarists thus tend to play down the importance of private sector shocks;

(b) that, in any event, in the face of these private sector shocks the economy is inherently resilient, absorbing these shocks with only minimal disruption;
(c) that, even though in the face of such shocks fine-tuning may, in principle, be effective, the reality is that policy makers are most unlikely to be able to achieve such stabilization.

Monetarists II contend, as we have seen, that systematic use of discretion in the short run will ultimately fail. So either the authorities act on the basis of a systematic rule, in which case their policies will fail, or they behave in a random fashion, in which case they will make a real impact but this, by definition, will be destabilizing. Thus the case for a CMGR is even stronger with monetarism II because, in their perception, fine-tuning is ineffective, even in principle.

We now consider, briefly, the case against discretion advanced by monetarism I. Proposition (a) has never been put to the test, at least in a global context. It is, however, certain that some private sector shocks (e.g. supply-side shocks, external shocks) will continue to buffet the economy. A constant CMGR is no guarantee that nominal income growth will be stabilized. Proposition (b) would be thought by antagonists to be altogether too optimistic. Consider, for example, Friedman's contention that a shock might produce only a ripple on the overall price level:

> It is essential to distinguish changes in relative prices from changes in absolute prices. The special conditions that drove up the prices of oil and food required purchasers to spend more on them, leaving less to spend on other items. Did that not force other prices to go down or to rise less rapidly than otherwise? Why should the average level of prices be affected significantly by changes in the prices of some things relative to others? (Friedman, 1974a, p.40.)

Consider now briefly proposition (c). It would be possible, in principle, to retain long-run control over money growth, with an eye on containing inflation, yet at the same time allow money growth within the year to respond, directly or indirectly, to emerging random shocks. Suppose a band were allowed around the target money growth. How can this band be exploited to achieve certain objectives such as minimizing fluctuations in output and/or prices?

It is convenient to distinguish three strategies here, all alternatives to the CMGR. First, money growth could be adjusted in the course of the year in response to *ex post* unanticipated shocks. Second, the authorities could follow a feedback rule, responding to unanticipated trends in prices and /or output. A variation on this theme is to target nominal income growth (Tobin, 1980b; Meade, 1978). The authorities would adjust money growth in line with observed deviations from this target. If the proxy for income indicated that income growth was running above (below) target, money growth would be allowed in the lower (upper) ranges of the band. For each unanticipated disturbance, adjustment now occurs after the event. Third, the authorities could follow a combination policy rule, whereby they adjust the growth in the money aggregate in line with unanticipated trends in a 'price' variable. This price could be the interest rate (Poole, 1970; Benavie and Froyer, 1983) or the exchange rate (Argy, 1984; Roper and Turnovsky, 1980). Such a policy amounts to having, at the same time, a quantity and a price target. In this respect it represents a compromise policy. The idea is to use the 'price' as an indicator for monetary policy with the objective ultimately of minimizing consumer price/output fluctuations. An extreme version of the third strategy is to use money growth policy to stabilize the exchange rate. This represents the hard currency option. A less extreme version is to stabilize the currency in the short run only (follow a purchasing-power-parity-type crawling peg rule).

How do the three strategies compare? The first is the most efficient in that it attacks the problem directly at its source. It is, however, by far the most difficult to implement. Shocks are not easily identifiable; moreover, they occur together making it difficult to know how to react. In addition, while for some disturbances (e.g. a money demand shock) the appropriate response is unambiguous (follow an accommodating money supply policy), for others (e.g. foreign interest rate or foreign price changes) the appropriate response is ambiguous depending on the authorities' objective function and the assumptions made about the behaviour of the economy (Argy, 1984). Finally, if some disturbances are not random, money growth may trend upward or downward.

The second and third strategies are easier to implement, in that they both involve the application of rules rather than discretion. There are, however, serious difficulties with both. For the second strategy to be effective one needs a good 'early-warning' proxy for income; moreover, with lags in adjustment it is not obvious that the policy response will be stabilizing. As regards the third strategy, Argy (1984) has demonstrated that the appropriate sign of the general coefficient of adjustment to the interest rate or the exchange rate is difficult to determine and depends on the sources of disturbances and the weights attaching to minimizing output and price fluctuations.

To conclude, then, while it is not difficult to demonstrate that alternative rules are superior in principle to the CMGR, they need not be so, faced with the hard realities of application.

*Supply-side economics and the adoption of a domestic gold standard*

Some supply-side economists (Laffer, 1980) would confront these issues quite differently. There would be no money growth target as such; thus there would be no problem about selecting a money aggregate. They would instead like to see the USA take the lead in fixing the dollar price of gold and then stand ready to buy and sell gold at the fixed price against certain Federal Reserve liabilities. After that the amount of base money in the system would bear some relationship, according to some agreed formula, to the amount of gold held by the monetary authorities.

The exact details surrounding the adoption of a domestic convertible gold standard vary greatly depending on the particular proposal advanced.[7] These differ greatly in terms of (a) the Federal Reserve liabilities to be convertible (all including base money but many also including official liabilities to foreign monetary authorities); (b) how the official price is to be set in the first place and how permanent this price is to be; (c) how the amount of base money is to be related to the amount of gold held by the authorities. It is impossible here to review the many variations on the basic theme. It is, however, worth outlining briefly one particular proposal (by Laffer), which did receive considerable attention.

In the Laffer plan (Laffer, 1980), the USA would announce its intention to return to a convertible dollar three–four months after enactment of legislation. The price of gold that would be adopted then would be the average price of gold bullion that prevailed in the five business days before such convertibility is resumed. At that point the value of gold would represent some proportion of the amount of base money in the system. Should the value of gold fall below 50 per cent of base money, the monetary base would be decreased by 1 per cent per month. Should it rise above 125 per cent, base money would be increased by 1 per cent per month. Within this range base money would be held fixed. Finally, if the gold reserve fell below 25 per cent or rose above 175 per cent of the base money, the Federal Reserve would suspend convertibility and reassure the situation, presumably with a view to setting a new price.

Criticisms of this type of proposal have centred around two issues: the difficulties inherent in fixing the initial price, and the potential fluctuations in gold stocks over time and their implication for money growth. It is difficult to see why the initial price of gold set in this way should be the right one, in the sense that it will be convincing to operators. If, in due course, the price were thought to be too high there would be massive sales of gold to convert into dollars, inflating the money supply. If the price were thought to be too low there would be purchases of gold and the money stock would fall sharply. Over time, too, there will be various pressures bearing on the market price of gold. With the price fixed, these pressures will ultimately fall entirely on the Federal Reserve. For example, an increase in international tension might sharply increase the world demand for gold. If the world market price rose there would be an immediate incentive to buy gold from the Federal Reserve at the official price and sell it at the market price. Gold stocks would fall and deflation might ensue. Again, if interest rates rose sharply there might be a switch out of gold, putting potential downward pressures on the gold price, now leading to sales of gold to the Federal Reserve, possibly forcing it in turn to inflate. To avoid at least some of these pressures, US residents would have to be prohibited from trading in world markets in gold and, in addition, monetary liabilities to foreign central banks would not be convertible. The first would be impossible to enforce and in any event would be inconsistent with concerns over economic liberties proclaimed by gold standard supporters. Thus in the end, in a very real sense, US monetary policy would be dictated by external pressures.

To sum up, then, it is clear that adoption of a gold standard would not ensure steady money growth. On the contrary, money growth, and hence short-run inflation, could be very erratic. As for the very long run, it is difficult to say whether a domestic gold standard would in fact stabilize money growth and hence offer protection against inflation. It is true that what evidence is available from the experience of gold standards in the past suggests that a gold standard may stabilize prices in the very long run. But (a) the historical gold standard was one that was very widely adopted by industrial countries, not, as now proposed, adopted by a single country; (b) with conditions now vastly different from the past it is difficult to know how it would work today; (c) in any event, the short-term costs appear to be very substantial without any guarantee of long-run gains; (d) instead of complex legislation to reintroduce the gold standard, there could be simpler legislation to ensure that the long-run growth of base money does not go outside certain bounds, thus also securing the long-run gains without exposure to the short-run costs.

## THE DESIGN OF LONG-RUN FISCAL POLICY

Monetarists and supply-side economists share the view that the public sector is too large and government involvement in the economy excessive (Friedman and Friedman, 1980; Gilder, 1981). In *Free to Choose* Friedman and Friedman (1980, p. 48) ask:

> In a society whose participants desire to achieve the greatest possible freedom to choose as individuals, as families, as members of voluntary groups, as citizens of an organized government, what role should be assigned to governments?

Their answer is that there are four duties only: to provide defence, police and certain (very limited) public works and institutions and to protect citizens who cannot be regarded as responsible individuals (p. 53). Since, in reality, governments have assumed functions far beyond this, the public sector and taxes need to be cut back. When the 'optimal' size of the public sector is reached, government expenditure and taxes will be allowed to grow over time at a rate equal to the normal growth of output.

## THE DESIGN OF SHORT-RUN FISCAL POLICY

Monetarism I holds strong views both about the real effectiveness of fiscal policy, given the money supply, and also about the use of discretionary fiscal policy for stabilization. Fiscal policy is assumed to have either no real effects or weak effects in the short run. Fiscal policy, therefore, cannot be used to offset shocks to the real economy. In support of this proposition monetarists have at various times spelt out various mechanisms that might make fiscal policy impotent. Nevertheless, there is no consensus amongst monetarists on the relative importance that attaches to these mechanisms.

It is convenient in spelling out crowding-out mechanisms to distinguish three time horizons: immediate crowding out, crowding out within one to one-and-a-half years, and crowding out in the longer run.

There are three potential mechanisms by which crowding out may be immediate. First, if fiscal policy takes the form of an increase in public expenditure that is directly in competition with private expenditure, there will be an offsetting cut in private expenditure. Second, if tax cuts or increases in public expenditure are matched by sales of debt and future taxes to service the debt are fully discounted to the present (the pre-Ricardian equivalence hypothesis), real crowding out could be immediate. Third, fully anticipated changes in fiscal policy may lead to immediate price–wage adjustment, ruling out real effects. Case 1 is only a special case. Case 2 has been extensively criticized on theoretical grounds; it is also inconsistent with the evidence

(Tobin, 1980a). Case 3 has already been criticized as being too inconsistent with the evidence.

Beyond the immediate horizon there are numerous potential mechanisms at work that might generate short-run crowding out. First, there may be some early wage–price effects, weakening the real effects. Second, if the exchange rate is flexible and capital mobility is high, the real exchange rate will rise and this will serve to dampen real private expenditure. Third, with money supply fixed, the interest rate will rise, forcing down private expenditure. Fourth, additional sales of debt will have to be absorbed and this may further force up the interest rate. A potentially offsetting consideration here is that, insofar as there are net wealth effects, there will be some increase in household expenditure. However, monetarists play down these wealth effects, asserting that the money demand effect is more powerful than the wealth expenditure effect (Stein, 1974). Whether or not these mechanisms combined are sufficient to make fiscal policy work in the short run is an empirical matter and the evidence appears to be against those monetarist outcomes. Nearly all econometric models show significant real effects for fiscal policy continuing for one–two years (OECD, 1982; Nevile, 1983). Nevertheless, to be fair to monetarists this evidence may be biased in that at least some crowding-out mechanisms are not fully incorporated in econometric models (Argy, 1983c).

In the long run, any model with a natural rate of unemployment (NRU), independent of real demand, will produce complete real crowding out. The reason is, of course, that, price–wage mechanisms will ultimately come into play that neutralize real effects. Significant qualifications to this long-run result are worth noting, however. All of these centre around the possibility that fiscal policy itself may alter the NRU. In the open economy, fiscal expansion may change the terms of trade (at least over the medium term) and, with wages fixed in relation to overall prices, this allows real domestic wages to fall and hence some increase in employment. Moreover, fiscal expansion accompanied by a prices and incomes policy that succeeds in lowering real wages (on a once-for-all basis) may also cause the unemployment rate to fall. Again, with public sector employment insensitive to considerations of profitability, fiscal expansion that takes this form may also succeed in lowering the unemployment rate. Finally, if a downward expenditure shock increases the NRU, offsetting fiscal policy will serve to reduce it.

Despite these qualifications, there is little doubt that, over longer-term horizons, price–wage adjustments will serve substantially to weaken the real effects. In this respect all models more or less converge. These conclusions are also consistent with the bulk of econometric evidence available.

To sum up, on the evidence available, fiscal policy can in principle have real effects in the short run; hence, fiscal policy could be used to speed up adjustment to the NRU. In itself, this does not necessarily justify fine-tuning; it does however weaken the case against fine-tuning.

## NOTES

1 The distinction between monetarism I and monetarism II follows Tobin (1981).

2 References for the neo-classical school are Lucas (1972), Sargent and Wallace (1975), Barro (1976), McCallum (1980), and Buiter (1980).

3 References on supply-side economics are Gilder (1981), Wanniski (1978), Meyer (1981).
4 This aggregate supply equation can be rationalized in many different ways. For details see, for example, McCallum (1980).
5 The only costs of high inflation here are assumed to be the effects on money balance (shoe-leather costs). So-called menu costs are disregarded. See Fischer and Modigliani (1978). Of course, many might argue that shoe-leather costs, widely diffused as they are, are simply not comparable to unemployment costs, which are much more concentrated. Also disregarded are 'search' costs associated with the differing timing at which prices of commodities will rise.
6 The inclusion of $Y$ with a negative term is intended to capture the notion that, other things being equal, as income increases there is an increase in the demand for currency, reducing bank reserves and hence the volume of money (Argy, 1983a).
7 For a review of such proposals see Schwartz (1982), Bordo (1981) and Cooper (1982).

## BIBLIOGRAPHY


Argy, V. E. (1983a), 'Choice of intermediate money target in a deregulated and an integrated economy with flexible exchange rates', *IMF Staff Papers*, 30, December.

Argy, V. E. (1983b), 'The design of monetary and fiscal policies – the experience of four "conservative" administrations', *Centre for Studies in Money, Banking and Finance*, Macquarie University, December, Working Paper Series A, no. 8315A.

Argy, V. E. (1983c), 'Targeting the budget deficit in the face of a downward expenditure shock', *Center for Studies in Money, Banking and Finance*, Macquarie University, June, Working Paper Series B, no. 8351B.

Argy, V. E. (1984), 'The optimal mix of monetary and exchange rate management in conditions of perfect asset substitution – a formal analysis, *Centre for Studies in Money, Banking and Finance*, Macquarie University, April, Working Paper Series B, no. 8450B.

Bacon, R. W. and Eltis, W. A. (1979), 'How growth in public expenditure has contributed to Britain's difficulties', *The Dilemmas of Government Expenditure, London, The Institute of Economic Affairs, 1–21.*

Barro, R. J. (1976), 'Rational expectations and the role of monetary policy', *Journal of Monetary Economics*, 2, January, 1–32.

Begg, D. K. (1982), *The Rational Expectations Revolution in Macroeconomics – Theories and Evidence*, Baltimore, Md., Johns Hopkins University Press.

Benavie, A. and Froyer, R. T. (1983), 'Combination monetary policies to stabilize price and output under rational expectations', *Journal of Money, Credit and Banking*, 15 (2), May, 187–198.

Bordo, M. D. (1981), 'The classical gold standard – some lessons for today', *Federal Reserve Bank of St. Louis Monthly Review*, 63, May, 2–17.

Buiter, W. (1980), 'The macroeconomics of Dr. Pangloss – a critical survey of the New Classical Macroeconomics', *Economic Journal*, 90, March, 34–50.

*Business Week* (1981), 'A return to the gold standard', 21 September, 58–62.

Clark, C. (1945), 'Public finance and changes in value of money', *Economic Journal*, 55, December, 371–389.

Commission on the Role of Gold (1982), 'Commission on Role of Gold in the Domestic and International Monetary Systems', II Annexes, March, Minority Report, Washington, DC, US Government Printing Office.

Cooper, R. (1982), 'The gold standard: historical facts and future prospects', *Brookings Papers on Economic Activity*, 1, 1–45.

Drazen, A. (1979), 'The optimal rate of inflation revisited', *Journal of Monetary Economics*, 5 (2), April, 231–248.

Feldstein, M. S. (1979), 'The welfare cost of permanent inflation and optimal short-run economic policy', *Journal of Political Economy*, 87 (4), August, 749–768.

Fischer, S. (1981), 'Towards an understanding of the costs of inflation: II', in K. Brunner and A. H. Meltzer (eds.), *The Costs and Consequences of Inflation*, Carnegie–Rochester Conference Series on Public Policy, 15, Amsterdam, North Holland, 5–42.

Fischer, S. and Modigliani, F. (1978), 'Towards an understanding of the real effects and costs of inflation', *Weltwirtschaftliches Archiv*, 114, 810–833.

Friedman, M. (1968), 'The role of monetary policy', *American Economic Review*, 58, March, 1–17.

Friedman, M. (1969), 'The optimum quantity of money', in M. Friedman (ed.), *The Optimum Quantity of Money and Other Essays*, Chicago, Aldine Publishing Co., 1–50.

Friedman, M. (1974a), 'Perspective on inflation', *Newsweek*, 24 June.

Friedman, M. (1974b), 'Using escalators to help fight inflation', *Fortune*, July.

Friedman, M. (1977), 'Nobel lecture: inflation and unemployment', *Journal of Political Economy*', 85 (3), June, 451–472.

Friedman, M. (1980), 'Memorandum – Treasury and Civil Service Committee', *Memoranda on Monetary Policy Session 1979/80*, London, HMSO, July.

Friedman, M. (1982), 'Monetary policy: theory and practice', *Journal of Money, Credit and Banking*, 14 (1), February, 98–118.

Friedman, M. and Friedman, R. (1980), *Free to Choose: A Personal Statement*, Ringwood, Victoria, Penguin Books.

Friedman, M. and Meiselman, D. (1963), 'The relative stability of monetary velocity and the investment multiplier in the U.S., 1897–1958, *Stabilization Policies – A Series of Studies prepared for the Commission on Money and Credit*, Englewood Cliffs, NJ, Prentice-Hall.

Gilder, G. (1981), *Wealth and Poverty*, New York, Bantam Books.

Gordon, R. J. (1976), 'Dynamic considerations in the choice of inflation and unemployment targets: a comment', in K. Brunner and A. H. Meltzer (eds.), *The Phillips Curve and Labor Markets*, Carnegie–Rochester Conference Series on Public Policy, 1, Amsterdam, North Holland, 149–159.

Gordon, R. J. (1982), 'Price inertia and policy ineffectiveness in the United States 1890–1980', *Journal of Political Economy*, 90, December, 1087–1117.

Gordon, R. J. and King, S. R. (1982), 'The output cost of disinflation in traditional and vector autoregressive models', *Brookings Papers on Economic Activity*, 1, 205–242.

Gregory, R. G. (1982), 'Work and welfare in the years ahead', *Australian Economic Papers*, 21, December, 219–243.

Hall, R. E. (1975), 'The rigidity of wages and the persistence of unemployment', *Brookings Papers on Economic Activity*, 2, 301–350.

Laffer, A. B. (1980), 'Reinstatement of the dollar: the blueprint', Economic Study by A. B. Laffer Associates, February.

Lucas, R. E. Jr. (1972), 'Expectations and the neutrality of money', *Journal of Economic Theory*, 4, April, 103–124.

McCallum, B. T. (1980), 'Rational expectations and macroeconomic stabilization policy: an overview', *Journal of Money, Credit and Banking*, Part 2, November, 716–746.

Meade, J. E. (1978), 'The meaning of internal balance', *Economic Journal*, 88, September, 423–435.

Meyer, L. (ed.) (1981), *The Supply-Side Effects of Economic Policy*, Federal Reserve Bank of St. Louis, May.

Meyer, L. H. and Raasche, R. H. (1980), 'On the costs and benefits of anti-inflationary policies', *Federal Reserve Bank of St. Louis Monthly Review*, 62, February, 3–14.

Minford, P. and Peel, D. (1981), 'Is the government's economic strategy on course?', *Lloyds Bank Review*, 140, April, 1–19.

Mishkin, F. S. (1982), 'Does anticipated monetary policy matter?: An econometric investigation', *Journal of Political Economy*, 90, February, 22–51.

Mullineaux, D. J. (1980), 'Unemployment, industrial production and inflation uncertainty in the United States', *Review of Economics and Statistics*, 62 (2), May, 163–169.

Nevile, J. (1983), 'The role of fiscal policy in the eighties', *The Economic Record*, 59 (164), March, 1–15.

OECD (1982), 'Budget financing and monetary control', *Monetary Studies Series*, Paris, Organisation for Economic Co-operation and Development.

Phelps, E. S. (1972), *Inflation Policy and Unemployment Theory: The Cost–Benefit Approach to Monetary Planning*, London, Macmillan.

Poole, W. (1970), 'Optimal choice of monetary policy instruments in a simple stochastic macro-model', *Quarterly Journal of Economics*, 84, May, 197–216.

Roper, Don. E. and Turnovsky, Stephen, J. (1980), 'Optimal exchange market intervention in a simple stochastic macro-model', *Canadian Journal of Economics*, 13, May, 296–309.

Sargent, T. J. and Wallace, N. (1975), ' "Rational" expectations, the optimal monetary instruments, and the optimal money supply rule', *Journal of Political Economy*, 83, April, 241–254.

Schwartz, A. J. (1982), 'Reflections on the Gold Commission Report', *Journal of Money, Credit and Banking*, 4, Part I, 19, November, 538–551.

Stein, J. L. (1974), 'Unemployment, inflation and monetarism', *American Economic Review*, 64, December, 867–887.

Summers, L. H. (1981), 'Optimal inflation policy', *Journal of Monetary Economics*, 7 (2), March, 175–194.

Tobin, J. (1980a), *Asset Accumulation and Economic Activity*, Chicago, Ill., University of Chicago Press.

Tobin, J. (1980b), 'Stabilization policy ten years after', *Brookings Papers on Economic Activity*, 1, 19–71.

Tobin, J. (1981), 'The monetarist counter-revolution today – an appraisal', *Economic Journal*, 91, (361), March, 29–42.

Wanniski, J. (1978), *The Way the World Works*, New York, Basic Books.

# 5 Some Macroeconomic Implications of Wage Indexation: A Survey

*JEFFREY CARMICHAEL, JEROME FAHRER and JOHN HAWKINS**

## I INTRODUCTION

Wage indexation affects macroeconomic stability through its impact on the variability of output and prices. Indexation can therefore be viewed from two perspectives: whether or not it raises economic welfare and whether or not it alters the effectiveness of stabilization policy. The major theorem of the literature on this topic is that wage indexation tends to stabilize output in response to nominal or demand-side disturbances, to destabilize output in response to real or supply-side disturbances, and to amplify the reaction in prices to all disturbances. The first formal statements of this proposition are usually attributed to Gray (1976) and Fischer (1977), although Fischer points out that the principle dates back a long way.[1] Despite considerable extension and refinement by the subsequent literature, this key result appears to have survived largely intact.

Whether or not indexation raises economic welfare can be considered only with respect to some benchmarks. One is the desired equilibrium that would obtain if all disturbances were known. Another is the equilibrium that would obtain if indexation were prohibited. The literature shows that indexation could replicate the desired equilibrium, although the complexity of the indexation rule and the information required to operate it make actual implementation impracticable. Within the class of indexing rules linked to the price level only, there is an optimal rule that balances expected deviations of output from its desired level. Since supply-side shocks require some adjustment of real wages and output in the desired equilibrium it is not surprising that the optimal rule lies somewhere between non-indexation and full indexation. The optimal rule balances the costs of expected shocks to both supply and demand. *Ex post*, of course, it should still be the case that highly indexed economies cope less well with realized supply-side shocks such as the oil crises in the 1970s.

The implications of the Gray–Fischer result for policy are interesting. Since wage indexation amplifies the reaction in the price level to all disturbances, it will tend to be inflationary if most disturbances, including policy shocks, are

* The views expressed in this chapter are not necessarily shared by colleagues at the Reserve Bank.

expansionary. At the same time, the tendency for indexation to increase the price reaction and reduce the output reaction to demand-side shocks should minimize the cost of a programme designed to reduce inflation through monetary contraction. The credibility of the policy might be expected to be less critical under indexation since workers have their nominal wages determined by the actual outcome of inflation, rather than by *ex ante* expectations about it.

While the tendency for wage indexation to amplify the effects of disturbances on the price level may be desirable under anti-inflationary policies, some see it as raising the magnitude of the task, indeed as a means of institutionalizing inflation. Whether indexation helps or hinders government in its efforts to control inflation depends very much on whether monetary policy accommodates or offsets the influence of other disturbances; in other words, it depends on how serious the authorities are about reducing inflation.

Section II of this chapter reproduces the important Gray–Fischer analysis and its main results. Their model is shown to have two critical features: the assumed nature of disequilibrium behaviour in the labour market and the process of forming contracts. These aspects are examined in more detail in Sections III and IV. Section V focuses on extensions of the Gray–Fischer analysis to an open economy. Section VI examines some international evidence on wage indexation.

## II THE GRAY–FISCHER ANALYSIS

This section presents the basic Gray–Fischer proposition that wage indexation stabilizes output in the face of demand disturbances and destabilizes it in the face of supply disturbances. Aggregate demand is derived from equations (1) and (2) representing, in log-linear form, equilibrium in the product market (*IS* curve) and the money market (*LM* curve) respectively:

$$y_t = c_1 y_t - c_2 i_t + \phi_{1t} \tag{1}$$

$$m_t + \phi_{2t} - p_t = z_1 y_t - z_2 i_t. \tag{2}$$

Here, $y$, $m$ and $p$ are the logarithms of real income, the nominal money stock and the price level respectively, $i$ is the level of the nominal interest rate[2] and $\phi_{1t}$ and $\phi_{2t}$ are independent random disturbances, each with zero mean. The elasticities in the expenditure and money demand functions are defined to be non-negative; this convention will be adopted throughout the chapter. Equations (1) and (2) can be solved for the aggregate demand schedule:

$$y_t^d = \beta_t - dp_t \tag{3}$$

where

$$\beta_t = [c_2 m_t + z_2 \phi_{1t} + c_2 \phi_{2t}]/[(1 - c_1)z_2 + z_1 c_2]$$
$$d = c_2/[(1 - c_1)z_2 + z_1 c_2].$$

The intercept term $\beta_t$ contains aggregate demand disturbances arising from shocks to real product demand ($\phi_{1t}$) as well as shocks to either money supply or demand ($\phi_{2t}$). Thus, $\beta_t$ includes the effects of both monetary and fiscal policy. Since all parameters are defined to be positive and $c_1 < 1$, the slope coefficient, $d$, will be positive. The denominator of $\beta_t$ is positive, so that $\beta_t$ will be positive for positive shocks to product demand and money supply, but negative for an increase in liquidity preference.

On the supply side of the economy, the capital stock is assumed to be fixed, so that aggregate output can be written as a function of total labour input and a stochastic productivity factor $\alpha$:

$$y_t = \alpha_t + \delta n_t \tag{4}$$

where $n$ is the log of employment and $\delta$ is the elasticity of output with respect to labour input.

The labour market is described by equations (5) and (6).[3] The supply and demand functions take familiar forms, with both depending on the real wage rate, $w_t - p_t$ (where $w$ is the log of the nominal wage rate), and demand also depending on the productivity factor $\alpha_t$:

$$n_t^d = \eta Ln\delta - \eta(w_t - p_t - \alpha_t) \tag{5}$$

$$n_t^s = \eta Ln\delta + \varepsilon(w_t - p_t). \tag{6}$$

The intercept term in the labour supply function ($\eta Ln\delta$) is chosen so that the log of the non-stochastic equilibrium real wage is zero. This assumption is convenient without restricting the generality of the results.

The critical features of the model are the nature of labour contracts and labour market behaviour. In the Gray–Fischer analysis, labour contracts are assumed to establish a base nominal wage rate, $w^*$, and an indexing parameter, $\gamma$. The analysis is simplified by assuming that the base wage rate is set at the level that corresponds to equilibrium in the labour market when the realized values of all disturbances ($\phi_{1t}$, $\phi_{2t}$ and $\alpha_t$) are zero. This assumption has the advantage that the base wage corresponds to a rational expectations forecast of the equilibrium wage, so that the results do not depend on an arbitrary process of forming expectations. Non-stochastic equilibrium values will be indicated by an asterisk.

The choice of the intercept term in the labour supply function leads to the condition that the log of the real wage rate associated with the base wage (i.e. the real wage corresponding to zero disturbances) is zero. This allows the indexing rule to be written in the convenient form:

$$w_t = \gamma p_t \tag{7}$$

where $\gamma = 0$ corresponds to non-indexation and $\gamma = 1$ corresponds to full indexation.

Once contracts are settled and production decisions made, employment becomes completely demand determined; i.e. labour supply is perfectly elastic with respect to the negotiated nominal wage ($w^*$ or $w^*$ plus a mechanical indexation adjustment). The aggregate supply schedule is obtained by substituting (5) and (7) into (4):

$$y_t^s = \alpha_t + \delta\eta Ln\delta + \delta\eta[(1-\gamma)p_t + \alpha_t].$$

To simplify notation, define $s = \delta\eta$ and $q = \delta\eta Ln\delta$. Thus, the aggregate supply schedule can be written as:

$$y_t^s = \alpha_t + q + s[(1-\gamma)p_t + \alpha_t]. \tag{8}$$

The aggregate demand and supply schedules, (3) and (8), can now be solved for the reduced-form expressions for real output and the price level:

$$y_t = \frac{dq}{d + s(I - \gamma)} + \left(\frac{s(1-\gamma)}{d + s(1-\gamma)}\right)\beta_t + \left(\frac{d(1+s)}{d + s(1-\gamma)}\right)\alpha_t \tag{9}$$

$$p_t = \frac{-q}{d + s(1-\gamma)} + \left(\frac{1}{d + s(1-\gamma)}\right)\beta_t + \left(\frac{1+s}{d + s(1-\gamma)}\right)\alpha_t. \tag{10}$$

The implications of wage indexation for the transmission of disturbances to real output and the price level can be seen clearly in the polar cases of non-indexation ($\gamma = 0$) and full indexation ($\gamma = 1$). The range of responses is shown in Table 5.1. Since all parameters ($d$ and $s$ in particular) are positive, $(1 + s) > d(1 + s)/(d + s)$, while $0 < s/(d + s)$. Thus, indexation increases fluctuations in output arising from aggregate supply shocks and reduces those fluctuations when shocks are predominantly demand oriented.[4] In contrast, wage indexation increases the response of the price level to all disturbances.

**Table 5.1** *Output and price responses to disturbances*

| | *Non-indexation* ($\gamma = 0$) | *Full indexation* ($\gamma = 1$) |
|---|---|---|
| $y_t$: | | |
| Supply shocks ($\alpha_t$) | $\frac{d(1+s)}{d+s}$ | $1 + s$ |
| Demand shocks ($\beta_t$) | $\frac{s}{d+s}$ | 0 |
| $p_t$: | | |
| Supply shocks ($\alpha_t$) | $\frac{-(1+s)}{d+s}$ | $\frac{-1(+s)}{d}$ |
| Demand shocks ($\beta_t$) | $\frac{1}{d+s}$ | $\frac{1}{d}$ |

The intuition behind these results can be developed with the aid of a diagram. Panel (A) of Figure 5.1 shows the initial aggregate demand schedule $y^d$ and the aggregate supply schedules $y^s_{n0}$ for (non-indexation) and $y^s_{i0}$ (for full indexation); the latter is vertical at the non-stochastic or full employment output level. The counterpart of the vertical aggregate supply schedule under full indexation is the perfectly elastic supply for labour, fixed at the non-stochastic real wage rate $w^* - p^* = 0$. This is shown in panel (C) of Figure 5.1. The labour supply function for the non-indexed economy initially coincides with that for the indexed economy but, unlike the latter, it shifts to the right with the fall in the price level and to the left with a rise in the price level. Panel (B) shows the production function $y(\alpha_0)$ from which the labour demand schedule $n^d(\alpha_0)$ in Panel (C) is derived.

The impact of demand disturbances is straightforward. Since the indexed aggregate supply function is vertical and is unaffected by shocks to aggregate demand, variations in $y^d$ impact fully on the price level but leave output unaffected. Since the non-indexed supply schedule is positively sloped, the

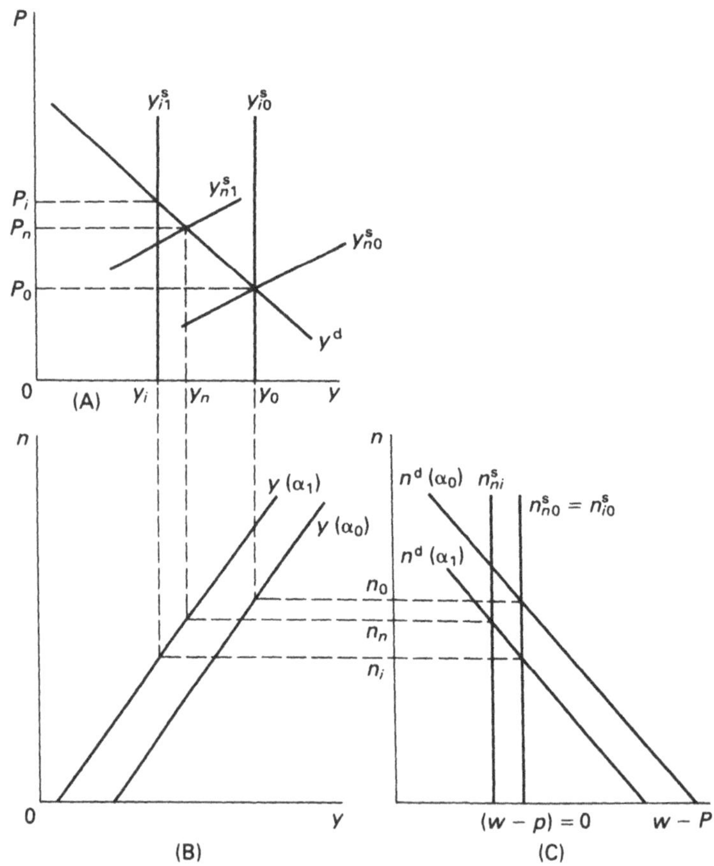


**Figure 5.1**

impact of variations in $y^d$ will be shared between responses in output and the price level.

The response to supply disturbances is less straightforward. Consider an exogenous fall in productivity (a decrease in $\alpha_t$ from $\alpha_0$ to $\alpha_1$). The production function shifts horizontally to the left. Similarly, the demand for labour schedule shifts horizontally to the left. Under full indexation, the real wage rate remains constant at $w - p = 0$. The full impact of the fall in labour demand falls on employment (from $n_0$ to $n_i$). The aggregate supply schedule shifts horizontally to the left from $y^s_{i0}$ to $y^s_{i1}$, resulting in a rise in the price level from $p_0$ to $p_i$. With non-indexation, the initial tendency is the same; employment falls, output falls and the price level rises. However, without indexation, the rise in price leads to a fall in real wages, thereby mitigating the fall in employment to $n_n$ and in output to $y_n$.

These results are derived here for impact multipliers only. In his paper, Fischer shows that the results are preserved in a fully dynamic model and also in its steady state. The Gray–Fischer theorem is intuitively appealing and, by and large, has survived the modifications and extensions of the subsequent literature. The following sections take up the various strands of this literature.

## III DISEQUILIBRIUM IN THE LABOUR MARKET

As pointed out in section II, an important feature of the Gray–Fischer model is the behaviour of its labour market. In that model, contracts are assumed to determine a base wage plus a level of automatic indexation at the start of the period. Once the contracts are settled, the supply of labour function is assumed to become perfectly elastic at the contracted nominal wage (or wage formula if some indexation is involved). With a perfectly elastic supply schedule, the labour market behaves in a standard neo-Keynesian fashion, with employment being completely demand determined.

The importance of this process of determining employment to the Gray–Fischer results is examined by Cukierman (1980). Cukierman follows Gray and Fischer in allowing contracts to determine a base wage and the degree of indexation. He points out, however, that there are no universally accepted principles of determining quantities in disequilibrium situations. Gray and Fischer assume that, in disequilibrium, employment is demand determined. Cukierman considers a more general formulation that includes the Gray–Fischer equilibrium as a special case. He assumes an eclectic rule for determining employment in disequilibrium situations under which, for any given real wage, employment is a weighted average of the underlying demand and supply quantities corresponding to the real wage rate:

$$n_t = \phi n_t^d + (1 - \theta) n_t^s, \tag{11}$$

where $n_t^d$ and $n_t^s$ are defined in equations (5) and (6). The Gray–Fischer assumption occurs for $\theta = 1$. At the other extreme, determination of employment along the supply curve occurs for $\theta = 0$. As noted by Cukierman, equation (11) also allows for more complex rules such as the short-end rule

($\theta = 1$ for $w - p > w^* - p^*$ and $\theta = 0$ for $w - p < w^* - p^*$). The general principle of equation (11), however, is that it allows both demand and supply to influence actual employment in disequilibrium.

Substituting (11) and (7) (the indexation rule) into the production function (4) defines the modified aggregate supply function:

$$y_t^s = \alpha_t + s\theta((1-\gamma)p_t + \alpha_t) - \delta\varepsilon(1-\theta)(1-\gamma)p_t, \tag{12}$$

where, for notational simplicity, the constant term $q$ is ignored.[5]

Setting aggregate supply (12) equal to aggregate demand (3) yields the following reduced-form solutions for output and the price level:

$$y_t = \left(\frac{(1-\gamma)[\theta s - \delta\varepsilon(1-\theta)]}{d + (1-\gamma)[\theta s - \delta\varepsilon(1-\theta)]}\right)\beta_t + \left(\frac{d(1+\theta s)}{d + (1-\gamma)[\theta s - \delta\varepsilon(1-\theta)]}\right)\alpha_t \tag{13}$$

$$p_t = \left(\frac{1}{d + (1-\gamma)[\theta s - \delta\varepsilon(1-\theta)]}\right)\beta_t - \left(\frac{(1+\theta s)}{d + (1-\gamma)[\theta s - \delta\varepsilon(1-\theta)]}\right)\alpha_t. \tag{14}$$

The impact multipliers for output and the price level for the polar cases of non-indexation and full indexation are reported in Table 5.2. The Gray–Fischer conclusion that aggregate demand disturbances have no impact on real

**Table 5.2** *Output and price responses with demand and supply influences on employment*

| | *Non-indexation* ($\gamma = 0$) | *Full indexation* ($\gamma = 1$) |
|---|---|---|
| $y_t$: | | |
| Supply shocks ($\alpha_t$) | $\frac{d(1+\theta s)}{d + \theta s - \delta\varepsilon(1-\theta)}$ | $1 + \theta s$ |
| Demand shocks ($\beta_t$) | $\frac{\theta s - \delta\varepsilon(1-\theta)}{d + \theta s - \delta\varepsilon(1-\theta)}$ | 0 |
| $p_t$: | | |
| Supply shocks ($\alpha_t$) | $\frac{-(1+\theta s)}{d + \theta s - \delta\varepsilon(1-\theta)}$ | $\frac{-(1+\theta s)}{d}$ |
| Demand shocks ($\beta_t$) | $\frac{1}{d + \theta s - \delta\varepsilon(1-\theta)}$ | $\frac{1}{d}$ |

output under full wage indexation is completely unaffected by altering the disequilibrium behaviour of the labour market. This much is immediately apparent from equation (12), where full indexation ($\gamma = 1$) once again eliminates the price term from the aggregate supply function.

Whether or not wage indexation exacerbates or dampens the output response to real disturbances, however, now depends on the sign and size of $\theta_s - \delta\varepsilon(1 - \theta)$. This term, of course, is simply the elasticity-weighted apportioning of the demand and supply influences on employment (recall that $s = \delta\eta$). When $\theta = 1$, the Gray–Fischer result obtains – wage indexation exacerbates real shocks. When $0 < \theta < 1$ several outcomes are possible.

The crux of the complication introduced by Cukierman is that supply determination (or even supply dominance) or employment makes the aggregate supply schedule negatively sloped[6] – the same as the aggregate demand schedule. The outcome then depends on the relative slopes of the two schedules.

Figure 5.2 reproduces Figure 5.1 for a negative real disturbance ($\alpha_t < 0$) in

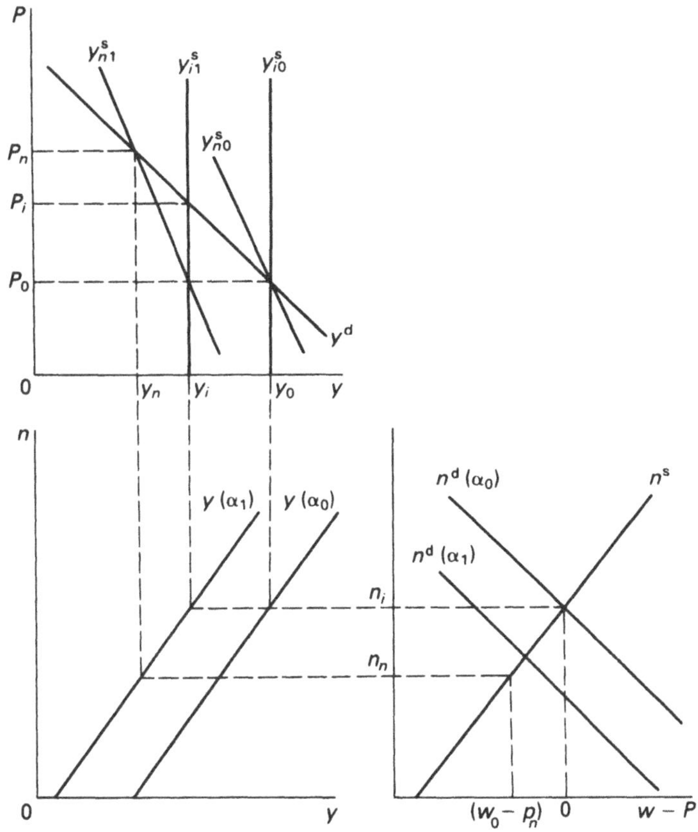


**Figure 5.2**

the case where the aggregate supply curve cuts the aggregate demand curve from above.[7] For simplicity, consider the polar case where employment is entirely supply determined ($\theta = 0$). With full indexation, the real wage remains constant, employment remains constant and the aggregate supply curve shifts to the left by the full amount of the disturbance, from $y^s_{i0}$ to $y^s_{i1}$; output falls from $y_0$ to $y_i$ and the price level rises from $p_0$ to $p_i$. Without indexation, the negatively sloped aggregate supply curve also shifts horizontally to the left by the full extent of the disturbance (from $y^s_{n0}$ to $y^s_{n1}$). Again, this forces the price level to rise but, in the process, real wages fall. The fall in real wages reduces employment by sliding down the labour supply schedule; the reduction in employment reduces output further to $y_n$ and increases the price level further to $p_n$.

Thus, so long as the aggregate supply schedule cuts the aggregate demand schedule from above, supply-side dominance reverses the Gray–Fischer result for supply disturbances. In this case, wage indexation dampens the impact of supply shocks on both output and prices. As supply-side dominance decreases ($\delta\varepsilon(1 - \theta)$ decreases towards $s\theta$), the non-indexed aggregate supply schedule steepens. When $\delta\varepsilon(1 - \theta) = s\theta$, the indexed and non-indexed schedules coincide and response patterns are identical. When demand influences dominate ($s\theta > \delta\varepsilon(1 - \theta)$), the non-indexed supply schedule again becomes positively sloped and the Gray–Fischer results obtain.

## IV THE NATURE OF CONTRACTS AND OPTIMAL INDEXATION

The previous section examined the importance of disequilibrium behaviour in the labour market to the Gray–Fischer results. This section turns to the second crucial aspect of labour market behaviour, namely the formulation of contracts. The role of labour market contracts for macroeconomic stability is one of the more recent and exciting areas of economic research. The simple version of the Gray–Fischer model presented so far raises a number of questions about the assumed wage contract: is it consistent with the information structure of the model? to what extent is the market likely to index contracts? and can the government improve welfare by imposing a predetermined level of indexation?

In the second part of her paper, Gray examines the process of determining the degree of indexation. Fischer also looks at this question and we shall return to his treatment shortly.

Gray assumes that firms and workers are risk neutral and (somehow) agree to set the degree of indexation so as to minimize the expected loss due to deviations of the log of actual output from the log of its desired level, $y_0$. Actual output is given in equation (9). Desired output is defined as the level of output that would occur if all disturbances were known. This is found by solving the labour demand and supply schedules (5) and (6) for equilibrium employment, then substituting into the production function (4) to get:

$$y_{0t} = q + \alpha_t + \left(\frac{\delta\varepsilon\eta}{\eta + \varepsilon}\right) \alpha_t. \qquad (15)$$

Gray defines the loss function $Z$ as:

$$Z = E(y_t - y_{0t})^2. \tag{16}$$

The loss function is obtained by subtracting (15) from (9), squaring the result and taking expectations:

$$Z = a_1^2 V_{\phi 1} + a_2^2 V_{\phi 2} + a_3^2 V_\alpha \tag{17}$$

where

$$a_1 = \frac{s(1-\gamma)z_2}{[d + s(1-\gamma)][(1-c_1)z_2 + z_1 c_2]}$$

$$a_2 = \frac{-s(1-\gamma)c_2}{[d + s(1-\gamma)][(1-c_1)z_2 + z_1 c_2]}$$

$$a_3 = \frac{s(d-(1-\gamma))}{d + s(1-\gamma)} - \frac{\delta\varepsilon\eta}{\eta + \varepsilon}$$

and $V_{\phi 1}$, $V_{\phi 2}$ and $V_\alpha$ are the variances of the independent disturbance terms $\phi_1$, $\phi_2$ and $\alpha$. The optimal degree of indexation is found by differentiating (17) with respect to $\gamma$, setting the resulting condition equal to zero and solving for the optimum value, $\tilde{\gamma}$. The optimal degree of indexing is a weighted average of the optima corresponding to the extreme cases of $V_\alpha = 0$ and $V_{\phi 1} = V_{\phi 2} = 0$; that is, the cases in which the aggregate supply and demand functions respectively are deterministic.

When $V_\alpha = 0$ (no supply-side shocks), full indexation ($\gamma = 1$) is optimal since this minimizes the impact of demand-side shocks. When $V_{\phi 1} = V_{\phi 2} = 0$ (no demand-side shocks), the optimal degree of indexation is still greater than zero since the desired equilibrium involves some output response to real shocks.

In Gray's simple model, in which the aggregate demand schedule is dominated by the extreme monetarist version of the quantity theory, the optimal degree of indexing, $\tilde{\gamma}$, depends on the elasticities of labour supply (positively) and demand (negatively). In addition, she shows $\tilde{\gamma}$ to be an increasing function of the variance of monetary shocks and a decreasing function of the variance of supply shocks. In the more general demand-side formulation suggested by Cukierman (and used in this paper), the optimal degree of indexation depends on these variables plus the income elasticity of consumption, the interest rate elasticity of aggregate demand and the variance of real demand shocks ($V_{\phi 1}$). He also finds that, so long as employment is demand dominated, allowing both supply and demand to influence employment does not alter the relationship between optimal indexation and the variance of monetary and real supply shocks. The variance of real demand shocks, not surprisingly, has the same effect as the variance of monetary shocks.

In a subsequent paper, Gray (1978) makes the contracting process more complicated by assuming that negotiating a contract entails a fixed cost. She also considers the effects of indexation costs (though it is not clear exactly how these costs are incurred) and the role of industry-specific real shocks on contracts.

An important characteristic of the contracts in Gray's models is that they are contingent contracts; i.e. the ultimate nominal wage is contingent on the actual outcome for the price level. This raises the question of whether other currently observed variables could be incorporated into the indexing formula to improve the outcome by increasing the range of contingencies allowed for. Pazner (1981) argues that Gray's indexation scheme is dominated by a contingent contract that is fully indexed to the price level and partially indexed to real income. Eden (1979) suggests that indexing nominal wages to the money supply would eliminate the response of real output to monetary disturbances. He copes with other disturbances by allowing for fully contingent contracts. Karni (1983) goes a step further. He points out that, given the structure of Gray's model, both the level of real output and the price level are current-period observed variables.

The contingent contracts involved, however, are extremely complicated and, as pointed out by Karni and Cukierman, they involve an element of moral hazard in that it will usually pay one party to the contract to default. In an interesting contribution, Blanchard (1979) points out that it would also be very costly to collect and treat all the information needed for fully contingent rules. He suggests that wages rules indexed only to the price level may be the optimal compromise. He also finds that policies that increase the correlation between the aggregate price level and relative price changes raise welfare by making the price level a better proxy for variables excluded from the indexing rule.

Another problem with the contingent rules discussed so far is timing. Indexing periods are assumed to be discrete, with the market equilibrium occurring at some unspecified point in the period. Current-period observations of price and output are needed for the indexing procedure, yet the indexing procedure is of crucial importance to the determination of price and output. In actual market situations, current values of aggregate variables are typically not known for some time. They usually involve measurement error and are often revised. Further, the necessary data are not always available with the same frequency; in many countries, some price data are available monthly, while output data are available quarterly or annually.

Barro (1976) analyses wage indexation in a rational expectations model with partial current information on prices. In his model, equilibrium is determined after shocks are realized but before the aggregate price level is known. Producers must infer the magnitude of shocks from market-specific information. Barro concludes that indexation has no implications for the determination of output across markets.

Barro's model, however, has some special assumptions. First, as pointed out by Karni, Barro's contract period coincides with the time lag in obtaining information. More importantly, indexation in Barro's model involves adjustment of all prices at the end of the period, with payments taking place at those prices. Thus, individuals use available current information to form expectations of final prices. Output decisions are then based on those expectations.

Under this set-up, indexation has no direct effect on output (other than through its influence on expectations). As a result, it can influence output only if it improves the information structure of the economy.

In practice, contracts often extend well beyond the information lag in data. More importantly, indexation usually takes the form of adjusting the wage for period $t + 1$ on the basis of price movements in period $t$. If contracts were written for the length of the data period only, the equilibrium would have the properties of the non-indexed case. That is, nominal wages in each period would be fully predetermined. Indexation starts to influence output fluctuations only when contracts extend over several data periods.

In this respect, Fischer's original contribution still stands as probably the most useful in terms of analysing the nature of indexation and labour contracts. In his model, contracts extend for two periods, with half the contracts coming due for renegotiation in each period.

He assumes that non-indexed contracts determine a wage rate at the beginning of period $t$ (before any disturbances are realized) so as to maintain real wages over periods $t$ and $t + 1$. Thus the contract involves expectations of the price level in periods $t$ and $t + 1$ formed on the basis of information available at the end of period $t - 1$. The indexed contract sets a wage for period $t$ in the knowledge that it will be adjusted in period $t + 1$ for price movements during period $t$.

The indexed and non-indexed models are very similar in that the nominal wage is predetermined in each period in both systems. The main difference is that indexation allows nominal wages to respond to actual rather than expected events. Fischer shows that, for an indexation rule that minimizes the variance of real wages, the model produces essentially the standard Gray–Fischer results. There is no differential response to a current disturbance because nominal wages are predetermined in both cases. Similarly, disturbances more than two periods old are known and fully incorporated into all contracts. The Gray–Fischer results show up in the response to disturbances in the last period before the current one.

Fischer is quick to point out, however, that the indexation rule that minimizes the variance of real wages is not the rule most seen in practice; namely, one in which the wage in period $t$ is the previous period's wage adjusted for the change in prices between the two periods. He argues that this latter rule will destabilize output if nominal disturbances are transitory. For example, if monetary shocks were completely random, a large monetary disturbance in period $t$ may raise nominal wages in period $t + 1$ by an excessive amount relative to the underlying structure of the model. Thus, indexation is more likely to be stabilizing when information is available at frequent intervals and indexing consists of a series of small adjustments; that is, as the system approaches the simple Gray–Fischer model in which wages are indexed to current rather than to lagged prices.

## V WAGE INDEXATION IN AN OPEN ECONOMY

Extending the analysis of wage indexation to an open economy raises two lines of inquiry: first, does the degree of openness and/or choice of exchange regime have any implications for the Gray–Fischer results, and, second, does the degree of wage indexation have any implications for traditional results in the open-economy literature? The answer is affirmative in both cases.

The importance of wage determination in generating standard results in international finance is analysed by Casas (1975), Sachs (1980), Argy and Salop (1979, 1983) and Marston (1982, 1983). They find wage behaviour to be of crucial importance in determining the extent to which a change in the exchange rate induces a change in the relative price of foreign and domestic goods and, through relative prices, a change in output.

The traditional view of the efficacy of policies under alternative exchange regimes is due to Mundell (1963) and Fleming (1962). Their main result is that, so long as there is at least some international capital mobility, fiscal policy is more effective in terms of altering output under a fixed exchange rate than under a flexible exchange rate, while the reverse proposition holds for monetary policy. Their analyses, however, are characterized by the assumption that domestic wages are constant, with the result that any change in the exchange rate changes both relative prices and the real wage rate. Once nominal wages are free to adjust to exchange rate changes, not only are the output responses to policy dampened, but the standard Mundell–Fleming results need substantial modification.

Following Sachs, we define the log of the overall (or consumer) price level, $p_c$, as:

$$p_{ct} = \lambda p_t + (1 - \lambda)(p_t^* + e_t), \tag{18}$$

where $\lambda$ is the weight of domestically produced goods in total consumption, $p^*$ is the log of the price of imports (in this section, an asterisk will denote foreign country variables) and $e$ is the log of the domestic currency price of foreign currency (a rise in $e$ is a depreciation of the domestic currency).

Since the choice between labour and leisure involves utility comparisons based on overall consumption, the real wage relevant to individuals is $w - p_c$. Correspondingly, indexation is redefined in terms of $p_c$.

$$w_t = \beta p_{ct}, \tag{19}$$

where, again, $\gamma = 0$ represents non-indexation and $\gamma = 1$ represents full indexation. While individuals regard $w - p_c$ as the relevant real wage, producers still face $w - p$ as the relevant real wage cost of employment. Real output effects will thus be possible under full indexation if exchange rate movements generate relative price changes between domestic and imported goods.

Substituting (18) and (19) into the labour demand function (5) and then into the production function (4) yields the open-economy aggregate supply schedule:

$$y_t^s = (1 + s)\alpha_t + q - s\gamma(1 - \lambda)(p_t^* + e_t) + s(1 - \gamma\lambda)p_t. \tag{20}$$

The condition for equilibrium in the goods market must also be modified to include the balance of trade. We assume a simple functional form in which the log of the balance of trade, $x$, depends negatively on the relative price of domestic goods and imports $(p - p^* - e)$ and positively on the log of foreign income, $y^*$:

$$x_t = -c_3(p_t - p_t^* - e_t) + c_4 y_t^*. \tag{21}$$

Most contributions to this literature introduce complex portfolio models of the asset markets. It is possible to illustrate the essence of their results, however, with a minimal specification of portfolio preferences. If we assume perfect capital mobility and perfect substitutability between domestic and foreign bonds, the bond market equilibrium condition is reduced to the uncovered interest parity condition – that the domestic interest rate equals the foreign interest rate, $i^*$, plus the expected rate of depreciation of the domestic currency. Further, without loss of generality, we can simplify the analysis by setting the expected rate of depreciation equal to zero. With these assumptions, the money market equilibrium condition becomes:

$$m_t + f_t + \phi_{2t} - p_t = z_1 y_t - z_2 i_t^*, \tag{22}$$

where $f$ is the long of 1 plus the domestic currency equivalent of the stock-shift change in the level of foreign reserves expressed as a ratio to the money stock. Under a fixed exchange rate, $f$ is associated with a swap of domestic holdings of bonds for domestic money. Under a flexible exchange rate, $f$ is identically zero.

The full model consists of the aggregate supply function (20), the money market equilibrium condition (22) and the goods market equilibrium condition (1) after including the balance of trade (21) and the assumptions of perfect capital mobility and substitutability:

$$y_t(1 - c_1) = -c_2 i_t^* - c_3(p_t - p_t^* - e_t) + c_4 y_t^* + \phi_{1t}. \tag{23}$$

The reduced-form solutions for $y_t$ and $p_t$ under a fixed exchange rate are:

$$y_t = s(1 - \gamma\lambda)(\phi_{1t} - c_2 i_t^* + c_4 y_t^*)/\Delta_1 + c_3[(1 + s)\alpha_t + q]/\Delta_1 + sc_3(1 - \gamma)(p_t^* + e_t)/\Delta_1 \tag{24}$$

$$p_t = [\phi_{1t} - c_2 i_t^* + c_4 y_t^* - (1 + s)(1 - c_1)\alpha_t - q(1 - c_1)]/\Delta_1 + [c_3 + s\gamma(1 - \lambda)(1 - c_1)](p_t^* + e_t)/\Delta_1 \tag{25}$$

where $\Delta_1 = c_3 + s(1 - \gamma\lambda)(1 - c_1) > 0$.

The corresponding reduced-form solutions for $y_t$ and $p_t$, and also for the exchange rate $e_t$, under a flexible exchange rate are:

$$y_t = c_3 s(1 - \gamma)(m_t + z_2 i_t^* + \phi_{2t})/\Delta_2 + s\gamma(1 - \lambda)(c_3 p_t^* - c_2 i_t^* + c_4 y_t^* + \phi_{1t})/\Delta_2 - c_3[s\gamma(1 - \lambda)p_t^* - (1 + s)\alpha_t - q]/\Delta_2 \tag{26}$$

$$p_t = [c_3 + s\gamma(1 - \lambda)(1 - c_1)](m_t + z_2 i_t^* + \phi_{2t})/\Delta_2 - z_1 s\gamma(1 - \lambda)(c_3 p_t^* - c_2 i_t^* + c_4 y_t^* + \phi_{1t})/\Delta_2 + c_3 z_1[s\gamma(1 - \lambda)p_t^* - (1 + s)\alpha_t - q]/\Delta_2 \tag{27}$$

**Table 5.3** *Indexation under fixed and flexible exchange rates*

| | *Fixed exchange rate* | | *Flexible exchange rate* | |
|---|---|---|---|---|
| | *Non-indexation* $\gamma = 0$ | *Full indexation* $\gamma = 1$ | *Non-indexation* $\gamma = 0$ | *Full indexation* $\gamma = 1$ |
| $y_t$: | | | | |
| Supply ($\alpha_t$) | $\frac{c_3(1+s)}{c_3+s(1-c_1)}$ | $\frac{c_3(1+s)}{c_3+s(1-\lambda)(1-c_1)}$ | $\frac{(1+s)}{1+z_1 s}$ | $\frac{(1+s)c_3}{c_3+s(1-\lambda)(1-c_1)}$ |
| Fiscal ($\phi_{1t}$) | $\frac{s}{c_3+s(1-c_1)}$ | $\frac{s(1-\lambda)}{c_3+s(1-\lambda)(1-c_1)}$ | 0 | $\frac{s(1-\lambda)}{c_3+s(1-\lambda)(1-c_1)}$ |
| Monetary ($\phi_{2t}$) | 0 | 0 | $\frac{s}{1+z_1 s}$ | 0 |
| Foreign ($p_t^*$) | $\frac{sc_3}{c_3+s(1-c_1)}$ | 0 | 0 | 0 |
| ($y_t^*$) | $\frac{sc_4}{c_3+s(1-c_1)}$ | $\frac{sc_4(1-\lambda)}{c_3+s(1-\lambda)(1-c_1)}$ | 0 | $\frac{c_4 s(1-\lambda)}{c_3+s(1-\lambda)(1-c_1)}$ |
| $p_t$: | | | | |
| Supply $\alpha_t$ | $\frac{-(1+s)(1-c_1)}{c_3+s(1-c_1)}$ | $\frac{-(1+s)(1-c_1)}{c_3+s(1-\lambda)(1-c_1)}$ | $\frac{-(1+s)z_1}{1+z_1 s}$ | $\frac{-(1+s)c_3 z_1}{c_3+s(1-\lambda)(1-c_1)}$ |

| | | | | |
|---|---|---|---|---|
| Fiscal ($\phi_{1t}$) | $\frac{1}{c_3 + s(1 - c_1)}$ | $\frac{1}{c_3 + s(1 - \lambda)(1 - c_1)}$ | 0 | $\frac{-z_1 s(1 - \lambda)}{c_3 + s(1 - \lambda)(1 - c_1)}$ |
| Monetary ($\phi_{2t}$) | 0 | 0 | $\frac{1}{1 + z_1 s}$ | 1 |
| Foreign ($p_t^*$) | $\frac{c_3}{c_3 + s(1 - c_1)}$ | 1 | 0 | 0 |
| ($y_t^*$) | $\frac{c_4}{c_3 + s(1 - c_1)}$ | $\frac{c_4}{c_3 + s(1 - \lambda)(1 - c_1)}$ | 0 | $\frac{-z_1 c_4 s(1 - \lambda)}{c_3 + s(1 - \lambda)(1 - c_1)}$ |
| $e_t$: | | | | |
| Fiscal ($\phi_{1t}$) | — | — | $\frac{-1}{c_3}$ | $\frac{-[1 + z_1 s(1 - \lambda)]}{c_3 + s(1 - \lambda)(1 - c_1)}$ |
| Monetary ($\phi_{2t}$) | — | — | $\frac{c_3 + s(1 - c_1)}{c_3(1 + z_1 s)}$ | 1 |
| Foreign ($p_t^*$) | — | — | $-1$ | $-1$ |

$$e_t = [s(1-\gamma\lambda)(1-c_1) + c_3](m_t + z_2 i_t^* + \phi_{2t})/\Delta_2 - [1 + s(1-\gamma\lambda)z_1] (c_3 p_t^* - c_2 i_t^* + c_4 y_t^* + \phi_{1t})/\Delta_2 + [z_1 c_3 - (1-c_1)][s\gamma(1-\lambda)p_t^* - (1+s)\alpha_t - q]/\Delta_2 \quad (28)$$

where $\Delta_2 = z_1 s c_3(1-\gamma) + c_3 + s\gamma(1-\lambda)(1-c_1) > 0$.

Table 5.3 gives the comparative statics solutions for output, the price level and selected exchange rate responses under fixed and flexible exchange rates, for both non-indexation and full indexation. The open-economy literature typically considers these response coefficients in terms of the efficacy of policy actions. In the rational expectations-type formulation of the wage indexation literature, the coefficients are interpreted as measuring (possibly undesired) reactions to random shocks. Thus, the observation that the response in output to a supply-side shock, $\alpha_t$, under a fixed exchange rate is greater when wages are indexed can be interpreted as meaning either that indexation exacerbates undesired supply shocks or that it increases the effectiveness of supply-side policies. We will use both interpretations.

The Mundell–Fleming results are contained in the second and third rows of Table 5.3 under non-indexation. With rigid nominal wages and a fixed exchange rate, monetary policy ($\phi_2$) is ineffective in expanding output; with perfect capital mobility, changes in the money supply are immediately offset by outflows of foreign exchange with no impact on output (or the price level). Fiscal policy ($\phi_1$), on the other hand, raises both output and the price level; with rigid money wages, the real wage falls to accommodate the expansion in output. Under a flexible exchange rate, the roles are reversed. Fiscal expansion leads to appreciation of the exchange rate, which crowds out the increase in demand through contraction of the trade balance. Monetary expansion is effective because it leads to depreciation of the exchange rate, which reinforces the expansion; the depreciation and rise in domestic prices reduce real wages, thus enabling a rise in employment and output.

The second and third rows of Table 5.3 also show the effect of wage indexation on the Mundell–Fleming results. Under a fixed exchange rate, monetary policy is still totally ineffective since there is no change in domestic or foreign prices, even without indexation. The impact of fiscal policy is reduced by indexation. Fiscal expansion raises the domestic price level, which raises nominal wages. With a constant exchange rate, import prices are unchanged, so that wages rise by less than the rise in domestic prices, with the result that output still rises but by less than in the non-indexed case. The impact of wage indexation under a flexible exchange rate is more dramatic, with the positions of monetary and fiscal policies being reversed. In this case, monetary expansion increases the domestic price level and depreciates the exchange rate. With full indexation, money wages rise equiproportionately and output is unaffected. Fiscal expansion leads to appreciation of the domestic currency and a fall in the domestic price level, but by less than the appreciation. With fully indexed wages, the real wage facing producers falls and some output expansion is possible.

The same rows of Table 5.3 also illustrate another point made by Marston

(1982) that, at least in relatively simple formulations of the model, the output responses to policy under full indexation are identical under fixed and flexible exchange rates. Thus, if the impact of policy on output is the major concern of the authorities, full wage indexation makes the choice of exchange regime irrelevant. In effect, a flexible exchange rate restores control over the money supply, but full wage indexation renders it ineffective as a means of stimulating output.

The model in equations (20), (22) and (23) is, of course, a very specialized model. The more general formulations used, for example, by Marston (1982) and Argy and Salop (1983) allow for wealth effects and limited substitutability among domestic and foreign assets. Although these extensions reduce the sharpness of some of the results in Table 5.3 (for example, monetary policy induces at least some response in output under both fixed and flexible exchange rates), the qualitative implications are unaltered, with one exception. As noted by Sachs (1980), the Mundell–Fleming results are altered by wealth effects in the long-run equilibrium. In the long run with non-indexation, both monetary and fiscal policy have positive output multipliers under a flexible exchange rate. Full indexation, however, leads to a negative output multiplier for fiscal policy. The complication is that fiscal expansion leads to appreciation of the domestic currency and a current account deficit over time. This reduces wealth, which reduces the long-run demand for goods. In the non-indexed case, equilibrium can be restored by subsequent devaluation, which leaves real wages lower. With fixed real wages, however, a fall in output is required to restore long-run equilibrium.

As noted above, Table 5.3 can also be used to evaluate the roles of wage indexation and exchange rate flexibility in protecting the domestic economy from various types of shocks. These are left to the reader.

Marston (1982) and Argy and Salop (1983) also look at the effect of indexation in the rest of the world. The degree of foreign indexation is crucial in the transmission of foreign disturbances. If the rest of the world is fully indexed, flexible exchange rates tend to insulate the domestic economy from foreign monetary disturbances. Argy and Salop argue that the situation of least conflict (in terms of being mutually beneficial) is monetary expansion by countries with nominal wage rigidity and fiscal expansion by countries with indexation.

## VI INTERNATIONAL EXPERIENCE WITH WAGE INDEXATION

Wage indexation has a long history. Friedman (1974) refers to a form of indexation mentioned by Fleetwood in 1707. It was discussed by nineteenth-century economists including Wheatley, Lowe and Marshall, and Humphrey (1974) describes how payments to soldiers in the American revolution were indexed. In the first half of this century, wages were indexed in Australia, Denmark, Iceland, Luxembourg and Norway. Wage indexation was adopted after World War II by Belgium, Finland, Israel and Italy. Indexation has since been adopted in Brazil and the Netherlands and escalator clauses have been used in Canada, Ireland and the United States. This section gives a brief overview of the experiences of these countries.

## MOTIVES FOR INDEXATION AND THE ROLE OF GOVERNMENT

While the theoretical literature generally discusses indexation in the context of private contracts between workers and firms, indexation in practice has been most common in countries with centralized systems of wage determination. In Australia, Belgium, Denmark, Ireland and Israel, the vast majority of wage movements (including those outside indexation schemes) have been the result of national bargaining between union and employer organizations. Generally the government has been involved in these negotiations, both as a major employer in its own right and as a 'social partner'. In countries such as the United States, where wage negotiations are decentralized, indexation provisions cover only a minority of employees.

The attitude of governments to indexation has varied from prohibition (France and West Germany) to virtual compulsion (Brazil and New Zealand). When Brazil introduced wage indexation in 1964 it was part of a programme of 'monetary correction' aimed at bringing down the inflation rate (which was running at over 100 per cent per annum). In contrast, the introduction of indexation in Israel appears to have been motivated by the idea of living with inflation by reducing some of the redistributive costs and inequities of high inflation. Both countries appeared to meet their aims: Brazilian inflation fell to 16 per cent by 1972; and output grew strongly in Israel despite rapid (and accelerating) inflation. These experiences are consistent with the Gray–Fischer results presented in section II.

## CHOOSING A PRICE INDEX

Indexation is generally viewed from the standpoint of maintaining the real purchasing power of wages. Reflecting this, indexation has generally been based on consumer price indices.[8] As argued in section V above, indexation in open economies tends to reduce the impact of exchange rate changes on real wages and output, thereby reducing the efficacy of exchange rate depreciation as a means of stimulating activity. Consistent with this observation, many countries made *ad hoc* adjustments to their indexation rules after the 1973 oil crisis and resulting inflation, in order to link them more closely to domestic rather than overall prices. The fear of an inflation/devaluation cycle led Finland to abandon indexation in 1968 and Luxembourg to suspend it in 1982. The effects of devaluation were excluded from indexation in Australia in 1977, Demark in 1980 and Israel in 1975. Iceland modified its indexation system in 1979 to allow for changes in the terms of trade. In 1979/80, Denmark and Iceland removed energy prices from the indices used for wage indexation and Australia discounted for the effect of higher oil prices, thus reducing the impact of the 1979 oil price rise.

Similar (relative price) considerations led Denmark, Israel, Italy and the Netherlands to exclude the effects of indirect taxes and/or government changes from the price indices used for indexation.[9]

## THE EFFECTS OF INDEXATION ON OUTPUT AND INFLATION

The ways in which wage indexation have been applied suggest that most countries, either explicitly or implicitly, have formed a view of indexation broadly compatible with the principles discussed in sections II–V. The adjustments of indexation rules for energy price rises and exchange rate changes are perhaps the best examples. Unfortunately, it is almost impossible to assess whether or not this view is supported by the actual experiences of these countries. In the first place, there are many differences across countries in terms of economic structure, institutions and so on. Second, any inter-country comparison needs to control for all sources of disturbances, in particular for the stance of government policies. Third, reliable information about wage indexation is available only for countries with government-initiated indexation; valid comparisons would need information about private indexation also.

Despite these difficulties, there is loose support for the theoretical analysis in the experience of countries like Brazil and Israel. There have also been some attempts to test these propositions empirically.

In terms of broad trends, there is little clear evidence. Real wages in countries that have adopted indexation have been neither higher nor necessarily more stable than in non-indexed countries. Inflation performances have been mixed: Belgium and the Netherlands wound back their inflation rates after the 1973 oil crisis more quickly than the average of non-indexed economies; Australia and Denmark were around that average; and in Italy, Israel and Iceland, the inflation rate stabilized above the average.

Fischer (1981) conducts a more formal cross-country analysis looking at various forms of indexation. Subject to the earlier caveats, he concludes that indexation neither helped nor hindered governments in their efforts to control inflation following the 1973 oil crisis. Two less formal surveys of international experience (Page and Trollope, 1974; Commission of the European Communities, 1974) also conclude that indexation seems to be inflation neutral. Goldstein (1975) and Cukierman (1977), on the other hand, find some evidence that indexation increases inflation. Gutierrez-Camara and Vaubel (1981) cautiously conclude that there is some evidence consistent with the hypothesis that indexation reduces the cost of reducing inflation.

In terms of the stability of output, there is little conclusive evidence from which to draw conclusions. The average growth rate of real GDP over the 1970s (around 3 per cent) in countries with sustained indexation does not appear to be greatly different from the average for other countries (around 3.5 per cent). The growth rate in indexed countries does, however, appear to have been more variable. Also, there does appear to have been an inverse relationship between economic growth and inflation (see Norton and McDonald, 1981, although indexation does not appear to have altered this relationship.

An alternative means of assessing indexation using econometric techniques is through simulation analysis. Phipps (1981) estimates a Phillips curve explaining wage determination prior to the introduction of indexation in Australia in 1975. The predictions from the model are then compared with the actual experience under indexation. He concludes that indexation probably reduced wage inflation for the first two years, but increased it in subsequent years. Caton, Evans and Johnston (1974) conduct a similar experiment with the NIF model of the Australian economy. They conclude that the accompaniment of wage indexation by moderate levels of wage claims outside the indexation system (less than 2 per cent per year) could have led to less inflationary situations than were observed in the early 1970s; in their analysis, the lower inflation is at the expense of some growth in real average earnings. In a simulation study using the MPS model of the US economy, Flannery and Johnson (1981) conclude that wage indexation appears to pose no significant threat to macroeconomic stability.

Overall, however, empirical analysis of the effects of wage indexation has not been very extensive. Notwithstanding the difficulties involved there appears to be considerable scope for productive work in this area.

## VII SUMMARY

There are two predominant views on the role of wage indexation. The first sees it as minimizing the distortions and inequities that arise from high and variable inflation. According to this view, wage indexation stabilizes output and, in particular, reduces the cost of policies designed to reduce inflation. The second view is that indexation destabilizes activity by reducing the responsiveness of the economy to disturbances requiring adjustment to real wages.

The major theorem of the theoretical literature on this topic encompasses both these views in arguing that wage indexation stabilizes output in the face of demand-side disturbances (e.g. monetary shocks) but destabilizes output in the face of supply-side disturbances (e.g. food and energy price shocks), while increasing the response in the price level to all disturbances.

The essence of the result is that wage indexation steepens the aggregate supply schedule of the economy. Since demand disturbances (monetary shocks, etc.) involve movements along this steeper schedule, they will, *ceteris paribus*, lead to smaller changes in output and larger changes in the price level than would occur without indexation. Supply disturbances (oil-price shocks, etc.), on the other hand, shift the aggregate supply schedule horizontally, In this case, a steeper schedule will, *ceteris paribus*, result in larger changes in both output and the price level; the failure of real wages to adjust to supply shocks causes employment to bear the full brunt of adjustment.

A cornerstone of the result is the assumption that employment is determined by labour demand in situations of disequilibrium. Thus, without indexation, a disturbance that reduces supply (e.g. an unexpected fall in productivity) raises the price level, which, in turn, reduces real wage costs, thereby partially offsetting the effect of the supply shock on labour demand and output. Alternatively, if disequilibrium employment is determined by labour supply, the fall in the real wage rate will decrease employment, thereby exacerbating the impact of the supply shock on output.

Another crucial aspect of the analysis is the nature of labour contracts, whereby workers and firms are assumed to agree on a base wage plus a degree of indexation linking current-period wages to current-period prices. Some have argued that use of current-period information should allow contingent contracts based on various pieces of information to dominate a simple indexation rule based only on the price level. However, the type of indexation contract seen most in practice (namely, a rule under which the current-period nominal wage equals last period's nominal wage adjusted for last period's price rise) utilizes very little information and is found by the literature to be inferior and potentially destabilizing even under demand disturbances. One reason for the existence of these contracts is the difficulty involved in sifting data for the information needed to implement more complex rules. Another is delays in data availability.

A critical factor in extending the analysis to the open-economy case is relative prices. The relevant price for labour supply decisions is the overall price level (a weighted average of domestic and import prices), while the relevant price for labour demand decisions is the domestic price level. A disturbance that changes the exchange rate will tend to have real effects by altering both the price of domestic goods relative to imports and the real wage cost to firms. Two interesting results come out of this literature:

- first, wage indexation alters the traditional theorems of international finance – by reducing the fall in real wages, indexation dampens the expansionary effect of fiscal policy under a fixed exchange rate, while it reverses the relative effectiveness of monetary and fiscal policies under a flexible exchange rate (monetary policy loses its impact because domestic prices and wages move equiproportionately with changes in the exchange rate); and
- second, full wage indexation tends to make the output responses to various shocks invariant to the choice of exchange regime (the differential impact of policies under fixed and flexible exchange rates depends critically on the effectiveness of the exchange rate in altering real wages – with full indexation, the exchange rate is unable to alter relative prices or the real wage).

The literature on wage indexation has extended the major theorem in some interesting directions without destroying its main message. At the same time, there appear to be some notable omissions. There is very little treatment of relative wages. If labour is immobile between sectors in the short run, widespread indexation will have different output effects across industries.[10] There is also very little treatment of the role of indexation in reducing uncertainty for both workers and firms, or of the implications for industrial relations. Finally, most of the practical problems encountered in actual indexation are given little coverage in the theoretical literature. These include: choice of an index; frequency of adjustment; problems of adjusting for wage relativities; choice of an appropriate base; choice of an equilibrium reference point; and how to adjust for known supply-side shocks.

In practice, there is evidence that countries have, in designing indexation schemes, behaved in a manner consistent with the principles raised in the theoretical literature; the adjustment of indexation rules for devaluation and commodity price shocks is probably the best example of this. The evidence on whether or not actual experience accords with theoretical priors is much more difficult to disentangle. In this area, empirical research has done little more than scratch the surface.

## NOTES

1 He refers to the report of an Israeli Committee of Experts in 1964 and to a conversation with Harry Johnson in which the result is attributed to Keynes.

2 Cukierman (1980) specifies investment more correctly as a function of the real interest rate. This complication, however, does not alter the conclusions presented below and is ignored in the interests of keeping the model as simple as possible.

3 The production function in levels underlying (4) is of the form $Y_t = e^{\alpha_t}N_t^{\delta}$. Labour demand is found by taking the derivative of this function with respect to $N_t$ and setting the resulting expression equal to the real wage rate. Solving this condition for $N_t$ and taking logs yields (5), in which $\eta = 1/(1 - \delta)$.

4 The original papers by Gray and Fischer use a very simple formulation of aggregate demand in which demand shocks are identified exclusively with monetary disturbances. This leads them to formulate their conclusion in terms of real and monetary shocks rather than demand and supply shocks. The difficulty with the Gray–Fischer dichotomy is that real shocks originating on the demand side induce the same responses as monetary shocks. The more correct statement above is due to Cukierman (1980). Cukierman also examines the impact of wage indexation on fluctuations in the real interest rate and investment. While interesting in their own right, the results are peripheral to the main themes being pursued here.

5 Since the constant term does not alter the response of output or prices to random shocks, it is of no real consequence to the analysis.

6 From (12), the slope of the aggregate supply schedule is $(1 - \gamma)[s\theta - \delta\varepsilon(1 - \theta)]$. For anything short of full indexation (i.e. $\gamma < 1$) this slope is positive or negative as demand influences, $s\theta$, or supply influences, $\delta\varepsilon(1 - \theta)$, dominate.

7 We will rule out the perverse case in which the supply curve cuts the demand curve from below.

8 For industrial relations reasons it is desirable to use a measure of inflation that is familiarly and widely accepted, available relatively quickly and not prone to revision. On these grounds the consumer price index is generally regarded as superior to the national accounts deflators or other indices.

9 In the Australian context, both these exclusions, and the treatment of import prices, represent divergences between the prices relevant to 'needs' and 'capacity to pay', the alternative concepts on which the Arbitration Commission has based its decisions. See Portus (1971).

10 While this issue is not treated explicitly as such (Gray looks at inter-industry differences in the context of contract costs), the main implications can be inferred from the open-economy analysis.

## BIBLIOGRAPHY

Argy, V. and Salop, J. (1979), 'Price and output effects of monetary and fiscal policy under flexible exchange rates', *International Monetary Fund Staff Papers*, 26(2), June, 224–256.

Argy, V. and Salop, J. (1983), 'Price and output effects of monetary and fiscal expansion in a two-country world under flexible exchange rates', *Oxford Economic Papers*, New Series, 35(2), July, 228–246.

Barro, R. J. (1976), 'Indexation in a rational expectations model', *Journal of Economic Theory*, 13, October, 229–244.

Blanchard, O. (1979), 'Wage indexing rules and the behavior of the economy', *Journal of Political Economy*, 87(4), August, 798–815.

Braun, A. R. (1975), 'Indexation of wages and salaries in developed economies', *International Monetary Fund Staff Papers*, 23(1), March, 226–271.
Casas, F. R. (1975), 'Efficient macroeconomic stabilisation policies under floating exchange rates', *International Economic Review*, 16(3), December, 682–698.
Caton, C. N., Evans, E. A. and Johnston, H. N. (1974), 'The inflationary process and the impact of wage indexation on the Australian economy', Fourth Conference of Economists, Canberra, August.
Commission of the European Communities (1974), 'Machinery for adjusting wages and salaries to the cost of living', mimeo, Brussels.
Cukierman, A. (1977), 'General wage escalator clauses and the inflation unemployment trade off', *Economic Inquiry*, 15(1), January, 67–84.
Cukierman, A. (1980), 'The effect of wage indexation on macroeconomic fluctuations', *Journal of Monetary Economics*, 6(2), April, 147–170.
Eden, B. (1979), 'The nominal system: linkage to the quantity of money or to nominal income', *Revue Economique*, 30(1), January, 121–143.
Fischer, S. (1977), 'Wage indexation and macroeconomic stability', in K. Brunner and A. H. Meltzer (eds), *Stabilization of the Domestic and International Economy*, Carnegie–Rochester Series on Public Policy, 5, Amsterdam, North Holland, 107–147.
Fischer, S. (1981), 'Indexing and inflation', National Bureau of Economic Research, Working Paper Series, No. 670, May.
Flannery, M. J. and Johnson, L. (1981), 'Indexing the United States economy', *Journal of Econometrics*, 15(1), January, 93–114.
Fleming, J. M. (1962), 'Domestic financial policies under fixed and floating exchange rates', *International Monetary Fund Staff Papers*, 9(3), November, 369–379.
Friedman, M. (1974), 'Monetary correction', in *Essays on Inflation and Indexation*, Domestic Affairs Study 24, Washington, DC, American Enterprise Institute.
Goldstein, M. (1975), 'Wage indexation, inflation and the labor market', *International Monetary Fund Staff Papers*, 22(3), November, 680–713.
Gray, J. A. (1976), 'Wage indexation: a macroeconomic approach', *Journal of Monetary Economics*, 2(2), April, 221–235.
Gray, J. A. (1978), 'On indexation and contract length', *Journal of Political Economy*, 86(1), February, 1–18.
Gutierrez-Camara, J. L. and Vaubel, R. (1981), 'Reducing the cost of reducing inflation through gradualism: preannouncement or indexation?', *Weltwirtschaftliches Archiv*, 117(2), 244–261.
Humphrey, T. M. (1974), 'The concept of indexation in the history of economic thought', *Federal Reserve Bank of Richmond Economic Review*, November/December, 3–16.
Karni, E. (1983), 'On optimal wage indexation', *Journal of Political Economy*, 91(2), April, 282–292.
Marston, R. C. (1982), 'Wages, relative prices and the choice between fixed and flexible exchange rates', *Canadian Journal of Economics*, 15(1), February, 87–103.
Marston, R. C. (1983), 'Stabilization policies in open economies', National Bureau of Economic Research, Working Paper Series, No. 117, May.
Mundell, R. A. (1963), 'Capital mobility and stabilization policy under fixed and flexible exchange rates', *Candian Journal of Economics and Political Science*, 29(4), November, 475–485.
Norton, W. E. and McDonald, R. (1981), 'Implications for Australia of cross-country comparisons of economic performance', *Economic Record*, 57(159), December, 301–318.
Page, S. A. and Trollope, S. (1974), 'An international survey of indexing and its effects', *National Institute Economic Review*, 70(4), November, 46–60.

Pazner, E. A. (1981), 'On indexation and macroeconomic stability', in M. J. Flanders and A. Razin (eds), *Development in an Inflationary World*, New York, Academic Press.

Phipps, A. J. (1981), 'The impact of wage indexation on wage inflation in Australia: 1975(2)–1980(2)', *Australian Economic Papers*, 20(37), December, 333–349.

Portus, J. H. (1971), *Australian Compulsory Arbitration 1900–1970*, Sydney, Hicks, Smith and Sons.

Sachs, J. (1980), 'Wages, flexible exchange rates and macroeconomic policy', *Quarterly Journal of Economics*, 94(4), June, 731–747.

PART II

# Experience in Developed Countries

# 6 Fiscal and Monetary Strategy in OECD Countries: A Review of Recent Experiences

*JEAN-CLAUDE CHOURAQUI and ROBERT PRICE**

## I INTRODUCTION

The aim of this chapter is to provide an assessment of the conduct of fiscal and monetary policies in OECD economies since the early 1970s. Four issues are discussed: first, the stance of policies up to the second oil shock; second, the current instrument–objectives setting; third, the rationale for the increasing adoption of medium-term budgetary and monetary objectives; and fourth, the problems of ensuring consistency between short-term actions and medium-term goals. Underlying these issues is the theme of monetary and fiscal policy management.[1] To the extent that central banks can contain the pressures stemming from the mix of restrictive monetary targets and expansionary budgets, monetary and fiscal policies might be assigned to different objectives: inflation control and short-term employment support respectively (although monetary restraint would not free expansionary action of short-run inflation consequences). However, persistent imbalance between the two 'instruments' may result in diminishing fiscal effectiveness because of cumulative budget financing difficulties; output and employment gains may be progressively eroded through upward pressures on interest rates, as a result of either the 'crowding out' of private demand or fears of future monetary accommodation and inflation. In this case the room for fiscal policy independence – i.e. for asymmetry between fiscal stance and monetary targets – may be limited. Fiscal and monetary policies may thus offer policy makers nearer one instrument than two.

## II THE MIX OF MONETARY AND FISCAL POLICIES UP TO THE SECOND OIL SHOCK

During the late 1960s fiscal and monetary policies, although constrained by interest rate and exchange rate objectives (which were sometimes in conflict),

* This chapter is based largely on 'Medium-term financial strategy: the co-ordination of fiscal and monetary policies', OECD Economics and Statistics Department Working Paper No. 9 (July 1983) prepared in collaboration with P. Muller. The views expressed do not necessarily represent those of the OECD or its member governments.

were usually mutually reinforcing. Periodic asymmetries emerged because monetary policies were considered to be quicker-acting in deflations than reflations, so that in some countries there may have been a tendency to 'loose budgets and tight money'. However, one of the main characteristics of the late 1960s was the monetary 'accommodation' of the United States budget deficit through relatively low interest rates. Given the then fixed exchange rate regime, there followed a growing US balance of payments deficit with the rest of the OECD and a build-up of world liquidity, which, in conjunction with accommodating monetary policies, served to underwrite a generalized monetary expansion within the OECD area in 1971/2. This was accompanied by fiscal reflation in the United States, Japan, West Germany, the United Kingdom and Italy, and by the transition to a managed floating exchange rate regime.[2] As may be seen from Figure 6.1, which compares real money supply changes and interest rates with indicators of budget stance, demand management policies were mutually supporting in 1971/2. The emphasis *ex post* (Figure 6.1(A)) appears to have been on monetary rather than budgetary expansion, but the cyclically adjusted budget indicator (Figure 6.1(C)) shows both fiscal and monetary stance to have been expansionary.[3]

In reaction to growing inflationary pressures, monetary conditions were tightened in 1973 and became more restrictive in response to the oil price shock. Budget stances also became more restrictive, as inflation-induced fiscal drag reduced government deficits.[4] Fiscal and monetary policies therefore remained synchronized (in the direction of restraint) in the immediate aftermath of the oil shock. However, while budgetary policies continued to be cautious for most of 1974, they became progressively more expansionary towards the end of that year and through 1975 as the authorities in several countries accepted the need to finance the external deficits relating to the oil shock through the public sector. With monetary restraint also easing, demand management policies remained mutually accommodating, becoming less so in 1976/7 as most countries turned towards fiscal retrenchment (Figure 6.1(C)).

As output continued to stagnate, unemployment increased and inflationary expectations persisted, the combined fiscal and monetary expansion of the early 1970s was perceived as having adverse results in terms of stabilization; attempts to 'fine tune' the economy to continuous high employment at the expense (*ex post* at least) of the inflation objective had proved unsuccessful. There were two dimensions to this failure. The 1970–5 experience suggested, first, that short-term discretionary action might be destabilizing because of forecasting and timing errors; in which case there was a need to frame monetary and fiscal policies in a more stable, medium-term framework, so that demand management would become 'steadier and more predictable' (OECD, 1977, p. 192). Secondly, the limited gains to output that followed monetary expansion demonstrated that governments should not – and in the end could not – acquiesce in high rates of monetary growth and inflation; countries that sought to achieve a high level of employment and rapid growth by means of 'easy money' and currency depreciation had, by the second half of the decade, to concede the failure of this policy. From late 1975 OECD countries, with exceptions among the smaller economies (Figure 6.1(B)), began to take corrective action to reduce budget deficits and public spending, this being

# FISCAL-MONETARY POLICY MIX IN THE OECD AREA

A. — REAL MONEY SUPPLY, REAL INTEREST RATES AND GENERAL GOVERNMENT BUDGET BALANCES: AGGREGATE FOR THE MAJOR SEVEN COUNTRIES 1971-1982

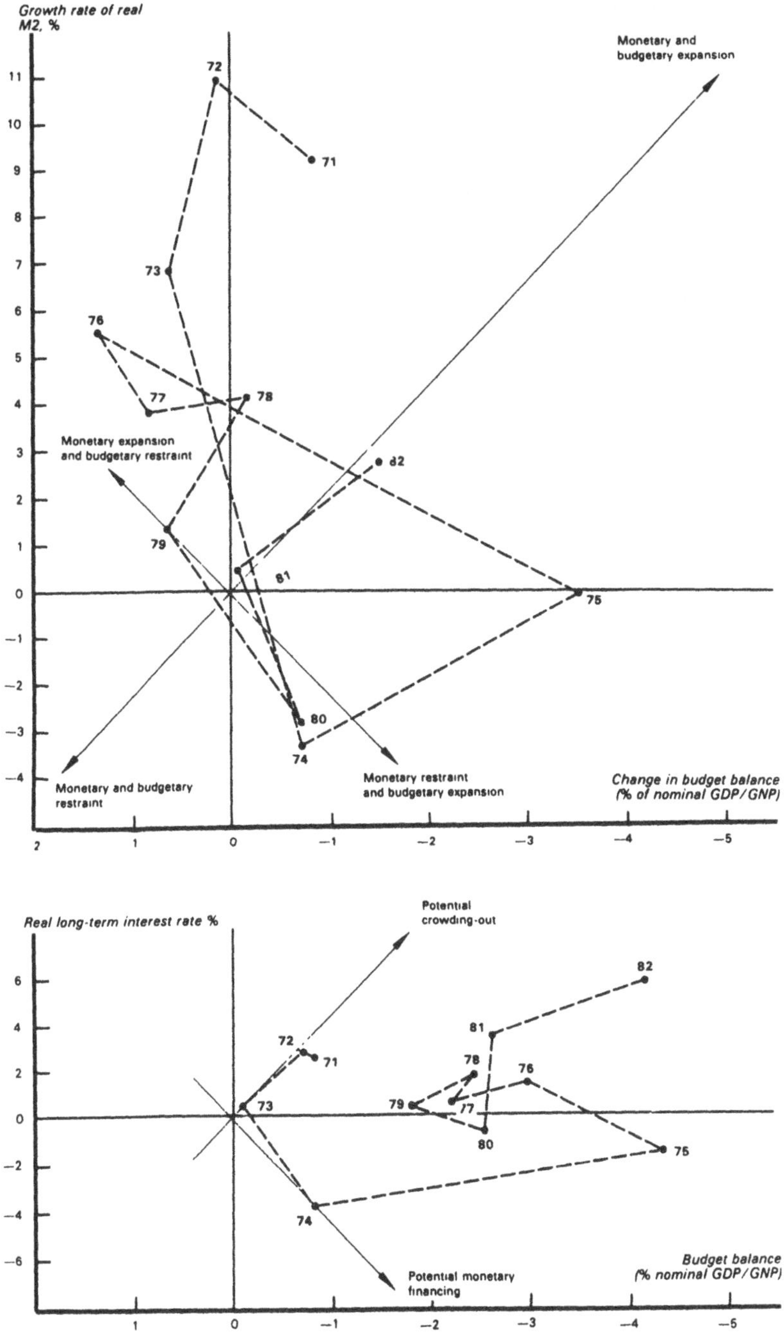


Figure 6.1

## FISCAL-MONETARY POLICY MIX IN THE OECD AREA

**B. — REAL MONEY SUPPLY, REAL INTEREST RATES AND GENERAL GOVERNMENT BUDGET BALANCES: AGGREGATE FOR SELECTED SMALLER COUNTRIES 1971-1982**

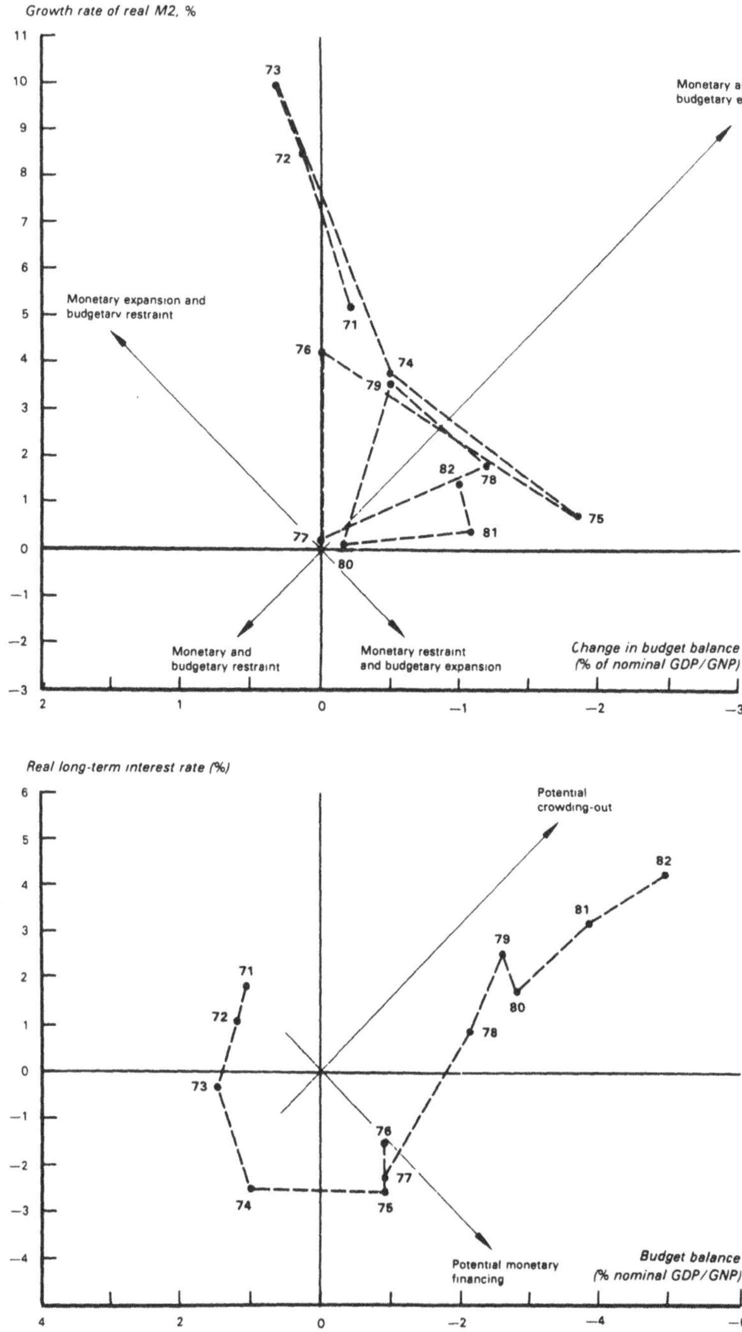


**Figure 6.1** (Contd.)

## FISCAL-MONETARY POLICY MIX IN THE OECD AREA

**C. — REAL MONEY SUPPLY, REAL INTEREST RATES AND CYCLICALLY-ADJUSTED BUDGET BALANCES: AGGREGATE FOR THE MAJOR SEVEN COUNTRIES 1971-1982**

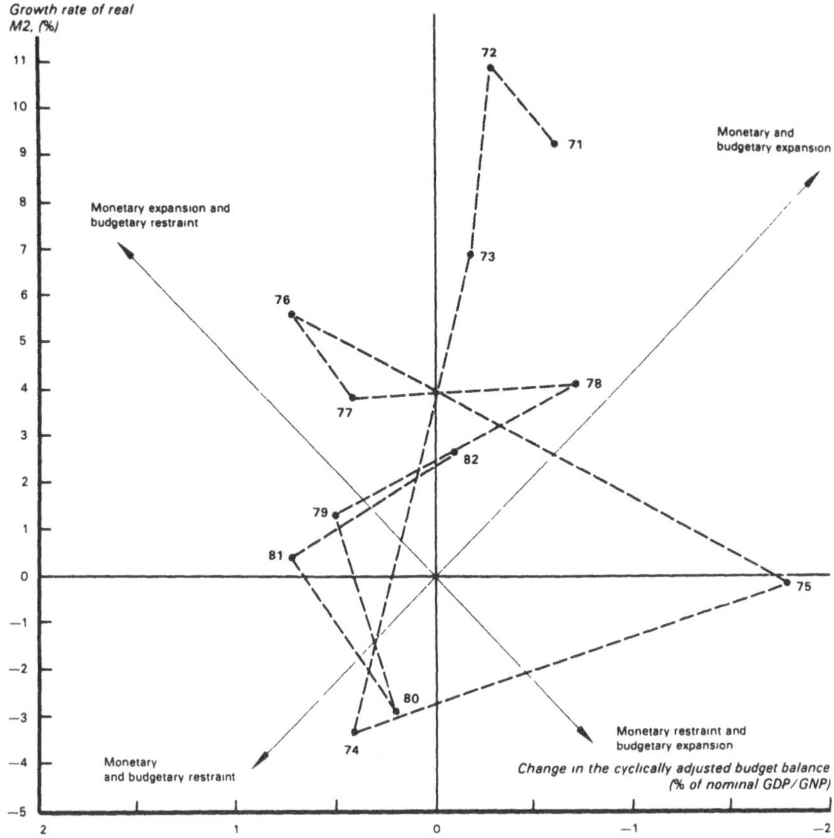


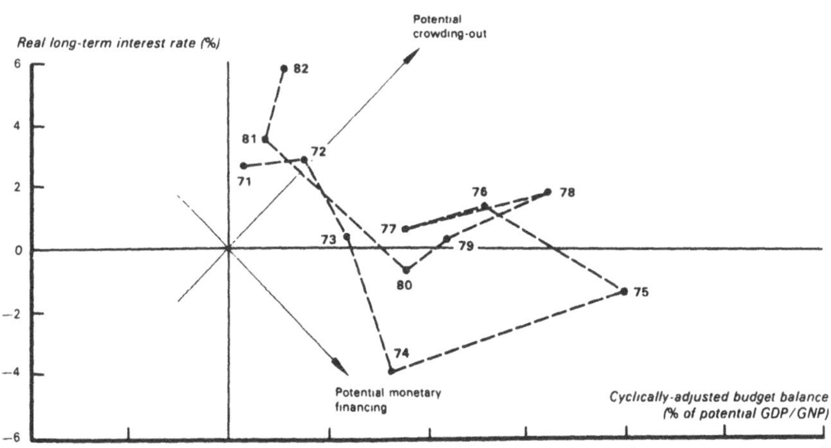


**Figure 6.1** (Contd.)

**Table 6.1** *Projected and actual growth rates of monetary aggregates*

| *Country* | *Aggregate* | *Period* | *Target* | | *Outcome* | |
|---|---|---|---|---|---|---|
| | | | *M1* | *M2* | *M1* | *M2* |
| United States | M1/M2[a] (% increase) | March 1975–March 1976 | 5.0–7.5 | 8.5–10.5 | 5.0 | 9.6 |
| | | 1975Q2–1976Q2 | 5.0–7.5 | 8.5–10.5 | 5.2 | 9.5 |
| | | 1975Q3–1976Q3 | 5.0–7.5 | 7.5–10.5 | 4.6 | 9.3 |
| | | 1975Q4–1976Q4 | 4.5–7.5 | 7.5–10.5 | 5.7 | 10.9 |
| | | 1976Q1–1977Q1 | 4.5–7.0 | 7.5–10.0 | 6.3 | 10.9 |
| | | 1976Q2–1977Q2 | 4.5–7.0 | 7.5– 9.5 | 6.6 | 10.7 |
| | | 1976Q3–1977Q3 | 4.5–6.5 | 7.5–10.0 | 7.8 | 11.0 |
| | | 1976Q4–1977Q4 | 4.5–6.5 | 7.0–10.0 | 7.8 | 9.8 |
| | | 1977Q1–1978Q1 | 4.5–6.5 | 7.0– 9.5 | 7.7 | 8.7 |
| | | 1977Q2–1978Q2 | 4.5–6.5 | 7.0– 9.5 | 8.2 | 8.4 |
| | | 1977Q3–1978Q3 | 4.0–6.5 | 6.5– 9.0 | 8.0 | 8.2 |
| | | 1977Q4–1978Q4 | 4.0–6.5 | 6.5– 9.0 | 7.2 | 8.6 |
| | | 1978Q1–1979Q1 | 4.0–6.5 | 6.5– 9.0 | 5.1 | 7.6 |
| | | 1978Q2–1979Q2 | 4.0–6.5 | 6.5– 9.0 | 4.8 | 7.7 |
| | | 1978Q3–1979Q3 | 2.0–6.0 | 6.5– 9.0 | 5.3 | 8.2 |
| | | 1978Q4–1979Q4 | 3.0–6.0 | 5.0– 8.0 | 5.5 | 8.3 |
| | | 1979Q4–1980Q4[b] | 4.0–6.5 | 6.0– 9.0 | 7.5 | 9.9 |
| | | 1980Q4–1981Q4 | 3.5–6.0 | 6.0– 9.0 | 5.5 | 8.7 |
| | | 1981Q4–1982Q4 | 2.5–5.5 | 6.0– 9.0 | 8.5 | 9.3 |
| | | 1982Q4–1983Q4[c] | 5.0–9.0 | 7.0–10.0 | — | — |
| Japan | M2[d] (% increase) | 1977Q3–1978Q3 | | 11.0–12.0 | | 12.0 |
| | | 1977Q4–1978Q4 | | 12.0 | | 12.6 |
| | | 1978Q4–1979Q4 | | 11.0 | | 9.1 |
| | | 1979Q4–1980Q4 | | 10.0 | | 7.2 |
| | | 1980Q4–1981Q4 | | 10.0 | | 11.0 |
| | | 1981Q4–1982Q4 | | 11.0 | | 7.9 |
| | | 1982Q2–1983Q2 | | 7.0 | | — |

| | | | | |
|---|---|---|---|---|
| West Germany | Central Bank money (% increase) | End-1974–End-1975 | 8.0 | 10.0 |
| | | Average 1975–1976 | 8.0 | 9.2 |
| | | Average 1976–1977 | 8.0 | 9.0 |
| | | Average 1977–1978 | 8.0 | 11.4 |
| | | 1978Q4–1979Q4 | 6–9 | 6.3 |
| | | 1979Q4–1980Q4 | 5–8 | 6.0 |
| | | 1980Q4–1981Q4 | 4–7 | 3.0 |
| | | 1981Q4–1982Q4 | 4–7 | 6.0 |
| | | 1982Q4–1983Q4 | 4–7 | — |
| France | M2 (% increase) | Dec. 1976–Dec. 1977 | 12.5 | 13.9 |
| | | Dec. 1977–Dec. 1978 | 12.0 | 12.2 |
| | | Dec. 1978–Dec. 1979 | 11.0 | 14.4 |
| | | Dec. 1979–Dec. 1980 | 11.0 | 9.8 |
| | | Dec. 1980–Dec. 1981 | 10.0[e] | 11.4 |
| | | Dec. 1981–Dec. 1982 | 12.5–13.5 | 12.0 |
| | | 1982Q4–1983Q4 | 9.0 | — |
| United Kingdom | Sterling M3 (% increase) | Fiscal year ending April 1977 | 9.0–13.0[f] | 7.8 |
| | | Fiscal year ending April 1978 | 9.0–13.0 | 14.9 |
| | | Fiscal year ending April 1979 | 8.0–12.0 | 10.9 |
| | | Oct. 1978–Oct. 1979 | 8.0–12.0 | 13.4 |
| | | June 1979–April 1980 | 7.0–11.0 | 9.7 |
| | | Feb. 1980–April 1981 | 7.0–11.0 | 19.9 |
| | | Feb. 1981–April 1982 | 6.0–10.0 | 13.6 |
| | | Feb. 1982–April 1983 | 8.0–12.0 | 10.8 |
| | | Feb. 1983–April 1984 | 7.0–11.0 | — |

**Table 6.1** *(Contd.)*

| *Country* | *Aggregate* | *Period* | *Target* | *Outcome* |
|---|---|---|---|---|
| | | | *M1* *M2* | *M1* *M2* |
| Italy | Total domestic credit (absolute increase) | March 1974–March 1975 | Lit. 21,800 bn | 19,600 bn |
| | | March 1975–March 1976 | Lit. 24,700 bn | 35,280 bn |
| | | Dec. 1975–Dec. 1976 | Lit. 29,500 bn | 33,280 bn |
| | | Dec. 1976–Dec. 1977 | Lit. 32,000 bn[g] | 35,652 bn |
| | | March 1977–March 1978 | Lit. 30,000 bn | 39,265 bn |
| | | Dec. 1977–Dec. 1978 | Lit. 46,000 bn | 49,013 bn |
| | | Dec. 1978–Dec. 1979 | Lit. 53,000 bn | 53,348 bn |
| | | Dec. 1979–Dec. 1980 | Lit. 59,300 bn | 62,141 bn |
| | | Dec. 1980–Dec. 1981 | Lit. 64,500 bn | 72,368 bn |
| | | Dec. 1981–Dec. 1982 | Lit. 73,000 bn | 98,430 bn |
| | | Dec. 1982–Dec. 1983 | Lit. 105,000 bn | — |
| Canada | M1 (% increase) | 1975Q2–1976Q2 | 10–15 | 12.06[h] |
| | | Feb./April 1976–1977Q2 | 8–12 | 7.0 |
| | | 1977Q2–1978Q2 | 7–11 | 9.5 |
| | | 1978Q2–1979Q2 | 6–10 | 8.1 |
| | | 1979Q2–1980Q3 | 5–9 | 3.3 |
| | | 1980Q3–1982Q4[i] | 4–8 | 3.1 |
| Australia | M3 (% increase) | June 1976–June 1977 | 10–12 | 10.5 |
| | | June 1977–June 1978 | 8–10 | 8.0 |
| | | June 1978–June 1979 | 6–8 | 11.8 |
| | | June 1979–June 1980 | 10.0 | 12.3 |
| | | June 1980–June 1981 | 9–11 | 12.7 |
| | | June 1981–June 1982 | 10–11 | 11.0 |
| | | June 1982–June 1983 | 11.0 | — |
| Netherlands | Domestic private sector M2 creation[j] (growth rate) | July 1977–March 1978 | 5.1[k] | 7.8 |
| | | April 1978–March 1979 | 5.2 | 4.6 |
| | | Jan. 1979–Dec. 1979 | 5.5 | 6.3 |
| | | Jan. 1980–Dec. 1980 | 4.5 | 4.7 |
| | | Jan. 1981–Dec. 1981 | 4.5 | 2.3 |

| | | | | |
|---|---|---|---|---|
| Switzerland | M1 (% increase) | Dec. 1974–Dec. 1975 | 6.0 | 5.9 |
| | | Average 1975–1976 | 6.0 | 8.0 |
| | | Average 1976–1977 | 5.0 | 5.4 |
| | | Average 1977–1978 | 5.0 | 16.2 |
| | Monetary base (% increase) | Average 1979–1980 | 4.0 | 0.2 |
| | | Average 1980–1981 | 4.0 | −1.5 |
| | | Average 1981–1982 | 3.0 | 2.6 |
| | | Average 1982–1983 | 3.0 | — |

*Notes:* a M3 targets, which have less operational meaning, are not shown.
b M1B in 1979 and 1980.
c 1983 M1 target is based on 1983Q2; M2 target is based on February–March 1983 average.
d Forecast. Including certificates of deposits from 1979.
e Raised implicitly to 12 per cent in the second half of 1981.
f Revised from 12 per cent target to be consistent with objective for domestic credit expansion.
g Revised from Lit. 36,600 billion.
h 1975Q2–Feb./April 1976 (excluding effects of postal strikes).
i No targets have been announced for 1983.
j Domestic private sector M2 creation targets were used to bring the 'liquidity ratio' (M2 in relation to national income) back from about 40 per cent in early 1977 to a desired level of 35 per cent in 1981. No targets were announced for 1982 and 1983.
k In percentage of total M2.

linked to the increasing adoption of either monetary targets (see Table 6.1) or the 'hard currency option', which implies that the exchange rate is tied to a strong currency like the Deutsche Mark. These policies were aimed at a gradual reduction in inflationary expectations, and a corollary of this was the need for public sector borrowing requirements to be explicitly linked to targets for monetary growth.

Another reason why the coincidence of high unemployment and inflation brought with it a reappraisal of policy trade-offs and the appropriate monetary–fiscal mix was that countries with the best inflation and balance of payments performance appeared to be those with the most successful output and employment records. To illustrate this, Figure 6.2 relates economic performance, in the form of inflation and real GDP growth, to the monetary policy instruments and intermediate targets used: monetary growth rates, real interest rates and exchange rate changes. The relationship between economic goals and the variability of monetary growth and interest rates is examined in Figure 6.2(C), since the case for stable medium-term policies has derived in part from a scepticism about the effectiveness of short-term activism, the unpredictability of which may be a destabilizing factor. In fact, both the link between monetary accommodation and inflation and that between real monetary growth and GDP growth emerge as positive, while greater stability in monetary conditions also seems to be significantly associated with better economic performance. The benefits of 'sound money' might also be inferred (*prima facie*) from the positive correlation between exchange rate appreciation and growth, although no strong conclusion emerges from the correlation of real interest rates with economic performance.[5]

An examination of the effectiveness of fiscal policies leads to similar conclusions about the beneficial impact of policy consistency and continuity: Figure 6.3(B) shows that the greater has been the discretionary variability of budgetary policy – i.e. the more the resort to 'fine-tuning' – the higher has been average unemployment.[6] Stable medium-term budgetary support may, on the other hand, be more beneficial, since the 'discretionary' budget indicator and government indebtedness (Figures 6.3(C) and 6.3(D)) do not display any significant negative longer-run correlation with employment and economic growth performance.[7]

Although 'fine-tuning' appears to have been discredited by the events of the early 1970s, the possibility of using selective discretionary action to steer OECD economies *gradually* back to higher employment emerged as an increasingly attractive strategy as activity stagnated in 1977/8.[8] With monetary targets acting as a medium-term prevention against excessive monetary financing of budget deficits, fiscal policy was still thought capable, in principle, of promoting a sustained increase in employment without engendering inflation. Nor were higher interest rates and 'crowding out' of private demand considered a necessary consequence of reflation, provided action was overtly temporary and governments correctly set their budget deficit targets to equate with the supply and demand for loanable funds over the (medium-term) budget period. The potential usefulness of fiscal policy as a means of stimulating OECD economies in a way consistent, *a priori*, with both monetary growth targets and balance of payments constraints was thus reasserted in the context of coordinated fiscal reflation – the 'concerted action programme' – in 1978.

## ECONOMIC PERFORMANCE AND INDICATORS OF MONETARY STANCE IN SELECTED OECD COUNTRIES 1973-1982

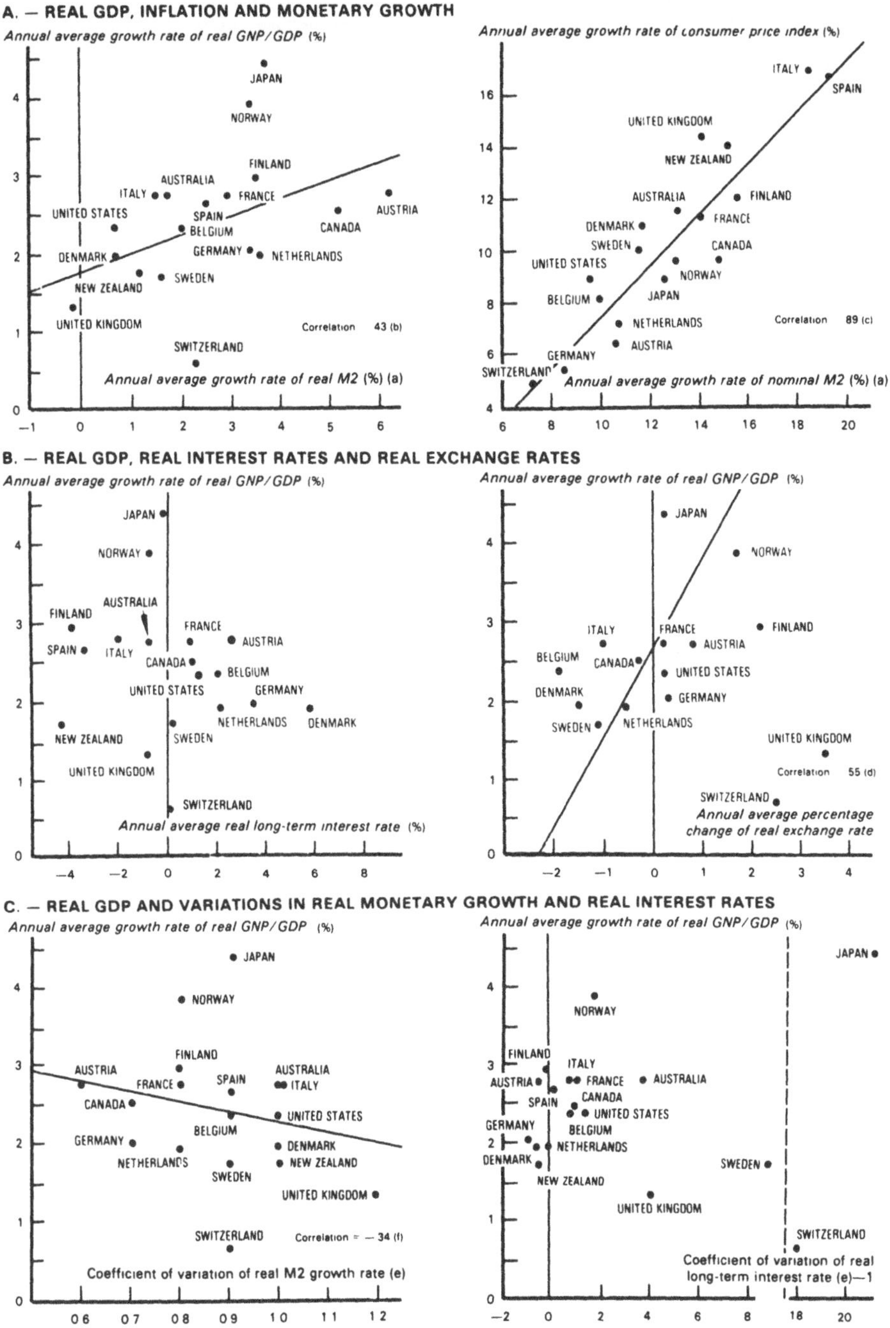


(a) M3 for Germany and £M3 for United Kingdom (b) Significant at 10% (c) Significant at 1% (d) Excluding United Kingdom and Switzerland, significant at 5% (e) Coefficient of variation = standard deviation/mean (f) Excluding Japan, United Kingdom and Switzerland, significant at 20%

**Figure 6.2**

## ECONOMIC PERFORMANCE AND BUDGETARY INDICATORS IN SELECTED OECD COUNTRIES 1971-1982 (a)

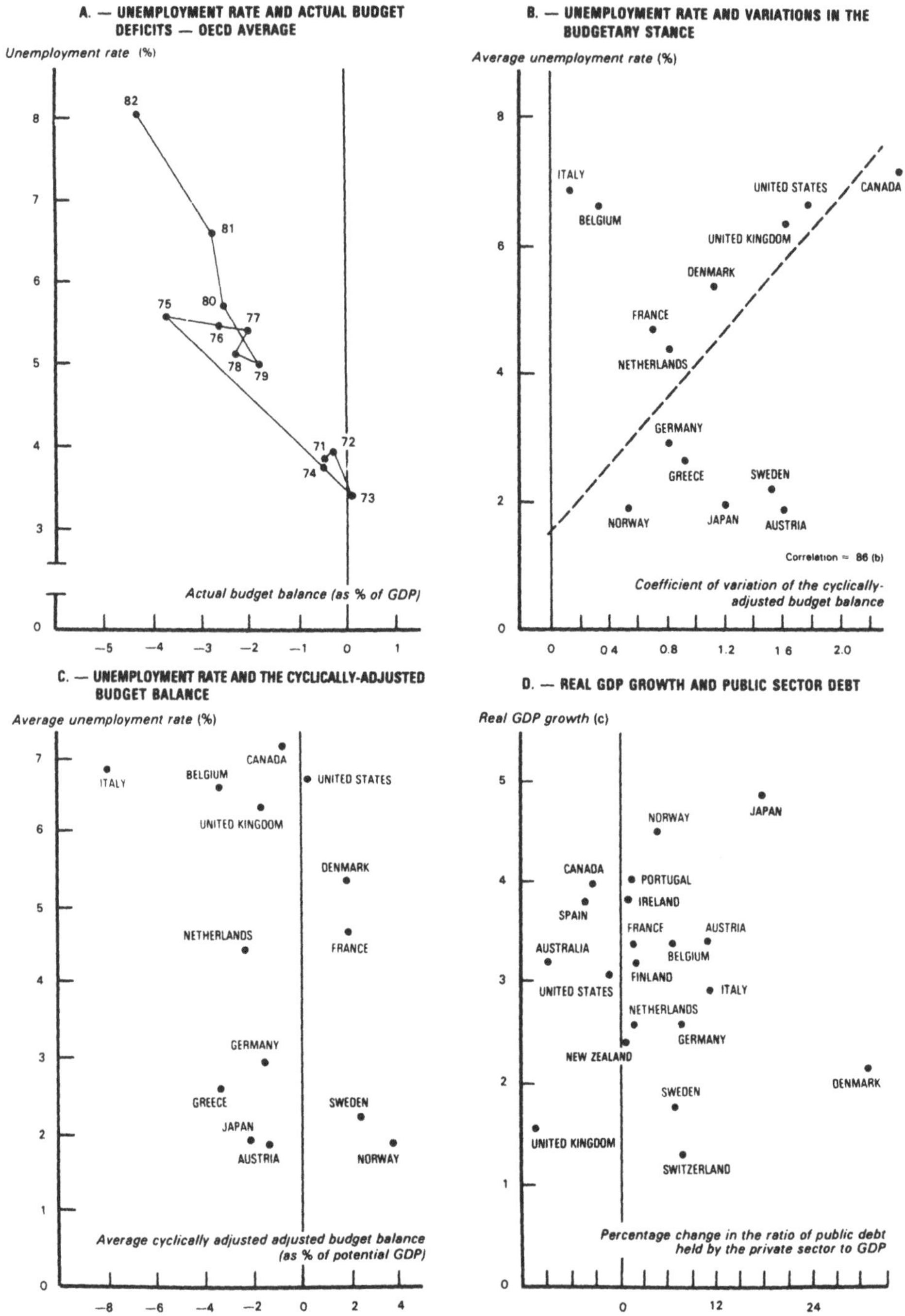


(a) See Annex 1 (b) Excluding Japan, Italy, Austria, Belgium and Sweden, significant at 5% (c) Average annual real GNP/GDP growth rate

**Figure 6.3**

## III THE CURRENT INSTRUMENT–OBJECTIVE SETTING

### POLICY STANCE

In the event, the second oil shock, which occurred at the end of 1979, meant that the expected growth of economic activity needed to finance budget deficits (through automatic increases in tax receipts) did not emerge, so that concerted reflation left OECD countries with a legacy of higher deficits and inflation. Given the inflationary consequences of the joint monetary–budgetary expansion after the first shock, and the restricted room for manoeuvre allowed by already large budget deficits, the response to OPEC II was non-accommodating. Fiscal policy became restrictive, as the maintenance of existing nominal money supply targets – lower in real terms because of higher inflation – called for deflationary budget action to prevent upward pressures on interest rates. However, 'automatic stabilizers' (in the context of a recession that turned out to be more severe than expected) have sustained budget deficits. Judged by the high level of government borrowing and real interest rates, policy stance might thus be characterized as one of relatively loose fiscal policy and monetary tightness (Figure 6.1(A)). However, 'discretionary' restraint – though less effective than announced – is reflected in the move towards surplus of the cyclically adjusted budget balance of the major seven countries between 1979 and 1981.[9] Fiscal policies have – on this measure – supported monetary tightness (Figure 6.1(C)). From 1982 the mix of high budget deficits and tight money in the United States has counterbalanced the combination of fiscal restraint and (less marked) monetary tightness applied elsewhere.

At the same time, the medium-term approach to fiscal policies has received a new impetus from the perceived need to plan for a gradual reduction in the size of the public sector to make room for expansion in private activity and create the 'supply-side' conditions for recovery (see Table 6.2). Tax incentives have been widely used to attempt to improve labour supply and investment, to reduce allocational distortions in labour and capital markets, and to correct perceived imbalances between wage and profit shares. In some countries, tax cuts have been linked to wage restraint and incomes policies. Again, because of short-term spending rigidities, governments have actually been forced to rely to a significant extent on tax increases to try to reduce budget deficits, and this development has run counter to their expressed aims of lowering taxation and enhancing the allocational soundness of the public sector. Attempts gradually to restructure and reduce public spending (so as to achieve a better balance between current and capital spending, or reform 'entitlement' programmes in particular) have, nevertheless, been significant factors determining budget stances in OECD countries. Fiscal policies have tended to be at least partially subordinated to both monetary and supply-side considerations in the process of medium-orientation.

The extent of the subordination varies, however, there being a range of attitudes towards the role of fiscal policies in creating the conditions for sustained non-inflationary recovery. In countries that have experienced relatively high inflation, such as the United Kingdom and Australia, the reduction in budget deficits has been seen as a *prior* requirement for the attainment of

**Table 6.2** *Medium-term budgetary objectives operative in 1983*

| *Country* | *Time-scale* | *Objective* |
|---|---|---|
| United States | FY1981–FY1988 | Achievement of federal budget balance by 1984, amended to a FY1988 federal deficit/GNP ratio of about 2 per cent; federal outlays to be reduced from 26 per cent of GNP in FY1983 to 23 per cent. |
| Japan | 1979/80–1984/5 | Seven-year plan to reduce public sector deficit from 11.25 per cent of GDP in 1978 to $5\frac{1}{2}$ per cent, implying the elimination of deficit-financed public consumption. Subsequently revised; objective still holds but no deadline at present operative. Original intention of raising taxation altered, in 1981, to policy of restraining public expenditure through a 'zero-ceiling' on most public consumption. |
| West Germany | 1983–1987 | Medium-term financial plan aimed at reducing the federal deficit from DM39 billion ($2\frac{1}{2}$ per cent of GNP) to DM22 billion (about 1 per cent), to be achieved by holding nominal public spending growth to about $2\frac{3}{4}$ per cent per annum. |
| France | 1982–3 | Aim to stabilize central government deficit at 3 per cent of GDP. |
| United Kingdom | 1980/1–1985/6 | 'Medium-term financial strategy' aimed at reducing PSBR from 5.7 per cent of GDP to 2 per cent; general public expenditure planned to fall from $47\frac{1}{2}$ per cent of GDP in 1981/2 to $43\frac{1}{2}$ per cent. |
| Italy | 1981–1983 | Freezing of PSBR at 1980 level; altered to stabilizing PSBR at 1982 level. |
| Canada | 1981/2–1986/7 | Reduction of federal deficit to 2 per cent of GNP in 1975/6 from over 5 per cent in 1978/9; revised to cutting deficit from nearly 7 per cent of GNP in 1982/3 to $3\frac{1}{2}$ per cent in 1986/7 via a reduction in the public expenditure/GNP ratio from 26 to $23\frac{1}{2}$ per cent. |
| Australia | 1975–1982 | General objective to reduce the central government deficit and size of public sector. Ceased to operate 1983. |
| Austria | 1978–1983 | Reduction of central government deficit to $2\frac{1}{2}$ per cent of GDP via expenditure restraint. |
| Belgium | 1979–1983 | Reduce general government deficit by about a half, to 7 per cent of GDP, through restriction on the growth of current spending. |

| | | |
|---|---|---|
| Denmark | 1980–1985 | Medium-term action programme to reduce the central government deficit through restriction on the growth of public spending and revenue-raising measures. |
| Finland | 1976–1982 | Growth in the volume of public consumption to be restricted to 1 per cent per annum below the annual average growth rate of GDP; tax burden to be stabilized. |
| Netherlands | 1978 onwards | Reduction in public sector deficit from 5.25 per cent to structural norm of 4–4.5 per cent of GDP, via expenditure restraint. |
| Norway | 1982–1985 | 'Long-term programme' to contain public expenditure growth and stabilize gross tax level. |
| Portugal | 1981–1984 | Stabilize or reduce the central government deficit. |
| Spain | 1979 onwards | Medium-term objective to control public sector deficit and curtail current expenditures. |
| Sweden | 1980–1990 | Reduction of central government deficit in line with the achievement of external current account balance. |
| Switzerland | 1980–1983 | Establish federal government budget balance by 1984, by restricting the growth of spending; altered to achieving deficit of 0.2 per cent of GDP by 1986. |

*Sources:* OECD, *Economic Surveys 1982–83* and national budget sources.

balanced medium term growth. 'Inflation-first' strategies have implied using fiscal policy as an instrument for the achievement of monetary targets, persistent budget deficits being regarded as an impediment to market-oriented economic recovery. Similarly in the United States the reduction of inflationary expectations via cuts in budget deficits and strict control of monetary growth, has also been ascribed an essential role in promoting recovery. 'Supply-side' considerations have, however, meant that tax cuts have been given priority (by the US administration) over budget deficit reductions. While a reduction in medium-term budget deficits is considered necessary for balanced recovery,[10] United States fiscal stance, from 1982, has actually been expansionary, so that high interest rates have borne the principal burden of suppressing domestic inflation.

In other OCED economies, the pursuit of budget deficit reductions also reflects the need for fiscal policy to support monetary restriction in order:

- to restore entrepreneurial confidence, lower interest rates and remove a source of potential inflationary pressure (West Germany[11] and Japan[12]);
- to contain government credit demands within the limit of domestic saving availability so as to free domestic capital resources for private investment (Belgium, the Netherlands); or, more generally,
- to prevent excess domestic liquidity.

In those countries that have had recourse to foreign borrowing (Sweden, Denmark, Norway, Ireland), the need is to prevent continuing pressures on the balance of payments, costs of credit and debt service charges (see *The Swedish Budget 1982/83*, 1982, pp. 33–4). In low-inflation countries generally, the interest costs of continuous government borrowing have become an actual and/ or prospective burden calling into question both the long-run effectiveness of supporting activity by budget deficits and the cost–benefit trade-off involved in maintaining domestic demand in the short term by this means.

The need to suppress inflationary expectations has thus been a strong motivation for budgetary restraint. It has derived both from the rationale that inflation tends – sooner or later – to undermine any immediately positive demand impact stemming from a money-accommodated budget deficit, and from the cumulating costs of avoiding the potentially inflationary consequences of persistent deficits. Such costs are seen in terms of domestic savings pre-emption, lower productive investment, higher debt service charges, and lower long-run revenue growth in exchange for a diminishing ability of budget deficits to sustain demand. For those OECD countries where market expectations are more favourable and budget cuts strategies credible, however, fiscal imbalance is something that can be corrected gradually, over a period of years. Correction is necessary for longer-run growth prospects, but this does not necessarily imply a belief in the sufficiency of budget balance to bring about recovery. Not only may a 'structural' budget *deficit* be necessary in equilibrium,[13] but progress towards deficit reduction may be tempered, in some cases, by short-term demand considerations: *temporary* employment-supporting measures have been judged necessary in economies such as Canada, Austria, and Switzerland.[14] Only in France, however, has a full-blown strategy of support for demand been attempted – unsuccessfully – in 1981–2 (see below).

## POLICY IMPLEMENTATION

### *Budgetary norms*

The majority of OECD economies have allowed, in their medium-term budget targets, for a structural budget *deficit* and a positive longer-run accumulation of government debt. Where public investment yields a return sufficient to cover debt interest payments, and where private savings have been high enough to warrant it, budgetary norms have been based on a positive role of the budget deficit in taking up excess domestic private savings. A *structural* (high employment) deficit has been planned, for example, in West Germany and the Netherlands,[15] where outstanding government debt grows in line with potential GDP. Such a positive role for fiscal policy in creating employment has been questioned, on the other hand, in countries (particularly the United States) where public expenditure is seen as consumption and where a longer-run balanced budget (implying a full employment *surplus*) appears to be more in line with the perceived self-equilibrating properties of a market economy.

Operational deficiencies have prevented budgetary norms from being achieved: in particular, the overestimation of potential GDP growth and the indexation of public sector wage and transfer costs to prices have both been responsible for some public sector overexpansion. Such conventions as indexation have been introduced to impart greater consistency to the medium-term evolution of public sector services and their costs; but in practice they have tended to make for perverseness and rigidity in responses to inflationary shocks, as they may prevent necessary adjustments in labour and exchange markets. In fact, indexation rules have frequently had to be suppressed for policy to be made more flexible.

### *Monetary targets*

Strategies designed to contain inflation expectations have implied a gradual reduction of monetary growth, and this has entailed a dominance of monetary over fiscal objectives. In general, monetary targets have been based on empirical evidence of medium-term stability in the relationship between money supply and nominal income (see OECD, 1979; Axilrod, 1982, pp. 16–17). On this ground, the narrow money aggregate (M1) was the principal target until recently in the United States and Canada, while a broader aggregate (variously defined) has been favoured by Japan, France, the United Kingdom, Australia, Spain and the Netherlands. Both West Germany and Switzerland (since 1980) target the 'central bank money stock'. This target has served as a proxy either for the broad money stock (M3 as in West Germany) or a monetary base target (the Swiss case). In Italy, considerations associated with both the financing of persistent public sector deficits and external disequilibria have led to the adoption of a quantitative target in terms of total domestic credit expansion.

The choice of the target variable also reflects the method of monetary control used.[16] The money stock may be controlled from the supply side via money market operations and/or central bank credit to the commercial banks, directly affecting banks' reserve positions. The use of such operating procedures (as in the United States, and to some extent in Canada, West Germany and Switzerland) tends to favour targets in terms of central bank money (which includes bank reserves) or narrow money supply (which is most closely related to bank reserves). Where the authorities attempt to control the money stock through its asset counterparts – influencing bank lending by altering private and government demands for credit (as in Japan, France, Italy and, to a certain extent, the United Kingdom) – attention has focused either on broad money aggregates, which cover most of the deposit liabilities of the banking system, or on domestic credit expansion.

It must be noted that the role of the public sector borrowing requirement (PSBR) in overall money creation (private credit demands and overseas capital flows being the other principal determinants) may be seen more explicitly by focusing on a broad money aggregate. This may allow for the use of the PSBR as an *instrument* of monetary control, as in the United Kingdom and Australia in particular, and in this sense the choice of a broad money aggregate may serve to strengthen the subordination of fiscal to monetary policy. In the process it may also give treasuries explicit leverage over monetary targets, and encourage centralization of monetary and fiscal decision making.

On the other hand, the experience of the United States has shown that fiscal and monetary policies can diverge if they are formulated and implemented autonomously, the respective authorities calling on the other to adjust. Such divergences may obviously affect market expectations about, and hence the achievement of, medium-term financial objectives. At root, there is in effect a choice between the merits of coordinated policy setting (but with the associated risk of monetary accommodation) on the one hand, and potentially uncoordinated policies (but with central banks acting as a bulwark against the monetary financing of budget deficits) on the other (see Fair, 1980).

In most countries, a degree of flexibility has also been found necessary with respect to monetary targets. The need to respond pragmatically to various types of shock and to allow for unforeseeable disturbances has led to the adoption of target ranges for monetary aggregates and – for the most part – to targets being formulated only for the short-term horizon. Moreover, experience with monetary targeting seems to have confirmed the need to monitor or target several monetary indicators rather than one. The institutionally induced instabilities in the demand for narrow money – owing to financial innovations – have, in fact, led to the de-emphasis of the M1 target in the United States and to its suspension in Canada, a closer attention being attached to broader aggregates. Conversely, uncertainty about the stability between the broad money stock and nominal income in the United Kingdom has led to the adoption of multiple monetary targets. In general, the monetary authorities have had to seek a balance between maintaining credibility through flexibility, or rigorous consistency, which may, at times, involve being locked into inappropriate and unrealistic targets.

## IV THE RATIONALE FOR MEDIUM-TERM POLICY MAKING

The increasing tendency towards the medium-term planning of budgetary and monetary policies has been based on the principle that, beyond the short run, such policies need to be harmonized. Independent assignment of instruments may be possible in the short run, but over a longer period the scope for persistent divergences between the stance of one instrument and another must be closely constrained so that adverse inflationary, allocational and financial repercussions are prevented. In this respect, medium-term budget and monetary strategy has three origins.

There was, first, a realization, following the inflationary consequences of the early 1970s reflation, that price stability cannot be sacrificed to the benefit of growth and unemployment goals, and that the monetary accommodation of budget deficits could not ensure that fiscal policy was effective. Given the perceived need to contain inflationary expectations through the control of monetary aggregates, a corollary was seen to be the pursuit of a compatible medium-term budget balance. This brought a reappraisal of the assignment of instruments to objectives, insofar as the necessity was recognized for fiscal policy stance to be set in concert with anti-inflationary monetary policies; governments could not rely on a long-run positive trade-off between inflation and output.

Secondly, the move towards long-range financial planning has reflected the attempt to stem what is seen as a piecemeal and uncontrolled expansion of the public sector over two decades. The adverse allocational and inflationary effects of this – reflected in the stagnation of private sector output in recent years – have created a general concern that public spending and taxation be brought into better long-run balance with available resources. This has been most marked where (as in the Netherlands, Belgium and Scandinavian countries) public sector expansion has been fastest (see Figure 6.4), where (as in the United Kingdom and Australia) there was a political reversion to greater belief in the efficacy of the market sector, and where (as in the United States and Canada) the degree of interference with private activities has been an issue.[17] Adverse trends in the composition of expenditure – in particular the growth of current transfers and the declining proportion of public investment in total spending (see Figure 6.5) – have, however, made concern about public sector imbalances more general; such a concern may be seen, particularly, in the budget cuts strategies of West Germany and Japan.

Thirdly, ensuring that high budget deficits are financed in a non-inflationary way – i.e. without money creation – has entailed increasing public sector borrowing from the non-bank private sector and cumulating debt interest payments. Continuation of such trends is seen as risking upward pressures on interest rates or forced tax increases, which would tend sooner or later to undermine the support given by budget deficits to demand.

This problem, however, has different dimensions and a different degree of immediacy between countries, depending on the extent to which (a) inflation has eroded outstanding government debt and/or such debt has cumulated; (b) prospective future budget trends are adverse or favourable; and (c) financial markets translate future deficit trends in terms of likely crowding out and inflation. In those economies where inflation is perceived by markets to be strongly linked to budget deficits and monetary creation, 'inflation-first' strategies have emphasized medium-term budget reductions from the point of view of controlling market expectations, reducing long-term interest rates and eliminating the danger of any future reimposition of an inflation tax. In the

## ECONOMIC PERFORMANCE AND THE EXPANSION OF THE GOVERNMENT SECTOR IN SELECTED OECD COUNTRIES, 1970-1982 (a)

### A. — GOVERNMENT EXPENDITURES ON GOODS AND SERVICES AND GROWTH PERFORMANCE

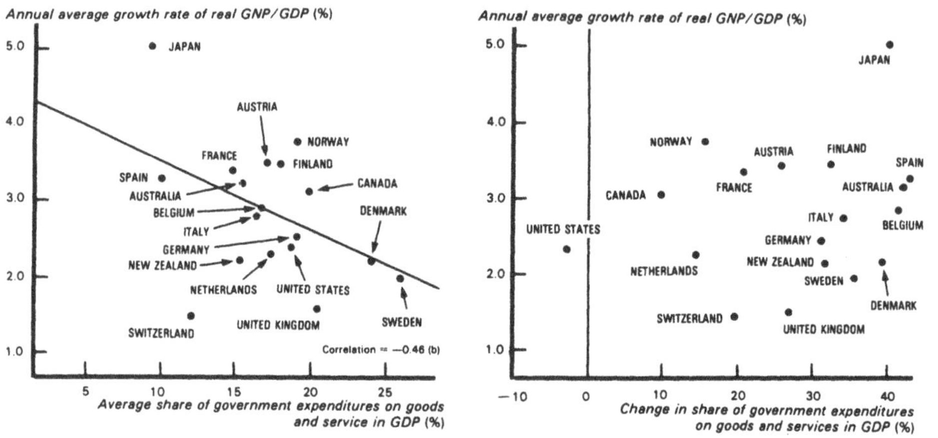


### B. — GOVERNMENT EMPLOYMENT AND GROWTH PERFORMANCE

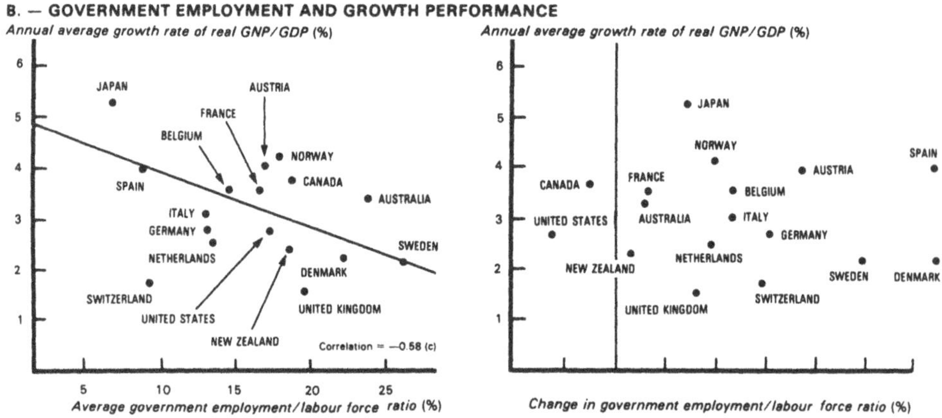


### C. — GOVERNMENT EXPENDITURES ON GOODS AND SERVICES, GOVERNMENT EMPLOYMENT AND INFLATION PERFORMANCE

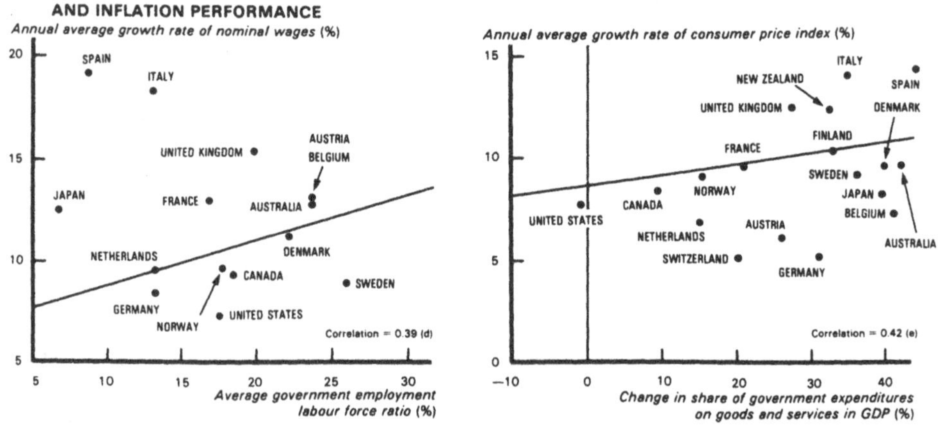


(a) See Annex 1 (b) Significant at 10 %. (c) Excluding Switzerland, significant at 5 %. (d) Excluding Japan, Italy and Spain, significant at 20 %. (e) Excluding Germany, Austria and Switzerland, significant at 20 %.

**Figure 6.4**

TRENDS IN GENERAL GOVERNMENT EXPENDITURES IN SELECTED OECD COUNTRIES

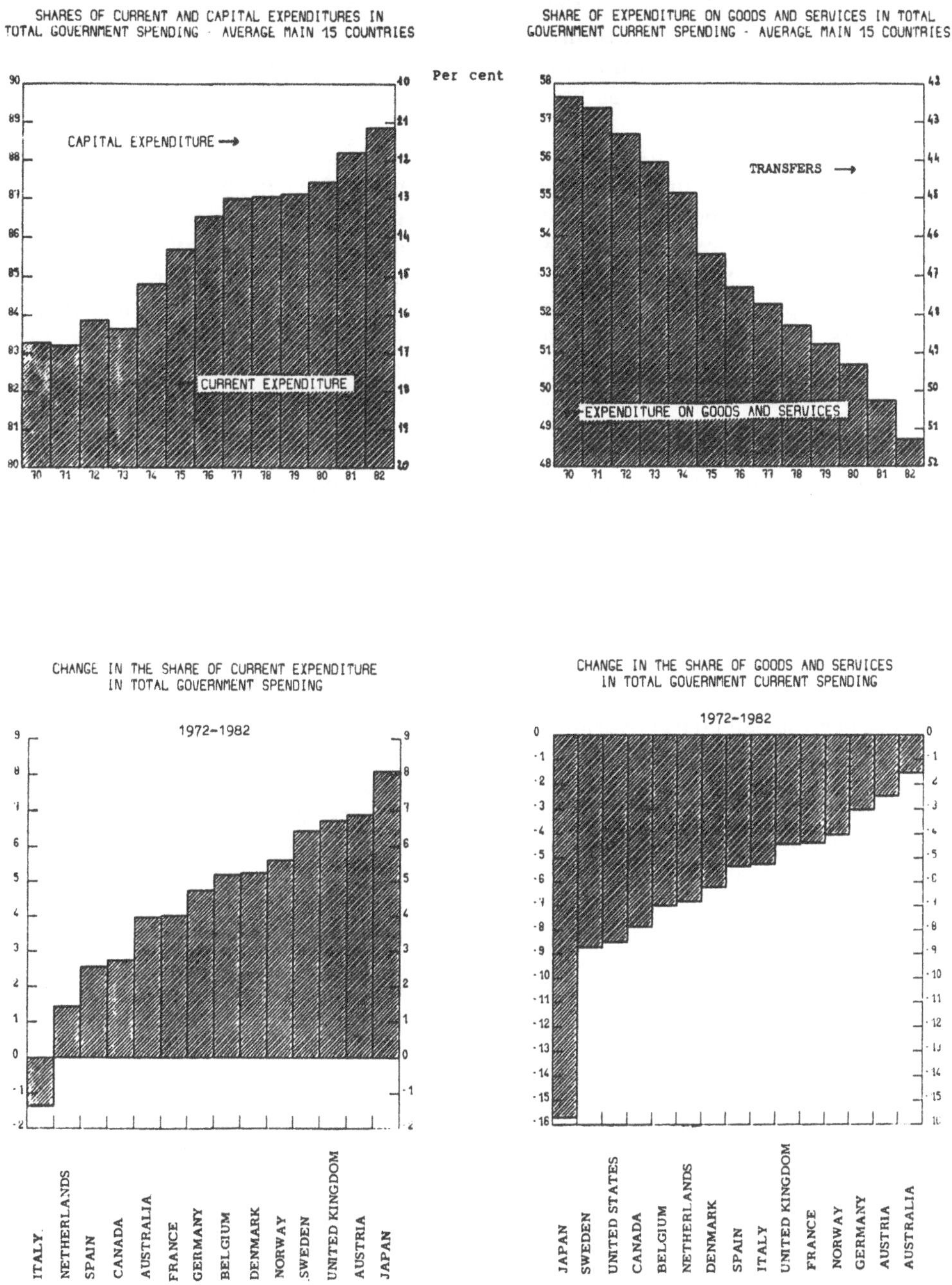


**Figure 6.5**

United Kingdom and Australia this problem has been seen as one calling for immediate correction, whereas in the United States the supply-side strategy has concentrated more on the correction of past tax – rather than debt – increases, accepting that future budget deficits must be reduced, but not (in recognition of the difficulties of achieving this) requiring immediate deficit cuts; future budget trends are seen as more important for the creation of business confidence.

Elsewhere, while there has been a general acceptance that the second oil-price shock called for fiscal retrenchment so as to relieve the burden on interest rates, such retrenchment has been only indirectly seen in terms of alleviating capital market pressures and inflationary uncertainty. In the Netherlands and Belgium, for example, the fact that public sector borrowing has reached the limits of private savings has meant that short-run corrective action has been necessary to prevent the emergence of upward pressures on interest rates. In addition, the link between business confidence and the budget deficit has required that short-term progress be made towards the reduction of this deficit in West Germany. But here, as in Japan, Canada, Austria and Switzerland, the need to take action to reduce government indebtedness is, perhaps, expressed more in terms of long-range fiscal prudence and the necessity to reverse the trend to debt accumulation and debt service pressures, rather than in terms of relieving actual crowding out of private expenditure or reducing inflationary expectations. It is, however, recognized that on present trends the capacity of budget deficits to support demand will diminish gradually, as refinancing problems and cumulating debt service obligations lead to mounting interest rate pressures and/or increased tax rates.

In countries such as Sweden, Denmark and Ireland, where domestic activity has been sustained by government external borrowing, the problem is linked to structural deficits in the current balance of payments; medium-term financial strategy is perceived as a means of preventing, by gradual adjustment, the real income transfers connected with overseas debt servicing from reaching a point where a deflationary domestic expenditure adjustment is ultimately needed.

France has been, in the very recent period, the principal exception to this medium-term concern: with a relatively small government debt, some room was seen, in 1981/82, for expanding the public sector deficit. However, this trend has had to be reversed (the deficit of the central government being limited to 3 per cent of GDP) because of increased monetary financing (owing to the narrowness of the domestic capital market), downward pressures on the exchange rate and larger borrowing abroad (associated with the emergence of a substantial current account deficit) – factors seen as implying a danger of crowding out and/or a worsening of inflationary expectations.

## V SHORT AND MEDIUM-TERM POLICY COORDINATION

### AUTOMATIC STABILIZERS AND MEDIUM-TERM BUDGETARY OBJECTIVES

In principle, once the appropriate medium-term budget and monetary targets have been set, monetary and fiscal stance could be allowed to change automatically with short-term demand conditions. The budget deficit would vary countercyclically owing to the operation of 'built-in stabilizers'.[18] For an economy on its long-run balanced growth path, but subject to short-run non-inflationary demand variations, such automatic budget responses would be consistent with the maintenance of balanced economic growth – in terms of public sector resource claims, public borrowing, monetary creation and price and interest rate stability. With such stabilizers in operation, the economy and the budget deficit might be self-correcting and as such market expectations would discount short-term increases in government demands for credit as transitory. Private sector demands for money and credit being lower in recession, no net pressure on interest rates need, in principle, arise either from current or expected public sector claims on private savings.

In practice, however, such stabilizers have tended to be imperfect and inadequate economic regulators. In the first place, tax and expenditure systems reflect social as well as economic objectives, so that their short-term stabilizing properties are to some extent arbitrary and not necessarily consistent with medium-term structural balance. Unemployment compensation may affect longer-run economic growth adversely by discouraging labour supply (increasing structural unemployment), although the evidence is not conclusive on this. Or, as noted above, where government transfers are indexed to prices, a degree of inflexibility in adjusting to supply-side (particularly terms-of-trade) shocks may be introduced, increasing real wage rigidity and decreasing labour mobility. 'Built-in stabilizers' may, in certain circumstances, reduce the long-run growth rate of the economy, thus becoming part of the structural budget problem.

Secondly, automatic stabilizers add to the stock of outstanding government debt insofar as they are not 'redeemed' through a budget surplus as the economy recovers. They will therefore have longer-run cumulative effects, which will help determine market expectations of future interest rates. The operation of automatic stabilizers is consistent with medium-term budgetary balance only insofar as they ensure that balanced economic growth is resumed; this raises questions of how automatic rules can facilitate the attainment of the longer-run growth on which they are predicated. Divergent opinions have been expressed in this respect.

Traditional short-run demand management, with its emphasis on active government support for demand, has stressed the view that the economic system is *not* necessarily self-regulating. If the economy is liable to diverge for long periods from its steady-state growth path, government intervention may be necessary to maintain a consistently higher level of employment and/or to speed recovery. If there is no way of distinguishing purely temporary from longer-run divergences demand management may need to be flexible in the short term – automatic stabilizers may not be sufficient for recovery (see Cairncross, 1981).

As has been described above, however, the tendency has been to question the effectiveness, feasibility and scope for countercyclical activism to aid economic recovery. Indeed, a corollary of 'inflation-first' strategies is generally a belief in the capacity of the private sector to achieve automatic recovery as a result of budget *cuts*. Three principal automatic mechanisms may be discerned:

- Lower inflation may mean a smaller erosion of the real value of private sector financial wealth (or a lower 'inflation tax'); private savers may then have to allocate a lower proportion of their income to maintaining the real value of their savings, so that personal spending may rise as a result. Given a constant monetary growth rate, a fall in the rate of inflation will cause an increase in the real money supply, allowing room for real demand to expand. This argument has been particularly prominent in the United Kingdom, where it has been associated with an emphasis on setting a fixed target for *nominal* GDP growth.
- Business investment may rise as lower interest rates and less inflationary uncertainty follow reductions in government credit demands and slower medium-term monetary growth.
- Investment may also be promoted by simultaneous tax and spending cuts. Either – as in the United States in particular – the 'supply-side' effects of lower taxation may be seen as reducing work and investment disincentives, or – as in the Netherlands – higher tax-financed public spending may be seen as leading to lower company profits and investment, so that simultaneous cuts in taxes and state spending may prompt higher net profits, more investment, faster longer-run growth and lower structural deficits.[19]

The idea that economic recovery may be facilitated by budget cuts goes further than neo-classical propositions about longer-run 'fiscal neutrality' (i.e. budget multipliers of zero). The stabilizing potential of the above mechanisms depends upon a reversal of the conventionally positive multiplier properties attaching to tax- and deficit-financed public spending. The combination of short-term fiscal and monetary restraint that followed the second oil-price rise may therefore be seen not just in terms of a trade-off between disinflation objectives and output, but as aiming to secure a viable and lasting increase in output and employment via *lower* public spending and inflation. Medium-term monetary and budgetary restraint has been seen as requiring a parallel restrictive coordination in the short run.

In the event, however, the combination of fiscal and monetary tightness has been associated with recession, stagnant investment and sustained government credit demands; public sector borrowing and interest rates have remained high, while the achievment of medium-term budgetary goals has had to be deferred. Because of increased unemployment-related transfers, lower tax receipts and higher public sector debt service costs, simultaneously tight fiscal and monetary policies have tended automatically to inflate budget deficits, frustrating – wholly or in part – attempted deficit reductions. In the process, economic recovery may also have been compromised: deflationary policies reducing demand while budget 'feedbacks' from lower growth prevented reductions in interest rates.

This problem has two (related) dimensions. In the first place, realized budget deficit cuts may be quite small in the short run when all countries are attempting *simultaneously* to reduce public borrowing by joint monetary and fiscal restriction. Indeed, in an international environment, failure to take account of the budgetary reaction in other economies may lead to an overestimate of likely budget deficit reductions (see OECD, 1981, pp. 30–1). Secondly, to avoid the 'feedback' on to the budget deficit from lower activity, interest rates need to fall in order to encourage interest-sensitive private spending and reduce debt service costs. In such a case, to the extent that crowding out of private demand may be virtually complete in the medium run, public sector deficits could be reduced without eventual loss in terms of activity and output: private spending would tend to substitute for public. However, if the realized budget deficit cut is small, or negligible, so will be the interest rate reduction and the increase in interest-sensitive private spending. Indeed, attempts to cut deficits, in conjunction with restrictive monetary targets, contain the danger that lower demand and sustained high interest rates will deter investment and risk locking OECD economies into a slow-growth impasse.

While cyclically corrected budget balances, which are better indicators of the thrust of fiscal policy, have generally shown a tendency towards surplus, or lower deficit, since the second oil crisis (OECD, 1983),[20] the overall level of actual budget deficits may still be maintaining expectations of monetary and interest rate pressures in the medium run. In the circumstances described above, a strategy of reducing interest rates by combined fiscal and monetary restraint may be slow to take effect because *ex ante* budget cuts may not lower the expected stream of future deficits, unless financial markets see the cyclical component of the deficit as temporary. If they do not, recovery may be pre-empted and medium-term structural budget balance be unattainable. Slow-growth expectations will be self-fulfilling, as high interest rates are sustained. Concerted short-term monetary and fiscal restriction might then be incompatible with the medium-term objectives of promoting growth and reducing the budget deficit.

Automatic stabilizers may therefore be a mixed blessing. They may be potentially beneficial in the face of demand shocks, and they may provide a more reliable source of fiscal support than 'fine-tuning'. However, they may contain structural biases that make for rigidities of response to inflationary supply-side shocks, reducing growth potential, sustaining long-term interest rate pressures and making structural budget deficit problems more intractable. In the process, they may – while supporting current demand – impede the implementation of recovery strategies based on reducing interest rates and inflation expectations. OECD economies have, therefore, been seeking to reshape such stabilizers through reforms to marginal tax and unemployment benefit rates and revisions to indexation commitments; in this way their impact may be made more consistent with longer-run structural budget balance. At the same time, budget cuts strategy has been seen to demand that at least part of the 'automatic stabilizer' element in the budget deficit be offset.

On the other hand, with non-accommmodating monetary targets (resulting in lower real monetary growth rates) the effects of offsetting such stabilizers in the cause of inflation control may prove deflationary and perverse. Their existence therefore demands a degree of autonomy in the setting of short-term fiscal stance, even if medium-term strategy needs to be based on the interdependence of fiscal and monetary policies and (currently) on the gradual reduction in structural budget deficits. Attempts to control monetary growth and reduce interest rates by cutting budget deficits appear (because of the dependence of the government deficit on economic activity) to be open to difficulties that may make the process self-defeating.

The difficulties of avoiding the short-term deflationary impact of attempted budget cuts, while assuring that excess spending is eliminated in the long run, has been accompanied by an increasing recognition of the need to distinguish between *structural* and *cyclical* budget deficits. Because continuous future deficits appear to affect present interest rates, these have needed (and still need in some cases) to be reduced. Concentrating budget cuts less on the present and more on following years is seen as allowing the aims of budget consolidation to be achieved without the adverse effects of fiscal deflation on demand. The extent to which short-run cuts in deficits are still needed, in order to instil confidence that budgets are under control, will vary; but in some cases (the 1983 Canadian budget for instance) controlling medium-term deficits may be seen as allowing greater scope for additional short-term demand support via overtly *temporary* budget measures. The proposition that budget cuts may raise activity and ensure recovery is more likely to be validated where *future* deficit cuts can be traded off for cuts in current interest rates.

## SHORT-TERM MONETARY TARGETS AND MEDIUM-TERM FINANCIAL STRATEGY

Although the problems entailed in expanded budget deficits and tight monetary policies are general to OECD economies, the conflicts have been particularly pronounced in the United States. Since, as noted above, fiscal monetary policies are set quasi-independently, their divergence might be looked on either as an expansionary fiscal stance conflicting with a given monetary constraint, or as a restrictive monetary target competing with a given fiscal stance. Critics of the American situation have based their case on the former interpretation – that fiscal policy should be tightened in order to reduce interest rates and the 'international crowding out' stemming from the transmission of high interest rates from the United States to Europe. The proposed readjustment of the policy mix is seen as a matter of meeting pre-set monetary targets by a different mix of interest rates and public sector deficits. Such a strategy would succeed in raising total OECD output if the fall in activity induced by tighter fiscal policies were more than offset by the effects of budget deficit cuts on interest-sensitive expenditures, in the United States and abroad. To the extent that the emphasis has increasingly been placed on cutting *future* deficits, and hence interest rates, rather than reducing current budgetary support for demand, this would be more likely to be the case.

Alternatively, and not confined to the United States, the monetary–fiscal mix issue may be seen as one of choosing the monetary growth rates most consistent with medium-term financial objectives, given an only marginally controllable fiscal policy course in the short run. Central banks can, in the short term, offset the monetary effects of budget deficits so that monetary targets may, in principle, be set independently of fiscal policy (as appears to be the case in the United States). For an economy on its medium-term growth path this poses few problems; but when the object of monetary targets is to reduce inflationary expectations, via negative real monetary growth, the question arises whether monetary restraint might, in the short run, prove too severe in order to achieve the monetary growth objectives (and hence stable prices). The higher the interest rates necessary to square monetary restriction with the fiscal stance, the greater the danger that they may feed – through automatic increases in budget deficits associated with lower economic activity and higher debt servicing costs – into expectations of future monetary accommodation.

It has been argued from this that, in the face of expanding budget deficits, short-term monetary tightness may be self-defeating, since cumulative interest payments and indebtedness will make longer-run financing of such deficits impossible, so that government debt will eventually be monetized (Sargent and Wallace, 1981). Two inferences might, once more, be drawn: either fiscal policy should be tightened or short-term monetary policy eased, the latter prescription being more consistent with medium-term budgetary objectives if financial markets put less weight on an undesirable upward revision of short-term monetary targets than on the prospective long-run benefits of reducing budget deficits. The issues involved here will have greater immediate relevance the more monetarist-rational are financial markets (though 'international crowding out' makes them of wider interest). Essentially, however, they concern the balance between gradualism and flexibility in monetary targetry on the one hand, and consistency and confidence in progress towards longer-run inflation goals on the other. In this respect, monetary targets may not constitute intermediate objectives that can be set independently of other economic factors, including the stance of fiscal policy, in the short or medium term.[21] Conversely, although it could display some degree of independence in the short run, the stance of fiscal policy should help the achievement of monetary targets in the long run.

The implications for the independence, or interdependence, of fiscal and monetary policies may therefore be summarized as follows. In the medium term, these policies need to be coordinated and cannot be considered as separate instruments. They may, however, constitute more than one instrument insofar as structural budget norms may be defined to take up excess private savings, provided government debt accumulation does not create imbalances in private portfolios. Moreover, the impact of 'built-in stabilizers' on budget deficits may imply that fiscal policy is relatively inflexible in the short run so that monetary stance needs to be framed with this partly in mind.

## NOTES

1 Aspects of these issues are discussed by Chouraqui and Price (1983). See also OECD (1982).

2 Reflation was associated in some cases with the belief that both monetary and fiscal policies could be more effective if they acted in concert, exchange rate depreciation preserving, where necessary, external competitiveness and payments balance.

3 The figure is drawn so that in the upper-right quadrant policies are mutually accommodating (budget expansion supported by monetary growth): see notes to the figure. The contrast between the *ex ante* thrust of fiscal policy, which was generally expansionary in 1971/2, and the *ex post* stance, which was roughly neutral, may be seen in the difference between Figures 6.1 (A) and 6.1 (C) (which show the budget deficit corrected for 'automatic stabilizers').

4 The influence of inflation-induced fiscal drag on budget stances is illustrated by the swing of the US cyclically adjusted federal government budget indicator towards surplus by \$9.2 billion (0.7 per cent of GNP) in 1974, all of which may be ascribed to automatic inflation-induced effects on government revenues: see de Leeuw and Holloway (1982).

5 The relationship between real interest rates, and their stability, and growth is ambivalent from Figures 6.2 (B) and 6.2 (C), again depending on the sub-set of countries chosen. Conflicts may, of course, occur between money stock and interest rate stability; hence the advantages of steady real interest rates and monetary growth may not be simultaneously available. The same applies to exchange rates. Moreover, cross-section correlations are not to be taken as expressing *causality* in any definitive sense.

6 'Discretionary' policy is here defined in terms of changes in the 'cyclically adjusted' budget balance. These incorporate announced policy changes, fiscal drag and estimating revisions. See Chouraqui and Price (1983), Annex I.

7 It should again be emphasized that the correlations depicted in the figure provide only *prima facie* evidence on the link between budget stance and economic objectives. Further research is needed in relating objectives to instruments in a multi-instrument setting taking account of incomes policies, monetary and exchange rate control etc. Moreover, a positive relationship between objectives and fiscal support may not be proof that such support is permanently sustainable.

8 See OECD (1977) which, while arguing for medium-term budgetary consistency, also diagnosed the need for active demand management to re-achieve the medium-term path (pp. 191–2).

9 OECD (1980) projected the aggregate change in the cyclically adjusted budget balance for the seven major countries for 1981 as +1.1 per cent. The outturn, as estimated in OECD (1983), was +0.7 per cent.

10 While 'supply-side' advocates have emphasized the allocative benefits of cutting tax rates, in the US case tax cuts have rather been designed to put pressure on the legislature to eliminate the ensuing budget deficit via reductions in public expenditure. It is the expenditure-cutting process that is hypothesized as freeing resources for private sector use, the switch from tax to deficit-financed spending being seen only as a choice in favour of deferred as opposed to current taxation.

11 Memorandum of the Deutsche Bundesbank, in UK House of Commons (1980), p. 13.

12 Japan, Budget Bureau, Ministry of Finance (1982). p. 12.

13 A 'structural' budget deficit is that component of the deficit that would remain, under unchanged policies, if the economy were to return to 'high employment' levels of activity. It is equivalent to the cyclically adjusted budget balance, which is used in this chapter to describe discretionary fiscal stance.

14 See OECD (1983), for a description of most recent fiscal policy actions.

15 The West German budget deficit is divided into two elements: (i) the 'cyclically neutral' deficit, composed of a normal structural borrowing requirement (of about $1\frac{1}{4}$ per cent of potential GDP) and automatic stabilizers (excluding unemployment transfers), which will be self-correcting as the economy returns to its long-run growth path; and (ii) the 'cyclical impulse' – this helps prevent discretionary fiscal support from spilling over into the medium term. Similarly in the Netherlands, short-term variations around the structural budget norm have been allowed up to a limit at which an 'emergency brake' has come into operation and fiscal policies would be subordinated to reducing actual deficits. See OECD (1978) and Den Dunnen (1981).

16 For a discussion of the two main systems of monetary control operating in OECD countries see OECD (1982).

17 As Figure 6.4 shows, public sector expansion has not been associated positively (i.e. beneficially) with economic growth and inflation performance in the past decade. The causality behind the negative relationship between growth performance and public sector expansion cannot, however, be inferred directly from the figure: slower growth may have prompted such expansion. Similarly, evidence that the public sector is a causal factor in inflation is inconclusive on a cross-country basis.

18 Automatic stabilizers have two dimensions: first, revenues fall in a recession, leaving a proportion of ongoing public expenditure to be financed through borrowing: the effectiveness of stabilizers is thus dependent partly on the composition of medium-term public spending

plans; second, unemployment-related transfers will tend to rise, increasing the consumption orientation of spending.

19 The proposition that simultaneous cuts in expenditures and revenues will tend to increase output and reduce government deficits (which inverts the conventional 'balanced budget multiplier' theory) relies significantly on the argument that taxes are borne, for the most part, by companies; reducing taxes is of more benefit to investment than cutting government borrowing and interest rates. See, for instance, Knoester (1983).

20 The United States federal budget has been *sui generis* in moving towards structural deficit since 1982.

21 See the memorandum by the Deutsche Bundesbank in UK House of Commons (1980), p. 13. It is the Bundesbank's conviction that 'control of the money supply for the sake of combatting inflation and ensuring steady economic growth can only be successful if the policies and behaviour of public authorities, enterprises and trade unions are guided by the same objectives'.

## BIBLIOGRAPHY

Axilrod, S. (1982), 'Monetary policy, money supply and the federal operating procedures', *Federal Reserve Bulletin*, 69, January, 13–24.

Cairncross, A. (1981), 'The relationship between fiscal and monetary policy, *Banca Nazionale del Lavoro Quarterly Review*, 34(139), December, 375–393.

Chouraqui, J. C. and Price, R. (1983), 'Public sector deficits: problems and policy implications', *OECD Occasional Studies*, June.

Den Dunnen, E. (1981), 'Long term fiscal and monetary policies in the Netherlands', Netherlands Central Bank, mimeo.

Fair, D. (1980), 'Relationships between central banks and the government in the determination of monetary policy, *Société Universitaire Européene de Recherches Financières*.

Japan, Budget Bureau, Ministry of Finance (1982), *The Budget in Brief 1982*, Tokyo.

Knoester, A. (1983) 'Stagnation and the invested Haavelmo effect: some international evidence', Dutch Ministry of Economics Affairs, Discussion Paper 8301, April.

de Leeuw, H. and Holloway, T. (1982), 'The high employment budget: revised estimates and automatic inflation effects', US Department of Commerce, *Survey of Current Business*, 62(4), April, 21–33.

OECD (1977), *Towards Full Employment and Price Stability*, a report by a group of independent experts, Chairman: P. McCracken, Paris.

OECD (1978), 'Budget indicators', *Occasional Studies*, July.

OECD (1979). 'Monetary targets and inflation control', *Monetary Studies Series*, Paris, Organisation for Economic Co-operation and Development.

OECD (1980), *Economic Outlook*, No. 28, December.

OECD (1981), *Economic Outlook*, No. 29, July.

OECD (1982), 'Budget financing and monetary control', *Monetary Studies Series*, Paris, Organisation for Economic Co-operation and Development.

OECD (1983), *Economic Outlook*, No. 33, July.

Sargent, T. and Wallace, N. (1981), 'Some unpleasant monetarist arithmetic', *Federal Reserve Bank of Minneapolis Quarterly Review*, Fall.

*The Swedish Budget 1982/83* (1982), Stockholm.

UK House of Commons (1980), *Memoranda on Monetary Policy*, Treasury and Civil Service Committee, Vol. II, London, HMSO.

# 7 Some Conclusions from Incomes Policy Experience in Industrial Countries[1]

*ANNE ROMANIS BRAUN*

## I INTRODUCTION

Harry Johnson used to say that incomes policy was vitiated by the closed-economy approach. This chapter investigates the nature of the problem of incomes policy in open, interdependent economies. It seeks to illustrate the incomes policy dimension of fiscal and monetary policy as well as experience with explicit incomes policies.

Clear, logically appealing prescriptions concerning the role of monetary and fiscal policy can be derived for a closed economy from a competitive equilibrium model based on drastic simplifying assumptions about the nature of product, labor and capital markets. However, the assumptions then ensure that there is a consistent, rapid and smooth response to financial management.

A world of two or more monetary authorities pursuing independent policies in open economies, with largely integrated product and capital markets but limited labor mobility, is not a world of two or more closed economies. Comprehensible, logically appealing prescriptions concerning monetary and fiscal policy, and their workings via interest rates and exchange rates, can be derived for two or more currency areas by making the same drastic simplifying assumptions as before, and predicating that those assumptions apply in each economy. (Essentially this means that, since profit-maximizing behavior is taken to apply in all markets – any apparent exceptions being ignored as transient phenomena – the forces of competitive equilibrium apply in similar fashion in each and every economy.) Hence general conclusions can be drawn about the consequences of differing national policy combinations, and it can be postulated that, apart from minor variations in the short run, policy outcomes will be consistent and predictable.

These are valuable thought experiments for gaining understanding of the interdependence of national fiscal and monetary policies. However, they provide little useful guidance concerning the medium-term consequences of government policies unless the insights gained are applied within a framework that captures the key elements of the actual economic system. This requires both some account of the changing relationship of national economies as 'planets' of the international system (see McCloskey, 1983), and a more realistic description of the process of wage and price determination within industrial economies than underlies neo-classical theory. These topics are treated in Sections II and III. Section IV outlines some implications of this account concerning the effectiveness of government policies, and the role of incomes policy in industrial countries. Section V discusses the recent incomes policy experience of the Netherlands, the United Kingdom, Austria and Norway. Section VI contains some concluding remarks.

## II THE CHANGING INTERNATIONAL CONTEXT FOR INCOMES POLICY

The economic experience of industrialized countries since 1945 represents a long swing from a fragmented system of isolated and distorted economies left by World War II, through a gradual reintegration and overcoming of extreme distortions within some economies, to the development of increasing strains within the system during the 1960s and of new distortions occasioned by exchange rate disequilibria. A sudden reversal of the pendulum followed, with the break-up of the fixed exchange rate system and greater independence of national policies, at least for the largest economies. One must bear this changing context constantly in mind when reviewing individual countries' experience in economic policy making, remembering especially that since 1973 the industrialized world has been in the throes of uncertain and protracted readjustments from another extreme disequilibrium situation, and that the change in the exchange rate system has impinged far more heavily on some economies than on others.

For much of the 1950s and early 1960s, the fixed exchange rate system actually served to limit inflation more strongly than had initially been foreseen because: (a) the United States' authorities were emphasizing domestic price stability rather than full employment; (b) some countries where abnormal conditions of excess labor supply *and* disorganization of labor unions prevailed after the war (e.g. West Germany, Italy and Japan) were favorably placed, at ruling exchange rates, to pursue export-led growth rather than domestic expansion; (c) so long as capital movements were restricted, any country that implemented a highly expansionary policy alone faced a rapid balance of payments deterioration caused by a worsening trade account, and this lessened the willingness of governments to seek a very rapid expansion of activity. Thus incomes policy, if used, was called upon to lessen domestic cost pressures in a situation where the conjuncture of national policies and operation of the payments system generally worked to prevent price inflation.

The reintegration of the industrial economies, rapid industrial growth and successful operation of the fixed exchange rate system over this period were not, however, the result of purely economic factors, but depended in large measure on politically inspired actions of US governments, anxious to restore a strong Europe and Japan as a counterbalance to the communist threat. This political context created a quite exceptional correspondence of US and other governments' policy objectives at this time.

By the mid 1960s, the industrial countries approximated to a unified economy with integrated product and capital markets. However, the difficulty of achieving the policy coordination now required for the operation of the fixed exchange rate system had increased with the freeing of capital movements and the weakening of US dominance by the emergence of the EEC and Japan as major economic powers. Before national authorities were fully aware of the change, the scope for independent policies had narrowed, while differences in objectives widened because of the way in which the payments system was being operated.

National policies had hitherto been conditioned by the marked differences between countries in labor market and wage bargaining conditions and in hourly wages at going exchange rates (wage differences being offset to a greater or lesser degree by differences in capital intensity and labor productivity). Countries faced with structural underemployment and totally inadequate export earnings to pay for imports were naturally disposed to seek export-led growth.[2] As the expansion of the export industries proceeded, the authorities were inclined to buttress the favorable wage-cost position by tight financial policies. The initial high wage-cost countries, on the other hand, tended to encounter increasing difficulty in maintaining output and investment in the open sector and in sustaining high post-war levels of employment as technology and productivity elsewhere improved. Thus some countries, notably West Germany, the Netherlands, Italy during the 1950s, and Japan, were inclined to follow strict policies; while others, such as the United Kingdom, Belgium, France during the 1950s, and the United States during the 1960s, were predisposed to deficit spending.

By the mid 1960s, the former group of European countries and neighboring countries were at, or close to, full employment and began to experience wage pressures under the influence of tighter labor markets and high export profits at going exchange rates. A growing tendency for wage increases to exceed overall productivity growth was essentially part of an equilibrating process by which domestic cost levels tended to be brought into line under full employment within the fixed exchange rate system, in the absence of exchange rate adjustments. Rapid industrial development within the EEC, under the stimulus of integration behind the common tarriff barrier and of heavy direct investment from outside the area, was also important in raising the general level of wages in some countries. Forces making for automatic upward adjustment of national costs strengthened with the development of international capital markets and the effects of inflationary US policies at the time of the Vietnam War. Sudden and unpredictable shifts of the US policy stance increased the difficulty of arriving at a compatible set of national policies and an appropriate adjustment of exchange rates.

A sharp deceleration of demand following a shift in US policies in 1969 led to sharp rise in unemployment with little change in inflation in North America and the United Kingdom, and vice versa in most other industrial countries, and provoked a still greater divergence of policy objectives between the two groups. Efforts to maintain the fixed exchange rate system under these conditions finally collapsed in 1973, when the control of inflation became of overriding concern in Japan and West Germany, where the rate of inflation was accelerating dramatically.

To understand the problems encountered in policy making after 1973 one must appreciate the consequences, in heightening social tensions and stiffening the attitudes of organized labor, of the prolonged efforts of many European countries to contain wage pressures generated by external factors with restrictive domestic demand policies. The industrial boom of the late 1960s (accompanied by heavy immigration or internal population movements) exacerbated the effect of earlier restrictive policies in limiting the supply of low-cost housing, public utility capacity, and educational and medical facilities. Pressures on the social infrastructure were compounded by demographic factors reflecting the post-war bulge in birth rates. The May 1968 uprising and subsequent wage increases in France marked the beginning of a wave of industrial and political unrest in Western Europe. The French crisis served to encourage public protests and unofficial strikes and to promote more aggressive union bargaining elsewhere, while employers and governments became less prepared to resist wage claims and pressures for higher public spending, for fear of provoking unrest. These conditions were a powerful stimulus towards rising public expenditures as a share of GNP. Increases in social security charges, tax reforms affecting earned incomes and 'fiscal drag' in countries relying on progressive taxes unadjusted for inflation, all contributed to provoke larger wage claims aimed at maintaining after-tax incomes.

As inflation took hold, there was increasing recourse to price escalation clauses in wage settlements, and indexation of pensions, social security benefits and minimum wages became general (Braun, 1976). Indexation was conceded by employers in the hope that it would avoid large, forward-looking wage claims when inflation was accelerating. It was seen by governments as a means of lessening the political divisiveness of inflation and of protecting weaker groups. Widespread indexation served to reinforce the momentum of inflation, aggravating the difficulty of securing a rapid deceleration of inflation after 1973.

Indexation was inappropriate in the context of the worsening of industrial countries' terms of trade and the need to adjust the balance of payments by an increased transfer of resources. Countries in which there was relatively little indexation, such as West Germany, Japan, the United States, Canada and Sweden, were less exposed than others to a sharp rise in nominal incomes and an ongoing momentum of wage increases, stemming directly from the commodity-price boom and oil-price shock. Hence the authorities could enforce a sharp deceleration of monetary growth and nominal demand with the likelihood of less adverse effects on output, profits and employment than in a highly indexed country. Where explicit or implicit indexation was pervasive (in Belgium, Denmark, France, Italy, the Netherlands, Norway and the United Kingdom, under the Heath government's 1973 incomes policy and the Labour government's Social Contract) governments were afraid to allow the exchange rate to depreciate and expose the economy to the risk of spiralling wage inflation and depreciation. Although the current account imbalances and the continuing disparity of inflation rates posed a need for further exchange rate adjustments after 1973, few countries were prepared to let the rate move freely downward (Braun, 1978).

One must distinguish three groups of countries when considering policies after 1973:

- countries least exposed to continuing inflation after the oil-price shock and best placed to pursue independent domestic policies under a flexible exchange rate regime: the three larger economies (USA, West Germany and Japan) and Switzerland;
- countries that, though more exposed to inflation, could aim to maintain a fixed exchange rate: France and five of the six small economies closely integrated with West Germany (Belgium, the Netherlands, Austria, Norway and Sweden), which chose to peg on the Deutsche Mark as a means of restraining domestic price movements and for practical convenience; Canada, which in effect supported the rate vis-à-vis the US dollar by its monetary policy;
- countries in the grip of surging inflation where the possibility of adopting a restrictive policy stance or of avoiding depreciation for long was virtually excluded: in the United Kingdom by the mandate under which the Labour government came to power in 1976; in Italy and Denmark by fragile coalitions.

None of the first group but all of the other countries (except Sweden and Italy), made some use of incomes policy after 1973. Austria, Canada, Denmark, Norway, the Netherlands and the United Kingdom implemented comprehensive policies over a period of years. Belgium and France adopted short-term measures, either to protect the balance of payments or, in France's case, to control price and wage movements after unpegging the exchange rate in 1976. The case for incomes policy under a pegged exchange rate remained much the same as under the fixed exchange rate system, but the problems of devising and implementing a policy were greatly increased when the value of the currency was fixed in terms of a currency whose value was changing against other major currencies.

The change in the international payments system constituted a favorable development for policy makers in the largest countries, who had secured greater control over developments in the economy. It was not unfavorable for 'satellite' economies, such as Austria and Canada, that were closely integrated with a single large economy, and marked by considerable similarities and interlinkages of the wage bargaining system with that of the major country. It presented formidable policy problems for small countries highly dependent on more than one large economy (Australia being a conspicuous case in point).

## III THE NATURE OF THE INCOMES POLICY PROBLEM: CHARACTERISTICS OF WAGE/PRICE DETERMINATION IN INDUSTRIAL ECONOMIES

To understand the nature of the problem of devising an incomes policy, one must relax the assumptions of general equilibrium analysis[3] and recognize that the economy is characterized by differing ease or difficulty of entry for new producers in various sectors. In other words, the system is not governed by pervasive and invariant forces of competition and will respond to change in sticky and erratic fashion. If the differences are considerable, changes in income distribution will be inherent in the system when the rate of monetary expansion changes, and will be much stronger than the 'accidental' short-term changes that can be supposed to occur under competitive conditions. Economic policy then is fraught with political consequences.

As a simplification, the private enterprise economy may be taken to comprise two sectors of easy and difficult entry – the former typically comprising small, labor-intensive enterprises, the latter large-scale and capital-intensive industry (as well as professions to which entry is restricted, and small enterprises exploiting techniques that are not generally available, etc.). One cannot assume that labor can move to equalize its earnings in the two sectors or indeed within the sector of difficult entry.

## WAGE BARGAINING AND PRICING IN THE LARGE-ENTERPRISE SECTOR

The difficulty of entry that gives the enterprise or the oligopolistic industry collectively the power to set and maintain prices for a time, though not indefinitely, also enables wage earners to maintain wages in the face of unemployment. Monopoly persists because, in a dynamic world of changing technique, the power to charge relatively high mark-ups over costs confers the power to perpetuate that situation in various ways.[4] The fact that adoption of advanced techniques or capital-intensive methods lessens the risk of competition from new entrants actually constitutes a powerful inducement for technical progress and the realization of economies of scale, under a high rate of investment and rapid replacement of capital. Limited entry is not an extraneous or an exclusively harmful 'rigidity' of the system.

The characteristics of product and labor markets are closely linked.[5] The conditions under which large, capital-intensive enterprises operate endow existing employees with considerable wage bargaining power,[6] in particular the power to prevent the hiring of new employees at less than the going wage rate. This situation, together with the limited threat of new concerns entering the industry, tends to insulate the level of wages in large enterprises from downward pressure caused by rising unemployment.[7]

Resistance to wage reductions naturally lessens firms' willingness to lower prices (in the inflationary context, resistance to real wage reductions lessens willingness to lower the rate of increase in prices). However, if the difficulty of entry has hitherto been associated with favorable mark-ups and a high rate of investment and capital turnover, the enterprise has the option of maintaining the same mark-up on smaller sales or of lowering the mark-up and prices in order to support sales.[8] Since the firm is concerned to maintain or expand its share of the market, wage earners need not fear that resisting a wage cut will pose a serious risk of losing their jobs in the near to medium term. The more probable first consequence is a cutback of the firm's investment and/or deterioration in its financial position, and a smaller net expansion or failure to maintain its real assets. If so, the reduction in employment occurs mainly outside the enterprise. By preventing a decline in wages, the wage earner secures an increased share in the gross receipts at the expense of shareholders. Even if employment in the enterprise is reduced, reduced hiring, natural wastage and early retirement may suffice to protect existing employees from redundancy.

It is not clear, therefore, how much weight employees should, or do, give to the short-term risk of unemployment if they insist on maintaining their wages. On the other hand, there is a clear risk of reducing their real wages if they accept a cut, or of securing a markedly smaller increase in wages than other wage earners. (Note that this suggests that incomes policy may be more effective than unemployment in moderating wage increases in the large-enterprise sector.) Some commentators seem to assume that, despite the postulate of maximizing behavior, wage earners or individual unions are altruists who care about the general level of employment (Gordon, 1981, p. 526). In practice, the general level of unemployment may be directly taken into account only in wage settlements under centralized bargaining (as in the Scandinavian countries), in national wage awards (Australia), or in coordinated wage rounds (on occasion in the Netherlands), or where industry-by-industry settlements are negotiated by individual unions within a strongly coordinated union movement (as in West Germany and Austria).

Faced with weaker demand and wage resistance, the large enterprise cuts back on investment and resorts to external financing, if feasible. Its financial position and technical competitiveness weaken. If some of its competitors are still maintaining high profit margins, high investment and rapid innovation, the enterprise may after a time, and perhaps suddenly, find itself unable to meet its financial obligations or unwilling to stay in business in the face of new competition from a cheaper or improved product. In general, marked changes in the competitive strength of large enterprises seem more likely to occur between different economies than in the same economy.[9] In the United States, the threat could come from non-unionized enterprises. However, that context seems less likely to pose a sudden threat, and more likely to exert a continuing influence on wage bargaining in the unionized sectors.

It is clear from this analysis that large enterprises are liable to become increasingly vulnerable to foreign competition after a period of restrictive monetary policy applied in the face of continuing wage resistance. It is also evident that the likelihood of large enterprises suddenly confronting an untenable position will be greatly increased in an international setting characterized by unforeseen changes in interest rates and real exchange rates induced by marked shifts in the mix of fiscal and monetary policies within, or between, major economies, or by autonomous shocks and events, etc.

This account suggests that governments should not be indifferent to the consequences of restrictive monetary policy and exchange rate appreciation in provoking the loss of major industries. Once lost, there is no certainty that sufficient incentives to promote establishment of other advanced enterprises will reappear when greater price stability is achieved. The developed country may then be at a disadvantage against the emergent low-income developing country that has recently been integrated in the international trading system through its access to private capital flows.

## OPEN ECONOMIES WITH SECTORS OF GREATER OR LESSER EASE OF ENTRY

The concept of a two-sector economy of this kind is helpful for understanding how a national economy will respond to government policies, and why the response may differ between large and small countries. It is especially important for understanding the scope for, and difficulty of achieving, an economically useful incomes policy.

In industrialized countries, small labor-intensive enterprises typically sell in localized markets and satisfy domestic demand; exports of goods and services are predominantly supplied by large enterprises. Large enterprises in small economies either specialize in exporting or sell a considerable part of their output abroad. In very large economies (e.g. the United States) large enterprises may not sell abroad, and exports will generally account for a relatively small proportion of their output.

As has been seen, organized labor in the large-enterprise sector possesses considerable power to insulate wages from the effect of weakening demands relative to labor supply in the economy. Thus, because small enterprises in the easy entry sector sell in localized markets, weak demand for labor, relative to supply, tends to cause the level of wages and real incomes in the small-enterprise sector to be such as to ensure that available manpower is absorbed in labor-intensive production to meet home demand, or that participation in the labor force is discouraged. So, in the absence of pervasive unionization outside the large-enterprise sector, a country that has experienced a lengthy period of weak labor demand relative to supply is likely to be one in which home demand, especially household spending, is satisfied by highly labor-intensive outputs sold under competitive conditions. The traditional pattern of consumption and the distribution system will be biased towards labor-intensive services and goods. In such an economy, large-scale enterprises, in which organized labor is able to secure and maintain a level of incomes more commensurate with that in comparable enterprises abroad, will be obliged to depend largely on exports to foreign markets, in which competition from the labor-intensive 'competitive' sector is weaker. Japan and Italy correspond to this prototype. The level of labor productivity in the small-enterprise sector relative to that of large enterprises selling in the world market is likely to vary widely between countries.

The inflation/unemployment response of an economy to a deflationary policy shift will be influenced by such factors as the relative size of the two sectors, the reduction in costs that can be brought about in the competitive sector, and the relative decline in incomes there that is politically tolerable. A more unequal distribution of income is an alternative to higher recorded unemployment.

In a Japanese-like case, the effect of restrictive demand management in moderating the rise in consumer prices via its effects on the small-enterprise sector can be important in lessening wage pressures in the large-economy sector.

## SPECIFIC CHARACTERISTICS OF NATIONAL LABOR MARKETS

Wage bargaining conditions differ between sectors of easy and difficult entry; but they also differ greatly between industrial countries, particularly with respect to the degree of labor organization and power of the unions to influence wages outside the large-enterprise sector. Such differences stem from many historical causes, although the pervasiveness of unionization is now related to the size of the country. Labor organization is weak outside the large-enterprise sector in the three geographically largest countries – the United States, Canada and Japan – and also in Italy. These four economies and, to a lesser extent, West Germany display greater divergence between income movements in the unionized large-enterprise sector and in the small-enterprise sector than occurs in geographically small, densely populated countries (such as the Netherlands, Belgium, Denmark and the United Kingdom), where resistance to widening disparities in earned income tends to be strong because they are highly evident. A concentration of small enterprises in the same locality facilitates the organization of national craft unions or general unions of unskilled workers cutting across industry lines. Such unions may be politically powerful even where their bargaining prerogatives are not great, although the small-enterprise context weakens their bargaining power. Hence, if the unions are unable to maintain wages in the weaker sectors, under rising unemployment, governments may intervene to support wages. For whatever reason, small industrialized countries are characterized by pervasive unionization and strong pressures for wages to move in line across the economy.

There is, however, an important difference between small economies with strongly coordinated union movements dominated by strongly coordinated employers and unions in the large-enterprise sector (e.g. Sweden, Norway, Austria) and those with pervasive unionization but uncoordinated employers' organizations and unions (e.g. the Netherlands, Belgium, Denmark and the United Kingdom). It would appear that a strongly coordinated union movement generally occurs in response to the need to face strongly coordinated employers, especially employers concerned to keep down wages in order to compete in world markets and not able to count on the influence of rising wages in creating lax pricing conditions in the home market (Romanis, 1967). Uncoordinated unions may be characteristic when unions develop in small enterprises serving a protected home market (Netherlands, Denmark, Australia) or at a time of commanding technical leadership in world markets (United Kingdom, Belgium).

Pervasive unionization with divided or uncoordinated bargaining by employers represents a difficult environment for the implementation of government economic policies. It provides the classic inducement for a statutory or government-inspired incomes policy.

## IV SOME IMPLICATIONS OF THESE CHARACTERISTIC FEATURES OF THE INDUSTRIAL ECONOMIES

This account suggests that deflationary policy is likely to be more effective in large economies than in small economies in bringing down the rate of wage increase with a limited rise in unemployment by virtue of the greater flexibility of relative incomes under less pervasive unionization and the greater effect of flexible prices in the small-enterprise sector in moderating upward pressures on wages and costs in the large-enterprise sector. When the major economies are seeking to bring down the rate of inflation, incomes policies will be needed in the small countries but hardly required in the large economies.

In a stable external environment, the small economy may have an advantage in achieving real growth without inflation, since it has a greater possibility of export-led growth if it can control wage movements, and the greater organization of the labor market may facilitate an effective incomes policy. However, under unstable external conditions, resulting from sharply changing or divergent policies in the major economies, no economically useful incomes policy may be feasible in a context of erratic and persisting changes in real exchange rates.

In economies with the characteristics that have been described here, there seems little reason to suppose that such changes in real exchange rates can be avoided under floating rates – still less so under a system of floating and pegged rates. That is to say, there are liable to be sudden unexpected changes in the comparative level of a country's domestic costs of producing open-sector output compared with world market prices for its exportables and import-competing goods. Such changes will mainly reflect changes in relative labor costs per unit of output in the open sector, converted to a common currency. Since wages are set in nominal terms in national currencies, or are subject to indexation adjustments made with considerable lags, relative levels of unit labor costs are changed when there is a change in nominal exchange rates (such as results from a sharp deceleration of money growth, or a change in the mix of fiscal and monetary policy, in a major economy). Unless the change in nominal rates is speedily reversed by speculators or monetary authorities' actions, the change in real rates has consequences that are not all automatic or predictable. There are really no grounds for confidently expecting that the pre-existing levels of exchange rates (or any other particular set of levels) will be restored in the near to medium term.

Very briefly, this is because of the differing responsiveness of wages to demand conditions and consumer price changes in different economies, and the scope for different policy responses of national authorities. To give an example, suppose that the USA adopts a restrictive monetary policy, and the dollar appreciates strongly; the yen and Deutsche Mark depreciate and would now seem undervalued compared to the previous period. The yen depreciation seems likely to be reflected in the maintenance of improved competitiveness. This would cause the yen to strengthen, were it not for the fact that the authorities, keen to maintain the advantage (especially in the new context of the lower prospective growth of the US market), counterbalance this tendency by reducing the budget deficit and easing monetary conditions. (Recall here that Japan still controls capital movements.) The West German authorities, on the other hand, are concerned to avoid an acceleration of inflation as a result of the depreciation, and tighten monetary policy to strengthen the exchange rate. This tends to crowd out private investment and create weaker domestic demand conditions coinciding with weak export markets. It is not excluded that the responsiveness of West German wage bargaining to these conditions is sufficient to ensure that the real exchange rate declines vis-à-vis the United States, even if the nominal dollar rate is restored to its initial level. It is also likely, in that case, that West Germany's real exchange rate will decline vis-à-vis the small countries pegging on the Deutsche Mark. This may be because the smaller countries are politically less inclined than West Germany to tighten their policies. Even if they do take comparable steps, however, the weakening of home and export markets is likely to have less effect on wage levels because of the greater pervasiveness of unionization and prevalence of indexation. (For example, if a depreciation versus the dollar persists for even a month or two, it may have the effect of inducing a rise in nominal wages under indexation, whereas there is no similar effect in West Germany.)

For a small economy in a closely integrated trading area, pegging (more or less firmly) on the major area currency may be the only feasible exchange rate policy. However, it would seem that small economies have a two-fold problem in a world of erratically changing exchange rates between major currencies – because of their greater institutional wage rigidity and because of their limited scope for an independent policy response to an exchange rate shock.

Incomes policy can be helpful if the objective is to moderate the rate of wage and price increase and satisfy considerations of equity, expressed in general support for the notion that all wages and salaries should go up broadly in line. However, this approach requires that exchange rates be generally stable, and world inflation fairly steady and predictable, so that the authorities and the wage bargaining organizations can gauge the influence of external forces and the conditions facing the open sector. Under those circumstances it is difficult, but not impossible, to devise and implement a broadly uniform wage guideline along with appropriate fiscal and monetary policies. Such an incomes policy is unlikely to survive, however, in a context of real exchange rate shocks. It would tend to cause price increases to accelerate, real wages to decline and export profits to rise in the large-enterprise sector, or, alternatively, result in increasing pressures on weaker enterprises and rising unemployment in the small-enterprise sector, and unforeseen gains in real wages, which it may be difficult to reverse.

## V RECENT INCOMES POLICY EXPERIENCE OF FOUR COUNTRIES

The two-sector approach outlined here is helpful in understanding the results achieved with recent incomes policies.

Despite the similarity of the wage bargaining framework, during the 1960s the context for incomes policy in the Netherlands was in many respects the antithesis of that in the United Kingdom. The Netherlands had a large small-enterprise sector and limited employment in a large-enterprise sector characterized by giant capital-intensive firms dependent on exports; the United Kingdom had a large proportion of employment in a large-enterprise sector marked by few giant firms and lesser (and declining) dependence on exports. The Dutch authorities were intensely concerned to maintain price stability, the British to maintain a very low unemployment rate in a closely balanced political situation where almost any rise was seen as a threat to the government.

In the United Kingdom, the avowed purpose of incomes policy during the 1960s was to secure a downward adjustment of relative labor costs, while avoiding an adjustment of the exchange rate. In practice, however, the effect was to make possible the maintenance of extremely low unemployment by fiscal measures, while using incomes policy to help the large-enterprise sector meet the immediate foreign competition and, by constraining the rise in nominal demand, to contain the effect of expansionary fiscal policy on the balance of payments. The large-enterprise sector was shielded from the effects of declining technical competitiveness as long as the home market was expanding and there were growing opportunities of selling to the public sector, where control over pricing was lax. This context was not one to encourage aggressive export efforts and the investment needed to maintain competitiveness vis-à-vis increasing up-to-date capacity abroad.

One can best understand the paradoxes of Dutch economic policy up to 1973 as reflecting the authorities' anxiety to reconcile the pursuit of price stability with protection of employment opportunities in the weak small-enterprise sector – a consideration that underlay the reluctance to appreciate. The Dutch authorities' refusal to accept the upward movement of relative costs at the going exchange rate or to revalue caused the economy to face an explosive wage bargaining situation, with pervasive indexation, an extraordinarily profitable export sector and a weak small-enterprise sector that was vulnerable to import competition.

In both countries, in the early 1970s governments fearful of losing control over wage movements under uncoordinated wage bargaining acted to hold down wages in the face of irresistible forces making for large wage increases. By doing so, each created an explosive wage bargaining and political climate that was only partially defused by a 'social contract' between the government and the unions, and which ultimately caused wage costs to go up much more rapidly than in most other countries after 1973.

In the United Kingdom, incomes policy was applied in an attempt to contain the consequences of an excessive monetary expansion, stemming from the Heath government's efforts to promote a rapid recovery from the 1971 recession at the same time as it relaxed long-standing credit controls. In November 1972, following depreciation of the pound, the government imposed a 90-day freeze of wages, prices and profits, succeeded by six months of strict controls. In the Autumn of 1973, agreement was reached with the Trades Union Congress for continuation of controls for one year, with provision for 'threshold' indexation arrangements (see Braun, 1976). The government was anxious to reach an agreement with the unions but, with the prospect of further depreciation, the provision for indexation, particularly in a form likely to set off wage/wage competition, was a dangerous move. After the defeat of the government in an election called over the miners' insistence on a large wage increase, Labour came to power, pledged not to rescind 'threshold' agreements or to reintroduce stricter controls. In July 1974 a system of voluntary wage restraint under the 'social contract' with the TUC was instituted in return for the government undertaking to improve welfare provisions and strengthen union prerogatives. During the twelve months to August 1975, wage increases not exceeding the rise in consumer prices were to be permitted, but many settlements were in fact much higher. For the next two years limits were agreed with the TUC. Having risen by 27.6 per cent over the preceding twelve months, average weekly earnings went up by 14 and then 9 per cent.

The chain of developments affecting wage movements between November 1973 and August 1975, combined with the maintenance of the pound by heavy public sector borrowing abroad, caused British unit labor costs to go up by 10 per cent compared with its competitors. Reduced competitiveness compounded the impact of world recession on the predominantly large-enterprise, industrial sector, where employment fell by 6.8 per cent between 1973 and 1976, while other employment rose by 3.4 per cent.

Dutch experience illustrates the difficulty of economic policy making in a small, highly open economy in a rapidly changing external environment. However, many of the problems encountered arose from adherence to theoretical principles more appropriate to a closed economy, and from efforts to maintain 'internal monetary equilibrium' in the face of external pressures on the level of domestic costs and prices. With the integration of the EEC market and the achievement of full employment in West Germany, the low level of Dutch wages at going exchange rates provided favorable openings for large-scale, export-oriented enterprises. The inherent wage bargaining power of large-enterprise unions resulted in considerable wage increases there; with the long-standing acceptance of the principle of uniform wage rounds, this induced similar claims in the small-enterprise sector, thus raising costs and prices and weakening competitiveness versus imports. Fiscal and monetary policies framed with the aim of maintaining price stability in the economy were bound to squeeze profits and limit investment in the small-enterprise sector catering to home demand, whereas investment by large export-oriented concerns was encouraged both by high profits and their ready access to foreign financing.

Under rather similar, but less extreme conditions, the Swedish and Norwegian authorities, who could count upon the constraint imposed by highly organized employers and coordinated bargaining, accepted the principle that wages should go up in line with the 'room' for wage increases in the large-enterprise open sector, although this implied that prices would rise and employment contract in open-sector enterprises of lower productivity growth (Braun, 1975, footnote 42). Less insistence than in the Netherlands on domestic price stability as a goal made it easier for small enterprises to respond to the need to raise productivity by investment; there was also extensive provision for retraining and relocating workers who lost their jobs. However, one may doubt whether this solution would have been adopted had the small-enterprise employers and unions been predominant in the wage bargaining system, and as politically powerful as they were in the Netherlands.

The strongly adverse development of Dutch relative costs between 1972 and 1976 was brought about by the combination of the pegging of the exchange rate to the Deutsche Mark and the provisions of officially sponsored, or imposed, wage settlements (which provided for real contractual increases and full indexation) together with cost-raising fiscal measures applied in panic in 1973.[10] Full indexation alone, when the West German authorities were pursuing restrictive policies in circumstances of greater real wages flexibility, implied a worsening of competitiveness vis-à-vis West Germany and other countries that were able to secure a lowering of real wages appropriate to the worsening of the terms of trade. 'Real' contractual increases (that is, nominal wage increases over and above full indexation) were based on calculations made in 1971, which were no longer valid as a guide to the scope for nominal wage increases when the external value of the currency was in fact changing. Rising gas income now contributed to support the rise in the external value of the currency and served to curb the rate of domestic price increase; it therefore did not provide the scope assumed in 1971 for wage increases in terms of guilders.

The consequences of the now relatively high cost of labor in the Netherlands were concealed, and the wage bargaining position of the unions was improved, by high investment and the strengthening of domestic demand associated with the development of gas resources. By the late 1970s however, the results were apparent in low profits and rising unemployment in labor-intensive enterprises (which were particularly hard hit by 'solidaristic' wage settlements giving larger wage increases to the lower paid). Rising unemployment led directly to higher budget deficits and to pressure for improved benefits, early retirement pensions and job protection. Increasing budget deficits and high public sector financing requirements then caused the apparent crowding out of private borrowers. In a more fundamental sense, however, this followed from the decision to enforce price restraint via the pegged exchange rate, when no corresponding restraint on the movement of small-enterprise costs was attainable, given the provisions of the officially sponsored wage settlements. The authorities had in effect decided to secure greater price stability at the cost of lowering profitability and raising unemployment, making higher unemployment feasible by high social provisions of the type mentioned.

The medium-term economic strategy adopted in 1978 aimed to relieve the pressure on profit margins and improve competitiveness by containing wage increases (permitting little or no increase in real wages), by stabilizing government revenues, including social security charges, as a share of the national income and by limiting the public sector deficit. It was expected that these policies would slow the growth of private consumption but enhance the growth of exports and productive investment over the next two or three years, promoting a faster rise in output, higher employment in the private sector and reduced unemployment.

In the event, despite favorable external demand conditions and higher exports, the slowing of private consumption and marked reduction of public investment in 1979 were associated with stagnating private investment and rising unemployment during the year, while import penetration of the home market intensified. After the 1979 oil-price increase, the government again intervened in wage settlements in order to prevent indexation provisions causing more rapid nominal wage increases, leading to a further erosion of profit margins. At the same time, the deflationary policies adopted by major countries (and in particular West Germany) so as to prevent the oil-price increase from being reflected in a renewed acceleration of inflation faced the Netherlands with an external environment of deepening recession and weak export market growth.

The statutory wages policy limiting indexation caused real wages per head to decline by 1 per cent in 1980 and 3 per cent in 1981. The consequent weakening of household demand, combined with little growth in export markets or exports, led to weakening output, employment and demand in the non-investment sectors of the economy, private consumption declining by 0.4 per cent in 1980 and by 2.6 per cent in 1981. Far from creating 'room' for a shift to profits, the reduction in real wages resulted in lower home demand, lower sales and reduced capacity utilization because there was very limited possibility for small enterprises to counteract declining sales to households by selling more abroad, or, by supplying demands met by imported products. (Despite improved competitiveness, import penetration continued and export market shares increased only very slightly.) This context was not one to encourage – or make possible – the financing of higher private investment.

In Norway after 1973, the government aimed to maintain full employment, taking advantage of the prospective increases in real national income and tax revenues from the oil sector to promote a more egalitarian distribution of income and to moderate wage increases by tax reductions, subsidies and other budgetary concessions granted in the process of annual 'combined' income settlements.[11] By this means, it was hoped to lessen domestic cost pressures and protect the competitive position of export industries under the pegged exchange rate. A fundamental object of the policies was to protect the traditional structure of the economy from disruption as a consequence of oil production. The complex character of the tripartite settlements, and the fact that measures aimed at maintaining employment in individual enterprises did not form part of the coordinated income settlements and did not enter into the Contract Committee's simulations, tended to obscure the inherent conflict between greatly raising real per capita incomes and consumption demand while at the same time seeking to maintain the pattern of employment associated with a previously greater dependence on foreign demand.

Norwegian experience illustrates certain inherent difficulties of such a system of coordinated income determination. Weaknesses such as conflicting policy objectives and tendencies to heavy wage drift cannot be treated as accidental failures, because essentially they represented the ways in which combined settlements were secured or preserved. A basic constraint was that the constituent unions of the union federation, especially the powerful unions of the large-enterprise sector, had to be satisfied if centralized bargaining was to continue. This necessitated measures to support employment in large enterprises selling in the world market. It also meant that wage drift, which tended to restore wage differentials between wage earners in the large-enterprise and other sectors and to compensate for increases in sheltered sector prices, represented a vital safety valve to avoid a break-up of the system. In the final analysis, the government participated as one of the parties in tripartite bargaining, and thereby sacrificed a considerable element of its authority for the formulation of economic policy.

In Austria there has been almost continuous close cooperation between the government and the highly structured organizations of management and labor since World War II. The 'social partnership' has enabled a trade-off to be achieved of industrial peace and some measure of control over wage bargaining in return for budgetary social expenditures, protection of employment opportunities in the nationalized sector by subsidization, and measures supporting employment in the private sector (notably investment subsidies to enterprises in areas of heavy unemployment). Its overall effect cannot be judged without an assessment of its impacts on the budgetary position and the allocation of investment. It is clear, however, that it provides the authorities with an invaluable channel for informing various groups about the changes in the economic situation and the government's intentions, and for obtaining the reactions of the economic 'constituencies' (in the process forcing them to reveal, and to some extent adjust, their positions). The system was useful in providing agreed procedures, which encourage the resolution of intra-union and employer–union issues out of the public eye, and which tend to discourage the adoption of extremist positions for their publicity value. Thus the 'social partnership' should probably be seen more as a means of securing and preserving consensus, and thereby ensuring the smooth operation of economic policies, rather than as an instrument of anti-inflationary policy *per se*.

## VI CONCLUDING REMARKS

The analysis sketched in this chapter has far-reaching implications. It is to be hoped that it may encourage others to study the issues raised. As a start, however, it suggests that before accepting any conclusions drawn from economic analyses as regards the prospective benefits and costs of policies in the medium term, one should begin by examining whether the underlying assumptions concerning the workings of the economy are reasonably realistic for the case in question.

The experience of the 1970s suggests that incomes policy has a necessary role (a) in extreme situations in order to avoid political disruption and make any economic policy feasible, and (b) to lessen persisting inflationary momentum and ease stagflation when the authorities impose a firm deceleration of monetary expansion.

The interdependence of policies is a running theme of this volume. Incomes policy, as illustrated here, is an adjunct to monetary and fiscal policies. This situation suggests that, for an understanding of countries' experience in policy making, one must adopt a 'systems analysis' approach to explain the joint effects of monetary, fiscal and incomes policies pursued *over time*, rather than attempt to describe their individual effects.

## NOTES

1 Australia is not included here because its export composition and protected home market sets it apart from other industrial countries and outside the framework of this analysis.

2 The exchange rates for the Deutsche Mark and the yen were expressly set with the aim of promoting exports and obviating the need for foreign aid.

3 For an excellent account see Reder (1982).

4 The enterprise earning high mark-ups (including sums to cover capital depreciation) can devote the proceeds to developing new products or investing in new technology, and is favored in raising capital in the market. Heavy expenditure on advertising can constitute a barrier to new entrants.

5 Reder (1982) points out that the Chicago view that monopoly is ephemeral, being eliminated by free entry, goes with the assumption that while 'prices may be set monopolistically in some subset of product markets, this does not appreciably affect equilibrium prices in the factor markets which are approximately competitive. Put differently . . . monopoly is not important enough to invalidate the contention that prices of factors are a good approximation to the opportunity cost of using them' (p. 15).

6 Contributing to this power are the high cost of idle capacity, the need for a cooperative work force to ensure quality control and avoid damage to equipment, the difficulty of replacing a numerous and experienced work force in the short term, and the fact that exceptional profits, to be made by leadership in innovation, incline management to concede wage increases in order to secure changes in the organization of production. (See Elbaum, 1983.)

7 It is misleading to suggest, as Gordon (1981) does, that 'heterogeneity of labor' and 'investments in training' (i.e. explanations consistent with the general equilibrium analysis) are the principal factors that confer 'a degree of monopoly power on *each* employed worker' and explain why 'unemployed workers cannot substitute for employed workers at a lower wage rate without costs'.

8 If there is a marked difference in the profitability and strength of enterprises, under industry-wide bargaining the pricing policy of stronger enterprises may force weaker enterprises out of business, tending to strengthen the market power of the survivors. Under deflationary conditions, wide differences in profitability will promote enterprise bargaining, as has recently been occurring in the United Kingdom and West Germany – a trend towards the wage bargaining pattern in the United States and Japan that weakens the wage bargaining position of the union movement in general.

9 For instance, because union members and managers are better informed about developments within the economy than abroad, and because enterprises within the same economy are subject to the influence of similar financial and demand conditions and exchange rate effects (Romanis, 1967).

10 The incomes policy system having effectively collapsed by 1965, the government unsuccessfully attempted to acquire greater control by new legislation enabling it to intervene in wage negotiations; it intervened under emergency powers to limit wage increases for six months in 1971. Similar interventions for six months to a year took place in 1974, 1976 and 1980. Price controls were in force from 1972 to 1982 (Flanagan, Soskice and Ulman, 1983). A 'social contract' between the government and the unions provided for agreed limits to wage increases in 1973 in return for tax concessions and improvements in social security, vacations, etc. The contract was hailed as the re-establishment of a consensus-based incomes policy. However, in the changed circumstances of 1973, the authorities' first concern was to adopt a restrictive policy stance in line with that of West Germany. A sharp increase in social security charges and direct taxes absorbed the whole increase in average gross wages, creating a renewal of tensions that led the government to impose an egalitarian incomes policy in 1974.

11 'Combined' income settlements involved the government in tripartite negotiations with the central union and employers' federations (LO and NAF), concerted with negotiations between the government and farmers' and fishermans' organizations concerning the development of their incomes under government price supports.

## BIBLIOGRAPHY


Arvig, Lars (1976), *Incomes Policy in Norway*, Oslo, Norwegian Employers' Confederation.

Braun, Anne Romanis (1974), 'Compulsory arbitration as a form of incomes policy: the Australian case', *IMF Staff Papers*, 21(1), March, 170–216.

Braun, Anne Romanis (1975), 'The role of income policy in industrial countries since World War II', *IMF Staff Papers*, 22(1), March, 1–36.

Braun, Anne Romanis (1976), 'Indexation of wages and salaries in developed countries', *IMF Staff Papers*, 23(1), March, 226–271.

Braun, Anne Romanis (1978), *Incomes Policies in Industrial Countries since 1973*, IMF Departmental Memorandum, 1978/8, January.

Braun, Anne Romanis (1979), *Some Reflections on Incomes Policy and the International Payments System*, Economic Council of Canada, Discussion Paper No. 132, September.

Braun, Anne Romanis (1981), *Inflation and Unemployment in Canada and Other Industrial Countries*, Center for the Study of Inflation and Productivity, Economic Council of Canada, Discussion Paper No. 184, January.

Braun, Anne Romanis (forthcoming), *Inflation and Incomes Policy in Industrial Countries*, Washington, DC, International Monetary Fund.

Brown, William (1983), 'Central coordination', *Oxford Bulletin of Economics and Statistics*, 45(1), February, 51–62.

Carew, Anthony (1976), *Democracy and Government in European Trade Unions*, London, Allen & Unwin.

Dean, A. J. H. (1980), 'Roles of governments and institutions in OECD countries', in Frank Blackaby (ed.), *The Future of Pay Bargaining*, London, Heinemann, 163–190.

Driscoll, David D. (1982), 'Wage and price policy in Austria', in Joint Economic Committee (1982).

Dunlop, J. T. and Galenson, W. (eds) (1978), *Labor in the Twentieth Century*, New York, Academic Press.

Elbaum, B. (1983), 'The internalization of labor markets: causes and consequences', *American Economic Review*, 73(2), May, 260–265.

Fallick, J. L. and Elliott, R. F. (eds) (1981), *Incomes Policies, Inflation and Relative Pay*, London, Allen & Unwin.

Flanagan, R. J., Soskice, D. W. and Ulman, L. (1983), *Unionism, Economic Stabilization and Incomes Policies: European Experience*, Washington, DC, The Brookings Institution.

Gordon, Robert J. (1981), 'Output fluctuations and gradual price adjustment', *Journal of Economic Literature*, 19(2), June, 493–530.

Gunter, Hans and Leminsky, Gerhard (1978), 'The federal reputation of Germany', in Dunlop and Galenson (1978).

Joint Economic Committee, Congress of the United States (1982), *Wage and Price Policies in Australia, Austria, Canada, Japan, the Netherlands and West Germany*, 97th Congress, 2nd Session, 24 June.

Korsnes, O. (1979), 'Duality in the role of unions and unionists in Norway', *British Journal of Industrial Relations*, 17(3), November, 362–375.

McCloskey, Donald N. (1983), 'The Rhetoric of economics', *Journal of Economic Literature*, 21(2), June, 481–517.

Mire, Joseph (1977), 'Income policy in Austria under the social partnership', *Monthly Labor Review*, 100, August.

*Norwegian Commercial Banks Financial Review* (1976), 'Prices and incomes policy in Norway', June.

Peston, Maurice (1981), 'The integration of monetary, fiscal and incomes policy', *Lloyds Bank Review*, 141, July, 1–13.
Reder, Melvin W. (1982), 'Chicago economics: permanence and change', *Journal of Economic Literature*, 20(1), March, 1–38.
Romanis, Anne (1967), 'Cost inflation and incomes policy in industrial countries', *IMF Staff Papers*, 14(1), March, 169–209.
Shirai, Taishiro, and Shimada, Hauro (1978), 'Japan', in Dunlop and Galenson (1978).

# 8 Government Policies towards Inflation and Unemployment in West Germany

*MANFRED WILLMS and INGO KARSTEN*

## I THE INFLATION PROBLEM

The problem of inflation dominated the discussion of economic policy issues in the Federal Republic of Germany during the 1970s, whereas it was not an important issue in the 1960s. On average, the cost of living index (for all households) increased between 1963 and 1973 by 3.1 per cent annually compared to 5.2 per cent between 1973 and 1982. Inflation reached its lowest level of 1.7 per cent during the recession in 1967 and 1968 (see Figure 8.1).

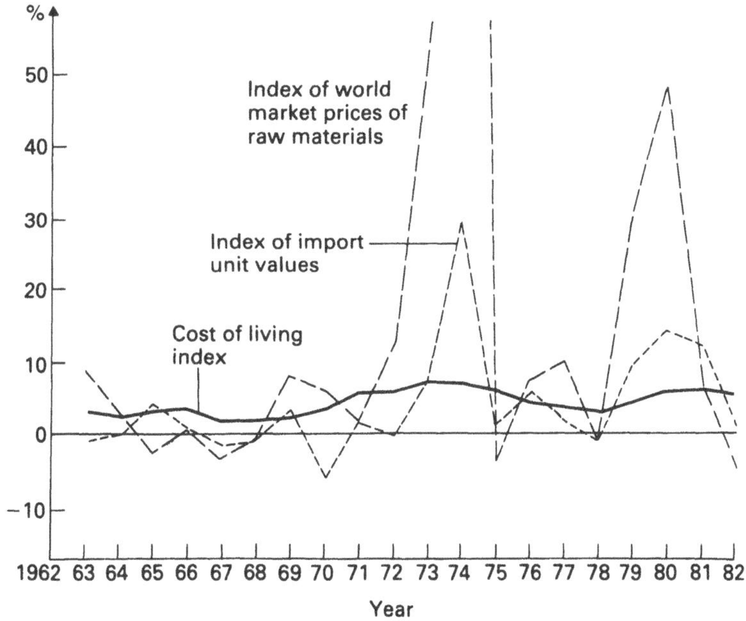


**Figure 8.1** Consumer prices, import prices and world market prices of raw materials, 1963–82 (*percentage* annual changes)

*Source:* Deutsche Bundesbank, *Monthly Reports* (various issues).

Peaks of 7 per cent were attained in 1973 and 1974 when world market prices of food and industrial raw materials on a dollar basis soared by more than 200 per cent in 1974. However, the surge in import prices (measured in terms of changes of the index of unit values of imports) on a Deutsche Mark basis was less than the price hike of raw materials on a dollar basis. The sharp revaluation of the Deutsche Mark following the breakdown of the Bretton Woods system to a large extent offset the adverse impact of the price increases of raw materials on the German price level. The second major increase in raw material prices in 1979 and 1980 had even greater repercussions on the cost of living index than the price shocks of 1973 and 1974.

Owing to high rates of inflation during the 1970s, real rates of interest (measured as the difference between the yield on total bonds outstanding in per cent per year and the change of the cost of living index for all households) were on average lower than in the period of low inflation rates of the preceding decade. Figure 8.2 shows that real interest rates reached peak levels of more than 5 per cent a year at the end of the 1960s. The average annual real interest rate amounted to 4.0 per cent from 1962 to 1972. For the period 1973–82 the average real interest rate was 3.4 per cent annually. The high levels of real interest rates in 1981 and 1982 of 4.7 per cent and 3.8 per cent, respectively, fell short of the levels attained in 1967 and 1968 of 5.3 per cent and 5.0 per cent, respectively.

Whereas real interest rates fluctuated more in the 1960s than in the 1970s, the reverse was true for the nominal rates of interest (see Figure 8.2). The standard

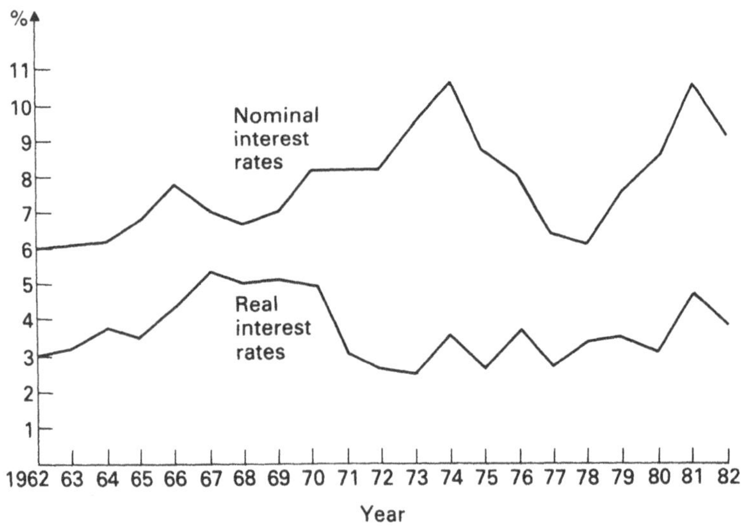


**Figure 8.2** Nominal[a] and real[b] interest rates, 1962–82 (per cent p.a.)

*Notes:* a Yield on total bonds outstanding in per cent p.a.
b Yield on total bonds outstanding in per cent p.a. less annual change in the cost of living index.

*Source:* Council of Economic Experts (1983); Deutsche Bundesbank, *Monthly Reports* (various issues).

deviation of nominal rates was 1.47 percentage points from 1973 to 1982 and 0.82 percentage points between 1962 and 1972. The corresponding standard deviations for real interest rates amounted to 0.62 percentage points and 0.94 percentage points.

Although inflation rates have been declining in the very recent past, it is much too early yet to assume that the inflation problem has been permanently solved, because uncertainty about the future course of monetary policy in the Federal Republic of Germany still remains. The slow decline of real interest rates at the beginning of the 1980s in spite of falling inflation rates seems to indicate that inflationary expectations or crowding-out problems due to high structural public deficits persist.

## II THE UNEMPLOYMENT PROBLEM

In the past few years attention has shifted from the inflation problem to the unemployment problem, because there has been a substantial increase in unemployment, unprecedented in post-war Germany. At the beginning of the 1960s, most refugees from former German territories in the East had found employment opportunities in the rapidly growing economy. Jobs were also provided for foreign workers from Mediterranean countries. From 1960 to 1976 the ratio of working persons (dependent wage and salary earners, self-employed and unemployed persons) to the number of inhabitants declined steadily owing to the increasing population (see Figure 8.3). Since then this ratio has increased slightly because the number of wage and salary earners showed an upward trend resulting from a more active participation of women in the labour market.[1] In 1981 and 1982 the number of wage and salary earners fell by about half a million from its peak level of almost 23 million in 1980 (Deutsche Bundesbank, 1983a, pp. 69ff). The recent reduction of employment opportunities can be observed in all industries, but especially in banking and

**Figure 8.3** Employment and unemployment, 1960–82

*Source:* Council of Economic Experts (1983).

insurance services as well as in the public sector (Council of Economic Experts, 1983, pp. 50–53).

In contrast with the (almost) full employment situation in the 1960s (with the exception of the 1967/8 recession), unemployment rates (defined as unemployed persons as a percentage of the dependent labour force) rose markedly after 1973 and reached a temporary peak in the recessionary period of 1975 (see Figure 8.3). Despite the economic revival of the following years, unemployment rates remained high in the rest of the 1970s. The unemployment ratio rose again in 1981 and 1982. At the beginning of 1983, 10 per cent of the labour force (or 2.5 million persons) were unemployed compared to average rates for the 1960s of 1 per cent and for the 1970s of 2.8 per cent. Unemployment has recently affected not only particular groups such as the elderly or handicapped, foreign workers and young people under 20 years of age (Council of Economic Experts, 1983, pp. 57–60), but also skilled workers.

Several reasons can be suggested for the pronounced rise in unemployment. Demographic factors, such as the more active participation of women in the work process and the higher entry of young people into the labour market in the late 1970s resulting, from high birthrates during the 1960s might have been of some importance.

However, more important are economic and policy-induced factors, such as the high level of real wages in relation to labour productivity and institutional rigidities in the German labour markets. If real wages increase by more than labour productivity, then employers replace expensive labour by capital in the medium term. In this case, demand for workers will decline and unemployment will go up. This tendency will be accentuated if trade unions do not include a deterioration of the terms of trade (defined as the ratio of the index of export unit values to the index of import unit values) in their wage demands and if the real cost of capital is reduced by high rates of inflation.[2] Both effects force employers to raise the capital intensity of the production process to remain competitive in domestic and world markets.

The movements of gross wages and salaries (in 1976 prices) per employee[3] of labour productivity (defined as GDP in 1976 prices per working person) and of the terms of trade are presented in Figure 8.4(A). As can be seen from Figure 8.4(B), real wages adjusted for productivity and terms-of-trade effects rose substantially in the 1970s. This was largely due to the sharp increases in real gross wages and salaries and to the remarkable decline in labour productivity in recent years. However, the most significant increase in adjusted real wages resulted from the deterioration of the terms of trade in 1973/4 and 1979. Because trade unions did not incorporate productivity and terms-of-trade developments in their wage demands, adjusted real wages increased to such an extent that labour markets were adversely affected. Even if terms-of-trade effects are not considered,[4] it is notable that the growth rates of wages and salaries (in real terms) have always exceeded annual changes in labour productivity. However, the gap was significantly larger in the 1970s than in the 1960s. This permanent increment in unit labour costs (defined as the ratio of gross wages and salaries in 1976 prices per employee to GDP in 1976 prices per working person) can be deemed one of the principal factors leading to the sharp rise in unemployment in the 1970s and at the beginning of the 1980s. Regional

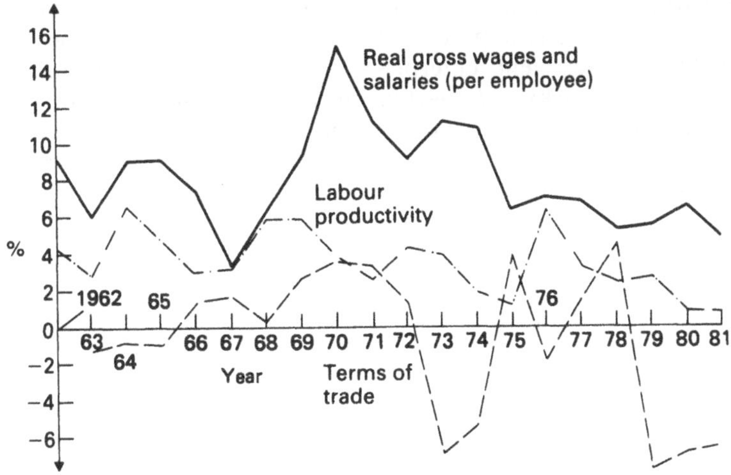


**Figure 8.4(A)** Real wages, labour productivity and terms-of-trade developments, 1963–81 (*percentage* annual changes)

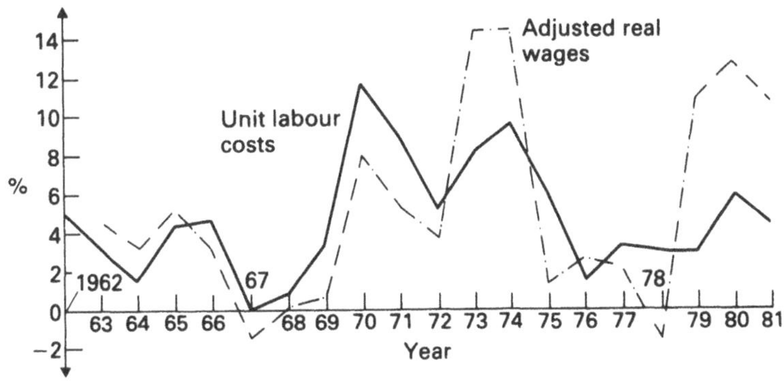


**Figure 8.4(B)** Adjusted real wages[a] and unit labour costs[b], 1963–81 (*percentage* annual changes)

*Notes:* a Annual change in gross real wages and salaries (in 1976 prices) per employee less annual change in labour productivity less annual change in terms of trade.
b Ratio of gross wages and salaries (in 1976 prices) per employee to GDP (in 1976 prices) per working person.

*Source:* Council of Economic Experts (1983); Deutsche Bundesbank, *Monthly Reports* (various issues).

and sectoral unemployment has been exacerbated by the German trade unions' strategy of demanding 'equal wages for equal work' (but not for equal productivity). Since increases in standard wages have not sufficiently taken into account the low profitability of weak industrial sectors (such as ship building and manufacturing of steel products), comprehensive government subsidies have been necessary to keep these sectors alive.

Apart from affecting demand for labour directly, rising unit labour costs have also had an adverse impact on profit margins. As a consequence of the low profitability of investment, enterprises did not have sufficient funds at their disposal to finance risky and novel investments. This slowdown of investment activity has delayed the growth of employment opportunities over time. Besides, the prospects of further rising labour costs might have clouded profitability expectations.

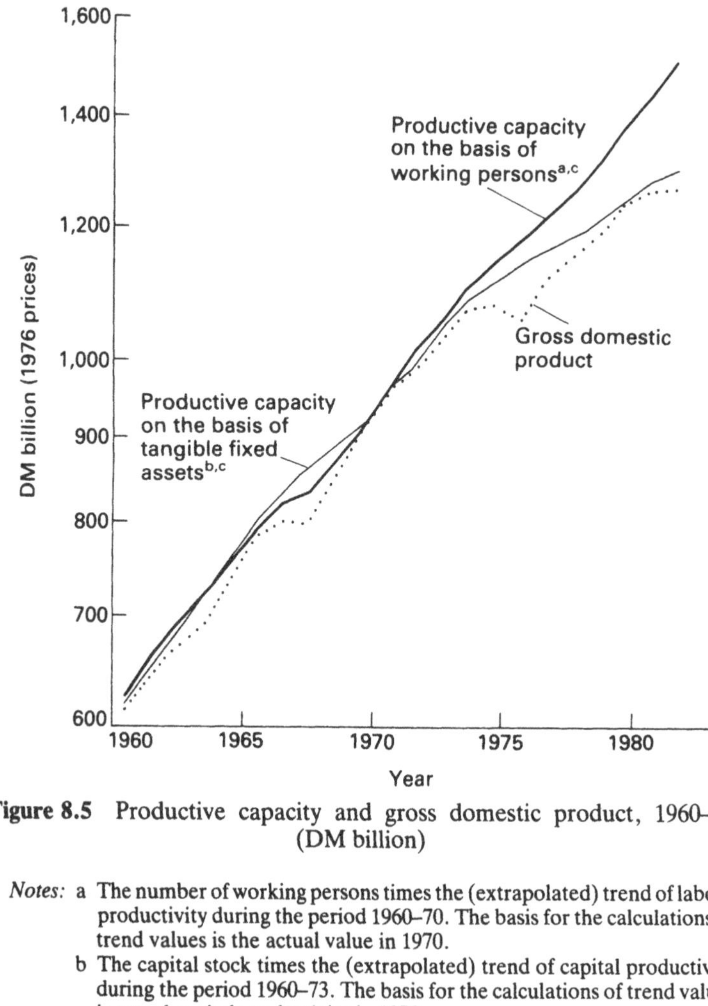


**Figure 8.5** Productive capacity and gross domestic product, 1960–81 (DM billion)

*Notes:* a The number of working persons times the (extrapolated) trend of labour productivity during the period 1960–70. The basis for the calculations of trend values is the actual value in 1970.

b The capital stock times the (extrapolated) trend of capital productivity during the period 1960–73. The basis for the calculations of trend values is actual capital productivity in 1970.

c Actual values were used for the flat-letting business, government private households, private non-profit organizations, non-deductible sales tax, import levies as well as for the adjustment for banking services.

*Source:* Wolter (1983), p. 27. Calculations based on Statistisches Bundesamt, Fachserie 18, Reihe 5.5, Revidierte Ergebnisse 1960 bis 1981 – Wirtschaft und Statistik, 11/1982.

In the Federal Republic of Germany some empirical evidence for the existence of unemployment caused by capital shortage has recently been provided (Wolter, 1983, pp. 25–28). This form of unemployment is calculated as the difference between productive capacity on the basis of working persons and productive capacity on the basis of the capital stock.[5]

Figure 8.5 and Table 8.1 show that since 1973 the job gap due to capital shortage has increased considerably, amounting to nearly 1 million persons in 1981. These calculations of the structural component of unemployment may be considered an underestimate, because, first, they are based on actual employment figures, whereas it may be assumed that, because of unfavourable labour market conditions during the 1970s, job-seekers stopped applying for jobs. Secondly, official capital stock figures overestimate the actual capital stock because supply shocks might have rendered some part of it obsolete. Thirdly, it is assumed that the marginal productivity of labour remains constant with increasing employment. It may be concluded from these calculations that unemployment due to capital shortage will persist unless positive supply shocks (such as a real fall in energy prices) occur or unless private investment activity is profoundly stimulated. A major contribution to the latter could be effected by moderate wage settlements.

Some institutional factors might also have contributed to rising unemployment, although these effects cannot be quantified. In the Federal Republic of Germany, unemployment benefits are probably too high in comparison with income earned. Thus, the unemployed might have been tempted to seek less wholeheartedly for a job. There are also several laws aimed at improving the social conditions of particular groups, e.g. young people (Young Persons Employment Act), women (Maternity Leave Law) or handicapped or elderly persons (Collective Bargaining Agreements on Protection against Dismissal). Despite their laudable objectives, one should not ignore the adverse employ-

**Table 8.1** *The job gap due to capital shortage, 1973–81 (per thousand persons)*

| *Year* | *Unemployed persons* | *Basic unemployment*[a] | *Reserve of job opportunities*[b] | *Job gap* |
|---|---|---|---|---|
| 1973 | 273 | 149 | 51 | 73 |
| 1979 | 876 | 149 | 17 | 710 |
| 1980 | 889 | 149 | 44 | 696 |
| 1981 | 1272 | 149 | 161 | 962 |

*Notes:* a Unemployed persons in the last boom year (1973).
b Vacancies still available in the existing capital stock, calculated as $[(P_K - B):(P_E - B)] \cdot (A-S)$, where $P_K$ = productive potential on the basis of the capital stock, $B$ = real GDP, $P_E$ = productive potential on the basis of working persons, $A$ = unemployed persons, $S$ = basic unemployment.

*Source:* Wolter (1983) p.27. Calculations based on Statistisches Bundesamt Wiesbaden, Fachserie 18, Volkswirtschaftliche Gesamtrechnungen, Reihe 5.5, Revidierte Ergebnisse 1960 bis 1981 – Wirtschaft und Statistik, 11/1982.

ment effects in the medium term. Furthermore, the problem of unemployment is then probably shifted to the less protected.

Finally, inflation might have contributed to the rise in unemployment. High rates of inflation during the 1970s could have led to a misallocation of resources in non-productive investment (such as gold, housing and real estate). Uncertainty about future price movements has adversely affected the willingness to undertake longer-term investments, such as the acquisition of financial claims or investment in plant and equipment. If the hiring of labour is also regarded as a long-term investment, the negative impact of high and variable inflation rates on employment cannot be ignored (International Monetary Fund, 1983, p. 37). Furthermore, attempts to combat inflation by restrictive monetary and fiscal policies could have led to a stabilization crisis with a slowdown of growth and employment. These issues will be dealt with in the following sections.

## III MONETARY POLICY

### MONETARY DEVELOPMENTS

In the past twenty years monetary policy has been quite discretionary. As can be seen from Figure 8.6 (B), annual growth rates of M1 (currency and demand deposits) ranged from nearly 14 per cent to 1 per cent.[6] However, the standard deviation of M1 growth rates during the period 1962–71 (2.5 percentage points) was lower than that for 1972–82 (4.1 percentage points). The growth rates of the central bank money stock (defined as currency in circulation plus minimum reserves on banks' domestic liabilities at constant reserve ratios) also exhibit marked fluctuations (see Figure 8.6(C)), although the standard deviations for the two periods considered were slightly lower (1962–71: 1.6 percentage points; 1972–82: 2.7 percentage points). Particularly strong growth rates of the central bank money stock occurred in 1972 and 1978, whereas relatively low annual rates were attained in 1967, 1980 and 1981.

At first glance, Figure 8.6 suggests that shifts in money supply led to corresponding changes in economic activity. In particular, a link between M1 growth and real GNP growth can be observed. The strong deceleration of M1 growth rates in 1973 and 1979–80 might have contributed (among other factors such as the oil-price hikes) to the pronounced reduction of GNP growth rates in 1975 and 1982. The subsequent acceleration of M1 growth in these recession years led to a recovery in 1976 and may have contributed to the economic revival in 1983. However, it is notable that from the mid-1970s large fluctuations of money supply growth effected only minor changes in real GNP growth rates in contrast to the previous decade.

Although the Bundesbank announced monetary targets from 1975 to stabilize money supply growth in the medium term, the high variance of central bank money growth indicates that the central bank might have had some difficulty in implementing effective control. In the following section, several factors explaining this high variability are examined.

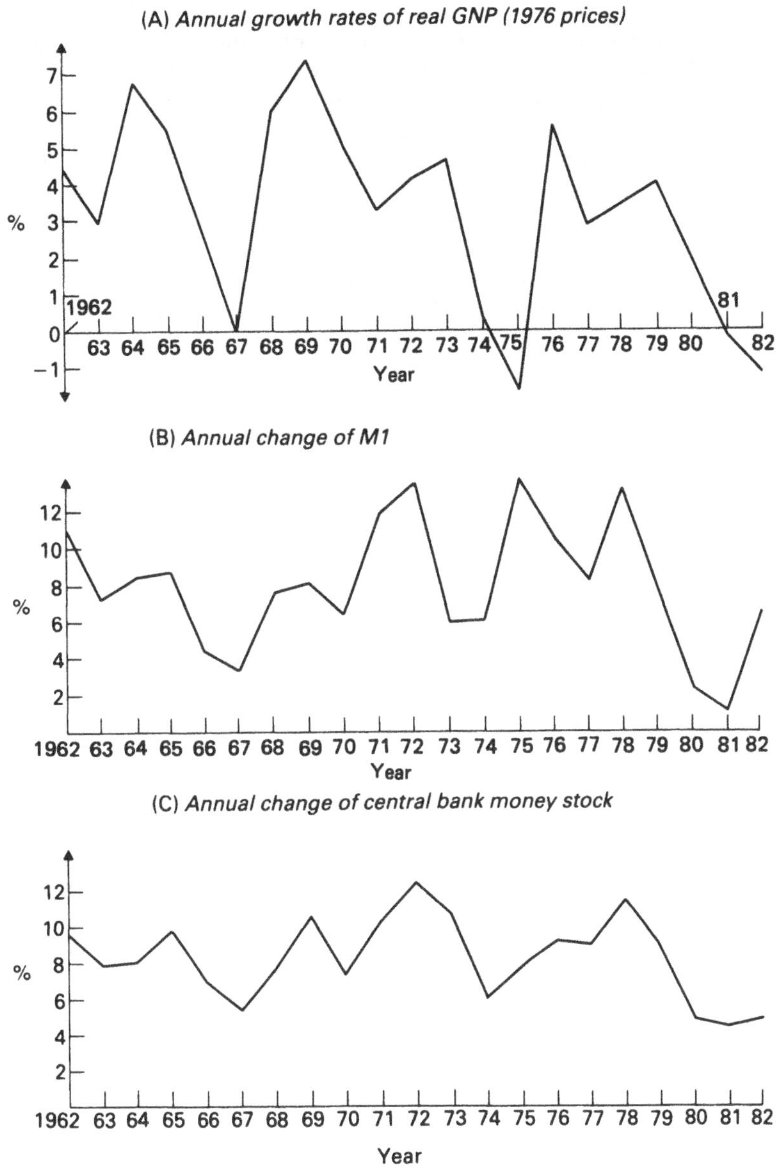


**Figure 8.6** Economic activity and monetary developments, 1962–82 (*percentage* annual changes)

*Sources:* Council of Economic Experts (1983); Deutsche Bundesbank, *Monthly Reports* (various issues).

## MONETARY POLICY INDICATORS AND TARGETS

The marked variations of central bank money and M1 growth raise the question whether and to what extent the German central bank has been capable of effectively controlling the money supply. Central bank money has been the primary control and target variable of monetary policy in Germany since 1973.[7] In December 1974, the Bundesbank announced a target growth rate of central bank money for the year 1975 for the first time. Since then the Bundesbank has annually declared a target rate in advance and since 1979 a target range ('corridor') for the planned annual rate of expansion of central bank money. The target rate or target range is based on a combination of the following four criteria (Deutsche Bundesbank, 1975, p. 11):

- the expected growth rate of production capacity;
- the expected change in capacity utilization;
- the 'unavoidable' increase in the price level; and
- the expected change in the velocity of circulation of money.

The annual target rates and the actual rates of growth of central bank money since 1975 are shown in Table 8.2. With the exception of 1978, actual growth rates have not deviated significantly from target rates. Although monetary targets have been achieved more or less precisely since 1979, the introduction of targets in terms of a corridor does not make the intentions of monetary policy as clear to the public as a single figure. By setting a target range, the

**Table 8.2** *Annual target rates of central bank money growth, actual growth rates of central bank money and growth rates of the money stock M1, 1975–83*

| *Year* | *Target rates of central bank money* % | *Actual rates of central bank money*[b] % | *Growth rates of M1*[b] % |
|---|---|---|---|
| 1975 | 8[a] | 7.8 | 13.7 |
| 1976 | 8[b] | 9.2 | 10.4 |
| 1977 | 8[b] | 9.0 | 8.2 |
| 1978 | 8[b] | 11.4 | 13.3 |
| 1979 | 6–9[a] | 9.1 | 7.5 |
| 1980 | 5–8[a] | 4.8 | 2.3 |
| 1981 | 4–7[a] | 4.4 | 1.1 |
| 1982 | 4–7[a] | 4.9 | 3.1 |
| 1983 | 4–7[a] | — | — |

*Notes:* a Target in the course of the year.
b Annual average growth rates.

*Sources:* Deutsche Bundesbank, *Monthly Reports* (various issues); Deutsche Bundesbank, *Statistical Supplements to the Monthly Reports, Series 4: Seasonally Adjusted Economic Data* (various issues).

Bundesbank makes it possible for monetary policy to react to unexpected disruptions of economic activity, prices and exchange rates during the year without jeopardizing its credibility. The Bundesbank also wants to be able to take account of short-term irregularities in the financial markets. Therefore, the Bundesbank has always outlined the conditions under which it would aim more at the upper or the lower floor of the target range depending on internal or external disturbances (Deutsche Bundesbank, 1982, pp. 86–7).

Despite the fact that monetary target ranges have been achieved, it is doubtful whether they increase the credibility of monetary policy. A target range varying from 50 to 75 per cent and dependent on future economic developments leaves the Bundesbank too much room for discretion. This is not likely to lead to the pursuit of a steady monetary policy that can be easily forecast by market participants.

Some evidence of a discretionary monetary policy is provided from the recent past. Between 1978 and 1982 the Bundesbank reduced the annual growth rate of central bank money from 11.4 per cent to 4.9 per cent in order to combat inflation. Although inflation rates have actually been contained recently, the Bundesbank has largely contributed to a stabilization crisis by decelerating money growth too fast and unexpectedly. Because market participants, in particular trade unions, did not adapt to the severe monetary policy stance, adverse output and employment effects could not be prevented.

At the beginning of 1983 there was again an unexpected and pronounced acceleration of high-powered money growth. The central bank money stock rose at an annual rate of 15.5 per cent in the first quarter and 5.25 per cent in the second quarter. From the fourth quarter of 1982 (which is the base period for the monetary target) to June 1983 the annual growth rate amounted to 9 per cent (Deutsche Bundesbank, 1983b, p. 6). Although the growth rate of central bank money significantly exceeded the upper bound of the target range in the first quarter, the Bundesbank appeared to be capable of achieving the monetary target in the course of the year by reducing central bank money growth abruptly again. However, it may be feared that such marked variability in the Bundesbank's behaviour not only endangers the credibility of monetary policy but may also contribute to decreasing real GNP growth rates, because market participants cannot reliably predict future policy actions.

This means that the Bundesbank should expand central bank money in line with the increase in productive capacity not only in the course of a year, but also within a period of three months or even less.

## CONTROLLING MONEY SUPPLY IN AN OPEN ECONOMY

The ability to control central bank money growth has increased in principle since the introduction of flexible exchange rates. However, the Bundesbank partly followed a monetary strategy conditioned by the movements of the dollar exchange rate. From the breakdown of the Bretton Woods system in 1973 until 1979 the Deutsche Mark appreciated in real terms compared with the dollar. During that period the Bundesbank intervened in the foreign exchange market to prevent a further (real) appreciation of the Deutsche Mark with the aim of protecting employment in export and import substitution industries.

Since 1979 the surge of the dollar induced the Bundesbank to sell dollars in the currencies market to prevent the Deutsche Mark from depreciating. The reason was that a far-reaching devaluation would not have improved the competitiveness of the export sectors, because, in the absence of money and exchange rate illusion, it would have induced nominal wage increases leaving real wages and employment unchanged. Besides, participation of the Federal Republic of Germany in the European Monetary System, which became effective in March 1979, obliges the Bundesbank to intervene in foreign exchange markets to support EMS member currencies. This might lead to inflows or outflows of foreign exchange that affect commercial banks' liquidity in a way not intended by the central bank.

This problem was particularly evident in March 1983, when large-scale interventions in the EMS led to the marked increase in central bank money growth mentioned above. Before the realignment in mid-March, the Deutsche Mark interventions within the EMS to support other currencies amounted to DM 12.6 billion (see Table 8.3). However, of these foreign exchange inflows, about DM 7.8 billion flowed out again between the realignment in mid-March and the end of March. During the same period the interventions in the Deutsche Mark/dollar market were negligible. Therefore, the net effect of foreign exchange inflows of DM 4.8 billion inflated liquidity to some extent only when compared with the absolute change of the central bank money stock of DM 1.3 billion during the first quarter of 1983.

Although there were considerable support operations for EMS currencies after the establishment of the EMS, their repercussions on the net external position and on liquidity were partly offset by interventions in the Deutsche Mark/dollar market and other foreign exchange movements (except for 1980). Despite the officially announced floating of the Deutsche Mark in relation to the dollar, the Bundesbank intervened to a larger extent in the Deutsche Mark/dollar exchange market (DM 39.1 billion between 1979 and 1982) than in the EMS (DM 16.4 billion for the same period) if the absolute amounts of interventions are considered. The same is true for the period 1973–9 when the so-called 'Snake' was in existence, although the total amount of interventions of DM 33.1 billion was only slightly lower than the dollar support operations of DM 36.5 billion. However, if one looks at the whole period from April 1973 to March 1983, EMS interventions led to a total inflow of foreign currencies amounting to DM 57 billion, whereas the Deutsche Mark/dollar interventions reduced the net external position by DM 2 billion because inflows before 1979 were compensated by outflows in subsequent years.

In the medium term, therefore, the system of 'managed' floating toward the dollar affects the net external position and liquidity more than a system of temporarily pegged exchange rates such as the 'Snake' or the EMS, whereas the reverse is true in the long run. The Bundesbank, however, has not lost potential control over central bank money growth because of either exchange rate system. No clear-cut link between the change in the net external position and the change in central bank money can be deduced. This seems to indicate that the Bundesbank is capable of sterilizing inflows or outflows of foreign exchange by domestic liquidity policy measures, at least in the course of a year.

**Table 8.3** *Changes in central bank money and in the net external position of the Bundesbank due to interventions in the foreign exchange markets, April 1973–March 1983 (DM billion)*

| *Period* | *Absolute change in central bank money*[a] | *Change in net external position*[b] | *Interventions* | | *Other foreign exchange movements* |
|---|---|---|---|---|---|
| | | | *DM/dollar Market* | *'Snake'*[c] *or EMS* | |
| 1973 | | | | | |
| April–December | +8.1 | +6.6 | −0.4 | +8.3 | −1.3 |
| 1974 | +5.8 | −1.6 | 0.0 | +0.2 | −1.8 |
| 1975 | +9.5 | −2.2 | −0.6 | −1.8 | +0.3 |
| 1976 | +7.5 | +8.9 | +2.5 | +17.0 | −10.6 |
| 1977 | +10.4 | +10.5 | +10.9 | +1.5 | −2.0 |
| 1978 | +14.1 | +20.1 | +24.1 | +7.9 | −11.8 |
| 1979 | +7.8 | −7.8 | +7.3 | +8.2 | −23.3 |
| 1980 | +6.5 | −25.4 | −18.3 | −10.5 | +3.4 |
| 1981 | +2.7 | −3.2 | −21.5 | +15.0 | +3.3 |
| 1982 | +7.5 | +3.2 | −6.6 | +3.7 | +6.2 |
| 1983 | | | | | |
| Jan.–mid-March | +2.7 | +17.1 | +0.4 | +12.6 | +4.1 |
| Mid-March–end-March | −1.4 | −7.2 | 0.0 | −7.8 | +0.7 |
| April 1973–March 1983[d] | +81.2 | +26.0 | −2.0 | +57.0 | −27.0 |

*Notes:* a Currency in circulation (as from March 1978 excluding the banks' cash balances of domestic notes and coins, which are deductible from required minimum reserves) and required reserves on the banks' domestic liabilities at current reserve ratios.

b The external position of the Deutsche Bundesbank comprises monetary reserves (gold, foreign currency balances, the reserve position in the IMF and SDPs and net claims on the European Monetary Cooperation Fund) minus external liabilities.

c From 1973 to March 1979.

d Discrepancies in the totals are due to rounding.

*Sources:* Deutsche Bundesbank (1983c), p.72; Deutsche Bundesbank, *Monthly Reports* (various issues).

## THE VELOCITY OF MONEY

In formulating the annual monetary target the Bundesbank explicitly takes account of the expected development of the velocity of circulation of money.

Movements in the velocities of circulation of various monetary aggregates are presented in Figure 8.7. Quarterly changes in the velocity of M1 (defined as the ratio of nominal GNP to M1) show a fairly clear cyclical pattern. The velocity of M1 decreased slightly from 1971 to 1982 at an average annual rate of –0.9 per cent. Over the same period, the average annual change in the velocity of central bank money amounted only to –0.7 per cent. In contrast, the velocity of the broadest money aggregate, M3, declined on average by almost 2 per cent a year. This downward trend in the velocity of M3 was interrupted only from the second half of 1979 to the second half of 1980. Furthermore, the quarterly changes in the velocity of M3 show a less clear-cut cyclical pattern than the two other velocity concepts considered.

Various factors could explain the different developments of the velocity of circulation of M1 and central bank money on the one hand and the velocity of M3 on the other hand. From Figures 8.7(A) and 8.7(B) it can be seen that the velocities of M1 and central bank money to some extent follow real economic activity. This relationship has become less clear-cut since 1977, and particularly since 1981, when both velocities rose temporarily but real GNP growth rates remained at low levels. No close link can be observed between quarterly changes in the velocity of M3 and quarterly changes of real GNP.

Recent ambiguous developments in the velocities of M1 and central bank money are probably due to the sharp increase in interest rates. As a result, market participants shifted their demand for money from non-interest-bearing cash holdings and demand deposits to interest-bearing time and savings deposits. Since the latter are included in M3, the velocity of this monetary aggregate declined almost in relation to the slowdown of real GNP growth rates since 1980. In contrast, soaring interest rates in 1981 led to marked increases in the velocities of M1 and central bank money, because higher opportunity costs induced a more efficient use of currency and of demand deposits.[8]

The gradual fall in interest rates since 1982 and the subsequent reduction in the velocities of M1 and central bank money might indicate the success of monetary policy in breaking inflationary expectations. Furthermore, the pronounced recession and uncertainty about future economic developments in the Federal Republic of Germany induce the public to hold more money as a precautionary measure.

Financial innovations have been rather limited in the Federal Republic of Germany. They have mainly occurred in the form of financial obligations issued by commercial banks. The so-called 'bank bonds' (*Bankschuldverschreibungen*) usually have a maturity of less than four years. These short-term papers are very close substitutes for savings deposits but, in contrast to the latter, they bear higher interest. The banks' financial obligations are not subject to reserve requirements and are not included in M3, the broadest monetary aggregate. In Figure 8.8(A) quarterly changes over the previous year of bank bonds issued since 1970 are presented. During 1970 and 1974 and between 1979 and 1982 increases of more than 20 per cent could be observed.

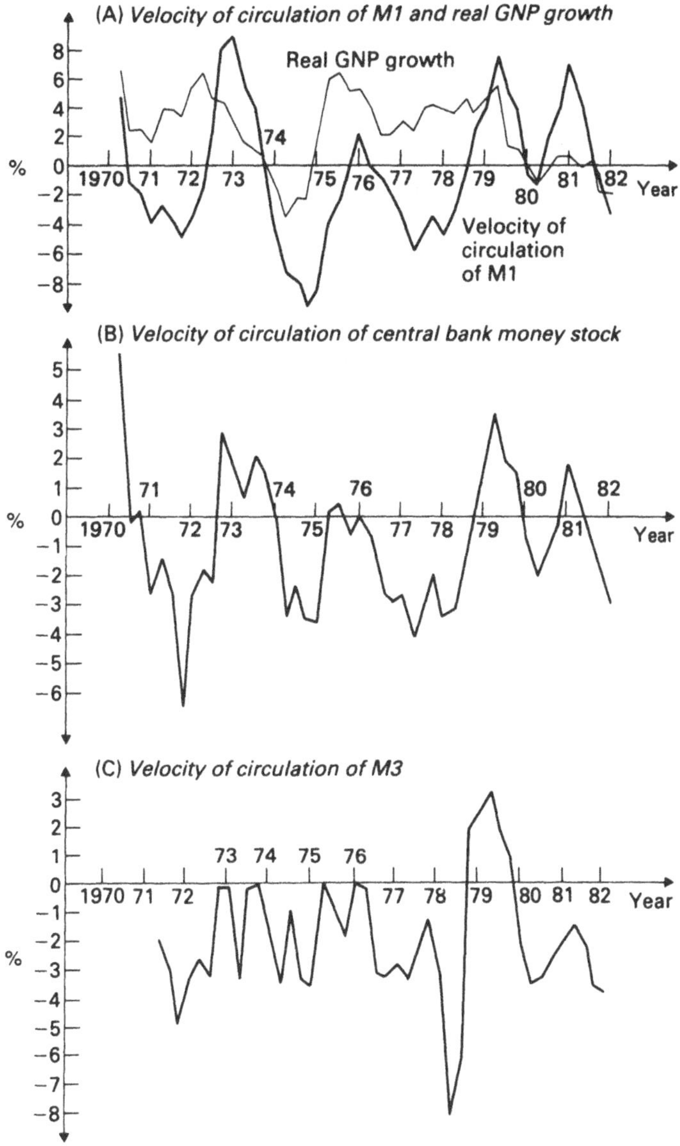


**Figure 8.7** Real GNP and velocities of circulation of money, 1970–82 (*percentage* quarterly changes over previous year)

*Sources:* Deutsche Bundesbank, *Monthly Reports* (various issues); Deutsche Bundesbank, *Statistical Supplements to the Monthly Reports, Series 4*; *Seasonally Adjusted Economic Data* (various issues).

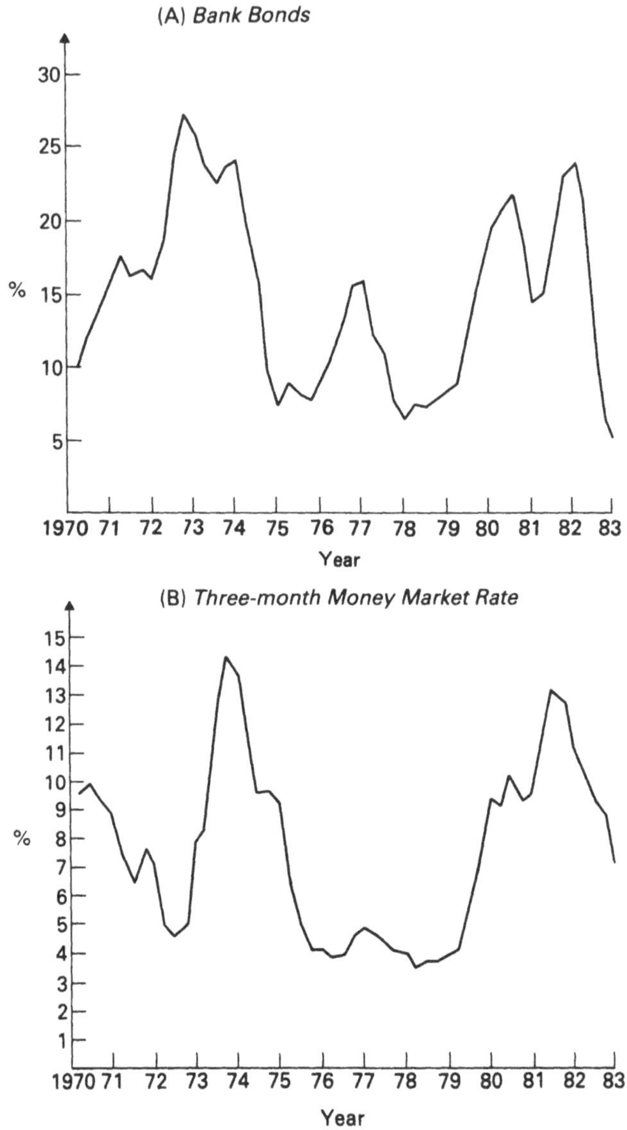


**Figure 8.8** Bank bonds and three-month money market rates, 1970–82 (*percentage* quarterly changes over previous year and quarterly averages in per cent p.a.)

*Sources:* Deutsche Bundesbank, *Monthly Reports* (various issues); Deutsche Bundesbank, *Statistical Supplements to the Monthly Reports*, *Series 4: Seasonally Adjusted Economic Data* (various issues).

The strong growth of financial obligations issued by commercial banks has occurred mainly at times of high interest rates (see Figure 8.8(B)). When interest rates were at relatively low levels, such as between 1975 and 1978, commercial banks did not have such an urgent need to compete for financial funds.

One can therefore presume that the velocity of money will move along the long-term trend when interest rates reach 'normal' levels again. In the very short run, the limited scope of financial innovation in the Federal Republic of Germany might render the demand for M1 and for central bank money at best unstable and unpredictable. In the medium term, however, both velocities seem to follow a foreseeable pattern that does not prevent the Bundesbank from conducting a non-discretionary monetary policy.

## IV FISCAL POLICY

### GENERAL TRENDS

Fiscal policy in the Keynesian sense was not practised in the Federal Republic of Germany before the middle of the 1960s. The first major recession of 1966/7, with a negative rate of real GNP growth (see Figure 8.9(A)), led to the introduction of the Stabilization Law in June 1967. By this law the federal government as well as the state governments were obliged to run their budgets in an anti-cyclical manner. The law enables the government to raise or lower income and corporate taxes by up to 10 per cent and to grant tax deductions for investment purposes.

The closer cooperation among the federal, state and local governments that was introduced by the Fiscal Reform Law of 1970 is also of great importance for stabilization policy in Germany. The purpose of this reform was to improve intergovernmental fiscal relations, especially concerning co-financing of public investment (Cooperative Federalism).

### PUBLIC EXPENDITURE

Public expenditure is implemented by all three levels of government according to their specific areas of responsibility. For the federal government, the areas are primarily defence, the social security system, unemployment insurance, federal railways, waterways and highways and foreign aid. For the state governments, major tasks are law enforcement (including police) and education. For the local authorities, they are social aid and infrastructure at the community level.

In the recent past the federal government's share of total public expenditure has on average been close to 40 per cent, while the shares of the states and the local communities have been about 35 per cent and 25 per cent, respectively.

According to the Stabilization Law, the federal government and the state governments should adjust their fiscal activity to the general economic situation, with the goal of stabilizing the price level and securing a high level of employment. The local communities are obliged to follow the same line of

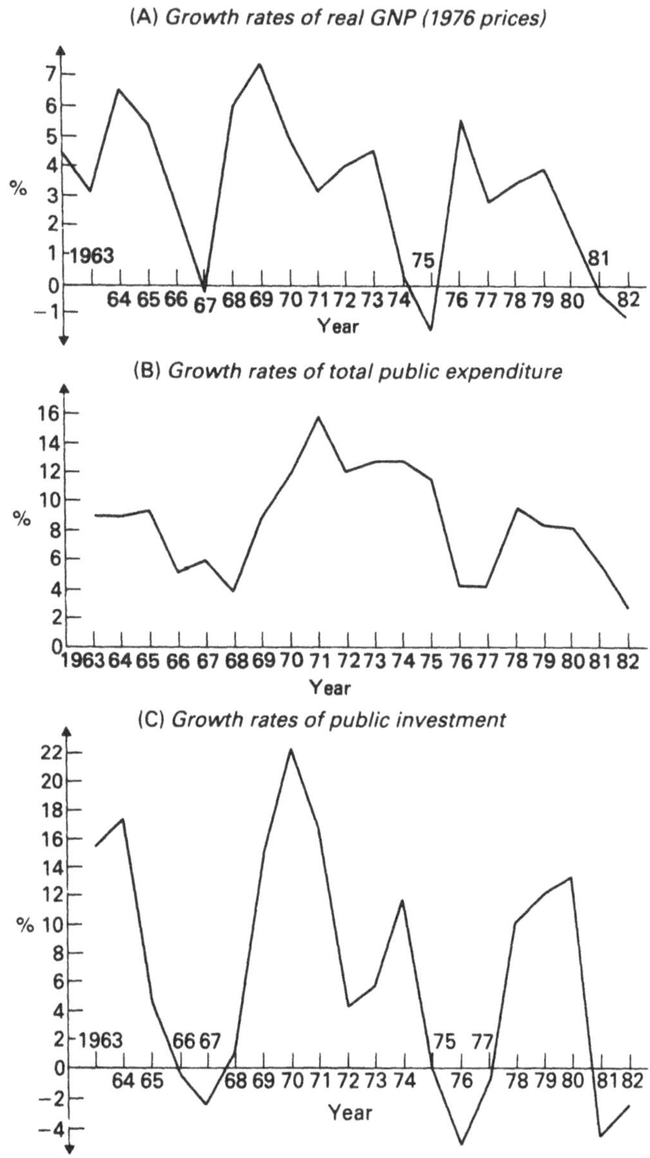


**Figure 8.9** Business cycles, public expenditure and public investment, 1962–82

*Source:* Council of Economic Experts (1983).

economic policy. The law requires that the states put into effect appropriate measures to induce the local communities to pursue an anti-cyclical policy. Thus, the intention of the Stabilization Law is to stabilize total demand. All levels of government are supposed to increase spending in recessionary periods and reduce spending in boom periods.

Since the early 1960s the cyclical situation would have required an acceleration of public spending in the recessionary periods of 1966/7, 1974/5 and 1980/82 and a deceleration of public expenditure in the boom periods of 1964, 1968/9, 1976 and 1979. Considering the actual growth rates of total public expenditure (Figure 8.9(B)), however, it can be seen that fiscal policy has hardly been carried out in an anti-cyclical way. For example, the growth rates of total government expenditure fell during the recessionary periods of 1966/7, 1974/5 and 1980/2 while they increased in the boom period of 1968/9. A moderate anti-cyclical policy took place only in the boom periods of 1964, 1976 and 1979.

The most important fiscal policy variable for the stabilization of employment, however, is not total public expenditure but public investment. The growth rates of public investment (Figure 8.9(C)) indicate a strong, if slightly delayed, pro-cyclical pattern. Most public investment programmes have taken place in the construction sector, and these investments are to a large extent carried out by local communities (in Germany, their share of total public investment is 65 per cent). However, the revenue of local communities typically declines in recessionary periods and thus induces a cut in public investment spending in such periods. The only advantage connected with this process is the reaction-lag, which leads to a relative stabilization of economic activity at the turning points of the business cycle. Obviously, it has been very difficult for the federal and state governments to neutralize or overcome the predominantly pro-cyclical investment behaviour of the local communities. Many of the federal government's anti-cyclical fiscal policy expenditure programmes in the late 1960s and the 1970s failed to induce anti-cyclical effects, despite the fact that most of these programmes were launched at the right time. A list of these programmes is presented in Table 8.4. Since nearly all programmes include a bundle of various investment incentives, it is not possible to identify or quantify their specific effects on investment or total economic activity.

While the cylical component of employment can partly be affected by the short-run behaviour of public expenditure, the long-run employment situation is governed by the structure of public expenditure, in particular by the growth of public expenditure relative to GNP and the structural division between consumption and investment spending. If public expenditure grows more than GNP and if an increasing portion is channelled into consumption instead of investment, unemployment will increase. The data in Table 8.5 indicate that from 1962 to 1981 public expenditure as a percentage of GNP grew almost continuously. The expansion is particularly strong if social transfer payments are included in public expenditure. This combined share increased from 35.2 per cent in 1962 to 48.1 per cent in 1981, whereas the share of public expenditure excluding the social security system grew only from 29.5 per cent to 35.1 per cent in the same period.

**Table 8.4** *Fiscal policy programs of the federal government, 1967–82 (DM million)*

| | | | |
|---|---|---|---|
| January | 1967 | Special Investment Programme | 2,500 |
| September | 1967 | Second Anti-Cyclical and Structural Programme | 5,300 |
| January | 1969 | Programme to Promote Structural Change | 600 |
| September | 1974 | Special Programme for Regional and Local Employment | 950 |
| December | 1974 | Programme for the Promotion of Employment and Growth | 2,600 |
| January | 1975 | Programme to Reduce Youth Unemployment | 200 |
| August | 1975 | Programme to Stimulate Housing and Investment | 5,750 |
| November | 1976 | Programme to Promote Employment | 430 |
| March | 1977 | Programme for High Technology Investment | 13,800 |
| May | 1977 | Programme to Support the Construction Industry | 600 |
| July | 1978 | Programme to Reinforce Demand and Support Economic Growth | n/a |
| November | 1978 | Programme to Support Research in Small Companies | 300 |
| May | 1979 | Special Employment Programme for Backward Areas | 200 |
| February | 1982 | Programme for Employment, Growth and Stability | n/a |
| December | 1982 | Programme for Economic Revival and Employment | n/a |

*Source:* Council of Economic Experts, *Annual Reports* (various issues).

## TAXES AND PUBLIC DEBT

Taxes are collected at all three levels of government. The most important taxes are income (personal and corporate) tax and value-added tax. These taxes account for more than two-thirds of total tax revenue. Revenues from these taxes are reallocated among the various government authorities. Other important taxes for the federal government are the gasoline tax, the cigarette tax and the liquor tax and for the states the property tax and the car tax. The main source of revenue for the local communities is the business tax and the real estate tax.

The most reliable anti-cyclical impact can be expected from the income tax, as progressive tax rates lead to an increase in revenue in boom periods and to a decrease in periods of declining economic activity.

In the past twenty years public revenue has grown much more slowly than public expenditure (columns 1 and 2 in Table 8.6). As a consequence, public debt has increased continuously (columns 3 and 4 in Table 8.6). However, during the 1960s growth rates were relatively moderate. In this period debt financing was constrained by the constitution to the volume of public investment. This restriction on public debt financing was removed in 1969 with an

**Table 8.5** *Total public expenditure and public investment as a percentage of GNP (in current prices), 1962–82*

| *Year* | *Public expenditure (incl. social transfers) as % of GNP* | *Public expenditure as % of GNP* | *Public investment as % of GNP* | *Public investment as % of public expenditure* |
|---|---|---|---|---|
| 1962 | 35.2 | 29.5 | 4.6 | 15.9 |
| 1963 | 35.3 | 30.4 | 5.0 | 16.4 |
| 1964 | 35.7 | 30.3 | 5.3 | 17.6 |
| 1965 | 36.5 | 30.4 | 5.1 | 16.9 |
| 1966 | 35.9 | 29.7 | 4.8 | 16.1 |
| 1967 | 36.6 | 31.2 | 4.6 | 14.8 |
| 1968 | 38.0 | 29.8 | 4.3 | 14.5 |
| 1969 | 38.9 | 29.4 | 4.4 | 15.1 |
| 1970 | 39.1 | 29.1 | 4.8 | 16.5 |
| 1971 | 39.9 | 30.1 | 5.0 | 16.6 |
| 1972 | 40.5 | 30.6 | 4.7 | 15.5 |
| 1973 | 41.4 | 30.5 | 4.5 | 14.7 |
| 1974 | 43.4 | 32.3 | 4.7 | 14.5 |
| 1975 | 45.7 | 35.0 | 4.5 | 12.8 |
| 1976 | 46.4 | 33.6 | 3.9 | 11.6 |
| 1977 | 46.7 | 33.0 | 3.6 | 10.9 |
| 1978 | 46.9 | 33.6 | 3.7 | 11.0 |
| 1979 | 47.7 | 33.7 | 3.7 | 11.3 |
| 1980 | 48.2 | 34.3 | 3.7 | 11.9 |
| 1981 | 48.1 | 35.1 | 3.6 | 10.6 |

*Source:* Council of Economic Experts (1983).

amendment to the constitution. The new formulation allowed the government to increase public debt beyond the level of public investment during economic downswings. However, in the amendment of the constitution a definition neither of an economic downswing nor of public investment is provided. Furthermore, no absolute or relative limit on public debt financing is specified.

The social–liberal coalition government made extensive use of the new law. In the recession year of 1975 the debt of the federal government grew at a record rate of 50.5 per cent while the state governments increased their net debt by 41.6 per cent. At the federal level the debt increase was almost five times higher than federal investment in tangible capital (*Sachinvestitionen*); at the state level it was twice as high. In the following years the fact that federal and state indebtedness was much higher than tangible capital investment was widely criticized as not being in accordance with the constitution. The federal government defended its policy by pointing out that the term public investment should also include public financial incentives to private investment or even public investment in human capital. The Council of Economic Experts at the Federal Ministry of Finance defines public investment more appropriately as investments in the public capital stock and public investment incentives as well

**Table 8.6** *Public Expenditure, Revenue and Debt 1962–82 (DM billion)*

| *Year* | *Expenditure* | *Revenue* | *Net increase in public debt* | *Total public debt* | *Ratio of total public debt to GNP* % | *Growth rate of total public debt* % |
|---|---|---|---|---|---|---|
| 1962 | 106.5 | 104.8 | 3.4 | 60.0 | 16.6 | 6.0 |
| 1963 | 116.3 | 110.9 | 6.7 | 66.7 | 17.5 | 11.2 |
| 1964 | 127.2 | 121.5 | 6.4 | 73.1 | 17.4 | 9.6 |
| 1965 | 139.3 | 129.9 | 9.9 | 83.0 | 18.1 | 13.5 |
| 1966 | 145.2 | 137.4 | 9.3 | 92.3 | 18.9 | 11.2 |
| 1967 | 153.8 | 141.7 | 14.9 | 107.2 | 21.7 | 16.4 |
| 1968 | 158.8 | 151.3 | 8.7 | 115.9 | 21.7 | 8.1 |
| 1969 | 174.6 | 176.9 | 0.2 | 116.1 | 19.4 | 0.2 |
| 1970 | 196.3 | 188.3 | 9.8 | 125.9 | 18.6 | 8.4 |
| 1971 | 226.5 | 211.2 | 14.5 | 140.4 | 18.7 | 11.5 |
| 1972 | 252.1 | 239.2 | 15.7 | 156.1 | 18.9 | 11.2 |
| 1973 | 280.5 | 271.5 | 11.7 | 167.8 | 18.3 | 7.5 |
| 1974 | 318.3 | 290.9 | 24.6 | 192.4 | 19.5 | 14.7 |
| 1975 | 360.5 | 296.6 | 64.0 | 256.4 | 24.9 | 33.3 |
| 1976 | 376.8 | 328.7 | 40.3 | 296.7 | 26.4 | 15.7 |
| 1977 | 395.2 | 364.0 | 31.8 | 328.5 | 27.5 | 10.7 |
| 1978 | 433.4 | 393.7 | 42.3 | 370.8 | 28.7 | 12.9 |
| 1979 | 469.9 | 423.5 | 43.1 | 413.9 | 29.7 | 11.6 |
| 1980 | 509.3 | 451.9 | 54.7 | 468.6 | 31.6 | 13.2 |
| 1981 | 542.2 | 465.6 | 77.0 | 545.6 | 35.4 | 16.4 |
| 1982 | 566.0 | 495.5 | 69.0 | 614.6 | 38.4 | 12.6 |

*Sources:* Council of Economic Experts (1983); Deutsche Bundesbank, *Monthly Reports* (various issues).

as public loans. Investment in human capital or in the military capital stock is excluded (Wissenschaftlicher Beirat, 1980).

To what extent have public authorities utilized the possibilities for an anti-cyclical debt policy provided by the constitutional amendment of 1969? Figure 8.10 shows that, measured by the ratio of debt financing to total investment, the federal government and the state governments carried out an anti-cyclical debt policy during the severe recession of 1974/5 and 1980/1. Similar action, though more moderate, is evident in the periods of economic upswing in 1973, 1976 and 1979. However, in 1977/8 and since 1982 the debt policies of the federal and state governments have been pro-cyclical. The local communities, apart from anti-cyclical behaviour in the 1974/5 and the 1980/1 recessions, acted either pro-cyclically or neutrally. Thus, the main burden of the anti-cyclical debt policy has been borne by the federal and state governments.

A severe problem with debt financing since 1975 has been its continuous high level, especially for the federal government. The ratio of federal debt financing to investment, which was close to 10 per cent in the early 1970s, reached peaks of more than 120 per cent in 1975 and 1981 and more than 100 per cent in 1982. Even in the periods of economic upswing in 1976 and 1979 the ratio did not fall

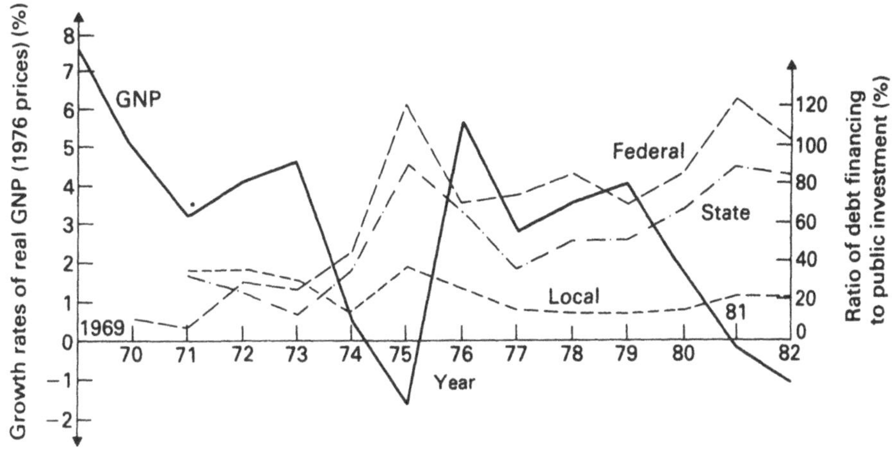


**Figure 8.10** Business cycles, debt financing and public investment, 1969–82

*Source:* Council of Economic Experts (1983); Federal Ministry of Finance, *Financial Reports* (various issues).

below 70 per cent. Similar, although more moderate, debt behaviour, can be observed for the state governments. Their ratio of debt financing to investment reached peaks of 90 per cent and 88 per cent in 1975 and 1981 and declined only slightly to 50 per cent in the boom period of 1979. Since 1975 only the local communities have been able to stabilize new debt in relation to investment at a relatively low level.

The primary motive for the rapid expansion of public debt by the federal government and the state governments has been the fight against unemployment, which was considered to be a cyclical phenomenon. In the meantime, however, it had become the result of a non-adjustment of real wages to lower productivity growth, increasing energy costs and deteriorating terms of trade. Public debt financing has not been and cannot be able to correct such a basic disequilibrium in the labour market. Therefore, it is not surprising that the unemployment rate continued to increase despite the rapid growth of public debt.

## FISCAL IMPULSE

The size and the growth rate of public debt as well as the ratio of debt financing to investment are not always reliable indicators of fiscal impact on the business cycle. One problem is that tax receipts that on the one hand influence the spending behaviour of public authorities and thus the business cycle are on the other hand themselves dependent on the business cycle. Another problem is that, independently from the business cycle, the three government levels traditionally finance a certain portion of their expenditure by debt. To the extent that the economy has adjusted to this 'normal' level of debt financing, no fiscal impact can be expected.

A concept of the fiscal impulse has been developed by the Council of

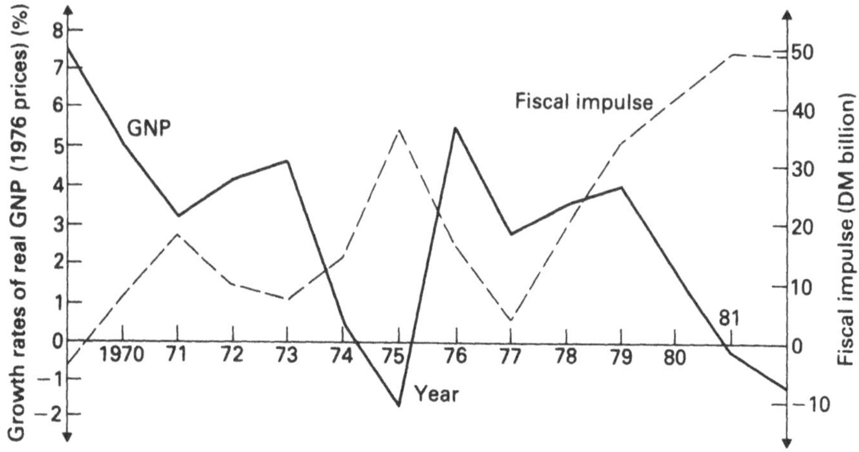


**Figure 8.11** Business cycles and fiscal impulse 1969–82

*Source:* Council of Economic Experts, *Annual Reports* (various issues).

Economic Experts. The Council defines the fiscal impulse as the difference between the actual budget deficit and a deficit that is neutral with respect to the business cycle. The neutral deficit is a hypothetical deficit based on normal deficit financing of the public budgets and on tax corrections for cyclical and inflationary impacts.

Figure 8.11 shows the fiscal impulse in relation to the business cycles of the period 1969–82. According to the figure, with the exception of 1977/8, fiscal policy has been precisely anti-cyclical: in periods of economic downswing, a positive fiscal impulse has been measured; in periods of economic upswing, a negative fiscal impulse. However, this anti-cyclical policy did not prevent severe cyclical fluctuations of economy activity. For example, the recessions of 1974/5 and 1980/2 took place despite the fact that the fiscal impulse indicated strongly anti-cyclical action by the government. A first possible explanation could be that the calculation of the 'neutral' deficit is somehow arbitrary (Thormählen, 1981). Secondly, the fiscal impulse is not so much exogenously determined as assumed, but is rather the result of predetermined policy implications. In recessionary periods, public debt, and thus the fiscal impulse, increase not because of an increase in public investment, but because of a quasi-indexed expansion of public consumption expenditure, while tax receipts are growing less or are even declining. Thirdly, increased public debt financing reflected by a strong fiscal impulse might have crowded out private investment. Without public demand for credit, interest rates would have been lower and the absorption of funds for private investment higher. Since the public sector has used the financial means mainly for consumption, total productive investment has been reduced and GNP growth rates have been lowered.

## V INCOMES POLICY

Incomes policy is defined here as public efforts to influence prices and wages directly in order to fight inflation and unemployment (Cassel and Thieme,

1977, 55–116). In West Germany, neither price and wage stops nor any type of indexation have taken place. During the 1950s, the government tried to influence the behaviour of trade unions and employers' associations mainly by moral suasion (*Maßhalteapelle*). In the early 1960s the 'social dialogue' was introduced. From time to time the Minister of Economics invited representatives of the various economic organizations to discuss general economic prospects and the necessary economic action of capital, labour and the government to facilitate long-run economic stability and growth.

Despite not very convincing results with the 'social dialogue', incomes policy was included in the Stabilization Law of 1967. According to this law, in a situation of economic disequilibrium the Minister of Economics is obliged to invite representatives of leading economic groups to discuss the economic situation and to try to reach an agreement on the necessary steps for adequate stabilization behaviour. The institutional arrangement of this type of incomes policy has been termed '*konzertierte Aktion*'. Meetings of the 'Konzertierte Aktion' were organized annually between 1967 and 1978. At these meetings representatives of the government, and the employers' associations very often tried to persuade union leaders to ask for lower wage increases than originally intended. Union leaders were under much more pressure to change their behaviour than were government officials and representatives of industry and trade. The unions therefore, felt that their interests were not adequately furthered in the 'Konzertierte Aktion', and they withdrew their participation in 1978. Since then no meetings have taken place and an official incomes policy is no longer practised.

Nevertheless, there are still efforts to inform the general public about the prospects for economic development and on the necessary policy behaviour to generate price stability and full employment. Apart from the government, the Council of Economic Experts and other notable bodies and individuals publish recommendations on issues of stabilization policy. To attain price stability, the Council of Economic Experts has demanded a monetary policy involving a growth rate of the money supply in accordance with the growth of productive potential. To ensure full employment, a policy that allows for more sectoral and regional wage differentiation and the introduction of more wage flexibility with respect to the cyclical nature of the economy is suggested.

German incomes policy seems to have had no significant effects on income distribution. Labour's share in the national income at factor cost (defined as the ratio of gross wage and salary income to national income) increased steadily from 60.4 per cent in 1960 to 73.6 per cent in 1981 (see Table 8.7). Although part of the increase in Labour's share is due to the decline in the proportion of employers in the total labour force (see column 2 of Table 8.7), the unions' bargaining power should not be ignored. In particular, the sharp rise of almost 5 percentage points in the unadjusted labour's share in the first half of the 1970s resulted from excessive wage demands.[9] During this period in particular, incomes policy was unable to exert a moderating influence on wage settlements. Another remarkable feature is that labour's share did not drop in recessionary periods (1974/5 and 1980/1). This may indicate inflexibility on the part of the trade unions, leading to an inability to react appropriately to economic changes in growth and unemployment.

The declining (unadjusted) share of entrepreneurial and property income as

**Table 8.7** *Distribution of income 1960–81 (per cent)*

| *Year* | *Labour's share*[a] | *Adjusted labour's share*[b] | *Share of entrepreneurial and property income* | | | |
|---|---|---|---|---|---|---|
| | | | *In total* | *Property income*[c] | *Self-employed*[d] | *Corporate profits*[e] |
| 1960 | 60.4 | 64.8 | 39.6 | 2.2 | 22.8 | 14.6 |
| 1965 | 65.6 | 67.3 | 34.4 | 2.6 | 19.9 | 12.0 |
| 1970 | 67.8 | 67.8 | 32.2 | 4.3 | 17.6 | 10.3 |
| 1971 | 69.1 | 68.7 | 30.9 | 4.2 | 17.4 | 9.4 |
| 1972 | 69.5 | 68.9 | 30.5 | 4.2 | 17.1 | 9.1 |
| 1973 | 70.7 | 69.8 | 29.3 | 4.3 | 17.1 | 7.9 |
| 1974 | 72.8 | 71.6 | 27.4 | 4.2 | 17.5 | 5.7 |
| 1975 | 72.3 | 71.4 | 27.7 | 4.7 | 17.6 | 5.4 |
| 1976 | 71.3 | 70.1 | 28.7 | 4.9 | 16.9 | 6.9 |
| 1977 | 71.5 | 70.0 | 28.5 | 5.1 | 16.5 | 6.9 |
| 1978 | 71.0 | 69.2 | 29.0 | 4.6 | 15.9 | 8.5 |
| 1979[f] | 70.9 | 68.6 | 29.1 | 4.3 | 15.4 | 9.3 |
| 1980[f] | 72.4 | 69.8 | 27.6 | 4.7 | 15.4 | 7.4 |
| 1981[f] | 73.6 | 70.7 | 26.4 | 5.0 | 15.4 | 6.0 |

*Notes:* a Defined as the ratio of gross wage and salary income to national income.
b Calculated at constant employment in 1970.
c Including interest and rents earned by dependent wage and salary earners.
d And their assisting relatives.
e Residual.
f Provisional figures.

*Source:* Institut der Deutschen Wirtschaft (1982).

a percentage of national income was borne primarily by the self-employed and the corporate sector. Their respective income shares fell from 22.8 per cent to 15.4 per cent and from 14.6 per cent to 6.0 per cent between 1960 and 1981. The share of income from property, which apart from capital and land also includes income from interest and rents earned by dependent wage and salary earners, remained relatively constant at close to 5 per cent. This marked decline in corporate profits and income for the self-employed should be seen in conjunction with unemployment due to capital shortage. Unless the profit situation significantly and permanently improves, investment activity is unlikely to recover and unemployment rates will remain high.

## NOTES

1 The number of foreign workers decreased from 1970 to 1978 and remained constant at about 2 million after 1980. See Sachverstandigenrat zur Begutachtung der gesamtwirtschaftlichen Entwicklung, Gegen Pessimismus, Jahresgutachten 1982/83 (Stuttgart, Mainz, Kohlhammer, 1982), in Council of Economic Experts (1983), p. 268.

2 From Figure 8.2 it can be seen that (*ex post*) real interest rates were lower in the 1970s than in the 1960s owing to higher inflation in the former period.

3 In calculating the level of wage and salary rates, lump-sum payments and across-the-board increases were added together and related to the entire duration of the wage agreements.

4 It could be argued that rising import prices could not be anticipated adequately in wage demands by trade unions.

5 The estimates for productive capacity are based on the product of the actual capital (actual number of working persons) and a hypothetical capital productivity (labour productivity) at full employment. The hypothetical productivities are derived by extrapolating the average increase in productivity during the period 1960–70 (on the basis of the last boom year before 1973) to 1981. Calculations refer to the corporate sector excluding flat-letting business. The productive capacity of the other economic sectors is equivalent to the actual real GDP.

6 Quarterly changes over the previous year, not presented here, fluctuated even more widely.

7 Up to 1973 the Bundesbank had focused on the liquidity ratio of commercial banks as the main monetary indicator and intermediate target variable. The central bank tried to control the 'free liquid reserves', which comprised the commercial banks' excess reserves, their stock of domestic money market papers, short-term foreign assets as well as their unutilized capacity to borrow through the discount window. The inadequacy of this concept as a target and indicator of monetary policy was shown by Neumann (1972) and Willms (1972).

8 Expected exchange rate changes might also have affected the demand for money to some extent, although the empirical support for currency substitution is ambiguous. For statistically significant empirical evidence of exchange rate expectations (measured as the relative differential of the forward and the spot rate), see Loef (1982). No statistically significant support for exchange rate expectations was found by Lehment (1982).

9 For real wage increases see Figure 8.4(A).

## BIBLIOGRAPHY


Cassel, D. and Thieme, H. J. (1977), *Einkommenspolitik*, Cologne, Kiepenheuer und Witsch.

Council of Economic Experts (1983), *Annual Report for 1982/83*, Washington DC.

Deutsche Bundesbank (1975), *Report of the Deutsche Bundesbank for the year 1974*, Frankfurt.

Deutsche Bundesbank (1982), *The Deutsche Bundesbank, Its Monetary Policy Instruments and Functions*, Special Series No. 7, Frankfurt.

Deutsche Bundesbank (1983a), *Monthly Report*, 35 (5), May.

Deutsche Bundesbank (1983b), *Monthly Report*, 35 (7), July.

Deutsche Bundesbank (1983c), *Report of the Deutsche Bundesbank for the Year 1982*, Frankfurt (German version).

Deutsche Bundesbank, *Statistical Supplements to the Monthly Report, Series 4: Seasonally Adjusted Economic Data*, various issues.

Institut der Deutschen Wirtschaft (1982), *Zahlen zur wirtschaftlichen Entwicklung der Bundesrepublik Deutschland*, Essen, Bacht.

International Monetary Fund (1983), *World Economic Outlook*, A Survey by the Staff of the IMF, Occasional Paper No. 21, Washington DC.

Lehment, H. (1982), 'Das Zinsniveau in einer offenen Wirtschaft', in W. Ehrlicher and D. Simmert (eds), *Geld- und Währungspolitik in der Bundesrepublik Deutschland*, supplement to *Kredit und Kapital*, 7, 404–406.

Loef, H.-E. (1982), 'Geldnachfrage in einer offenen Volkwirtschaft: Bundesrepublik Deutschland 1970–1979', *Kredit und Kapital*, 15, 524–526.

Neumann, M. J. M. (1972), 'The Deutsche Bundesbank's concept of monetary theory', in K. Brunner (ed.), *Proceedings of the First Konslanzer Seminar on Monetary Theory and Monetary Policy*, supplement to *Kredit und Kapital*, 1, 165–218.

Thormählen, Th. (1981), 'Kritische Anmerkungen zur Berechnung des Strukturellen Defizits', *Wirtschaftdienst*, 61, 389–396.

Willms, M. (1972), 'An evaluation of monetary indicators in Germany', in K. Brunner (ed.), *Proceedings of the First Konstanzer Seminar on Monetary Theory and Monetary Policy*, supplement to *Kredit und Kapital*, 219–242.

Wissenschaftlicher Beirat beim Bundesministerium der Finanzen (1980), *Gutachten zum Begriff der öffentlichen Investitionen*, Bonn, Stollfuss.

Wolter, F. (1983), 'Kapitalmangel und Unterbeschäftigung in der Weltwirschaft', in *Kapilalbildung und Wachstum in den achtziger Jahren* (Report of the Scientific Section of the 46th Assembly of the Working Group of the German Economic Science Research Institute, Bonn, 5 and 6 May 1983), in supplement to *Konjunkturpolitik*, 25–28.

# 9 Lessons from the Macroeconomic Performance of the Japanese Economy*

*KŌICHI HAMADA*

## I INTRODUCTION

The two oil crises of the 1970s brought serious hardship to the Japanese economy. Japan relies on imports for 90 per cent of her energy sources and almost 100 per cent of her petroleum consumption. The first oil crisis worsened the terms of trade by about 30 per cent in the two years 1973–75 and the second oil crisis led to deterioration by more than 30 per cent between 1978 and 1980. Even though there was a slight recovery in the terms of trade during the period 1976–78, the purchasing power of Japanese exports was almost halved between 1972 and 1980.

Although the magnitude of these external supply shocks was about the same in each case, macroeconomic performance following the two crises differed to a considerable extent. A situation of excess liquidity due to the attempt to prevent further appreciation of the yen had existed before the first oil crisis. The first supply shock then induced the worst inflation since the post-war recovery period. The inflationary period was followed by a long adjustment process of stagflation. After the second oil crisis, on the other hand, external pressures were contained by an appropriate combination of macroeconomic policies. The contrast between the effects of the two oil crises is worth close attention.

In the midst of the worldwide recession that started in 1979 because of the radical experiments of major industrial countries to curb inflation, the Japanese economy too was drawn into a long recession. The recovery of the world economy – particularly the economy of the United States – and the hope of improving terms of trade as a result of the weakening of the OPEC cartel have generated better prospects for the Japanese economy. Japanese macroeconomic policies are generally conceived to be restrained by two important barriers: (i) the difficulty of mobilizing fiscal policy because of the huge accumulated debt of the public sector, and (ii) the difficulty of reducing

* A substantial part of this chapter is based on my joint work with Fumio Hayashi (Hamada and Hayashi, 1983) and with Yoshio Kurosaka (Hamada and Kurosaka, 1983). I am much indebted to both of them for allowing me to utilize the results of the joint work.

interest rates in a world environment where real rates of interest are extremely high.

This chapter is designed to give a bird's-eye view of the course of macroeconomic development of the Japanese economy and the role of macroeconomic policies since the late 1960s. By comparing the experience of various countries, one can learn how institutional differences affect the macroeconomic performance of industrialized economies; at the same time, one can assess the universal applicability of laws or tendencies concerning economic activities that have been found in major countries.

In section II, I sketch the historical course of development of the Japanese economy. Then in sections III and IV I discuss the role of monetary and fiscal policy, their effectiveness and limitations. In Section V, I take up the aggregate supply relationship, notably Okun's law and the Phillips curve. In the final section the international aspects of Japan's macroeconomic performance are considered.

## II AN OVERVIEW OF THE POST-WAR EXPERIENCE OF THE JAPANESE ECONOMY

Before describing the macroeconomic performance of the Japanese economy during the worldwide inflationary period since 1968, it seems appropriate to review briefly the pattern of development over the whole post-war period. In particular, it is useful to point out the difference between the *modus operandi* of monetary policy during the period under fixed exchange rates and that under flexible exchange rates.

The Japanese economy started its recovery after the end of World War II in 1945. Inflation and scarcity of goods then prevailed. At first, economic progress was very slow, but in 1951 the Korean War broke out; ironically, as a result of this unfortunate development, the Japanese economy was set on a path of self-sustaining growth and became strong enough to maintain the exchange parity between the yen and the dollar at 360 yen per dollar – the exchange parity set in 1949 during the Occupation period. At that time, surplus labour in the agricultural sector was abundant; the spurt in industrial growth was yet to come.

Figure 9.1 shows the Phillips curve in post-war Japan. During the 1950s the curve was quite steep. The trade-off between employment and inflation, if it existed, was unfavourable to policy makers, probably because of the inflationary expectations that became entrenched during the period of very rapid price increases in the process of reconstruction immediately after World War II and during the boom that followed the Korean War. The 1950s can be regarded as the period when conditions were established for the remarkable growth of the 1960s.

The following decade was the most prosperous period for the Japanese economy: the unemployment rate was low, around 1.1–1.3 per cent, except for 1960 when it was 1.6 per cent; the real GNP growth rate varied from 5.7 per cent (1965) to 14.5 per cent (1961), averaging more than 10 per cent. In 1961, Prime Minister Ikeda announced a plan – which many people at that time

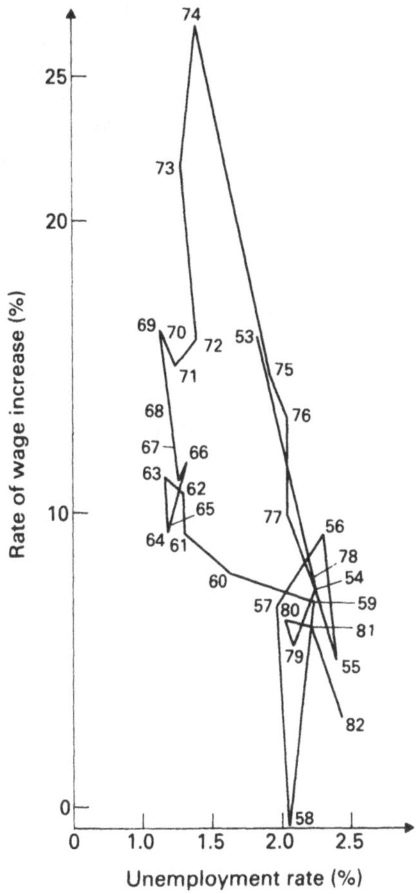


**Figure 9.1** The Phillips relationship in Japan

regarded as mere wishful thinking – to double national income in ten years. In the event, to the surprise of many, this target was surpassed, with real per capita GNP almost tripling between 1960 and 1973. In spite of unwelcome by-products of growth such as polluted air and water, the 1960s can be regarded as the golden decade of the Japanese economy.

Until August 1971, when the New Economic Policy was announced by President Nixon, the 360-yen-per-dollar exchange parity was kept constant and monetary policy was conducted in such a way as to limit the loss of international reserves under the fixed parity. Monetary policy thus reacted to the current account of the balance of payments, as was shown by Kaizuka (1967). As soon as the current account went into deficit, a contractionary monetary policy was adopted. This stop–go policy enabled the price level in Japan to follow a relatively stable path.

Under the fixed exchange rate, the price level of traded goods at home was linked to that in foreign countries. Fortunately, until around 1967, the monetary policies of the major industrial countries, particularly the United States, succeeded in containing price inflation within a low range. Accordingly, the wholesale price index (WPI) which was closely linked to the price level of traded goods, remained quite stable (see Figure 9.2). The consumer price index (CPI) gradually rose because there was a difference between the rate of technological progress in manufacturing and that in consumer goods or service industries.

After about 1968, however, partly because of the Johnson administration's ambitious policy of seeking both butter and guns, price levels abroad began to move upwards. The policy of maintaining a stable domestic price level in Japan thus started to imply a substantial surplus on the current account. Theoretically, Japan could have appreciated the yen in order to keep her domestic price level stable; however, the monetary authorities, for the most part, were for a long time obsessed by the advantage of the fixed exchange rate, and the possibility of appreciating the yen was never seriously considered as a feasible alternative for Japan.

If the exchange rate was to be kept intact, the choice was either to keep the price level stable while accumulating surpluses in the balance of payments, or to inflate the economy in line with world inflation. The first alternative was taken until the adoption of President Nixon's New Economic Policy. After the interlude of the Smithsonian realignment of exchange rates, the Japanese monetary authorities adopted the second alternative. They turned to inflationary policy to prevent the yen from appreciating further.

This policy, combined with Prime Minister Tanaka's ambitious plan for remodelling Japan, created excess liquidity within the financial system even before the supply shock hit the Japanese economy. Owing to the cartel activities of OPEC, Japan's terms of trade declined by 25 per cent between 1973 and 1974. The first oil crisis brought the Japanese economy to the brink of catastrophe.[1] In 1974 the wholesale price index rose by 31.4 per cent, the

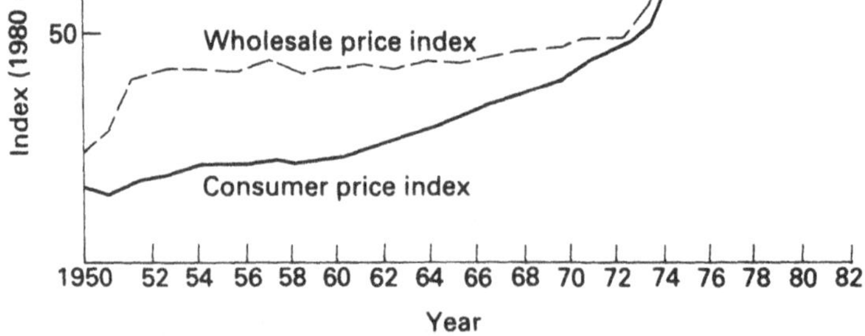


**Figure 9.2** Movements of the domestic price level

consumer price index by 24.5 per cent and nominal wages in the manufacturing sector by 26.2 per cent.

The period after 1974 can be regarded as one of adjustment of the Japanese economy to the supply shock. The Bank of Japan suddenly contracted the money supply and the Japanese economy suffered from a long period of stagflation. In 1978 real GNP declined for the first time since World War II. The rate of unemployment jumped to 1.89 per cent in 1975 and kept increasing until 1978. From this bitter experience, which can be seen as a failure that had its origins in the creation of excess liquidity, the Bank of Japan learned a great deal; in particular, it learned the danger of sacrificing the objective of stable prices for other objectives such as stable parity of the yen. The labour union leaders, who won a wage increase of 26.2 per cent in the 1974 Spring Labour Offensive (*shuntō*), learned the possible cost of big wage increases in terms of the loss of jobs. Probably because of this learning process, the effect of the second oil crisis was rather mild. The terms of trade again declined by approximately 30 per cent between 1978 and 1980. The wholesale price index increased by 17.8 per cent from 1979 to 1980; the consumer price index, however, rose only 8.0 per cent over the same period. Moreover, the trough of the recession was shallower than that after the first oil crisis.

Thus, in the 1970s the Japanese economy was exposed to various external disturbances: that is, two oil crises and the realignment of international monetary rules. We may call the 1970s a decade of *Sturm und Drang*. In particular, in 1973 Japan adopted the system of flexible exchange rates, along with other industrialized economies. Naturally, monetary policy gained more autonomy. The Bank of Japan bgan to focus on control of the money supply, and in 1978 the Bank of Japan started announcing the forecast, though not the target, for the rate of increase in money supply for the next quarter.

## III THE ROLE OF MONETARY POLICY

Figure 9.3 shows the path of the growth rate of M2 + CD and the rate of change in nominal GNP and in the GNP deflator in Japan. One can deduce from the figure that nominal GNP is influenced by money growth. But the lag is rather irregular. The forecast of money supply by the Bank of Japan, initiated in 1978, is drawn with vertical solid segments because the forecast is made with confidence intervals.

Here let me explain the concepts underlying the various measures of the monetary aggregates used in Japan. The narrow money stock measure, M1, consists of currency held by the public, and demand and ordinary deposits. The use of personal cheques has not been popular in this country, and 'ordinary' deposits are not subject to drawing through cheques but are payable on demand at the bank counter or by use of a cash card at any branch of the bank. (In Japan, major 'city' banks have branches all over the country.) The Japanese financial system has shifted from a cash society directly to a cash-card and credit-card society without passing through the stage where cheque accounts are important. A broader concept of money, M2, includes time and other types of deposits in addition to M1. In 1979 the certificate of deposit (CD) was

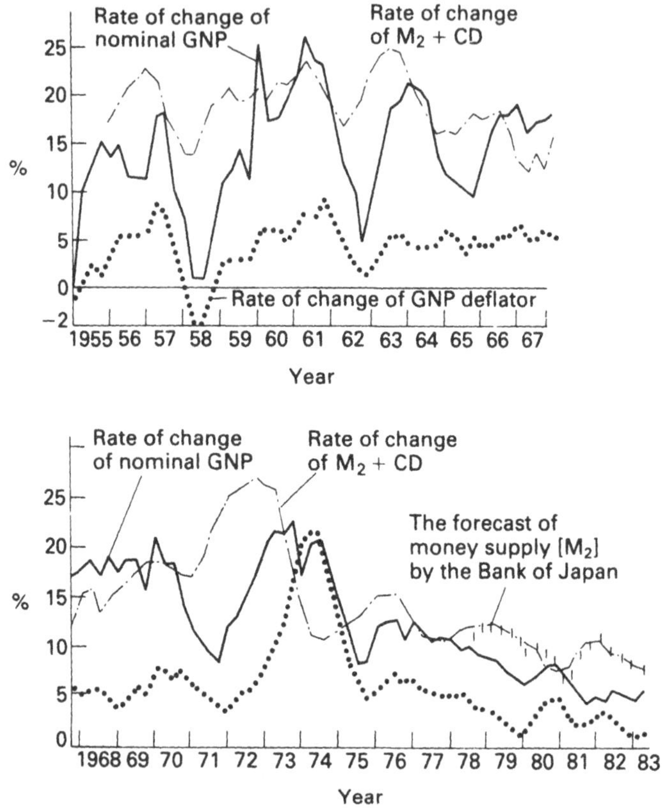


**Figure 9.3** The growth rate of money supply

introduced. We shall pay attention to the concept of M2 + CD instead of M2 after 1975. An even broader money concept is M3, which includes also the deposits of agricultural, fishery and credit cooperatives, of labour credit associations, money and loan trusts, and notably postal savings deposits. Post offices all over the country provide postal (ordinary and savings) deposits that are highly competitive with and often preferable to bank deposits. In 1980 the expectation that postal savings deposits would have *de facto* preferential tax treatment caused a sudden shift of deposits from banks to the postal savings system.

From the data in Table 9.1, one can see that the demand for M1 is less stable than the demand for M2. The growth rate of M1 dropped from its trend in 1977 and sharply declined again in 1980. The first drop is attributed to the increase in interest sensitivity of the public, and the second to the shift of funds from banks to postal savings deposits. Accordingly, M2 or M2 + CD moves more smoothly, and this is why in Figure 9.3 the growth rate of M2 was taken. Of course, one cannot neglect the movements of M3 because of the importance of the postal savings deposits.

For a long time, Japanese households put a major portion of their savings into ordinary and time deposits at the commercial banks. At the end of 1980, M2 held by households constituted about 65 per cent of the total financial assets of households. My guess is that the comparable figure for the United States would be below 40 per cent. Recently, however, new savings instruments have been introduced in order to compete with the postal savings deposits. A new loan trust with a compound interest rate feature called 'big', new bank debentures with a compound interest rate feature called 'wide', a new unit-type bond trust called 'jumbo', and so forth, have been introduced. The commercial banks have also introduced a new type of deposit whose maturity can be designated by depositors. Mitsubishi Money Capsule (MMC) – a bank account that manages funds in long-term public bonds – is the most recent innovation. At the same time, information concerning interest differentials has become more readily available to the general public. Accordingly, Japanese households have started to shift their savings from one form of savings instrument to another. In addition, a large volume of existing long-term government bonds will provide close substitutes for bank deposits as their maturity shortens.

These new developments in financial instruments have been and will be an important factor in opening the possibility of sudden shifts in the public's portfolio. The coexistence of regulated interest rates and market-determined interest rates is another factor (bank deposit rates and the rates for newly issued public bonds are, respectively, under a regulation similar to regulation Q in the United States and under government guidance). Thus we have already observed volatile movements in the velocity of money, particularly in that of M1. However, the pace of financial innovation has not been as rapid as in the United States, where very high and volatile movements in interest rates are a promoting factor; and, since the Ministry of Finance and the Bank of Japan will act to prevent a very sudden change in the Japanese financial system, the velocity of money will not move wildly in the near future. The factors mentioned above, however, will create a difficult problem for the monetary authorities because the concentration on a single monetary aggregate will not be sufficient to maintain a stable price level as well as a stable level of economic activity.

As already mentioned, the Bank of Japan emphasizes a broader money concept, M2, whose demand has been more stable; it also takes into consideration M3. Under the flexible exchange rate regime since 1973, the autonomy of monetary control has naturally been reinforced; the political environment for pursuing independent monetary policy has also been improved, simply because the cost of excessive expansion of money before the first oil crisis is now well understood by the public. The Bank of Japan conducted its monetary policy during the 1960s with the emphasis on the total amount of credit extended by the commercial banks as well as the call rate (the interest rate for short-term inter-bank funds, similar to the federal fund rate in the United States). In the 1970s, it shifted the emphasis to money supply by making M2 an operational target. In the third quarter of 1978 is started to publish a forecast of money supply for the succeeding quarter. As is shown in Figure 9.3, the actual path of money supply does not deviate from the forecast path by a great deal.

**Table 9.1** *Indicators of economic activity in Japan*

| *Year* | *Real GNP growth* | *Unemploy-ment rate* | *Job offers applicants ratio* | *Rate of increase in nominal wages* | *Rate of increase in CPI* | *Rate of increase in WPI* | *Rate of money supply, M1* | *Rate of money supply M2 (+CD)* |
|---|---|---|---|---|---|---|---|---|
| 1953 | 6.3 | 1.85 | — | +12.1 | — | + 0.4 | — | — |
| 1954 | 5.8 | 2.25 | — | + 5.4 | — | − 0.7 | — | — |
| 1955 | 8.8 | 2.38 | 0.22 | + 4.1 | — | − 1.8 | — | — |
| 1956 | 7.3 | 2.29 | 0.33 | + 9.1 | — | + 4.4 | — | — |
| 1957 | 7.5 | 1.96 | 0.39 | + 3.6 | — | + 3.0 | — | — |
| 1958 | 5.6 | 2.04 | 0.32 | + 2.3 | — | − 6.5 | — | — |
| 1959 | 8.9 | 2.23 | 0.44 | + 7.5 | — | + 0.9 | — | — |
| 1960 | 13.3 | 1.62 | 0.58 | + 7.9 | + 3.6 | + 1.1 | +21.7[a] | +21.1[a] |
| 1961 | 14.5 | 1.30 | 0.74 | +11.8 | + 5.3 | + 1.1 | +21.6[a] | +20.2[a] |
| 1962 | 7.0 | 1.28 | 0.68 | + 9.2 | + 6.8 | − 1.6 | +18.1[a] | +20.2a |
| 1963 | 10.5 | 1.16 | 0.70 | +10.2 | + 7.6 | + 1.6 | +26.5[a] | +24.0[a] |
| 1964 | 13.1 | 1.18 | 0.79 | +10.9 | + 3.9 | + 0.4 | +17.4 | +15.3[a] |
| 1965 | 5.7 | 1.22 | 0.64 | + 8.4 | + 6.6 | + 0.7 | +14.6 | +18.0[a] |
| 1966 | 10.6 | 1.31 | 0.73 | +11.8 | + 5.1 | + 2.4 | +15.3 | +16.3[a] |

| | | | | | | | | |
|---|---|---|---|---|---|---|---|---|
| 1967 | 10.8 | 1.26 | 1.00 | +13.0 | + 4.0 | + 1.7 | +15.3 | +15.5[a] |
| 1968 | 12.7 | 1.18 | 1.12 | +14.7 | + 5.3 | + 1.0 | +16.9 | +15.6 |
| 1969 | 12.3 | 1.12 | 1.30 | +16.6 | + 5.2 | + 2.0 | +19.4 | +17.3 |
| 1970 | 9.9 | 1.15 | 1.41 | +17.5 | + 7.7 | + 3.7 | +20.7 | +18.3 |
| 1971 | 4.7 | 1.23 | 1.12 | +14.0 | + 6.1 | − 0.8 | +22.6 | +20.5 |
| 1972 | 9.0 | 1.39 | 1.16 | +15.7 | + 4.5 | + 0.8 | +22.4 | +26.5 |
| 1973 | 8.8 | 1.27 | 1.76 | +23.4 | +11.7 | +15.8 | +27.8 | +22.7 |
| 1974 | −1.2 | 1.38 | 1.20 | +26.2 | +24.5 | +31.4 | +13.4 | +11.9 |
| 1975 | 2.4 | 1.89 | 0.61 | +11.5 | +11.8 | + 3.0 | +12.2 | +13.1 |
| 1976 | 5.3 | 2.01 | 0.64 | +12.3 | + 9.3 | + 5.0 | +13.5 | +15.1 |
| 1977 | 5.3 | 2.03 | 0.56 | + 8.5 | + 8.1 | + 1.9 | + 7.0 | +11.4 |
| 1978 | 5.1 | 2.24 | 0.56 | + 5.9 | + 3.8 | − 2.5 | +10.1 | +11.7 |
| 1979 | 5.2 | 2.08 | 0.71 | + 7.4 | + 3.6 | + 7.3 | +10.7 | +11.9 |
| 1980 | 4.8 | 2.01 | 0.75 | + 8.1 | + 8.0 | +17.8 | + 2.6 | + 9.2 |
| 1981 | 3.8 | 2.21 | 0.68 | + 6.2 | + 4.9 | + 1.4 | + 3.3 | + 8.9 |
| 1982 | 3.0 | 2.36 | 0.61 | + 4.8 | + 2.7 | + 1.8 | + 5.8 | + 9.2 |

*Notes:* a End-of-year comparison.

During and after the first oil crisis, monetary management aggravated inflation and unemployment, because supply shocks were transmitted to Japan in an amplified form. In coping with the second oil crisis, the Bank of Japan succeeded in preventing the deteriorating terms of trade from being translated into domestic inflation. Following this successful performance, the Bank of Japan, in my opinion, now conducts its monetary policy too cautiously. Bank of Japan officials are afraid of the possible effect of declining interest rates on the yen exchange rate. The Bank of Japan thus did not reduce the official discount rate, as was widely expected around the end of 1982.

I shall now comment briefly on the question of whether or not the Bank of Japan is able to control the monetary aggregates. In Japan, the main channel of financial intermediation used to be the commercial bank sector. This gave rise to the idea that economic activity could be controlled by controlling the total amount of loans extended by commercial banks. This may be regarded as a forerunner of the credit paradigm now popular in the United States (Modigliani and Papademos, 1980; B. Friedman *et al.*, 1980). According to this view, M2 is determined by extension of credit by commercial banks and then M1 is determined by the endogenous demand for currency and deposits by the public. Thus, control of the amount of commerical bank loans through 'window guidance', a form of moral suasion by the Bank of Japan, was considered the most important means of monetary control (see Ueda, 1982). A Granger test suggests that, during the period under the fixed exchange rate, causation may have run from M2 to M1 (Hamada and Hayashi, 1983).

This view may have contributed to the excess supply of money before the first oil crisis: by emphasizing the role of commercial loans, the Bank of Japan seems to have overlooked the effect of the increase in international reserves on the money supply. At present, the Bank of Japan possesses various means of influencing financial markets: *tegata* operations (market operations in the commercial bills market), 'window guidance', changes in the official discount rate and changes in the reserve requirement ratio. As noted by Horiuchi (1980), the money multiplier is not constant over time but moves according to a regular pattern. The change in reserve requirement and the cyclical pattern of cash (and deposit) holding by the public determine the movement of the money multiplier. Thus I do not foresee any serious problem in controlling the money supply in Japan. More difficult will be to predict changes in the velocity of money due to shifts in the portfolio behaviour of the public.

## IV THE ROLE OF FISCAL POLICY

The ruling party in Japan throughout the post-war period has been the Liberal Democratic Party (LDP), except for a short interlude just after the war when a coalition government was in charge. The LDP, despite its name, is more or less conservative. The nature of government policy has thus tended to be influenced by the characters of individual prime ministers rather than by major shifts in the policy attitudes of government. Prime Minister Ikeda, for example, was noted for his optimistic and growth-oriented policy; Tanaka was associated with an ambitious plan for remodelling Japan; and the present prime minister,

Nakasone, is known for his support of administrative reform (*gyōsei kaikaku*) directed towards less expensive and more efficient government.

Fiscal policy before 1965 would now be described as supply-side policy. When the high rate of nominal as well as real economic growth increased tax revenue, realignment of the individual income tax schedule was made in such a way as to contain public expenditure within one-fifth of GNP. A built-in stabilizer was working through the corporate income tax (Ishi, 1976). By the Government Budget Act (*zaisei hō*), the issuance of public bonds to finance current expenditure had been prohibited. When a recession hit the Japanese economy in 1965, the government introduced a special statute enabling it to issue long-term bonds; however, it was not until fiscal 1976 that a large volume of public bonds was issued.

To cope with the prolonged stagflation after the first oil crisis, the government greatly expanded deficit-financed spending. Figure 9.4 shows the movement of public capital formation with the movement of GNP. From the figure

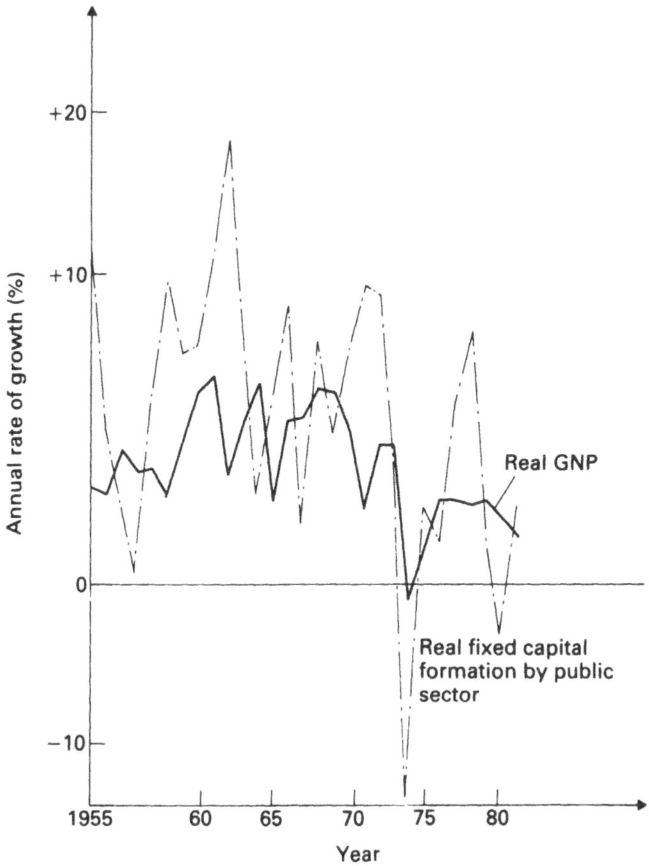


**Figure 9.4** The relationship between the annual rate of growth, real GNP and real fixed capital formation

one can see that, after 1976, public expenditure was made to counteract the recession. It is a matter of dispute whether or not fiscal policy was really effective in sustaining the economy and then saving it from the recession. There seems to be a kind of robustness in the method of tracing the effectiveness of monetary and fiscal policy. Estimations of the St Louis Federal Reserve Bank type applied to the Japanese data give results that deny the efficacy of fiscal policy, while the Keynesian-type macroeconometric models suggest that the multiplier effect was at work.

At any rate, as a result of substantial deficit spending, the public has accumulated a large amount of government debt. At the end of May 1983, the level of outstanding public debt reached 100 trillion yen, equivalent to more than 37 per cent of the GNP of fiscal 1982 (which ended in March 1983). This huge amount of outstanding debt creates a difficult problem of debt management and future debt refunding for the Japanese monetary authorities. The long-term interest rate for government debt actually increased substantially in 1979 and 1980, indicating the possibility of portfolio crowding out. All these factors work as a restraint on any further use of discretionary fiscal policy at present.

The national consensus now seems to favour administrative reform aimed at smaller and more efficient government. Public expenditure is under strict scrutiny. This may be regarded as a healthy reaction against excessive expansion of government activities. But, in my opinion, fiscal conservatism is being carried a little too far; Japanese fiscal policy now works as a built-in destabilizer because expenditure is adjusted to tax revenue, which has fallen owing to the current recession.

## V THE AGGREGATE SUPPLY RELATIONSHIP IN JAPAN

Let us now turn to aggregate supply in Japan. I shall mention two important relationships in aggregate supply: the Okun law and the Phillips curve. The former relates unemployment to excess output capacity; the latter,unemployment to wage increase.

Before going on to describe these relationships, it is appropriate to point out the nature of unemployment statistics in Japan. Column 2 of Table 9.1 (pp. 188–189) shows the rate of unemployment since 1953. The level of unemployment is low and the variance of the statistics is quite small; this coincides with the general impression that the employment situation in Japan has been generally favourable. In order to assess the situation in the Japanese labour market in comparative perspective, however, I must call attention to the quite rigorous definition of unemployment used in Japan. In Japanese statistics, 'completely unemployed workers' are defined as those among the population over 15 years of age who are not employed, are able to work, who want to work and who search for jobs during the last seven days of the month. If one compares this definition with those of other countries – for example, with that of the United States – one finds several differences (see Taira, 1983; Yashiro, 1982; Hamada and Kurosaka, 1983). The most significant factor tending to reduce the Japanese unemployment rate below the rate that would be derived using the more common international definition is the treatment of those who search for jobs during a four-week period but not during the testing period – that is, the last week of the month. In US statistics such people are counted as unemployed. In Japanese statistics they are not, and this tends to exclude housewives or students who are looking for part-time jobs but not frequently enough to meet the statistical requirement. In particular, during the recession many women workers have been more or less discouraged from regularly seeking jobs.

There have been a few attempts to put the Japanese unemployment figures in comparative perspective. Taira (1983) and Yashiro (1982) claim that, if adjusted to the US standard, male unemployment would increase by about one-quarter while female unemployment would perhaps even triple. Although some controversial problems still remain with these attempts, they seem to indicate that official figures for unemployment may underestimate the degree of excess supply in the labour market.[2] Japan managed to cope rather well with the second oil crisis, but perhaps not quite as well as the official unemployment figures suggest.

Now let us turn to Okun's law in Japan. With Yoshio Kurosaka, I found that there is a positive correlation between the unemployment rate and the potential GNP gap in Japan (Hamada and Kurosaka, 1983). Surprisingly, a 1 per cent increase in unemployment widens the GNP gap by about 28 per cent; this is in strong contrast to the US case, where a 1 per cent change in the unemployment rate is associated with a 3 per cent change in the GNP gap. This high value of the Okun coefficient reflects partly, of course, the limited variability of unemployment statistics in Japan. It also indicates that adjustment behaviour in the Japanese labour market is different from that in the United States. Changes in working hours and changes in the labour participation rate (particularly of female workers owing to discouragement) contribute to the high value of the coefficient. This certainly indicates that output loss due to recessions is much greater than the low unemployment figures suggest.[3]

Figure 9.1 (p. 183) shows the Phillips curve linking wage increases and unemployment in Japan. One can easily explain the shape of the curve by appealing to the expectations-augmented Phillips curve introduced by Phelps (1967) and M. Friedman (1968). After the rapid inflation of the post-war reconstruction period, and after the boom caused by the Korean War, expectations of a high rate of inflation prevailed; accordingly, the Phillips relationship between wages and unemployment was steep, and unfavourable for policy makers. An abundant supply of labour from rural areas still existed, so the curve was located to the right.[4] Then came a period of rapid growth and rapid technical progress. With more or less stable prices due to monetary policy aimed at keeping the exchange rate constant, price expectations were stabilized and one can observe the hyperbolic shape originally discovered by Phillips himself for British data. Next came a period of excess liquidity followed by the supply shock that caused the severe inflation known as 'frenzied prices'; the Phillips curve shifted upwards because of high inflationary expectations. Whether the current relationship – say, after 1980 – can be regarded as a demonstration of the vertical Phillips curve, or as a segment of a short-run Phillips curve along which one can exploit the trade-off between inflation and unemployment, is a difficult issue to which I shall return briefly.

In addition to the vertical shift of the Phillips curve, we should consider the horizontal shift as well. Rigidity or inertia in the growth rate of real wages in the context of declining productivity growth and worsening terms of trade would shift the Phillips curve horizontally to the right, creating 'classical' instead of 'Keynesian' unemployment. Despite declining productivity due to the first oil crisis, the Japanese wage bargaining process kept real wages constant or even increased them. This was owing partly to the inflationary expectations prevailing in 1974 and partly to the unhappy coincidence that, at the time of the 1974 Spring Labour Offensive (when annual wage increases are determined), firms were recording very high, if only nominal, rates of profit. Thus, after 1974, the Phillips curve shifted to the right. The supply shock was then an unexpected one; it took time for the parties involved in wage bargaining to notice the adverse effect of the decline in terms of trade, and the adverse effect on employment of maintaining high real wages.

Japanese labour union leaders seem to have learned a lesson from the experience of the first oil crisis; thus, after the second oil crisis, the Phillips relationship did not shift to the right. Figure 9.5 indicates the relationship between the rate of wage increase minus the rate of labour productivity increase, on the vertical axis, and the job offers/applicants ratio, on the horizontal axis. This figure appears to indicate that real wages respond fairly flexibly to excess demand in the labour market. In FY 1980, real wages in the non-agricultural sector did in fact decline by 1.7 per cent; the real wage per efficiency unit of labour also declined in fiscal 1978 and 1979.

The process of wage determination in the Japanese economy still allows for real wage flexibility. The favourable performance of the aggregate supply relationship after the second oil crisis is based on real as well as nominal wage flexibility. The Spring Labour Offensive practice – that is, the system of simultaneous wage determination for all the leading sectors of the economy – allows firms to adjust wages annually for most workers. Furthermore, if unexpected changes in productivity occur during the year, firms may alter labour compensation through adjustments in semi-annual bonuses.

What, then, is the natural rate of unemployment in Japan? If real wages are perfectly flexible in response to excess demand, all the observed unemployment should be frictional and not involuntary. However, even in Japan the labour market is not that efficient. The Spring Labour Offensive determines wages on the basis of the information available at the time of negotiation, and the wages thus determined are effective for approximately one year. By looking at the Phillips curve in Figure 9.1 (p. 183), one may deduce that the natural rate of unemployment was around 1.2–1.3 per cent during the 1960s and that after the first oil crisis it rose to more than 2 per cent.

In Figure 9.5, where the rate of real wage increase per efficiency unit of labour is plotted against the job offers/applicants ratio,[5] one can also guess the values of the non-accelerating inflation rate of unemployment (NAIRU) in Japan. Where the graph intersects the horizontal axis, the rate of unemployment will not accelerate inflation. The job offers/applicants ratio correspond-

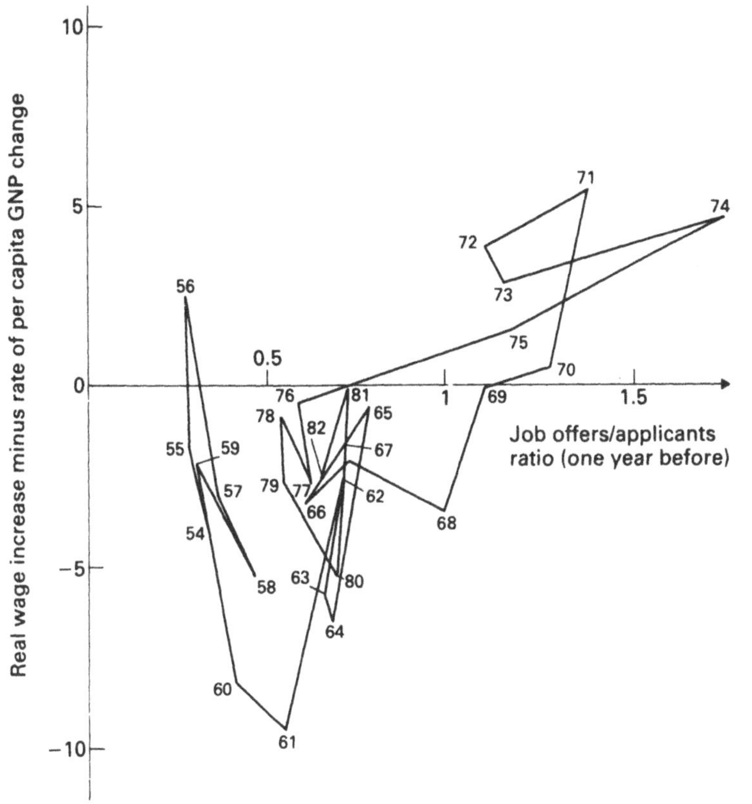


**Figure 9.5** The relationship between the rate of wage increase minus the rate of labour productivity increase and the job offers/applicants ratio

ing to NAIRU seems to have been about 1.2 at the end of the 1960s but now seems to be approximately 0.8. Figure 9.6 is shown in order to relate the unemployment rate to the offers/applicants ratio. From this figure one might roughly guess that NAIRU was about 1.2 per cent in the 1960s, and that it became about 2.0 per cent after 1978 or so.

Thus real wages have become quite flexible. However, actual unemployment still seems to be higher than the natural rate or the NAIRU. Is there, then, still some room for discretionary monetary policy to affect unemployment? There are several studies concerning the effects of anticipated and unanticipated money supply in Japan. Pigott (1978), using quarterly data, arrived at the conclusion that anticipated money supply does not matter in Japan; however, studies using more recent data (e.g. Seo and Takahashi, 1982; Katō, 1979; Hamada and Hayashi, 1983) indicate that, although unanticipated money is more important in explaining output behaviour, anticipated money also matters. Taniuchi, in his interesting work (1982), took into account the institutional framework of the Spring Labour Offensive and formulated a model in which nominal wages are determined on the basis of information

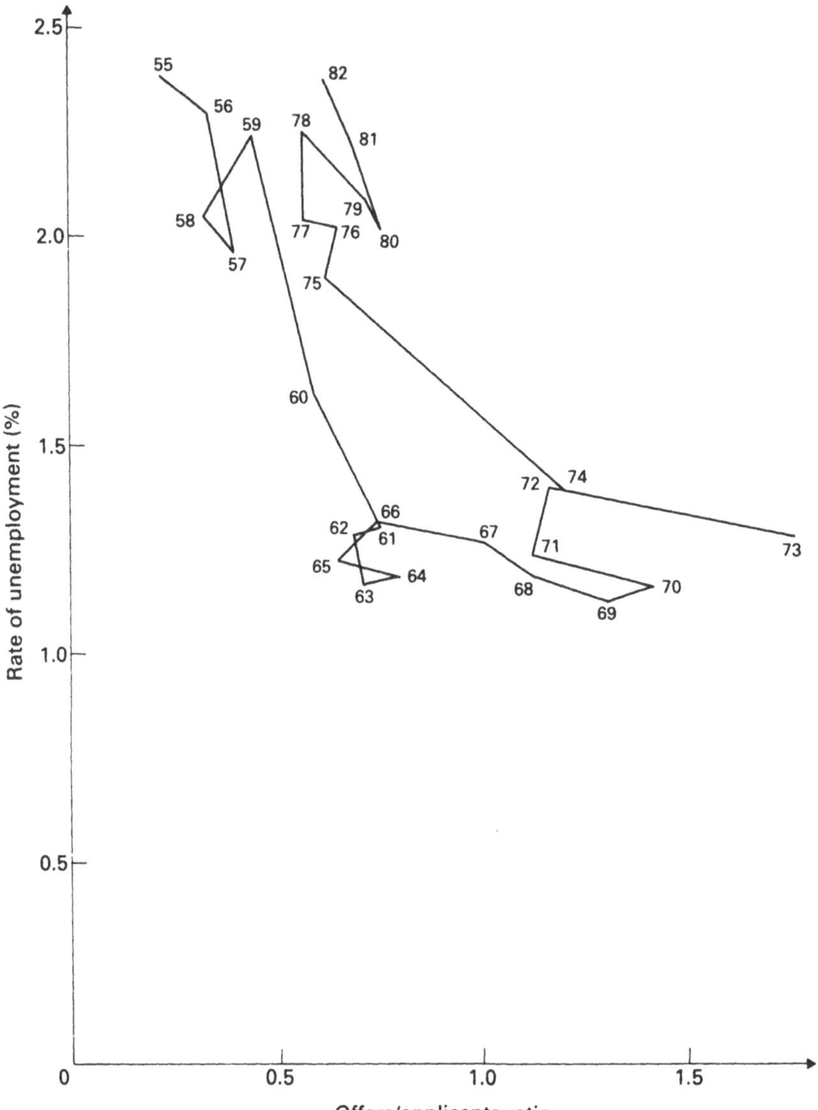


**Figure 9.6** The relationship between the rate of unemployment and the job offers/applicants ratio

available at the time of the Spring Offensive. Thus the neutrality hypothesis in his model is that anticipated money influences output for only three quarters.

In summary, real wages have become quite flexible since the second oil crisis. This is probably due to the fact that labour unions are organized on a company-by-company basis – there were more than 34,000 unions in 1981 – and that some community-oriented cooperative attitudes are held by both employers and employees. Yet there is some inertia in nominal wages, at least for three quarters and probably longer, that makes discretionary monetary policy effective. In addition, as has probably been found in many countries, the recent radical experiment in containing inflation revealed that price expectations are not immediately altered downward in the face of contractionary monetary policy, as the strong form of the macro rational expectations hypothesis suggests. This makes monetary policy effective in counteracting recessions.

Needless to say, the above remarks do not imply that discretionary monetary policy always works in the same manner. Expectations play an important role, and so the impact of a particular policy on output behaviour may vary depending on the expectations it creates in the public. In my opinion, however, there is still a case for more active demand management policy to foster domestic demand in the present state of the Japanese economy than the current policy of 'just wait and see'.

## VI CONCLUDING REMARKS

Instead of summarizing the content of this chapter, let me comment on the international side of Japanese macroeconomc policy.

The scope of monetary policy is constrained, or at least is conceived by the monetary authorities to be constrained, by the high levels of real interest rates throughout the world. The extreme policy combination of tight money and (forecast) large budget deficits in the United States has created unprecedentedly high real interest rates that are transmitted to other countries even under flexible exchange rates. Therefore, it is feared that an expansionary monetary policy, particularly a policy of lowering the interest rate, would depreciate the value of the yen still further, which would in turn aggravate trade conflicts.

The present task for Japanese macroeconomic policy is to find a way to foster economic recovery not only through export demand accompanying recovery abroad but also through domestic demand. Some economists of the OECD or the Group of Thirty recommend that Japan adopt a combination of tight monetary and easy fiscal policy. Such advice implies, however, that Japan should follow the worldwide trend towards low-growth-oriented policy. Instead, the first-best policy for Japan would be to pursue her domestic objectives. This might lead to further improvements in the current account of the balance of payments. In the long run, if the Japanese people have high saving propensities, it would not be unnatural for Japan to channel her ample savings to the world. Export surpluses are just a by-product of the saving/investment balance of the domestic economy.

However, this first-best policy would create more trade conflicts under current world economic conditions. In addition, in the short run, there seems to be excess capacity that can be utilized to produce more if stimulated by demand. Therefore, I would like to suggest the following eclectic policy combination. First, instead of the present practice of fiscal policy that works as a built-in destabilizer because expenditure is adjusted to tax revenue, which is reduced by recession, fiscal policy should be conducted in a more flexible manner. Second, if more flexible fiscal attitudes create some crowding-out effect, then it will be easier for the Bank of Japan to relax its monetary policy without fear of depreciating the yen further. Finally, it may be useful for the Bank of Japan to test the effect of lowering the official discount rate. Lowering the interest rate might not affect the value of the yen very much if the policy was already built in to the expectations of the public.

## NOTES

1 As an example of panic buying, housewives rushed grocery stores to buy toilet paper out of fear of a shortage of paper products.
2 Needless to say, I do not mean that the US standard for unemployment is the most desirable one, but merely that some adjustment is needed to compare unemployment statistics in different countries.
3 Quite recently, the monthly figures for the Japanese unemployment rate have begun to show record high levels. In December 1982 the seasonally adjusted unemployment rate was 2.41, and it has remained high, at around 2.6 to 2.8, since February, 1983. It is explained that reshuffling of samples makes this difference. Though the new figures seem to reflect the situation more realistically, some puzzles still remain.
4 Incidentally, the effect of inflationary expectations during the inter-war period was strong.
5 The job offers/applicants ratio indicates the ratio of job offers to applicants (excluding new graduates but including part-timers) through public employment security offices. Even though the actual number of jobs located through the offices is limited, this ratio serves as a responsive indicator of the labour market.

## BIBLIOGRAPHY


Friedman, Benjamin M., Friedman, Milton and Clausen, A. W. (1980) 'Postwar changes in the American financial markets', in Martin Feldstein (ed.), *American Economy in Transition*, Chicago, Ill., University of Chicago Press, 9–100.

Friedman, Milton (1968), 'The role of monetary policy', *American Economic Review*, 58, March, 1–17.

Friedman, Milton (1977), 'Nobel lecture: inflation and unemployment', *Journal of Political Economy*, 85(3), June, 451–472.

Hamada, Kōichi and Hayashi, Fumio (1983), 'Monetary policy in postwar Japan', paper presented at the First Internatioal Conference on Monetary Policy in Our Times, organized by the Bank of Japan, June.

Hamada, Kōichi and Kurosaka, Yoshirō (1983), 'The relationship between output and unemployment in Japan: Okun's law in comparative perspective', paper presented at the International Seminar on Macroeconomics, Maison de Sciences de l'Homme, Paris.

Horiuchi, Akiyoshi (1980), *Nihon no kin'yū seisaku* [monetary policy in Japan], Tōyō Keizai Shimposha.

Ishi, Hiromitsu (1976), *Zaisel kōzō no antei kōka* [the built-in stabilizer effect], Keiso Shobō.

Kaizuka, Keimei (1967), 'Keizai antei to kin'yū seisaku' [Economic stabilization and monetary policy], in K. Kinoshita (ed.), *Keizai antei to zaisei kin'yū seisaku* [economic stabilization and fiscal and monetary policy], Nihon Keizai Shimbun.

Katō, Hirotaka (1979), 'Keizai riron ni okeru gōriteki kitaikeisei no saikentō' [rational expectations in economic theory], *Kindai keizaigaku*, series 49–54, Tōyō Keizai Shimpōsha.

Komiya, Ryūtarō (1976) 'Shōwa 48–49 nen no infureeshon go gen'in' [the causes of the 1973–74 inflation], *Keizaigaku ronshū*, 46, April.

Komiya, Ryūtarō and Suzuki, Yoshio (1977), 'Inflation in Japan', in L. Krause and W. S. Salant (eds), *World-Wide Inflation*, Washington, DC, Brookings Institution.

Modigliani, Franco and Papademos, L. D. (1980), 'The structure of financial markets and the monetary mechanisms', in *Controlling Monetary Aggregates*, III, Federal Reserve Bank of Boston, Conference Series No. 23.

Phelps, Edmund S. (1967), 'Phillips curve, expectations of inflation and optimal unemployment over time', *Economica*, 34(5), August, 254–281.

Pigott, C. (1978), 'Rational expectations and counter-cyclical monetary policy: the Japanese experience', *Federal Reserve Bank of San Francisco Economic Review*, Summer, 6–22.

Seo, Jun'ichirō and Takahashi, Wataru (1980), *Gendai Nihon kin'yū ron*, Tōyō Keizai Shimpōsha, 1974; English translation, *Money and Banking in Contemporary Japan*, New Haven, Conn., Yale University Press.

Seo, Jun'ichirō and Takahashi, Wataru (1982), 'Gōriteki kitai to manee sapurai seisaku' [rational expectations and the money supply policy], *Kin'yū kenkyū shiryō*, 11, Bank of Japan, February, 37–70.

Taira, Kōji (1983), 'Labor markets in Japan: how unemployment is minimised', BEBR Discussion Paper No. 916, University of Illinois (Champaign–Urbana).

Taniuchi, Mitsuru (1982), *Atarashii manetarizumu no keizaigaku* [the new economics of monetarism], Tōyō Keizai Shimpōsha.

Taniuchi, Mitsuru and Hatanaka, Michio (1982), 'Nichibei ryōkoku ni okeru kaheijuyō kansu no anteisei ni tsuite' [the stability of the money demand function in Japan and the United States], *Gendai keizai*, autumn, 124–135.

Ueda, Kazuo (1982), 'Kashidashi shijō to kin'yū seisaku' [the loan market and monetary policy], paper presented at a Bank of Japan research meeting on monetary policy.

Yashiro, Naohiro (1982), *Josei rōdō no keizai bunseki: mō hitotsu no meizaru kakumei* [an economic analysis of women workers: another subtle revolution], Tōyō Keizai Shimpōsha.

# 10 Inflation in the United Kingdom

*M. J. ARTIS and M. K. LEWIS**

## I INTRODUCTION

Inflation experience in the United Kingdom in the past decade or so affords a rich variety of economic pathologies. Figure 10.1 plots the time series of inflation rates over the period 1970–82, calculated for three different price indices – the GDP deflator, the consumer price index (implicit deflator of consumers' expenditure) and the deflator of total final expenditure (TFE). Each one of the series tells a similar story, in that inflation peaks in the mid-1970s, then falls to a trough in the late 1970s, only to re-emerge strongly at the end of the decade, before dying away to a new low late in 1982. Current forecasts suggest that while this new low will give way to some resurgence of inflation, the acceleration this time may not be very great.[1] There are, it will be seen, some differences in both levels and timing between the three series. In particular, the mid-1970s' increase in inflation is apparent first in the TFE deflator, although the eventual peak rate is highest in terms of the GDP deflator, whereas the reduction in inflation through the late 1970s is somewhat more pronounced in the TFE and CPI deflators than it is in the GDP deflator. Finally, in the most recent disinflationary phase, the TFE deflator can be seen to lead the downturn.

Very roughly, these differences seem to coincide with the outlines of an inflation 'story' that focuses on the import price explosion of the mid-1979s, closely followed by an induced wage explosion, and then by a deceleration due in part to domestic incomes policies, pursued in turn by a rebound (assisted by a further oil-price rise in 1979) and ending up with the severe disinflation of the Thatcher period, during which exchange rate appreciation was a significant factor, along with steeply rising unemployment, in reducing inflation. Figure 10.2 plots, on an annual basis, the 'Phillips curves' observations for the period 1969–82 along with forecast values for 1983 and 1984; of this, more later.

The richness of this inflation experience would justify tomes of explanation, but the plan of this chapter is necessarily more modest. In Section II, we discuss a 'proximate accounting' of inflation (measured by the consumers' expenditure deflator), by way of introduction to Sections III and IV, where we examine the evolution of ideas about acceptable explanations of price and wage developments. Drawing on and integrating that work, we go on to present new estimates of price and wage equations for the United Kingdom. We then look

* We gratefully acknowledge the assistance of Helen Wickens and John McLaren in the preparation of this chapter.

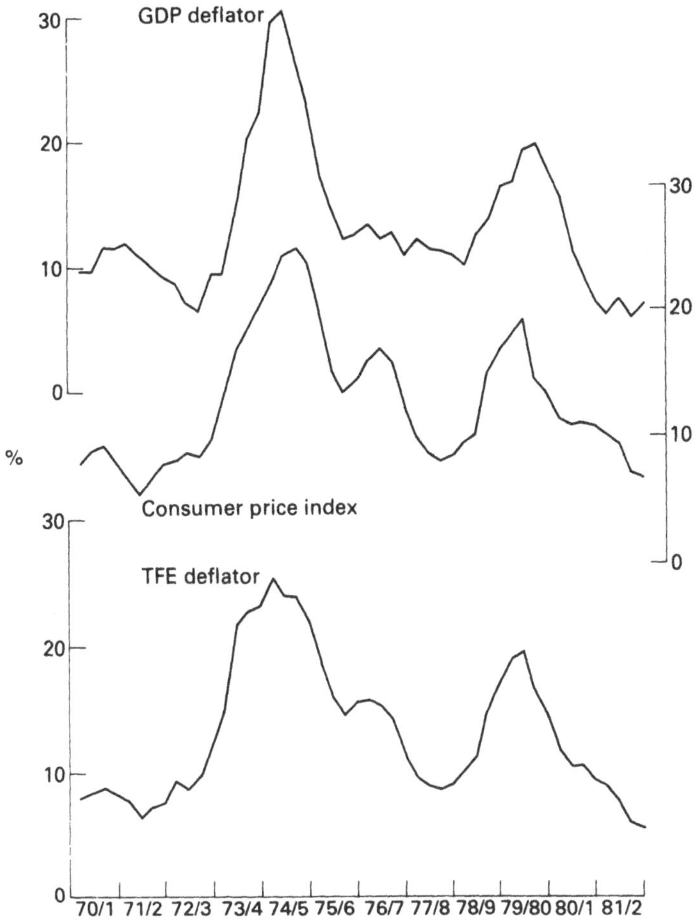


**Figure 10.1** Inflation in the UK.

at aspects of the monetary approach for purposes of comparison. In the final section there are a few conclusions.

## II A 'PROXIMATE ACCOUNTING' FRAMEWORK

In Table 10.1, we show figures that account for consumer price inflation over the period in a proximate sense. The table is based on weighting together rates of increase in employment costs, non-employment costs (including profit margins), import prices and indirect taxes, using as weights the coefficients given in the government's summary input–output tables for 1973.[2] These tables show the breakdown of the final output category consumers' expenditure in terms of income from employment, gross profits and other trading incomes, imports of goods and services, taxes on expenditure less subsidies and a final category 'sales by final demand'. The weight of the last category is very small

**Table 10.1** *Proximate accounting for inflation[a] in the United Kingdom, 1970/1–1980/1 (per cent)*

| | *1970/1* | *1971/2* | *1972/3* | *1973/4* | *1974/5* | *1975/6* | *1976/7* | *1977/8* | *1978/9* | *1979/80* | *1980/1* |
|---|---|---|---|---|---|---|---|---|---|---|---|
| Increase in CPI[b] | 8.4 | 6.6 | 8.6 | 17.3 | 23.6 | 15.7 | 15.2 | 8.8 | 12.8 | 16.0 | 10.9 |
| *Contribution to inflation:* | | | | | | | | | | | |
| Increase in employment costs | 2.5 | 4.1 | 2.7 | 7.2 | 11.2 | 3.5 | 3.2 | 3.9 | 5.6 | 7.4 | 3.8 |
| Increase in non-employment costs | 3.2 | 3.9 | 2.6 | 0.8 | 4.3 | 5.0 | 7.4 | 3.4 | 2.6 | 3.4 | 2.5 |
| Increase in import prices | 0.8 | 0.6 | 5.0 | 9.0 | 3.0 | 4.7 | 3.0 | 0.6 | 1.6 | 2.1 | 1.1 |
| Increases in indirect taxes | 0.2 | 0.4 | –0.1 | –0.3 | 3.8 | 3.1 | 4.4 | 1.6 | 4.7 | 4.2 | 2.6 |
| Unidentified | 1.7 | –2.4 | –1.6 | 0.6 | 1.3 | –0.6 | –2.8 | –0.7 | –1.7 | –1.1 | 0.9 |

*Notes:* a For details see text.
b Implicit deflator of the consumers' expenditure series.

*Source:* Central Statistical Office, *Economic Trends*, Annual Supplement.

and it has been ignored for the purposes of Table 10.1. Price indices corresponding to the several input categories were constructed from data on factor incomes and expenditures. The former were used to yield employment costs per unit of output and, as a residual, non-employment factor costs; the latter yield the implicit deflator of imports of goods and services and an index of indirect taxes, measured as the ratio of indirect tax revenues at current prices to real output.[3] The explicand was the rate of change of the implicit deflator of consumers' expenditure.

The framework used is thus not itself an identity, and although the 'explanation' is certainly only proximate, it does not exactly exhaust the identified rate of increase in consumer prices. However, it seemed close enough to merit attention.

What does the table show? First of all, it does seem to tally with the outlines of the story already mentioned in the introduction. The import price surge of 1972/3 and 1973/4 is clearly identified, for example, as is the wage explosion of 1974/5 and the rebound in 1979/80. A profit 'push' seems indicated in the wake of the wage explosion, as might be expected. Perhaps more surprising is the contribution to inflation identified with net indirect taxes, which is substantial in the three years 1975–7 and again in 1979 and 1980. It may be recalled that, by construction, our index of indirect taxes would demonstrate a positive contribution to inflation even if tax rates were only indexed, and on these grounds alone we would expect to see indirect taxes contributing 15 per cent of yearly CPI inflation (this being the input–output weight of indirect taxes in consumers' expenditure). It is evident, however, that in many of the years in question the contribution of indirect taxes was in fact much greater than this: this is particularly true of 1979, but also of 1976, 1977, 1980 and 1981. In each of these years except 1976, conventional indirect tax rates were increased, in 1979 substantially; and in 1976 the national insurance surcharge was introduced, which, by a quirk of British national accounting procedures, is treated as an indirect tax (even though the regular national insurance contributions are not so treated).

Evidence from a proximate accounting framework should not be pushed too far: inflation, after all, is a general rise in prices (costs), and in steady inflation all costs and prices will be rising in line with one another without implying causality. Stein (1982) has recently strictured 'Keynesians' for falling into the trap of merely redescribing inflation by resorting to explanations of this type.

With this observation, we turn to a consideration of wage and price equations. These purport to be more than 'mere accounting identities', although the determinants may be proximate ones standing in for many factors. However, we want to try to sidestep these issues and concentrate on the way the modelling of wage and price behaviour has changed in response to the course of inflation over the past decade. We begin with pricing equations.

## III PRICING EQUATIONS

Standard practice in specifying and estimating pricing equations was set, not long ago, by the 'normal-cost' hypothesis, first clearly set out by Nield (1963).

According to this hypothesis, firms would set prices on the basis of a mark-up over the unit cost of producing a 'normal' rate of output. In the specification of the hypothesis, a good deal of care was typically expended on the measurement of normal output levels; as an alternative, coefficients were imposed – rather in the style of the proximate accounting exercise of the previous section – on the basis of information derived from the input–output tables. The latter approach was embodied in the wholesale price equation used in HM Treasury's macroeconometric model as late as 1982 (see Whittaker and Davis, 1983).

Within the normal-cost paradigm, the chief area of dispute was whether or not size of the normal mark-up reflected demand influences.[4] The strong form of the hypothesis held that such influences were insignificant and, in a series of apparently exhaustive tests, Godley and Nordhaus (1972) and Coutts, Godley and Nordhaus (1978) sought to show that the strong form of the hypothesis was supported. Later, Smith (1982) argued that these investigations had neglected crucial specifications of the hypothesis and that, when these were tested, demand influences were found to be statistically significant, though not numerically powerful.

The dominance of the normal-cost paradigm has been on the wane for the last decade, however. The course of output, since 1973, and the onset of the unparalleled post-war recession in 1979–80 made the estimation of 'normal' levels of output an increasingly difficult and arbitrary business. As a result, investigators appear to have all but abandoned the practice of normalizing output levels and the two-stage procedure whereby costs were first normalized and only then entered in the price equation. Instead, the prevailing practice is to enter actual unit cost variables in the price equation – albeit at various lags. The results, on a suitable interpretation of the coefficients obtained, may still be interpreted within the normal-cost paradigm, but necessarily in a more open manner than heretofore: it is clear, for example, that the lag distributions of prices on costs represent a convolution of expectational, normalizing and administrative or institutional features; it is also clear that variations in foreign cost variables tend to be dominated by the exchange rate and this makes it difficult to distinguish between the contribution of complementary and of competitive import prices to UK price formation. A second main feature of applied econometrics in this area that has helped reduce the dominance of the normal-cost hypothesis is the power exercised over empirical work by the 'law of one price'/'global monetarist'/'Scandinavian model' prejudice that domestic price setting in a small(ish) open economy should closely reflect the influence of international competition.

The high-water mark of fascination with this idea has now been passed. Indeed, experience has dealt its more extreme manifestations a decisive blow. The law of one price starts from the undeniably reasonable proposition that (but for transport costs and border taxes) the price of identical goods will be the same everywhere in the world in common currency; it moves, in the applications we are concerned with, to the refutable propositions that, for the export price measures actually available for a country like the UK, the 'weight' on world prices will be very high, if not unity, and that on domestic costs small, if not negligible, and further to the proposition that, by way of a transmission process linking traded goods, world prices will also play a key role in the formation of domestic price indices such as wholesale and retail prices. The London Business School, among the major forecasting bodies in the UK, has been particularly closely associated with this general line of argument.

In 1980, the Bank of England released a discussion paper (Brown, Enoch and Mortimer-Lee, 1980) that summarized the state of knowledge in the UK at that time on the interrelationships between costs and prices.[5] It focused particularly on the role of foreign prices and the exchange rate in domestic price formation. Table 10.2 lists in the 1980 column the weights on foreign and domestic price or cost[6] variables appearing in the pricing relationship used by the major UK modellers at that time, upon which the Brown *et al.* study focused. This is complemented, in the 1983 column, by comparable information drawn from more recent model manuals. Comparison of the two columns shows evidence of a reduction in the weight given to the law of one price in the modellers' price equations, much the most marked in the case of the London Business School. The reason is not difficult to find: the rise in *relative* UK export prices that was so marked a feature of 1980 and 1981 took them, at the peak, to a level more than 40 per cent above that of 1976, hardly confirmation of the law of one price!

In retrospect, there seems little reason for the special fascination that the law of one price held in this period. A speculation that would have provided a rationalization would be that the influence of foreign competitive prices became greater over the 1970s; when this proposition has been studied, however, it has been shown to be unsupported. Ormerod (1980), for example, finds that, if anything, the post-floating period features higher domestic and lower foreign weights in export price equations than the earlier fixed exchange

**Table 10.2** *Foreign and domestic cost/price weights in the modellers' pricing equations*

| | *1980* | | *1983* | |
|---|---|---|---|---|
| | *Foreign* | *Domestic* | *Foreign* | *Domestic* |
| *Export prices:* | | | | |
| Treasury | 0.52 | 0.48 | 0.50 | 0.50 |
| LBS | 1.00 | 0 | 0.70 | 0.30 |
| NIESR | 0.48 | 0.49 | 0.50 | 0.47 |
| *Wholesale prices:* | | | | |
| Treasury | 0.37 | 0.76 | 0.23 | 0.77 |
| LBS | 0.69 | 0.28 | 0.48 | 0.45 |
| NIESR | 0.50 | 0.43 | 0.42 | 0.58 |

*Sources:* 1980 – as reported in Brown, Enoch and Mortimer-Lee (1980). Model manuals for 1979. 1983 – for Treasury, export prices are from HM Treasury *Macroeconomic Model Technical Manual 1982* (London, HMSO), wholesale prices from Whittaker and Davis (1983); for NIESR, see listing of *National Institute Model 6*, February 1983; and for LBS, see *The London Business School Quarterly Econometric Model of the United Kingdom Economy: Relationships in the Basic Model as at December 1982.*

rate period. It cannot of course be denied that foreign competition is significant; the course of inventories, output and employment in the 1979–82 period cannot be understood without assigning it great weight (e.g. Buiter and Miller, 1981) and there is evidence that the declining share of profits may be due to the interaction of foreign competition and domestic wage behaviour.[7] The difficulty seems to be that modellers, some of them anyway, misunderstood what are essentially conditions of equilibrium for behavioural parameters. It is particularly ironic that modelling of this kind was often typified as a 'Scandinavian' or 'Nordic' model, since the normative origin of this model as a means of preserving internal and external equilibrium through the use of incomes policies is so clear.

## IV THE WAGE EQUATION

The observations plotted in Figure 10.2 suggest that, whatever else the so-called 'monetarist experiment' of the 1980s may have done, it has restored the Phillips curve. As Nickell (1982) recently put it, 'few would deny that the recent fall in the rate of change of nominal wages is related to the unprecedented rise in unemployment'; although this in itself does not establish whether it is the level or the *change* in the level that people think is important, at least some effect of the pressure of demand now seems plainly visible.

**Figure 10.2** Unemployment and inflation: United Kingdom, 1968/9–1982/3 and forecasts for 1983/4

This was not always so, even in quite recent British experience. Not even when the observers were predisposed to the view that the pressure of demand was highly significant was it possible to establish this with great conviction. The work of the Manchester Inflation Workshop is a case in point. Perhaps the most sophisticated statement of the augmented Phillips curve to emerge in the mid-1970s was that by Parkin, Sumner and Ward (1976), but even here the significance of the unemployment term was tenuous.[8] Nor did Sumner's later work (Sumner, 1978) do much to remove the suspicion that finding a significant pressure of demand term was a difficult and laborious exercise, the true significance tests on the results of which should have been accordingly far more stringent than those implied by conventional t-tests. Elsewhere, Malcolm Sawyer (1982) has already noted that the predictive ability of the Parkin–Sumner–Ward (PSW) equation left much to be desired. Omitting irrelevant variables and rounding off, the PSW equation can be reduced to

$$\dot{w} = 6.00 - 2.00\ u + \dot{p}_c,$$

where $\dot{w}$ is the rate of wage inflation, $u$ is the unemployment rate and $\dot{p}_c$ is the expected rate of inflation. So with stylized 1982 values of $u$ (12 per cent) and $\dot{p}_c$ (10 per cent), wage inflation would be predicted to proceed at a rate of *minus* 8 per cent. The same point can be re-expressed in a different way, in terms of the required increase in the natural rate of unemployment. Treating the coefficient on $u$ as an unbiased estimate of that on the natural rate,[9] it is easily calculated that the natural rate must have risen by some 9 points since the period of estimation to generate a wage inflation of 10 per cent when prices are expected to rise by something of the same order. Since the natural rate of unemployment was estimated by PSW at 1.7 per cent,[10] this implies a 1982 value of about 11 per cent.

Difficulty in estimating pressure of demand terms continued to dog empirical work on the determination of wages through the mid to late 1970s (Artis, 1981). One response questioned the status of unemployment as an index of excess demand, arguing in particular that changes in the unemployment benefits regime exerted significant effects on unemployment, producing an unstable mapping over time. The work of Sumner (1978) and more recently that of Minford (1981) is in this vein, introducing the ratio of unemployment benefits to earnings to shift the Phillips curve to the right. Another reaction to the 'breakdown' of the Phillips relation was work on the rival 'real wage target hypothesis', which traced wage inflation to a discrepancy between the real wage aspirations of the labour movement and actual real wage achievement. Its hallmark is the inclusion of the lagged real wage as a determining variable, rather than the absence of unemployment (which may, after all, play a role in bargaining models); but the presence of the lagged real wage can alternatively be rationalized as providing a supplementary indicator of excess demand (Henry, 1981). A third reaction, exemplified in the work of Wren-Lewis (1983), attempts to dispense with the excess demand indicator approach, substituting for it a reduced form of supply and demand variables. In this context, output has been shown to exert significant negative (but long-lagged) effects on wage inflation.

## Table 10.3 *Wage equations – some recent examples*

| *Study* | *Sample period and dependent variable*[b] | *Expected inflation* | *Lagged Endogenous* | *Pressure of Demand* | *Retention ratio, tax terms* | *Real wages* | *Other terms* | *Statistics of fit* |
|---|---|---|---|---|---|---|---|---|
| | | *Independent variables*[a] | | | | | | |
| Capella and Ormerod (1981), equation (4) | 1971Q3–1980Q2 (quarterly) $\Delta lnERPR$ | $+0.599\Delta lnP^{e}_{R}$<br>(4.11) | $+0.401\Delta lnEPR_{-1}$<br>(imposed) | $-0.150\Delta\Delta lnU_{-1}$<br>(2.72)<br>$-0.063lnU_{-1}$<br>(3.80) | $+0.273\Delta lnRR$<br>(2.00)<br>$-0.329\Delta lnRR_{-1}$<br>(2.62) | $-0.375\ ln(ERPR/P_R)_{-1}$ | $+0.0015t$<br>(1.86) | $\bar{R}^2 = 0.516$<br>DW = 2.57<br>LM (4) = 9.30 |
| Sumner and Ward (1983), equation (15) | 1958Q3–1980Q4 (quarterly) $\Delta lnw_w$ | $+0.71\hat{P}^{e}$<br>(8.59)[c]<br>$+0.29\Delta lnP_{e-1}$<br>(imposed) | | $-0.96\ U\%$<br>(3.49) | $-0.32\Delta ln(1-t_e)$<br>(3.38)<br>$-0.68\Delta lnRR$<br>(imposed) | | $-9.79\ I$<br>(4.85)<br>$+28.00D7802$<br>(7.27) | $\bar{R}^2 = 0.77$<br>DW = 1.71 |
| Grubb, Jackman and Layard (1982), Table 1 | 1957–1980 (annual) $\Delta lw_h$ | $+0.92\Delta lnP_{c-1}$<br>(2.9) | $+0.08\Delta lnw_{h-1}$<br>(imposed) | $-2.01\ U\%^*$<br>(2.3) | | | | $\bar{R}^2 = 0.33$<br>DW = 1.49<br>SE% = 3.75 |
| Grubb (1983), Table 4, equation (4) | 1966–1980 (annual) $\Delta lnw_w$ | $+0.57\Delta lnP_{A-1}$ | $+0.43\Delta lw_{w-1}$<br>(imposed) | $-5.44$ | | $-0.50\ (W_w/P_A)_{-1}$<br>(2.2) | $+0.028t$<br>(3.4) | SE% = 2.7 |
| | | | | Output | | | | |
| Wren-Lewis (1983) equation (7) | 1966Q1–1978Q4 (quarterly) $\Delta\ ln\ ERPR$ | $+0.32\Delta lnP_{c-2}$<br>(1.9)<br>$+0.22\Delta ln(P_R-RR)_{-1}$<br>(1.7)<br>$\Sigma = 0.54$ | $-0.46\Delta lnERPR_{-1}$<br>(3.1)<br>$-0.32\Delta lnERPR_{-2}$<br>(2.1)<br>$-0.35\Delta lnERPR_{-3}$<br>(2.3)<br>$-0.27\Delta lnERPR_{-4}$<br>(2.0)<br>$\Sigma = -1.40$ | $+0.10lnY_{p-6}$<br>(0.5)<br>$+0.54lnY_{p-7}$<br>(2.8)<br>$+0.35lnY_{p-8}$<br>(1.9)<br>$+0.13lnY_{p-9}$<br>(0.8)<br>$\Sigma = 1.12$ | | $-0.37ln(ERPR.t'_e/P_c)_{-6}$<br>(2.6)<br>$-0.15ln\ (ERPR.t'_e/P_c)_{-7}$<br>(1.0)<br>$+0.04ln(ERPR.t'_e/P_c)_{-8}$<br>(0.3)<br>$-0.12ln\ (ERPR.RR/P_R)_{-8}$<br>$\Sigma = 0.60$ | | $\bar{R}^2 = 0.51$<br>$\chi$ (4) = 7.0 |

*Definitions:* Variable definitions are as follows. *Wages*: *ERPR* = average private sector earnings per head, $w_w$ = weekly earnings and $w_h$ = hourly earnings; *prices*: $P_R$ = retail price, $P_c$ = deflator of consumers' expenditure, $P_A$ = average of consumers' and producers' prices, $P_e$ = employers' (wholesale domestic sales) prices, $P_s$ = implicit deflator of private sector (non-oil) output; [a] indicates a forecast value, a superscript 'e' a Carlson–Parkin expectation (based on CBI data) and * in Sumner–Ward means the value of this variable is set to zero up to end–1969; *unemployment*: $u$ = unemployment in 000s, $U\%$, the percentage rate of unemployment and * in Grubb, Jackman and Layard indicates a transformation in which $u$ is taken as the sum of its 1960–72 average value plus deviation from trend; *retention ratio, tax terms*: *RR* is the retention ratio, $t_e$ is the ratio of employers' national insurance contribution to average wages and * in Sumner–Ward indicates value set to zero up to end-1970, while $t'_e$ is the ratio of private sector labour costs (inclusive of NIS, etc.) to private sector wage costs; *output*: $Y_p$ is private sector (non-oil) output; *other terms*: *D7802* is a dummy variable for 1978Q2, *I* an incomes policy dummy for 1976Q3–1977Q2, *t* a time trend. t-ratios are given in brackets.

*Notes:* a Constant and seasonals are omitted.
b The dependent variable in estimation is in ΔΔ form for Capella and Ormerod, Grubb, Jackman and Layard and Grubb, and statistics of fit relate to this.

Examples of these approaches to wage equations are shown in Table 10.3. Those due to Grubb (1983) and Grubb, Jackman and Layard (1982) and also to Sumner and Ward (1983) are representative of the augmented Phillips curve approach. The latter represents an attempt to update the Parkin–Sumner–Ward equation. Unemployment has a negative and significant sign in the revised version, although the homogeneity of the total sample period appears to be in doubt. The new estimate of the natural rate of unemployment emerges at less than 4 per cent! The Capella–Ormerod (1981) equation represents an avowedly more eclectic approach. Once again, unemployment has significant negative effects. Finally, the Wren-Lewis (1983) equation demonstrates the reduced-form approach in which output exerts significant negative effects with a lag of two years.

The constraint that wage inflation be homogeneous in expected inflation is now widely accepted in empirical work (although not confirmed in Wren-Lewis' case); and the role of the lagged real wage is also now widely recognized (although Sumner and Ward, somewhat exceptionally, report finding no role for it). Notably though, in this recent crop of wage equation estimates (itself a parsimonious selection from a wider field), pressure of demand terms are once again significant.

## V A WAGE–PRICE SYSTEM

The wage equations reported above were estimated to 1980 and we wished to take advantage of the additional observations since then to see how well they survive the disinflation experience of 1981 and 1982. At the same time, it seemed a worthwhile exercise to try to integrate the wages work with some features of the prices equations. These considerations prompted us to estimate a 'compromise' wage equation,[11] employing inflation expectations derived in each of two ways – from an autoregressive equation and from a cost-based price equation.

Figure 10.3 plots the basic data used, prices being the retail price index while the wages series is hourly earnings in manufacturing. The approach, as we have said, is necessarily eclectic, with the independent variables being expected inflation, pressure of demand terms, the lagged real wage and the retention ratio. An additional feature of the equation to be estimated is inertia, represented by the lagged dependent variable; in order to preserve homogeneity of wage and price inflation, the coefficient on the inertia term is imposed at 1 *minus* that on the inflation expectations term. Thus the wage equation to be estimated can be represented as

$$\dot{w} = \alpha_0 + \alpha_1\dot{p} + (1 - \alpha_1)\,\dot{w}_{-1} + \alpha_2(w/p)_{-i} + \alpha_3 x_{-i} + \alpha_4 RR_{-i},$$

where $\dot{w}$ stands for four-quarter overlapping logarithmic differences, $\dot{p}$ is an expected inflation rate, $p$ is the retail price index, $x$ a vector of variables representing excess demand and $RR$ the retention ratio. Because of the inertia term $\dot{w}_{-1}$ the equation can be estimated with $\Delta\dot{w}$ as the dependent variable. The general-to-specific methodology followed here involves a testing-down from an

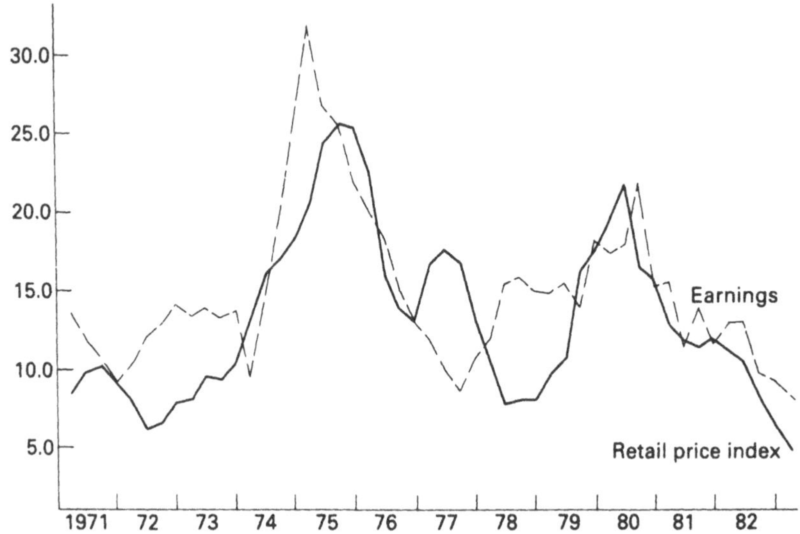


**Figure 10.3** Wage and price inflation, 1971Q1–1983Q1 (*percentage* increase on same period in previous year)

*Source:* Data are from OECD *Main Economic Indicators*, wherein old and new series of average hourly earnings (mfg.) have been linked.

initial specification, which makes generous allowance for the determining variables to appear at various lags and in two orders of difference.

Inflation expectations are determined simultaneously and a systems method of estimation (NL3SLS) is employed. We consider first the results obtained for the equation determining the inflation expectations term. Table 10.4 presents the results of OLS and NL3SLS estimation of an unrestricted fourth-order autoregressive equation as well as those derived from a more standard 'cost-based' approach. The estimate of the autoregressive scheme provides a tolerable representation of the inflation process, although most of the weight is taken by the first lagged term. In principle, a restricted form of the equation would be more desirable, with $\beta_0 = 0$, and the sum of $\beta_{1i}$ $\beta_4 = 1$; these restrictions would enable a steady-state interpretation of the equation to be given and, indeed, appear data-acceptable.[12] However, the unrestricted estimate provides an acceptable 'rule of thumb' inflation forecasting equation for use in conjunction with the wage equation. In earlier work, Ormerod (1982) showed that there was little gain in using quasi-rational inflation forecasts (drawn from a large model) over the predictions of such a rule of thumb. However, in part B of Table 10.4, we present the results of a cost-based inflation equation, which might be seen as quasi-rational, with a view to using its prediction in the wage equation as an alternative. The equation provides a better explanation (in terms of SEE%) of inflation than the autoregressive scheme and has stationary steady-state properties that appear reasonable, although in a growth state the coefficients estimated appear to imply a steady reduction in profit margins. The earnings variable has not been scaled by

**Table 10.4** *Equations for inflation expectations*

(A) *Autoregressive scheme*

$\dot{p} = \beta_0 + \beta_1\dot{p}_{-1} + \beta_2\dot{p}_{-2} + \beta_3\dot{p}_{-3} + \beta_4\dot{p}_{-4}$

| | $\beta_0$ | $\beta_1$ | $\beta_2$ | $\beta_3$ | $\beta_4$ | SEE% |
|---|---|---|---|---|---|---|
| OLS | 0.03<br>(2.39) | 1.33<br>(7.47) | −0.34<br>(1.25) | −0.24<br>(0.88) | 0.08<br>(0.50) | 12.8 |
| NL3SLS | 0.02<br>(2.50) | 1.35<br>(8.60) | −0.45<br>(1.60) | −0.13<br>(0.40) | 0.06<br>(0.36) | |

(B) *Cost-based approach*

$$\dot{p} = \beta_0 + \beta_1 w_{-4} + \beta_2 p_{m_{-4}} + \beta_3 t_{-4} + \beta_4\Delta_4 w_{-1} + \beta_5\Delta_4 w_{-3} + \beta_6\Delta_4 p_{m_{-1}} + \beta_7\Delta_4 t_{-1} + \beta_8\frac{(p)}{w_{-4}} + \beta_9\Delta_4 p_{-1}$$

| | $\beta_0$ | $\beta_1$ | $\beta_2$ | $\beta_3$ | $\beta_4$ | $\beta_5$ |
|---|---|---|---|---|---|---|
| OLS | 0.42<br>(2.73) | −0.13<br>(2.17) | 0.07<br>(1.61) | 0.02<br>(0.53) | 0.26<br>(2.70) | −0.18<br>(1.75) |
| NL3SLS | 0.38<br>(3.43) | −0.09<br>(2.26) | 0.04<br>(1.44) | 0.01<br>(0.58) | 0.32<br>(4.11) | −0.26<br>(3.47) |

| | $\beta_6$ | $\beta_7$ | $\beta_8$ | $\beta_9$ | SEE% |
|---|---|---|---|---|---|
| OLS | 0.009<br>(0.27) | −0.02<br>(0.83) | −0.75<br>(4.50) | 0.50<br>(4.42) | 10.60 |
| NL3SLS | 0.02<br>(0.84 | −0.03<br>(1.43) | −0.73<br>(5.77) | 0.54<br>(5.71) | |

*Notes:* Estimation period: 1972Q3–1982Q2; $\dot{p} = \Delta_4 ln\ p = \Delta_4 p$; all variables in logs. $w$ = earnings; $p_m$ = import prices; $t$ = index of indirect tax (ratio of GDP at factor costs *minus* GDP at market prices to GDP at factor cost). SEE% = equation standard error in per cent of mean.

output or trend output, but the results suggest that such scaling is unnecessary (and there is indeed essentially no trend in output over the period in question).

Table 10.5 gives the results for the wage equation using each of the inflation expectations schemes. The parameter values obtained compare closely, whichever scheme is employed. It will be observed that, among the pressure of demand terms, the coefficient on lagged unemployment is estimated to be positive. This must be read, however, in conjunction with the significant right-signed estimates obtained for the parameter values of the vacancy variables ($V$). Taken together, the vacancy and unemployment terms clearly provide, for example, a negative influence on wage inflation in the 1980–2 disinflation period.[13] The lagged real wage term is significantly negative throughout. The retentions ratio is also significant in differenced form, and its negative sign is consistent with the reasoning that variations in the retention ratio affect the supply price of labour.

The stability of the system was tested by re-estimation over a truncated

**Table 10.5** *Wage inflation estimates, 1972Q3–1982Q2 (NL3SLS)*

$$\Delta\Delta_4 w = \alpha_0 + \alpha_1(\dot{p} - \Delta_4 w_{-1}) + \alpha_2(w/p)_{-4} + \alpha_3 U_{-4} + \alpha_4 \Delta\Delta U + \alpha_5 V_{-4} + \alpha_6 \Delta_4 V + \alpha_7 \Delta\Delta_4 V + \alpha_8 \Delta_4 RR_{-1}$$

| Inflation expectations | $\alpha_0$ | $\alpha_1$ | $\alpha_2$ | $\alpha_3$ | $\alpha_4$ | $\alpha_5$ | $\alpha_6$ | $\alpha_7$ | $\alpha_8$ |
|---|---|---|---|---|---|---|---|---|---|
| Autoregressive | –1.90 | 0.70 | –0.73 | 0.11 | –0.40 | 0.21 | 0.03 | 0.06 | –0.40 |
| | (4.28) | (4.87) | (4.00) | (4.18) | (2.00) | (3.85) | (1.69) | (0.91) | (2.81) |
| Cost-based | –1.41 | 0.85 | –0.95 | 0.10 | –0.28 | 0.13 | –0.002 | –0.01 | –0.29 |
| | (6.13) | (6.17) | (6.26) | (5.80) | (2.31) | (5.34) | (0.14) | (0.19) | (3.73) |

**Table 10.6** *Out-of-sample forecasts*

| | *Predictions, by expected inflation model* | | |
|---|---|---|---|
| | *Autoregressive* | *Cost-based* | *Actual* |
| *Prices:* | | | |
| 1981 Q1 | 211.0 | 210.9 | 208.0 |
| Q2 | 218.7 | 217.0 | 218.1 |
| Q3 | 222.6 | 223.5 | 221.9 |
| Q4 | 227.2 | 227.2 | 227.4 |
| 1982 Q1 | 234.6 | 236.4 | 231.1 |
| Q2 | 243.0 | 241.4 | 238.5 |
| Correlation coefficient | 0.988 | 0.981 | |
| Regression coefficient[a] | 0.921 | 0.907 | |
| Theil's inequality coefficient[b] | 0.005 | 0.006 | |
| *Wages:* | | | |
| 1981 Q1 | 197.2 | 195.6 | 196.9 |
| Q2 | 207.7 | 201.7 | 200.5 |
| Q3 | 208.4 | 206.3 | 212.0 |
| Q4 | 209.5 | 208.0 | 216.9 |
| 1982 Q1 | 212.3 | 215.6 | 222.2 |
| Q2 | 223.6 | 224.7 | 226.5 |
| Correlation coefficient | 0.874 | 0.950 | |
| Regression coefficient[a] | 1.212 | 1.090 | |
| Theil's inequality coefficient[b] | 0.014 | 0.012 | |

*Notes:* a Actual on predicted.
b = $[\Sigma(P_i - A_i)^2/\Sigma A_i^2]$, where $P_i$, $A_i$ are actual and predicted values, respectively.

period (1972Q3–1980Q2), with 'out-of-sample' forecasting for the remaining eight quarters. Summary forecasting statistics are reported in Table 10.6.

Despite these 'predictions' and the general reappearance of pressure of demand variables in these and the earlier equations, we consider it naive simply to 'welcome back' the Phillips curve. It is hardly a satisfactory state of affairs when twenty or so years of wage-modelling experience turns out to suggest that the shifts in the relationship are more important than the slope of the Phillips curve itself. It may be instructive to consider this experience, though, in the light of the anticipations of the earliest architects of the Keynesian revolution: economists like Kalecki (1944), Robinson (1937), Worswick (1944). With a little licence, their view on the wage equation may be restated as follows: when the market is left to itself, unemployment exerts a clear influence on wage settlements (there is a Phillips effect); but when, as was then in prospect, the state takes upon itself the role of securing full employment, wages move into a state of quasi-'neutral equilibrium'. Full employment policies determine the real wage, given capital and state of technique, but the real wage is a quotient of nominal variables whose value is left without an anchor. Viewed in this light, recent experience is a retrogressive transition, reflecting the suspension of goverment support for full employment, back to a 'pre-Keynesian' environment. Transitions of this kind are necessarily confused and ambiguous, because simple 'announcements' do not change matters overnight and, in practice, the transition needs the support of a series of 'exemplary episodes'.[14] Put more shortly, all this is just to say that 'regime anticipation' is a forceful variable in wage determination. Since this has not been convincingly modelled, it seems more than likely that wage and price equations will continue to provide work for modellers in the years ahead.

## VI MONEY AND PRICES

The explanations of inflation we have considered so far are conventional 'Keynesian' accounts, and monetary influences have been excluded. There is no necessary contradiction between allowing a substantial role to 'money' in inflation and describing its determinants in the conventional way. The conventional account in essence comprises the intermediate variables or transmission mechanism, and is not necessarily in conflict with a 'monetarist' account. Monetary conditions need not even be the initiator of inflation. One-time changes in the price level coming from large changes in oil prices, devaluation of the currency, variations in indirect taxes or imposts and the removal of subsidies become inflation, as monetarists define it (as a sustained rate of increase of prices generally), if accommodated by increases in the quantity of money.

Before looking to the UK evidence, there is one aspect of the doctrine that 'money matters' with which we readily concur. Upheavals to the international monetary system in the early 1970s and the ultimate breakdown of fixed exchange rates severed the nexus that had previously existed in the longer run between domestic and international prices, so removing what probably was the anchor for nominal variables and altering the character of price and wage determination. In the more 'flexi-price' world ushered in, we should expect expectations of inflation to be more volatile so that relationships forged when those expectations were considered by the balance of payments position would break down. Domestic prices are potentially more susceptible to influence via domestic policies but they are also potentially more responsive to wages shocks and influences of the type modelled in earlier sections.

Of course, too, the transition to an average inflation rate of 14.0 per cent per annum in the decade after 1971 (compared with 4.6 per cent per annum in the decade before) would have been difficult to sustain unless accompanied by a nearly equivalent growth in the money supply.[15] However to take the monetary explanation further than this requires that monetary factors feature prominently in the two major cycles 1973–6 and 1979–82, which dominate the inflation experience shown in Figure 10.1. In terms of the quantity equation, the underlying requirements are that the demand for money and the real economy both be stable. Our own work (Artis and Lewis, 1984) suggests that the long-run stability of the demand for money seems to be as assured a fact as empirical economists can hope to get, provided that it is M2 that is in question. It does seem clear that short-run stability, especially that of M3, is in greater doubt.

Evidence submitted by the UK Treasury to the House of Commons Select Committee on the Treasury and Civil Service (HM Treasury, 1981), which sought to promote the 'monetary' explanation, ran in terms of M3 and contained admissions that long-run homogeneity of prices in money was not observed, and that additional variables (particularly 'world' variables) had to be relied upon. As in the earlier work of Coghlan (1980), a convincing correlation between money and incomes or prices necessitates assuming a substantial time lag – in the order of two years or more. Figure 10.4 shows that two years did indeed elapse between the peak rate of monetary growth in 1973 and the subsequent peak rate of increase in retail prices. Although both Coghlan and the Treasury included data for earlier years, it is fair to say in the light of Tarling and Wilkinson's (1977) earlier regressions that 'conformity to the monetarist hypothesis' rests heavily on the observations for 1972–6.

Since these studies pre-date the second inflation cycle, we endeavoured to replicate the Treasury's reduced-form relationship. The Treasury estimates, supplied to the House of Commons Committee in 1980, referred to an observation period comprising 'the last 15 years or so'. Our own sample period uses quarterly data for 1970Q1–1982Q2, with a subsample comprising data from 1970Q1–1979Q4. The money supply figures (£M3) were adjusted for disturbances caused by the supplementary Special Deposit ('corset') scheme and the Civil Service strike;[16] prices are represented by the retail price index. A slavish replication of the Treasury specification produced the following result for the full sample period:

$$\begin{aligned}\Delta lnP = &-0.25 + 0.04lnM_{-1} - 0.05lnP_{-1} + 0.37lnP_{-1} + 0.01\Delta lnM_{-4}\\ &(1.05) \quad (1.24) \qquad (1.5) \qquad (2.40) \qquad (1.15)\\ &+ 0.26\Delta lnM_{-12} + -0.001\Delta lnM_{-14} + \text{Seasonals}\\ &(2.16) \qquad (.71) \qquad\qquad \bar{R}^2 = 0.46\end{aligned}$$

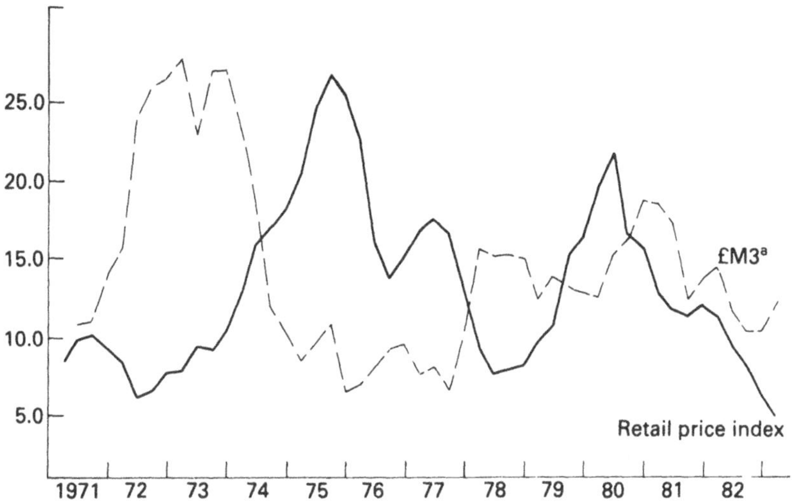


**Figure 10.4** Monetary growth and inflation, 1971Q1–1983Q1 (*percentage* increase on same period in previous year)

*Note:* a £M3 has been adjusted for a break of definition in 1981Q4, otherwise such breaks have been ignored.

Over the shorter sample period, the same specification produced a better fit, with higher levels of significance, viz:

$$\underset{}{\Delta lnP} = \underset{(3.04)}{-1.25} + \underset{(2.14)}{0.18 lnM_{-1}} - \underset{(3.13)}{0.14 lnP_{-1}} + \underset{(2.06)}{0.30 \Delta lnP_{-1}} - \underset{(1.40)}{0.28 lnM_{-1}}$$

$$+ \underset{(2.16)}{0.31 \Delta lnM_{-12}} - \underset{(.41)}{0.01 \Delta lnM_{-14}} + \text{Seasonals} \qquad \bar{R}^2 = 0.59$$

However, in neither case were the Treasury parameter values closely approached and the levels of significance and overall fit were certainly lower. A more liberal experimentation, testing down from a general to a more specific form using a mechanical criterion (based on their *t*-values) for eliminating variables, tended to produce results with the inertia term displaying instability. The results, in any case, inspire little confidence and suggest only that, although careful data mining can produce nice results, these are unlikely to be at all robust.

This rather confirms the experience of those who, relying on sterling M3, have recently made some poor inflation forecasts as a result. Such results are typically excused away by monetarists (e.g. Meltzer, 1981) because of distortions to sterling M3 induced by the 'corset' and, somewhat surprisingly for monetarist reasoning, shifts in the demand for that aggregate. Appeal is made, instead, to narrow money.

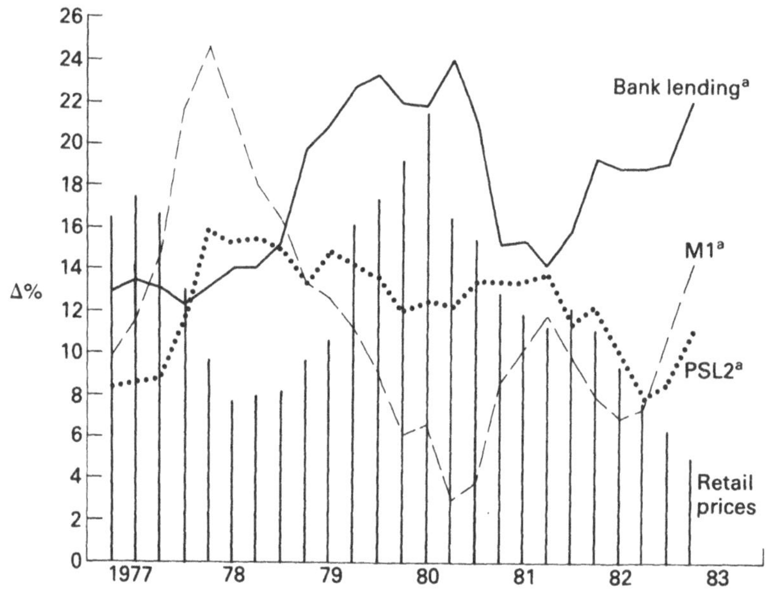


**Figure 10.5** Inflation and monetary indicators, 1977Q1–1983Q1 (*percentage* increase on same period in previous year)

*Note* a M1, private sector liquidity (PSL2) and bank lending to the UK private sector have all been adjusted for the break in definition in 1981.

Figure 10.5 graphs three altenative monetary indicators against inflation, concentrating on the 1977–82 cycle. The indicators are M1, private sector liquidity (PSL2) and bank lending to the UK private sector. PSL2 tells much the same story as sterling M3, except for the absence of a surge in 1980/1. For M1, a two-year lag must once again be advanced. On this interpretation, the accelerating rate of inflation of retail prices in 1979/80 is traced back to the 20 per cent per annum growth of money in 1977/8, in advance of the 1978/9 pay round. Disinflation in 1982 is presumably a delayed result of the marked slowing down of M1 growth in 1980. Only with the bank lending series is it possible to discern evidence of a shorter lag, but that aggregate is on the wrong side of the balance sheet for monetarists.

Thus it would seem that the monetary explanation of inflation in the UK continues to rely upon acceptance of a two-year or more lag between monetary growth and inflation, about which we remain to be persuaded. In the 1972–6 cycle, we see a case for viewing money supply injections as 'surprising' financial markets so that the portfolio rearrangements set in train by the excess money balances took time to feed through to commodity prices and wage settlements (Artis and Lewis, 1981, chs 2 and 3). It is another thing to expect a two-year lag to be repeated in an environment in which financial markets are more responsive and people are more watchful of monetary surprises, without any appeal to the influence upon prices of other arms of economic policy.

Here we would look to the arguments of the demand for money function and see monetary factors acting in a general way to constrain, or at least not sustain, inflation in the early 1980s – what the Bank of England (1983) recently called 'constrained Keynesianism': ' . . . a published M3 target as an overriding constraint upon policies which might otherwise fail to stop inflation reaccelerating to 20 per cent per annum and more' (p. 203). Certainly what began as an intended monetary disinflation by the Thatcher government in 1979 via sterling M3 became a 'Keynesian' fiscal and interest rate deflation since these were (much to Friedman's disgust) the instruments of monetary control.

On this view, the point of adopting and persevering with monetary targets was to make known, in a manner that was deliberately slightly obscure and roundabout, that the name of the government's counter-inflation game was 'no accommodation'. Monetary targets made it possible to slip this message in without pre-announcing the likely unemployment costs of the policy, a clear statement of which might have prevented it from ever being implemented.

## VII CONCLUSIONS

Our examination of inflation in the UK has been largely in terms of the recent history of experimentation with pricing and wage equations, with a background given by our 'proximate accounting' approach exploiting input–output and national accounts data. As well as reviewing the standard explanation of inflation in terms of the econometric work on both wage and price equations, we presented a system of our own incorporating elements of both. It would seem that price and wage equations can be estimated that have plausible properties, but past history holds out little hope about their durability. They involve little innovation in economic theory, but do incorporate some innovations in econometric practice. Indeed, in retrospect the deviant theoretical paths of the 'law of one price' in price equations, the neglect of demand in wage equations – seem to have been mistaken. General practice has on the whole returned to the *status quo ante*, though not without some important lessons having been learnt ('learning by losing' as Sumner and Ward, 1983, have pithily put it). The survival power of the conventional approach seems proof also against the rival monetary approach, though we argue that the explanations are not properly to be thought of as mutually exclusive.

Finally, we can see that the rationalization of monetary targets offered by the Bank of England has something in common with the early 'Keynesian' thinking about inflation and incomes policy, which we identified with Kalecki, Robinson and Worswick, among others. These architects of the Keynesian Revolution saw very clearly that the commitment of governments to use Keynesian techniques to maintain full employment left money wages and prices in a limbo by substantially removing wage determination from the economic arena and making it into a political issue. They saw that the appropriate solution is also political, in the form of an incomes policy. In practice, this advice has been only fitfully adopted. One way of resolving the problem is for governments to withdraw the full employment commitment, which is what, under cover of monetary targets, they have done. Then 'the market' will invent its own incomes policy in the form of the dole queue. Something like this seems to have happened.

## NOTES

1 In its May 1983 *Economic Review*, the National Institute of Economic and Social Research predicted consumer price inflation of 6.3 per cent through 1983 rising to 7.6 per cent through 1984. (By February 1984, the actual rate of inflation through 1983 was put at 6.5 per cent, and the 1984 forecast trimmed to 7.4 per cent.)
2 *Economic Trends*, June 1978, Summary Input–Output Table for 1973, Table 8, p. 109.
3 This measure in effect treats all indirect taxes 'as if' they were specific duties, so that if all indirect taxes were indexed to inflation it would increase *pari passu* with the CPI, and show a 'contribution to inflation' equivalent to its weighted value.
4 Given the procyclical behaviour of productivity and thus the countercyclical variation in actual unit labour costs, the hypothesis already allowed for the *actual* mark-up to vary with demand.
5 The Bank's interest was presumably not accidental. Soon afterwards the Medium Term Financial Strategy was unveiled to the public. Prophetically, the authors of the discussion paper consider the question of the *symmetry* of response of prices (and wages) to exchange rate changes, commenting, 'It may still be true, however, that wages may respond more slowly to an appreciation and the attendant slowing of inflation than to a quickening of inflation consequent upon depreciation. This . . . would suggest that, whilst the gain in cost competitiveness following depreciation might be short-lived, the deterioration in competitiveness resulting from appreciation could be painfully long' (Brown *et al.*, 1980, p. 25).
6 Although the definition of these variables differs between the modellers, the variation in definition between 1980 and 1983 for a given model is small and in all probability inconsequential.
7 An alternative hypothesis appeals to the recession as a force making for cuts in profit margins. Cowling (1983), however, has examined this with as much care as the data allow, and comes to the conclusion that recession effects on profit margins are likely to prove only transitory, and indeed that recessionary conditions are likely to make for an increase in the degree of monopoly in the longer run.
8 Unemployment was not significant in the unrestricted forms of the preferred equation, though it became so when restrictions were applied to the price and tax expectation terms.
9 This would be reasonable if the natural rate were constant during the estimation period and if we think of the equation as $\dot{w} = \alpha + \beta(u^* - u) + \gamma x$, because then the estimated constant term contains $\beta u^*$ and the coefficient on $u$ is an estimate of $\beta$.
10 About which they remark: 'This point estimate is hardly consistent with the common assertion that the cost of price stability is massive unemployment' (Parkin, Sumner and Ward, 1976, p. 12).
11 These estimates are a further development of results presented in Artis and Ormerod (1983).
12 In a revised version of Artis and Ormerod (1983) such a restricted version (for a slightly different sample period, however) has been estimated and found to be data-acceptable.
13 Nevertheless, it did not prove possible to represent the work done by the vacancy terms solely by added terms in unemployment without losing significant explanatory power.
14 Thus in the United Kingdom there have been a number of 'defeats' for the labour movement in recent years.
15 The growth rate of M1 increased from a decade average of 4.0 per cent per annum to an average of 12.6 per cent per annum after 1971.
16 The money stock figures were very kindly supplied to us by Adam Bennett of HM Treasury.

## REFERENCES

Artis, M. J. (1981), 'Is there a wage equation?', in A. S. Courakis, (ed.), *Inflation, Depression and Economic Policy in the West*, London, Mansell.

Artis, M. J. and Lewis, M. K. (1981), *Monetary Control in the United Kingdom*, Oxford, Philip Allan.

Artis, M. J. and Lewis, M. K. (1984), 'How unstable is the demand for money in the UK?', *Economica*, 51, May.

Artis, M. J. and Ormerod, P. (1983), 'Wage inflation in Western Europe', Henley Centre for Forecasting, Discussion Paper.

Bank of England (1983), 'Setting monetary objectives', *Quarterly Bulletin of the Bank of England*, 23(2), June.

Brown, R. N., Enoch, C. A. and Mortimer-Lee, P. D. (1980), 'The inter-relationships between costs and prices in the United Kingdom', Bank of England Discussion Paper No. 8, March.

Buiter, W. H. and Miller, M. H. (1981), 'The Thatcher experiment: the first two years', *Brookings Papers in Economic Activity*, 2, 315–367.

Capella, P. and Ormerod, P. (1981), 'Earnings and the pressure of demand in the UK', mimeo.

Coghlan, R. T. (1980), *The Theory of Money and Finance*, London, Macmillan.

Coutts, K., Godley, N. and Nordhaus, W. (1978), *Industrial Pricing in the United Kingdom*, Cambridge, Cambridge University Press.

Cowling, K. (1983), 'Excess capacity and the degree of collusion: oligopoly behaviour in the slump', *Manchester School of Economic & Social Studies*, 51, December, 341–359.

Godley, W. and Nordhaus, W. D. (1972), 'Pricing in the trade cycle', *Economic Journal*, 82, September, 853–882.

Grubb, P. (1983), 'Lagged output in the wage equation', mimeo, London School of Economics.

Grubb, P., Jackman, R. and Layard, R. (1982), 'Causes of the current stagflation', *Review of Economic Studies*, 99, July, 707–730.

Henry, S. G. B. (1981), 'Incomes policy and aggregate pay', in J. C. Fallick and R. F. Elliott, (eds), *Incomes Policy, Inflation and Relative Pay*, London, Allen & Unwin, 23–44.

HM Treasury (1981), 'Background to the government's economic policy', Third Report of the House of Commons Treasury and Civil Service Committee, *Monetary Policy*, Vol. III, Appendices.

Kalecki, M. (1944), 'Employment in the United Kingdom during and after the transition period', *Bulletin of the Oxford Institute of Statistics*, December.

Meltzer, A. H. (1981), 'Tests of inflation theories from the British laboratory', *The Banker*, July.

Minford, P. (1981), 'Labour market equilibrium in an open economy', *SSRC–University of Liverpool Research Project on the International Transmission of Fluctuations in Economic Activity, Secular Growth and Inflation*, Working Paper No. 8103.

Nickell, S. (1982), 'Wages and unemployment – a general framework', *Economic Journal*, 92, March, 51–55.

Nield, R. R. (1963), *Pricing and Employment in the Trade Cycle*, National Institute of Economic and Social Research, No. 21, Cambridge, Cambridge University Press.

Ormerod, P. (1980), 'Manufactured export prices in the United Kingdom and the "law of one price"', *The Manchester School*, September.

Ormerod, P. (1982), 'Rational and non-rational expectations of inflation in wage equations for the United Kingdom', *Economica*, 49(196), November, 375–388.

Parkin, M., Sumner, M. and Ward, R. (1976), 'The effects of excess demand, generalized expectations and wage–price controls on wage inflation in the UK: 1956–71', in K. Brunner and A. H. Meltzer (eds), *The Economics of Price and Wage Controls*, Carnegie–Rochester Conference Series on Public Policy, 2, Amsterdam, North Holland, 193–221.

Robinson, J. (1937), *Essays in the Theory of Employment*, London, Macmillan.
Sawyer, M. (1982), 'The non-Keynesian nature of the Phillips' curve', mimeo.
Smith, G. W. (1982), 'The normal cost hypothesis: a reappraisal', in M. J. Artis *et al.* (eds), *Demand Management, Supply Constraints and Inflation*, Manchester, Manchester University Press.
Stein, Jerome R. (1982), *Monetarist, Keynesian and New Classical Economics*, Oxford, Blackwell.
Sumner, M. T. (1978), 'Wage determination', in M. Parkin, and M. T. Sumner, (eds), *Inflation in the United Kingdom*, Manchester, Manchester University Press and Toronto University Press.
Sumner, M. and Ward, R. (1983), 'The reappearing Phillips curve', *Salford Papers in Economics*, 83(1).
Tarling, R. and Wilkinson, F. (1977), 'Inflation and the money supply', *Economic Policy Review*, Cambridge, No. 3, March, 56–61.
Whittaker, R. and Davis, G. (1983), 'The wholesale price equation', HM Treasury, mimeo.
Worswick, G. D. N. (1944), 'The stability and flexibility of full employment', in Oxford University Institute of Statistics, *The Economics of Full Employment*, Oxford, Blackwell.
Wren-Lewis, S. (1983), 'A model of the behaviour of private sector earnings from 1966 to 1980', mimeo.

# 11 Inflation and Unemployment in the United States: Recent Experience and Policies

*PETER B. CLARK**

## I INTRODUCTION

The period of the 1970s and early 1980s in the United States was characterized by much higher inflation and unemployment, and lower real output growth, than the 1960s. What were the causes of this deterioration in economic performance? How much of the higher inflation can be attributed to excessive stimulation by government policies, and how much to possibly exogenous food and energy price increases? What policies were proposed and implemented to reduce inflation, and how successful were they? These are some of the questions addressed in this chapter. While the analysis and evidence given here shed some light on these questions, definitive answers are beyond the scope of this chapter.

Section II provides a brief overview of the data for key economic variables. This is followed in Section III by a discussion of some of the factors generating high inflation, with attention focused on the effect of monetary policy on aggregate demand and inflation, and the role of the rise in the price of energy as an independent contributor to inflation. Section IV describes and evaluates the main government policies – monetary, fiscal and incomes – designed to reduce the inflation rate.

## II MAIN FEATURES OF THE US ECONOMY: 1970–83

Table 11.1 presents data on some of the key macroeconomic variables during the 1970s and early 1980s. Compared with the 1960s, this period was characterized by a low real growth rate, on average, and low productivity growth,

* The views expressed are those of the author and do not necessarily represent those of the Board of Governors or the staff of the Federal Reserve System. I am indebted to many colleagues at the Board for providing data and comments and suggestions for the text. These include Jerry Enzler, Bob Anderson, Eileen Mauskopf, Don Kohn, Darrel Cohen, Steve Braun, Dave Lindsey and Wolf Rahm. The research assistance of Mike Leahy and Katie Merrell is also gratefully acknowledged. Excellent typing under pressure of a deadline was provided by Ann Smith, Cindy Wheaton and Ruby Boone.

**Table 11.1** *Key economic variables, 1970–82 (per cent)*

| | *1970* | *1971* | *1972* | *1973* | *1974* | *1975* | *1976* | *1977* | *1978* | *1979* | *1980* | *1981* | *1982* | *Average 1970–82* | *Average 1960–9* |
|---|---|---|---|---|---|---|---|---|---|---|---|---|---|---|---|
| GNP (72$) | –0.1 | 4.7 | 7.0 | 4.2 | –2.8 | 2.2 | 4.4 | 5.7 | 5.8 | 1.4 | –0.8 | 2.0 | –1.7 | 2.5 | 4.1 |
| Unemployment rate | 5.0 | 6.0 | 5.6 | 4.9 | 5.6 | 8.5 | 7.7 | 7.1 | 6.1 | 5.9 | 7.2 | 7.6 | 9.7 | 6.7 | 4.8 |
| Capacity utilization in manufacturing | 79.5 | 78.4 | 83.4 | 87.5 | 83.8 | 72.9 | 79.6 | 82.2 | 84.7 | 86.0 | 79.6 | 79.4 | 71.1 | 80.6 | 84.9 |
| Implicit consumption deflator | 4.6 | 3.8 | 3.7 | 7.4 | 11.0 | 6.1 | 4.8 | 5.8 | 7.9 | 9.5 | 10.2 | 7.5 | 4.9 | 6.7 | 2.4 |
| CPI | 5.6 | 3.5 | 3.4 | 8.3 | 12.1 | 7.4 | 5.1 | 6.6 | 9.0 | 12.8 | 12.5 | 9.6 | 4.5 | 7.7 | 2.5 |
| CPI less food and energy | 6.5 | 3.4 | 3.0 | 4.6 | 10.9 | 7.0 | 6.4 | 6.2 | 8.4 | 10.7 | 12.2 | 10.2 | 5.2 | 7.3 | 2.6 |
| Hourly earnings index | 6.6 | 6.7 | 6.6 | 6.3 | 9.1 | 7.4 | 7.3 | 7.5 | 8.4 | 8.0 | 9.6 | 8.3 | 6.0 | 7.5 | n.a. |
| Compensation per hour | 6.8 | 5.9 | 7.4 | 7.9 | 10.9 | 8.1 | 8.4 | 7.6 | 8.9 | 9.2 | 10.8 | 9.0 | 7.2 | 9.0 | 5.0 |
| Federal funds rate | 7.2 | 4.7 | 4.4 | 8.7 | 10.5 | 5.8 | 5.0 | 5.5 | 7.9 | 11.2 | 13.4 | 16.4 | 12.3 | 8.7 | 4.2 |
| Federal funds rate less CPI | 1.6 | 1.2 | 1.0 | 0.4 | –1.6 | –1.6 | –0.1 | –1.1 | –1.1 | –1.6 | 0.9 | 6.8 | 7.8 | 1.0 | 1.7 |
| Aaa utility recently offered bond rate | 8.7 | 7.7 | 7.3 | 7.7 | 9.4 | 9.4 | 8.5 | 8.2 | 9.0 | 10.0 | 12.7 | 15.6 | 14.4 | 9.9 | n.a. |
| Civilian labor force | 2.4 | 2.2 | 2.8 | 3.3 | 2.3 | 1.7 | 3.0 | 3.3 | 3.2 | 2.4 | 1.5 | 1.5 | 1.7 | 2.4 | 1.7 |
| Total employment | 0.1 | 2.0 | 3.5 | 3.9 | 0.4 | –0.1 | 3.6 | 4.5 | 4.0 | 2.3 | –0.1 | 0.6 | –1.0 | 1.8 | 1.9 |
| Productivity in non-farm business sector | 1.0 | 3.8 | 4.7 | 0.2 | –2.7 | 3.8 | 2.2 | 2.6 | 0.3 | –2.1 | 0.2 | 1.2 | 0.8 | 1.2 | 2.5 |
| M1 | 4.9 | 6.7 | 8.5 | 5.8 | 4.8 | 5.0 | 6.1 | 8.2 | 8.2 | 7.4 | 7.2 | 5.1 | 8.5 | 6.6 | 3.8 |
| M2 | 5.9 | 13.5 | 12.8 | 7.2 | 5.9 | 12.1 | 13.3 | 11.2 | 8.0 | 8.1 | 9.0 | 9.4 | 9.3 | 9.7 | 7.1 |
| M3 | 9.2 | 14.8 | 14.0 | 11.6 | 8.6 | 9.2 | 11.0 | 12.3 | 11.2 | 9.6 | 9.7 | 11.7 | 10.1 | 11.0 | 7.4 |
| US oil import unit value | 5.2 | 4.6 | 9.3 | 23.0 | 166.0 | 0.3 | 7.3 | 8.7 | –0.3 | 77.4 | 36.2 | 0.5 | –4.5 | (–12.9) | |
| Weighted average US exchange rate | –1.1 | –5.7 | –3.5 | –10.6 | 2.0 | 2.7 | 2.7 | –5.0 | –12.6 | –0.5 | 1.8 | 18.5 | 16.0 | (7.1) | |

*Note:* The unemployment, capacity utilization and interest rates are annual averages. All other variables are Q4/Q4 rates of change. Data definitions and sources are given in the data appendix. ( ) = change 1982Q4–1983Q3.

together with high unemployment and high inflation. Average real GNP growth declined from 4.1 per cent to 2.5 per cent, whereas inflation, as measured by the implicit consumption deflator, rose from 2.4 per cent, on average, in the 1960s to 6.7 per cent, on average, from 1970 to 1982. The more familiar consumer price index (CPI) shows a somewhat larger increase in inflation between the two periods. Associated with the lower real growth was a higher average unemployment rate (6.7 per cent versus 4.8 per cent) and a lower rate of growth of productivity (1.2 per cent compared with 2.5 per cent). If one included in the earlier period the years 1970–3, which were before the first large increase in oil prices, the comparison would have been even less favorable for the 1970s.

In comparing the two periods it is noteworthy that the average growth in the civilian labor force was larger in the latter period (2.4 per cent) than in the 1960s (1.7 per cent). Despite the lower real output growth in the 1970s, the growth in total employment (at 1.8 per cent) was almost the same as in the earlier period (1.9 per cent). The counterpart to the higher ratio of growth in employment to output was reflected primarily in the lower growth in productivity noted above.

One of the main features of the 1970s was the sharp rise in food and energy prices. As shown by the difference between the CPI and the CPI less food and energy in Table 11.1, this rise was particularly important in 1973 and 1974, and in 1978 and 1979.

The price of imported oil is shown separately in Table 11.1. The first oil-price rise was concentrated in 1974, one year after the burst in other commodity prices, whereas the second price rise was spread out over the two years 1979 and 1980. Also shown in the table is the change in the weighted average foreign exchange value of the dollar. One factor raising US non-oil import prices in 1973 and 1977/8 was the depreciation of the dollar in those years. By the same token, the dollar's large appreciation during 1981/2, in addition to the drop in commodity prices, was responsible for the decline in import prices, on average, during these years.

The figures for unemployment and average hourly earnings show an inverse relationship. Tight labor markets in 1973 and early 1974, combined with rapidly rising inflation during both years, generated the high growth in nominal earnings in 1974. Similarly, relatively low unemployment in 1978 and 1979, together with growing inflation, led again to accelerated growth in earnings at the end of the 1970s. The sharp increase in the unemployment rate in the early 1980s, along with the decline in inflation and the squeeze on the traded goods sector of the US economy resulting from the appreciation of the dollar, generated a dramatic drop in the growth in earnings through the third quarter of 1983.

On the monetary side, what is striking is that monetary restraint during the 1980s is manifested not so much in a slowdown in M1 growth, but much more in the rise in real short-term interest rates.

One appealing and widespread explanation for the decline during the 1970s in the macroeconomic performance of the United States, and other industrial countries as well, is the stagflationary effect of the two sharp oil-price increases during the last decade. Many economists (e.g. Bruno and Sachs, 1979, 1982) have analyzed this case. Although the effects of oil-price increases depend in an important way on policy makers' reactions, in the event, under the range of policy reactions usually considered, an increase in the price of an important intermediate input such as petroleum will for a time increase inflation and unemployment rates and reduce real output growth and productivity. Certainly this supply-side shock represents part of the story, and estimates of the effects on the US economy of this shock are given in the next section. However, the sharp rise in the price of oil reflected both demand and supply conditions, so that the level of aggregate demand in both the United States and other industrial countries must be taken into account in appraising the causes of inflation and unemployment in the 1970s. This point is discussed in more detail below.

## III CAUSES OF INFLATION

In discussing and analyzing inflation and unemployment in the recent past it is essential to take a view about the underlying determinants of the inflationary process. The view taken here is basically the approach described by Perry (1978) as the 'mainline model', and is similar to that adopted by Tobin (1980) and Gordon (1982).[1] Such an approach is embodied in the Federal Reserve Board's quartly econometric model of the US economy (which is the same as the MPS model), and a number of simulations of this model are reported below.

In this mainline model a Phillips curve augmented by a variable representing price expectations plays a key role: wages respond to some measure of tightness or slack in the labor market – typically the measured unemployment rate – as well as some proxy for inflationary expectations, which is often taken to be past rates of inflation. In the Board's model, prices are determined in a two-step procedure. First, a behavioral equation is used to explain the deflator for value added in the non-farm business sector excluding energy. In this equation, the mark-up over unit labor costs depends on the inverse of the unemployment rate, the price ratio of US goods to foreign goods, and the change in import prices. Second, prices of raw materials are added to this deflator (with a weight equal to the share of raw materials in the private, non-agricultural sector) to get an index for final sales prices. A feature of this approach is that both prices and wages display considerable inertia. However, both can be ratcheted sharply upward in response to increases in commodity, e.g. oil, prices. Particularly important is the fact that the simultaneous increase in wage inflation and the unemployment rate – which occurred, for example, in 1974 and 1980 – can be explained fairly well by models of this kind.[2]

A feature of the mainline model is that monetary policy has a substantial impact on wage and price inflation that occurs by means of changes in aggregate demand and, in models with endogenous exchange rates, through shifts in demand from the external sector and changes in prices of imported inputs.[3] Monetary policy does not have a direct effect on actual prices and wages or on price expectations in models of this type. The indirect channel by which monetary policy affects prices and wages through interest rates, aggregate demand and the unemployment rate will be a maintained hypothesis, so to speak, throughout this chapter.[4]

Nevertheless, it is not clear whether mainline models that emphasize the aggregate demand channel to explain inflation take full account of demand pressures on prices of raw materials and semi-finished goods that are traded on world markets. Part of the upward movement in commodity prices during the 1970s was no doubt due to pure exogenous supply shocks, but some portion was related to demand pressures as well. The importance of aggregate demand is perhaps most readily apparent in the case of the price of petroleum. Before the two oil-price hikes in the 1970s, both aggregate demand and the demand for oil were growing strongly in the industrial countries and the developing countries. To take the price of oil as exogenous for a country that looms as large in the world economy as the United States may not be appropriate. To make the price of oil endogenous of course poses substantial modeling problems. The point remains that mainline models provide an incomplete description of the inflationary process because they tend to ignore the linkage between aggregate demand and commodity prices. This point will be addressed again in connection with the analysis of the impact on US inflation of the second oil-price increase in the 1970s.

In this section some of the causes of the inflation of the 1970s are examined. First, the role of aggregate demand, as influenced by monetary policy, is discussed. Then two estimates are provided of the macroeconomic impact on the US economy of the second oil-price hike, one estimate using the standard 'unchanged money' assumption, and another based on a monetary policy reaction function. A brief discussion of the role of fiscal policy in affecting aggregate demand completes this section.

### MONETARY POLICY

There is an obvious, trivial sense in which one can say that monetary policy was the cause of the inflation of the 1970s. One can always assert that, if monetary policy had been sufficiently tight, the observed increase in inflation could have been avoided. This is no doubt true, and the experiments reported below provide an estimate of the effects of a tighter monetary policy during the 1970s. However, if one examines the stance of monetary policy, as revealed in the minutes of the Federal Open Market Committee, one finds that the intent of policy was by and large to restrain the growth in demand at the time when inflation was increasing. As Table 11.1 shows, in periods of rising inflation from 1972 to 1974 and from 1977 to 1980, rates of growth in the monetary aggregates declined on balance, interest rates rose, and the ensuing reduction in aggregate demand brought about a decline in inflation. During these periods monetary policy was not directed at pushing aggregate demand to the limits of capacity, but rather toward controlling inflation. It would therefore be inaccurate to identify monetary policy as the cause of double-digit inflation in the 1970s.

None the less, in hindsight one might well conclude that it would have been preferable if the growth of real GNP in 1972 and 1977/8 had been less robust, and if monetary policy had been somewhat less expansionary in the years following the recessions of 1970 and 1974/5. It is desirable, therefore, to appraise the effect of monetary policy on the economy and examine the costs, in terms of initially lower output and higher unemployment, of a tighter monetary policy designed to reduce the inflation rate. With such information one can evaluate the desirability of alternative policies.

One estimate of the impact of monetary policy on the US economy, computed as the effects of a 1 per cent lower growth rate in M1, is given in Table 11.2. The results were derived by simulating the Board's quarterly econometric model over the period 1975Q1–1982Q4, with the money supply (M1) constrained to expand one percentage point less each quarter (at an annual rate) than it actually did. The impact of this particular change in monetary policy is equal to the simulated value of the endogenous variables in the model minus the actual historical value, which corresponds to the control solution of the model. The control solution of the model tracks history because the residuals have been added back into each equation. The same residuals are, of course, also added back into each equation in the deviation from the control solution, and consequently do not affect the multiplier.

The channel through which the lower money supply growth affects the economy is higher short- and long-term interest rates. The demand for money function (specifically, the demand–deposit equation) includes as one of its determinants the federal funds rate. When, as in this simulation, the supply of M1 is exogenous, the demand–deposit equation is used to solve for the level of the federal funds rate that equates the demand with the (lower) supply of money. In the first eight quarters, the federal funds rate rises 44 basis points, on average, and the long-term rate (determined by a term structure equation) rises on average by half that amount, 22 basis points. The higher interest rates reduce both inventory and fixed investment as well as expenditures on consumer durables. The higher interest rates also raise the dividend/price ratio, thereby reducing the value of stock market wealth, which leads to lower consumption spending. Also, under a regime of floating exchange rates the foreign exchange value of the dollar rises (assuming foreign central banks do not also increase their interest rates in lockstep with the rise in US rates) and real net exports are reduced. The induced decline in real GNP raises the unemployment rate and reduces wage and price inflation. Not shown in Table 11.2 is an appreciation of the dollar, generated by higher dollar interest rates (in nominal and real terms) and an improved trade balance position, which also puts downward pressure on prices. At the end of two years the 1 per cent decline in money growth results in a fairly modest 0.5 per cent decline in price and wage inflation, which is associated with a 0.5 percentage point increase in the unemployment rate and a roughly 1.7 per cent decline in real GNP.

After four years, however, the interaction of wages and prices, combined with an unemployment rate that rises by almost 1 percentage point, results in a reduction in inflation that approaches 2 percentage points. The lower price level, together with the reduction in real GNP, results in a substantial decline in nominal GNP. Because this variable is an important determinant of the demand for nominal money balances, nominal interest rates decline appreciably after the second year relative to the control solution. These lower interest rates in turn generate a rebound in real GNP so that, beginning in the sixth year after the tighter monetary policy, real output is above the control solution and

**Table 11.2** *Effects of a 1 per cent lower growth rate in M1 (deviation from control solution)*

| *Quarter of simulation* | | *Real GNP* *$ 1972 bn* | *Civilian unemployment rate* % | *Federal funds rate* % | *Consumption deflator (annual percentage rate of change)* |
|---|---|---|---|---|---|
| 1975Q1 | 1 | −2.8 | 0.04 | 0.70 | 0.11 |
| | 2 | −2.1 | 0.06 | −0.02 | −0.09 |
| | 3 | −6.1 | 0.11 | 0.92 | 0.12 |
| | 4 | −7.1 | 0.16 | 0.17 | −0.01 |
| 1976Q1 | 5 | −13.1 | 0.27 | 0.98 | −0.04 |
| | 6 | −15.2 | 0.36 | 0.08 | −0.24 |
| | 7 | −20.6 | 0.47 | 0.72 | −0.24 |
| | 8 | −22.7 | 0.56 | −0.01 | −0.47 |
| 1977Q4 | 12 | −29.8 | 0.86 | −0.70 | −1.46 |
| 1978Q4 | 16 | −27.0 | 0.90 | −1.13 | −1.93 |
| 1979Q4 | 20 | −9.7 | 0.55 | −1.24 | −1.93 |
| 1980Q4 | 24 | 11.0 | 0.03 | −1.27 | −1.53 |
| 1981Q4 | 28 | 20.5 | −0.34 | −0.76 | −1.03 |
| 1982Q4 | 32 | 16.7 | −0.44 | −0.00 | −0.49 |

*Note:* Simulation covers the period 1975Q1–1982Q4. The money supply (M1) was set exogenously at a level each quarter corresponding to a growth rate that was 1 per cent lower (at an annual rate) than the historical value.

eventually the unemployment rate falls below its historical value. Because of lags in adjustment in the real side of the economy and between wages and prices in the Board's econometric model, a simulation of this sort (money path fixed) has a built-in tendency to cycle up and down around the pre-existing path of real GNP. In the longer run, a 1 per cent decline in money growth results in a 1 per cent decline in inflation.

From a shorter-run perspective, the results in Table 11.2 indicate that, if the Federal Reserve had engineered a growth rate in M1 1 per cent lower than in fact occurred between 1975 and 1982, real output would have been higher, and unemployment and inflation would have been lower at the end of 1982. These gains come at the cost of higher unemployment and lower output earlier in the period.

The money multiplier results in Table 11.2 provide an estimate of the effects of a monetary policy different from that actually pursued in the latter half of the 1970s. Many other alternative policies can, of course, be contemplated. One particular monetary policy that was simulated involved the use of a policy reaction function that has been developd at the Board by Anderson and Enzler (1983). The basic idea is not to try to mimic how the Federal Reserve actually set policy, but rather to develop an equation that specifies the setting of a policy instrument so as to damp fluctuations in output and inflation and put the economy on a path toward long-run targets for inflation, real output growth and unemployment. Thus the approach involves going from ultimate target objectives to setting a path for an instrument of monetary policy. The targets are the non-accelerating inflation rate of unemployment (NAIRU), as computed by the model for the unemployment rate, the natural rate of growth of real output (equal to the sum of the growth in productivity and the labor force), and, for this chapter, the long-run inflation target has been set arbitrarily at 4 per cent.[5]

The reaction function assumes that the policy maker would like, other things equal, to keep the unemployment rate at its natural rate, but is willing to deviate from that target level as inflation deviates from its target. In other words, if inflation is above its target rate, the target level of unemployment is set above the natural rate, and vice versa. The policy maker does not control unemployment directly, but rather attemps to influence it through the rate of growth of output.

Finally, it is assumed that the real after-tax short-term interest rate (the federal funds rate adjusted for inflation and taxes) is moved up and down to bring output growth toward its target value. In addition, the interest rate is adjusted if there are cumulative departures of actual values from target levels of output, unemployment and inflation. Thus the federal funds rate is set higher, the higher is the growth in output relative to the natural rate, the higher the cumulative sum of output growth from the target rate (this takes care of permanent shifts in the *IS* curve), the lower the cumulative deviation of unemployment from the target rate (this adjusts for shifts in the relationship between real GNP and unemployment), and the higher the cumulative inflation rate from its target (this adjusts for shifts in the Phillips curve).

Initial parameter values for the reaction function were obtained by guessing. Interim parameter values were then obtained by conducting long simulations of the quarterly model under various parameter settings and choosing values that 'best succeeded' in keeping the economy near its natural rate while simultaneously keeping inflation low. To obtain reasonable parameters for the terms involving cumulative departures from targets, large shocks to taxes, productivity and the Phillips curve were created and the parameters were chosen to minimize the effects of these shocks. Parameter values were generally found to be quite robust in the sense that outcomes were not sensitive to small changes in parameters.

Table 11.3 shows the effects of using this reaction function with a 4 per cent inflation target over the period 1975–82. Because there are no restrictions on the magnitude of changes in the federal funds rate generated by the reaction function, this interest rate can jump sharply from quarter to quarter, and did so in 1975 and 1976. This feature of the reaction function is probably somewhat unrealistic, but it does illustrate the kinds of changes in short-term interest rates needed to achieve inflation and other targets, all of course conditional on the structure of the Board's model.

From 1975 to 1977 the impact of the reaction function is roughly the same as the effects of the 1 per cent lower money growth reported in Table 11.2. The major difference lies in 1978–80. The reaction function significantly dampens the economy, trading considerably higher unemployment for substantial reductions in the inflation rate. By restraining the forces of inflation earlier, the reaction function generates benefits in the form of a considerably lower unemployment and price level at the end of 1982, and a level of real GNP roughly 10 per cent higher than actually occurred. Obviously, many other outcomes are possible with different settings for the parameters in the reaction function. These results should be regarded as only illustrative of the behavior of the economy in the face of a rather determined effort by the monetary authorities to achieve an inflation target.

Two aspects of the economy's deviation from its historical path generated by the reaction function are worth noting. First, the economy demonstrated remarkable recuperative powers: over a period of three years, from the end of 1979 to the end of 1982, the economy recovered from a position of $100 billion (in 1972 dollars) below its historical level to a position nearly $150 billion above its actual value. These major shifts in the economy's path reflect both a fairly rapid response in the private sector to variables such as interest rates and a monetary authority that is not shy in manipulating interest rates to achieve its basically anti-inflationary aims. Second, the reaction function generated a drastically tight monetary policy roughly two years before it actually occurred, i.e. in 1978 rather than in 1980, which was before the second oil-price rise. This timing of the onset of significant tightening in policy suggests that there were already forces generating an increasing rate of inflation before the sharp rise in oil prices in 1979 and 1980.

Finally, it is useful to compare these results with those reported by Gordon (1982, p. 134) with regard to the reduction in inflation associated with a given increase in the unemployment rate. Using five-equation model, Gordon simulated the impact of a monetary policy beginning in 1975 that set the money supply (M1B) growth rate each year 2 percentage points below the growth rate of natural real GNP. Taking the average of his results for 1979 and 1980 one

**Table 11.3** *Effects of a reaction function with 4 per cent inflation target (deviation from control solution)*

| *Quarter* | *Real GNP* *$ 1972 bn* | *Civilian unemployment rate* % | *Federal funds rate* % | *Consumption deflator* *(annual percentage rate of change)* | *M1 (level)* |
|---|---|---|---|---|---|
| 1975Q1 | 0.6 | –0.01 | –0.26 | 0.00 | 0.02 |
| 2 | –11.2 | 0.16 | 3.28 | 0.27 | –4.11 |
| 3 | –22.6 | 0.42 | 4.67 | 0.34 | –9.62 |
| 4 | –17.0 | 0.44 | –0.34 | –0.68 | –9.56 |
| 1976Q1 | –24.5 | 0.55 | –0.12 | –0.20 | –8.30 |
| 2 | –16.4 | 0.54 | –3.62 | –0.66 | –1.31 |
| 3 | –6.5 | 0.35 | –3.36 | –0.63 | 3.40 |
| 4 | –0.9 | 0.21 | –1.73 | –0.39 | 5.63 |
| 1977Q4 | –29.0 | 0.76 | 0.76 | –1.23 | –17.98 |
| 1978Q4 | –96.4 | 2.26 | 4.93 | –2.36 | –44.00 |
| 1979Q4 | –101.8 | 2.95 | –2.41 | –4.96 | –40.47 |
| 1980Q4 | –34.1 | 1.69 | –0.05 | –4.63 | –36.13 |
| 1981Q4 | 58.8 | –0.38 | –4.36 | –3.34 | –47.30 |
| 1982Q4 | 146.0 | –2.92 | –1.16 | –0.09 | –40.59 |
| 1983Q1 | 150.6 | –3.38 | 2.65 | 0.74 | –45.04 |

*Note:* Simulation covers the period 1975Q1–1983Q1.

finds that a 1 percentage point increase in the unemployment rate reduces the inflation rate (GNP deflator) by 2.4 percentage points. This figure is not too far from our results, where the average for 1979/80 indicates that a 1 percentage point increase in the unemployment rate reduces the inflation rate (consumption deflator) by 2.1 percentage points.

### OIL-PRICE INCREASES

As already noted in Section II, the 1970s were characterized by large increases in commodity prices, and particularly the price of petroleum.[6] Some investigators find, or argue, that the inflation during the last decade was primarily caused by increases in food and energy prices (e.g. Gordon, 1982, and Blinder, 1982). Others find that rising oil prices have made a rather modest contribution to inflation (e.g. Nordhaus, 1980). Little or no contribution to inflation by oil-price increases is espoused by a few (e.g. Parkin, 1980), who tend to regard monetary policy as the sole or main cause of inflation.

Here, attention is focused on a rather narrow aspect of this topic, namely, the impact of the second oil-price increase on the US economy. Tables 11.4 and 11.5 provide two estimates of the impact of the oil-price increase. First, the Federal Reserve Board's econometric model was simulated over the period 1979Q1–1983Q1, holding the real price of oil constant and the money supply (M1) at its actual historical value. Such a simulation has the virtue that it makes a strict 'money supply constant' assumption and therefore the estimated effects are not contaminated by any changes in monetary policy. This standard type of simulation has the disadvantage, however, of being quite unrealistic in assuming that the monetary authorities would desire the same money supply in the absence of the oil-price increase.

This assumption was therefore relaxed and a second simulation was run where it was assumed that the monetary authority was operating under the same reaction function described above. In order to ensure that the effects of the oil-price rise would not be contaminated by the impact of shifting to the reaction function, a baseline simulation was run using the reaction function over the period 1975–1983Q1. The results of this simulation, which was used as the control simulation, were already reported in Table 11.3.

There are two main channels through which a higher oil price affects the US economy. First, there is a deterioration in the terms of trade and a transfer of income from the United States to oil-exporting countries. This loss in real income is approximated by the increased real cost of the initial level of oil imports. Sachs (1982) has estimated this real cost as 0.5 per cent of GNP in 1979 and 2 per cent of GNP in 1980. This loss in real income results in a decline in spending on domestic goods and services. Second, the higher price level leads to an increase in the demand for money; with an unchanged money supply, this results in higher interest rates, which reduce interest-sensitive expenditure. In addition to these two automatic deflationary effects, the policy makers might undertake explicit policy measures to offset the inflationary impulse generated by the oil-price increase.

Table 11.4 shows that with the unchanged monetary policy assumption the second oil-price increase is estimated to have had a major impact on the

**Table 11.4** *Oil shock–money exogenous (deviation from control solution)*

| *Quarter* | *Real GNP* *$1972 bn* | *Civilian unemployment rate* % | *Federal funds rate* % | *Consumption deflator* *(annual percentage rate of change)* |
|---|---|---|---|---|
| 1979Q1 | 0.1 | 0.00 | 0.12 | 0.03 |
| 2 | 1.1 | 0.01 | 0.03 | 0.38 |
| 3 | 0.6 | 0.06 | 0.01 | 1.11 |
| 4 | –5.6 | 0.14 | 0.16 | 1.25 |
| 1980Q1 | –9.8 | 0.26 | 0.57 | 2.50 |
| 2 | –19.2 | 0.42 | 1.04 | 3.59 |
| 3 | –31.4 | 0.65 | 0.87 | 2.77 |
| 4 | –39.2 | 0.86 | 0.79 | 2.65 |
| 1981Q1 | –52.9 | 1.16 | 1.95 | 3.99 |
| 2 | –59.1 | 1.39 | 0.27 | 1.12 |
| 3 | –64.2 | 1.50 | –0.13 | –0.56 |
| 4 | –67.3 | 1.61 | 0.81 | 0.88 |
| 1982Q1 | –68.6 | 1.72 | 0.26 | –0.03 |
| 2 | –64.8 | 1.70 | –0.70 | –1.23 |
| 3 | –57.0 | 1.62 | 0.11 | –1.42 |
| 4 | –52.4 | 1.52 | –0.07 | –1.71 |
| 1983Q1 | –43.5 | 1.35 | –0.48 | –2.48 |

*Note:* The real price of oil was held constant at its 1978Q4 value.

economy: the inflation rate is raised by over 2.5 per cent in 1980, interest rates are 0.5–1.0 percentage points higher, and real GNP is reduced by 1.7 per cent on average for the year. The longer-run effects of the deflation, however, are to reduce the inflation rate and interest rates below what they otherwise would have been in 1982, but the real income loss continues to be substantial, running at about 4 per cent of GNP.

In Table 11.5, because the reaction function involves an explicit monetary policy response to the higher inflation generated by the oil-price rise, interest rates increase much more rapidly. Therefore the unemployment rate is higher and the inflation rate and level of real GNP are lower in 1979–1981 as a consequence of the induced tighter monetary policy. However, beginning in 1982, monetary policy acts to counteract the higher unemployment and lower output generated by the oil-price shock, and the money supply is increased above the baseline level in order to reduce interest rates.

Table 11.5 suggests that the high interest rates observed in 1980 and 1981 cannot be ascribed primarily to the effects of the higher oil price. The simulated effects on the federal funds rate indicate that, without the oil-price rise, this short-term interest rate would nevertheless have been near its peak rate of about 19 per cent in mid-1981. Furthermore, the CPI less food and energy increased by 10.7 per cent and the consumption deflator by 9.5 per cent in 1979, i.e. before the major impact of the oil-price increase was manifiested. Thus, the oil-price increase can by no means explain or account for all of the run-up in inflation. Consequently, the tightness in monetary policy not explained by the rise in the price of oil in 1979/80 is perhaps attributable to inflationary impulses from other sources, particularly the high capacity utilization and low unemployment rates 1978/9.

It has been assumed up to this point that the sudden spurt in oil prices was strictly exogenous to the US economy. One can, however, make the case that expanding aggregate demand in the United States has both direct and indirect effects (working through the stimulating impact on other countries' GNP) on the supply–demand situation in the world oil market, and therefore has some influence on the price of oil charged by OPEC.[7] Rapid growth in the United States in 1971–3 and 1977–9, together with fairly vigorous expansion in the other major industrial countries, generated a demand for oil that put OPEC close to its production capacity of 30–31 million barrels per day at the end of both periods of rapid growth. If the United States had not run at peak capital and labor utilization rates during 1972/3 and 1978/9, the run-up in oil prices might have been less sharp.

## FISCAL POLICY

The role of fiscal policy has not been assigned a high weight in recent discussions as a factor generating inflation during the 1970s. Table 11.6 gives estimates of the full employment federal budget surplus/deficit in level form and as a percentage of potential GNP. One measure of the thrust of fiscal policy is the change in the latter ratio, given in column 3 of the table. It is hard to see from this measure any expansionary stimulus in a procyclical direction, except perhaps in 1980. An example of countercyclical policy occurred in 1975. The

**Table 11.5** *Oil shock–reaction function with 4 per cent inflation rate (deviation from simulation with reaction function)*

| *Quarter* | *Real GNP $1972 bn* | *Civilian unemployment rate %* | *Federal funds rate %* | *Consumption deflator (annual percentage rate of change)* | *M1 (level)* |
|---|---|---|---|---|---|
| 1979Q1 | −0.1 | 0.01 | 0.05 | 0.06 | −0.09 |
| 2 | −0.5 | 0.03 | 0.40 | 0.44 | −0.71 |
| 3 | −6.9 | 0.11 | 0.78 | 1.11 | −1.78 |
| 4 | −8.3 | 0.20 | 0.42 | 1.23 | −2.17 |
| 1980Q1 | −16.3 | 0.36 | 1.42 | 2.49 | −3.10 |
| 2 | −28.5 | 0.60 | 1.84 | 3.40 | −3.87 |
| 3 | −40.4 | 0.85 | 0.63 | 2.34 | −2.89 |
| 4 | −54.6 | 1.16 | 1.49 | 2.30 | −3.58 |
| 1981Q1 | −74.2 | 1.62 | 3.06 | 3.51 | −6.12 |
| 2 | −79.2 | 1.91 | 0.19 | −0.36 | −7.33 |
| 3 | −79.0 | 1.98 | −1.41 | −2.00 | −6.73 |
| 4 | −68.4 | 1.93 | −2.98 | −0.64 | −0.95 |
| 1982Q1 | −55.0 | 1.78 | −4.49 | −1.13 | 6.09 |
| 2 | −41.2 | 1.52 | −4.24 | −1.89 | 10.50 |
| 3 | −25.7 | 1.22 | −2.13 | −1.74 | 11.58 |
| 4 | −10.5 | 0.86 | −1.47 | −1.77 | 10.74 |
| 1983Q1 | 3.9 | 0.46 | −0.27 | −1.94 | 7.39 |

*Note:* The real price of oil was held constant at its 1978Q4 value. The baseline, or control, solution for this experiment is the simulated path of the economy reported in Table 11.3.

**Table 11.6** *High employment surplus/deficit*

| *Calendar year* | (1) *Surplus/deficit (–1)* $ bn | (2) *Percentage of potental GNP* | (3) *Change in (2)* |
|---|---|---|---|
| 1970 | –11.8 | –1.2 | –1.0 |
| 1971 | –19.2 | –1.8 | –0.6 |
| 1972 | –20.6 | –1.8 | 0.0 |
| 1973 | –18.2 | –1.4 | 0.4 |
| 1974 | –9.9 | –0.7 | 0.7 |
| 1975 | –39.8 | –2.5 | –1.8 |
| 1976 | –29.4 | –1.7 | 0.8 |
| 1977 | –34.3 | –1.8 | –0.1 |
| 1978 | –31.2 | –1.5 | 0.3 |
| 1979 | –19.4 | –0.8 | 0.7 |
| 1980 | –36.7 | –1.4 | –0.6 |
| 1981 | –17.9 | –0.6 | 0.8 |
| 1982 | –54.5 | –1.6 | –1.0 |

*Note:* High employment surplus/deficit computed at 6 per cent unemployment rate, and potential GNP computed as the level of GNP that generates a 6 per cent unemployment rate.

*Source:* Federal Reserve staff estimate.

Tax Reduction Act of 1975, which included temporary reductions in personal income taxes, liberalization of the investment tax credit and a lower corporate income tax on earnings of less than $50,000, generated considerable fiscal stimulus that year, which was one factor in the sharp recovery in output from the low level early in 1975. More important is the fact that in 1971–3 and 1977–9 – years of rapid growth and a declining unemployment rate – the high employment budget shifted toward surplus. Thus, it would appear correct to absolve fiscal policy of the high inflation of the 1970s.

## IV GOVERNMENT POLICIES FOR DEALING WITH INFLATION

Section III dealt with the major factors causing inflation during the 1970s. This section describes the main policies designed to control inflation that were either implemented or seriously considered during this period. The primary policy tool used to reduce the inflation rate in 1973–5 and 1978–81 was monetary policy. A few of the issues relating to the implementation of monetary policy are described below. There follows a brief description of the Reagan administration's fiscal policy package passed by Congress in 1981, which was designed to increase savings and investment, and, in conjunction with reduced rates of growth in monetary aggregates, lead to strong economic growth and declining inflation. The current problem of the monetary–fiscal policy mix is also discussed. Finally, the direct measures to reduce wage and price inflation during the 1970s – wage–price controls under President Nixon and the pay–price standard under President Carter – are described.

## MONETARY POLICY

The issues relating to the goals of monetary policy, the setting of intermediate targets and the techniques for achieving intermediate targets are broad, important topics, but within the confines of this chapter only a small subset of issues will be addressed. These include the reasons for the change in operating procedures in October 1979, the success of the Federal Reserve in achieving its monetary growth rate targets, the use of credit controls in March of 1980, and recent problems and issues relating to financial innovations and shifts in demands for the monetary aggregates.

In the late 1960s the Federal Open Market Committee (FOMC) began to allow decisions regarding money market conditions to be affected by objectives stated in qualitative fashion for various measures of monetary aggregates.[8] The impetus to use long-term intermediate monetary and credit targets became more concrete under HR133, passed in March 1975 by the House and the Senate. Under this resolution, Congress requested that targets be set by the Federal Reserve for a four-quarter horizon and that they be restated each quarter. The most formal embodiment of the intent of Congress that the Federal Reserve adopt monetary and credit aggregates as intermediate targets is the Full Employment and Balanced Growth Act of 1978 (Humphrey–Hawkins). This act amended the Federal Reserve Act to require the Federal Reserve to submit to Congress twice a year '. . . the objectives and plans of the Board of Governors and the FOMC with respect to ranges of growth or diminution of the monetary and credit aggregates'. The February report gives ranges for the current year and the July report gives ranges for the current year and, on a preliminary basis, ranges for the following year.

A significant change in the operating procedures of the Federal Reserve occurred on 6 October 1979. In the face of growth rates in monetary aggregates above those consistent with the targets and of inflation rising rapidly during the year, the Federal Reserve shifted its focus from the federal funds rate to reserve aggregates as a guide for open market operations. Under the old procedure, the level of the federal funds rate was set to produce the targeted money stock, given specific forecasts of nominal GNP. The level of non-borrowed reserves was the endogenous variable that was adjusted to maintain the predetermined federal funds rate. The problem with this approach was that, if there were an unexpected change in money demand, adherence to a funds rate target would mean that the change in demand would be fully accommodated, at least in the short run, by a change in non-borrowed reserves that would support a money stock that deviated from the target.

To achieve better money stock control, the Federal Reserve shifted to using non-borrowed reserves as the operating target. Under this procedure, the level of non-borrowed reserves was set in advance to achieve the targeted level of the money stock. For a given level of non-borrowed reserves, the impact on the money stock of an unanticipated shift in either money demand or the money supply function would be muted by partially offsetting movements in interest rates. This change in procedure represented a technical innovation and did not encompass a change in either the broader objectives of monetary policy or the use of monetary aggregates as intermediate targets.

A major assessment of the new operating procedure was undertaken by the Board staff fairly soon after the procedure was implemented (Federal Reserve Staff Study, 1981). The basic finding of this study was that the shift to using non-borrowed reserves to control the money stock was indeed beneficial in attaining the desired growth rate in money aggregates. The task of evaluating the new procedure was complicated, however, by the fact that other factors also affected the supply and demand for money during 1980; these resulted in increased variability in the money stock during the year and added to the volatility in interest rates beyond even the greater range of fluctuations expected to result from the new techniques.

An important influence on the money stock was the program of credit restraint announced by the Federal Reserve Board on 14 March 1980.[9] This program, which was part of a general government policy to curb inflation, included as its major elements the following:

- a voluntary special credit restraint program for all domestic commercial banks;
- a program of restraint on certain types of consumer credit, including credit cards;
- increases in reserve requirements on the managed liabilities of large banks; and
- restraints on the expansion of money market mutual funds.

This program had drastic short-run effects on the economy: real GNP, money growth rates and interest rates fell dramatically in the second quarter of 1980. The inflation rate, as measured by the CPI, continued unchanged, however, at 1 per cent per month. The lowering of credit costs, coupled with removal of the special credit restraints at the end of the second quarter, helped bring about a recovery in economic activity in the second half of 1980 that was unexpectedly early and strong. During this period of recovery, the public's demand for money retraced most of the downward shift in the first half of the year. By the end of the year, the growth rates of the monetary aggregates were slightly above the upper end of their target ranges.

The program of credit restraint can perhaps be regarded as the financial analogue of an incomes policy. It substituted government controls for the market mechanism – interest rates – that allocates credit. The aim of the program appears to have been to reduce costs in unemployment of fighting inflation using the traditional policy of demand restraint generated by high interest rates. The program was unsuccessful in achieving this objective; interest rates in fact fell considerably, but only because real aggregate demand dropped precipitously, and inflation did not budge. Moreover, by distorting the usual economic relationships, it complicated the interpretation of incoming economic data and made more difficult the administration of monetary and fiscal policies. Thus, this experiment had results that were similar to two experiments with income policies during the 1970s described below: the wage–price controls under President Nixon and the wage–price standards under President Carter.

In recent years, the development of new financial instruments and the deregulation of the interest rates that banks and savings institutions can pay on numerous categories of deposits have greatly complicated the task of setting intermediate monetary targets and the interpretation of current monetary data. For M1, the major change has been the introduction of interest-bearing checking accounts. Table 11.7 shows the components of the change in M1 since the beginning of 1977. The importance of interest-bearing checking accounts (OCDs) rose dramatically in 1981 when regular negotiated order of withdrawal (NOW) accounts became available on a nationwide basis in January of that year. The rapid growth of M1 in 1982, which was associated with an unprecedented decline in M1 velocity, was accounted for primarily by a continued expansion in OCDs. It is likely that these deposits responded considerably more to precautionary and other savings motives than did demand deposits. Their growing proportion in M1 has been one factor upsetting the previous relationship between this aggregate and nominal GNP.

M2 has also been heavily influenced by innovation and deregulation. The share of the non-transactions part of M2 that has market-determined yields has grown from 1.4 per cent at the beginning of 1977 to 76 per cent in 1983. This development reduces the sensitivity of the broader aggregates to interest rate changes because own rates adjust to market rates. This reduced sensitivity increases the difficulty of achieving targets for these aggregates without wide swings in interest rates and income.

As a result of these changes and the unusual demand for money associated with the deep recession in the United States, the income velocities of both M1 and M2 fell in 1982 by record amounts. Moreover, the pace of deregulation accelerated toward the end of 1982, bringing even greater uncertainties about the relationships of measured aggregates to ultimate goals. In December, deposit institutions were permitted to offer an account with limited transactions capability but without any ceiling on interest rates for accounts with an average balance over $2,500 (the MMDA, or money market deposit account). In early January 1983 deposit institutions were permitted to offer an account with unlimited transactions and with no interest ceiling for accounts with average balances over $2,500, but subject to Federal Reserve transaction account reserve requirements (the Super NOW). Growth of the Super NOW has been good; that of the MMDA has been spectacular, with the level of MMDAs reaching $367 billion in June 1983.[10]

As a result of these developments, the Federal Open Market Committee moved the base for measuring the M2 target to February–March after much of the initial shift into MMDAs had passed. M1 was downgraded in importance as a target because of distortions arising from the massive rearrangement of asset portfolios along with continuing uncertainties about longer-run M1 behavior in light of the growth of NOW accounts. In July 1983, the FOMC decided to move the base for monitoring M1 growth from 1982Q4 to 1983Q2. This decision reflected a judgement that the rapid growth in M1 should be treated as a one-time phenomenon.

**Table 11.7** *M1 and its principal components (changes in $ bn, not seasonally adjusted)*

| | *M1* | *Currency plus travelers checks* | *Demand deposits* | *OCD*[a] | *Super NOWs* |
|---|---|---|---|---|---|
| 1977Q1 | 7.3 | 1.8 | 5.0 | 0.5 | |
| Q2 | 5.5 | 2.0 | 3.3 | 0.2 | |
| Q3 | 5.5 | 2.1 | 3.0 | 0.4 | |
| Q4 | 6.9 | 2.2 | 4.3 | 0.4 | |
| 1978Q1 | 6.8 | 2.2 | 4.1 | 0.4 | |
| Q2 | 7.4 | 2.3 | 4.9 | 0.4 | |
| Q3 | 7.0 | 2.1 | 4.5 | 0.3 | |
| Q4 | 6.1 | 2.6 | 1.8 | 1.7 | |
| 1979Q1 | 4.9 | 2.4 | –1.9 | 4.5 | |
| Q2 | 8.7 | 2.2 | 3.8 | 2.5 | |
| Q3 | 9.7 | 2.6 | 4.9 | 2.3 | |
| Q4 | 3.5 | 2.3 | 0.6 | 0.6 | |
| 1980Q1 | 6.6 | 2.3 | 2.8 | 1.5 | |
| Q2 | –3.8 | 1.9 | –6.8 | 1.0 | |
| Q3 | 15.6 | 3.0 | 8.3 | 4.3 | |
| Q4 | 9.5 | 2.7 | 3.9 | 2.9 | |
| 1981Q1 | 5.1 | 1.8 | –22.0 | 25.3 | |
| Q2 | 9.4 | 2.2 | –6.5 | 13.7 | |
| Q3 | 3.3 | 1.5 | –3.6 | 5.5 | |
| Q4 | 3.5 | 1.6 | –1.5 | 3.4 | |
| 1982Q1 | 11.5 | 2.5 | 0.4 | 8.7 | |
| Q2 | 3.6 | 2.7 | –3.2 | 4.0 | |
| Q3 | 7.0 | 2.3 | 0.0 | 4.7 | |
| Q4 | 14.9 | 2.3 | 4.9 | 7.8 | |
| 1983Q1 | 16.7 | 3.5 | 1.6 | 11.5 | 20.8 |
| Q2 | 14.9 | 4.0 | 2.4 | 8.5 | 9.7 |
| Q3 | 11.2 | 2.7 | 2.7 | 5.8 | 3.2 |
| Amount outstanding, September 1983 | 517.1 | 147.7 | 243.4 | 126.0 | 33.7 |

*Note:* a OCD = other checkable deposits, which include negotiable order of withdrawal (NOW) and automatic transfer service (ATS) accounts at banks and savings institutions, credit union share draft accounts, and demand deposits at mutual savings banks.

More generally, since 1983 it has been necessary to place greater reliance on a variety of incoming economic and financial data when making decisions on the provision of reserves, and somewhat less reliance exclusively on one or another of the monetary or credit aggregates. This change in emphasis would appear to reflect a judgement by the Federal Reserve that strict adherence to monetary targets, at least in the short run, will not necessarily achieve its ultimate objectives for the economy. Nevertheless, the Federal Reserve recognizes that the long-run goal of price stability can be achieved only by means of reductions in the growth rates of the monetary aggregates.

FISCAL POLICY

The brief examination of fiscal policy in Section III revealed that during the 1970s fiscal policy did not play a major role in the fight against inflation. The major innovation in fiscal policy occurred shortly after the Reagan administration assumed office in January 1981. The Economic Recovery Tax Act, passed by Congress in August 1981, embodied in part some of the notions that have been identified as 'supply-side' economics. The central idea is that cuts in marginal personal income tax rates will increase both savings and the supply of labor. The line of reasoning embodied in this view is given in the *Economic Report of the President, 1982* (p. 120):

> To discuss the effects of the tax cuts on labor supply and saving decisions, it is necessary to understand the various incentives on household behavior created by reductions in marginal tax rates. Cutting tax rates increases an individual's after-tax wage rate. With the Federal Government taking a smaller share of the last dollar of earnings, the return to an individual from an extra hour of work or a more demanding job will increase, strengthening the incentive to work more hours, or accept a more demanding job.
>
> Similarly, cutting tax rates increases after-tax interest rates. The higher the after-tax interest rate, the higher the level of future consumption possible for a given reduction of current consumption. The increase in after-tax interest rates resulting from the tax cuts will thus tend to decrease present consumption, including consumption of leisure as well as goods. In other words, households will tend both to work more and to save more.

The Economic Recovery and Tax Act also made significant changes in the taxation of business income. The most important change was the accelerated cost recovery system, which provided a more generous treatment of the way in which capital can be depreciated for tax purposes. Other changes included leasing provisions that would encourage investment by firms with low taxable income, an increase in the investment tax credit for some types of equipment, and allowing small businesses to count as current expenditure up to $5,000 of new investment in 1982 (rising to $10,000 in 1986 and thereafter). These changes were designed to increase business investment substantially by raising the after-tax return on new projects.

The tax changes were designed to shift the composition of output from consumption to investment, and increase total output by raising the incentive for labor to work more. In addition, substantial cuts in expenditure, relative to those planned by the previous administration, were intended to mitigate the deficit-expanding effects of the tax cuts. Finally, the administration endorsed gradual reductions in the rates of growth in the monetary aggregates to reduce the rate of inflation.

These fiscal policy changes and a monetary policy designed to reduce inflation were projected to generate rapid growth in 1982 and 1983 and sharp reductions in inflation and unemployment rates, and to eliminate the federal deficit by 1984. They presumed that it would be possible to achieve simultaneously a rapid expansion of the economy and a significant reduction in inflation. Seen in this light, the administration's 1981 policies had the same objective as standard incomes policies, i.e. a reduction in the inflation rate through means other than demand deflation.

The promise of rapid growth was unfulfilled, at least in the short run. In 1982, real GNP fell rather than rising by 5 per cent, as the administration had forecast in 1981. It did, however, start to rise strongly in 1983. In addition, the administration's fiscal policies did not have the intended effect of shifting the composition of output from consumption to investment. On the contrary, consumption rose and investment fell: between 1981Q2 and 1983Q2, consumption (1972 dollars) rose from $955 billion to $1,011 billion, an increase of nearly 6 per cent, whereas gross private fixed non-residential investment (1972 dollars) declined from $173 billion to $163 billion, a decline of nearly 6 per cent. Moreover, after rising from 6 per cent in 1981Q2 to 7.5 per cent in 1981Q4, the personal saving rate declined continuously to 4.0 per cent in 1983Q2.

The stimulus to the economy provided by the huge actual and prospective federal government deficits (which are also very large when computed on a full employment basis) poses certain problems for the domestic and international economy. The strong fiscal stimulus combined with the natural rebound of inventories from their recession lows reduce the scope for the economic recovery to be generated by interest rates lower than those that have been observed so far this year. On the contrary, given the Federal Reserve's targets for the monetary aggregates and its desire to achieve a moderate, sustained recovery, the fact that the recovery is led by fiscal expansion means that real and nominal interest rates are higher than they would be if the federal deficit were in balance.

The result of this mix of fiscal and monetary policies is that the interest-sensitive sectors of the US economy get hurt. These sectors include not only the usual domestic categories of spending – consumer durables, housing and business fixed investment – but the foreign sector as well. On purely theoretical grounds, one cannot assert that a larger government budget deficit, with monetary policy unchanged, will necessarily appreciate a country's currency. Nevertheless, under current conditions, the high federal deficit and the continuing high nominal and real interest rates may well be a factor explaining the dollar's strength on world currency markets. The dollar's high value has already resulted in a record US trade deficit of $73 billion (seasonally adjusted annual rate) in the third quarter of 1983.

The ramifications of high US real and nominal interest rates and the high value of the dollar obviously extend beyond the US economy. High interest rates on dollar-denominated instruments exacerbate the debt-repayment problems of many developing countries. Moreover, central banks in several industrial countries, concerned about the inflationary effects on their economies of a depreciation in their currencies against the dollar, have at times felt constrained to raise interest rates, or not lower them as fast as they otherwise would, for fear of further depreciation of their currencies. Thus, the federal deficit has had worldwide repercussions.

## EXPERIMENTS WITH INCOME POLICIES

The decade of the 1970s spawned numerous programs and proposals (both in the United States and in other industrial countries) to restrain the upward movement of wages and prices by means other than contraction of aggregate demand, thereby avoiding the losses in real output associated with demand deflation. There were two programs of this type during the 1970s – the wage–price control program that was part of President Nixon's New Economic Policy, and the voluntary pay and price standards that were part of President Carter's anti-inflation program. These are described and evaluated in turn.

In the first part of 1971, unemployment continued high at about 6 per cent, and although the inflation rate had declined somewhat it still remained at what was then a high rate of roughly 5 per cent. In addition, there was a large deterioration in the US balance of payments position. Wanting to reduce inflation without exacerbating the unemployment problem, the Nixon administration announced on 15 August 1971 a 90-day wage and price freeze, which subsequently became known as Phase I of the wage–price control program.[11] After the freeze on wages and prices came Phase II, which was a more flexible program for controlling prices and wages. The upper limit on wage increases was 5.5 per cent per year, with special allowances for low-paid workers and gross inequities. Increases in costs could be passed along into prices, and agricultural and imported commodities were exempt from the wage–price controls.

Phase II extended from November 1971 to January 1973, when it was replaced by Phase III, which embodied an even more flexible arrangement of controls, until June, when President Nixon announced a new freeze on prices. This freeze lasted until August, when Phase IV was implemented, which was stricter than Phase II in some respects, but certain industries were decontrolled. With support for the control program waning, it was terminated on 30 April 1974.

There have been numerous attempts to measure the impact on wages and prices of this very comprehensive controls program.[12] The general verdict appears to be that, although the controls may have reduced inflation below what it otherwise would have been, when controls were eliminated inflation was above what it otherwise would have been. Thus, the average inflation rate was probably little affected by the controls program.

On 14 October 1978, President Carter announced a program of voluntary wage and price standards. Firms were asked to restrain their average price increase to 0.5 percentage points below their average annual rate of increase during 1976–7. The pay standard was 7 per cent during the first year of the program (October 1978 – September 1979). President Carter also proposed a program of real wage insurance that would help protect workers who complied with the program from suffering losses in real income, but this proposal was not adopted by Congress.

Evaluation of this program of pay and price standards has been less extensive than that of the controls program. Evidence is cited in the *Economic Report of the President, 1981* (p. 59) that annual wage increases were 1.0–1.5 percentage points lower during 1979 than they would have been without the standards, and that these reductions in labor costs were passed on to consumers through lower prices. This reduction in wage and price inflation could well have been offset, however, by higher inflation later on.

The period of the 1970s generated many experiments in incomes policies, such as those described above, as well as a great deal of discussion of such policies, including tax-based incomes policy (TIP).[13] Other policies – credit controls and supply-side approaches described above – were also tried in an attempt to reduce inflation without incurring the costs of deflation. None of these policies was successful in achieving this objective. Inflation was ultimately brought down in 1975–6 and 1981–3 by means of traditional deflationary policies.

## VI CONCLUSION

This chapter has not established a single cause for the high inflation in the United States during the 1970s. Oil-price shocks clearly played a role, but it has been argued here that it would be inaccurate to characterize the two sharp increases in petroleum prices in the 1970s as purely exogenous. The high level of aggregate demand relative to potential output in the United States contributed directly and indirectly to tight oil market conditions. In addition, although not discussed in this chapter, demographic and other factors raised the NAIRU to a level that was probably higher than was realized at the time, so that in retrospect the growth in aggregate demand was perhaps too rapid in 1972 and 1977/8. The simulation experiment with the monetary policy reaction function gave some indication that greater restraint in the early phase of the recovery in the second half of the 1970s could have paid off in terms of higher output and lower unemployment in the early 1980s.

A number of different policies were implemented between 1970 and the present in an attempt to reduce inflation and keep to a minimum the costs of unemployment associated with a policy of demand deflation. These policies – wage, price and credit controls, and an experiment with supply-side economics – were not successful in reducing the average rate of inflation for a given level of unemployment for an extended period of time. One lesson of the US experience is that such policies will not be successful if aggregate demand is excessive. Nevertheless, the verdict is still out on the questions of whether some form of incomes policies accompanying an aggregate demand policy could ratchet down wage and price inflation and thereby reduce some of the unemployment costs of demand deflation.

## APPENDIX: DATA DEFINITIONS AND SOURCES (Table 11.1)

**Gross national product** (1972 dollars) – quarterly data, seasonally adjusted at annual rates.

*Source:* National Income and Product Accounts, *Survey of Current Business*, Bureau of Economic Analysis, US Department of Commerce.

**Unemployment rate** – number unemployed as a percentage of the civilian labor force, quarterly averages of monthly data, seasonally adjusted.
*Source:* Household Survey, Bureau of Labor Statistics, US Department of Labor.

**Capacity utilization** – manufacturing total capacity utilization rates, quarterly averages of monthly data, seasonally adjusted.
*Source:* Federal Reserve Board.

**CPI** – concatenation of two series: from January 1978 to June 1983 it is the Consumer Price Index for All Urban Consumers, and prior to January 1978 it is the Consumer Price Index for Urban Wage Earners and Clerical Workers; after 1982, based on a rental equivalence for owner-occupied housing; all items, quarterly averages of monthly data, seasonally adjusted.
*Source:* Bureau of Labor Statistics, US Department of Labor.

**CPI less food and energy** – same as CPI above, except it is all items less food and energy.

**Hourly earnings index** – average hourly earnings for production or non-supervisory workers on private non-agricultural payrolls, 1977 = 100, quarterly averages of monthly data, seasonally adjusted.
*Source:* Bureau of Labor Statistics, US Department of Labor.

**Compensation per hour** – private non-agricultural sector, 1967 = 100, quarterly data, seasonally adjusted.
*Source:* Bureau of Labor Statistics, US Department of Labor.

**Federal funds rate** – 'effective' rate on federal funds. Until 25 July 1983, this rate represents a consensus of major market participants in New York City on the rate at which most transactions in these funds were executed during the day. Since then, the daily effective rate is an average of the rates on a given day weighted by the volume of transactions at these rates. Quarterly averages of daily data, not seasonally adjusted, per cent per annum.
*Source:* Federal Reserve Board.

**Yields on recently offered Aaa utility bonds – Federal Reserve Series.** This series represents estimates for a standard bond, which is defined as a new, straight-debt, long-term (20 years or longer) utility issue, rated Aaa by Moody's Investors Service, Inc., and AAA by Standard and Poor's, Inc., that carries 5-year call protection and is underwritten by a process of competitive bidding. This series is derived from quotas at the close of trading on Fridays. The yields included are those on such bonds for the first four weeks after the termination of underwriter price restrictions. Quarterly averages of monthly data, not seasonally adjusted, per cent per annum.
*Source:* Federal Reserve Board.

**Civilian labor force** – all employed or unemployed persons in the civilian non-institutional population, quarterly averages of monthly data, seasonally adjusted.
*Source:* Household Survey, Bureau of Labor Statistics, US Department of Labor.

**Total employment** – quarterly averages of monthly data, seasonally adjusted.
*Source:* Household Survey, Bureau of Labor Statistics, US Department of Labor.

**Productivity** – output per hour in the non-farm business economy. Computed with GDP rather than GNP. Hours include estimates of non-farm and farm proprietor hours. 1977 = 100, quarterly data, seasonally adjusted.
*Source:* Bureau of Labor Statistics, US Department of Labor.

**M1** – averages of daily figures for (1) currency outside the Treasury, Federal Reserve banks, and the vaults of commercial banks; (2) travelers checks of non-bank issues; (3) demand deposits at all commercial banks other than those due to domestic banks, the US government, and foreign banks and official institutions less cash items in the process of collection and Federal Reserve float; and (4) other checkable deposits (OCD) consisting of negotiable order of withdrawal (NOW) and automatic transfer service (ATS) accounts at depository institutions other than credit unions, credit union share draft accounts, and demand deposits at savings institutions. The currency and demand deposit components exclude the estimated amount of vault cash and demand deposits, respectively, held by savings institutions to service their OCD liabilities. Quarterly averages of monthly data, seasonally adjusted.
*Source:* Federal Reserve Board.

**M2** – M1 plus overnight (and continuing contract) repurchase agreements (RPs) issued by all commercial banks and eurodollars issued by foreign (principally Caribbean and London) branches of US banks, MMDAs, savings and small denomination time deposits (time deposits – including retail RPs – in amounts of less than $100,000), and balances in both taxable and tax-exempt general purpose and broker/dealer money market mutual funds. Excludes IRA and KEOGH balances at depository institutions and money market funds. Also excludes amounts held by US commercial banks, money market funds (general purpose and broker/dealer), foreign governments and commercial banks, and the US government. M2 will differ from the sum of components by a consolidation adjustment that represents the estimated amount of demand deposits and vault cash held by savings institutions to service time and savings deposits. Quartly averages of monthly data, seasonally adjusted.
*Source:* Federal Reserve Board.

**M3** – M2 plus large-denomination time deposits and term RPs (in amounts of $100,000 or more) issued by commercial banks and savings institutions, excluding those held by depository institutions, the US government, money market funds, and foreign banks and official institutions. M3 will differ from the sum of components by a consolidation adjustment that represents the estimated amount of overnight RPs held by institution-only money market mutual funds. Quarterly averages of monthly data, seasonally adjusted.
*Source:* Federal Reserve Board.

**Petroleum import unit value index,** 1972 = 100, quarterly data, not seasonally adjusted.
*Source:* Bureau of the Census, US Department of Commerce.

**US exchange rate** – an index of the weighted average exchange value of the US dollar. A geometric weighted average of the dollar against ten major foreign currencies. The weight of each currency in the index is equal to that

country's share of total trade (imports plus exports) for the five years 1972–76. March 1973 = 100; quarterly averages of monthly data.
*Source:* Federal Reserve Board.

## NOTES

1 Gordon has written voluminously on this topic. The paper cited in the text is among the more recent, and it has citations for many others.
2 For explicit examination of the extent to which a mainline model (such as the MPS model) can replicate the experience of the 1970s, see Ando and Kennickell (1983).
3 The former channel, working through interest rates, is well known. The latter channel of monetary policy working through induced exchange rate effects has recently been highlighted by Gordon (1982). It is also heavily featured in Stevens *et al.* (1983). The Board's econometric model also has an endogenous exchange rate.
4 For tests of the two competing hypotheses, see Gordon (1982) and Ando and Kennickell (1983).
5 In the simulations, the price target was represented by a fixed-weight deflator for gross domestic sales net of indirect business taxes. This price index has the advantage over a value added deflator, such as the GNP deflator, in that it is not affected perversely in the short run by movements in the inputs, e.g. oil.
6 For analysis and estimates of the effects of the first round of commodity price increases in the early 1970s, see Cagan (1980), Pierce and Enzler (1974) and Berner *et al.* (1975). A useful compendium of results obtained from fourteen models describing the macroeconomic effects of the US oil-price increases is given in a paper by the Energy Modeling Forum (1983).
7 OPEC, of course, does have a major influence on the price of oil through its decisions regarding oil production. The view taken here, however, is that both spot and contract prices for crude oil reflect the supply and demand for oil, so that the causation goes from the spot market price to contract prices. See Verleger (1982) for evidence on this point.
8 For descriptions of the Federal Reserve's monetary policy and operating procedures, see Wallich and Keir (1979), Axilrod (1982) and Davis (1981).
9 A description of the monetary and credit restraint actions undertaken by the Federal Reserve in March 1980 is contained in the *Federal Reserve Bulletin*, April 1980.
10 An extensive description of these new instruments is contained in the article, 'new deposit instruments', *Federal Reserve Bulletin*, May 1983.
11 This program is described in the *Economic Report of the President, 1972–1974*.
12 See, for example, Gordon (1982), Blinder and Newton (1981) and Russell (1982).
13 See, for example, *Economic Report of the President, 1981*, pp. 57–68, and *Brookings Papers on Economic Activity*, vol. 2, 1978, special issue, *Innovative Policies to Slow Inflation*.

## BIBLIOGRAPHY


Anderson, Robert, and Enzler, Jared (1983), 'Stabilizing policy reaction functions', unpublished paper, Federal Reserve Board, July.

Ando, Albert, and Kennickell, Arthur (1983), 'Failure of Keynesian economics and "direct" effects of money supply: a fact or a fiction?', unpublished paper, Federal Reserve Board, March.

Axilrod, Stephen (1982), 'Monetary policy, money supply and the Federal Reserve's operating procedures', in Paul Meek (ed.), *Central Bank Views on Monetary Targeting*, Federal Reserve Bank of New York, May.

Axilrod, Stephen, and Lindsey, David (1981), 'Federal Reserve System implementation of monetary policy: analytical foundation of the new approach', *American Economic Review*, 71(2), May, 246–252.

Baily, Martin Neil (1982b), 'Labor market performance, competition, and inflation', in M. N. Baily (ed.), *Workers, Jobs and Inflation*, Washington, DC, The Brookings Institution, 15–48.

Bartlett, Bruce (1981), *Reaganomics – Supply Side Economics in Action*, Westpoint, Conn., Arlington House Publishers.

Berner, Richard, *et al.* (1975), 'International sources of domestic inflation', Joint Economic Committee, *Studies in Price Stability and Economic Growth*, 94th Congress, 1st Session, paper no. 3, 5 August.

Blinder, Alan (1982), 'The anatomy of double-digit inflation in the 1970s', in Robert E. Hall (ed.), *Inflation: Causes and Effects*, Chicago, Ill., University of Chicago Press, 261–282.

Blinder, Alan, and Newton, W. J. (1981), 'The 1971–1974 controls program and the price level: an econometric post-mortem', *Journal of Monetary Economics*, 7, July, 1–23.

Bruno, Michael, and Sachs, Jeff (1979), 'Macroeconomic adjustment with import price shocks: real and monetary aspects', Working Paper No. 340, National Bureau of Economic Research, April.

Bruno, Michael, and Sachs, Jeff (1982), 'Input price shocks and the slowdown in economic growth: the case of UK manufacturing', Working Paper No. 851, National Bureau of Economic Research, February.

Cagan, Phillip (1980), 'Imported inflation 1973–74 and the accommodation issue', *Journal of Money, Credit and Banking*, 12(1), February, 1–16.

Davis, Richard (1981), 'Monetary aggregates and the use of intermediate targets in monetary policy', in *New Monetary Control Procedures*, Federal Reserve Staff Study, Washington, DC, Board of Governors of the Federal Reserve System.

*Economic Report of the President to Congress* (USA), various years.

Energy Modeling Forum (1983), 'Macroeconomic effects of energy price shocks: EMF 7 working growth report', Energy Modeling Forum, Terman Engineering Center, Stanford University, Calif., July.

*Federal Reserve Bulletin*, Washington, DC, Board of Governors of the Federal Reserve System, various issues.

Federal Reserve Staff Study (1981), *New Monetary Control Procedures*, Washington, DC, Board of Governors of the Federal Reserve System.

Gordon, Robert (1982), 'Inflation, flexible exchange rates, and the natural rate of unemployment', in M. N. Baily (ed.), *Workers, Jobs and Inflation*, Washington, DC, The Brookings Institution, 89–152.

Hall, Robert E. (1979), 'Labor markets in recession and recovery', in National Bureau of Economic Research, *1979 Research Conference: A Summary*, 5–8.

Nordhaus, William (1980), 'Oil and economic performance in industrial countries', *Brookings Papers on Economic Activity*, 2, 341–388.

Okun, A. M. and Perry, G. L. (eds) (1978), 'Innovative policies to slow inflation', *Special Issue of Brookings Papers on Economic Activity*, 2.

Parkin, Michael (1980), 'Oil and push inflation', *Banca Nazionale del Lavoro Quarterly Review*, No. 133, June, 164–185.

Perry, George (1978), 'Slowing the wage–price spiral: the macroeconomic view', *Brookings Papers on Economic Activity*, 2, 259–291.

Pierce, James, and Enzler, Jared (1974), 'The effects of external inflationary shocks', *Brookings Papers on Economic Activity*, 1, 13–54.

Russell, R. Robert (1982), 'Can incomes policies work?', Economic Policy Papers, C. U. Starr Center for Applied Economics, New York University, February.

Sachs, Jeff (1982), 'The oil shocks and macroeconomic adjustment in the United States', *European Economic Review*, 18, May/June, 243–248.

Stevens, Guy, *et al.* (1983), *The US Economy in an Interdependent World: A Multi-country Model*, Washington, DC, Federal Reserve Board.

Tobin, James (1980), 'Stabilization policy ten years after', *Brookings Papers on Economic Activity*, 1, 19–71.

Verleger, Philip K. (1982), 'The determinants of official OPEC crude prices', *Review of Economics and Statistics*, 64(2), May, 177–183.

Wallich, H. C. and Keir, P. M. (1979), 'The role of operating guides in US monetary policy; a historical review', *Federal Reserve Bulletin*, 65(9), September, 679–691.

# 12 Adjustment Performance of Small, Open Economies: Some International Comparisons

*W. D. McCLAM and P. S. ANDERSEN**

## I INTRODUCTION

The adjustment problems of small, open economies have been a focal point of analysis for many years. Up to the early 1970s discussion proceeded against a background of international developments dominated by demand shocks, which often originated in divergent and overambitious demand management policies and ultimately led to breakdown of the Bretton Woods regime. Thereafter, attention shifted as the world economy became subject mainly to supply shocks, including the commodity boom of 1972/3, the two oil shocks, fluctuations in real and nominal exchange rates and, in the early 1980s, the emergence of unusually high interest rates internationally. Whereas in the first period demand disturbances from abroad had affected inflation and unemployment in opposite directions, the second period brought an increase in inflationary pressures and a rise in unemployment at the same time.

Two further developments that have strongly conditioned policy formation in small, open economies have been the generalized move to more flexible exchange rates in the early 1970s and the subsequent adoption in some major countries of targets for the growth of the monetary aggregates. In this environment, and given their openness both as price takers and in regard to capital movements, small, open economies have, with certain exceptions, generally preferred to fix their currencies in relation to that of some larger trading partner rather than to adopt a monetary target. Although the hard-currency option tends to provide a stabilization pivot for their policies, it may also set constraints that are at times too stringent for the country to cope with.

The stylized model of the small, open economy has been the subject of a great deal of theoretical analysis. At the empirical level, of course, there are important differences in the economic position and policy experience of individual countries. At least four differences seem to be of major importance:

* The authors are from the Bank for International Settlements, but the views and conclusions presented in this chapter are their own and are not necessarily shared by that Bank.

degree of openness, vulnerability to particular kinds of external shocks, institutional factors, and policy responses. Obviously, it is of considerable potential interest to compare the experience of different countries with a view to learning the lessons of developments over the past fifteen years. In particular, it is useful to see to what extent rigidities – caused by institutional factors, behavioural patterns or past policy measures – have influenced the adjustment process and thereby either hampered or facilitated the implementation of effective policies. We have chosen for this purpose four countries: Austria, Belgium, Canada and Sweden – a more or less random selection of open economies whose experience, though similar in some respects, has differed widely in others.

## II ECONOMIC DEVELOPMENTS IN AUSTRIA, BELGIUM, CANADA AND SWEDEN

### SOME GENERAL FEATURES

*Austria* belongs to the group of countries with the best overall economic performance even though the initial conditions were not particularly favourable. Thus, Austria has a large share of its labour force employed in agriculture and in industries (particularly textiles and steel) that have been hard hit by recession and international competition. A unique feather has been the Austrian approach to macroeconomic policies ('Austro-Keynesianism') which, within the framework of the 'social partnership', combines a hard-currency option with an active fiscal policy and a relatively accommodating monetary policy. Until recently, Austria was comparatively little affected by the international recession and the rate of unemployment – also helped by a high degree of wage flexibility – has remained near 2 per cent, with an inflation rate well below the OECD average. Public sector deficits have not been a major concern and the monetary authorities have only occasionally encountered difficulties in meeting the twin targets of accommodating the nominal income gains as determined within the social partnership and of setting interest rates at levels that prevent capital outflows.

*Belgium* is one of the countries to record a pronounced deterioration in economic performance. Belgium entered the 1970s with low inflation and unemployment rates and a large surplus on external account, although it was also among the few countries that were already experiencing problems in financing public expenditure. By the early 1980s, however, both unemployment and the public sector deficit had increased to record levels in international as well as historical terms, the external balance had moved into substantial deficit and the rate of inflation was accelerating in the middle of a global disinflationary process. It is true that Belgium's industrial structure made it particularly vulnerable to adverse international trends, but, in addition, high labour costs and extremely rigid wage behaviour have hampered the adjustment process.

*Canada*, unlike most other industrialized countries, experienced a terms-of-trade improvement in the 1970s but, like the USA, also saw a pronounced deterioration in productivity growth. Canada was among the first countries to adopt money supply targets in the implementation of monetary policy, and another feature of policies in Canada has been the use of wage and price controls. Until recently, fiscal policy was not constrained by concerns about public sector deficits, and the unemployment rate, although high by international standards, rose only moderately during the 1970s, and mainly as a result of unusually strong growth in the labour force.

*Sweden* is a representative of the 'Scandinavian group' with its traditional emphasis on the full employment target. Sweden also has a long tradition of active use of fiscal policy and it was in a favourable position by the time of the first oil-price rise, with both public sector finances and external account in large surplus and the economy recovering from a mild recession. However, like Belgium – though for different reasons – Sweden encountered problems in maintaining international competitiveness and the authorities chose to replace the previous hard-currency policy with frequent and large exchange rate adjustments. Another feature of Swedish policies has been the very extensive use of labour-market measures and subsidies to weak firms, which have helped to keep the registered unemployment rate low but at the expense of a growing public sector deficit and slumping productivity growth.

## ADJUSTMENT POLICY PROFILES: FOUR APPROACHES

The four economies have faced common problems of adjustment deriving from the emergence of worldwide inflation, recurrent oil and commodity shocks, high international interest rates and tendencies towards large-scale unemployment. Beyond these similarities, however, these economies are representative of quite different choices in policy priorities and approaches.

### *Austria*

In many respects the most unusual – and successful – case was that of Austria. Demand management policies in that country – although timely in terms of the business cycle – have not only aimed at fine tuning the economy but, more importantly, have attempted to affect expectations in a stabilizating way. In this context the policy makers have been able consistently to start from the basis of an established, continuing incomes policy of an effective kind. In brief, the wage/price outcome is the result of the voluntary, informal cooperation of labour and business working within the confines of the so-called 'social partnership', a highly institutionalized system of political and social consensus that evolved out of Austria's harsh experiences leading up to and following World War II. Price adjustments over a wide range of goods and services are subject to approval by a subcommittee of the Joint Commission for Prices and Wages, and wage bargains must be acceptable to the Wage Subcommittee.[1]

The achievement of satisfactory wage/price results is said to be facilitated by Austria's pursuance of a hard-currency policy, which aims at minimizing fluctuations between the schilling and the Deutsche Mark. Wage bargaining looks for guidance to the outcome of negotiations in West Germany, particularly in the metal-working industry, and prices are adjusted, on the basis of rises in costs, with an eye to international competitiveness. In this respect, much as had been hoped of monetary targets in other countries, the hard-currency policy has been a basis for helping to stabilize the expectations of domestic economic agents. The Austrian hard-currency policy also lends a new twist to the Scandinavian theory of inflation: in a highly competitive environment, with prices in the exposed sector leaving little margin for advantageous bargaining, incomes policy has focused largely on the importance of exercising reasonable restraint on wage increases in the sheltered sector in order not to upset historical wage relativities.

Freed from any overriding concern about autonomous wage/price pressures, the Austrian authorities through most of the 1970s were able to follow a countercyclical budget policy. Moreover, with real wages being kept under reasonable restraint, the maintenance of high levels of employment was possible without an unduly large growth of public sector expenditure, particularly of transfer payments.[2] Thus, unlike most countries, Austria was able to meet the oil-price shocks through a combination of incomes and exchange rate policies to offset the cost-push effect and of fiscal policies to offset the deflationary effect. Some budgetary support was given to structurally weak industries, but for this purpose the authorities preferred to rely on accelerated investment allowances and credits to sustain real capital formation. More recently, in the context of deep world recession, unemployment has risen significantly for the first time. Moreover, there are indications that the effectiveness of fiscal policy has declined and the budget deficit has increased to disquietening proportions, leading the authorities, as in other countries, to introduce measures designed to reduce the structural component of the deficit.

Against this background, monetary policy was basically accommodating, with interest rates being kept in line with those in West Germany (see next section). True, to keep credit to the private sector within bounds, ceiling limitations were in effect over most of the period, backed up by the condition that, if not observed, central bank refinancing facilities could be restricted. However, although direct and indirect central bank lending to the government is, in principle,[3] forbidden in Austria, there was no question of not making available adequate sources of finance to the public sector. To avoid excessive recourse to domestic credit markets, and to alleviate any inconsistency between domestic and external objectives, the government itself sought as far as possible to borrow from the capital market and from abroad.

Austrian adjustment policies have not been without their difficulties. On occasion, as in 1975/76, real wages have been allowed to increase excessively, contributing in 1977 to an unusually rapid expansion of domestic credit. Another difficulty emerged in 1979 when interest rates were kept too low, leading to a large outflow of reserves. Moreover, the usefulness of the hard-currency policy has been questioned. Some critics feel that this policy tends over long periods to weaken competitiveness, undermine domestic industry and contribute to a long-persisting current account deficit, whereas others maintain that it enforces greater cost effectiveness on the exposed sector and helps to dampen import prices, wages and inflationary expectations. What is noteworthy is that, when difficulties emerged or mistakes were made, Austrian adjustment policies were sufficiently flexible to remedy the situation in due course. It might also be fair to characterize Austrian policy as constituting a policy-mix approach to monetary control. In other words, by focusing their adjustment efforts so successfully on incomes and fiscal policies in the context of a hard-currency policy, the Austrian authorities tend indirectly to achieve a satisfactory path of money growth.

*Belgium*

Like Austria, Belgium consistently opted for a hard-currency policy but, in terms of policy objectives, Belgium's emphasis on combating inflation sharply contrasted (formally at least) with the priority given in Austria to low unemployment. In practice, moreover, there were several fundamental weaknesses that in the Belgian environment accentuated the problems of both full employment and inflation. First, in terms of openness, Belgium's exposed sector is more than twice as large, measured relative to GNP, as that of our other three countries. Secondly, the structure of Belgian industry, with its emphasis on older traditional industries, was ill-suited to the changed competitive environment of world trade in the 1970s and 1980s. Thirdly, in sharp contrast to the consensus incomes policy ingrained in the Austrian setting, Belgium was burdened from the beginning with a comprehensive system of wage and salary indexation, in both private and public sectors. In the context of the kinds of external shock experienced in the 1970s, the key problem that emerged was that of high real wages combined with strong built-in rigidities.

Belgium, much like the other three countries, sought by means of fiscal policy to alleviate the growing problem of unemployment, although its measures appear to have been ill-timed and worked in a procyclical way. Moreover, given its cyclical and structural competitive weakness (both abroad and at home), budget deficits mounted sharply over the years (see Table 12.1). Expenditure increased virtually across the board: indexed public sector wages, educational and social outlays, other transfer payments and not least – with its relatively large public sector debt – interest payments. By the advent of the second oil shock and in its aftermath, the public sector deficit had emerged as a major problem in its own right.

Despite these cumulating difficulties, the authorities considered it vital to adhere determinedly to a hard-currency policy, backed up by a dual exchange rate system and, as appropriate, an adjustment of domestic interest rates. Although, apart from periods of exchange market pressures, the central bank sought to keep interest rates as low as possible, rates generally tended to move much closer to US interest rates than to West German ones (see Table 12.2 below) – a reflection, perhaps, of Belgium's high degree of financial openness. Even so, the maintenance of the exchange rate parity required heavy intervention, supported by growing recourse over recent years to borrowing abroad by both the private and the public sector.

Despite Belgium's progressive deterioration in economic performance, the authorities resisted a devaluation of the Belgian franc until 1982. The view taken was that, given Belgium's extreme dependence on imports and the existence of comprehensive incomes indexation, devaluation would be inflationary and ineffective unless accompanied by appropriate stabilization measures. On the basis of emergency legislation in early 1982, permitting economic measures by decree, the franc was devalued in February by $8\frac{1}{2}$ per

**Table 12.1** *Indicators of fiscal policy*

| *Countries and items* | *1960* | *1970* | *1973* | *1975* | *1978* | *1980* | *1981* | *1982*[a] |
|---|---|---|---|---|---|---|---|---|
| | | | *as a percentage of GNP/GDP* | | | | | |
| *Canada:* | | | | | | | | |
| Public expenditure | 28.5 | 35.0 | 35.1 | 39.7 | 40.3 | 40.2 | 41.0 | 45.6 |
| Goods and services | 16.5 | 21.7 | 20.7 | 22.4 | 22.2 | 21.4 | 21.3 | 23.0 |
| Transfers | 12.0 | 13.3 | 14.4 | 17.3 | 18.1 | 18.8 | 19.7 | 22.6 |
| of which: interest | 2.8 | 3.8 | 3.9 | 4.0 | 4.9 | 5.3 | 6.2 | 7.2 |
| Revenue | 26.7 | 35.9 | 36.1 | 37.3 | 37.3 | 38.1 | 39.8 | 40.3 |
| Deficit (+) | 1.7 | -0.9 | -1.0 | 2.4 | 3.0 | 2.1 | 1.2 | 5.3 |
| Public debt | — | 64.5 | 56.9 | 55.3 | 60.4 | 58.5 | 59.4 | 65.8 |
| *Austria* | | | | | | | | |
| Public expenditure | 32.1 | 38.2 | 38.6 | 44.2 | 48.3 | 46.9 | 48.2 | 48.3 |
| Goods and services | 19.4 | 19.8 | 20.4 | 22.8 | 23.3 | 22.4 | 22.6 | — |
| Transfers | 12.7 | 18.4 | 18.2 | 21.4 | 25.0 | 24.5 | 25.6 | — |
| of which: interest | — | 1.1 | 1.1 | 1.4 | 2.2 | 2.5 | 2.7 | 3.2 |
| Revenue | 31.0 | 39.7 | 41.9 | 42.8 | 46.2 | 45.9 | 47.4 | 46.2 |
| Deficit (+)[b] | 1.1 | -1.0 | -1.3 | 2.5 | 2.8 | 2.0 | 1.8 | 2.2 |
| Public debt | — | 19.4 | 17.5 | 24.0 | 33.9 | 37.1 | 39.2 | 41.0 |
| *Belgium* | | | | | | | | |
| Public expenditure | 30.3 | 37.0 | 39.7 | 45.3 | 49.1 | 52.7 | 58.9 | 60.0 |
| Goods and services | 14.7 | 17.4 | 18.4 | 20.5 | 21.5 | 22.5 | 21.8 | 21.2 |
| Transfers | 15.6 | 19.6 | 21.3 | 24.8 | 27.6 | 30.2 | 37.1 | 38.8 |
| of which: interest | 2.9 | 3.4 | 3.4 | 3.6 | 4.6 | 6.3 | 8.0 | 9.5 |
| Revenue | 27.5 | 35.7 | 37.0 | 41.2 | 43.5 | 44.1 | 46.7 | 48.8 |
| Deficit (+)[b] | — | 3.7 | 5.3 | 6.4 | 8.2 | 12.2 | 16.5 | 16.1 |
| Public debt | — | 65.2 | 61.9 | 58.7 | 65.5 | 76.0 | 88.2 | 97.4 |
| *Sweden* | | | | | | | | |
| Public expenditure | 31.3 | 43.8 | 44.9 | 49.1 | 59.0 | 61.6 | 65.9 | 68.2 |
| Goods and services | 20.2 | 28.2 | 27.7 | 28.1 | 32.6 | 33.3 | 33.8 | 33.7 |
| Transfers | 11.1 | 15.6 | 17.2 | 21.0 | 26.4 | 28.3 | 32.1 | 34.5 |
| of which: interest | 1.7 | 1.9 | 2.0 | 2.2 | 2.7 | 4.1 | 5.7 | 7.4 |
| Revenue | 32.2 | 47.0 | 47.9 | 50.7 | 57.9 | 56.8 | 60.6 | 61.1 |
| Deficit (+)[b] | -1.1 | -4.7 | -4.0 | -2.7 | 0.5 | 4.0 | 5.3 | 7.1 |
| Public debt | — | 33.6 | 35.6 | 35.6 | 41.7 | 52.3 | 60.3 | 69.1 |

*Notes:* a Preliminary data.
b Including lending transactions.
*Source:* OECD and national statistics.

cent within the European Monetary System (EMS), accompanied by a temporary price freeze and suspension of incomes indexation arrangements, with a relaxation to take place only gradually. In consequence, an effective devaluation along textbook lines proved possible, accompanied by a substantial reflux of capital but a relatively small change in relative prices.

*Sweden*

In Sweden, and in Canada as well, relatively heavy dependence on exports of primary industry imparts an extra dimension to openness, as does a tendency for domestic activity to lag behind economic developments abroad. Broadly speaking, these countries fall somewhere between Austria and Belgium in terms of their susceptibility to external disturbances. At the same time, Sweden is much like Austria in the importance it attaches to the maintenance of low levels of unemployment. It cannot be said, on the other hand, that incomes policy has been a very helpful instrument in adjusting real wages to changing external conditions. In practice, therefore, Sweden's commitment to exchange rate stability has proved to be weak, and it has relied primarily on fiscal policy, together with several exchange rate adjustments, to keep unemployment low while seeking to preserve external competitiveness. In the circumstances, monetary policy has been aimed mainly at liquidity control, exercised largely by means of credit ceilings, liquidity ratios and investment quotas for banks and other financial institutions. As in Belgium, the monetary authorities have consistently argued that the demand for money was unstable, relying instead on a credit market approach. In contrast to Belgium, however, efforts have been made in Sweden to channel credit towards priority sectors, particularly to the central government and housing. Interest rates, though still subject to supervision, have over the years been increasingly adapted to international market conditions and the domestic scope for market-determined rates has increased.

On grounds of openness and as a counter to inflation, Sweden has viewed a stable exchange rate as being, in principle, a desirable aim of policy. From 1973 to 1977 it adhered to a hard-currency policy as a member of the European 'Snake' arrangement. A strong current account balance of payments position, together with a marked increase in profits in 1973/4, enabled Sweden to weather the initial phase of the first oil shock quite well. Expecting that the world recession would be short-lived, the authorities deliberately chose expansionary demand management policies, both fiscal and monetary, in an effort to sustain output and employment. However, wage pressures were mounting in response to the strong profit rise in 1973/4 while, at the same time, the bridging policy weakened employers' resistance, leading to a 40 per cent rise in nominal wage costs in only two years. In consequence, external payments difficulties began to build up in 1976 and the international competitiveness of Swedish firms deteriorated sharply. These developments led, despite a tightening of policies, to a sizeable devaluation in April 1977 (6 per cent against the Deutsche Mark) and subsequently, in August, to a withdrawal from the 'Snake' arrangement, a further 10 per cent devaluation and a decision to fix the krona in terms of a weighted currency basket. As external conditions eased, and as a moderation of wage settlements was achieved, expansionary policies were again put into effect on domestic grounds. Thus, when the second oil shock set in, Sweden found itself, with a sharply weakened public sector balance and relatively low interest rates, facing a renewed deterioration in its payments position. In the course of 1981 a new programme of wage restraint was agreed upon and fiscal and monetary policies were tightened. However, the appreciation of the US dollar within Sweden's currency basket caused the krona to appreciate relative to the Deutsche Mark, and growing competitive pressures led the authorities to devalue the krona by 10 per cent in October. Subsequently, when despite this move the current account deficit did not decline, the new government decided on competitive grounds to devalue by a further 16 per cent in October 1982.

Thus, Sweden's exchange rate difficulties started around the middle of the 1970s and to a considerable extent reflected a progressive weakening in the current account. As time went on, it became apparent that the deterioration was partly of a structural nature, stemming much as in Belgium from excessive dependence on traditional industries such as steel, textiles, shipbuilding and paper products. However, the difficulties were also largely attributable to discretionary policy efforts to compensate for external disturbances and to keep employment high. This resulted in a strong 'stop–go' cycle in which every easing of the external constraint was followed by a move to more expansionary domestic policies, mainly of a budgetary nature, leading to an acceleration of domestic credit expansion and price inflation, widening external deficits and increased recourse to foreign borrowing.[4]

Among our four countries, therefore, Sweden stands out for its heavy emphasis on fine-tuning by way of compensatory fiscal policy. Expansionary measures were taken in the wake of the first oil shock and, despite occasional tightening, fiscal policy remained strongly expansionary over the rest of the decade, with the central government's borrowing requirement rising from about 2 per cent of GNP in 1976 to about 11 per cent in 1980. Total expenditure and taxation (already comparatively burdensome) accelerated rapidly after 1973, being higher relative to GNP than in most other OECD countries. One feature in Sweden was the growth of industrial subsidies during the 1970s, the aim being to 'bridge' the weakness in world demand in order to keep down unemployment. However, as this involved substantial assistance to declining industries, such as shipbuilding, steel and wood and paper products, policy in the early 1980s turned towards reducing these subsidies. Another feature of budgets was the substantial size of social expenditure and benefits, in some cases (e.g. pensions) indexed in such a way as to provide a gradual improvement in real terms. By 1980 it had become widely appreciated that the large size of the public sector, and the heavy financing requirement, were tending to crowd out private investment activity and impede external adjustment. In conjunction with the two devaluations, fiscal policy became more restrictive, involving some cuts in public consumption and investment, lower subsidies and curbs on transfer payments.[5]

### *Canada*

In contrast to the other three countries, Canada was alone in placing reliance mainly on monetary policy for stabilization purposes, with the exchange rate in principle floating freely after 1970. After the first oil shock, it is true, an expansionary budget policy was pursued in order to sustain activity. Moreover, and even more than in Sweden, the commodity boom of 1972/3, combined with low domestic interest rates to limit exchange rate appreciation, helped to stimulate inflationary pressures and to move the current account into substantial deficit beginning in 1974. By late 1975 inflation had assumed top priority, and the authorities introduced a mandatory programme of price and wage controls, which continued in effect until 1978. In addition, the Bank of Canada adopted a target for the trend growth of M1, with an ensuing rise in interest rates relative to those abroad being accompanied by a sharp appreciation of the nominal and real effective exchange rate. An easing of inflation in 1977 and 1978 led to a lowering of interest rates, a dismantling of price/wage controls and a sharp depreciation in the nominal and real effective exchange rate – not, however, with any significant improvement in the current account deficit.[6] Partly as a result of this experience, the authorities appear thereafter to have given more attention to the exchange rate, although continuing to fix monetary targets aimed at gradually reducing the rate of monetary growth. A further phase in exchange rate policy emerged as the US dollar strengthened. High domestic interest rates, together with a desire to limit any further depreciation in US dollar terms, contributed to a rise in the real effective exchange rate and some loss of competitiveness.

As already mentioned, monetary targeting seems to have little appeal for the typical small, open economy. For this reason, the Canadian experience is of particular interest and, as an approach, is based on some rather special features. At the same time, one fairly positive development was that fiscal policy, although expansionary after the first oil shock, did not get out of hand in the following years (see Table 12.1 above). Tax subsidies and high interest rates might also help to explain a quite remarkable increase in household saving in the latter half of the 1970s. Since fixed capital investment remained relatively strong in Canada until the early 1980s, mainly because of resource and energy development, the buoyancy of final demand also helped to keep budget deficits within bounds. Another factor, of course, is that budgetary policy was not used as actively as, for example, in Sweden, although labour market measures were also very important in the Canadian case.

In the course of 1982/3 Canada was hit by its worst recession of the post-war period. Reflecting its external exposure, including high international indebtedness, the main causal factors were disproportionate wage increases, high interest rates, weak world markets, low commodity prices and, to some extent, the strengthening of the currency in line with the US dollar. However, given that inflation in Canada, although steadily declining, is still higher than in the United States, Canada has kept the exchange rate vis-à-vis the US dollar very stable. At the same time, the Spring 1983 budget, while providing a moderate fiscal stimulus (higher public investment, tax concessions and measures to promote job creation), reflected a major effort to reduce the budget deficit over the medium term and to encourage private investment and exports.

## MONETARY DEVELOPMENTS AND POLICY

### *Interest rates and exchange rates*

Turning now to monetary implications, we first look broadly at comparative developments in terms of interest rate differentials, effective exchange rates and official reserve movements. In the small, open economy, disturbances

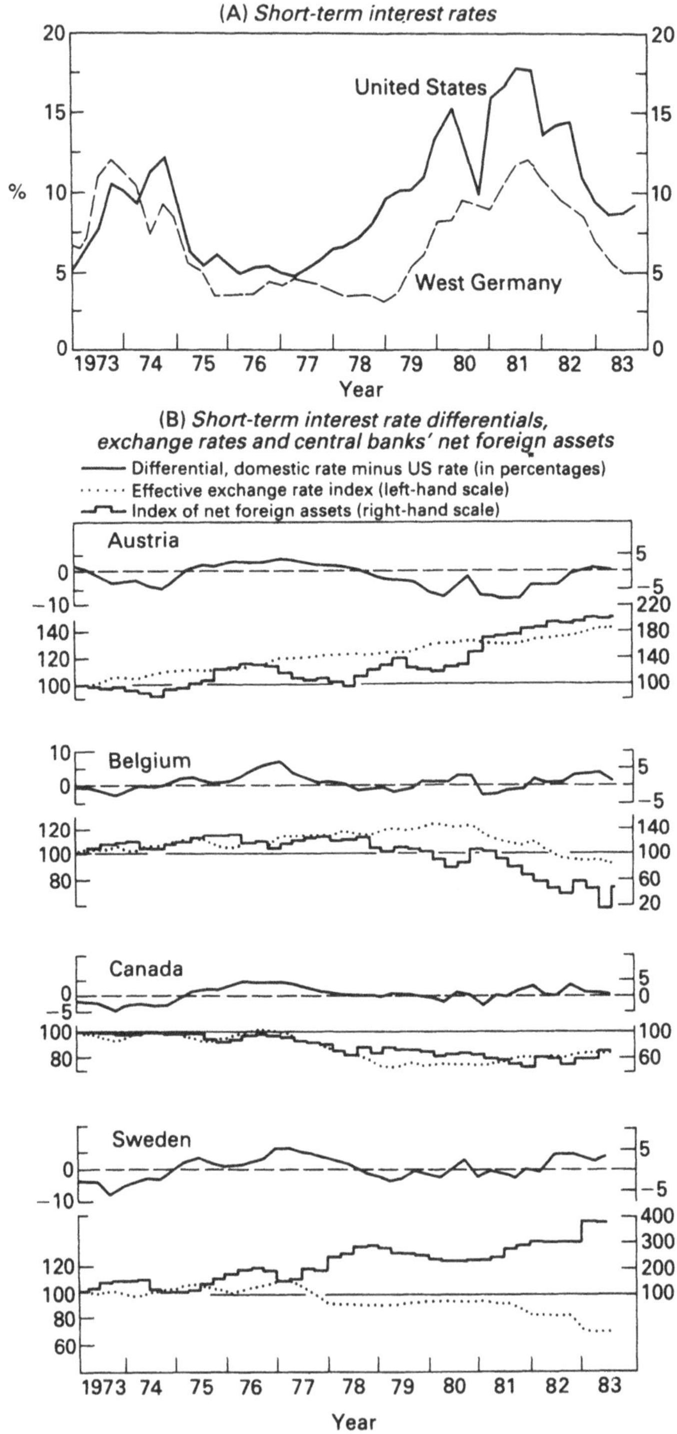

(A) Short-term interest rates
United States
West Germany
%
Year
(B) Short-term interest rate differentials, exchange rates and central banks' net foreign assets
Differential, domestic rate minus US rate (in percentages)
Effective exchange rate index (left-hand scale)
Index of net foreign assets (right-hand scale)
Austria
Belgium
Canada
Sweden
1973 74 75 76 77 78 79 80 81 82 83
Year


**Figure 12.1**

from abroad, in their monetary guise, present the authorities essentially with a choice in terms of interest rate adjustment, exchange rate adjustment and intervention, singly or combined. Broadly speaking, the outcome in these respects is shown in Figure 12.1.

Table 12.2 provides a tentative assessment of how closely interest rates in the four countries are related to international rates, with West Germany and the United States having been selected as representative of rates in key financial centres. Although there are some indications of mis-specified equations, the table points to a high degree of capital and money market integration but also to some interesting differences in the sources and strengths of the international influences:

- *Austria* is the only country in which West German rates have any significant influence[7] and, reflecting the hard-currency policy, the discount rate is more strongly influenced than the three-month market rate. As regards the bond rate, the impacts of changes in German and US bond rates are of about equal size. Interestingly, compared with the other three countries, Austrian rates are relatively independent, as only around one-half of international changes is reflected in domestic rates;
- *Belgium* and *Sweden* are very similar in that 70–75 per cent of changes in US rates are reflected in domestic short-term rates while for bond rates this proportion increases to 85 per cent. In both countries movements in the bond rate are almost entirely explained by international trends, while in the shorter run unexplained deviations from international trends account for 36–43 per cent of the variations;
- in *Canada* the bond rate follows the US rate one-for-one. The three-month rate is less well determined and appears to have been subject to some instability.

*Domestic credit expansion, external balance and money growth*

Domestic credit expansion (DCE) via the banking system accelerated from the early 1960s onwards in all the countries. Moreover, the balance of payments, as measured by changes in the banking system's net foreign assets (i.e. approximately the 'basic' balance), shifted from a surplus in the years 1960–5 to a deficit in 1976–80. In terms of its percentage point contribution to acceleration in the broad money stock, DCE increased much more in Canada and Sweden than in Austria and Belgium. However, whereas credit to the public sector accounted for about one-half of the increase in Sweden, credit to the private sector was much the predominant influence in Canada. In part, this was a reflection of the better fiscal performance in Canada, but it was also due to the fact that public sector financing in Canada occurred to a greater extent outside the banking system. In both countries the fast expansion of domestic credit was also associated partly with the external impulses feeding through the export sector. In Austria and Belgium, credit to the public sector accounted for about one-third or more of total DCE over the two periods.

*Sweden* Viewing the financial balance sheet as a whole, credit expansion in Sweden has accelerated over the last fifteen years. A particularly sharp

**Table 12.2** *Domestic and foreign interest rates (average annual data)*

| *Country* | *Dependent variable* | | *Explanatory variables* | | | | |
|---|---|---|---|---|---|---|---|
| | | *Constant* | *West German rate*[a] | *US rate*[a] | $\bar{R}^2$ | *DW* | *Period* |
| Austria | Discount rate | 3.40 (6.0) | 0.20 (2.1) | 0.04 (0.4) | 0.32 | 2.2 | 1965–82 |
| | 3-month rate | 3.35 (4.0) | 0.14 (1.2) | 0.42 (3.4) | 0.66 | 1.8 | 1968–82 |
| | Bond rate | 4.13 (4.7) | 0.24 (1.9) | 0.30 (4.9) | 0.73 | 0.9 | 1965–82 |
| Belgium | 3-month rate | 2.49 (2.5) | 0.02 (0.1) | 0.70 (3.8) | 0.57 | 2.0 | 1961–82 |
| | Bond rate | 1.86 (3.1) | 0.02 (0.2) | 0.86 (18.5) | 0.96 | 1.4 | 1961–82 |
| Canada | 3-month rate | –0.42 (0.8) | — ([b]) | 1.21 (14.6) | 0.90 | 0.9 | 1961–82 |
| | Bond rate | 0.56 (2.9) | — ([b]) | 1.02 (40.7) | 0.99 | 1.6 | 1961–82 |
| Sweden | 3-month rate | 1.54 (1.9) | — ([b]) | 0.75 (6.4) | 0.64 | 1.7 | 1961–82 |
| | Bond rate | 1.88 (5.2) | — ([b]) | 0.86 (18.4) | 0.94 | 0.9 | 1961–82 |

*Notes:* a 3-month rate and bond rate respectively, according to dependent variable.
[b] Excluded from final estimates as coefficient was found to be negative.
$\bar{R}^2$ = coefficient of determination corrected for degrees of freedom; *DW* = Durbin–Watson statistic; t-statistics given in brackets.

increase occurred around 1976–7, when monetary policy was relatively loose and the general government sector shifted into financial deficit and first began to borrow abroad. From 1977 to 1982 total funds raised by non-bank domestic sectors rose from about 19 to well over 25 per cent of GNP. The proportion of total borrowing accounted for by public sector borrowing went up at the same time from about 27.5 per cent to over 50 per cent. From the monetary standpoint, the most critical problem became that of controlling the liquidity creation stemming from the growing public sector borrowing needs. The external deficit itself tended continuously to drain off domestic liquidity, but this was more or less replaced by borrowing abroad, at first by the central government but later by local authorities and other borrowers. However, although foreign borrowing increased rapidly from 1977 onwards, its proportion of total borrowing rose only from 27 to 29 per cent, reflecting the sharp concurrent rise in borrowing from the domestic market as well.

Monetary policy in Sweden traditionally put its main emphasis on liquidity control and credit availability to particular sectors. However, the role of 'credit rationing' changed around the middle of the 1970s. A two-tier credit market began to develop, with an organized sector subject to controls and another relatively free one. The free sector consists mainly of finance companies (numbering about 150), of which those associated with banks constitute the great majority, with loans being made at market-determined interest rates instead of regulated ones. Moreover, foreign borrowing proved to be another means of circumventing limits on credit availability: lending abroad was permitted if financed abroad, while domestically it was possible to obtain additional krona credit if this could be indirectly financed abroad.

In short, the emergence of a large public sector deficit, together with the ease with which it could be financed, increasingly became a source of massive liquidity creation.

*Belgium* Like Austria and Sweden, Begium has consistently rejected the idea of using a money stock target. It is believed that the demand for money, however defined, is too unstable to permit such a target to be a practicable tool of policy. The reasons that have been given are several: the high degree of openness and related shifts of funds internationally (especially changes in leads and lags); the large scope domestically for shifts between different types of deposit and between different types of financial institution; the importance of the government securities market and the role of expectations; and, finally, the extensive use of overdraft facilities in the Belgian economy. From the outset of the floating rate era, therefore, Belgium opted for a hard-currency policy, to which it steadfastly adhered, first under the European 'Snake' arrangement and subsequently under the European Monetary System. Owing to the variable, and sometimes large, degree of monetary financing of budget deficits, much attention has focused on the control of credit expansion to the private sector. In this context, bank liquidity is considered a key indicator, and the authorities have on occasion had recourse to reserve requirements, credit ceilings and portfolio investment ratios for financial institutions. However, considering the whole of the period under review, the adjustment of interest rates, supported at times by large-scale intervention (including government borrowing abroad) has been the principal instrument for keeping the exchange rate stable in relation to the currencies in Belgium's main trading partners. Another supporting element has been the continuing use of a dual exchange market system – a regulated market for current transactions and most transfer payments and a free market for most transactions of a capital nature.

Taking the private sector as a whole, financial asset formation exceeded financial liabilities after 1973. However, as the public sector's financing requirement rose from 4 per cent of GNP to over 16 per cent in 1982, it absorbed the increase in the private sector's net financial assets and formed the financing counterpart of the external deficit as well.

*Canada* Canada stands out among the four countries for the relatively strong emphasis that it placed on monetary policy for stabilization purposes. Although this was perhaps more evident from about 1975 onwards (following the introduction of an M1 growth target), targeting did not change operating procedures in any fundamental way. Monetary policy had traditionally relied for its effects on generalized interest rate influences stemming from its actions to influence the banks' cash reserves, and this approach remained more or less intact. The purpose of targeting was seen more in avoiding cumulative errors through biased reactions to short-term developments, in helping to avoid procyclical monetary responses and in influencing market expectations. The main difference, however, lay in the emergence of inflation as a persisting, growing problem and the recognition that monetary policy would have to assume a major role in combating it.

The intensification of inflation around the middle of the 1970s was an outgrowth of the international commodity boom of 1972/3 followed by the first oil shock. At first, from about 1970 to early 1973, Canada's balance of payments was strong, interest rates could be kept low on domestic grounds and exchange rate appreciation was avoided. However, both M1 and M2 went up quite sharply over the two years to mid-1974. Discretionary fiscal measures were used to sustain activity after the oil-price shock, contributing their part to the emergence of a substantial external current account deficit. In consequence, given the large external deficit, the introduction of a monetary target presented no problem of conflict with the exchange rate, although it contributed to a widening of interest rate differentials in favour of Canada in 1975.

However, in 1976 and 1977, interest rate differentials dropped fairly steadily and the Canadian dollar depreciated substantially over the two years 1977/8. Up to a point this was consistent with the perceived need to improve competitiveness, but, by the time price and wage controls were dismantled, fears had grown that progressive depreciation might only be the forerunner of new inflationary pressures. Against this background, and with the second oil shock exacerbating the inflationary problem, the authorities began to give more attention to keeping the exchange rate stable, particularly vis-à-vis the US dollar. However, it could still not be said that there was any conflict between monetary and exchange rate considerations.

Against the background of a high inflation rate, the first setting of the M1 target in 1975 established a growth range of 10–15 per cent, which was to be brought down gradually from year to year. In this respect the authorities were quite successful, and the target for 1982 (prior to its being dropped as no longer workable) was 4–8 per cent. Except for several cases of undershooting (particularly in 1976/7 and 1981/2), the technical performance in hitting the target was noteworthy. None the less, Canada experienced an acceleration in the rate of consumer price inflation from 1976 to the end of 1981 before a decline finally set in.

The possible reasons for this disappointing outcome present an interesting puzzle. It may be pointed out that the choice of M1 was based on its earlier stability characteristics and its substantial elasticity with respect to interest rates, but it is interesting to note that, as a share of total financial assets, M1 in Canada is very small compared with that in other countries, including the United States. In fact, its control was based on a 'feed back' approach under which, because of the closeness of its relationship with final demand, it could serve as an indicator of the need for adjustments in interest rates. However, there was never any ambiguity about the underlying view that it was interest rates that served as the cutting edge of the transmission process, not the quantity of M1 as such. Moreover, given that the M1 target was set in terms of a *trend* growth rate, there was considerable built-in flexibility with respect to interest rate and exchange rate considerations. Thus, the authorities have not paid attention to M1 to the exclusion of other guides to policy. In particular, in the case of higher import prices, exchange rate depreciation would tend to lead any corrective signals that might subsequently come from new inflationary pressures and an induced rise in M1. The same would be true in the case of an improvement in the terms of trade that stimulated increased demand for wages in the export sector.

Canada's abandonment of its M1 target in late 1982 did not signify any change in monetary stance; the predilection for targeting remains, as it is seen to provide the central bank with a 'place to stand'. The reason, rather, was that rapid financial innovation, resulting in changes in the forms in which money balances are held, was rendering M1 unusable. In the Canadian case, the underlying factors were inflation, high interest rates, computer technology and financial competition. Interestingly, in contrast to developments in the United States, financial deregulation was not a factor (see Freedman, 1983). To illustrate: banks have on an increasing scale been offering business firms cash management facilities involving the daily consolidation of all their current account balances on a country-wide scale. In some instances this has involved the elimination of business holdings of M1, or, alternatively, arrangements that encourage M1 holdings on the basis of negotiated rates of return. For individuals, the banks began in 1979 to offer savings accounts with interest rates calculated on a daily basis. Another development has been the offer of chequing privileges as well as a market rate of interest on accounts above a certain level. All these developments have contributed, if not to economies of M1, to uncertainties in interpreting its movements. The authorities hope in time to devise a transactions aggregate that would be a reliable substitute.

**Table 12.3** *Money supply and price inflation, 1964–81*

| *Country* | *Main determinant % change* | *Independent variables* | | | | | *Summary statistics* | |
|---|---|---|---|---|---|---|---|---|
| | | *Current* | *1 lag* | *2 lags* | $\Delta \frac{IMP}{EXP}$ | *Dummy* | $\bar{R}^2$ | *DW* |
| *Austria:* | | | | | | | | |
| GDP deflator | M1 | 0.11 (1.9) | 0.16 (2.6) | 0.12 (1.9) | 0.36 (1.9) | | 0.37 | 0.8 |
| | M3 | — | 0.08 (0.4) | 0.09 (0.5) | 0.22 (0.7) | | –0.17 | 0.4 |
| | ULC | 0.08 (1.0) | 0.28 (3.5) | — | — | | 0.57 | 1.4 |
| Consumption deflator | M1 | — | 0.13 (1.7) | 0.13 (1.6) | 0.40 (1.7) | | 0.17 | 1.1 |
| | M3 | 0.10 (0.5) | 0.01 (0.2) | — | 0.33 (1.1) | | –0.11 | 0.5 |
| | ULC | 0.16 (2.0) | 0.28 (3.4) | — | 0.34 (2.2) | | 0.66 | 1.3 |
| *Belgium:* | | | | | | | | |
| GDP deflator | M1 | — | 0.21 (1.5) | 0.52 (3.3) | — | | 0.49 | 1.4 |
| | M3 | — | 0.19 (1.4) | 0.57 (3.9) | — | | 0.56 | 1.4 |
| | ULC | 0.15 (2.1) | 0.45 (5.9) | — | –0.27 (1.2) | | 0.80 | 1.4 |
| Consumption deflator | M1 | — | 0.32 (2.3) | 0.44 (2.9) | 1.01 (3.2) | | 0.59 | 1.7 |
| | M2 | — | 0.23 (1.6) | 0.50 (3.2) | 0.73 (2.3) | | 0.57 | 1.3 |
| | ULC | 0.23 (2.8) | 0.38 (4.5) | — | 0.23 (1.0) | | 0.78 | 1.5 |

| | | | | | | | | |
|---|---|---|---|---|---|---|---|---|
| *Canada:* | | | | | | | | |
| GDP deflator | M1 | — | 0.30 (1.4) | 0.57 (3.7) | −0.20 (1.0) | — | 0.56 | 0.8 |
| | M2 | — | 0.36 (2.6) | 0.50 (3.4) | −0.26 (1.5) | −3.83 (1.7) | 0.66 | 1.9 |
| | LIAB | — | 1.02 (4.6) | — | −0.45 (2.6) | −1.80 (0.8) | 0.62 | 1.2 |
| | ULC | — | 0.60 (8.2) | — | −0.59 (5.5) | 3.00 (2.5) | 0.85 | 1.9 |
| Consumption deflator | M1 | — | 0.33 (1.4) | 0.47 (2.4) | 0.21 (1.0) | — | 0.34 | 0.6 |
| | M2 | — | 0.35 (2.5) | 0.48 (3.1) | 0.15 (0.8) | −3.91 (1.7) | 0.50 | 1.6 |
| | LIAB | — | 1.00 (4.5) | — | — | −2.21 (1.2) | 0.55 | 1.2 |
| | ULC | — | 0.55 (5.5) | — | — | 1.80 (1.3) | 0.66 | 1.4 |
| *Sweden:* | | | | | | | | |
| GDP deflator | M1 | 0.26 (2.3) | 0.16 (1.4) | — | −0.23 (1.3) | | 0.31 | 1.3 |
| | M2 | — | — | 0.70 (2.6) | −0.18 (1.0) | | 0.26 | 0.7 |
| | ULC | 0.13 (1.2) | 0.52 (4.9) | — | −0.11 (0.9) | | 0.70 | 2.4 |
| Consumption deflator | M1 | 0.28 (3.0) | 0.11 (1.2) | — | — | | 0.39 | 1.3 |
| | M2 | — | — | 0.67 (2.9) | — | | 0.32 | 0.6 |
| | ULC | 0.13 (1.1) | 0.42 (3.5) | — | 0.10 (0.7) | | 0.53 | 1.3 |

*Notation:* M1 = percentage change in narrow money stock; M2/M3 = percentage change in broad money stock; ULC = percentage change in unit labour costs; LIAB = percentage change in banking system's total liabilities; Δ(IMP/EXP) = year-to-year change in ratio between import and export prices; Dummy = 0.5 for 1976, 1 for 1977 and 1978, otherwise 0 (proxy for wage and price controls introduced in Canada in October 1975); $\bar{R}^2$ = coefficient of determination corrected for degrees of freedom; *DW* = Durbin–Watson statistic; t-statistics given in brackets. All equations contain a significant intercept term, which is not shown in the table.

MONETARY POLICY AND INFLATION

Although few would question the proposition that in the long run inflation is a monetary phenomenon, it is far more difficult to say whether monetary policy has *directly*[8] affected inflation during the shorter periods considered in this chapter. This is particularly so in small and open economies, because international price developments are bound to have a major impact regardless of the current stance of monetary policy.[9]

None the less, changes in the money supply (whether induced by domestic credit expansion or by changes in foreign reserves) may still act as a determinant of inflation. Without any claim to deliver 'the final verdict', Table 12.3 presents some tentative estimates for the period 1964–81. First, for each country, changes in the GDP and private consumption deflators were regressed on changes in the broad and narrow monetary aggregates (subject to various lags) and in foreign prices.[10] Secondly, this simplistic monetarist approach was replaced by a mark-up hypothesis as the change in unit labour costs (current and lagged) was entered and tested as the main determinant of prices.

For all four countries there is a significant and positive impact of either current or lagged changes in the money supply on prices: in both Canada and Belgium this approach explains 50–60 per cent of the observed movements in prices,[11] while for Sweden and Austria the share that can be related to the money supply is considerably smaller. Except in the case of M1 in Sweden, lagged changes in the money supply are more important than current changes, and in Belgium and Canada the broad aggregates give far better results than M1.[12] However, in several cases the estimates are suggestive of 'missing variables', and for all four countries – but least for Canada – the mark-up hypothesis yields more satisfactory results, although the constant terms (which may be interpreted as the unexplained change in prices) tend to be uncomfortably large.

Given the long-run relationship between money and prices, changes in nominal wages cannot permanently influence the rate of price inflation unless subsequently validated by faster growth in the money supply. Hence unit labour costs may only be acting as a proxy for a monetary policy that is accommodating with respect to nominal wages. However, the empirical evidence does not support this hypothesis, as a regression of changes in the domestic credit supply on current and lagged changes in nominal wages produced very low $R^2$s and no significant coefficients. It would therefore appear that, in all four countries, price changes in the short to medium run are mainly determined by unit labour costs and other input prices. In the longer run, price changes are constrained (but not necessarily 'caused') by money supply growth and there is little evidence that 'the reaction function' of the monetary authorities involves an automatic accommodation of preceding changes in wages. In turn, these findings have important implications for wage behaviour (which will be further pursued in the following section): first, in the short to medium term, which is frequently the relevant time horizon for policy decisions, inflation will be closely related to – and sometimes caused by – nominal wage changes; and secondly, to the extent that the money supply and changes in domestic credit are independent of preceding movements in nominal wages, the flexibility of nominal and real wages will greatly influence the degree to which external shocks have repercussions on real output trends and unemployment.

## WAGE BEHAVIOUR AND THE ADJUSTMENT TO EXTERNAL SHOCKS

### *Nominal and real wage behaviour*

As a result of the type of shocks occurring in the 1970s, policy makers in virtually all countries have been faced with the problem of enforcing lower real income growth. Failure to achieve such an adjustment would result in imbalances, which – depending on built-in rigidities and the policies adopted – might appear as inflationary pressures, loss of international competitiveness, changes in the distribution of factor income and/or higher unemployment.

The supply shocks experienced have differed in both size and nature, with Austria and Belgium being exposed to large and adverse terms-of-trade shifts while in Canada and Sweden supply shocks mainly took the form of lower productivity growth. There were also major differences in the extent to which the response to these shocks led to shifts in the distribution of factor income and in relative unit labour costs measured in domestic currencies:

- in Belgium, the distribution of factor income changed in favour of wage earners as real wages rose faster than productivity; however, unit labour costs increased less than in other countries and the rate of inflation was relatively low;
- in Austria, there was only a small change in factor income shares and this was achieved with low inflation and an improvement in relative unit labour costs that was even more pronounced than in Belgium;
- in Canada, factor incomes also remained relatively stable but this occurred against a background of high inflation and an unfavourable cost development;
- in Sweden, there was a marked decline in competitiveness and profit shares up to around 1977 and a partial reversal of these trends in subsequent years.

Exchange rate fluctuations have been as important for international competitiveness as domestic factors, but in the following we shall focus on the latter and take the behaviour of nominal and real wages as a central element of the adjustment process in the four countries. Unfortunately, there is no generally agreed measure of wage flexibility, although the extent to which countries are likely to achieve a smooth adjustment would seem to depend on the following aspects of the wage formation process:

- the response of real and nominal wages to changes in productivity growth, since in the absence of a complete absorption there will be changes in the distribution of factor income and in inflationary pressures;
- the cyclical sensitivity of nominal and real wages, which affects the effectiveness of anti-inflationary policies;

- the existence of time lags in the wage and price formation process, which not only creates a difference between the short- and the long-run slope of the Phillips curve but also affects the speed with which restrictive policies will reduce the rate of inflation;
- the extent to which nominal wages are linked to current price changes or to past wage changes (wage/price vs. wage/wage links), which has a major influence on the impact of terms-of-trade changes as well as on the average time lags.

Tables 12.4 and 12.5 present some regression results in an attempt to identify major wage determinants. For each country, five equations are shown with the following specifications:

(i) in the first equation, nominal wage changes in manufacturing are regressed on current or lagged values of the rate of unemployment,[13] changes in consumer prices, changes in productivity and the ratio between export prices and import prices. The terms of trade were included in both level and rate-of-change form, but for all countries the level specification produced the most satisfactory results. This may reflect the fact that only major changes in the terms of trade lead to adjustments in wage behaviour, while the influence of minor changes is captured by consumer prices;
(ii) in the second equation, current price changes are replaced by one-period lagged price changes as a proxy for inflationary expectations;[14]
(iii) the third equation adds lagged wage changes to capture wage/wage links;
(iv) in the fourth equation the sum of the coefficients on prices and lagged wages is constrained to unity as an approximate test for the existence of a long-run vertical Phillips curve;
(v) finally, the real wage equations shown in Table 12.5 were based on the specification of the first nominal wage equation except that a measure of unanticipated inflation (defined as actual price changes less inflationary expectations as measured above) was added.

In *Austria* current wage changes seem to be influenced by price expectations and by lagged wages in the ratio of 2:1. The significant influence of lagged nominal wage changes may reflect the bargaining pattern, with the exposed sectors often acting as wage leaders, and the negative coefficient on terms of trade (TOT) could be interpreted in a similar way, as it suggests that higher import prices lead to wage moderation whereas higher export prices result in an acceleration of wage claims. Approximately 40 per cent of productivity changes is reflected in nominal wage gains, and the coefficient with respect to unemployment would imply that a 1 percentage point rise in the rate of unemployment leads to a 3.5 point reduction in the rate of wage inflation. However, this coefficient is likely to be biased and not representative of recent trends because, for the estimation period, the rate of unemployment ranged only between 1.5 and 2.9 per cent, while by the end of 1982 it had reached 4.4 per cent.[15] The estimates are not inconsistent with a vertical long-run Phillips curve but, given the large sensitivity of nominal wages to foreign price trends, it is probably more relevant to interpret the 'trade-off' as a single point or a very

**Table 12.4** *Wage equations: nominal wages*

| *Country* | *Constant* | $\dot{p}$ | $\dot{p}_e$ | $u$ | $\dot{q}$ | *TOT* | $\dot{w}_{-1}$ | *Dummy* | $\bar{R}^2$ | *DW* |
|---|---|---|---|---|---|---|---|---|---|---|
| Austria | 10.50 (1.6) | 0.70 (1.7) | | −2.79 (1.2) | 0.11 (0.4) | −0.65 (2.4) | | | 0.47 | 1.7 |
| | 8.10 (1.4) | | 1.19 (2.5) | −3.56 (2.2) | 0.39 (1.4) | −0.71 (2.9) | | | 0.56 | 1.2 |
| | 7.60 (1.4) | | 0.70 (1.2) | −3.50 (2.2) | 0.41 (1.5) | −0.56 (2.1) | 0.32 (1.3) | | 0.59 | 1.5 |
| | 7.86 (2.5) | | 0.67 (2.9) | −3.54 (2.6) | 0.40 (1.7) | −0.55 (2.3) | 0.33 (—) | | (0.48) | 1.5 |
| Belgium | 5.43 (2.5) | 1.31 (8.3) | | −0.76 (3.6) | 0.12 (0.6) | — | | | 0.84 | 1.1 |
| | 3.65 (0.7) | | 1.18 (2.7) | −0.70 (1.6) | 0.45 (1.0) | — | | | 0.33 | 0.8 |
| | 5.95 (2.1) | 1.39 (4.4) | | −0.86 (4.2) | 0.10 (0.4) | — | −0.06 (0.3) | | 0.83 | 1.2 |
| | 8.36 (2.8) | 0.96 (4.4) | | −1.17 (2.3) | 0.35 (1.3) | 0.20 (0.8) | 0.04 (—) | | (0.62) | 1.4 |
| Canada | 17.70 (6.6) | 0.01 (0.0) | | −0.64 (1.7) | — | −0.63 (5.9) | | −2.54 (2.3) | 0.85 | 1.8 |
| | 16.78 (5.3) | | 0.13 (0.5) | −0.71 (1.9) | — | −0.57 (4.1) | | −2.27 (2.2) | 0.82 | 1.6 |
| | 9.10 (2.8) | | 0.16 (0.7) | −0.58 (2.0) | — | −0.30 (2.3) | 0.58 (3.2) | −3.65 (3.9) | 0.91 | 2.1 |
| | 6.17 (3.1) | | 0.35 (2.7) | −0.56 (2.0) | 0.12 (1.3) | −0.22 (3.4) | 0.65 (—) | −3.88 (4.3) | 0.83 | 2.4 |
| Sweden | 9.26 (3.7) | 0.71 (4.3) | | −0.42 (0.4) | — | −0.42 (3.0) | | −2.38 (2.4) | 0.55 | 3.1 |
| | 12.67 (3.4) | | 0.70 (2.5) | −2.59 (1.5) | — | −0.29 (1.6) | | −1.53 (1.2) | 0.39 | 2.7 |
| | 15.91 (4.4) | | 1.01 (3.6) | −2.72 (1.8) | — | −0.36 (2.9) | −0.46 (2.1) | −1.83 (1.7) | 0.47 | 1.6 |
| | 13.30 (3.7) | | 1.35 (5.9) | −3.13 (1.9) | — | −0.40 (2.5) | −0.35 (—) | −2.16 (1.8) | (0.70) | 1.9 |

*Notation:* $\dot{p}$ = percentage rate of change in consumer prices; $\dot{p}_e$ = expected percentage rate of inflation; $u$ = percentage rate of unemployment; $\dot{q}$ = percentage rate of change in output per hour; *TOT* = ratio between export and import prices, unit values except for Austria; $\dot{w}_{-1}$ = dependent variable, lagged; $\bar{R}^2$ = coefficient of determination corrected for degrees of freedom; *DW* = Durbin–Watson statistic; t-statistics given in brackets.

**Table 12.5** *Wage equations: real wages*

| *Country* | *C* | *u* | $\dot{q}$ | *TOT* | $\dot{p}-\dot{p}_e$ | *Dummy* | $\bar{R}$ | *DW* |
|---|---|---|---|---|---|---|---|---|
| Austria | 9.40 (2.7) | –3.48 (2.0) | 0.31 (1.1) | 0.68 (2.9) | –0.82 (1.8) | | 0.36 | 1.3 |
| Belgium | 7.35 (3.6) | –0.66 (3.4) | 0.06 (0.3) | — | 0.56 (2.5) | | 0.61 | 1.7 |
| Canada | 9.22 (3.8) | –0.93 (2.6) | | 0.15 (1.6) | –0.81 (3.1) | –1.07 (0.8) | 0.56 | 0.9 |
| Sweden | 8.11 (2.7) | –1.28 (0.8) | 0.20 (1.3) | 0.45 (3.1) | –0.41 (1.7) | –2.55 (2.5) | 0.69 | 3.2 |

*Note:* $\dot{p}-\dot{p}_e$ is included as a proxy for unanticipated inflation.

narrow range on a negatively sloped Phillips curve.[16] The sensitivity to foreign prices as well as the importance of wage/wage links are also apparent in the real wage equation: there is a large positive coefficient with respect to TOT and expectational errors are almost fully reflected in real earnings. The cyclical sensitivity would again appear to be overstated, while the elasticity with respect to productivity changes implies cost pressures and declining profit shares in periods of below-average productivity gains.

The estimates for *Belgium* show a marked contrast to those obtained for Austria, with nominal wages dominated by current price changes and neither the terms of trade nor lagged wages appearing to have any influence. This result can probably be explained by the indexation scheme in effect until 1982 (although the simultaneity bias is likely to overstate the influence of prices) and the implied rigidity of real wages with respect to 'external shocks' is confirmed in Table 12.5, as there is a positive coefficient with respect to unanticipated inflation. Both nominal and real wages display some cyclical sensitivity and the estimates might be interpreted as giving relatively strong support to a vertical long-run Phillips curve.

A main feature of wage formation in *Canada* appears to be the predominance of wage/wage links, while changes in consumer prices have only a small and insignificant influence.[17] The cyclical sensitivity is relatively small and productivity does not appear to affect either nominal or real wages. As in Austria, terms-of-trade shifts have a marked influence on wage behaviour and the improvement in the terms of trade has contributed to the post-1973 surge in wages.[18] Moreover, because of the apparently strong wage/wage links, the rise in raw material and oil prices is likely to have added to wage-cost pressures for manufacturers of finished goods. On the other hand, and assuming that export prices rose less than import prices, the flexibility in relation to foreign prices may have helped to improve firms' international competitiveness in periods when the Canadian dollar was depreciating.

Following a suggestion made by Fortin and Newton (1982), a dummy variable with the values 0.5 for 1976 and 1 for 1977 and 1978 was included as a proxy for the wage and price controls introduced in October 1975. Judging by the size of the coefficients, these measures on average reduced nominal wage gains by 2.5–3.9 per cent and the rise in real earnings seems to have fallen by 1 per cent per year, giving some support to the charge made by unions that the policies were biased in favour of profits.[19] The equation is considerably improved when the dummy variable is included and the estimated impact is in line with those obtained in other studies (see Auld *et al.*, 1979; Reid, 1979; Fortin and Newton, 1982). Moreover, the pattern of residuals does not point to any post-control surge in wages, as it is dominated by negative figures (i.e. estimated increases exceeding actual increases).[20] On the other hand, the income policy proxy is a very crude one and the dummy variable may in part be capturing the effect of slower productivity gains, thus biasing the estimated impact of both variables. Furthermore, with nominal wage increases in most countries peaking in 1975, the negative coefficient on the dummy variable may in part be measuring a deceleration that would have occurred in any case.[21]

The equations obtained for *Sweden* seem to represent an intermediate case. On the one hand, as in Austria and Canada, terms-of-trade shifts affect wage behaviour in line with the assumptions of the Scandinavian theory of inflation, and unanticipated increases in the rate of inflation tend to reduce real wage gains. On the other hand, as in Belgium, there is no indication of wage/wage links, which suggests that centralized agreements rather than the exposed sectors have been 'setting the pace'.[22] Productivity changes do not appear to affect nominal wages (which is also inconsistent with the Scandinavian hypothesis) and have only a minor effect on real earnings.[23] The cyclical sensitivity of both nominal and real wages is relatively high, but these coefficients are likely to be biased because the rate of unemployment has been kept artificially low through employment measures and publicly financed training programmes, thus making the measured rate of unemployment an increasingly inappropriate indicator of labour market pressures. A dummy variable was included and assigned the value of 1 for years with a general wage settlement[24] as a very approximate test of the possibly dampening effect of tax concessions granted prior to several general settlements during the 1970s. The negative coefficient obtained suggests that some moderation of nominal and real wages has been achieved, but this result should be interpreted with caution as the statistical evidence is not very strong and the dummies could be capturing other influences specific to the settlement years. Moreover, the dummies were not scaled according to the size of the tax concessions,[25] and, to the extent that the implied stimulus to demand was not offset by other factors, part of the wage moderation would subsequently be 'lost' through a lower rate of unemployment.[26]

Generally, nominal and real wages in all four countries have only partly adjusted to the external shocks and cyclical responsiveness as well as wage/price and wage/wage links differ widely. This implies that all four countries, though Austria less than others, were faced with rising inflationary pressures in the 1970s and also that there were large differences in how effectively and quickly these pressures could (in theory, and even more so in practice) have been met by more restrictive policies.

## III CONCLUSIONS

To some extent, the differences in economic performance observed among the four countries examined are rooted in differences in their openness and their vulnerability to particular kinds of external shock. The more important factor, however, has been differences in policy approaches and institutional rigidities and constraints. In these respects several conclusions seem to stand out:

(1) The experiences of the four countries suggest that a heavy emphasis on any particular aspect of policy – hard currency, incomes, fiscal or monetary – will generally lead to unsatisfactory results. This conclusion, though perhaps obvious, seems particularly important in the case of small, open economies, where a high degree of responsiveness to change is desirable. Conceptually ideal, however difficult in practice, is a full policy-mix approach. Austria has come closest to achieving this, whereas Belgium has put most weight on a hard-currency policy, Canada on monetary policy and Sweden on fiscal policy.

(2) Efforts to keep to a stable exchange rate, if not backed up by appropriate adjustment policies, imply a need for exchange market intervention. This has occurred on a significant scale in all four countries and was supported in Belgium and Sweden by substantial borrowing abroad.

(3) The lessons for monetary policy are several-fold. As the Canadian experience shows, and as the other three countries have insisted, monetary targets of the conventional sort are difficult to apply in a small, open economy. Interest rates are more clearly relevant, given the fact of openness, the importance attached to exchange rate stability and the general relevance of changing levels of rates in international markets. However, it was also seen that some attention could usefully be given (in a 'monetary approach' to the balance of payments) to some broad concept of domestic credit expansion. Owing to financial innovation, it is not enough to look simply at credit expansion via the banking system. Account has to be taken of flows outside the banks as well as of recourse to borrowing abroad. In this context, financial innovation has been seen to reflect not merely market initiative but also new debt management techniques applied by governments. It is also evident that financial innovation in both these senses – market induced and policy induced – can be disturbing both to countries pursuing monetary aggregate targets (such as Canada) and to those emphasizing liquidity control.

(4) Broadly speaking, four phases of fiscal policy may be identified: strongly expansionary measures to offset the deflationary impact of the first oil shock; fiscal restraint between 1975 and 1978; moderately expansionary measures to meet the second rise in oil prices; and, most recently, retrenchment efforts as budget deficits got out of control. In all four countries, fiscal policy changes have played an important role in 'filling in', or compensating, for concurrent changes in private sector credit demand and in the external account. None the less, and regardless of whether or not targets for monetary aggregates are used in implementing monetary policy, some limitations of fiscal policy have become clearly visible:

- automatic stabilizers may be destabilizing in conditions of external supply shocks, of structural as opposed to cyclical changes, and of protracted and deep recession;
- as noted above, an unbalanced policy approach is generally inefficient, and fiscal ease is subject to particular difficulties in the current situation of monetary restraint and high nominal interest rates;
- although all four countries have been able to finance fiscal deficits without any excessive growth in the money supply, various strains and imbalances have developed, not least because of the growing burden of interest payments on the public debt. To some extent this development reflects the fact that small, open economies have only a limited degree of policy independence, but it also underlines a fundamental implication of the 'government budget constraint' (see Christ, 1968; Hansen, 1973), which is that at least one policy variable is determined endogenously and therefore can get out of control. Whatever the

immediate or underlying causes, all four countries have felt compelled to pay more explicit attention to the financial imbalance of the public sector and to introduce restrictive measures despite high and growing rates of unemployment.

(5) In this context, it is also useful to separate fundamental adjustment policies – those affecting real wages, profitability, productivity and competitiveness – from those of an adaptive, accommodating or defensive nature – such as exchange market intervention and foreign borrowing, government assistance and subsidies to industry, and transfer payments to the unemployed. With the onset of the second oil shock, national authorities became much more attuned to the need to emphasize adjustment rather than adaptive policies.

(6) A particular obstacle to adjustment by a small, open economy is indexation, especially of wages and budgetary expenditure, including welfare benefits. Austria has always specifically rejected indexation as inimical to a flexible incomes policy and even to harmonious wage/price negotiations, while Belgium (comprehensive wage and salary indexation), Sweden (indexation of pensions and certain other welfare benefits and periodic use of threshold schemes for wages) and Canada (indexation of taxes, transfers and in part also wages and salaries) have had to suspend indexation, either wholly or partially, during certain periods. Although it is possible to imagine benign versions, involving limits and conditionality, indexation has tended to be an enemy of adjustment.

(7) This is particularly evident in periods of large external shocks such as terms-of-trade deteriorations and lower productivity growth. For a given change in money supply or nominal income, the way in which such shocks are 'split' between lower output growth and higher inflation depends importantly on the degree of wage flexibility, and in this respect Belgium and Austria represent two 'opposite poles'. In Belgium, as a consequence of the indexation scheme, the terms-of-trade deteriorations were fully reflected in higher nominal wages, which, combined with a relatively low cyclical responsiveness of wages, meant a marked rise in the non-accelerating inflation rate of unemployment (NAIRU); i.e. the maintenance of a stable inflation rate would have required an even steeper increase in unemployment than actually occurred. In Austria, by contrast, wage earners appear to have accepted the need for wage moderation in phases of external disturbance, and given, also, a high cyclical responsiveness of wages there has been very little change in either the actual unemployment rate or the NAIRU. A similar cyclical responsiveness is also characteristic of Sweden, but Canada is in an analogous position to Belgium owing to the absence of wage moderation in face of a marked decline in productivity growth.

## NOTES

1 The social partnership, which has attracted considerable attention outside Austria, has a number of features that bear on the adjustment process. It is not a narrowly defined incomes

policy but rather a broadly based set of institutions that encompasses virtually all aspects of economic policy making. On occasion (1967 and 1975), tax/wage bargains have been concluded within this framework and the hard-currency option (endorsed by the trade unions as a means of preserving international competitiveness) is one of its cornerstones. Negotiations are highly centralized, with both employees and employers being represented by parallel organizations (Chambers (compulsory) and Associations (voluntary)), and decisions in the centralized bodies – including the subordination of specific income claims to common economic targets – are largely accepted at the sectoral and individual company levels. While the Price Subcommittee can control most prices, the Wage Subcommittee can influence only the timing of wage increases. None the less, the impact of direct price control seems small compared with the more indirect inducement to wage restraint provided by the principle of cost-based price increases. For more details concerning the social partnership (or economic partnership as the labour representatives prefer), see OECD, *Economic Survey of Austria*, 1982, Farnleiter and Schmidt (1982).

2 However, in assessing employment trends in Austria, the following features should be noted: (a) there has been a large reduction in the number of foreign workers, although not on the same scale as in Switzerland and West Germany; (b) vacations were extended from three to four weeks in 1972 and the average working week was reduced from 42 to 40 hours in 1975; and (c) the bulk of employment growth during the recession has taken place in the service sectors and in the nationalized industries.

3 The central bank may rediscount Treasury bills up to a maximum corresponding to 5 per cent of the previous year's tax revenue.

4 Mention should also be made of a specific structural or institutionalized problem. Traditionally, trade unions have aimed at a 'solidaristic wage policy' whereby rapidly growing industries set the pace while weak firms went out of business. This worked satisfactorily as long as world trade was expanding and the exposed sectors could absorb labour from the weak firms. However, with the slump in world trade and the deterioration in competitiveness, the 'solidaristic wage policy' came into conflict with full employment policy. With the latter still given high priority and unions unwilling to accept productivity-based bargaining, the government has had to 'absorb' an increasing part of employment in one form or another, thus contributing to the rapid growth of public sector spending.

5 In the 1950s and 1960s, anti-cyclical investment fund schemes in Sweden constituted another important element of fiscal policy that helped to stabilize investment, particularly in manufacturing (see Taylor, 1982). For most of the period since 1975 firms have been able to draw freely on these funds, but investment has declined none the less.

6 The National Energy Programme also contributed to the weakening of the currency and to the rise in the external debt.

7 However, more recent evidence suggests that in the period after 1979 the influence of West German interest rates increased following the decision by the authorities in several European countries – particularly members of the EMS – only partly to follow the rise in US rates and accept a depreciation of their exchange rates against the US dollar.

8 As distinct from indirect effects stemming from changes in the level of economic activity.

9 It is, of course, possible to offset external influences through changes in monetary policy and exchange rates, but for the 1970s this would have required a very severe tightening of the monetary policy stance. In this respect, Jonung's (1976a) study for Sweden is of interest. Thus, for longer periods (more than 200 years in the case of Sweden) there is a positive correlation between changes in prices and in the money supply. However, over shorter periods, and especially after World War II, Jonung finds a negative correlation between contemporaneous changes in the money stock and in prices; he interprets this result as indicating a timely countercyclical policy on the part of the Swedish monetary authorities.

10 This variable was measured as changes in the ratio between import and export prices (national accounts deflators), but in a number of cases coefficients were not very well determined. Using separate export and import price indices rather than their ratio might have been more appropriate.

11 For Canada, the estimates obtained for M1 are quite close to those reported by Bordo and Choudhri (1982), who find a coefficient with respect to M1 (lagged twelve quarters) of 1.1 and an $R^2$ of 0.6. It may also be noted that the incomes policy dummy gives rather different results depending on which hypothesis is tested. According to the mark-up hypothesis, price changes

during this period were higher than predicted by unit labour costs, supporting the view (see the following section) that real wages were squeezed. However, according to the monetarist hypothesis, price rises were slower than would have corresponded to the rate of growth of M2, whereas they were in line with the growth of M1. This may suggest that monetary policy, as measured by M2, was not fully consistent with the inflation target during this period.

12 In the case of Canada, however, there was a shift in the demand for M1 in 1976/7, which has not been taken into account, and the relatively high explanatory power of M2 may reflect a reverse causal relationship between nominal income and M2.

13 Equations entering the inverted rate of unemployment were also tested, but in all cases the results obtained seemed less satisfactory.

14 This is, of course, a very simplistic scheme, but at the very least it serves to remove the simultaneity bias contained in the first equation.

15 Frisch (1982), on the other hand, using a very similar specification except that TOT is excluded, finds a coefficient of 2.9 when the number of unemployed is measured net of vacancies and expressed as a percentage of total employment.

16 The same argument applies to the Canadian and Swedish results reported below.

17 A similar result is obtained by Fortin and Newton (1982) for the period 1954–79.

18 In addition, the high volatility of foreign prices and domestic producer prices in the 1970s may have lent an inflationary bias to the wage formation process.

19 In this context, it should be noted that import prices, which account for some 40 per cent of the CPI, were not subject to controls.

20 The residuals for nominal wages, equations 2 and 3, and real wages were as follows:

| | NW 2 | NW 3 | RW |
|---|---|---|---|
| 1979 | –0.1 | 0.2 | –0.9 |
| 1980 | –2.0 | –1.0 | –1.6 |
| 1981 | –0.4 | –0.1 | –0.9 |

21 Leaving out the dummy variable, equation 3 yields a residual of only 0.25 for 1976, suggesting that some 85 per cent of the deceleration was due to other factors. See also Auld *et al.* (1979).

22 In the case of Sweden, however, lagged wage changes may be a particularly poor proxy for wage/wage links, and the negative coefficients obtained in equations 3 and 4 could imply that a general settlement that is too low (high) relative to current labour market conditions subsequently leads to higher (lower) wage drift.

23 By estimating separate equations for exposed and sheltered sectors, Calmfors (1978) finds a significant impact of productivity in the exposed sectors, but the coefficient is only 0.17.

24 Years of general settlements (with length of contracts in brackets) were: 1966 (3 years), 1969 (2), 1971 (3), 1974 (1), 1976 (2), 1977 (1), 1978 (2), 1980 (1) and 1981 (2).

25 Neither the tax concessions nor their likely demand impact are easy to quantify because they have frequently consisted of reductions in personal taxes accompanied by increases in payroll taxes paid by employers (on the assumption that these would be met by a corresponding reduction in nominal wages) and/or the introduction of measures aimed at reducing post-tax profits or constraining their availability to firms.

26 In addition, if the coefficient on lagged wages is taken at face value, the moderating effect of tax concessions would be reduced through subsequent catch-ups.

## REFERENCES

Auld, D. A. L., Christofides, L. N., Swidinsky, R. and Wilton, D. A. (1979), 'The impact of the Anti-Inflation Board on negotiated wage settlements', *Canadian Journal of Economics*, 12 (2), May, 195–213.

Bordo, M. D. and Choudhri, E. M. (1982), 'The link between money and prices in an open economy: the Canadian evidence from 1971 to 1980', *Federal Reserve Bank of St. Louis Review*, 64, August, 13–23.

Calmfors, L. (1978), 'Prices, wages and employment in the open economy', Institute for International Economic Studies, Stockholm University, Monograph series, 10.

Calmfors, L. (1982), 'Cost adjustment in smaller OECD countries', Skandinaviska Enskilda Banken, *Quarterly Review*, 111–119.

Christ, C. F. (1968), 'A simple macroeconomic model with a government budget restraint', *Journal of Political Economy*, 76, February, 53–67.

Christ, C. F. (1979), 'On fiscal and monetary policies and the government budget restraint', *American Economic Review*, 69, September, 526–538.

Courchene, T. J., Fortin, P., Sparks, G. R. and White, W. R. (1979), 'Monetary policy in Canada: a symposium', *Canadian Journal of Economics*, 12 (4), November, 590–646.

Deutsches Institut für Wirtschaftsforschung (1983), 'Oesterreichs Wirtschafts- und Finanzpolitik im internationalen Vergleich', *Wochenbericht*, 185–202.

Farnleiter, J. and Schmidt, E. (1982), 'The social partnership', in S. Arndt (ed.), *The political economy of Austria*, Washington, DC, American Enterprise Institute, 87–100.

Fortin, P. and Newton, K. (1982), 'Labour market tightness and wage inflation in Canada', in M. N. Baily (ed.), *Workers, jobs and inflation,* Washington, DC, Brookings Institution.

Freedman, C. (1983), 'Financial innovation in Canada: causes and consequences', *American Economic Review*, 73, May, 101–106.

Frisch, H. (1982), 'Macroeconomic adjustment in small open economies', in S. Arndt (ed.), *The political economy of Austria*, Washington, DC, American Enterprise Institute, 42–60.

Hansen, B. (1973), 'On the effects of fiscal and monetary policy: a taxonomic discussion', *American Economic Review*, 63, September, 546–571.

Jonung, L. (1976a), 'Money and prices in Sweden, 1732–1972', *Scandinavian Journal of Economics*, 78, 40–58.

Jonung, L. (1967b), 'Sources of growth in the Swedish money stock, 1871–1971', *Scandinavian Journal of Economics*, 78, 611–627.

OECD, *Economic surveys* of Austria, Belgium, Canada and Sweden, Paris, 1983 and earlier years.

OECD (1983), 'The present unemployment problem', paper presented to Working Party No. 1 of the Economic Policy Committee, June.

Reid, F. (1979), 'The effect of controls on the rate of wage change in Canada', *Canadian Journal of Economics*, 12, May, 214–227.

Sneessens, H. R. (1981), 'A macroeconomic rationing model of the Belgian economy', unpublished working paper, London School of Economics.

Taylor, J. B. (1982), 'The Swedish investment funds system as a stabilising rule', *Brookings Papers on Economic Activity*, 1, 57–106.

PART III

# The Particular Case of Australia

# 13 The Australian Economy in the 1930s and the 1980s: Some Facts

*P. D. JONSON and G. R. STEVENS**

## I INTRODUCTION

On most criteria, the economic devastation of the 1930s was far more serious than anything experienced in the current episode. After fluctuating in the range 3–6 per cent between 1910 and 1929, the Australian rate of unemployment reached 20 per cent (almost 30 per cent amongst trade unionists) in 1932. Unemployment did not subsequently fall much below 10 per cent until World War II. Since 1973, the unemployment rate has moved in two major steps from around $1\frac{1}{2}$ per cent to over 10 per cent. Figure 13.1 puts current experience into a long-term perspective. However, for many individuals, and especially perhaps in relation to the expectations built up in the earlier period, the recent deterioration may in some relative sense be on a similar scale.

This chapter compares the main economic developments leading to and resulting from the high rates of unemployment in the 1930s and the 1980s. Developments in the world economy, in economic policies in Australia and in the main economic aggregates are examined. The statistics, particularly in the 1930s, are imperfect, and only a thumbnail sketch can be offered here. The references listed at the end of the chapter provide a wealth of detail and interpretation.

The data in this chapter are largely presented in the form of graphs. Mostly there is a comparison of data for two fifteen-year periods – 1921/2–1935/6 and 1971/2–1985/6. The latter period, of course, is partly in the future. The figures for 1983/4–1985/6 are taken from the projections presented to the National Economic Summit Conference (1983).[1] Although these data are only illustrative of one out of a large number of possible sets of developments,[2] in one fundamental aspect the projections parallel earlier experience: the unemployment rate is assumed to remain high after the sharp lift in recent years.

* The views expressed in this chapter are solely those of the authors, and are not necessarily shared by the Reserve Bank of Australia. This chapter was originally prepared for a plenary session at the Twelfth Conference of Economists held in Hobart in August 1983. Helpful suggestions on the issues have been made by many economists. Particular acknowledgement must go to Bob Gregory, who also spoke on the subject at the conference. Thanks also go to John Broadbent, William Coleman, Paul Johnson and Richard Wood for help on particular issues. The data base, which is available on request, owes a good deal to an earlier Research Discussion Paper by Matthew Butlin (Butlin, 1977).

Appendices with further information can be found in Research Discussion Paper No. 8303 of the Reserve Bank of Australia.

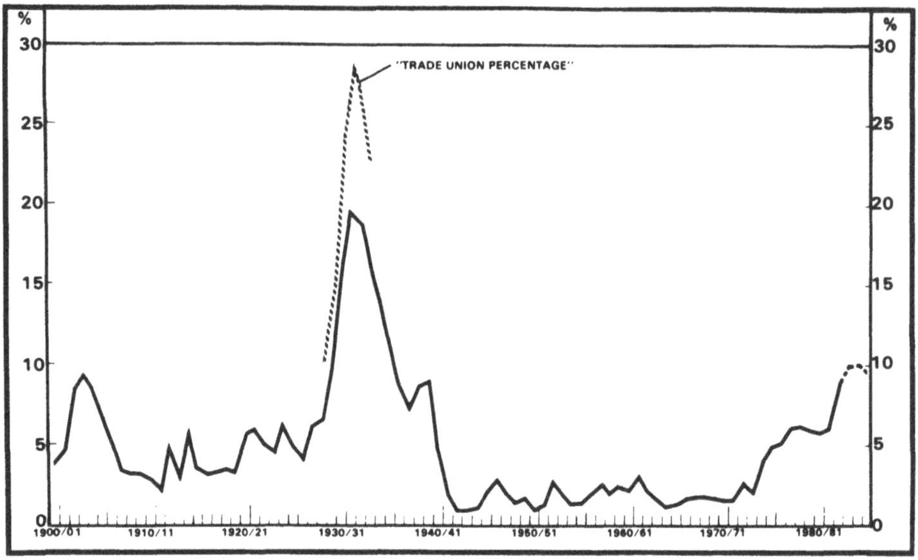


**Figure 13.1** Unemployment rate

## II MAIN ECONOMIC INDICATORS

### SHARE PRICES

Share prices are one of the most general economic indicators, with particular relevance for the health of the corporate sector. Figure 13.2 shows indices of share prices in the United States and Australia in the 1920s and 1930s and the 1970s and 1980s. In both countries share prices generally rose through the 1920s. The rise and subsequent fall was much greater in the United States.[3] Movements in share prices have generally been much smaller in the 1970s and the 1980s.[4] Share prices generally fell in the early 1970s. There was a strong rise in Australia in the late 1970s with a peak in November 1980. Share prices in New York have risen by about 50 per cent from their trough in August 1982 to their value in mid-August 1983.

### GROWTH IN REAL GDP

Figure 13.3 shows growth in real GDP and Table 13.1 shows a breakdown into its major components.

For the first half of the 1920s growth of real GDP was, except in one year, fairly strong. Domestic demand grew at a high rate (note the high growth rates of consumption and imports). In the second half of the decade Australia's growth performance deteriorated considerably. Boehm (1979) attributes the slowdown in the late 1920s to a conjunction of events including a sharp fall in the price and value of exports and a big reduction in capital formation financed by overseas borrowing. The big drop in export receipts reflected the disastrous

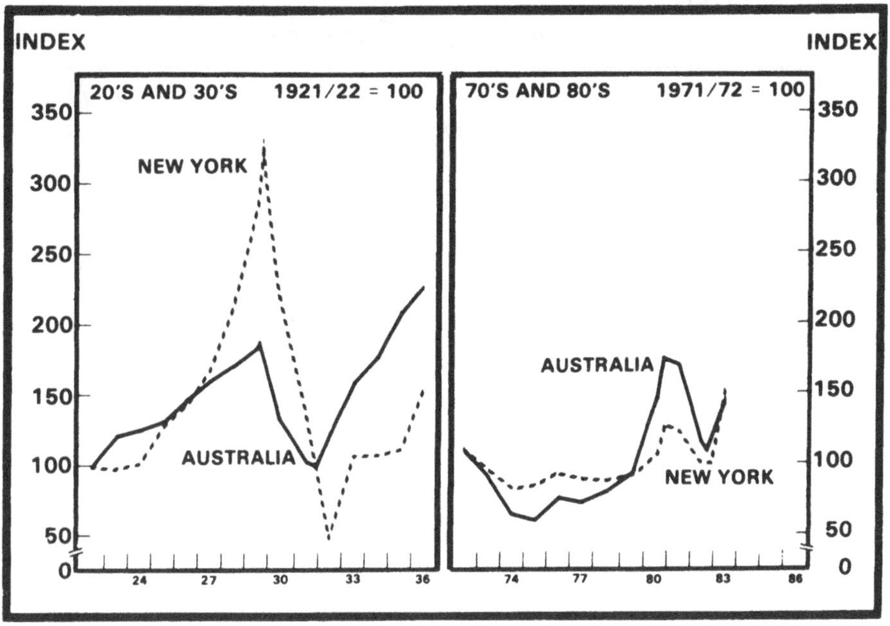


**Figure 13.2** Share prices

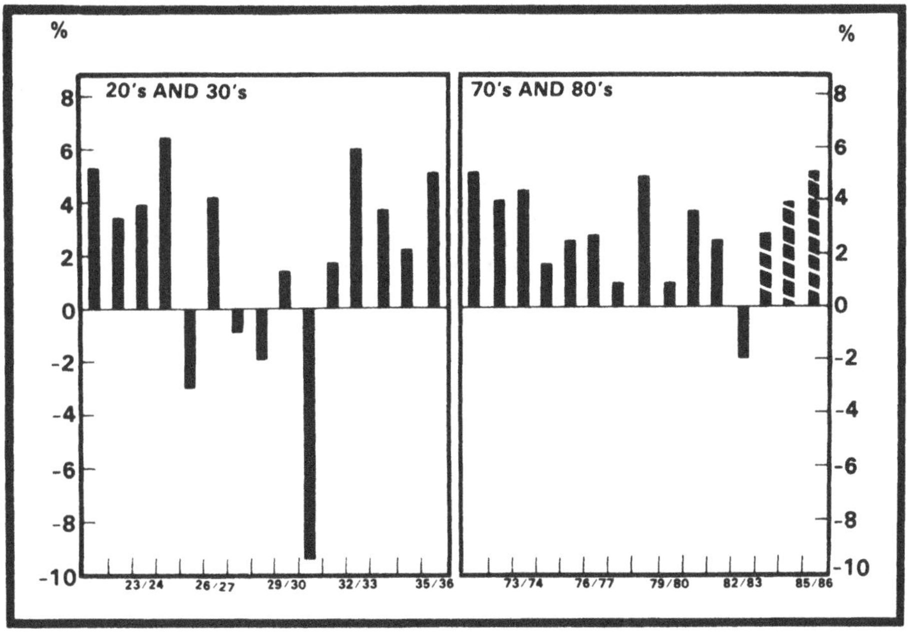


**Figure 13.3** Growth in real GDP

**Table 13.1** *Components of gross domestic product (average annual growth rates, per cent)*

| | *Private consumption* | *Private investment* | *Public expenditure* |
|---|---|---|---|
| 1921/2–25/6 | 6.1 | 8.2 | 4.8 |
| 1926/7–30/1 | -3.0 | -13.5 | -3.7 |
| 1931/2–35/6 | 4.4 | 11.7 | 5.4 |
| 1971/2–75/6 | 4.2 | -0.6 | 5.4 |
| 1976/7–80/1 | 2.5 | 5.3 | 2.2 |
| 1981/2 | 3.6 | 8.3 | 2.6 |
| 1982/3 | 0.8 | -17.1 | 3.5 |
| | *Exports* | *Imports* | *Total GDP* |
| 1921/2–25/6 | 4.2 | -(7.8) | 3.2 |
| 1926/7–30/1 | 3.5 | -(-11.5) | -1.4 |
| 1931/2–35/6 | 1.8 | -(11.4) | 3.7 |
| 1971/2–75/6 | 3.3 | -(4.0) | 3.5 |
| 1976/7–80/1 | 3.5 | -(4.3) | 2.7 |
| 1981/2 | 1.0 | -(12.1) | 2.5 |
| 1982/3 | 1.4 | -(-10.3) | -2.0 |

reduction in world trade and the associated drops in commodity prices, which are examined below. The falling away in capital inflow was partly due to a tightening in overseas financial markets, and partly due to the increasing concern of overseas lenders about the financial situation in Australia. According to the estimates used in Figure 13.3, real GDP fell by almost 10 per cent in 1930/1. Subsequently growth of real GDP resumed, albeit from a very low base.

Growth of real GDP was strong in the first three years of the 1970s, with both private consumption and public expenditure growing quickly. Performance for the rest of the decade was, in general, more subdued. There was a pick-up in real growth at the start of the 1980s, followed by a very sharp slowdown – at least by post-war standards: in 1982/3, real GDP fell by 2 per cent. The Treasurer indicated in his Budget speech that growth of around 3 per cent in 1983/4 might be achievable. Scenario A in the Economic Summit projected growth of 3.9 per cent and 4.8 per cent, respectively, in 1984/5 and 1985/6.

## GROWTH IN POPULATION AND LABOUR MARKET

Table 13.2 sets out average rates of growth of population, the work force and employment.

In the 1920s and 1930s, population growth was generally low. In the first half of the 1920s, the participation rate increased strongly but the work force nevertheless grew less quickly than total employment. The second half of the 1920s saw a big drop in employment, falling participation and generally rising

**Table 13.2** *Population and labour market (average annual growth; per cent)*

| | *Population* | *Work force* | *Employment* | *Unemployment rate* |
|---|---|---|---|---|
| 1921/2–25/6 | 1.0 | 2.3 | 3.0 | 5.4 |
| 1926/7–30/1 | 1.6 | 1.2 | -2.5 | 8.7 |
| 1931/2–35/6 | 0.7 | 1.7 | 4.0 | 15.9 |
| 1971/2–75/6 | 1.5 | 2.3 | 1.6 | 4.0 |
| 1976/7–80/1 | 1.2 | 1.5 | 1.3 | 5.9 |
| 1981/2 | 1.7 | 1.6 | 1.2 | 6.2 |
| 1982/3 | — | 1.6 | -1.4 | 9.0 |

unemployment. In the three years 1929/30–1931/2, employment fell disastrously (by 17 per cent from the 1928/9 level). There was then a period of strong employment growth (again from a very low base).[5]

Growth of population, the work force and employment were all much steadier in the 1970s, and the participation rate generally increased. Employment fell by about $1\frac{1}{2}$ per cent in 1982/3.

## GROWTH IN PRICES AND WAGES

Figure 13.4 compares three measures of inflation in the two periods. The solid lines show growth in consumer prices, the thin lines growth in a measure of product prices, and the striped lines growth in average weekly earnings.[6]

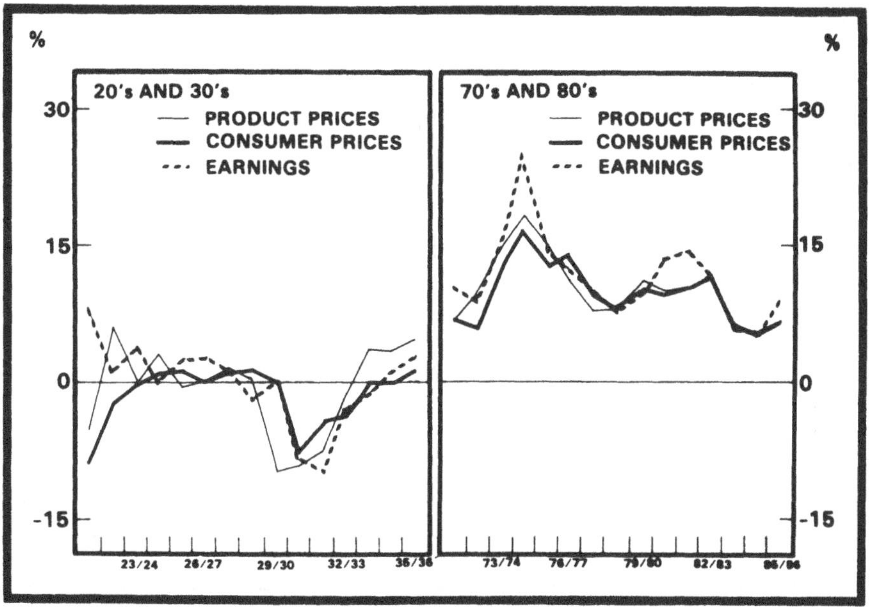


**Figure 13.4** Growth in prices and wages

There was a large rise in real wage incomes early in the 1920s, but thereafter wages and consumer prices moved fairly closely together until the cut in real wages in 1931/2 (reflecting the January 1931 decision by the Arbitration Commission to reduce wages by more than the fall in consumer prices). The general tendency of the GDP deflator to rise in the early 1920s meant that wages as a cost to the employer rose more slowly than real wage incomes. In 1929/30, however, a big fall in product prices, reflecting the large decline in export prices, preceded the fall in consumer prices and earnings. Real labour costs, therefore, increased sharply; they rose a bit more in 1930/31 before declining in subsequent years.

The 1970s and 1980s, of course, have experienced strong inflationary pressures. For the period shown in the right-hand panel of Figure 13.4 (including the projections up to 1985/6), the average rate of increase in consumer prices was 10 per cent, and the maximum (in 1974/5) was 16.7 per cent. In the early 1970s, growth in wages outstripped that of prices. Then real wages were fairly flat until the early 1980s, when real wages once again grew strongly. Scenario A does not foresee any significant reduction of real wages up to 1985/6.

## OUTPUT EMPLOYMENT AND PRODUCTIVITY

Figure 13.5 shows real GDP, employment and a measure of productivity. GDP grew quickly in the first half of the 1920s, while slightly slower growth in employment implied a modest rise in productivity. In the middle of the decade,

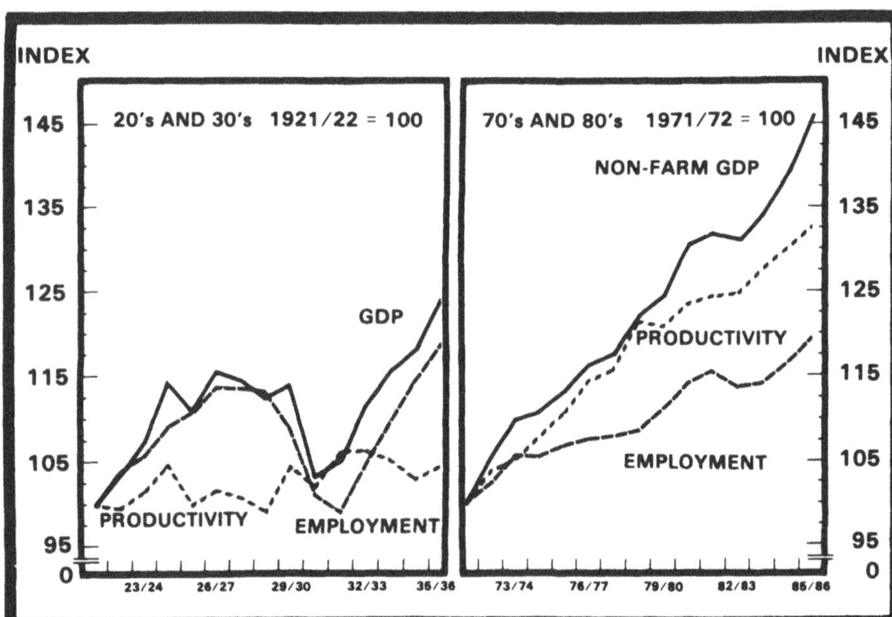


**Figure 13.5** Output, employment and productivity

productivity tended to decline as GDP grew more slowly than employment. Through the depression years, productivity generally rose as employment fell faster than GDP. Over the fifteen-year period as a whole, however, productivity did not show much growth.

Experience in the 1970s and 1980s has been very different. Productivity showed relatively strong growth throughout, with both real non-farm GDP and employment generally increasing. This experience is projected in Scenario A to continue after the downturn of 1982/3.

## COMPONENTS OF REAL UNIT LABOUR COSTS

The indices in Figure 13.6 attempt to measure real unit labour costs.[7] They show real labour costs (measured as nominal wages deflated by the GDP deflator) adjusted for movements in labour productivity from Figure 13.5.

Real unit labour costs fell in the early 1920s as a result of strong productivity gains. They then rose sharply with the cut in productivity in 1925/6, then more gradually until 1929/30, when the GDP deflator fell by 10 per cent, but average weekly earnings were more or less unchanged. By 1930/1, real unit labour costs were 10 per cent above the 1921/2 level. In that year, real GDP dropped by almost 10 per cent and unemployment rose from around 10 per cent to 16 per cent. The effect on real labour costs of the 10 per cent drop in real wages implemented by the Arbitration Commission at the start of 1931 is illustrated fairly clearly.[8] With some increases in productivity, and further falls in real wages, unit labour costs declined more or less continuously from 1930/1 to the

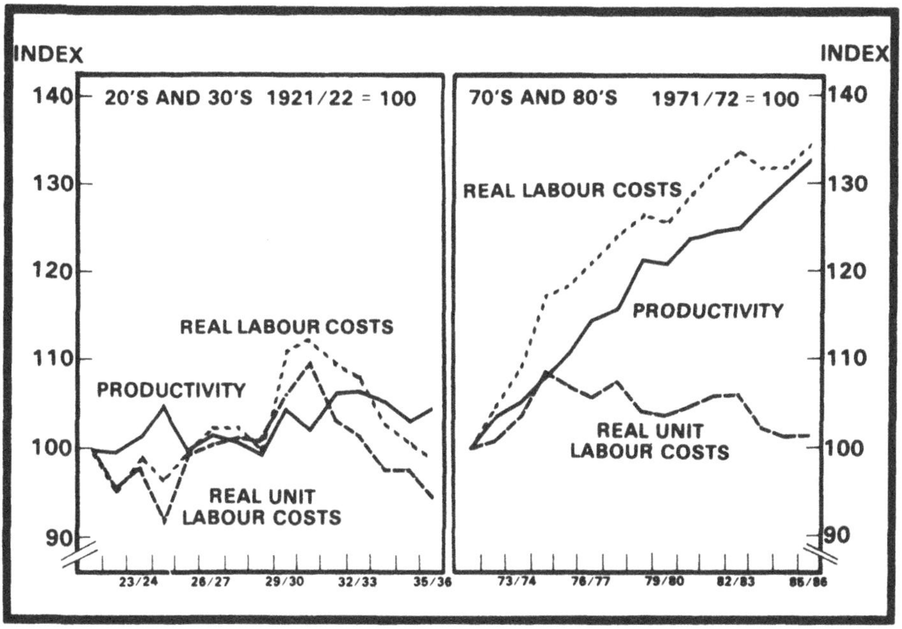


**Figure 13.6** Components of real unit labour costs

mid-1930s. By 1935/6, real unit labour costs were about back to their level at the start of the 1920s. As this implies, the share of profits in national income had also been restored to its level of the early 1920s.

In contrast to experience in the early 1920s, real labour costs and real unit labour costs rose sharply in the early 1970s. On the measure used in this graph, real unit labour costs peaked in 1974/5 around 8 per cent above the level at the start of the decade. There was then a gradual net fall of around 5 per cent over the next five years (as productivity rose more quickly than real labour costs), followed by another rise around the turn of the decade. By 1982/3 unit labour costs were about 6 per cent above the level at the start of the 1970s. Scenario A implies that unit labour costs will decline to the 1970/1 level by 1985/6, basically as a result of increases in productivity.

## III EXTERNAL INFLUENCES

### COMMODITY PRICE INDICES

Figure 13.7 shows indices of the prices of commodities of particular importance to Australia. For the early experience, prices (in Australian pounds) of wool, wheat and gold are given. For the later episode, prices of wool and wheat are again given, but an index of the price of metals replaces that of gold.

The 1920s was a period of generally falling prices. Wool prices rose strongly in the early 1920s, but then declined over the rest of the decade. The price of wheat also declined over the second half of the decade, with a very sharp drop

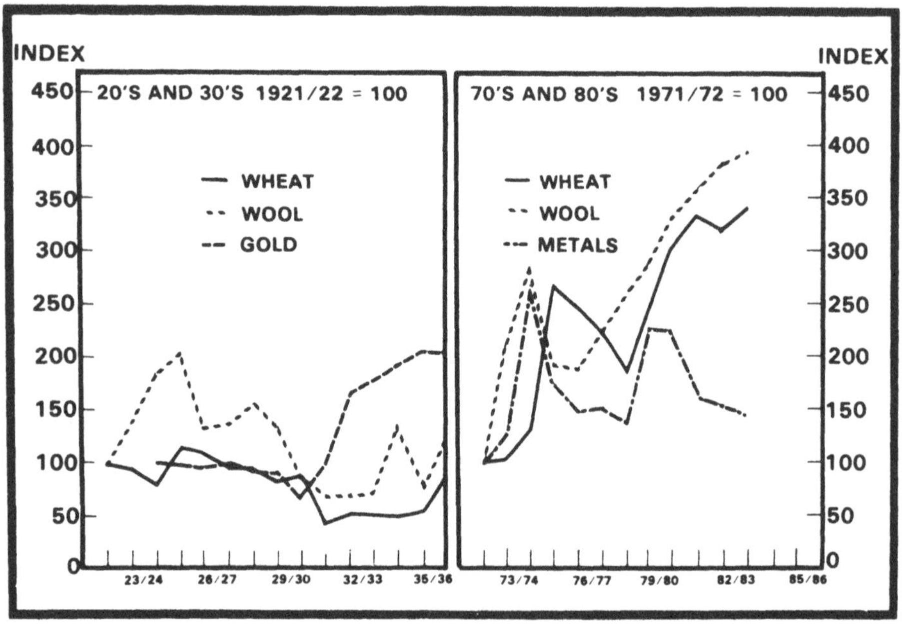


**Figure 13.7** Commodity price indices

in 1930/1. The price of gold was more stable, although this too declined slightly during the 1920s. During the recovery period of the mid-1930s, the prices of gold and, to a lesser extent, wool rose. The price of wheat did not rise appreciably until later in the decade.

The 1970s and the 1980s have been periods of generally rising prices. After a sharp rise in the years 1972–4, commodity prices declined as the world's economies moved into recession. The prices of wool and wheat are nevertheless now almost double that at their respective troughs in 1975/6 and 1978/9. Metal prices fell sharply in the mid-1970s, rose strongly in 1979 and 1980, but have since fallen to levels not much above those of the mid-1970s.

## IMPORT PRICES

Figure 13.8 shows indices of the price of imports (for the later period there is a division into the price of oil and other import prices). A general downward trend is evident for the 1920s and 1930s. Experience in the 1970s has been dominated by the two major hikes in the price of oil. The price of other imports has shown a general upward trend during the 1970s and 1980s.

## TERMS OF TRADE

The implications of these and other price movements for Australia are most simply summarized in the terms of trade, shown in Figure 13.9. For each period

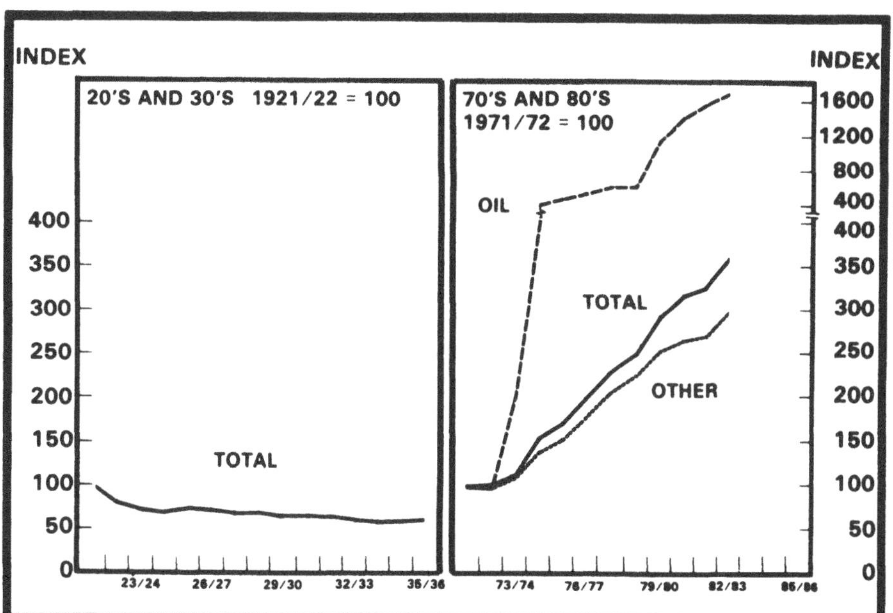


**Figure 13.8** Import prices

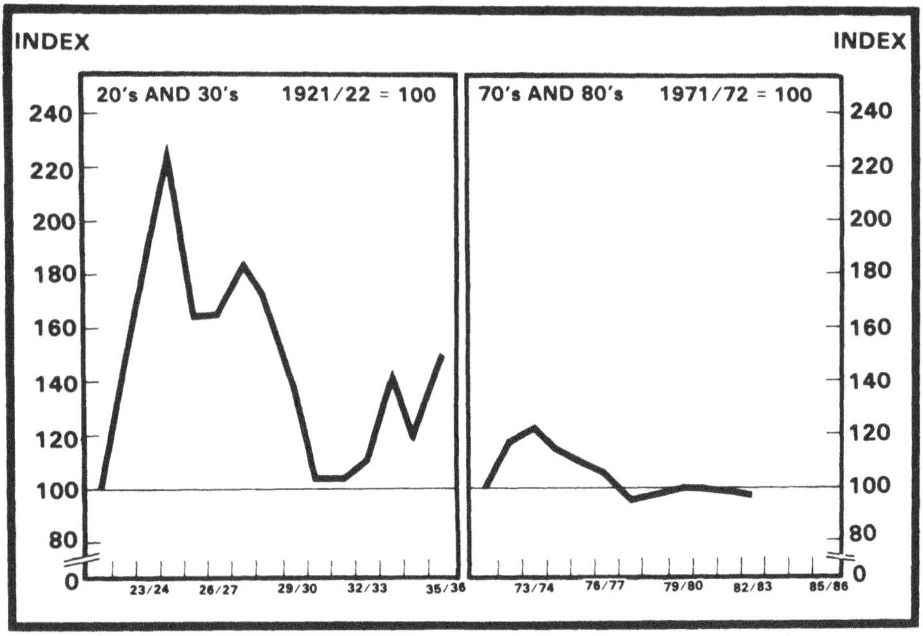


**Figure 13.9** Terms of trade (*export price deflator/import price deflator*)

the index is defined as the average price of exports in relation to the average price of imports.

Mainly as a result of an increased price of wool, export prices rose (while import prices fell) in the early 1920s and the terms of trade rose by over 100 per cent in the five years to 1924/5. Beginning with a sharp fall in 1925/6, there was then a long period in which export prices generally fell more quickly than import prices, so that the terms of trade fell by 50 per cent in the next six years (bringing them by 1930/1 roughly back to the same level as in the early 1920s).

Although recent experience has been qualitatively similar, the magnitudes of the movements have been very much smaller. There was a 20 per cent rise in the terms of trade in the early 1970s and then a fall of similar magnitude in the next three or four years as the average price of imports rose by more than those of exports. Australia's terms of trade have been roughly constant since the late 1970s, although there was a $2\frac{1}{2}$ per cent drop in 1982/3.

## WORLD TRADE VOLUME

Figure 13.10 shows indices of world trade. (This graph is in calendar years, reflecting the available data.) The volume of trade expanded strongly through the 1920s, before the sharp slump around the turn of the decade. By 1934, world trade was once again growing. Apart from the sharp setback in 1975,

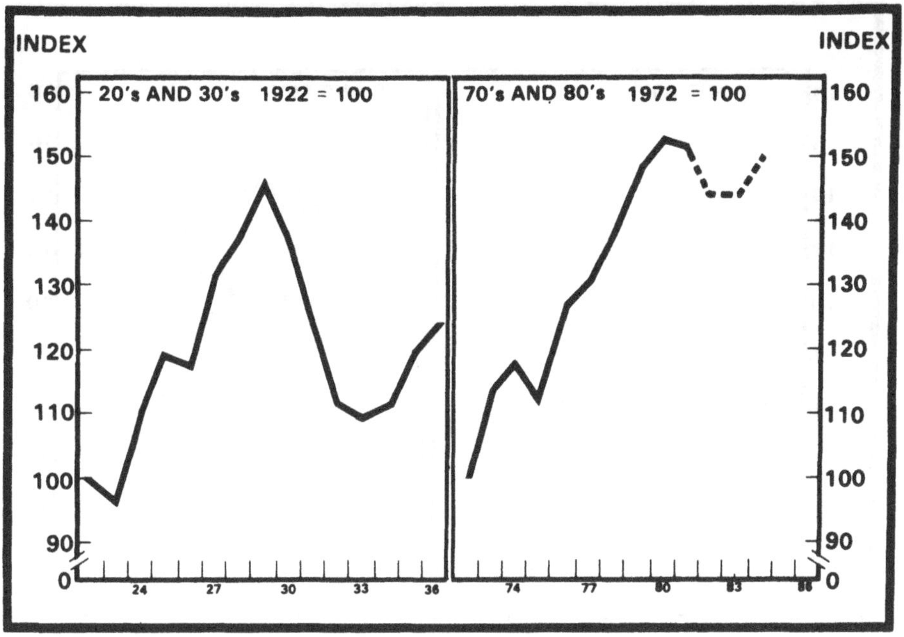


**Figure 13.10** World trade volume

trade expanded strongly in the 1970s. The sizeable declines in 1981 and 1982 went with reduced demand for Australia's exports. Current indications are, however, that some sort of recovery has commenced. (The graph includes the latest OECD forecasts for 1983 and 1984.)

## INTEREST RATES

Figure 13.11 shows interest rates in Australia and in a major overseas centre – London for the 1920s and 1930s and the United States for the 1970s and 1980s. The London 'Bank rate' peaked in June 1928, and then declined substantially, stabilizing at around 2 per cent by the mid-1930s. The rate on Australian government securities rose from the mid-1920s to 1930/1, reflecting, at least towards the end of this period, declining confidence in the solvency of Australian government finance. The lessening of these fears, with the advent of the Premiers' Plan and the legislated reduction in domestic interest rates associated with that Plan, led to a fall in market yields from late in 1931.

In the 1970s and early 1980s, interest rates around the world generally rose, peaking during 1981/2. This was due to a number of factors, including large budget deficits, high rates of inflation and the use of tough monetary policies to control that inflation. There has since been a slight decline.

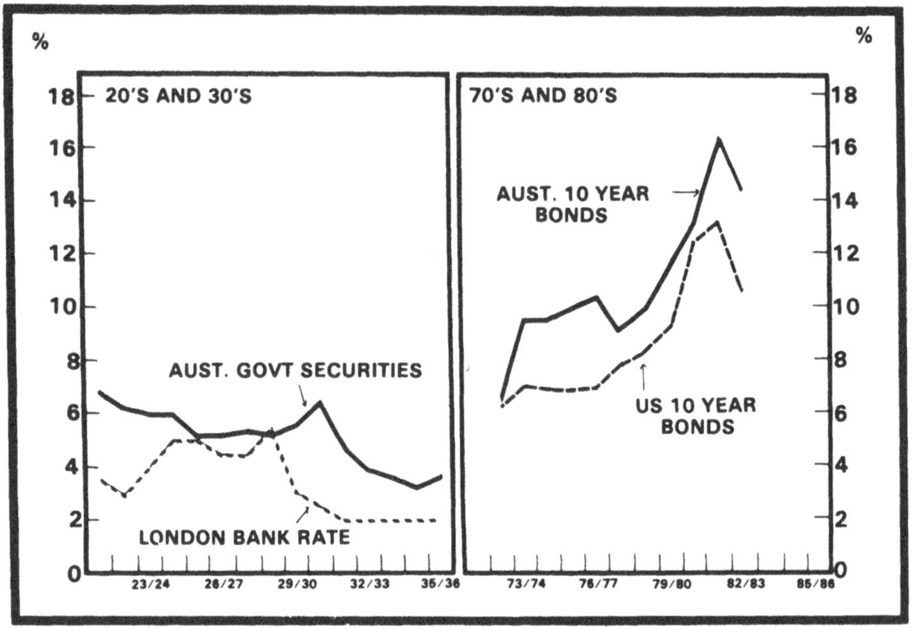


**Figure 13.11** Interest rates: Australia and abroad

## IV BALANCE OF PAYMENTS

### RATIO OF BALANCE OF PAYMENTS TO GDP

In Figure 13.12, the solid lines show current account deficits (occasionally surpluses), the dashed lines show net capital inflows and the bars show changes in international reserves (all in relation to GDP).

During the periods of relatively strong growth in the early 1920s, the current account deficit fluctuated between 0 and 6 per cent of GDP. Current account deficits were financed by large overseas borrowings, mainly by state governments and government authorities. Most of this borrowing was in London, in some cases in the form of overdrafts.[9] With the decline in world trade and the fall in commodity prices, the current account deficit increased substantially in the second half of the 1920s, peaking at over 10 per cent of GDP in 1929/30 (with real GDP growing by only 2 per cent). With a virtual drying up of capital inflow, there was a large drop of reserves in the same year. In the next two years, the rapid weakening of activity in Australia, large increases in protection and devaluation of the exchange rate produced a sharp move to surplus in the current account. Schedvin (1970a, p. 9) notes that this combination of factors 'successfully restored payments balance around mid-1931, although this was achieved without the exhaustion of international reserves by the barest margin'.

The 1970s opened with a strong current account. From 1973/4 on, however,

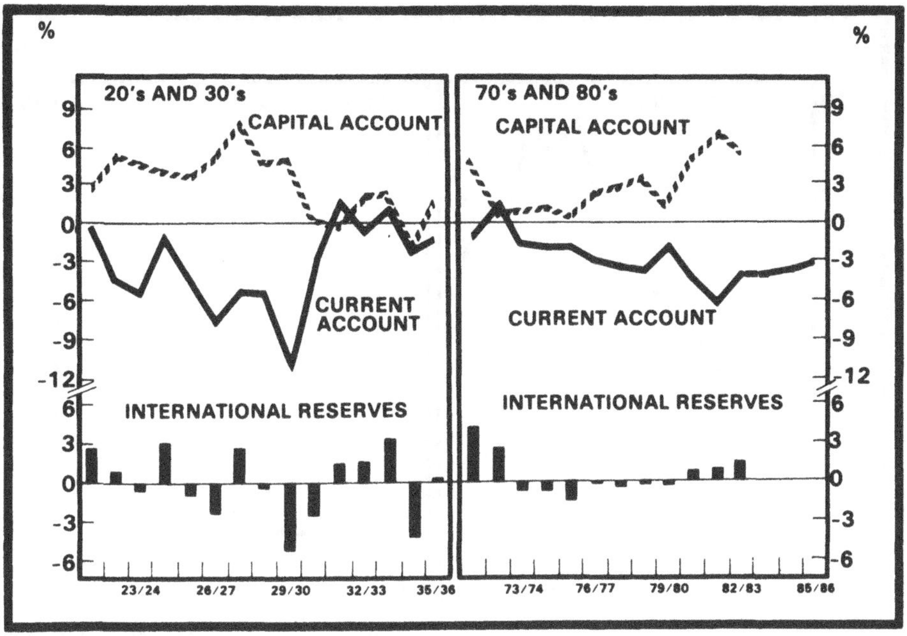


**Figure 13.12** Balance of payments (*ratio to GDP*)

the rest of the 1970s saw current account deficits of 2–4 per cent of GDP. The deficit widened substantially in 1980/1 and 1981/2. There was some cutback during 1982/3 and this trend is projected in Scenario A to continue until 1985/6.

Capital inflows were very strong in the early 1970s and then weakened considerably for the rest of the decade. In the early 1980s, net capital inflows increased even more in relation to GDP than did the current account deficit, so that overall balance of payments has shown sizeable surpluses since 1980/1.

## DEBT SERVICING BURDEN

Figure 13.13 shows interest payments on overseas borrowings as a ratio of export receipts. Table 13.3 gives some figures.

The large overseas borrowings (as noted above, predominantly by governments) in the late 1920s meant that interest payments increased substantially in the face of generally falling export prices. Export earnings collapsed in 1929/30. As a ratio of exports, interest payments jumped from 14 per cent in the early 1920s to almost 30 per cent in 1930/1. There was subsequently a modest reduction.

In the 1970s, the corresponding ratio has been much smaller (generally 3–5 per cent), although the outcome for 1982/3 may be nearer 10 per cent. The sizeable increase since 1980/1 mainly reflects the increased use of offshore borrowing at high interest rates. In contrast to earlier experience, overseas borrowing in the 1970s and 1980s has been mostly on private account.

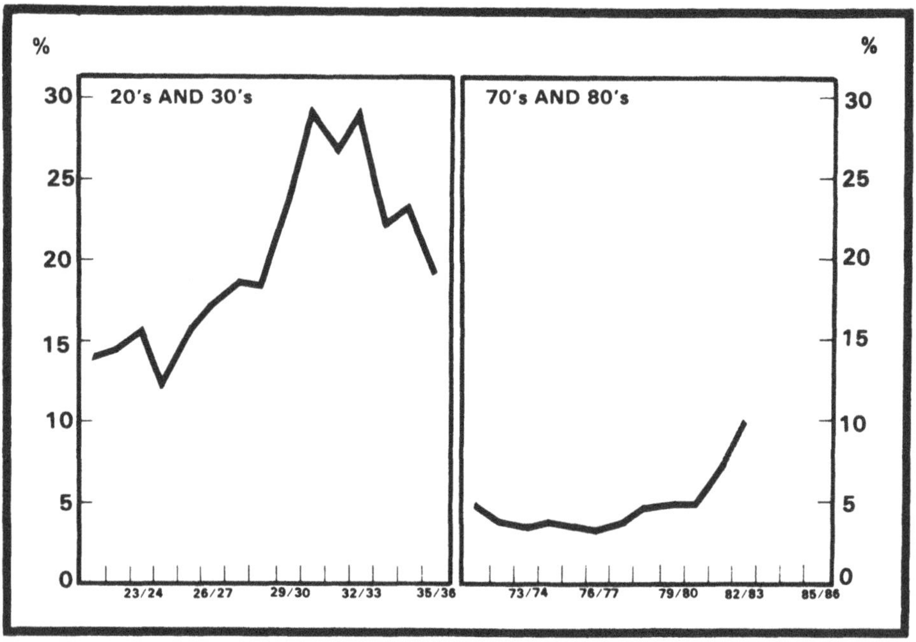


**Figure 13.13** Debt servicing burden (*interest payments on foreign debt/export receipts*)

**Table 13.3** *Interest payments and export receipts ($m.)*

| | *Interest on overseas debt*[a] | *Export receipts*[b] *(current prices)* | *Ratio* (%) |
|---|---|---|---|
| 1921/2–24/5 | 40 | 284 | 14.1 |
| 1925/6–28/9 | 52 | 297 | 17.5 |
| 1929/30 | 53 | 216 | 24.5 |
| 1930/1 | 59 | 201 | 29.4 |
| 1931/2–34/5 | 60 | 237 | 25.3 |
| 1971/2–75/6 | 323 | 8,257 | 3.9 |
| 1976/7–80/1 | 769 | 17,455 | 4.4 |
| 1981/2 | 1,669 | 22,663 | 7.4 |
| 1982/3 | 2,300[c] | 24,559 | 9.4[c] |

*Notes:* a For 1920s and 1930s, interest on government debt domiciled overseas. For 1970s and 1980s, includes interest payable on private overseas borrowing.
b National Accounts basis.
c Estimated.

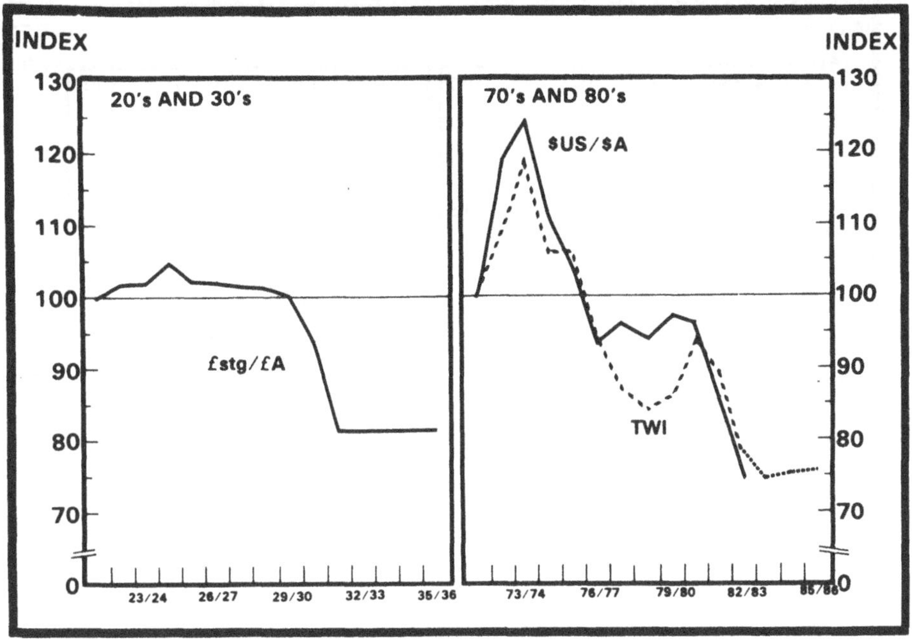


**Figure 13.14** Exchange rates

EXCHANGE RATES

In Figure 13.14, the exchange rate against sterling is shown to have been fairly stable until the large devaluation in 1931, after which it again held constant. In the 1970s, exchange rates were much more volatile after the breakdown of the system of fixed exchange rates that had operated since shortly after World War II. The Australian dollar appreciated against other currencies early in the decade. The effects of the subsequent devaluations are clearly seen. After the November 1976 devaluation, the trade weighted index (TWI) tended to appreciate for several years. Between 1980/1 and 1982/3, however, the value of the Australian dollar fell by around 17 per cent.

INDICES OF COMPETITIVENESS

Competitiveness is shown in Figure 13.15. Many measures of competitiveness can be constructed: those shown by the dotted lines are the ratio of unit labour costs in Australia to those in the United Kingdom in the 1920s and the 1930s and in major OECD countries in the 1970s and the 1980s; the solid lines adjust the ratios of unit labour costs for movements in the exchange rate (against sterling in the early episode and the other relevant currencies for the recent experience). In this graph a movement down indicates an increase in competitiveness (and vice versa).

For much of the 1920s, the competitiveness of Australian industry declined relative to that of the United Kingdom. However, the large cut in real unit

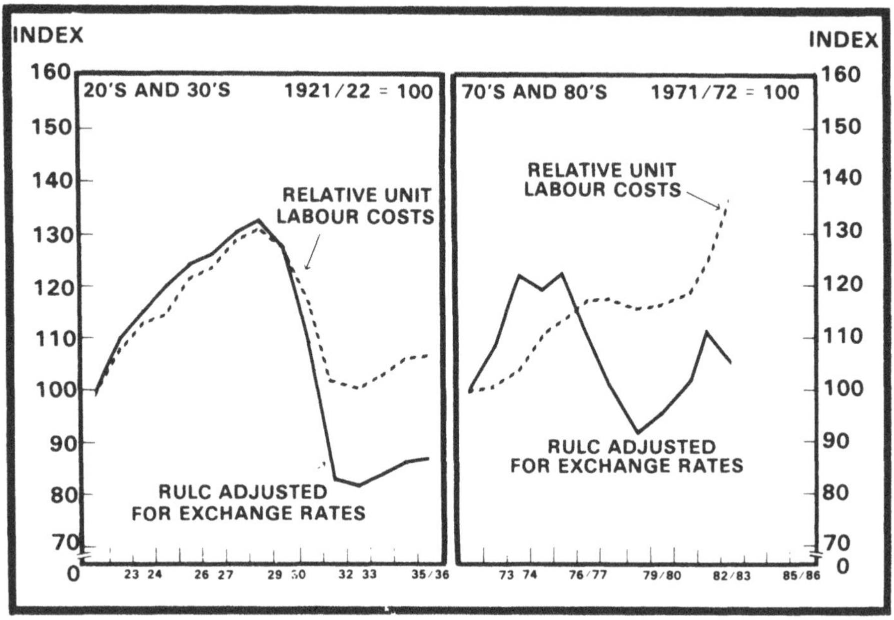


**Figure 13.15** Indices of competitiveness

labour costs from 1931/2 onwards produced a substantial improvement in competitiveness. When the effects of devaluation were added, there was a very large increase in competitiveness in the early 1930s.[10] Giblin (1936, p. 17) provides a nice summary of the situation:

> With the depression came a gradual but strong improvement of competitive power by Australian factories, so that even when duties remained unchanged, less protection was used. This came about partly as a result of greater economy and efficiency induced by the depression and the keen competition of Australian factories for the reduced market.
>
> A still more powerful factor was the fall in wages relative to wages abroad. This came about primarily through our peculiar method of adjusting wages to prices. The 10 per cent additional cut imposed by the Federal Court affected perhaps half the field of wages, but was offset by the slowness of some of the States, particularly New South Wales, to allow wages to be adjusted to lower prices. The net effect over all Australian wages has been a reduction almost exactly equal to the fall in prices. Wages in the three years 1930 to 1932 fell 21 per cent, and retail prices 22 per cent. In England, in the same time, the cost of living fell 15 per cent, and wages only 5 per cent. Wages now in Australia are 18 per cent lower than in 1930, but in England only 2 per cent lower. This fall in wages relative to the movement in England took place in the face of a depreciation of the currency in relation to sterling; it may be said at the present time that sterling wages have fallen 34 per cent in Australia since 1930, and practically not at all in England.

Australian unit labour costs rose by considerably more than those in OECD countries during the 1970s and 1980s. However, this has been largely offset by the substantial net devaluation of the exchange rate over this period. It should also be noted that other measures – e.g. those based on relative prices of *commodities* – show a less unfavourable picture for competitiveness in recent years.

## V INDICATORS OF GOVERNMENT POLICY

### INDICES OF TARIFF RATES

A considerable debate occurred in the 1920s over protection of Australian industry. Figure 13.16 shows indices of rates of protection.[11]

A gradual upward trend through the early and mid-1920s was followed by sharp increases when the foreign exchange crisis of 1929–31 forced policy makers to act to reduce imports sharply. In the 1970s and 1980s, overall rates of protection have been much more stable.

### PUBLIC SECTOR OUTLAYS

The size of government budgets was another big issue in the 1930s. Figure 13.17 shows public sector outlays by type and relative to GDP. While capital spending on goods and services was roughly the same proportion of GDP in both periods, current spending in the 1920s and 1930s was about half that in the

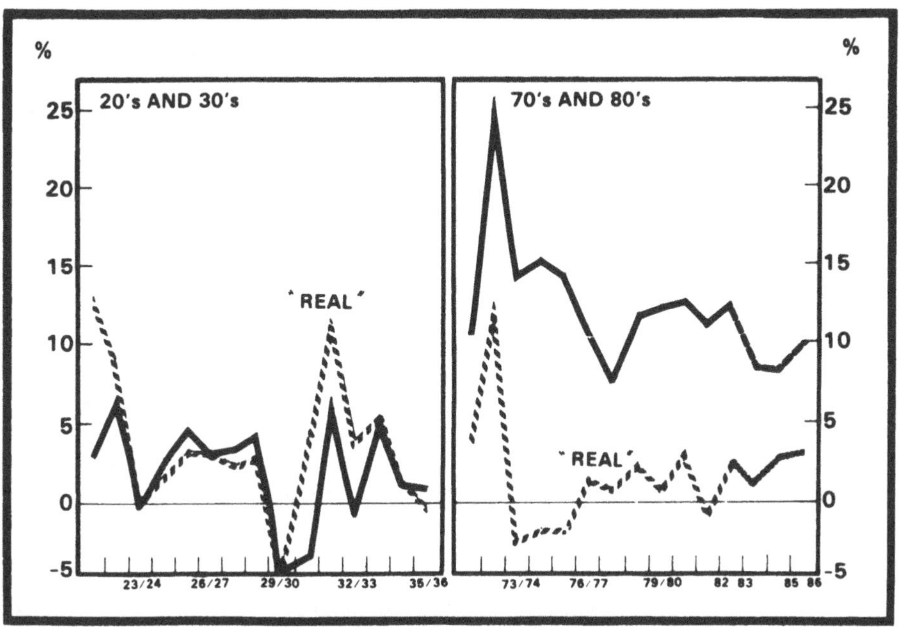


**Figure 13.16** Indices of tariff rates

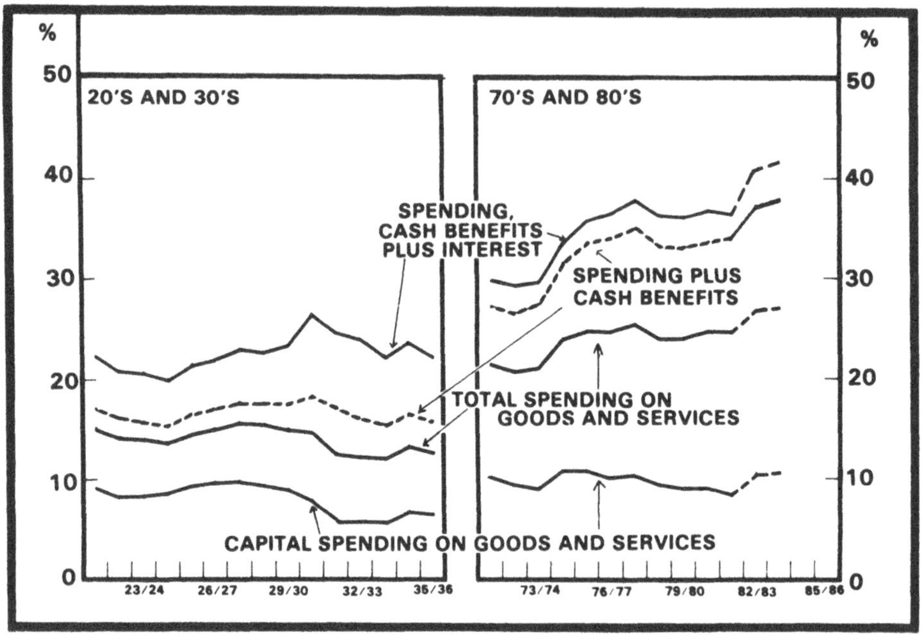


**Figure 13.17** Public sector outlays (*ratio to GDP*)

1970s and 1980s. Cash benefits accounted for a much smaller share of total government outlays in the 1920s and 1930s than in the 1970s and 1980s, but interest payments were relatively larger in the former period.

Relative to GDP, there was a steady upward trend in public sector outlays from the mid 1920s until 1930/1, with a sharp acceleration in the latter year. Early on this mainly reflected rising expenditure on capital goods and rising interest payments, but later a sharp increase in interest payments and cash benefits combined with falls in GDP were the main influences. The rise in total outlays was, however, moderated by a rapid fall in capital spending after 1928/9. This reflected severely restricted opportunities for overseas borrowing.

In the early 1970s, total government outlays were about 32 per cent of GDP. There was a sharp increase in government outlays beginning in 1974/5 and due mainly to increased current spending on goods and services and increased cash benefits. Total outlays continued to increase relative to GDP until 1977/8, when they fell slightly before levelling out.

The combination of weakening economic activity and expansionary policies (both of the Commonwealth and the non-Commonwealth authorities) contributed to a marked increase in public sector outlays in 1982/3. As shown in Figure 13.17, this increase is reflected in all the categories of outlays.

## BUDGET DEFICIT

The left-hand panel of Figure 13.18 shows measures of public sector deficits (relative to GDP) during the 1920s and 1930s. There was a gradual rise in public sector revenues relative to GDP over this period, due mainly to growth in

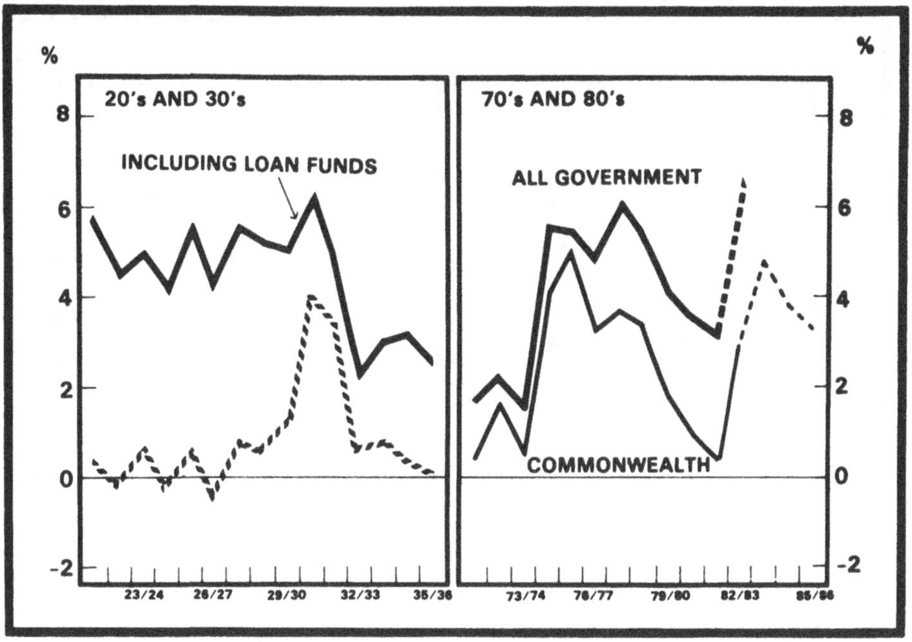


**Figure 13.18** Budget deficit (*ratio to GDP*)

indirect taxation revenues (relative to GDP). Consequently, the rise in the deficit at the onset of the depression is much less pronounced than that in outlays. The fall in capital spending in the late 1920s also moderated the increase in the deficit. This is shown in Figure 13.18 by the fact that the deficit including loan funds (shown by the black line) increased by much less than the consolidated revenue deficit (represented by the striped line). The policy, adopted in the Premiers' Plan, of balancing (or at least trying to balance) budgets is clearly reflected in the sharp fall in the size of both measures of budget deficits by 1932/3.

Public sector deficits in the 1970s and 1980s are shown in the right-hand panel of Figure 13.18. The thick line in this panel shows the consolidated deficit of all public authorities. In the early 1970s this deficit amounted to about 2 per cent of GDP. It subsequently increased sharply with the expansion of Commonwealth outlays in the middle of the decade. The relative size of deficits was gradually pegged back in the late 1970s, but the increase in spending by non-Commonwealth authorities, financed mainly by borrowing, prevented the consolidated deficit from falling to the same extent as the Commonwealth deficit. Both deficit measures increased sharply in 1982/3 and this trend continued in 1983/4. Scenario A projects further large Commonwealth deficits up to 1985/6, but with some declines (especially relative to GDP).

## INTEREST RATES

Figure 13.19 shows nominal and 'real' interest rates.[12] Nominal rates were fairly stable in the earlier period. The volatility in real rates was caused mainly

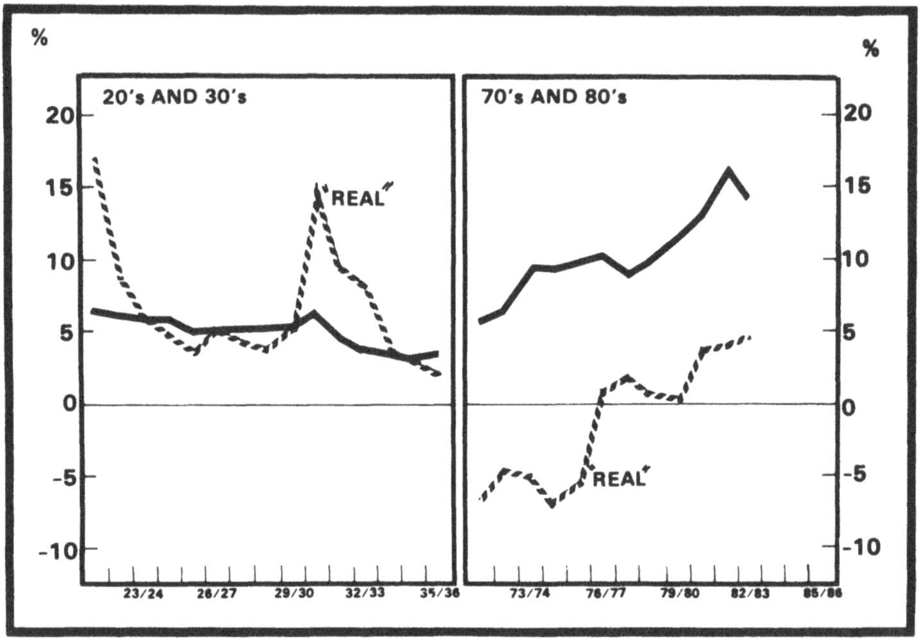


**Figure 13.19** Interest rates

by fluctuations in inflation. With prices falling, real rates of interest reached over 15 per cent in 1930/1. The Premiers' Plan included a cut in interest rates; the effects of this cut are seen in the latter part of the early period.

In the early 1970s, high and persistent rates of inflation exceeded nominal rates of interest, implying negative real interest rates (as measured) for some years. In the last few years, nominal rates have exceeded inflation, implying positive real rates, which approached 5 per cent in 1981/2 and 1982/3. For the 1970s and 1980s, however, real rates of interest have, on average, been much lower than in the 1920s and 1930s.

## GROWTH IN M3

Figure 13.20 shows the rate of growth in the supply of money, in nominal and real terms. Both measures of money fell substantially in 1929/30. In the following year, money again declined but by less than the general level of prices. This implied growth in real terms, which continued in the next two years. Towards the middle of the 1930s, growth rates (on both real and nominal measures) again declined.

In the early 1970s, there was a sharp acceleration of monetary growth, associated with large foreign exchange surpluses. This was followed by almost as sharp a deceleration in 1973/4, and a further reduction in 1977/8. In subsequent years, monetary growth was generally between 10 and 13 per cent. After adjustment for inflation, monetary growth in real terms has (since 1972/3) been a good deal more stable than in the 1920s and 1930s.

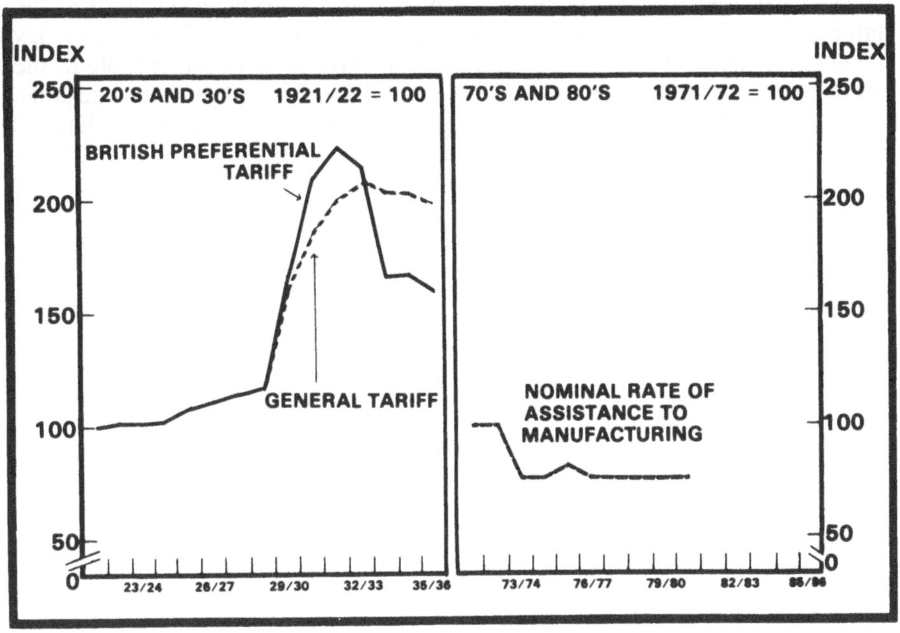


**Figure 13.20** Growth in M3

## VI CONCLUDING COMMENTS

In comparing the 1920s and 1930s with the 1970s and 1980s, it is quickly evident that there are both similarities and differences. Both periods saw a sharp rise in unemployment. Prices were generally falling in the 1920s and 1930s, whereas most prices have risen (in some cases by a large amount) in the 1970s and 1980s.

World trade fell much more severely from the late 1920s than seems likely in the current episode. The rise and fall in Australia's terms of trade was much larger in the earlier episode. Although Australia is still a small, open economy, its economic base is now much wider; also the external shock has been much smaller in the current episode.

Overseas borrowings in the 1920s were on a much vaster scale in relative terms than in the 1970s. The debt servicing burden is consequently much smaller in the 1980s than it was in the 1930s. Moreover, in the late 1920s, capital inflow dried up (forcing large adjustments to eliminate the current account deficit), whereas in recent times capital inflow has tended to exceed the large current account deficits.

Although the timing and mechanisms differed, both periods saw a noticeable rise in real unit labour costs. The rise was larger in the earlier episode and strongly influenced by the enormous fluctuations in the terms of trade. Helped by a once-for-all cut in real wages, there was a sharp fall in unit labour costs in response to the economic crisis of the 1930s. A more gradual reduction has been predicted for the 1980s.

The responses of general economic policy have also been different in the later episode. Budget deficits were cut back strongly in the 1930s, whereas they have expanded in the 1980s. Levels of protection were raised sharply in the 1930s and the exchange rate was cut relatively late. In the 1980s, the exchange rate was devalued early and average levels of protection have not changed much. Monetary policy has been more stable and, on average, less deflationary in the recent episode (whether measured by real rates of interest or by the growth of monetary aggregates).

## NOTES

1 The figures used are those from the so-called 'Scenario A'. In presenting the Scenarios, the Treasurer stressed that they were not forecasts and that 'surprises will inevitably occur'. The figures from Scenario A, however, provide a set of numbers that indicate one way in which economic developments might unfold up to 1985/6.

2 'Scenario C' assumed slightly lower unemployment, while 'Scenario B' assumed that unemployment would be noticeably higher than in Scenario A (peaking at 12.2 per cent in 1985/6). The uncertainties involved are illustrated by projections for the rate of unemployment. The average rate of unemployment projected for 1983/4 in Scenario A was 10 per cent. Another recent set of projections (by Blandy and Harrison, 1983), suggested that the rate of unemployment might be as low as 11 per cent or as high as 14 per cent in December 1983.

3 Figures for June in each year are given, with figures for other months given as required to indicate peaks and troughs.

4 In 1971/2 the Australian index was 15 times above its level in 1921/2, while the New York index was 17 times its 1921/2 level. Over the same period, Australian consumer prices rose 3.7 times, while US prices rose 2.5 times.

5 Research Discussion Paper No. 3303 of the Reserve Bank of Australia examines the composition of employment in each episode. Employment in manufacturing and construction was most volatile in both episodes, with much greater fluctuations in the 1920s and 1930s.

6 Deflation of earnings by consumer prices gives information about spending power, while deflation by product prices is relevant for calculations of labour as a cost of production.

7 Real unit labour costs are calculated by dividing average earnings by product prices and productivity (output per employed worker). In theory, this equals the wage share of output. In practice, differences in methods of measurement and the existence of taxes make this only approximately true. The series graphed here for the 1980s incorporates payroll tax as a cost to the employer. For further discussion of these issues see 'The measurement of real unit labour costs' in a Supplement to Department of the Treasury (1978).

8 The following extract from the Award of the Commonwealth Court of Arbitration, 22 January 1931, from Shann and Copland (1931b) is of considerable interest:

> Great and increasing unemployment is strongly symptomatic of a wage level too high for our present capacity. The national loss of spending power synchronizes with the recent aggravated increase of unemployment; after analysis of other suggested causes elsewhere in this judgment, the conclusion is unavoidable that the present wage level is above that which can be supported by the marketable productivity of the Commonwealth and that a lowering of that level is one of the essential means of checking a further increase of unemployment, of gradually restoring employment and of restoring a proper economic balance.

9 Schedvin (1970a, p. 5) gives a succinct account of sources of instabilities to the market for overseas loan funds in the 1920s.

10 It would be possible to adjust the measures of competitiveness shown here to allow for the additional effects of the changes in tariffs on the competitiveness of manufacturing industry, as done for the 1973 changes by Gregory and Martin (1976). Such a procedure would suggest an even bigger improvement in competitiveness (for manufacturing) than that shown for the early 1930s in Figure 13.15.

11 The average level of protection in the 1970s was around 17 per cent for manufacturing, compared with average tariff rates of up to 50 per cent in the 1920s for non-UK goods. The

figures for the 1970s and 1980s include Industries Assistance Commission estimates of protection through quotas and other restrictions as well as tariffs, while the early figures do not allow for non-tariff barriers to trade. For some discussion of the latter see Schedvin (1970b), ch. 8.

A feature of recent changes to protection policy has been the increase in the *dispersion* of levels of protection. This increase means that the stability shown in the right-hand panel of Figure 13.16 is more apparent than real.

12 The 'real' rate of interest is defined for this graph as the yield on government bonds adjusted for movements in the linked C-series retail price index for the 1920s and 1930s and in the GDP deflator for the 1970s and 1980s.

## BIBLIOGRAPHY

Bambrick, Susan (1970), 'Australian price indexes', unpublished PhD thesis, Australian National University.

Barnard, A., Butlin, N. G. and Pincus, J. J. (1977), 'Public and private sector employment in Australia 1901–1974', *Australian Economic Review*, 37(1), 43–52.

Blandy, R. J. and Harrison, D. (1983), 'The Australian labour market March 1983', *Australian Bulletin of Labour*, 10, March, 75–92.

Boehm, E. A. (1979), *Twentieth Century Economic Development in Australia*, 2nd edn, Melbourne, Longman Cheshire.

Butlin, M. W. (1977), 'A preliminary annual database 1900/01 to 1973/74', Research Discussion Paper 7701, Sydney, Reserve Bank of Australia, May.

Butlin, N. G. (1962), *Australian Domestic Product, Investment and Foreign Borrowing 1861–1938/39*, Cambridge, Cambridge University Press.

Butlin, S. J., Hall, A. R. and White, R. C. (1971), *Australian Banking and Monetary Statistics 1817–1945*, Occasional Paper No. 4A, Sydney, Reserve Bank of Australia.

Campbell, K. O. (1956), 'Current agricultural development and its implications as regards the "utilisation of resources"', *Economic Record*, 22, May, 119–134.

Commonwealth Bureau of Census and Statistics (1950), *The Australian Balance of Payments 1928/29 to 1948/49*, Canberra, Commonwealth Bureau of Census and Statistics.

Copland, D. B. (1933), *Australia in the World Crisis, 1929–33*, Melbourne, Cambridge University Press.

Cowles, Alfred and Associates (1938), *Common Stock Indexes, 1871–1937*, Cowles Commission for Research in Economics, Monograph No. 3, Bloomington, Ind., Principia Press.

Department of the Treasury (1978), *Round-up of Economic Statistics*, September.

Feinstein, C. H. (1972), *National Income, Expenditure and Output of the United Kingdom 1855–1965*, Cambridge, Cambridge University Press.

Forster, C. (1965), 'Australian unemployment 1900–1940', *Economic Record*, 41, September, 426–450.

Giblin, L. F. (1930), 'Australia 1930', Inaugural Lecture, Melbourne.

Giblin, L. F. (1936), 'Some economic effects of the Australian tariff', Joseph Fisher Lecture in Commerce, Adelaide.

Giblin, L. F. (1951), *The Growth of a Central Bank*, Melbourne, Melbourne University Press.

Gregory, R. G. and Martin, L. D. (1976), 'An analysis of relationships between import flows to Australia and recent exchange rate and tariff changes', *Economic Record*, 52, March, 1–25.

Keating, M. (1973), *The Australian Workforce 1910/11–1960/61*, Canberra, Australian National University Press.

Lamberton, D. M. (1960), *Securities Prices and Yields 1875–1955*, Sydney Stock Exchange Research and Statistical Bureau.

League of Nations (1945), *Industrialisation and Foreign Trade*, Geneva.

Lewis, W. A. (1952), 'World production, prices and trade, 1870–1960', *Manchester School of Economics and Social Studies*, 20, May, 105–138.

McLean, I. W. (1968), 'The Australian balance of payments on current account 1901 to 1964/65', *Australian Economic Papers*, 7(2), June, 77–99.

National Economic Summit Conference (NESC) (1983a), *Projections of the Australian Economy to 1985/86*, Canberra, Australian Government Publishing Service.

National Economic Summit Conference (1983b), *Information Paper on the Economy*, Canberra, Australian Government Publishing Service.

OECD (1983), *Economic Outlook*, June.

Pope, D. (1982), 'Wage regulation and employment in Australia 1900–1930', *Australian Economic History Review*, 22(2), September, 103–126.

Schedvin, C. B. (1970a), 'The long and short of depression origins', in R. Cooksey (ed.), *The Great Depression in Australia*, special issue of *Labour History*, 17, 1–13.

Schedvin, C. B. (1970b), *Australia and the Great Depression*, Sydney, Sydney University Press.

Shann, E. O. and Copland, D. B. (1931a), *The Battle of the Plans*, Sydney, Angus & Robertson.

Shann, E. O. and Copland, D. B. (1931b), *The Crisis in Australian Finance 1929 to 1931*, Sydney, Angus & Robertson.

Swan, P. L. (1968), 'The Australian balance of payments and capital imports, 1914/15 to 1923/24', *Australian Economic Papers*, 7(2), June, 90–103.

Valentine, T. J. (1978), 'The battle of the plans: an econometric analysis', papers presented to Seventh Conference of Economists, Sydney.

Wilson, R. (1931), *Capital Imports and the Terms of Trade*, Melbourne, Melbourne University Press.

# 14 Monetary and Fiscal Policy in Australia

*J. R. HEWSON and J. W. NEVILE*

## I INTRODUCTION

The first half of the 1970s saw quite violent changes in the stance, first of monetary policy then of fiscal policy. The large expansionary change in fiscal policy in the financial years 1974/5 can be explained (though not necessarily excused) by the rapid rise in unemployment in that year; but the very rapid rise in the money supply in 1972/3 was due to a desire to maintain a grossly undervalued exchange rate for the Australian dollar – a desire that may have had some political rationality, but certainly had no economic rationality.

After the very expansionary year 1974/5, fiscal policy was tightened significantly in 1975/6 and again in 1976/7. Over the next two years it did not change much and was roughly neutral in an absolute sense. Then in 1979/80 fiscal policy was abruptly tightened. It was even more contractive in 1980/1 and 1981/2, but in 1982/3 there was another violent change, this time in an expansionary direction.

The very expansionary monetary policy of 1972/3 was followed by a severe credit squeeze in 1974, but since 1975/6 monetary policy has been much more stable and more often than not mildly contractive. The rate of growth of the money supply in real terms varied between –2.5 per cent and +2.5 per cent. In most years it was less than the rate of growth of the labour force. Real interest rates appear to have increased substantially over the period.

The course of monetary and fiscal policy is examined in detail in Sections IV and V below. Before that, Sections II and III set the scene by sketching out the movements in inflation and unemployment and commenting on the influences on these movements.

Our own conclusions on different issues are included in the relevant sections. Five general points can be made here. First, the political attitudes to macroeconomic policy have changed over the last decade. There is now a more disciplined approach to both monetary and fiscal policy, and this disciplined approach has become a political objective in itself. Moreover, the government has become much more interested in and concerned about the overall policy mix.

Secondly, as always in Australian history, the balance of payments has been important. Since unemployment increased rapidly in 1974/5 it has served as a constraint on expansionary policies.

Thirdly, the dominant factor on the policy scene since the early 1970s has been wage developments. Inability to contain wage increases when economic activity improves has led to increased debate about the need for incomes policy.

Fourthly, monetary and fiscal policies alone were not effective in reducing inflation, given the extent to which they were applied in Australia. Contractive policies did reduce inflation from the peak in 1974, but from 1978/9 to 1981/2 the rate of inflation rose despite generally consistent contractive macro policy.

Finally, over the last ten years there has been increasing emphasis on the medium term and on the need to avoid violent swings in policy.

## II INFLATION IN AUSTRALIA

Table 14.1 shows two measures of the annual (year-on-year) rate of inflation in Australia in the 1970s and early 1980s. To put these figures in context it should be noted that in the 1960s inflation in Australia was below 4 per cent in every year until 1969/70, when it was 4.7 per cent. The rise in inflation to 1971/2 was perceived as a sharp increase at the time, and did represent a doubling of the rate over a period of three years, but it was dwarfed by the rise from 1972/3 to 1974/5. Inflation fell quite sharply between 1974/5 and 1978/9, then drifted upwards. So far, the effects of the current deep recession on inflation have not been very noticeable, but this is not very surprising. On past experience one would not expect them to show up before the middle of 1983.

How important have changes in the level of unemployment been, vis-à-vis other factors, as proximate determinants of changes in the rate of inflation in Australia? Many economists have estimated short-run Phillips curves for

**Table 14.1** *Measures of inflation in Australia, 1970/1–1981/2*

| *Year* | *Consumer price index % increase* | *Implicit gross national expenditure deflator %increase* |
|---|---|---|
| 1970/71 | 4.8 | 7.0 |
| 1971/72 | 6.8 | 7.0 |
| 1972/73 | 6.0 | 6.8 |
| 1973/74 | 12.9 | 13.2 |
| 1974/75 | 16.7 | 19.6 |
| 1975/76 | 13.0 | 16.0 |
| 1976/77 | 13.8 | 11.6 |
| 1977/78 | 9.5 | 9.5 |
| 1978/79 | 8.2 | 7.7 |
| 1979/80 | 10.1 | 10.4 |
| 1980/81 | 9.4 | 10.1 |
| 1981/82 | 10.4 | 10.1 |
| 1982/83 | 11.5 | 11.4 |

*Sources:* Calculated from figures in Australian Bureau of Statistics, *Monthly Review of Business Statistics*, Cat. No. 1304.0, various issues; and *Australian National Accounts: National Income and Expenditure*, Cat. No. 5204.0, various issues.

Australia, but all these curves include other explanatory variables besides unemployment. Generally the other variables have been more important than unemployment in influencing the rate of inflation in Australia.

To illustrate this, consider the version of the Phillips curve estimated in Nevile (1975). Very briefly, the theoretical derivation of this curve is as follows. One starts with the truism that a certain proportion of prices in Australia is determined in the first instance by overseas prices and the rest are determined, in the first instance, by domestic factors:

$$P = hP_f + (1 - h)P_d,$$

where $P$ is the rate of growth of the general price level, $P_f$ the rate of growth of overseas prices, $P_d$ the rate of growth of prices determined by domestic factors, and $h$ is a parameter, greater than 0 and less than 1.

The equation for domestically determined prices is

$$P_d = W_{en} - Q + aD,$$

where $W_{en}$ is the rate of growth of average weekly earnings net of changes in overtime earnings, $Q$ is the long-run rate of productivity growth and $D$ is the level of excess demand. Changes in weekly earnings net of changes in overtime earnings and the long-run rate of growth of productivity are used because of the belief that pricing decisions are made on the basis of costs at normal levels of output.

Changes in net average earnings are determined by changes in award wage rates plus two sources of earnings drift. One is the level of excess demand and the other is the difference between the expected rate of increase in prices and the rate of increase in award wage rates less productivity growth. Hence the equation for $W_{en}$ is

$$W_{en} = bW_a + c(P_e - W_a + Q) + dD,$$

where $W_a$ is the rate of growth of award wage rates, and $P_e$ the expected rate of growth of prices.

The rate of growth of award wage rates is assumed to be determined partly by the expected rate of growth of prices and partly by other factors, i.e.

$$W_a = P_e + A,$$

where $A$ is an adjustment or loading in recognition of productivity increases, social goals such as equal pay for women, and amounts dictated by the goal of industrial peace. It also, of course, includes any variations in the rate of growth of award wage rates caused by changes in the composition of the bench hearing the national wages case and similar factors.

Combining these equations and adding an extra term to allow for the existence of indirect taxes gives

$$P = hP_f + b(1-h)P_e + (b-c)(1-h)A - (1-h)(1-c)Q + (1-h)(a-d)D + fT,$$

where $T$ is the rate of change of an index of indirect tax rates.

If the long-run Phillips curve is vertical, the coefficient $b$ must be equal to 1. When our Phillips curve is estimated with no constraints on the size of $b$, that coefficient is significantly smaller than 1 (at the 5 per cent level). However, there are undoubtedly measurement errors in the two relevant variables, $P_e$ and $P_f$, which would bias downwards the estimate of the coefficient $b$. Hence, we have had the courage of our theoretical convictions and imposed the condition that $b$ equals 1. If one assumes that the long-run rate of growth of productivity is constant, and hence that its effects are included in the constant term, this gives the following equation, which was estimated from annual data for the period 1954/5–1978/9:[1]

$$\underset{1.12}{P = -5.69} + .15P_f + \underset{.05}{.85P_e} + \underset{.04}{.22A} + \underset{.04}{.11T} + \underset{10.73}{(52.78)/u} + 7$$

$$R^2 = 0.96 \qquad DW = 1.58$$

where $u$ is the unemployment rate.

On the assumption that the long-run rate of productivity growth is 2.5 per cent and that this is normally passed on in wage rises, the inflation-stabilizing rate of unemployment implied by the above equation is 3.28. The equation was estimated from data ending in 1979/80 because of a desire to see how well it performed in 1980/1 and 1981/2 without being influenced in any way by the data for those years. In fact, although it predicted well in 1980/1, it performed very badly in 1981/2, underpredicting the rate of inflation by over 2 percentage points. However, 1981/2 was a difficult year for all the traditional explanations of inflation in Australia – as they all underpredicted inflation in that year.

This has led Gregory (1982) to argue that the relationship between the level of unemployment and inflation is more apparent than real. If anything, he argues, the relationship is between changes in the level of unemployment and inflation; but even this is only a reflection of the true relationship, which is between the profitability of firms and wage growth.

Substituting the change in unemployment for the level of unemployment in the equation for inflation is not a precise test of Gregory's hypothesis, it is probably the nearest one can get to a quick direct statistical test. The equation for inflation is less satisfactory (by the usual statistical tests) when the change in unemployment is used instead of the level of unemployment. However, the equation using the change in unemployment does not underpredict inflation in 1981/2. Thus, one should treat with caution any application of our estimated equation to the 1980s, although it does fit data for the 1970s reasonably well. Gregory's hypothesis explains 1981/2, but it does not fit the data of the 1970s particularly well.[2]

In the light of this we have used our estimated Phillips curve to analyse the proximate causes of changes in the inflation rate in the 1970s and early 1980s. The results are set out in Table 14.2.[3] Judging from this table, fluctuations in the level of unemployment have been relatively unimportant in causing changes in the inflation rate. One possible exception to this generalization is the year 1970/1 when over-full employment was an important proximate cause of the rise in the inflation rate. Over much of the period, high levels of

**Table 14.2** *Proximate causes of changes in the inflation rate in Australia, 1970/1–1981/2*

| | *Change due to:* | | | | | |
|---|---|---|---|---|---|---|
| *Year* | *Differences between expected rate of inflation and last year's actual rate* % points | *Differences between rate of growth of import prices and last year's actual rate of inflation* %points | *Increase in award wage rates above prices plus productivity* % points | *Increase in indirect tax rates* % points | *Difference between the level of unemployment and the inflation-stabilizing level* % points | *Random factor* % points |
| 1970/71 | –0.6 | 0.6 | 0.6 | 0.6 | 1.0 | 0.4 |
| 1971/72 | –1.4 | –0.1 | 1.0 | 0.4 | 0.8 | –0.2 |
| 1972/73 | –1.1 | –1.0 | 0.6 | – | 0.4 | 0.5 |
| 1973/74 | 1.1 | 0.7 | 2.2 | 0.9 | 0.6 | 0.3 |
| 1974/75 | 1.5 | 2.4 | 3.7 | 0.6 | 0.3 | –1.0 |
| 1975/76 | –2.8 | –1.4 | –0.6 | 0.8 | –0.7 | –0.1 |
| 1976/77 | –2.6 | 0.1 | 0.4 | 0.1 | –0.6 | –0.2 |
| 1977/78 | 1.4 | 0.2 | –1.5 | 0.2 | –1.0 | –1.5 |
| 1978/79 | –1.4 | – | –0.9 | 1.1 | –1.2 | –0.3 |
| 1979/80 | 1.6 | 1.6 | –0.7 | 0.9 | –1.2 | 1.8 |
| 1980/81 | –0.2 | –0.4 | –0.4 | 1.1 | –1.1 | –0.3 |
| 1981/82 | –1.1 | –1.1 | 0.1 | 0.7 | –1.0 | 2.3 |

unemployment had a restraining influence on inflation, but the influence was not all that great. It never reduced inflation as much as 1.5 percentage points. The large fall in inflation from 1974/5 to 1978/9 was mainly due to wage moderation, just as the large rise in the years 1973/4 and 1974/5 was due more to the wage explosion than any other factor. Indeed, over the 'indexation' years 1975/6–1980/1 inclusive, increases in award wage rates reduced inflation by 0.6 of a percentage point a year on average, compared with an increase of 3 percentage points a year over the previous two years.

It could be argued that excessive increases in award wage rates, on the one hand, and moderation in award wage rates, on the other, are themselves simply the results of changes in levels of unemployment. In fact, over the period in question, the level of unemployment is a good predictor of the rate of growth of award wage rates in all years but two. However, these two years are 1973/4 and 1974/5, when social and political factors – the equal pay for women movement and the use of the public service as a pace-setter in wage bargains – produced very large rises in award wage rates – indeed, about as much variation in award wage rates as there was in all the other years combined. What is equally important is that, even in the years in which unemployment was highest, the effect of unemployment on award wage rate growth, as estimated in a regression equation, was only large enough to reduce inflation by about one-third of a percentage point.

Overall it is clear that by far the most important factor in the big rise in inflation in 1973/4 and 1974/5 was the very large rises in award wage rates, which can be ascribed to social factors. The fall in inflation over the next three years can be ascribed to increases in unemployment, award wage rates increasing less rapidly than prices plus productivity, and the fact that the expected rate of inflation did not reach the heights that the actual rate reached. Over the period as a whole, the difference between expected and actual inflation had a moderate downward effect and rising import prices had a slight upward effect. Increases in indirect tax rates added 0.6 of a percentage point to the inflation rate on average and, although the size of increases in award wages varied greatly on average, they added only 0.4 of a percentage point to the rate of inflation each year. Unemployment had an upward effect in the first half of the period, but this was more than outweighed by the downward effect in the second half.

The rate of growth of the money supply does not appear in the equation explaining the rate of inflation. In fact, one can get a moderately high $R^2$ if one regresses the inflation rate on past rates of growth of the money supply. Using the same data period as for the previous regression one gets:

$$P = -1.63 + .53DM_{-1} + .39DM_{-2}$$
$$1.19 \quad .15 \quad + .14$$
$$R^2 = .71 \qquad DW + .62$$

where $DM$ is the (year-on-year) rate of growth of M3. If $DM_{-3}$ is included, its coefficient is completely insignificant, but all the explanatory variables are fairly highly correlated. It is interesting that our result is much better than the result one gets in regressing the rate of nominal gross domestic product on changes in the money supply,[4] which might be thought to be a more appropriate regression. It is presumably a somewhat degenerate reduced-form equation, reflecting a hidden transmission mechanism that could well work through a Phillips curve such as the one that we estimated. In this connection it is interesting to note that the econometric model in Nevile (1983) contains a Phillips curve very similar to the one in this chapter. If that model is simulated to show the effects of a sustained 10 per cent increase in the money supply, the long-run result (after ten years) is that the price level rises by 9 per cent and the rate of interest falls slightly.

There is considerable other evidence of a long-run link between money and prices. Although the estimates are the subject of some debate (for example, Davis and Lewis, 1978, seem more sceptical), Porter (1982), looking at the period 1952–78, concludes that the overall elasticity of prices to money (M1) was not significantly different from unity, using either annual or quarterly data, and that the pattern of adjustment was roughly 15 per cent within 12 months, with per-quarter elasticity at a peak two–three years later. Using annual data Porter also explained about 70 per cent of variation in inflation by monetary growth, but with quarterly data this dropped to only 16 per cent. It appears that short-term fluctuations in money growth have little effect on prices; what matters is long-term trend growth.

This relationship between money and prices was generally thought to be stronger for M3 and M1. However, more recent evidence (Valentine, 1983a, using the period 1968Q3–1981Q3) suggests that broader or narrower aggregates or a credit aggregate are providing better explanations of the rate of inflation than M3 (Goodhart's law).

The analysis so far suggests that, while of some importance in combating inflation, monetary and fiscal policy were not of overwhelming importance, either in the rapid rise in inflation in the 1970s or in the subsequent fall. If our Phillips curve is correct, the way monetary policy affects inflation is through exchange rate variation and the level of unemployment. Exchange rate variations had only a small part to play in changes in the inflation rate. The high level of unemployment was a significant factor in reducing the rate of inflation below its peak, but it was not of overwhelming importance. Fiscal policy affects inflation both through unemployment and through changes in indirect tax rates. The increasingly contractive fiscal policy between 1975/6 and 1981/2 played some part in moderating inflation over that period, but the increases in indirect tax rates that were part of contractive fiscal policy had a small, but immediate, impact in increasing the rate of inflation.

## III UNEMPLOYMENT IN AUSTRALIA

Trends in unemployment are summarized in Table 14.3. Average unemployment improved temporarily with the boom in 1973/4 but deteriorated quite rapidly from 1974/5 onwards, although it did not peak again until 1978/9, which was more than four years after the economy moved into recession. In 1979/80, rapidly expanding domestic activity was reflected in a noticeable fall in the rate of unemployment. However, the fall was short-lived and (in average terms) confined to 1980/1; unemployment has since risen rapidly. There has, of course, been considerable debate on the causes of unemployment, and, rather than fully reflect that debate, observations here will be confined to three areas – money supply, structural factors and real wages.

Movements in the money supply are shown in Table 14.5 below. While in the early to mid-1970s there was some correlation between the pace of money growth and the rate of unemployment, this seems to have shifted noticeably in the late 1970s and so far in the 1980s. The monetary acceleration from early 1970s to 1973–4 is at least consistent with the fall in the unemployment rate in 1973–4, as perhaps is the second acceleration of money growth between 1974 and 1976 consistent with the more moderate rise in the rate in 1977/8; the lag in each case could be a year or so. However, the persistence of reasonably high growth rates of money since 1978/9 has occurred along with the significant upward shift in unemployment.

In general, evidence on the effect of money on economic activity suggests that only sustained variations matter and, particularly in a downward direction, activity effects occur somewhat quicker than price effects. Davis and Lewis (1978), however, would suggest a somewhat stronger link with real activity.

**Table 14.3** *Unemployment rates (%)*[a]

| Year (August) | Total actual | Total 1969/70 labour force weights | Males | | | | | | Females | | | | |
|---|---|---|---|---|---|---|---|---|---|---|---|---|---|
| | | | 15–19 | 20–24 | 25–34 | 35–44 | 45–54 | 55+ | 15–19 | 20–24 | 25–34 | 35–44 | 45+ |
| 1969 | 1.5 | 1.5 | 2.3 | 1.3 | 0.6 | 0.8 | 0.7 | 0.9 | 3.6 | 3.1 | 3.5 | 2.5 | 1.2 |
| 1970 | 1.4 | 1.4 | 2.9 | 1.3 | 0.8 | 0.6 | 0.7 | 0.9 | 3.6 | 2.0 | 2.2 | 2.8 | 1.3 |
| 1971 | 1.7 | 1.7 | 3.2 | 1.8 | 0.7 | 0.9 | 0.8 | 0.9 | 4.3 | 2.6 | 2.9 | 2.5 | 1.6 |
| 1972 | 2.5 | 2.5 | 5.6 | 2.6 | 1.5 | 1.3 | 1.4 | 1.5 | 5.9 | 3.8 | 4.1 | 3.1 | 2.1 |
| 1973 | 1.8 | 1.8 | 4.6 | 2.1 | 0.8 | 0.9 | 0.7 | 0.9 | 4.9 | 2.5 | 2.3 | 3.2 | 1.6 |
| 1974 | 2.9 | 2.3 | 5.0 | 2.9 | 1.3 | 1.3 | 1.2 | 0.8 | 6.7 | 3.6 | 3.5 | 3.4 | 1.6 |
| 1975 | 4.6 | 4.5 | 10.8 | 5.2 | 2.4 | 2.3 | 2.2 | 2.5 | 15.1 | 6.9 | 5.5 | 4.5 | 3.0 |
| 1976 | 4.7 | 4.7 | 12.7 | 6.5 | 2.8 | 2.3 | 2.3 | 1.9 | 15.8 | 6.3 | 5.1 | 4.0 | 2.9 |
| 1977 | 5.7 | 5.6 | 15.8 | 7.2 | 3.2 | 2.9 | 2.5 | 2.5 | 20.3 | 8.0 | 5.3 | 4.5 | 2.7 |
| 1978 | 6.3 | 6.1 | 15.9 | 8.6 | 4.0 | 3.1 | 3.1 | 3.4 | 18.7 | 9.1 | 6.6 | 4.6 | 3.4 |
| 1979 | 6.2 | 6.0 | 15.8 | 8.6 | 3.8 | 2.6 | 2.6 | 3.2 | 20.6 | 9.1 | 6.8 | 4.4 | 3.4 |
| 1980 | 6.1 | 5.9 | 15.3 | 8.5 | 4.0 | 2.6 | 2.6 | 2.8 | 19.1 | 9.4 | 6.6 | 4.0 | 3.2 |
| 1981 | 5.8 | 5.3 | 13.6 | 7.7 | 3.9 | 2.4 | 2.7 | 3.2 | 17.9 | 8.8 | 6.3 | 4.5 | 3.0 |

*Note:* a Disaggregated figures are available only until 1981. In 1982 and 1983 the total figures were 6.7 and 9.9 respectively.

Although sufficient work has not yet been done, it is possible that structural factors have been of lesser importance in Australia than in other countries. To take one simple example, shifts in the age/sex composition of the work force do not seem to have had a significant effect on unemployment; unemployment rates of each (age/sex) group seem to have dominated the trend, as revealed in Table 14.3.

In this regard, changes in the unemployment experiences of males and females are markedly different. In every age group the position of the males deteriorated proportionately more than that of females, as is shown in Table 14.4. There was not a big difference in the case of teenagers, but for adults the proportionate increase in male unemployment was twice that for females. Moreover males in the age group 20–35 fared proportionately as badly as male teenagers but this was not the case for females. Although the data only extend up until 1981, the differences between males and females would have become much more marked since 1981, because the rapid rise in unemployment in 1982/3 was particularly heavy among adult males.

Finally, there is the question of real wages. Despite many studies, it is not possible to give a definitive answer to the question about the importance of high real wages in increasing unemployment in Australia; there are various pieces of evidence, but they are far from clear-cut.

It is true, for example, that real wages increased rapidly from June 1973 to December 1974 and that this was followed by a rapid increase in unemployment from June 1974 to March 1975. However, this does not prove that the rise in real wages caused the rise in unemployment. When output declines – or even when its rate of growth slackens significantly – profits fall, and hence real wages rise, and also, after a lag, unemployment increases. It is quite feasible, indeed likely, that some third factor caused both the rise in real wages and the rise in unemployment in Australia in the mid-1970s. Moreover, after 1975 there was no clear relationship between real wages and unemployment up until 1981. Then, with a sudden increasing of the worldwide recession, real wages and unemployment both again significantly increased in Australia. It is no easier to sort out cause and effect in the case of 1981/2 and 1982/3 than it is when

**Table 14.4** *Increases in unemployment by age and sex, 1969/70–1980/1*[a]

| | *Sex* | |
|---|---|---|
| *Age* | *Male* | *Female* |
| 15–19 | 5.6 | 5.1 |
| 20–24 | 6.2 | 3.6 |
| 25–35 | 5.6 | 2.3 |
| 35–44 | 3.6 | 1.6 |
| 45 to pensionable age | 3.7 | 2.0 |

*Note:* a Average in August for 1980 and 1981 combined with the average for the same two months in 1969 and 1970.

analysing the events of the mid-1970s, although this time the 'boom' had ended before real wages started to rise.

It is, of course, possible to use multiple regression methods to try and disentangle the importance of various factors that influence unemployment. The results obtained by different researchers, using different time periods and different definitions of variables, are somewhat contradictory, but the majority of studies do find that real wages have some influence on unemployment. However, the effects are not large, and overall the studies do not lead one to disagree with the conclusion reached by Gregory and Duncan (1979) as a result of their own analysis: 'The important variable for employment, as it always has been, is the rate of growth of output'.

Even if one accepts Gregory and Duncan's conclusion, this is not the end of the matter. It is possible, especially in a less than fully employed economy, that real wages, while not having a large direct influence on unemployment, may have a substantial indirect effect by affecting output growth. One way of tracing both the direct and indirect effects of one economic variable on another is by simulating an econometric model. Several attempts have been made to answer the question about the effects of wages on employment in Australia through the use of econometric models (for example, Coghlan, 1978; Dixon, Parmenter and Powell, 1979; and Nevile, 1983). These generally show that cuts in real or money wages have a significantly favourable effect on employment. However, the results depend more on assumptions that have been built into the models than on features or coefficients that have been estimated empirically.

Perhaps a more fruitful way of looking at this question is to examine what economic theory has to say about it and to use other features or assumptions of the theory to decide whether or not the theory is trustworthy. The two competing theoretical systems that throw light on this question are, of course, the classical and Keynesian. Both give some reasons for believing that a large rise in real wages may cause unemployment.

The classical system tends to think of the labour market in terms of an aggregate demand and supply curve for labour, with the amount of labour demanded falling as the real wage rises. There is an equilibrium, or full employment position, where the real wage is such that the amount of labour demanded equals the amount supplied. If the real wage rises above this full employment position, the amount of labour demanded will fall, causing unemployment. An essential part of the argument is that the amount of labour demanded falls as the real wage rises; given the whole classical system, this implies that labour productivity falls as employment and output increase.

There was intense investigation in Australia of the question of whether labour productivity rose more rapidly than usual following the large real wage rise in 1973–4. Some researchers (for example, Gruen, 1979b) think that productivity behaved to some extent in the way predicted by the classical model, but the evidence is very weak. Keynesians have no difficulty in rejecting it, and even such a sympathetic observer as Snape, after examining his table of productivity movements by industrial sectors, concludes that 'There does not appear to be a very clear pattern in the table' (1981, p. 32). The empirical evidence just does not give strong support to the classical position.

In the Keynesian system, a large rise in real wages can also cause unemployment. If real wages rise faster than productivity, the share of profits must fall. In a Keynesian world, and also, many believe, in the real world, the level of profits is the major factor determining the level of private investment (Nevile, 1980). If real profits fall, investment will fall and, as a result, output and employment will fall. In the short run the fall in private investment could perhaps be offset by increased public expenditure, but if the trends go on for long, with private investment continuously falling or even staying constant at a low level, productivity will almost certainly fall; this will reduce profits still further (unless real wages fall), starting a vicious circle. Profits certainly fell after 1973/4, mainly no doubt owing to the recession caused by worldwide factors, but it is plausible to believe that the rapid rise in real wages in Australia had an additional effect, reducing investment, and hence output and employment in the following years.

There is one final point to be made about real wages and employment. There seems little doubt that real wages that are inflexible downwards limit the ability of government policy to reduce unemployment. This is because of balance of payments considerations. Nevile (1979) argues that, if the economy is stimulated and unemployment reduced, along with other types of increased spending there will be increased spending on imports. A big fall in unemployment will result in a big increase in imports, which will probably cause a devaluation. If real wages cannot be reduced significantly, the likely effects of that devaluation will negate the employment-creating effects of the expansionary policy. Devaluation will raise the prices of imports and also possibly the prices of goods that compete with imports. If this rise in prices is not passed on in higher wages, industry will be more competitive; things produced at home will be cheaper relative to imports and rather more will be produced domestically, less will be imported, and perhaps more will be exported. However, if money wages are increased to preserve the standard of living of wage earners after devaluation, any competitive advantage of Australian industry will be short-lived, a further devaluation will be necessary, leading to a further price rise, and so on, giving a devaluation–inflation spiral that will erode the gains in employment of the expansionary policy as well as increasing the inflation rate. In present circumstances we would judge this to be the most important point in the relationships between real wages and unemployment.

To summarize: there is no doubt that large rises in nominal wage rates are inflationary, and have some adverse effects on unemployment. High real wages also probably increase unemployment, both for the reasons discussed and also because they may increase participation rates. Real wages that are rigid downwards certainly limit the ability of government policy to reduce unemployment.

The policy conclusion is clear: limit the rise in wage rates as much as possible. This does not mean striving for zero wage increases for a prolonged period. If too ambitious a programme of wage restraint is pursued, it will break down and probably be followed by a wage explosion, which will increase inflation and unemployment. The appropriate policy is not to strive for the impossible but to see that genuine wage restraint is achieved.

## IV MONETARY POLICY

There have been a number of significant developments in the conduct of monetary policy in the last decade.[5] The first half of the 1970s saw a distinct lack of monetary stability, which, in large measure, has resulted in a somewhat more disciplined process of monetary management with somewhat greater flexibility of interest and exchange rates as monetary policy has increasingly relied on more market-based techniques.

The most significant developments in the conduct of monetary policy included: a shift to a sort of *de facto* monetary targeting since early 1976, the introduction (1972) and then subsequent abolition (1977/8) of capital controls, a shift to more flexible, managed but non-market exchange rates with the introduction of a fixed peg to a trade weighted basket in 1974 and then management of that link to the basket since late 1976,[6] a process of gradual deregulation of the banking system, especially since 1977/8, and a somewhat greater reliance on more market-oriented methods of marketing government securities with the introduction of the 'tap' system (April 1980) and tender systems for Treasury notes (December 1979) and other government securities (July 1982).

Table 14.5 shows movements in three aggregates, M1 (currency plus demand-deposits), M3 (M1 plus deposits with trading and savings banks) and M6 (M3 plus deposits of major non-bank financial institutions). M1 and M3 moved broadly together in the early to mid-1970s, with the most notable differences being in the much greater decline in M1 in 1974 (the so-called credit

**Table 14.5** *Growth rates of monetary aggregates*[a]

| *Year* | *M1* | *M3* | *M6* |
|---|---|---|---|
| 1970 | 4.9 | 6.2 | |
| 1971 | 6.6 | 6.3 | |
| 1972 | 9.1 | 11.4 | |
| 1973 | 26.3 | 29.5 | |
| 1974[b] | 2.3 | 18.0 | |
| 1975 | 12.6 | 17.2 | |
| 1976 | 14.1 | 13.3 | |
| 1977 | 8.4 | 11.4 | |
| 1978 | 8.6 | 6.1 | |
| 1979 | 16.7 | 13.3 | 14.2 |
| 1980 | 12.9 | 16.5 | 13.7 |
| 1981 | 12.0 | 15.2 | 15.7 |
| 1982 | 1.6 | 13.9 | 13.8 |
| 1983 | 5.8 | 8.0 | 10.7[c] |

*Notes:* a Percentage growth over the twelve months ended in June in the year shown.
b Papua New Guinea figures are excluded from 1974 onwards.
c Preliminary.

squeeze), the much greater acceleration in M1 in 1978/9 and the much slower growth rate in M1 in 1981/2 and 1982/3 (due primarily to deregulation of savings bank deposit rates in December 1980 and other refinements in 1982). The broader aggregates have generally grown faster (by 2–3 percentage points) than M3 since the mid-1970s. Differences in the growth of M3 and broader financial aggregates have fluctuated with the cycle – the faster growth of the broader aggregates occurring when product growth was strongest, these differences being accentuated by the relative competitive positions of controlled and uncontrolled financial institutions. The domestic component of M3 tended to grow somewhat faster in the last half of the 1970s as the contribution of the balance of payments to monetary growth declined.

Focusing on M3 (the targeted aggregate) reveals a rapid expansion to mid-1973, with a peak rate of increase of some 25 per cent, and a noticeable, but volatile downward trend thereafter, with two significant declines in 1973/4 and 1977/8. Since 1978/9 M3 has grown annually within a fairly narrow range of 11.0–12.5 per cent.

There was a substantial contribution to money growth from private sector foreign exchange transactions (PSFET) in two periods, the early 1970s and the early 1980s, but balance of payments developments served to reduce money growth in 1975/6, 1977/8 and 1978/9. The turnaround in the balance of payments (private sector) from surplus to deficit in the mid-1970s followed a couple of revaluations of the Australian dollar, a tariff cut and use of exchange controls. The subsequent pick-up in PSFET owes much to the two devaluations of the exchange rate in 1974 and 1976 and exchange rate management since then. In the period 1974/9, the budget deficit contributed the bulk of the change in M3. However, in the early 1970s and again the first few years of the 1980s, the domestic surplus drained liquidity from the system. Throughout the period, bank lending made significant contributions to money formation. This was particularly the case in the early and late 1970s when activity was generally accelerating. The non-bank take-up of Commonwealth securities has fluctuated markedly over the period, with sizeable net sales (relative to M3) in 1975–8 (due largely to the Australian Savings Bonds) and again in 1982/3 (reflecting in large measure the significant success of the bond tender system).

Interest rates lifted sharply in two periods 1972–4 and 1978–82, both of which were associated with some moderation in money growth rates. With the exception of the mid-1970s and the early 1980s, the yield curve has been reasonably flat. Thus, any relationship between money and interest rates is quite complex and seems to depend importantly on expectations. Porter (1982, pp. 61–4) suggests that a rise in actual and expected money growth (proxied by actual money growth in the next period) can generate a temporary fall in interest rates, but this decline is likely to be short-lived, and to be followed by a fairly steady rise in nominal interest rates. The short-term effect was also more pronounced at the short end of the yield curve: long rates did not respond at all, as expected. There is also evidence that these relationships appear to have shifted in the course of the 1970s, with the responsiveness now greater.

The exchange rate was formally (i.e. discretely) revalued in 1972 and 1973 and devalued in 1974, 1976 and again in 1983. Since 1977 the rate has been managed downward in virtually three main phases. First, the index was devalued from 1977 to 1979 – through most of this period the upward thrust of the weak US dollar on the mid rate was slightly more than offset by the downward adjustment in the index. Then the index was revalued through to late 1981 – the downward thrust of the strengthening US dollar on the Australian mid rate was slightly more than offset (on average) by the upward adjustment of the index. In 1980 and 1981 the exchange rate was held at an overvalued level as an anti-inflation initiative. Finally, the index has generally been reduced since late 1981, with the practical effect of accentuating the downward thrust of the ever-strengthening US dollar on the mid rate as Australia's competitive position and the balance of payments deteriorated quite markedly. Nevertheless, the thrust of policy was still to moderate this fall by holding on to the index virtually 'as much as the market would bear' on anti-inflation grounds.

Although monetary aggregates were monitored in earlier periods, specific monetary aggregate objectives were first announced in 1976. Nevertheless, monetary targeting as such is not officially endorsed. Budget papers announce conditional 'monetary projections' annually in terms of a desirable movement in M3. Rigid M3 objectives have been eschewed on several grounds.[7] Any given growth of M3 can be achieved by different mixes of money formation factors, each of which is difficult to estimate, and rigid adherence to an M3 objective in the face of an external shock (like the 1978/9 shift in the terms of trade owing to the oil-price hike) could have unacceptable consequences for the ultimate objectives of policy (e.g. especially activity in 1978/9 given the 'fight inflation first' strategy). Moreover, smooth achievement of short-term monetary objectives might require large and erratic variations in instruments. As a result, even if such variations were politically possible and the monetary objective were achieved, they still might impair economic performance. Finally, control of one aggregate may only lead to offsetting movements in others.

In short, because the aggregates cannot readily be controlled, and because there is considerable uncertainty about the precise nature of the link between them and ultimate objectives, rigid targets have been seen as neither feasible nor desirable. However, because projections have not been formally altered during the year as economic conditions and prospects have changed, they have quickly become the focus of both public debate and the internal policy advisory process, such that they have in effect been treated as at least flexible targets against which monetary performance has been measured.

The main advantages of such targeting have been (officially) claimed to be: first, the demonstration of how aims of monetary policy fit within the broader policy framework; secondly, the indication of medium-term 'steadiness' in monetary management without abandoning an appropriate degree of discretionary responsiveness; and, thirdly, the provision of a 'peg of stability' in an attempt to exert a direct influence on inflationary expectations.

The targets set have generally been seen to imply restrictive monetary policy in that the 'target' (taken as the mid-point of the range) is set slightly below the forecast increase in nominal product over the year minus the trend increase in velocity. The political justification is to 'bear down on inflation' while providing sufficient funds to sustain 'desired' economic growth.

The 'targets' were successfully met in the first three years, but were significantly exceeded in 1978/9, 1980/1 and 1981/2. Outcomes were only slightly above the top end of the projected ranges 1982/3 and 1983/4. In the period 1975/6–1977/8, 'targets' were successfully achieved (despite the large budget deficits) for a number of reasons, but most importantly because of offsets via private sector foreign exchange transactions, large bond sales to the public and, to a lesser extent, some quantitative restraint on bank lending.

The failure to achieve the 'targets' in more recent years is due to a number of factors. First, there have been conflicting objectives of government policy, particularly interest rate and exchange rate objectives. On several occasions since 1978/9 the government could be said to have had a well-developed interest rate objective (e.g. late 1980) that in the circumstances contributed to a sizeable blow-out in monetary aggregates. This rigidity has been reduced with the additional interest flexibility that has come with the development of more market-based methods of marketing government securities. Potentially more important has been the conflict in objectives with exchange rate management. The most notable occasion was, of course, 1972. Since then the persistent anti-inflationary bias of exchange rate management, at times clearly against growing market expectations, has served interest rates. However, it could be said that on other occasions the anti-inflationary bias of exchange rate management has served to complement domestic monetary restraint and to have assisted in pegging domestic inflationary expectations.

Secondly, it has been difficult to achieve a June-on-June 'target' in the context of a pronounced intra-year liquidity cycle, whereby heavy net budgetary injections are concentrated in the first half to three-quarters of the financial year relative to the last part of the year.

Thirdly, the policy authorities have encountered difficulties in identifying and reacting to adverse monetary developments. The major problems here have included budget over-runs (the budget deficit outcome exceeded initial estimates in every year between 1976/7 and 1982/3 except 1976/7 and 1979/80); shifting interest rate expectations, which have often compounded the bond selling task under prevailing marketing arrangements; shifting exchange rate expectations – in part the result of management of the mid rate – and fluctuations in interest differentials, which had considerable influence on private foreign exchange transactions; excessive bank lending (outside quantitative restrictions), in large measure due to the vagueness of the directives and/or failure to back up such initiatives with changes in the Statutory Reserve Deposit ratio; and deviations from forecast in the actual growth and inflation rates in the course of the year. Because 'targets' were not changed in the course of the year, effective maintenance of the 'target' would at times have implied a significant tightening of monetary policy.

There has been debate in Australia about various aspects of the monetary targeting. Many of the issues are the same as those debated worldwide – for example, the appropriate monetary variable to target, multiple targets, whether monetary growth or the interest rate is the appropriate target, and whether intermediate targets have any validities. Although many of these issues remain unresolved at the academic level, governments of either persuasion are likely to remain committed to a disciplined monetary policy for the foreseeable future and to continue to express this discipline in terms of a conditional projection on M3. In an environment where inflation remains a problem and where the focus of debate is on the strength of their policy resolve, they have little choice, irrespective of whether they believe in them. In these circumstances, it seems desirable to make maximum use of the target in terms of the purposes described above, but perhaps most importantly in terms of influencing inflationary expectations.

## V FISCAL POLICY

Fiscal policy in Australia in the 1970s showed all possible variations from widely expansionary to very contractive, with periods of steady consistent policy and periods of large swings from one year to the next. In assessing the stance of fiscal policy it is not enough, of course, just to look at the size of the deficit. The size of the deficit is determined by a mixture of two things. One is the stance of fiscal policy, e.g. whether tax rates are high or low and whether expenditure is relatively large or not. The other is the state of economy. This has a considerable effect on the level of taxation receipts and also affects budget outlays, particularly, of course, unemployment benefits. The figures for the deficit must therefore, be corrected for changes due to changes in the state of the economy, or to cyclical variation, before they can be used as a measure for the stance of fiscal policy. Thus, rather than look at actual deficits, in this context it is more useful to examine the structural or residual deficit, or the deficit net of effects caused by cyclical variations in economic activity.

The size of the structural deficit in any year is very sensitive to the level of economic activity chosen as the norm, although year-to-year variations are less affected by this. Not only is the closeness to full employment characteristic of 'normal' levels of economic activity a matter of assumption, but the determining of the trend rate of growth of the economy, and hence of the 'normal' level of activity, is heavily dependent on judgemental factors. There are good reasons to believe that the trend rate of growth, which held when the economy was reasonably close to full employment, no longer holds now that the economy has been below full employment for many years. Moreover, in Australia, farm income creates additional problems. In many years, farm income in Australia is unusually high or unusually low, owing both to factors connected with the weather and to large movements in the prices received for farm exports. If one is estimating the potential gross domestic product that could be produced in a 'normal' year, one needs to estimate 'normal' farm income. However, to know whether actual farm income in a particular year is greater or smaller than normal, one must know whether the export prices are normal or abnormally good or bad. Hence, any estimates of the structural deficit involve a position on the terms of trade.

The size of the structural deficit is also fairly sensitive to the elasticity employed to relate changes in economic activity (measured say by gross domestic product) and changes in government receipts. In principle, this can be estimated empirically, but different investigators often produce quite different estimates. For example, Blandy and Creigh (1983) estimate it to be 1.114, whereas the National Economic Summit Conference document *Projection of the Australian Economy to 1985–86* (1983) implies an estimate of about 0.7.

Table 14.6 gives estimates of the federal government's structural budget deficit for the years 1970/1–1982/3. Payments of profits from the Reserve Bank to the government are treated as part of the deficit and a correction is made for the prepayment of $216 million to the states for hospital operating costs in June 1976. The elasticity of receipts is assumed to be unity and the potential rate of growth of the economy is assumed to be 4.3 per cent in the mid 1970s, declining to 4 per cent by the end of the decade. This is perhaps a somewhat optimistic estimate of potential growth, and, for comparison, figures based on a very pessimistic potential growth rate estimated by Blandy and Creigh (1983) are given as well. Blandy and Creigh assume a potential rate of growth of 3.41 per cent, which they obtain by fitting a time trend to the period 1971/2–1982/3. Since the first year of this period was one of 2 per cent unemployment, and the last year one in which unemployment averaged 9 per cent, this results in a very low rate of growth. For example, Blandy and Creigh show 1975/6 as a year of above-normal activity, although in that year unemployment was 5 per cent and elsewhere in their article they suggest that 2 per cent unemployment should be assumed to correspond to the 'normal' level of activity. Thus it is not surprising that Blandy and Creigh's estimates of the structural deficit are greater than ours, although it should be noted that our estimate of the elasticity of receipts is more conservative than theirs, which increases the size of the structural deficit.

In the first four years of the 1970s, those responsible for fiscal policy indulged

**Table 14.6** *Structural components of the Australian federal government deficit, 1970/71–1983/4*

| *Year* | *Corrected deficit $(000)m.* | *Structural deficit $(000)m.* | *Structural deficit as proportion of GDP %* | *Blandy and Creigh estimate of the structural deficit as proportion of GDP %* |
|---|---|---|---|---|
| 1970/71 | 0.1 | 0.1 | 0.2 | – |
| 1971/72 | 0.2 | 0.1 | 0.2 | 0.8 |
| 1972/73 | 0.7 | 0.5 | 1.2 | 2.2 |
| 1973/74 | 0.3 | 0.3 | 0.6 | 1.4 |
| 1974/75 | 2.6 | 1.7 | 2.8 | 4.5 |
| 1975/76 | 3.4 | 1.7 | 2.3 | 5.0 |
| 1976/77 | 3.0 | 0.8 | 1.0 | 2.5 |
| 1977/78 | 3.5 | 0.3 | 0.3 | 2.7 |
| 1978/79 | 3.7 | 0.1 | 0.1 | 3.0 |
| 1979/80 | 2.3 | –2.9 | –2.5 | 0.5 |
| 1980/81 | 1.3 | –4.7 | –3.6 | –0.3 |
| 1981/82 | 0.9 | –6.9 | –4.7 | –1.2 |
| 1982/83 | 5.1 | –5.0 | –3.1 | –0.5 |
| 1983/84[a] | 9.0 | –2.7 | –1.5 | 1.5 |

*Note:* [a] Projected.

in fine tuning. Changes that seemed large at the time seem small in the perspective of what happened later in the decade. In as much as (as often as not) the changes were in the wrong direction, it was fortunate that they were relatively restrained in magnitude.

In 1974/5 there was a very large expansionary change in fiscal policy. The change was even more violent than is shown in the annual figures, because most of it occurred in the second half of the financial year. The seasonally adjusted actual deficit was $300 million in the first half of the financial year and $2,200 million in the second. Unemployment was, of course, much greater in the second half of the year, but nowhere near enough to explain the difference in the size of the deficit. Given the lags in the system, the large deficit continued for nearly twelve months before the measures instituted by Mr. Hayden when he became Treasurer started to restrain it. This large expansionary change in fiscal policy had only a modest effect on output and virtually none on unemployment. However, it is true that contractive forces were very strong, with the downswing of the cycle greatly reinforced by the extremely severe monetary squeeze in the September quarter of 1974, and that there was an incipient upswing by the June quarter of 1975, which may well have been killed by the uncertainty surrounding the constitutional crisis in the second half of 1975.

From 1976/7 to 1978/9 inclusive, the deficit looked large but the structural component was very similar as a proportion of gross domestic product to what it had been in the 1960s and early 1970s. In this period there were no dramatic changes in fiscal policy and fiscal policy did not seem to have a big impact on the economy.

This was not true over the next three years. In 1979/80, fiscal policy was abruptly tightened. This was followed by further large contractive moves in fiscal policy in each of the succeeding years. The immediate effect on output and unemployment was not great, although the mini-boom of 1981 might have been rather larger if fiscal policy had not been so contractionary.

In 1981, unemployment rose steadily from January to August, and then increased dramatically. The timing of this is what one would expect if the rise in unemployment were due mainly to the extremely contractive fiscal policy in 1981/82, but the delayed effects of the international recession must have been at least equally important. It is interesting to note that, over the three years that fiscal policy was so contractive, the rate of growth of the gross national expenditure deflator rose by about $2\frac{1}{2}$ percentage points. Virtually all of this was due to rises in indirect tax rates. Over the same three years, the consumer price index rose by a little over 2 percentage points; and, according to the Institute of Applied Economic and Social Research, indirect tax increases and reductions in health insurance subsidies added about 2 percentage points each year to the rise in the consumer price index. Increasing indirect tax rates, to combat inflation through contractive fiscal policy, appears to have been counterproductive, at least in the short to medium run.

## NOTES

1 The price expectations series is defined as in Nevile (1975), i.e. as equal to $2\frac{1}{2}$ per cent for years prior to 1970/1, and equal to the June-on-June rate of change of the consumer price index in the

previous year for 1970/1 and subsequent years. Changes in foreign prices are represented by changes in the implicit deflator for imports. The increase in indirect tax rates is the rate of growth of the index in indirect tax rates described in Nevile (1975) and the level of excess demand is proxied by $K - (1/u + k)$. The dependent variable is the rate of growth of the implicit gross national expenditure deflator.

2 The conventional wisdom is that the talking up of the 'resources boom' by government spokesmen for election purposes greatly strengthened the bargaining position of unions and led to a mini-explosion in over-award payments in 1981/2. The virtual abandoning of centralized wage fixing may have aided this process.

3 The random factor is, of course, the error term in the estimated equation. Each row sums to the change in inflation in that year. The changes thus arrived at are not exactly the same as the changes in the gross national expenditure deflator in Table 14.1, because Table 14.1 uses the most recent and heavily revised data.

4 If one does this, while the coefficient on $DM_{-1}$ is 0.57 and is three times its standard error, the $R^2$ of 0.54 is of the same order of magnitude as the $R^2$ between $DM$ and $DM_{-1}$. It is likely that the actual relationship reflected in the regression is that between nominal income and the volume of money.

5 For useful summaries of monetary policy over this period see Jonson (1979), Poole (1981), Porter (1982), Statement No. 2 in the annual *Department of the Treasury Budget Statements* and the *Report and Financial Statements* of the Reserve Bank of Australia.

6 This shift was completed with the adoption of a floating rate of exchange in 1984.

7 See Statement No. 2, 1982/3 *Budget Statements*, p. 46.

## BIBLIOGRAPHY


Australian Financial System Inquiry (1982), *Final Report*, Canberra, Australian Government Publishing Service.

Barry, P. (1978), 'An indicator of central bank policy in an open economy', in M. G. Porter (ed.), *The Australian Monetary System in the 1970s*, Melbourne, Melbourne University Press.

Blandy, R. and Creigh, S. (1983), 'The Australian labour market June 1983', *Australian Bulletin of Labour*, 9(3), June, 159–189.

Burns, M. E. (1980), 'Interest rates or monetary aggregates: some aspects of monetary control', *Economic Papers*, 63, February, 41–57.

Butlin, M. W. and Ryan, C. J. (1982), 'The causal relationship between money base and money supply in Australia: 1960–1979', Reserve Bank of Australia, Research Discussion Paper 8203.

Coghlan, P. L. (1978), 'Simulation with the NIF model of the Australian economy', paper presented to the Simulation Special Interest Group, Canberra.

Davis, K. and Lewis, M. K. (1978), 'Money and income: evidence from simple models', in M. G. Porter (ed.), *The Australian Monetary system in the 1970s*, Melbourne, Melbourne University Press, 128–141.

Davis, K. and Lewis, M. K. (1983), 'Monetary tactics and monetary targets: a guide to post-Campbell monetary policy', *Economic Papers*, special edition, April, 82–100.

Department of the Treasury, *Budget Statements*, Canberra, Australian Government Publishing Service, various issues.

Dixon, P. B., Parmenter, B. R. and Powell, A. A. (1979), *Structural Adaptation in an Ailing Macroeconomy*, Melbourne, Melbourne University Press.

Gloster, G. and Matrenza, R. (1978), 'The Australian monetary system – the need for a sound theoretical framework', in M. G. Porter (ed.), *The Australian Monetary System in the 1970s*, Melbourne, Melbourne University Press, 187–194.

Gregory, R. G. (1982), 'Work and welfare in the years ahead', *Australian Economic Papers*, 21(39), December, 219–243.

Gregory, R. G. and Duncan, R. C. (1979), 'The labour market', in Reserve Bank of Australia, *Conference on Applied Economic Research*, 256–319.

Gruen, F. H. (1979a), 'Australian economics 1967–1977', *Australian Economic Papers*, 18(32), June, 1–20.

Gruen, F. H. (1979b), 'Comment', in Reserve Bank of Australia, *Conference on Applied Economic Research*, 236–239.

Horne, J. (1983), 'Choice of monetary aggregate as intermediate targets in Australia: the message in the innovations', paper presented to the twelfth Conference of Economists, University of Tasmania.

Jonson, P. (1979), 'Some aspects of Australian monetary experience in the 1970s', paper presented to Money Study Group, Oxford University.

Jonson, P. and Trevor, R. G. (1981), 'Monetary rules: a preliminary analysis', *Economic Record*, 57(157), June, 150–167.

National Economic Summit Conference (1983), *Projections of the Australian Economy to 1985–86*, Documents and Proceedings, Vol. I, Government Documents, Canberra, Australian Government Publishing Service.

Nevile, J. W. (1975), *Fiscal Policy in Australia: Theory and Practice*, Melbourne, Longman–Cheshire.

Nevile, J. W. (1979), 'Macroeconomic policy issues in Australia', *Australian Economic Review*, 45(1), 16–21.

Nevile, J. W. (1980), 'Inflation and the incentive to invest', Working Paper No. 16, Centre for Applied Economic Research, University of New South Wales.

Nevile, J. W. (1983), *Monetary and Fiscal Policies Against Stagflation*, CAER Paper No. 19, Centre for Applied Economic Research, University of New South Wales.

Poole, W. (1970), 'Optimal choice of monetary policy instruments in a simple stochastic macro model', *Quarterly Journal of Economics*, 84(2), May, 197–216.

Poole, W. (1981), 'Australian monetary policy: an outsider's view', paper presented to 51st ANZAAS Congress, Brisbane, May.

Porter, M. G. (1982), 'Monetary targeting', Australian Financial System Inquiry, Commissioned Studies and Selected Papers, Part I, Canberra, Australian Government Publishing Service.

Reserve Bank of Australia, *Report and Financial Statements*, Sydney, Reserve Bank of Australia, various issues.

Sharpe, I. G. and Volker, P. A. (1978), 'The selection of monetary policy instruments: evidence from reduced form estimates of the demand and supply of money in Australia', in M. G. Porter (ed.), *The Australian Monetary System in the 1970s*, Melbourne, Melbourne University Press.

Sharpe, I. G. and Volker, P. A. (1979), 'The trade-off between improved monetary controls and market interest rate variability', *Australian Journal of Management*, 4(2), October, 119–134.

Snape, Richard J. (1981), 'Australian unemployment – is it created by costs or demand', *Growth*, 31, April, 20–35.

Valentine, T. J. (1983a), 'Growth in monetary and credit aggregates', Centre for Studies in Money, Banking and Finance, Macquarie University, Working Paper series A, No. 8301A.

Valentine, T. J. (1983a), 'Monetary targeting revisited', *Bulletin of Money, Banking and Finance*, 1982/3, No. 2, 1–41.

# 15 Unemployment, Inflation and Job Creation Policies in Australia

*R. G. GREGORY and RALPH E. SMITH*

## I INTRODUCTION

Before the economic upheavals of the early 1970s it was quite acceptable to think of a natural rate of unemployment in Australia of somewhere between 1.5 per cent and 2.5 per cent without being too precise about what exactly was meant by the concept. This unemployment range encompassed the average unemployment rate around which the economy could be expected to fluctuate, the estimates of the natural rate of unemployment derived from the Phillips curve and even the 'full employment' level of unemployment.

Over the last seven or eight years there has been a dramatic change. It is difficult to believe, in the current environment of 10 per cent unemployment, that the natural rate is between 1.5 and 2.5 per cent. Furthermore, it is probable that the empirical counterparts of the different concepts of the natural rate of unemployment cover a sufficiently large range that it is no longer a convenient shorthand to talk loosely of an all-embracing estimate. More precision is needed. (See, for example, Trivedi and Baker, 1982.)

In section II we document that there has been an increase in the natural rate of unemployment that has evolved from the Phillips curve literature. We also offer a labour market analysis for this increase. This analysis emphasizes the distinction between labour utilization rates within the firm and labour utilization rates within the economy as a whole. We argue, over the range of unemployment experience in Australia to date, that it is the labour utilization rate within the firm that is particularly important for wage negotiations rather than the labour utilization rate within the economy. During the 1950s and 1960s these labour utilization rates moved closely together but since the late 1970s they have diverged, causing the displacement of the Phillips curve as it is usually defined. We show, however, that if wage increases are related to the labour utilization rate within the firm then the Phillips curve has not shifted. If labour utilization rates within the firm are more important for wage outcomes than the utilization rate of labour in the economy as a whole, then the natural rate of unemployment, as it is usually defined in a Phillips curve context, is not a particularly useful concept.

There has also been an increasing divergence between capacity utilization rates within the average firm and the potential output of the economy. We define potential output as the output level that would fully employ labour if the trend relationships between output and unemployment that prevailed before

1975 had continued. The Australian economy now reaches 'full employment' capacity utilization rates *within* the average firm well before labour is fully utilized in the economy as a whole.

This dislocation has important implications for the likelihood of the economy being able to return to low unemployment rates in the future. It suggests that there may be a ratchet effect operating, because each unemployment increase, associated with a long recession, tends to create economic conditions that make it difficult to return to full employment. We argue that this ratchet effect is primarily related to wage increases rather than the physical limitations of capacity *per se*.

Within this framework of analysis the economic policy problem can be thought of as consisting of two parts. The major part is to devise policies to bring the full employment utilization rates of factors within the firm more closely into line with the full employment utilization rates of labour in the economy as a whole. These policies, of course, go to the heart of the macroeconomic policy debate that is the subject matter of a number of the other chapters in this volume. The other part of the policy response is the range of measures that might be introduced to cope with the larger unemployment pool that has accompanied the dislocations mentioned earlier and that will exist for a considerable time into the future. It is to this part of the policy response that we offer a number of comments in Section III.

## II A LABOUR MARKET EXPLANATION FOR THE INCREASE IN THE NATURAL RATE OF UNEMPLOYMENT[1]

### THE RECENT HISTORY OF THE PHILLIPS CURVE

A casual glance at figures for unemployment and inflation shows that there is no stable relationship between wage increases and the level of unemployment. If a trade-off exists between wage increases and unemployment then it has shifted to the right and become worse.

The Phillips curve should be adapted to make some allowance for expected rates of inflation. Presumably partners to the wage negotiation process are bargaining over real wage outcomes. Once allowance is made for expectations of future price increases, some of the instability of the Phillips curve disappears. For example, M. Kirby (1981) makes a special point of emphasizing that there is little evidence of instability in the Australian Phillips curve, at least until mid-1978, which is the end of his data period. Kirby also estimates that the natural rate of unemployment defined in a Phillips curve context is somewhere around the 1.7–2.2 per cent mark. Examples of his equations, along with other equations showing wage changes as a function of labour utilization rates, are given in Table 15.1.

If we take one of Kirby's stable Phillips curves (equation 1, Table 15.1) and add the post-1978 data (equation 2), it is immediately obvious that the relationship is no longer stable.[2] Over the period 1966Q4–1982Q4 the unemployment coefficient has halved and is no longer a statistically significant variable.[3] The estimated price expectation coefficient has also fallen considerably.

The Phillips curve estimated by Kirby completely misses the upturn in the rate of inflation during 1979 and continues to underestimate the rate of inflation throughout the 1979–82 period. This is easily seen in equation 3, where we have divided the unemployment rate into two periods. The first period coincides with that of Kirby's analysis and the second encompasses the data period 1978Q3–1982Q4. Unemployment is clearly losing its impact upon the rate of change of wages. The estimated coefficient attached to the unemployment rate since 1978Q3 is much less than that attached to unemployment for the earlier period. It is our conjecture that similar considerations apply to most Phillips curves during this period.

## THE ACCELERATION OF WAGE INFLATION DURING 1979

There are a number of hypotheses that may explain the sudden acceleration of wage increases during a period when unemployment averaged 6 per cent.

The first hypothesis relates to the price expectation term of the augmented Phillips curve. Perhaps there were factors, unrelated to the past rate of increases of prices, that led employers and employees to believe that the rate of price inflation was suddenly about to accelerate. Under these circumstances, unions will seek in advance, and be successful at obtaining, wage increases that are larger than otherwise. We refer to this hypothesis as an *expectations explanation* of the increase in the rate of inflation.

The second hypothesis is that there was excess demand for labour during 1979–82 but unemployment was no longer an appropriate measure of the gap between the demand for and supply of labour. Although unemployment was high, perhaps there were severe labour shortages. We refer to this hypothesis as *labour market mismatching*.

The third hypothesis is that wage increases were never causally related to the level of unemployment *per se*. Perhaps wage increases are primarily related to the rate of labour utilization within the average firm and this utilization rate is no longer strongly correlated with the rate of labour utilization in the economy as a whole. For reasons that will become clear later, we refer to this hypothesis as an *implicit contract* explanation.

### *The expectations hypothesis*

The Kirby equations, along with most empirical work in this area, measure price expectations as a weighted sum of past price increases. Perhaps past price increases are no longer an adequate indication of the community's expectations of future price increases.

One way to test this hypothesis is to examine a direct measure of price expectations. Such a measure can be constructed from a quarterly survey undertaken for the Institute of Applied Economic and Social Research of the University of Melbourne. In this survey about 2,000 respondents are asked whether they expect prices to rise, fall or stay the same over the next twelve months.[4] A further question asks those respondents who expect a price change to express a percentage estimate.

The arithmetic mean of this series of expected inflation is given in Figure 15.1 as the broken line. The broken line is the actual rate of inflation that

**Table 15.1** *Wage changes[a] and labour utilization rates, 1966Q4–1978Q2: 1966Q4–1982Q4*

| | | | Labour utilization within the economy | | | | | | | | | | |
|---|---|---|---|---|---|---|---|---|---|---|---|---|---|
| *Period* | *Equation* | *Constant* | $U$ | $U_1$ | $U_2$ | $V$ | $V_1$ | $V_2$ | $P^e$ | $P^c_1$ | $P^e_2$ | $R^2$ | DW |
| Short | | 2.803 | −.507 | | | | | | .807 | | | .16 | 1.64 |
| 1966Q4–1978Q2 | 1 | (5.06) | (1.95) | | | | | | (2.86) | | | | |
| Long | | 2.352 | −.148 | | | | | | .523 | | | .10 | 1.52 |
| 1966Q4–1982Q4 | 2 | (5.18) | (1.18) | | | | | | (2.61) | | | | |
| Long | | 2.783 | | −.489 | −.260 | | | | .788 | | | | |
| 1966Q4–1982Q4 | 3 | (5.46) | | (2.12) | (1.87) | | | | (3.17) | | | .15 | 1.71 |
| Long | | 2.656 | −.380 | | | | | | | .685 | 1.169 | | |
| 1966Q4–1982Q4 | 4 | (5.40) | (1.94) | | | | | | | (3.04) | (2.50) | .14 | 1.64 |
| Short | | −.689 | | | | 1.773 | | | .688 | | | | |
| 1966Q4–1978Q2 | 5 | (0.68) | | | | (2.97) | | | (3.52) | | | .24 | 1.93 |
| Long | | .633 | | | | .995 | | | .584 | | | | |
| 1966Q4–1982Q4 | 6 | (0.89) | | | | (2.32) | | | (3.27) | | | .15 | 1.71 |
| Long | | −.453 | | | | | 1.625 | 3.70 | .669 | | | | |
| 1966Q4–1982Q4 | 7 | (0.50) | | | | | (3.01) | (2.45) | (3.70) | | | .20 | 1.88 |
| Long | | −.521 | | | | 1.681 | | | | .663 | 1.160 | | |
| 1966Q4–1982Q4 | 8 | (0.58) | | | | (3.11) | | | | (3.71) | (3.45) | .21 | 1.92 |

*Labour utilization within the firm*

| *Period* | | *Constant* | *O/T* | $O/T_1$ | $O/T_2$ | $P^e$ | $P^e_1$ | $P^e_2$ | $R^2$ | DW |
|---|---|---|---|---|---|---|---|---|---|---|
| Short | | –4.356 | 3.928 | | | .824 | | | .27 | 1.92 |
| 1966Q4–1978Q2 | 9 | (2.23) | (3.36) | | | (3.94) | | | | |
| Long | | –4.372 | 3.928 | | | .814 | | | | |
| 1966Q4–1982Q4 | 10 | (2.53) | (3.79) | | | (4.39) | | | .25 | 1.97 |
| Long | | –4.398 | | 3.959 | 3.867 | .823 | | | | |
| 1966Q4–1982Q4 | 11 | (2.53) | | (3.77) | (3.64) | (4.35) | | | .26 | 1.99 |
| Long | | –4.413 | 3.968 | | | | .826 | .759 | | |
| 1966Q4–1982Q4 | 12 | (2.53) | (3.78) | | | | (4.35) | (3.15) | .26 | 1.99 |

*Note:* Figures in parenthesis are t-statistics.

a Wage change = rate of change of average weekly earnings for employed male unit. (Australian Bureau of Statistics (ABS), *Average Weekly Earnings, States and Australia*, Cat. No. 6302.0. Seasonally adjusted. The new series has been applied to the old series as described in ABS Cat. No. 6302.0, May 1983.)

*Notation:* $U$ = unemployment rate (ABS, *The Labour Force*, Cat. No. 6204.0, seasonally adjusted); $U_1$ = unemployment rate 1966Q4–1978Q2; $U_2$ = unemployment rate 1978Q3–1982Q4; $V$ = vacancy rate (CES series until 1979Q3, then ABS series applied – ABS, *Job Vacancies, Australia*, Cat. No. 6231.0; $V_1$ = vacancy rate 1966Q4–1978Q2; $V_2$ = vacancy rate 1978Q3–1982Q4; $P^e$ = the rate of change of the consumer price index, from one quarter to the next (ABS, *Consumer Price Index*, Cat. No. 6401.0, lagged four quarters); $P^e_1$ for 1966Q4–1978Q2. $P^e_2$ = $P^e$ for 1979Q3–1982Q4. *O/T* = overtime rate (pre-1979, Department of Employment and Industrial Relations, *Monthly Review of Employment*; Post-1979, ABS, *Average Weekly Earnings, States and Australia*, Cat. No. 6302.0).

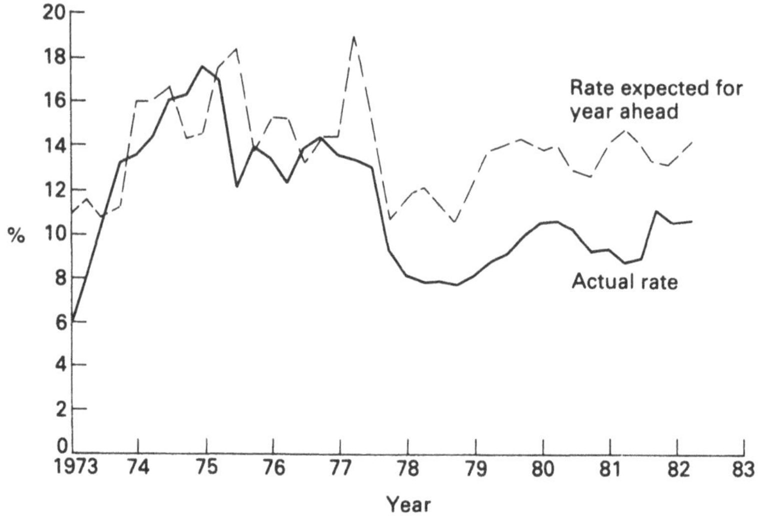


**Figure 15.1** Annual inflation rates, 1973–82

eventuated. The expected and actual rates of inflation are fairly well correlated although, since 1977, the expected rate of inflation has been continually above the actual rate of inflation.[5] It appears that during the recessions of 1975/6 and 1977/8 expectations about future price changes were slower to adjust downwards than actual prices changes.[6] It also appears that the upward movement in expectation that is observed in 1979–82 pre-dated the increase in actual inflation.

For our purposes the Melbourne Institute series is not long enough to include in our regressions. Consequently in equation 4 of Table 15.1 we split the Kirby measure of price expectations into the same two periods as earlier: the Kirby data period (1966Q4–1978Q2) and the subsequent data period. The estimated coefficients on the price expectations terms are different. The estimated coefficient for the post-1978 period is about 50 per cent larger than the coefficient for the pre-1978 period. The significance level of the unemployment variable improves and it now borders upon statistical significance at the 5 per cent level.

The data appear to be consistent with a shift upwards in the link between past price increases and expectations of future price increases. The improvement in the fit of the Phillips curve is marginal, however. There is also still some decline in the effect of unemployment upon wage agreements. We shall return to the price expectations term later.

*Mismatching in the labour market*

It is sometimes suggested that one reason why the Phillips curve has shifted to the right is that the relationship between unemployment and the excess demand for labour in the economy as a whole has changed. Consequently, there may be no need to adjust or jettison the basic underlying model that relates wage increases to the excess supply of labour. What may be needed is a more adequate measure of the excess demand for labour.

This hypothesis is tested by considering three sets of data. First, we consider the relationship between unemployment and vacancies. Then we look at a survey of manufacturers' opinions on the degree of labour shortages over the last few years. Finally we include the vacancies series in the Phillips curve regressions.

Most writers date a noticeable outward shift in the unemployment–vacancy relationship sometime around the middle of 1973 (see Hughes, 1975; Harper, 1980; Trivedi and Baker, 1982; Gregory and Paterson, 1983). To account for this shift they turn to the changing flows of immigration, the real level of unemployment benefits and wages, and an index of the changing structure of industry. Most of these variables are statistically significant but their changing levels during the 1970s suggest that the outward shift is quite small.

Trivedi and Baker (1982) suggest that the equilibrium rate of CES unemployment (where unemployment equals vacancies) increased from 1.02 per cent to 1.60 per cent to 1.79 per cent in 1968/9, 1976/7 and 1980/1 respectively. These are very small shifts indeed, especially when placed against the change in the rate of unemployment from 1.6 per cent in August 1968 to 5.6 per cent in August 1981. These estimates seem to suggest that for practical purposes the shift in the unemployment–vacancy relationship can be ignored at least until 1979Q3, which is the end of their data period.[7] What has happened since then?

In Figure 15.2 we plot the unemployment–vacancy relationship over the period 1966Q4–1982Q4. It is quite clear that the relationship has moved outwards between 1966Q3–1971Q3 and 1971Q4–1974Q3. After 1975, however, it is difficult to measure the extent of any shift because almost all the data

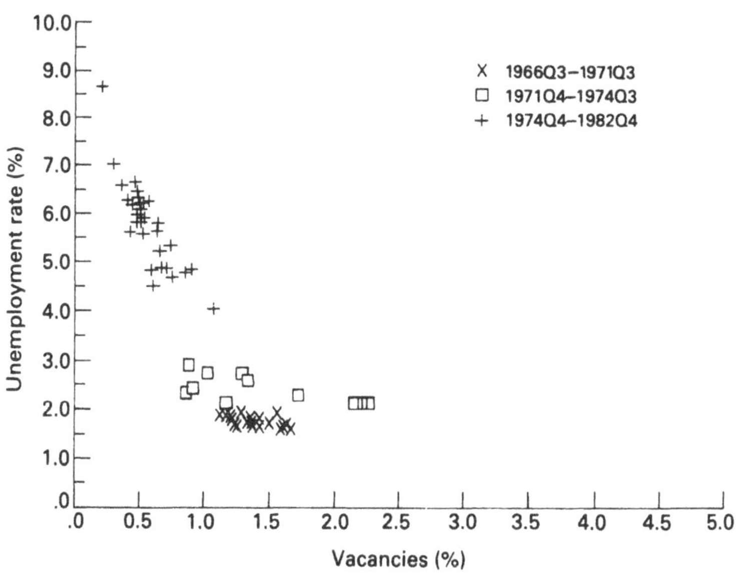


**Figure 15.2** Unemployment and vacancies, 1966–82

observations are outside the previous range of experience. However, given the low level of vacancies and high rates of unemployment after 1979, there does not appear to be any excess demand for labour that might explain the wage acceleration.

It may be worth looking at the question of labour shortages in a little more detail. There may have been shortages that are not easily detected in an aggregate unemployment–vacancy relationship. Given the nature of Australian wage-fixing procedure, wage increases to special groups (which may be in short supply) spread quickly to other sections of the labour force and therefore generate across-the-board wage changes.

There are a number of surveys that can help us to determine whether there were severe shortages of labour in particular areas of the economy. The Bank of New South Wales and the Confederation of Australian Industry (CAI) conduct a survey of manufacturers that includes the question, 'What single factor, if any, is most limiting your ability to increase production?' The percentage of respondents who replied that labour was the most limiting factor acting as a constraint on production show that there have been three periods of acute labour shortages in Australia since 1960: the years 1965, 1970 and 1973. There is no evidence of a comparable shortage during the period 1979–82.

It has been suggested that there were particular skill shortages in the metal manufacturing areas of the economy (Department of Labour Advisory Council, 1980). Since metal workers were the group that began the recent wage round, the data have been disaggregated to include those establishments involved in basic and fabricated metal products. These data are plotted in Figure 15.3. The broken line represents the percentage of respondents who reported capacity shortages as the constraining factor and the unbroken line is the sum of the percentage that reported capacity shortages and the percentage

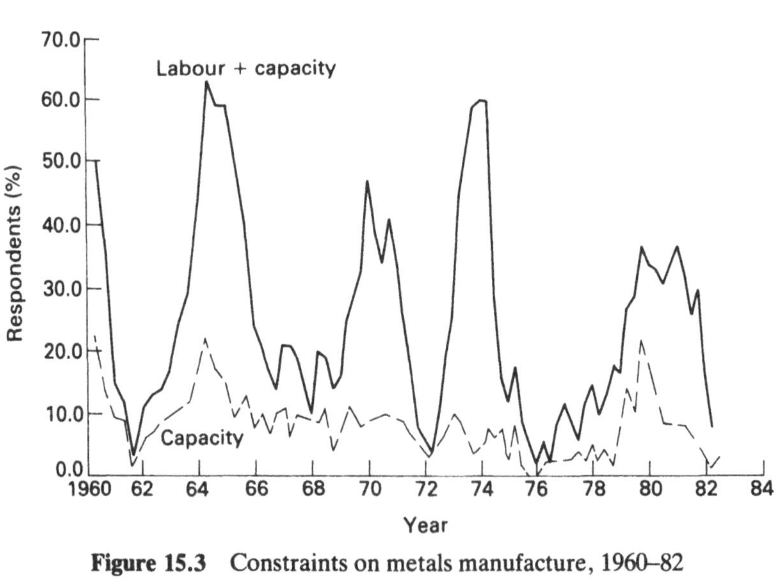


**Figure 15.3** Constraints on metals manufacture, 1960–82

that reported labour shortages. The proportion of respondents who reported labour as a constraint is measured by the vertical gap between the two lines.

The same story is evident as before, except that there is evidence of capacity constraints similar to that of 1965. Any shortage of labour, representing a constraint on production in the metal manufacturing industries, is much smaller than that during the previous three boom periods. There does not seem to be any significant evidence in these data to suggest that we should discard the unemployment rate as a measure of excess supply in the labour market and to argue that despite the level of unemployment there was excess demand during 1979–82.

Finally, we experimented with various combinations of vacancies and unemployment in the Kirby equations. The best results were obtained from using the vacancy series divided by the labour force. In general the vacancy series performed better than the unemployment rate, but the same pattern of results is evident (see Table 15.1, equations 5–8). The coefficient attached to the vacancy variable is unstable and approximately twice as large in the second period as in the first. The coefficients are statistically significant and significantly different from each other. Just as a given level of unemployment exerts a smaller downward influence upon wage increases after 1978, a given level of vacancies exerts a larger upward influence. The Phillips curve has clearly shifted.

The same results with respect to price expectations are apparent. If the vacancy series is included in the regressions for the whole and the price expectations coefficient allowed to differ before and after 1978, then the coefficient is larger in the second period.

*Implicit contract theories*

The idea that a significant part of wage increases is not related to excess demand or supply in the aggregate labour market is not a new idea. Indeed, before the advent of the Phillips curve it was probably the most common view.

This view of the labour market has been presented in a number of guises. It is sometimes called a real wage maintenance theory, or a trade union pushfulness theory of wage changes. The latest form of this general idea has been called the Implicit Contract Theory and the basic arguments have been developed by Okun (1981) and a number of others (Solow, 1980; Hall, 1980; Hicks, 1973). In Australia, similar ideas can be found in Gregory (1982, 1983a), Blandy and Richardson (1982) and Isaac (1981).

These arguments are not developed here. Instead we shall take a slightly different tack and develop a more general argument to emphasize that a long period during which the economy operates well below its productive capacity will set in train forces that make it increasingly difficult to return to full employment without reactivating the wage inflation process.

The basic idea is that not all resources adapt at the same rate to long periods of low utilization rates. As a recession continues, *employed* resources of labour and capital tend to get placed back at their full utilization rates while labour as a whole may remain at a low utilization rate; i.e. unemployment may be high. As employed labour and capital approach their normal utilization rates, normal conditions with regard to wage negotiations tend to reapply without regard to the unemployed. The initial shock of the recession (when there are falling utilization rates of labour within the firm and for the economy as a whole) wears off as the utilization of labour within the firm returns to normal. It is at this stage that the implicit contracts between the employer and the employee begin to deliver normal rates of real wage increases independent of the state of labour market outside the firm.

There are a number of reasons why unemployed labour resources outside the firm fail to exert much influence upon the wage negotiation process. One reason is that unemployed labour is very different from employed labour and the two types of labour are not very close substitutes. The employed labour force, for example, can expect a job tenure with the current employer in the current geographical location of about twelve years. Furthermore, about 20 per cent of the employed labour force can expect a job tenure of more than twenty years. For most of the employed work force, therefore, their dominating workforce experience relates to employment with a particular firm during which time they not only build up firm-specific capital but are able to develop and reinforce many non-economic relationships between members of the firm that will affect economic decisions. By contrast, most of the unemployed have either not had a job, or their last job has been of very short tenure. For example, in May 1976 approximately one-half of the unemployed had not been employed in a full-time job in the previous eighteen months and of those who had held a full-time job about half had held that job for less than twenty-six weeks. The unemployed tend to be young, inexperienced and unskilled. There is thus a large degree of separation of the employed and unemployed. The implications of this separation for wage determination are discussed more fully in Gregory (1982).

## LABOUR UTILIZATION WITHIN THE FIRM

Figure 15.4 presents the level of unemployment in the Australian economy and a measure of overtime hours worked, which we use as an indication of labour utilization within the firm. Before 1975 these two labour utilization rates moved together. Since 1975, however, the utilization rate of employed labour has tended to go back towards the average of the pre-1974 levels whereas the utilization rate of the labour force as a whole has not adjusted. In 1979 and 1980, when unemployment was over 5 per cent, the average level of factory overtime had returned to be close to previous long-run and normal levels. For the employed labour force, economic conditions within a firm during 1980 and 1981 did not appear to be that different from a decade earlier, when full employment in the economy as a whole prevailed.

In equations 9–12 of Table 15.1 we replace the unemployment rate by the level of overtime hours worked.[8] For the pre-1979 period this variable appears to be far superior to the unemployment rate as a measure of the labour utilization rate in a Phillips curve. The degree of statistical significance of the coefficients of the variables is greater and the $R^2$ has almost doubled.

When the equation is fitted to the long period there is an almost undetectable change in each of the coefficients. The contrast with the equations that include the unemployment or the vacancy variable is very marked. *There appears to be*

**Figure 15.4** Unemployment and overtime hours, 1966–82

*no instability of the Phillips curve when it is defined with respect to labour utilization rates within the firm.*

Earlier, we discussed the possibility that the relationship between price expectations and lagged prices had changed and that this might explain the shifting Phillips curve. In equation 12, we include the lagged price variable for the two periods along with the overtime hours worked variable. Both lagged price expectation terms are statistically significant and, unlike the equations that included unemployment or the vacancy series, the coefficients are *not* significantly different from each other. It appears that once the switch-over is made from the unemployment rate to the overtime variable there is no evidence of a changing relationship between price expectations and past price changes. To repeat, the wage change–labour utilization relationship is stable if defined with respect to labour utilization rates within the firm.

## CAPACITY UTILIZATION AND THE CAPITAL SHORTFALL

A dislocation similar to that between labour utilization rates within the firm and for the economy as a whole would seem to be occurring between the rate of capacity utilization within the firm and the rate of utilization of labour in the economy. The CAI and Bank of New South Wales publish an indicator of capacity utilization for the manufacturing sector that can be used to illustrate this point. In 1970, when 45 per cent of respondents reported a satisfactory rate of capacity utilization (the second highest proportion so responding since that time), the level of unemployment was 1.6 per cent. In 1974 a similar response rate was associated with about 3.3 per cent unemployment. By 1981, the same response rate was associated with 5.5 per cent unemployment. The comparison between 1977 and 1981 is also striking. The level of unemployment was the same in both years – about 5.5 per cent – but the proportion of factories reporting acceptable rates of capacity utilization almost doubled, increasing from 26 to 46 per cent.

### AN EQUILIBRIUM UNEMPLOYMENT RATE

A dislocation between factor utilization rates within the firm and labour utilization rates within the economy suggests that we can define an equilibrium unemployment rate as the unemployment rate that is associated with normal rates of factor utilization within the firm. Unemployment rates lower than this will be associated with above-average utilization rates of factors within the firm and therefore above-average wage increases. Given this definition, there is clearly a move upwards in the equilibrium unemployment rate. If we define 1.4 hours as a normal rate of overtime, then the equilibrium unemployment rate has moved upwards from about 1.7 per cent for 1970 to 2.4 per cent for the 1970–4 period and about 5.8 per cent for the 1979–82 period.

If this analysis is correct, it has important implications for policy in the current economic environment. It suggests the following line of thought, which is very different from much of the official thinking. If the economy grows *very* quickly as from now, so that the normal utilization rates within firms are restored quickly, then the equilibrium unemployment rate may not increase very much. In other words, the economy may reverse its step along a relationship not very different from that between 1981 and 1982. If, as we suggest, wage inflation is related to utilization rates of factors within the firm, then the inflationary implications of such an expansion should not be too serious.

On the other hand, the economic recovery is a long drawn out process, the equilibrium unemployment rate will drift upwards and a recovery of the length of the 1974/5–1978/9 recession, for example, should establish a new equilibrium rate of about 9.5 per cent. There will be a very serious ratchet effect.

## III JOB CREATION SCHEMES TO REDUCE THE LEVEL AND CONCENTRATION OF UNEMPLOYMENT

Job creation schemes may be designed to meet a number of different objectives. One may be to change the relative costs of labour inputs to employers, thereby increasing employment in the subsidized market at the expense of employment in the unsubsidized market. This may permit a higher level of aggregate employment to be achieved, for a given rate of inflation, if certain conditions are satisfied. Baily and Tobin (1977) and others have developed the theoretical underpinning for private sector wage subsidies and public sector job creation schemes along these lines. They say, 'The basic strategy is simple: Shift labor demand to types of workers who are – because of high unemployment, weak bargaining power, rigid wages, or other characteristics – on relatively flat Phillips curves' (p. 512). Their approach, however, assumes a wage determination process different from the one suggested in section II. In any event, this approach is not particularly relevant in a world characterized by *general* excess capacity in the labour market for the economy as a whole in which there are no markets where there is a danger of excess demand.

Improving the Phillips curve trade-off has never been an important objective of job creation programme in Australia. Job creation programmes have been primarily concerned with two objectives. One objective has been to increase employment quickly and to generate more jobs for a given degree of fiscal stimulus. In this context, job creation schemes have been part of an anti-cyclical policy. The other objective has been to provide jobs for particular groups in the labour force. These groups have been identified on welfare or equity grounds, such as long duration of unemployment.

## THE AUSTRALIAN PROGRAMMES

There have been three discernible stages in Australia's history of job creation schemes since the 1970s.[9]

The first stage was the operation of the controversial Regional Employment Development Scheme (REDS), which lasted for a little over a year. This scheme was primarily aimed at those who were eligible for unemployment benefits and had dependants. Few women and young people were admitted to the programme. During the first five months of its operation it was also oriented towards geographical areas of high unemployment.[10]

The second stage, beginning in late 1976, saw the introduction of the Special Youth Employment and Training Program (SYETP).[11] The emphasis of this scheme was almost the opposite of the RED scheme. It was aimed at those *without* dependants and primarily involved subsidies to private enterprise to induce them to hire and train long-term unemployed youth.[12] Extensive information has been collected on the characteristics of the SYETP-subsidized workers. Throughout its history, over 300,000 jobs have been subsidized. Most of these jobs have gone to teenagers, with the greatest concentration among persons between the ages of 15 and 17. The majority of subsidized workers have been female. Both characteristics appear to be associated with the terms of the subsidy, rather than the eligibility criteria. Since firms receive a fixed amount per week, they can recover a higher percentage of wages by hiring low-wage workers, who are disproportionately young and female.

The third stage, which began during 1983, involves extending private sector employment subsidies to adults and the introduction of new public sector job creation schemes.[13] One public sector job creation scheme was introduced in January 1983 by the Liberal government. Under the Wage Pause Program, $200 million was to be allocated to the states for job creation activities in 1982/3 and 1983/4. The programme guidelines call for labour-intensive projects to be funded through governmental and community-based organizations. The Labor government has continued the Wage Pause Program and introduced the Community Employment Program.[14] The purpose of this programme is to create up to 70,000 full-time jobs, with an average duration of six months, with an expenditure by the Commonwealth of $300 million in 1983/4. Preference is to be given to those who have been unemployed at least nine months, to persons who have never worked, and to others considered to be disadvantaged in the labour market, such as Aboriginals.

## PROGRAMME EXPENDITURES AND IMPACTS

Although job creation programmes have been part of the Australian landscape throughout the past decade, their size has varied considerably. Tables 15.2 and 15.3 provide estimates of the expenditures made by the Commonwealth on the major job creation schemes described above and of the numbers of people who have participated in them. Table 15.2 also reports the number of people who were unemployed and the number who received unemployment benefits. Three patterns are worth noting.

First, as a response to unemployment, job creation schemes have always played a minor role relative to income support by unemployment benefits. After REDS was disbanded and unemployment continued to increase through 1976–8, expenditure on job creation schemes was about 4 per cent of the expenditure on unemployment benefits. Even the large initiatives over 1983/4 cost only about 15 per cent of the expenditure on unemployment benefits.

Second, there have been enormous fluctuations in programme expenditures and participation during the decade. Under REDS, the Commonwealth government went from spending virtually nothing to $123 million within twelve months, to almost nothing again the following year. Under SYETP, there was a major reduction in 1979/80 and a gradual build up since, though never back to the level of spending of 1978/9. In real terms the expenditures planned for 1983/4 were the largest yet.

Third, although there are large numbers of people passing through the programmes, they are not in them for very long. For example, the maximum duration in SYETP for most of its history has been seventeen weeks. Thus, when converted into person-years, the participation rate is not so impressive. The total number of person-years of subsidized employment between 1974/5 and 1981/2 was a little over 100,000. Even at the peak of REDS, the number of subsidized jobs was less than 10 per cent of the unemployment level. In recent years, subsidized employment levels have equalled 2–5 per cent of aggregate unemployment levels.

Thus, it is clear that, no matter how effective these schemes might have been, their direct impacts on aggregate unemployment must be very small. This point is further illustrated in Table 15.4, which provides the actual employment and unemployment statistics for Australia during this period together with two alternative sets of statistics based on different assumptions about the direct impact of the schemes. It shows that, even under the most generous assumptions about the impacts of the job creation schemes – in which every subsidized job is a net addition to aggregate employment – the aggregate unemployment rate would have been only 0.1–0.4 percentage points higher had the programmes not existed. A more realistic assumption is that about one-third of the subsidized jobs were net additions to employment.[15] Under this assumption, the impact on the aggregate unemployment rate throughout the decade was negligible. The hypothetical unemployment rates shown in the table are within 0.1 percentage points of the actual rates in every year.

Targeted job creation schemes are intended to change the distribution of employment and unemployment, even if the levels are not changed. Examination of the impacts on employment and unemployment of the target groups

**Table 15.2** *Expenditure on major job creation schemes, 1974/5–1983/4 ($'000)*

| *Programme* | *1974/5* | *1975/6* | *1976/7* | *1977/8* | *1978/9* | *1979/80* | *1980/1* | *1981/2* | *1982/3* | *1983/4* (est.) |
|---|---|---|---|---|---|---|---|---|---|---|
| Regional Employment Development Scheme (REDS)[a] | 60,400 | 123,400 | 460 | | | | | | | |
| Special Youth Employment Training Program (SYETP)[b] | | | 6.600 | 47,100 | 82,600 | 24,200 | 41,300 | 53,700 | 63,600 | 74,700 |
| Adult Wage Subsidy[c] | | | | | | | | | 375 | 10,000 |
| Wage Pause Program[d] | | | | | | | | | 100,000 | 100,000 |
| Community Employment Program (CEP)[c] | | | | | | | | | | 300,000 |
| Private Sector Assistance Program (PSAP)[c] | | | | | | | | | | 22,000 |
| Total | 60,400 | 123,400 | 7,060 | 47,100 | 82,600 | 24,200 | 41,300 | 53,700 | 163,975 | 506,800 |
| Total (in 1982/3 dollars)[e] | 137,700 | 247,400 | 12,300 | 75,300 | 122,600 | 32,600 | 51,000 | 59,600 | 163,975 | 471,400 |
| Unemployment benefits[f] | 251,740 | 513,923 | 618,074 | 794,144 | 910,012 | 925,195 | 995,748 | 1,224,343 | 2,249,000 | 3,261,000 |

*Notes:* a From Department of the Treasury, *Budget Statements* (annual) and P. Kirby (1981).
b From P. Kirby (1981) up to 1978/9 and National Economic Summit Conference (1983) thereafter.
c Based on Department of Employment and Industrial Relations news releases and budget estimates.
d $200 million was to be allocated to the states in 1982/3 and 1983/4.
e 1974/5–1981/2 inflated using the December quarter six-city weighted CPI. 1983/4 estimate based on 7.5% increase.
f From Department of Social Security data and Department of the Treasury (1983).

**Table 15.3** *Participants in major job creation schemes, 1974/5–1983/4*[a]

| *Programme* | *1974/5* | *1975/6* | *1976/7* | *1977/8* | *1978/9* | *1979/80* | *1980/1* | *1981/2* | *1982/3* | *1983/4 (est.)* |
|---|---|---|---|---|---|---|---|---|---|---|
| REDS | | | | | | | | | | |
| New approvals | n.a. | n.a. | | | | | | | | |
| Person-years[b] | 7,000 | 23,000 | | | | | | | | |
| SYETP | | | | | | | | | | |
| New approvals | | | 9,600 | 66,000 | 66,300 | 44,300 | 61,400 | 51,700 | 66,300 | 33,200 |
| Person-years | | | 3,000 | 20,000 | 22,000 | 11,000 | 15,000 | 15,000 | 16,700 | n.a. |
| Adult Wage Subsidy | | | | | | | | | | |
| New approvals | | | | | | | | | 1,600 | 2,800 |
| Person-years | | | | | | | | | n.a. | n.a. |
| Wage Pause Program | | | | | | | | | | |
| New approvals | | | | | | | | | 10,000 | 10,000 |
| Person-years | | | | | | | | | n.a. | n.a. |
| CEP | | | | | | | | | | |
| New-approvals | | | | | | | | | | 40,000 |
| Person-years | | | | | | | | | | n.a. |
| PSAP | | | | | | | | | | |
| New approvals | | | | | | | | | | 38,200 |
| Person-years | | | | | | | | | | n.a. |
| Total approvals | n.a. | n.a. | 9,600 | 66,000 | 66,300 | 44,300 | 61,400 | 51,700 | 77,900 | 124,200 |
| Total person-years | 7,000 | 23,000 | 3,000 | 20,000 | 22,000 | 11,000 | 15,000 | 15,000 | n.a. | n.a. |
| Total unemployed | 247,100 | 301,600 | 325,100 | 394,700 | 405,400 | 403,900 | 392,800 | 419,700 | 622,100 | n.a. |
| Unemployment recipients | 116,603 | 191,723 | 216,856 | 265,828 | 306,200 | 306,300 | 310,000 | 332,000 | 540,000 | 680,000 |

*Notes:* a See Table 15.2 for sources. 1982/3 and 1983/4 participant estimates from Department of Employment and Industrial Relations (1983).
b Estimates based on information in P. Kirby (1981) and Department of the Treasury, *Budget Statements*.

**Table 15.4** *Direct impacts of job creation schemes on Australian employment and unemployment, 1974/5–1981/2 (in thousands, except as indicated)*

| | *1974/5* | *1975/6* | *1976/7* | *1977/8* | *1978/9* | *1979/80* | *1980/1* | *1981/2* |
|---|---|---|---|---|---|---|---|---|
| Persons, aged 15 and over | | | | | | | | |
| Employed | 5,856.0 | 5,929.3 | 5,965.6 | 5,980.5 | 6,019.3 | 6,156.8 | 6,326.0 | 6,404.1 |
| Unemployed | 247.1 | 301.6 | 325.1 | 394.7 | 405.4 | 403.9 | 392.8 | 419.7 |
| Unemployment rate (%) | 4.1 | 4.9 | 5.2 | 6.2 | 6.3 | 6.2 | 5.8 | 6.2 |
| Subsidized employment | 7.0 | 23.0 | 3.0 | 20.0 | 22.0 | 11.0 | 15.0 | 15.0 |
| Hypothetical labour force status in absence of schemes: | | | | | | | | |
| *Assumption 1:* no displacement or labour force response | | | | | | | | |
| Employed | 5,849.0 | 5,906.3 | 5,962.6 | 5,960.5 | 5,997.3 | 6,145.8 | 6,311.0 | 6,389.1 |
| Unemployed | 254.1 | 324.6 | 328.1 | 414.7 | 427.4 | 414.9 | 407.8 | 434.7 |
| Unemployment rate (%) | 4.2 | 5.2 | 5.2 | 6.5 | 6.7 | 6.3 | 6.1 | 6.4 |
| *Assumption 2:* one-third net job creation | | | | | | | | |
| Employed | 5,853.7 | 5,921.6 | 5,964.6 | 5,973.8 | 6,012.0 | 6,153.1 | 6,321.0 | 6,399.1 |
| Unemployed | 249.4 | 309.3 | 326.1 | 401.4 | 412.7 | 407.6 | 397.8 | 424.7 |
| Unemployed rate (%) | 4.1 | 5.0 | 5.2 | 6.3 | 6.4 | 6.2 | 5.9 | 6.2 |

themselves provides a somewhat more optimistic impression of these schemes. For example, in 1978/9 (the peak year of subsidized employment under SEYTP), about 18,000 of the 22,000 subsidized employees were between the ages of 15 and 19. During that year, the average levels of teenage employment and unemployment were 644,000 and 138,000 respectively. If all of the 18,000 subsidized teenagers would otherwise have been unemployed, the teenage unemployment rate would have been 19.9 per cent, rather than 17.6 per cent. If one-third of the subsidized jobs were net additions to the job stock, the rate would have been 18.4 per cent. A similar exercise shows that the potential impacts of the scheme on long-term unemployed teenagers and on persons between the ages of 15 and 17 (the majority of the teenage participants) were much larger.

## THE FUTURE ROLE OF JOB CREATION SCHEMES

The major lesson to be learned from the preceding exercise is that job creation schemes on the scale of those mounted in Australia during the past decade cannot have a significant direct impact on the aggregate unemployment rate, although they can redistribute employment and unemployment. In so far as their impact on the aggregate statistics is concerned, the programmes in operation would need to have been increased by a factor of ten to have reduced the aggregate unemployment rate by 1 percentage point.[16] The administrative problems involved in scaling programmes up to that size cannot be ignored.

It is important to stress that these results have nothing to do with whether such schemes have been cost-effective and worthwhile. No cost–benefit analyses have been performed. However, the theory and the overseas experience suggest that job creation schemes can play a useful role, both as a countercyclical instrument and as a structural instrument to provide work experience to people for whom this might be a good investment in human capital. On the latter basis, some mix of training, private sector employment subsidies and public sector schemes may pay off in terms of raising the subsequent earnings of the participants. None the less, one simply cannot expect these schemes to play a major role in bringing Australia back to full employment.

## NOTES

1 This section draws heavily upon Gregory (1982, 1983a).
2 Kirby uses seasonally unadjusted data. The new average weekly earnings series introduced during the September quarter of 1981 does not have a seasonal pattern. Therefore to extend the data period it was necessary to use seasonally adjusted data.
3 The very low $R^2$'s of Table 15.1 may require comment. They arise because the dependent variable is defined as the rate of change of earnings from one quarter to the next. Most studies use a four-quarter rate of change, which smooths the series considerably and thereby increases the $R^2$. The estimated values and significance level of coefficients do not seem to be affected to any degree by the choice of the period over which the rate of change of wages is defined. The very high $R^2$'s in the Kirby equations arise from the seasonal dummy variables.
4 During the early years of the survey, which began in 1973, the sample size was much smaller. As a result the mean of the series is more volatile.

5 Considerable difficulties are encountered when using a direct measure of price expectations. For example, what should be done about the outlying observations that appear to arise by mistake? Many people in the survey forecast 100 per cent inflation. It is also not clear whether arithmetic means are better a measure than medians.

6 There may be a statistical bias upwards in the expectations series. If there is, however, it needs to be explained why this bias has increased since 1978.

7 There is, however, a small problem associated with calculating the equilibrium unemployment rate and using this as an indicator of change of the extent of the shift. Harper (1980) suggests that the move outwards in the relationship has not been uniform.

8 The Treasury wage equation (Department of the Treasury, 1981) includes overtime hours worked in the wage equation. They also note the changing relationship between overtime hours worked and the utilization rate of labour in the economy as a whole. See Gregory (1983b).

9 See P. Kirby (1981) for a history of Australia's employment and training programmes up to 1980.

10 The only analysis of REDS (Department of Employment and Industrial Relations, 1976) focused on administrative issues; its key findings are reported by P. Kirby (1981).

11 Descriptions and analyses of SYETP are provided in Hoy (1983), Bureau of Labour Market Research (1983), and Smith (1983).

12 Under the current rules for the main part of the scheme ('Standard SYETP'), private employers can receive $75 per week for up to 17 weeks of employment of an eligible worker. The new worker must be between the ages of 15 and 24 and be unemployed and away from full-time education for at least four of the preceding twelve months. Under 'Extended SYETP', introduced in 1981, firms receive $100 per week for the first 17 weeks and $75 per week for the next 17 weeks for hiring someone between the ages of 18 and 24 who has been unemployed and away from full-time education for at least eight of the preceding twelve months.

13 The adult employment subsidies and the Wage Pause job creation schemes are described in news releases by the Minister of Employment and Industrial Relations in December 1982 and January 1983.

14 The Community Employment Program is described by the Minister for Employment and Industrial Relations in his Second Reading Speech on the Bill, 19 May 1983.

15 This is consistent with fiscal substitution estimates for public sector job creation schemes in the USA and with displacement estimates for targeted private sector employment subsidies in the OECD countries recently surveyed (Palmer, 1978; Haveman and Palmer, 1982; OECD 1982). Moreover, when samples of employers who hired people under the SEYTP scheme were asked how the job opening arose and what they would have done in the absence of the scheme, they indicated that about one-third of the positions existed because of the subsidy and otherwise would not have been filled. The extent to which these were net additions to total employment, of course, also depends on the employment that could have been generated through alternative uses of the funds and on the impacts of the subsidy on firms that did not participate.

16 Projected programme expenditures in 1983/4 were almost eight times their real level in 1981/2 and double the real level in 1975/6 (the peak expenditure year). It will be interesting to see what impact this will have on Australian unemployment.

## REFERENCES

Baily, M. N. and J. Tobin, (1977), 'Macroeconomic effects of selective public employment and wage subsidies', *Brookings Papers on Economic Activity* 2, 511–544.

Blandy, R. and Richardson, S. (eds) (1982), *How Labour Markets Work: Case Studies in Adjustment*, Melbourne, Longman-Cheshire.

Bureau of Labour Market Research (1983), *Employment and Training Programs for Young People: Analysis of Assistance in 1980–1981*, Research Report No. 2, Canberra, Australian Government Publishing Service.

Department of Employment and Industrial Relations (1976), 'Evaluation of the Regional Employment and Development Scheme', Parts I and II, unpublished.

Department of Employment and Industrial Relations (1983), *Department of Employment and Industrial Relations Programs, 1983–4*, Canberra, Australian Government Publishing Service, August.

Department of Labour Advisory Council (1980), *Prospective Demand for and Supply of skilled labour 1980–83, with particular reference to major development projects: Report*, Canberra, DOLAC Working Party.

Department of the Treasury, *Budget Statements*, Canberra, Australian Government Publishing Service, various issues.

Department of the Treasury (1981), *The NIF-10 Model of the Australian Economy*, Canberra, Australian Government Publishing Service.

Department of the Treasury (1983), *Budget Statements, 1983–4*, Canberra, Australian Government Publishing Service.

Gregory, R. G. (1982), 'Work and welfare in the years ahead', *Australian Economic Papers*, 21(39), December, 219–243.

Gregory, R. G. (1983a), 'The slide into mass unemployment: labour market theories, facts and policies', Annual Lecture, The Academy of the Social Sciences, Australia.

Gregory, R. G. (1983b), 'Comments on the NIF-10 model', mimeo.

Gregory, R. G. and P. R. Paterson, (1983). 'The impact of unemployment benefit payments on the level and composition of unemployment in Australia', in D. Trewin (ed.), *Statistics in the Labor Market*, New York, Marcel Dekker Inc., 5–31.

Gruen, F. H. (1978), 'Structural unemployment as a rival explanation – a survey of an inconclusive argument', Working Papers in Economics and Econometrics, No. 63, Canberra, Australian National University.

Hall, R. E. (1980), 'Employment fluctuations and wage rigidity', *Brookings Papers on Economic Activity*, 1, 91–123.

Harper, I. (1980), 'The relationship between unemployment and unfilled vacancies in Australia: 1952–78', *Economic Record*, 86(154), September, 231–243.

Haveman, R. and Palmer, J. (eds) (1982), *Jobs for Disadvantaged Workers: The Economics of Employment Subsidies*, Washington, DC, The Brookings Institution.

Hicks, J. R. (1973), *The Crisis in Keynesian Economics*, London, Basil Blackwell.

Hoy, M. (1983), *Review of Five Years Operation of the Special Youth Employment Training Program*, Bureau of Labour Market Research, Conference Paper No. 18, Canberra.

Hughes, B. (1975), 'The *U–V* displacement', *Australian Bulletin of Labour*, 1(4), September, 1–23.

Isaac, J. E. (1981), 'Equity and wage determination', *Australian Bulletin of Labour*, 7(4), September, 205–218.

Kirby, M. (1981), 'An investigation of the specification and stability of the Australian aggregate wage equation', *Economic Record*, 57(156), March, 35–46.

Kirby, P. (1981), 'An overview of Australian experience with manpower programmes', in C. Baird, R. Gregory and F. H. Gruen (eds), *Youth Employment, Education and Training*, Canberra, Australian National University.

National Economic Summit Conference (1983), *Addendum*, Canberra, Australian Government Publishing Service.

Okun, A. (1981), *Prices and Quantities: A Macroeconomic Analysis*, Washington, DC, The Brookings Institution.

OECD (1982), *Marginal Employment Subsidies*, Paris, Organisation for Economic Co-operation and Development.

Palmer, J. (ed.) (1978), *Creating Jobs: Public Employment Programs and Wage Subsidies*, Washington, DC, The Brookings Institution.

Smith, R. E. (1983) *Employment Subsidies in Theory and in Practice: The Special Youth Employment Training Program*, Discussion Paper No. 69, Centre for Economic Policy Research, Canberra, Australian National University.

Solow, R. (1980), 'On theories of unemployment', *American Economic Review*, 70(1), March, 1–9.

Trivedi, P. K. and Baker, G. M. (1982), *Equilibrium Unemployment in Australia: Concepts and Measurement*, Discussion Paper No. 59, Centre for Economic Policy Research, Canberra, Australian National University.

# 16 Wages, Unemployment and Inflation

*D. W. CHALLEN**

## I INTRODUCTION

The Australian Parliamentary *Hansard* of 3 May 1983 records a short question without notice by the Leader of the Opposition to the Prime Minister. Mr Peacock asked: '. . . what would be the effect on the level of unemployment of a 3 to 4 per cent wage increase this year?' This chapter examines one way in which an answer might be provided to Mr Peacock's question (broadened perhaps to encompass the effects on the inflation rate and employment as well as unemployment), namely by recourse to any one of the five major macroeconometric models of the Australian economy currently available. These models are the Commonwealth Treasury's NIF model, the Reverse Bank's RBII family, the IMPACT Project's ORANI model, the IMP model from the Institute of Applied Economic and Social Research at the University of Melbourne and NEVILE, the modelling product of Professor John Nevile. This chapter is a companion to Challen (1983), which includes background material that will be of interest to readers unfamiliar with the Australian modelling scene. A more detailed discussion of model specification issues than is possible within the present space constraints is also provided there.

The structure of this chapter is as follows. The rest of this section attempts to place the models in a broad context. Section II deals rather briefly with the main relevant aspects of model specification, the models being dealt with in roughly ascending order of complexity. Section III quantifies the linkages between the variables of interest and provides an answer to Mr Peacock's question.

Two points of clarification are appropriate before proceeding. Output appears in the list of variables of interest because it is a central variable in all the models in the response channels through which wage changes impinge on employment and unemployment. It is therefore difficult to understand the wages–employment linkage without bringing output into the picture. Another reason for including output in the list is that neither employment nor unemployment appears among the endogenous variables of NEVILE. Output is the obvious choice of real variable to permit across-model comparisons involving NEVILE.

* The Bureau of Labour Market Research provided financial support for some of the model simulations reported in this chapter. Assistance, which is gratefully acknowledged, has been received from John Nevile, Neil Johnston, Chris Murphy, David Chessell, John Taylor, Peter Jonson, Peter Brain, Cosima McPhee, John Madden, Alf Hagger, Mark Kerslake and Anne Oakford.

The other point of clarification concerns the choice of the *money* wage variable rather than *real* wages, given that much of the existing literature focuses attention on the link between real wages and unemployment. However, it is *money* wages that are of importance to the policy debate. Notwithstanding the theoretical importance of the real wage concept, it is of little *immediate* policy relevance, since it is by no means clear in most instances what mechanism can be used to bring about a specified real-wage change.

NEVILE, NIF and IMP are members of the Keynes–Klein (KK) class (see Challen and Hagger, 1979a, 1983, and Powell, 1981). Consistent with their membership of this class, all three are non-linear, formulated in discrete time, stochastic and dynamic. Their broad emphasis is on the determination of the major expenditure aggregates, they are demand dominated and oriented to adjustment processes in disequilibrium. NIF and IMP both provide a significant role for relative prices, and IMP, in particular, pays some attention to the supply side, modelling in this area being more rudimentary in NIF. NIF features a well-developed and carefully specified monetary sector. IMP also includes a financial block that explains the major monetary aggregates and the asset holdings of a range of agents, as well as providing channels of influence of the main monetary policy instruments. Notwithstanding these similarities, NIF and IMP are very different models. Aside from major differences in modelling philosophy, the most obvious point of contrast is the level of aggregation at which modelling takes place, IMP being very much more highly disaggregated. The consequence of this is a dramatic difference in size, NIF being in the medium-size category amongst KK models with 234 equations whereas IMP is in the very large category with about 6,000 equations.

NEVILE is in a class apart. Unlike NIF and IMP, it has not followed the worldwide trends in KK model-building and has more in keeping with the antecedents of today's KK models. It was conceived with a specific purpose in mind – analysis of the consequences of fiscal policy – and, consistent with that purpose, has remained small throughout its existence. The current version comprises 26 equations.

The RBII models (including the current version, RBA79) are members of the Phillips–Bergstrom (PB) class. Such models are formulated in continuous time and emphasize the role of adjustment processes in disequilibrium. Steady-state behaviour is an important consideration in model specification. RBA79 includes reaction functions for such policy variables as the bond rate and the exchange rate. Imposition of theoretically supported within-equation and across-equations restrictions is a feature of its estimation. PB models are typically very small. RBA79 is no exception, comprising only 26 equations.

ORANI is a general equilibrium model of the Johansen type, linear in the percentage changes of the variables in its working form. It has some similarity with IMP in that the level of disaggregation is high, modelling taking place at industry and commodity level. Unlike any of the other models (which are all dynamic), however, ORANI relates to an equilibrium situation. ORANI imposes perfect competition, assuming all firms and consumers are price takers, and views all economic agents as optimizers in some sense.

NEVILE and IMP are annual models, while NIF and RBA79 are quarterly. NEVILE, NIF and IMP are non-linear models and are used in their non-linear form. Such non-linearities as are present are not, however, of great significance to the dynamic responses of these models, and, aside from the technical complication arising from their presence, non-linearity can be ignored for practical purposes in the interpretation of simulation results from the model.[1] The structures of both RBA79 and ORANI are highly non-linear but the working form of both models is linear.

All five models are working systems that are the subject of on-going development effort. The versions of the models referred to here are those current at the time of writing. That of NEVILE is the late-1982 version of the model, which appears in Nevile (1983). The member of the RBII family chosen for discussion is RBA79, which appears in Jonson and Trevor (1979) and Jonson, McKibbin and Trevor (1981), for instance. The version of ORANI considered is ORANI78, which is fully documented in Dixon, Parmenter, Sutton and Vincent (1982). The 1982 version of IMP has been chosen (Brain, forthcoming). Fairly general discussions of the IMP model appear in Brain (1977), Brain, Smith and Schuyers (1979) and Brain and Schuyers (1981). The current version of NIF is NIF-10, documented in Department of the Treasury (1981). However, the variant dealt with here is NIF-10S(F), the simulation version of the model formulated in mid-1982.[2] Complete specifications of the models are provided in the sources given. More general and comparative discussions of the models are provided in Challen and Hagger (1979a, b, and 1983), Freebairn (1980), McKibbin (1982) and Challen (1983).

## II SPECIFICATION ISSUES

The available space precludes any more than the briefest overview of the specification of the five models under discussion. Naturally, attention is focused on the determination and the linkages between wages, output, employment, unemployment and inflation.

### NEVILE

NEVILE is essentially a Keynesian commodity market system with a number of minor extensions and with the addition of a wage–price sector. No labour market is provided in the model, the consequence of which is that neither an employment nor an unemployment variable appears. The general structure of the model is depicted in a highly stylized manner in schematic form in Figure 16.1. The central Keynesian core, built around the output–income–expenditure loop, is the main feature of the model, accounting for 22 of the 26 equations.

The wage–price sector of the model comprises three equations, which explain the inflation rate, expected inflation and award wage growth. A conventional Phillips curve specification, implying absence of a long-run inflation–activity trade-off, forms the basis for the specification of the inflation rate equation. The award wage growth equation provides an excess demand influence and requires that award wages fully reflect expected inflation. A simple treatment is given to inflation expectations, which ensures that, in

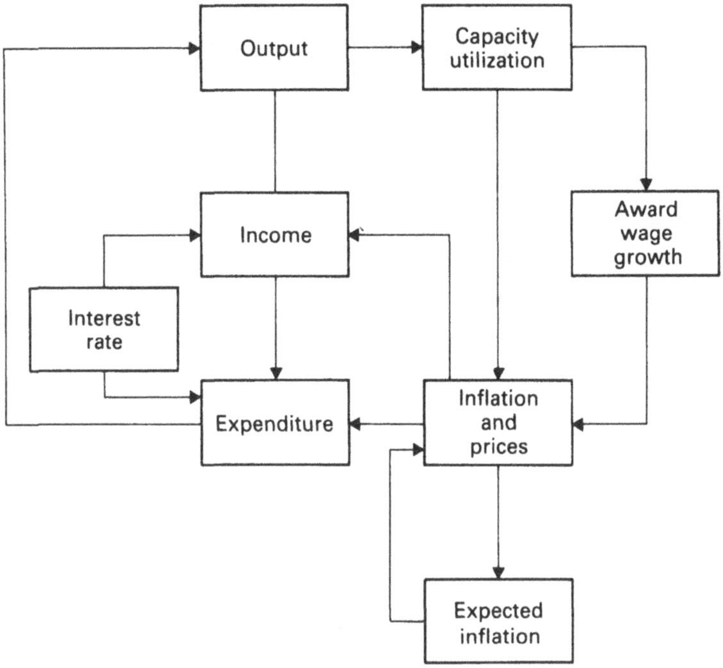


**Figure 16.1** Schematic presentation of major linkages, in NEVILE

simulation, expected inflation will deviate from control by the lagged deviation from control of actual inflation.

NIF/10

Although NIF-10 is a fully integrated model that includes a quite extensive monetary sector and in which considerable attention has been paid to supply-side influences, the determination of real output remains very much demand dominated.[3] Given (expenditure-determined) output, desired employment is obtained by inverting a production function in which effective capital input and capacity utilization are the other major 'inputs'. Actual employment adjusts relatively slowly towards desired employment. Given wages, actual employment determines the wage bill, which in turn feeds in to household disposable income, a major determinant of real consumption expenditure and dwellings investment. This central income–expenditure loop, illustrated in Figure 16.2, is one of the key ingredients in the output–employment–wages linkage in NIF-10. The other, also shown in Figure 16.2, centres around the determination of wages. Potential output is exogenous in NIF-10, so output solely determines capacity utilization. This, together with real wages, determines the unemployment rate. Both the unemployment rate and desired employment influence the determination of vacancies. Unemployment and the labour force are simultaneously determined, given employment, the unemployment rate and certain

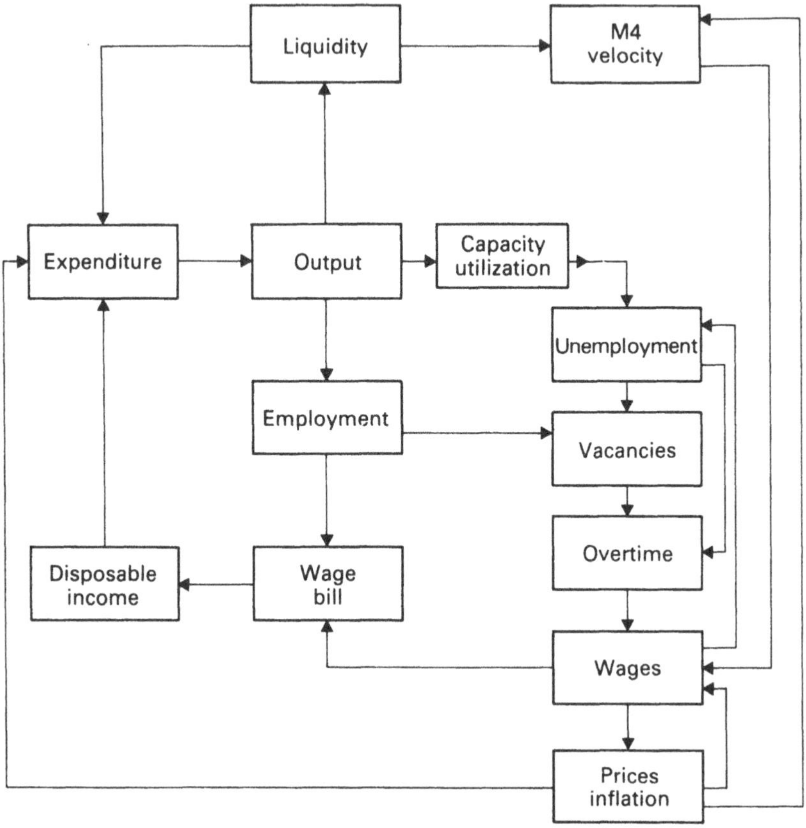


**Figure 16.2** Schematic presentation of major linkages in NIF-10

exogenous labour force components. The difference between the vacancy and unemployment percentages then forms a labour market demand pressure measure that is the sole determinant of overtime per employee. All this amounts to a tightly specified channel linking output and overtime, the importance of which lies in the fact that overtime plays a major role as the activity variable in the determination of wages, which feed back via the wage bill, prices and inflation on the income–expenditure loop described earlier.[4]

A quasi-reduced-form approach is taken to the explanation of unemployment in NIF-10. The actual unemployment rate adjusts towards a desired unemployment rate, which depends upon capacity utilization and real wages. Given the close link between capacity utilization and non-farm output, the unemployment rate in NIF-10 is more responsive to an output stimulus than is employment.

NIF-10 includes a formidable array of price equations. Although these exhibit considerable variety in the details of their specification, most are based on the idea that the actual price level adjusts towards a desired price level, the latter being proportional to normal unit labour cost. Given this structure, the inflation rate in NIF-10 depends upon the extent to which the *real* wage differs from the average product of labour or, equivalently (in view of the Cobb–Douglas production function), from the marginal product of labour.

RBA79

RBA79 focuses attention on adjustment processes in disequilibrium, with the burden of short-run adjustment being placed on quantity change. The model therefore has a central role for buffer stocks of goods, money and labour. The model also accommodates adjustment of prices, especially in the presence of excess demand in the relevant market (Challen and Hagger, 1979a).

Figure 16.3 provides a highly stylized schematic presentation of the major linkages in RBA79 that bear on the variables under discussion. Notwithstanding the level of abstraction implicit in the diagram, it provides an indication of

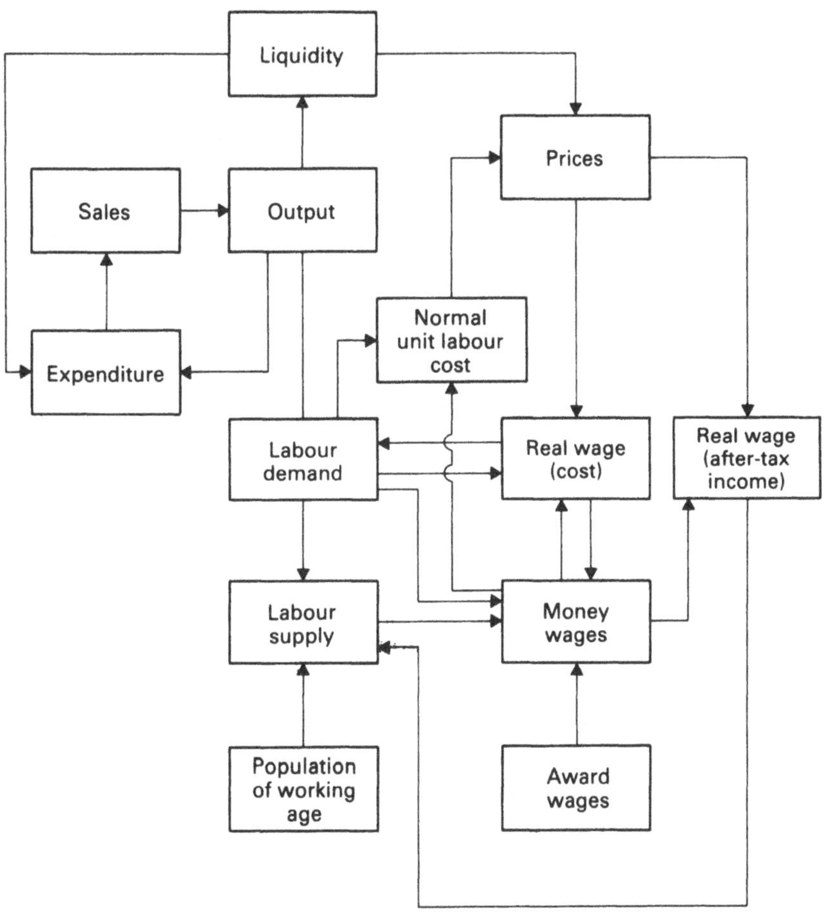


**Figure 16.3** Schematic presentation of major linkages in RBA79

the high degree of simultaneity of the labour market and related areas of the RBA79 specification. The centrepiece of the labour market specification of RBA79 is a two-input, constant returns to scale Cobb–Douglas production function, subject to Hicks-neutral technical progress, defining normal output. This production function provides the basis for the factor demand relationships of RBA79 and for labour demand in particular, as well as playing a part, consistent with its role in the determination of factor demands, in the explanation of money wages and prices.

As regards labour demand, an identity is provided to link the proportionate change in employment with the level of employment. The latter variable is then explained by a desired adjustment equation pair. Although various refinements appear, the desired proportionate change in employment equation essentially requires that the change in labour demand adjust in response to the gap between the marginal product of labour and the real wage. The adjustment equation that completes the pair makes the actual proportionate change in employment adjust towards its desired value at a rate that depends, among other lesser influences, on the extent to which actual and normal output differ.

Labour supply is also endogenous in RBA79, the labour force participation rate depending principally on the after-tax real wage.

The condition for profit maximization applied to the aggregate firm, requiring the quality of labour's marginal product and the real wage, forms the basis for both the desired money wage and desired price of output equations in RBA79. These 'desired' equations are very simple and mutually consistent. An adjustment equation is also provided in each case. That for money wages incorporates a modification of the partial adjustment process to reflect the extent of labour market disequilibrium and the deviation of real award wage growth from trend. Similarly, the price of output adjustment equation admits a direct expectational effect, proxied by excess nominal money balances, as well as a direct goods market short-run disequilibrium influence in the form of the discrepancy between desired and actual inventories.

### IMP

Although very much larger than more familiar KK models, IMP is nevertheless conceptually quite similar to other members of this class. Its size is a direct consequence of the level of disaggregation that has been adopted for modelling purposes. The model is based on a 72-industry classification, most industries producing a single homogeneous commodity. Labour market variables are also dealt with at industry level.

Nine modules form the complete IMP model. For present purposes, the Industrial Activity module is of most interest since it is here that the determination of industry outputs, employment, prices and wage rates occurs. At the heart of this module is a standard input–output identity, which requires that, for each industry, output equal the sum of intermediate demands and of nine final demand categories, net of aggregate imports. A set of conventional behavioural relationships, one for each of the relevant industries, is provided to explain the elements of final demand. The final demand components are in turn linked to the input–output subsystem by a set of identities that allocate to each industry a fixed share of a specified expenditure aggregate as final demand of the appropriate type. Given all final demand components for all industries, the input–output subsystem then determines output industry-by-industry.

Aggregate output is determined by an identity that forms GDP as the sum of the components of final expenditure not, as might be thought, as the sum of individual industry outputs. Consequently, final demands are explained in a conventional Keynesian manner by an aggregate level output–income–expenditure loop that has similar features to those described in NEVILE and NIF. An integral part of this loop is the fairly detailed treatment of income determination provided in IMP. For the most part, this runs in terms of aggregate variables. However, at its most basic level, the income determination process is linked to the input–output subsystem through the wage bill and gross operating surplus of individual industries. In this respect there is a

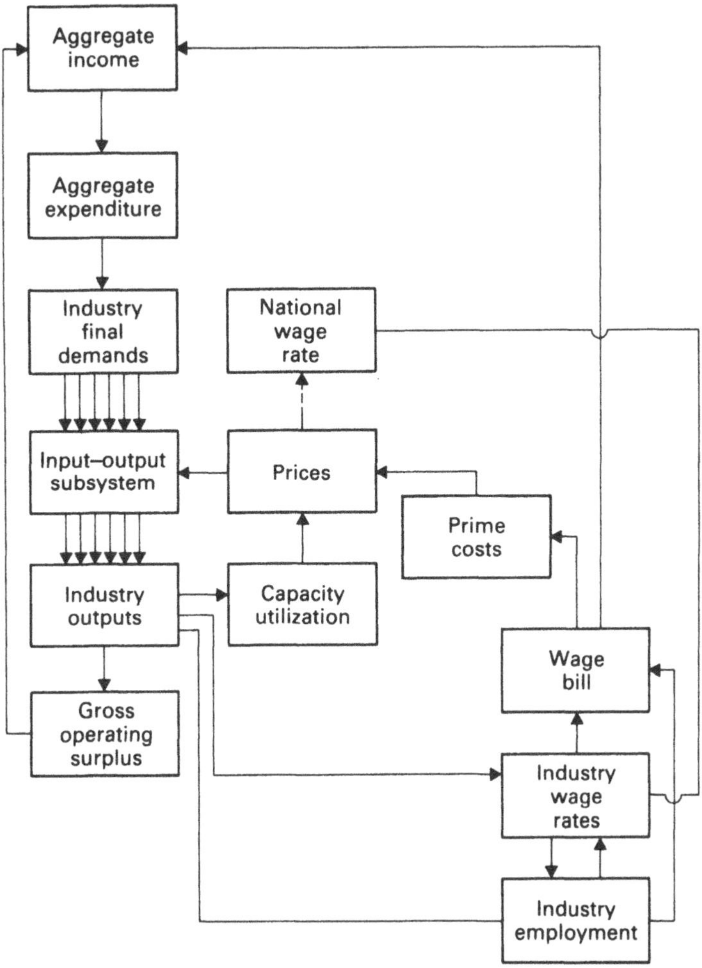


**Figure 16.4** Schematic presentation of major linkages in IMP

feedback of the input–output subsystem on the output–income–expenditure loop which gives the former a central role in the model's response channels.

Factor demands are derived by a process of cost minimization from a three-input production function, the specification of which leaves the degree of returns to scale free to be estimated and which permits free substitution between capital, labour and material inputs. The outcome is a demand for labour function in which the demand by an industry for total standard hours worked by labour as a ratio of its gross output depends on the price of labour relative to that of other inputs, industry output and installed capital in the industry.

The determination of industry wage rates in IMP is based upon a generalized neo-classical model according to which the ratio of the industry wage rate to the national wage rate adjusts to equate the industry supply of labour with its demand for labour. The national wage rate is linked to average earnings, which are explained by a Phillips-type relationship.

As regards prices, a basic distinction is made between home and export prices. In each case, prices are modelled at industry level. Home prices are explained as a variable mark-up on industry prime costs, which, in turn, are defined in terms of materials outlays and the industry wage bill. Export prices are explained in terms of a vector of relative domestic-currency tradeables–goods prices, export incentives to the industry and capacity utilization. Only the levels of prices are explained; no inflation rate appears in the model.

Figure 16.4 presents the major linkages in IMP schematically.

## ORANI

While there are some obvious similarities between the models already considered, ORANI stands apart. It is, in the strict sense, a numerical general equilibrium model of the Australian economy. The other models are dynamic models, but ORANI is a static model; it portrays an economy in which current and past exogenous change has been fully absorbed, so that no adjustments are taking place.

ORANI is a truly large-scale model, its basic structure consisting of several million equations and variables. It encompasses 113 domestic industries producing 115 commodities. Every commodity, whether domestically produced or imported, potentially serves as an input to its own production process and that of every other commodity. Other inputs are the services of nine separate labour skills, the services of fixed capital, the services of agricultural land and other services such as the holding of inventories.

Because of the size of the basic structure and its non-linearity, the model in its basic form is unsuitable for use in policy analysis. To produce a usable model two steps are required. The first is to apply the technique of logarithmic differentiation to produce the linearized model, which is linear in the percentage rates of change of the variables. A much smaller, *final model* is then produced by a process of substitution.

Each of ORANI's industries is governed by a constant-returns production technology. The basic relationship in this technology is that between different material inputs, between material inputs and primary factors in general, and between either of these types of input and other services. This relationship is of the Leontief form. That is, in the absence of technical change, inputs must be used in fixed proportions – there is no possibility of substitution, irrespective of relative price changes. Nested into this overall Leontief production function there are, however, a number of lower-level non-linear functions that allow substitution between sub-classes of inputs within the broader input types. The material inputs of a given commodity from domestic and imported sources follow a CES production function, while the different types of primary inputs (the services of labour, of fixed capital and of agricultural land) follow a CRESH production function.[5]

A set of input demand functions is provided for each ORANI industry – one for each of the available productive inputs into current production. These are derived by a process of cost minimization in which the production functions constitute the constraints and in which input and output prices are taken as parameters. One group of these equations, the demands for labour, will be considered further below. Each ORANI industry also has a set of input demand functions relating to inputs into capital creation.

ORANI features five distinct types of commodity price variable:

- the prices *paid by* domestic users for ORANI's 115 commodities from domestic sources and from foreign sources (purchaser prices);
- the prices *received by* the domestic producers of the 113 industries in respect of domestic sales and the prices in *Australian currency* received by the importers of 115 imported commodities (basic prices);
- the prices of the fixed capital equipments that are constructed for ORANI's 113 domestic industries;
- the fob foreign-currency prices *received by* the exporters of the 115 domestically produced commodities;
- the cif *foreign-currency* prices *paid by* the importers of the 115 domestically produced commodities.

Linking the equilibrium levels of these five sets of price variables are five groups of price equations. Two important assumptions underly these equations. The first is that there are no pure profits either in the production of current commodities or in the production of capital. The second assumption is that all basic prices are uniform across users; that is, domestic producers and importers receive the same price regardless of whether they are selling to domestic firms, to households, to other domestic users or to foreigners. However, the prices paid for commodities will vary from one class of user to another because of differences in margins costs and in indirect taxes.

A set of labour market clearing equations is provided, each of which equates the aggregate employment of a particular labour skill with the sum of the quantities of that skill used as an input into the production of current commodities by each industry commodities by each industry. ORANI also includes a set of miscellaneous macro equations, an important subset of which are 'indexing' equations that allow a variety of 'scenarios' to be imposed on the basic ORANI system. Among these is an indexing equation for each of the nine labour skills in each industry. Each of these equations has the following form:

$$w_{lj} = h_{lj}p_c + f + f_{lj} \qquad l = 1, \ldots, 9; \quad j = 1, \ldots, 115.$$

Here $f$, $f_{lj}$ and $h_{lj}$ are at-choice parameters, $f$ is a wage-shift variable; $w_{lj}$ and $p_c$ denote, respectively, the percentage change in the money wage rate paid for labour skill class $l$ by industry $j$ and the percentage change in the consumer price index.

As was noted above, the productive technology on which the input demand equations of ORANI are based takes the form of a set of nested production functions that allow substitution between inputs at some levels but not at

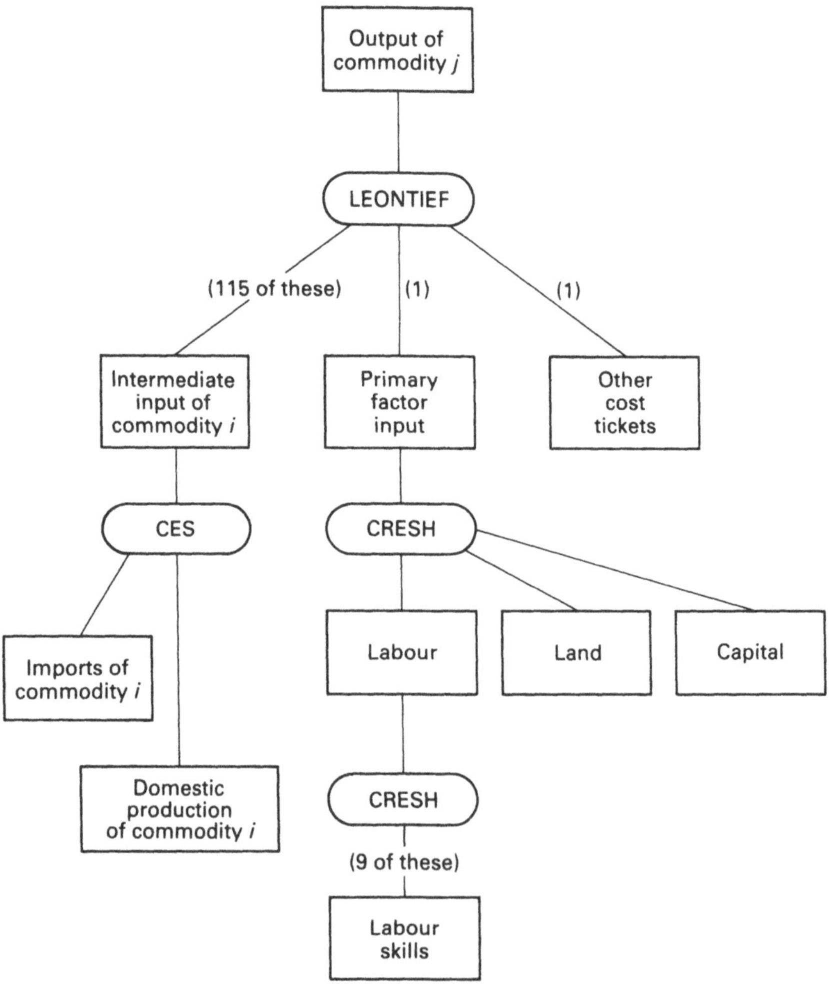


**Figure 16.5** Schematic representation of the ORANI production technology

others. Figure 16.5 provides a schematic representation of this general structure that helps to clarify the explanation of input demands in general and of the demands for labour in particular. The demand for a specific labour skill by a given industry depends upon that industry's demand for labour in *general* and on the wage rates applicable to each of the labour skill classes. In the absence of changes in relative wage rates paid to different skill types, the demand for labour of a specific skill type by an industry will increase at the same rate as its demand for labour in general. However, if the wage rate for a particular skill increases relative to a weighted average of the rate payable to all skills, the demand for labour of that skill class by industry will rise at a slower rate than the industry's demand for labour in general. Moving up one level, a given industry's demand for labour *in general* depends on its output and on the prices of each of the three primary inputs. If the relative prices of the three primary factors (labour, capital and agricultural land) do not change, an industry's demand for labour in general will rise at the same rate as its output. A rise in wage rates in general relative to a weighted average of the prices of the three primary factors will, however, lead to substitution away from labour so that the industry's demand for labour in general will rise at a lower rate than its output.

One important aspect of the flexibility of ORANI arises from the fact that the computing is so organized that the model user is free to choose which 3,452 of the full set of 3,844 variables are to be treated as exogenous. The values allotted to the exogenous variables in an ORANI simulation serve to define: (a) the economy-wide shock that is under examination and (b) the conditions in which the shock is assumed to take place – the environment or 'scenario' underlying the experiment.

## SOME COMPARISONS

NEVILE, the smallest of the models, is also the one with the simplest structure, calling essentially only on a Phillips-type response channel from output to wages and prices, with feedbacks on real-sector variables via the effects of inflation on expenditure. Employment is not explained in the model. None of the other models ranks clearly first in terms of the richness of specification of the linkages between the variables of interest. RBA79, IMP and ORANI have an edge over NIF-10 in terms of supply-side responses, relative price effects being well-specified in all three models. Such influences on employment do not play a part in the short-run dynamics of NIF. ORANI, in stand-alone mode, lacks any aggregate-level macroeconomic linkages such as those that operate through wages to income and expenditure and through liquidity influences. Both linkages are present in IMP, where the modelling approach adopted for employment is similar in conception though quite different in execution from those of RBA79 and ORANI, factor demands being modelled in a consistent way in each case.

Although the underlying philosophies differ, the three 'big' models and RBA79 each deal carefully with the modelling of prices and wages. Some similarities can be found in the theoretical underpinnings of the price equations of NIF and RBA79. Wages are dealt with in RBA79 in a manner entirely consistent with the treatment of prices, while NIF adopts a more 'Phillips-like' treatment of wages of the same general type as that present in NEVILE. No individual commodity price equations or equations for the wages of particular skill classes in individual industries are to be found in ORANI. In view of the general equilibrium nature of the model, it is the clearing equations and the zero pure profits conditions that are the central elements of the determination of prices and wages in ORANI. A mark-up treatment is adopted for domestic prices in IMP, while the treatment of wages is somewhat eclectic, lacking the tightness of specification of RBA79 and ORANI in particular. NEVILE, NIF and RBA79 provide explicit expectational influences on wages and prices, RBA79 exhibiting much the richest specification in this area.

## III MODEL RESPONSES TO A WAGE SHOCK

In this section, the dynamic response of each of the models to a wage shock is considered and these responses are used to provide an assessment of the linkages in each model between wages, unemployment and inflation. In principle, the same shock should be imposed on each of the models. In practice, however, this requirement cannot be met. Because specifications differ and because the definitions of the wage variable differ between models, the shocks cannot be regarded as strictly comparable. Nevertheless, the shocks have been chosen to minimize comparability problems. Another problem arises from the fact that sample periods differ between models, making it difficult (sometimes impossible) to introduce the wage shock at the same point in time and to provide simulation results for the same period. The importance of this problem depends on the degree of non-linearity of models. Although all the models except ORANI are non-linear in their working form, only RBA79 is highly so and, even in that case, a linearized form of the model is used for simulation purposes. Consequently, differences in timing should not detract to any significant extent from the comparability of the dynamic responses to the wage shock.

Ideally, the wage shock to be imposed on the models would have been chosen with Mr Peacock's specific question in mind. Unfortunately this was not possible, so that it was necessary to 'make do' with simulation results obtained with another purpose in mind. Results were available from all five models for a sustained 10 per cent reduction in the level of money wages[6] and it is this shock that forms the basis for the discussion of the present section.

### NEVILE

The wage shock simulation was performed in NEVILE over the ten-year period 1970/1–1979/80, the shock being introduced in the first of those years. The only wage variable that appears in NEVILE is $w_a$, the rate of award wage growth. A sustained 10 per cent reduction in the level of award wages can be achieved by an appropriately gauged *impulse* change in the rate of award wage growth.[7] In this case, a reduction by 0.1 in the intercept of the $w_a$ equation in the first year only of the simulation period is required. The results of this experiment are shown in Figure 16.6.

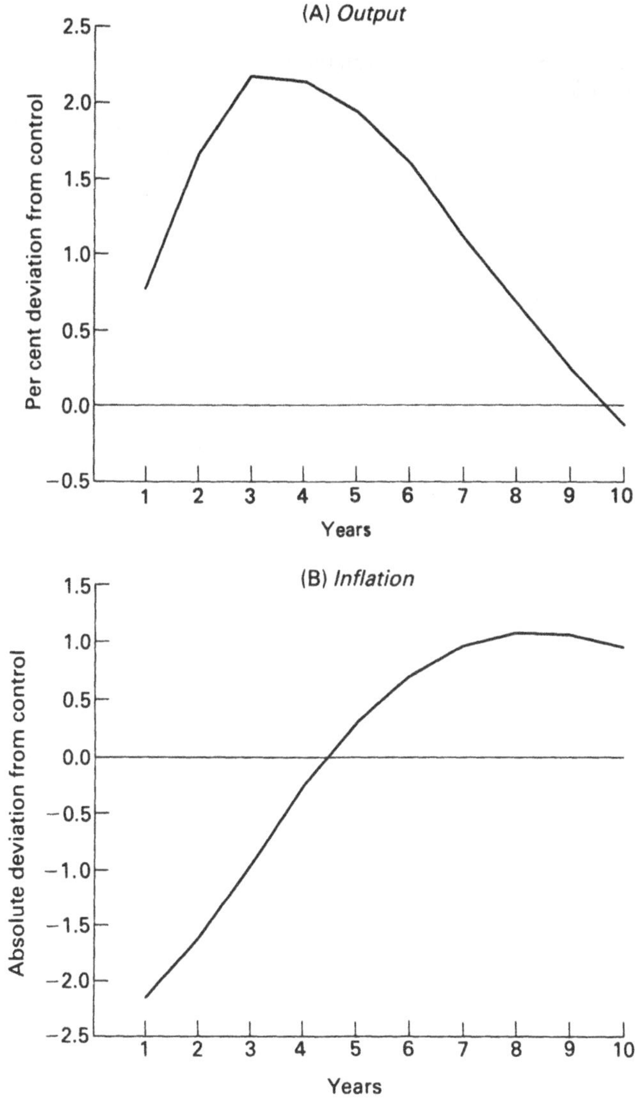


**Figure 16.6** NEVILE: dynamic response to wage shock

The impact effect of the wage shock in NEVILE is to raise real output by 0.77 per cent and to reduce the inflation rate by 2.15 points. Output rises to a peak of 2.18 per cent higher than control after three years and remains around 2 per cent above control for a further two years, before declining fairly rapidly to be back near control at the end of the ten-year simulation period. Inflation remains below control for four years before entering a cyclical path that takes it above control but falls back towards control after ten years.

NIF-10

NIF-10 simulations were undertaken over the ten-year period 1970/1–1979 Q4, the wage shock being introduced in the first quarter of the period.[8] The particular form of the wage shock in the NIF-10 cases is a sustained 10 per cent decrease in the level of *desired* wages (WAR$*). Since the dependent variable in the desired wage equation is the rate of change of desired wages, the shock is implemented simply by lowering the constant of that equation by 0.1 for the first quarter of the simulation period. The results of this experiment are shown in Figure 16.7.

The impact effect of the shock is to reduce the level of money wages, as intended, by 10 per cent of their control value. However, the dynamics of the system quickly dominate the shock and, after declining to a trough of about 14 per cent below control six quarters into the simulation period, money wages recover to be near control after about ten quarters. Subsequently, money wages decline again to settle at about 7 per cent below control in the last three years of the simulation period.

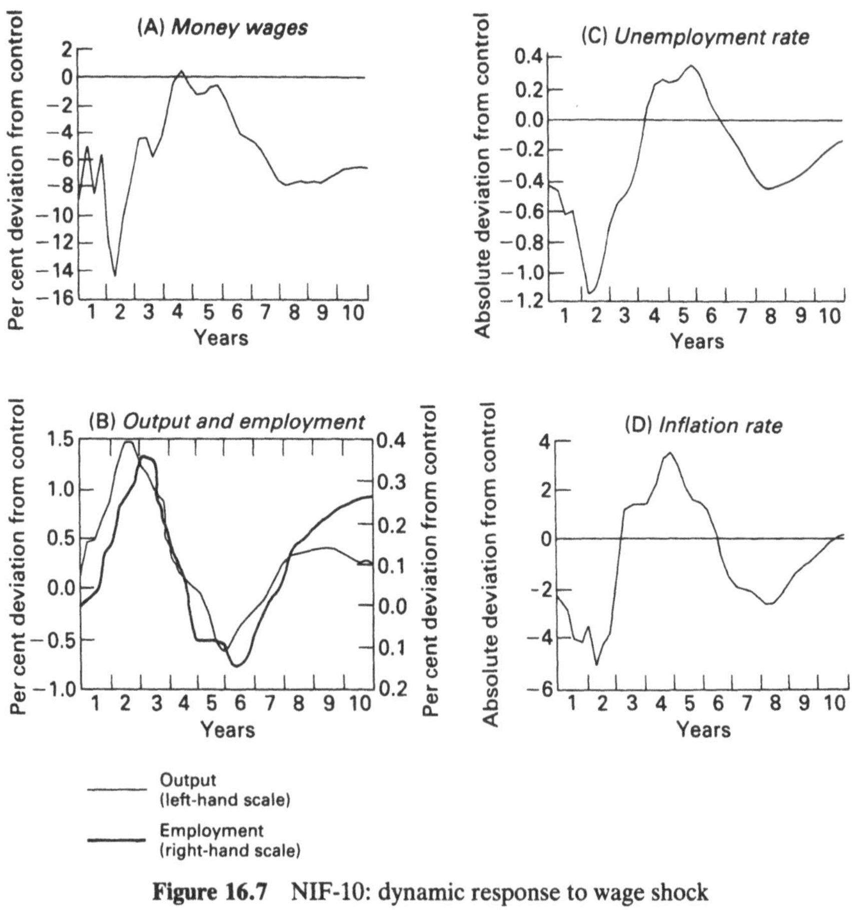


**Figure 16.7** NIF-10: dynamic response to wage shock

Although the wage shock sets in train a rapid and quite strong money wage response, the activity responses are by no means strong. Output rises quickly to a peak response of about 1.5 per cent above control after seven quarters, the peak coinciding closely with the trough in the response of money wages and prices. Output declines rapidly from the initial peak to reach a trough of about 0.5 per cent below control half way through the simulation period. Subsequently the output response is dominated by a heavily damped cycle around control. The response of employment is not dissimilar, although it is significantly weaker than that for output. Employment rises to a little less than 0.4 per cent above control and the mid-period trough is only 0.15 per cent below control.

The response of the unemployment rate is, for the most part, dominated by the output response. This is accentuated in the early part of the simulation period by the fall in real wages as money wages deviate below control by more than prices. In the later part of the simulation period, real wages deviate little from control and the response of the unemployment rate is completely determined by that of output.

The inflation rate responds in a manner that is broadly consistent with money wages. Initially, the money wage cut pushes inflation below control to a trough of –4.13 points. As money wages begin to rise again back towards control, the levels of prices also rise and, as a consequence, inflation very quickly rises above control, to peak some sixteen quarters after the shock at 3.57 points above control.

## RBII

The simulation period for the RBA79 experiment was 1966Q3–1975Q2, comprising forty quarters. The wage shock is implemented in RBA79 by holding average weekly earnings at 0.9 of their control value throughout the simulation period. Results are shown in Figure 16.8.

Output rises rapidly in response to the wages shock, from an impact effect of 0.2 per cent above control to a peak of about 2.4 per cent higher than control eight quarters into the simulation period. The output response then enters a very long-period cyclical path. The response of employment is generally stronger than that for output, but with a somewhat shorter-period cycle and with much less of a tendency to die away. The effects of relative price adjustment in RBA79 account for virtually all of the difference between the output and employment responses to the wage shock. Prices fall in response to the wage shock, but they do so relatively slowly and never by as much as the fall in money wages. The consequent decline in real wages produces labour for capital substitution in production in the model and employment therefore rises more than proportionally to output. Although much less important quantitatively, the real wage influence on labour supply partially offsets this boost to employment, the decline in real wages bringing about a reduction in labour force participation. The consequence is that the unemployment rate response is dominated by that of employment, the labour supply effects of the induced decline in real wages being of little importance.

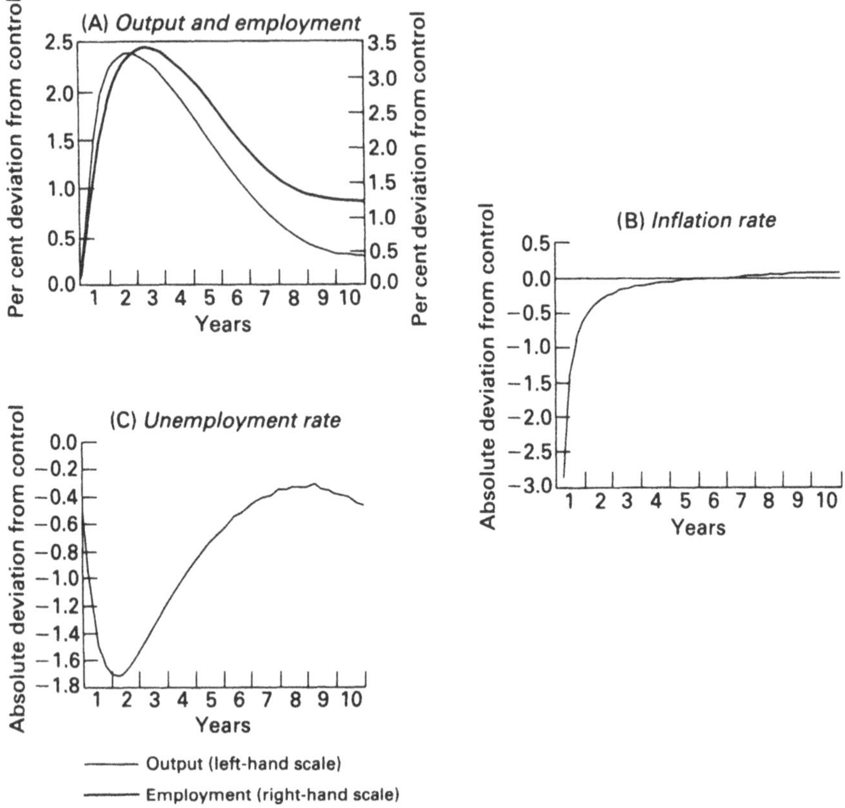


**Figure 16.8** RBA79: dynamic response to wage shock

IMP

The simululation with IMP was performed over the eight year period, 1975–1982. Implementation of the wage shock took the form of a reduction, in the first year, of the constant term in the Phillips relationship of the model by 0.0639. This has the effect of lowering the economy-wide nominal wage rate by the required 10 per cent of control. However, as was the case in NIF, the system dynamics quickly dominate the shock and the effect is for the wage rate to decline rapidly. The processes that halt this decline are very slow acting, and only in the last year of the simulation period does the wage rate begin to recover. The shock is clearly much stronger than in the other models, making comparisons difficult between the IMP responses and those of the other models.

Figure 16.9 shows that output initially declines before growing steadily and quite strongly, even taking due account of the strength of the shock. Employment grows consistently away from control throughout the simulation period and, like output, shows no sign of any turn-down even after eight years.

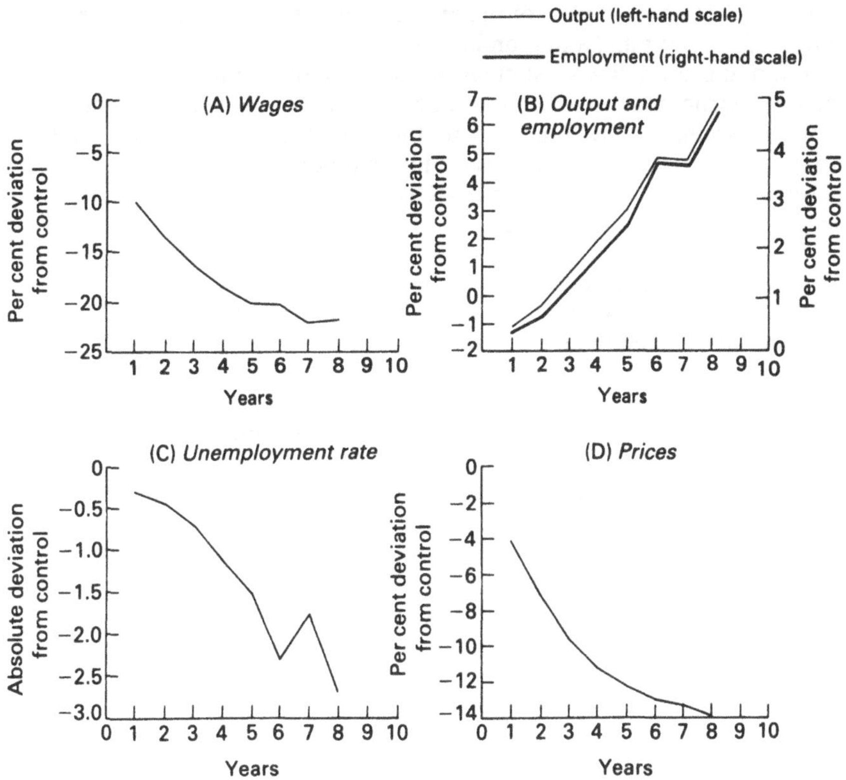


**Figure 16.9** IMP: dynamic response to wage shock

Consistent with the employment response, the unemployment rate falls strongly below control.

The price level falls below control throughout the simulation period, but by less than wages, so that a real wage cut occurs of about 6–8 per cent of control throughout. Relative to this real wage effect, the response of both output and employment is very strong by comparison with the other models.

ORANI

ORANI's indexing equations for wage rates paid to labour skills provide the vehicle for introducing a wage shock into ORANI. These equations have the following form:

$$w_{lj} = h_{lj}p_c + f + f_{lj} \qquad l = 1, \ldots, 9 \quad j = 1, \ldots, 115.$$

What is required in the present context is a 10 per cent cut in money wages that is uniform across industries and across labour skill classes; that is, to set $w_{lj} = -0.1$. It is clear from the indexing equations that this can be achieved in a number of ways but, in view of the endogeneity of $p_c$, the simplest means is to set $h_{lj} = f_{lj} = 0$ for all $l$ and $j$, and $f = -0.1$.

Underlying an ORANI simulation is a set of assumptions defining the general environment on which the shock impinges. These assumptions, which form the scenario, are reflected in the values allotted to the exogenous variables and to those ORANI parameters that are at the user's choice. The chosen scenario was the standard ORANI neo-classical, short-run scenario,[9] the main elements of which are:

- real domestic absorption exogenous and fixed;
- initial capital stocks in all industries exogenous and fixed;
- nominal exchange rate exogenous and fixed.

The results of the ORANI wage shock simulation are shown in Table 16.1. The effect of the shock is to raise employment by a little over 3 per cent and output by about 2 per cent. The ORANI consumer price index falls by about 6.4 per cent. Since this is less than the 10 per cent fall in money wages, real wages fall by about 4 per cent.

In interpreting these ORANI results, it is important to note that, as simulated here in its stand-alone mode, ORANI lacks any genuine macroeconomic linkages such as those between expenditure, incomes and wages. As a result, the effects on such output and employment shown in Table 16.1 arise solely as the consequence of the effects of relative price change on individual industry's demand for factor inputs and on industry outputs.

Because ORANI is a general equilibrium model, it is silent on the question of the timing of the output and employment changes. Nevertheless, a general indication of the length of time involved in the ORANI 'short run' is helpful in interpreting the simulation results. The view of the ORANI model-builders is that the ORANI short run can be regarded as a period of one–two years.[10]

**Table 16.1** *ORANI: response to wage shock*

| | *Percentage change in economy-wide variables* |
|---|---|
| Money wages[a] | –10.000 |
| Real wages[b] | –3.621 |
| Consumer price index | –6.379 |
| Investment price index | –6.056 |
| Gross domestic product | +2.336 |
| Employment (hours) | +3.177 |
| Employment (persons) | +3.279 |

*Notes:* a Defined as the common value of the $w_{lj}$, $\overset{*}{w}_{lj}$

b Defined as $\dot{w}_{lj} - p^c$.

## RESPONSES TO THE WAGE SHOCK: COMPARISONS BETWEEN THE MODELS

Some interesting comparisons can be made between the responses of the models to the respective wage shocks, although considerable care must be exercised in so doing. The need for caution arises, of course, because the shocks are, to an extent, model-specific. Comparisons between ORANI and the other models are particularly difficult because of the considerable difference in conceptual basis and model-building objectives, and because the question of the timing of ORANI short-run effects is one that depends largely on the model-builder's intuition and on information external to the model. Those between IMP and the other models are risky in view of the problem of the comparability of the magnitude of the wage shock.

Another problem affecting the inter-model comparisons is that the RBA79 shock is conceptually dissimilar to that of the other dynamic models. In the RBA79 case, money wages have been held at 90 per cent of control, thus eliminating the dynamic feedbacks of other endogenous variables on wages, such feedbacks originating in the wage shock itself. By contrast, the wage shock in NEVILE, NIF-10 and IMP has been implemented by a one-period reduction in the intercept of an equation on which the rate of money wage change depends. In these cases, the equations that determine money wages continue to operate and, in particular, feedbacks of the kind eliminated in the RBA79 implementation impinge on money wages. The implication is that shock of uniform intensity is applied to RBA79, whereas in the other dynamic models the intensity of the shock is to an extent dependent on the dynamics of the process of money wage determination. An illustration of this point can be readily gained from the response of wages shown in Figures 16.7 and 16.9 for NIF-10 and IMP, respectively.

The validity of inter-model comparisons of dynamic responses to any shock is also dependent on the similarity of the policy mix between models. Broadly speaking, the historical settings of the policy instruments and, where applicable, the estimated reaction functions apply in each case. In practice, however, there are two departures from this generalization that should be noted. The wage shock in NIF-10 impinges on an environment in which the estimated bond rate reaction function is replaced with the rule that the bond rate adjust so as to maintain holdings of government securities by the non-financial private sector at their control level. Since the rule reflects an accommodating monetary policy stance, this modification does not materially change the policy mix from the historical experience. In implementing the wage shock in IMP, real interest rates have been held constant. The effect is to amplify the effects of the wage shock on activity, in a manner similar to a policy mix in which a less restrictive monetary policy applied.

As regards both the magnitude and the timing of the peak response of output, there is a considerable degree of agreement between the models in the subset of four that omits IMP. From Table 16.2, it can be seen that the peak output responses are all in the vicinity of 2 per cent above control, although that for NIF-10 is distinctly on the low side. While the peak output response occurs a

**Table 16.2** *Response to wages shock – model comparisons*

| | *NEVILE* | *NIF-10* | *RBA79* | *IMP* | *ORANI* |
|---|---|---|---|---|---|
| *OUTPUT:* | | | | | |
| Impact effect[a] | 0.77 | 0.11 | 0.23 | -1.08 | |
| Peak response[a] | 2.18 | 1.48 | 2.39 | 4.9 | 2.34 |
| Delay (years) to peak response | 3 | 1.75 | 2 | 6 | 1–2[b] |
| First trough | n.p.[c] | -0.63 | 0.32 | 4.8 | n.a. |
| Delay (years) to first trough | n.a. | 5 | 10 | 7 | n.a. |
| Effect after 10 years[a,d] | -0.12 | 0.24 | 0.32 | 6.71 | n.a. |
| *Employment:*[e] | | | | | |
| Impact effect[a] | n.a. | 0.01 | 0.34 | 0.32 | |
| Peak response[a] | n.a. | 0.36 | 3.43 | 3.71 | 3.28 |
| Delay (years) to peak response | n.a. | 2.25 | 2.5 | 6 | 1–2[b] |
| First trough[a] | n.a. | -0.15 | 1.26 | 3.71 | n.a. |
| Delay (years) to first trough | n.a. | 5.50 | 9 | 7 | n.a. |
| Effect after 10 years[a,d] | n.a. | 0.26 | 1.31 | 4.7 | n.a. |
| *Unemployment:* | | | | | |
| Impact effect[f] | n.a. | -0.44 | 0.36 | -0.31 | n.a. |
| Peak response[f] | n.a. | 0.35 | -0.31 | -2.31 | n.a. |
| Delay (years) to peak response | n.a. | 5 | 8.25 | 6 | n.a. |
| First trough[f] | n.a. | -1.15 | -1.72 | -1.76 | n.a. |
| Delay (years) to first trough | n.a. | 1.5 | 1.50 | 7 | n.a. |
| Effect after 10 years[d,f] | n.a. | -0.15 | -0.47 | -2.7 | n.a. |
| *INFLATION:* | | | | | |
| Impact effect[f] | -2.15 | -2.39 | -2.87 | n.a. | n.a. |
| Peak response[f] | 1.06 | 3.57 | n.p. | n.a. | n.a. |
| Delay (years) to peak response | 8 | 4 | n.a. | n.a. | n.a. |
| First trough[f] | n.p. | -5.06 | n.p. | n.a. | n.a. |
| Delay (years) to first trough | n.a. | 1.50 | n.a. | n.a. | n.a. |
| Effect after 10 years[d,f] | 0.93 | 0.28 | 0.08 | n.a. | n.a. |

*Notes:* a Per cent deviation from control, percentage change for ORANI.
b See text for discussion.
c Not present.
d 8 years for IMP.
e Persons in each case.
f Absolute deviation from control, percentage points.

year later in NEVILE, that for the other models is around two years. NIF-10 is the fastest to achieve its peak response in output.

In other respects, there is much less agreement between the models as regards the response of output to the wage shock. The impact effect is strongest for NEVILE and weakest for NIF-10, although this comparison is of little importance given the sensitivity of the impact effect to relatively minor differences in dynamic specification. While the output response of both NIF-10 and RBA79 enters a cyclical path, NEVILE shows no signs of doing so over the available simulation period. For practical purposes, the same remark applies to

IMP. The cycle is much longer in RBA79 than in NIF-10, the first trough being reached in ten and five years respectively, taking output below control in NIF-10 but remaining above in RBA79. After ten years, output is around 0.3 per cent above control in NIF-10 and RBA79 but is a little below in NEVILE.

Less information is available on which to base a comparison of the employment responses of the models because employment does not appear in the list of endogenous variables in NEVILE. ORANI, RBA79 and (somewhat surprisingly) IMP produce very similar peak employment responses, in the general vicinity of 3.5 per cent above control. NIF-10 is very much weaker at only 0.36 per cent; the reasons for this are, however, well understood (Challen and FitzGerald, 1983). RBA79, NIF-10 and ORANI achieve their peak response (bearing in mind the caveats discussed above on the timing of the ORANI short run) after about two years, while that for IMP occurs very much later at six years. In both NIF-10 and RBA79 this is two quarters later than the output peak, while in IMP it coincides with the (local) output peak.

The picture as regards the unemployment rate response to the wage shock is very similar to that for employment, a reflection of the fact that labour supply responses are weak in all three of the models for which the unemployment variable is the magnitude of the impact effect and the magnitude and timing of the first trough. In these respects the three models tell much the same story. The impact effects lie in the range 0.3–0.4 per cent below control, coinciding in RBA79 and NIF-10 at six quarters into the period but arriving only after seven years in IMP.

In the case of the inflation rate response, there is very little to go on, the only useful comparison being between impact effects. Here, however, there is some agreement between the models. NEVILE exhibits the weakest impact effect at 2.15 points below control, RBA79 is the strongest at 2.87 points, while at 2.39 points below control, NIF-10 is close to their mean.

Perhaps the most surprising conclusion that can be drawn from these comparisons is the remarkable degree of unanimity between the models as regards the impact of wages on the four variables considered. For output, the only variable that is represented in all five models, a reasonable conclusion would be that a 10 per cent money wage cut will raise output by something in excess of 2 per cent over a period of about two years, but that this peak response will fade away moderately quickly. In drawing this conclusion, the IMP results have been put to one side. For employment the conclusion would be a peak response of around 3.5 per cent occurring after about 2.0–2.5 years. Here, the NIF-10 result has been disregarded, although this is entirely appropriate given the weak output–employment linkage in that model. A reasonable conclusion for the unemployment rate response is that in less than two years a decline of nearly 2 points might be achieved, relying here mainly on the NIF-10 and RBA79 results. Leaving aside IMP, the models suggest that both the employment and unemployment rate responses will fade away to a considerable degree, but it is by no means clear that there will not be lasting employment/unemployment effects of the wage cut. Finally, in respect of the inflation rate there is little to say except that an impact effect of something between 2 and 3 points might be expected.

## NOTES

1 The only member of this model group that has been subjected to a test of the extent of non-linearity present is NIF. Experiments by Johnston, Murphy and Perazzelli (1983) show that those non-linearities present have no significant effect on the dynamic response of the model.
2 See Johnston, Murphy and Perazzelli (1984) for details.
3 See Department of the Treasury (1981), pp. 35–7, Challen and FitzGerald (1983), section 3.
4 See Challen and FitzGerald (1983) for further discussion.
5 CRESH (constant ratio of elasticities of substitution, homothetic) functions are a generalization of CES (constant elasticity of substitution) functions, allowing for more than one elasticity of substitution among inputs.
6 See, however, the remarks below concerning the NIF-10 results.
7 See McKibbin (1980) for a proof of this proposition.
8 In the case of NIF-10, the available simulation results were for a 10 per cent wage *increase* analogous to that described as a *decrease* in the text. With comparability between models in mind, the results shown in the text were obtained by reversing the sign of all deviations from control from those of the 10 per cent wage increase. As noted previously, experiments with NIF-10S performed by Johnston, Murphy and Perazzelli (1983) demonstrate that the non-linearities present in the model are of little significance. Consequently, the magnitude of the responses of NIF-10S will be largely independent of the sign of the shock.
9 See Dixon *et al.* (1982), section 44.
10 See Dixon *et al.* (1982), pp. 39, 65–6, 289; and Cooper and McLaren (1981).

## BIBLIOGRAPHY

Brain, P. J. (1977), 'The Institute multi-purpose model: an outline', *Australian Economic Review*, 37(3), 47–64.

Brain, P. J. (forthcoming), *The Structure of the Australian Economy*, Melbourne, Longman-Cheshire.

Brain, P. J. and Schuyers, G. P. (1981), *Energy and the Australian Economy*, Melbourne, Longman-Cheshire.

Brain, P. J., Smith, R. L. and Schuyers, G. P. (1979), *Population, Immigration and the Australian Economy*, London, Croom-Helm.

Challen, D. W. (1983), *The Wages–Employment Relationship in Australian Macro-Econometric Models*, Canberra, Bureau of Labour Market Research.

Challen, D. W. and FitzGerald, V. W. (1983), 'Dynamical features of the NIF-10 model of the Australian economy', in *Proceedings of the Conference on the NIF-10 Model*, Canberra, Australian Government Publishing Service.

Challen, D. W. and Hagger, A. J. (1979a), *Modelling the Australian Economy*, Melbourne, Longman-Cheshire.

Challen, D. W. and Hagger, A. J. (1979b), 'Economy-wide modelling with special reference to Australia', paper given at the Eighth Conference of Economists, Melbourne.

Challen, D. W. and Hagger, A. J. (1983), *Macro-Econometric Systems: Constructions, Evaluation and Applications*, London, Macmillan.

Cooper, R. J. and McLaren, K. R. (1981), 'The ORANI-MACRO interface: an illustrative exposition', *IMPACT Preliminary Working Paper*, No. IP-10.

Department of the Treasury (1981), *The NIF-10 Model of the Australian Economy*, Canberra, Australian Government Publishing Service.

Dixon, P. B., Parmenter, B. R., Sutton, J. and Vincent, D. P. (1982), *ORANI: A Multisectoral Model of the Australian Economy*, Amsterdam, North-Holland.

Freebairn, J. (1980), 'The IMPACT project: a review', *Economic Record*, 56(152), March, 17–35.

Johnston, H. N., Murphy, C. W. and Perazzelli, P. A. (1983), 'Simulation experiments with the NIF-10S model', five instalments, mimeo.

Johnston, H. N., Murphy, C. W. and Perazzelli, P. A. (1984), 'A simulation version of NIF-10', in *Proceedings of the Conference on the NIF-10 Model*, Canberra, Australian Government Publishing Service.

Jonson, P. D., McKibbin, W. J. and Trevor, R. G. (1981), 'External and domestic interactions: a sensitivity analysis (further results)', Research Discussion Paper 8104, Reserve Bank of Australia, Sydney.

Jonson, P. D. and Trevor, R. G. (1979), 'Monetary rules: a preliminary analysis', Research Discussion Paper 7903, Reserve Bank of Australia, Sydney. Also in *The Economic Record* (1981) 57(157), June, 150–167.

McKibbin, W. J. (1980), 'Macroeconometric models of the Australian economy: a comparative study', Research Discussion Paper 8001, Reserve Bank of Australia, Sydney.

McKibbin, W. J. (1982), 'A comparison of four macroeconometric models of the Australian economy', *The Economic Record*, 58 , September, 263–282.

Madden, J. R., Challen, D. W. and Hagger, A. J. (1981), 'ORANI-ORES: a method for determining the effect on the state economies of national economic shocks', CREA Paper No. SB-01, Centre for Regional Economic Analysis, Hobart.

Nevile, J. W. (1970), *Fiscal Policy in Australia, Theory and Practice,* Melbourne, Longman-Cheshire.

Nevile, J. W. (1977), *Tax Cuts as an Anti-Inflationary Weapon*, CAER Paper No. 3, Centre for Applied Economic Research, University of New South Wales.

Nevile, J. W. (1983), *Monetary and Fiscal Policies Against Stagflation*, CAER Paper No. 19, Centre for Applied Economic Research, University of New South Wales.

Powell, A. A. (1981), 'The major streams of economy-wide modelling: is rapprochement possible?', in J. Kmenta and J. B. Rasmey (eds), *Large Scale Macro-Econometric Models*, Amsterdam, North-Holland.

# 17 Indexed Securities

*T. J. VALENTINE**

The possibility of issuing indexed securities has received considerable attention in the 1970s and 1980s. In 1981 the Campbell Committee recommended that 'both "variable rate" and "inflation linked" government securities should be viewed as ongoing policy options and should be introduced in appropriate market circumstances' (Australian Financial System Inquiry, 1981, p. 193). Until very recently the Australian Government had not issued indexed securities. In December 1983 it was announced that a small offering of indexed securities was to be made through the tender system. These bonds were to offer an indexed interest rate, but the real rate was to be determined in the tender. The objective of offering these bonds was to provide insurance companies and superannuation funds with assets they could use as a backing for indexed annuities. The government wanted to encourage the issue of these annuities to reduce criticism of their decision to increase the tax on lump-sum superannuation payments. This tender had not taken place up to the time of writing.

There have been only a small number of examples of other borrowers issuing indexed securities. A partially indexed security was issued by the Industries Assistance Commision in 1977. This security paid a variable interest rate (a margin above a bank deposit rate) that was increased by the rate of inflation. Only a small amount was raised by this security, apparently because investors found the terms of the security to be too complex. Recently, indexed securities have been issued by two groups. The Ramsay Trust in South Australia offered bonds with a face value tied to the consumer price index but with a zero coupon. Insufficient subscriptions were received and the issue had to be withdrawn. The State Electricty Commission of Victoria also issued an indexed security; in this case the security had an indexed capital value but paid an interest rate of 2.9 per cent. This issue was not received enthusiastically, but it was eventually oversubscribed.

The major objective of this chapter is to explain the absence of indexed securities in Australia. The first step in this explanation is to consider the advantages of indexed securities to holders. This is taken up in Section I. The reasons for the non-existence of indexed securities in the Australian financial system are examined in Section II. This section includes some empirical results on the formation of interest rate expectations. Section III takes up the question of whether the government should have taken the lead in issuing indexed securities.

*I am grateful to Dick Clout, Andre Cohen, Bob Daly, Peter Mair, Chris Warrell and Jeff West for helpful discussions on the topic of this chapter and to K. O'Neill for assistance with the statistical calculations reported below.

## I THE ADVANTAGES OF INDEXED SECURITIES

In this discussion an indexed security is taken to be one on which the nominal return is equal to a stated real return plus the rate of inflation. This is equivalent to a loan in which the real value of the principal is maintained throughout the course of the loan.

An important problem in setting up an indexed loan is choosing the price index to which the nominal interest payments are to be tied. In this discussion I shall assume that the consumer price index is used for this purpose. This means that the value of the principal is maintained in terms of its ability to purchase a representative basket of goods. A holder whose pattern of consumption differs from this average basket will find that the purchasing power of his principal varies over time.

The major impact of inflation on financial transactions is that, unless some compensation is provided for it, it leads to a redistribution of wealth from lenders to borrowers. Inflation causes a fall in the purchasing power of a lender's funds that can more than offset the interest payment he receives. Conversely, the borrower benefits from an equivalent reduction in the real burden of the debt that he has taken on. It is argued that this redistribution is inequitable and that the financial system should react to inflation so as to prevent the redistribution from occurring. It is not always clear why this redistribution is automatically regarded as undesirable. After all, it may be from the richer and more conservative members of society to the poorer and more entrepreneurial. Nevertheless, there are some reasons for accepting that it is undesirable. For example, it has been suggested that it will reduce the level of saving in the economy.[1] Parkin (1975) argues that the redistribution will not in fact be away from the wealthy because they have more opportunities to invest in hedges against inflation.

One way in which the financial system can prevent this redistribution is for nominal interest returns to increase with the rate of inflation. Let us assume to begin with that nominal interest rates are determined by the 'Fisher relationship', i.e. changes in the anticipated rate of inflation produce equivalent changes in nominal interest rates. At this stage I shall ignore the complications introduced by the fact that nominal interest receipts are taxed. In this situation, the lender receives compensation for the effect of inflation on the value of his funds.

The amount of compensation he receives is not, however, certain. The anticipated real rate of interest is

$$r = R - \Pi, \tag{1}$$

where $R$ is the nominal rate of interest and $\Pi$ is the anticipated rate of inflation.[2] However, the realized real rate of interest is

$$rr = R - p, \tag{2}$$

where $p$ is the actual rate of inflation. There is still a redistribution from lenders to borrowers that depends on the extent to which the actual rate of inflation differs from its expected value. If, for example, the actual rate of inflation is always underestimated, there will be a redistribution from lenders – at least in the sense that the real value of their principal will be below the value they had anticipated.

A more important problem is that the real return that lenders earn is uncertain. Some lenders might favour an indexed loan that would yield them a certain real return and make it unnecessary for them to bear the price-level risk involved in a nominal bond that pays a return determined by the Fischer relationship. In fact, it seems likely that some lenders would be willing to accept a real return on an indexed bond below that which they would anticipate receiving on a nominal bond because of the removal of the uncertainty. This would in turn provide an incentive for borrowers to issue indexed securities.

This possibility has received detailed consideration from Fischer (1975). He shows that, in a consumption model with three financial assets (an indexed bond, a nominal bond and an equity), the real return on an indexed bond is more likely to be below the anticipated return on a nominal bond if there is a negative correlation between the real return on equities and the rate of inflation. If the correlation is positive, equity serves as a hedge against inflation and the need for the indexed bond to act as a hedge is reduced. Fischer goes on to show that human capital (wage income) can also act as a hedge against inflation and that this would increase the real return on indexed bonds relative to the anticipated real return on nominal bonds.

So far we have assumed that the Fisher relationship holds. In fact it has been a noticeable characteristic of the Australian financial system that the Fisher relationship does not appear to have been borne out by interest rates. Certainly realized real rates were negative through much of the 1980s. One explanation for this is that the anticipated rate of inflation has substantially underestimated the actual rate of inflation over the period in question. This seems unlikely. Horne (1981) shows that, although the PE1 series constructed by Defris and Williams (1979) underestimated inflation up to 1977, the underestimation was not substantial in 1975, 1976 and 1977 and it overestimated inflation from then on. Moreover, statistical analyses of interest rates using empirical price expectations series have also shown that a change in the anticipated rate of inflation has not been passed on in full to nominal interest rates (see Volker, 1980; Crowley and Vlastuin, 1981; and Stammer and Valentine, 1983). Some explanations for this failure have been discussed in Carmichael and Stebbing (1983) and Stammer and Valentine (1983).

If the interest rate does not fully reflect the anticipated rate of inflation, lenders will be even more anxious to obtain indexed loans to avoid the loss that would be imposed on them by inflation. On the other hand, borrowers would avoid issuing indexed loans. This point is discussed in the next section.

The final question to be discussed in this section is the impact of taxation on indexed bonds. At the moment, nominal interest rates are fully taxed, although a large proportion of interest income is simply compensation for the erosion of the principal caused by inflation. It must be assumed that all income received from an indexed bond in excess of the initial investment will also be taxable.

One outcome of this is that the introduction of an indexed bond would not in fact remove uncertainty about the *after-tax real return* on the loan. For

**Table 17.1** *The real rate of interest: 1974/75–1982/83*

| *Quarter* | | *Realized real rate* | *After-tax realized real rate* |
|---|---|---|---|
| 1974/75 | D | –2.2 | –6.2 |
| | M | –5.0 | –8.1 |
| | J | –5.1 | –7.9 |
| 1975/76 | S | 5.8 | 3.0 |
| | D | –14.1 | –16.7 |
| | M | –4.1 | –6.9 |
| | J | –1.7 | –4.4 |
| 1976/77 | S | 1.7 | –1.7 |
| | D | 3.4 | 0.4 |
| | M | 0.2 | –2.8 |
| | J | 0.4 | –2.8 |
| 1977/78 | S | 3.4 | –0.2 |
| | D | 1.2 | –2.2 |
| | M | 4.9 | 1.7 |
| | J | 2.2 | –1.2 |
| 1978/79 | S | 3.1 | –0.4 |
| | D | 0.9 | –2.2 |
| | M | 1.9 | –1.0 |
| | J | –1.4 | –4.4 |
| 1979/80 | S | 1.3 | –2.1 |
| | D | –2.1 | –5.3 |
| | M | 1.4 | –1.9 |
| | J | 1.6 | –2.5 |
| 1980/81 | S | 6.2 | 1.7 |
| | D | 3.2 | –0.5 |
| | M | 3.3 | –0.7 |
| | J | 5.8 | 1.1 |
| 1981/82 | S | 7.9 | 2.8 |
| | D | –1.4 | –6.3 |
| | M | 8.8 | 3.7 |
| | J | 10.1 | 3.8 |
| 1982/83 | S | 5.0 | –1.0 |
| | D | 2.1 | –2.5 |
| | M | 1.2 | –2.0 |

*Notes:* The data in this table are based on the 90-day bill rate (*R*90). The rate of inflation has been calculated on a quarterly basis from the consumer price index and then multiplied by 4 to put it on an annual basis. The realized real rate of return is defined as the value of *R*90 at the end of the previous quarter ($R90_{-1}$) minus the rate of inflation in the present quarter. The realized after-tax real rate of return is defined as $(1 - t)R90_{-1}$ minus the current rate of inflation. $t$ is taken (conservatively) to be the lowest personal tax rate (0.32).

example, assume that the base return on the indexed bond is 2 per cent and that the relevant marginal tax rate is 50 per cent. Then, if the inflation rate is 5 per cent, the after-tax real return is –1.5 per cent, while, if the inflation rate is 15 per cent, the after-tax real return is –6.5 per cent. Clearly, the after-tax real return varies with the inflation rate and the uncertainty remains. The final column of Table 17.1 indicates the type of variation that occurred in realized real after-tax rates of return over the 1970s.

## II THE ABSENCE OF INDEXED SECURITIES IN AUSTRALIA

The purpose of this section is to discuss the reason why the private sector in Australia has not issued indexed securities. The discussion can be conveniently divided into two parts – the reasons why lenders did not demand indexed securities, and the reasons why borrowers were unwilling to issue them. A final subsection will consider some other impediments to the introduction of indexed bonds.

### LENDERS

In discussing lenders' demand for indexed securities, it is important first of all to reiterate the point made above that the evidence of empirical price expectations series suggests that lenders were aware of the likely magnitude of future inflation. They would, therefore, have been looking for investments for their savings that would have insulated them against inflation. The important question, raised by Fischer's work mentioned above, is whether, in the absence of indexed bonds, such an investment was available to them. Three assets will be considered – shares, human capital and real estate.

Earlier studies (Stammer and Valentine, 1983; Saunders and Tress, 1981) suggest that shares are at best a long-term hedge against inflation.[3] For example, Stammer and Valentine found that the impact effect of the rate of inflation on share prices is negative. Davies (1982) surveys some of the evidence on this question and also concludes that shares are not good short-term hedges against inflation. In addition, purchase of shares might not be an option that is actually available to many savers because of transactions costs and because shares involve risks (e.g. company failure) apart from the basic risk that the nominal return on them will not fully reflect inflation over a given period.

Wage income has been a hedge against inflation because increases in nominal wages have been highly correlated with the rate of inflation, i.e. there has been wage indexation in Australia for some time. In addition, some wage earners are able to save through contributions to superannuation funds that provide benefits that are indexed in some way.

Obviously, this hedge is not available to retired people. However, it is well known that many retired people in Australia do not attempt to obtain the maximum interest return on their savings. Instead they invest in non-income-earning assets so as to retain their eligibility for various social security benefits. The importance of this influence is unknown.

It seems that housing investment provided a satisfactory long-term hedge against inflation in the 1970s. Davies (1982) argues that this is one of the major explanations of the move out of share investment by individuals. The return on investment in housing is increased by the benefits it receives through the taxation system. Specifically:

- capital gains are tax-free;
- imputed rental income of owner-occupied housing is not taxed; and
- interest charges incurred to purchase a house to rent out can be charged off for taxation purposes against any income received.

It is true that there are substantial transactions costs involved in this form of investment and that, like shares, it carries some risks. It is obvious, however, that the return to investment in housing was high in the late 1970s even when the transactions costs were taken into account. In reference to the second point, it is quite likely that investors did not attach a high weight to these risks over the 1970s.

Weiner (1983) argues that housing investment was unlikely to have been an adequate hedge against inflation in the United States because of high transactions costs and divisibility constraints. Transaction costs have been considered above. The indivisibility of housing investment has been overrrated because an investor can increase his holdings of the asset by carrying out some relatively inexpensive improvements to a house he already owns.

There is another alternative open to lenders. They can lend on a very short basis so that the interest rates received can be adjusted rapidly to changes in the market interest rate. This involves lenders in transactions costs. It also reduces the extent to which borrowers can spread fixed costs (such as the cost of prospectus preparation and advertising) over the term of the loan. Nevertheless, there has been a marked shortening of the average maturity of outstanding debt. For example, the weighted average period to maturity of non-official holdings of marketable government securities was 126 months in June 1970, 105 months in June 1975, 78 months in June 1980 and 59 months in June 1982.

This process has not, however, removed uncertainty about the real return to be received by lenders. This is illustrated by Table 17.1, which shows the real return produced by the 90-day bill rate. It is clear that considerable variability exists in these realized real returns and that an indexed bond would have substantially reduced the uncertainty about real returns.

The Australian Savings Bond (ASB) is another way for household investors to obtain a security that effectively pays a variable rate of interest. In fact, it is even better than this because holders are able to exchange their bonds for a new series if the latter carries a higher interest rate, but they can continue to hold the older bonds if interest rates have fallen. Investors therefore have a 'one-way bet', although, as Poole (1981) points out, many holders do not take advantage of this option when interest rates increase. Some commentators have criticized this bond on the grounds that it is excessively generous to holders and, therefore, imposes an unnecessary cost on taxpayers. It has also been criticized by the Martin Committee (Australian Financial System

(Review Group), 1984) on the grounds that the option that holders have to surrender it reduces the authorities' control of the liquidity of the economy.

The conclusion of this section is that, although Australian lenders did not have access to an asset that did not involve uncertainty about the real return they would receive, they had at least one creditable alternative long-term hedge against inflation available to them in the 1970s in the form of investment in housing. The attraction of this asset was enhanced by the favourable taxation treatment it receives. This contrasts with the treatment that an indexed bond would have received.

### BORROWERS

Table 17.1 shows that a borrower who offered an indexed security with a positive real return attached would have lost throughout the 1970s. Borrowing with a succession of short-term instruments would have allowed him to raise the funds at a considerably lower cost. It is, of course, the borrower's expectations about future interest rates that affect his decision whether to issue indexed securities or not. It will be worthwhile, therefore, to examine the factors affecting interest rate expectations.

It is now generally agreed that overseas interest rates have a substantial influence on domestic interest rates, particularly at the short end of the maturity spectrum. It would be reasonable, therefore, for borrowers to form their expectations on the basis of developments in overseas interest rates and views on likely changes in the value of the Australian dollar. Inflationary expectations would play a role in this process only in so far as they influence exchange rate expectations. It would not be surprising, however, if expectations were not based on overseas influences because the present high degree of integration of the Australian and overseas financial sectors is a fairly recent development arising out of such institutional changes as the growth of the hedge market and weakening in the force of exchange controls. If overseas factors are ignored, interest rate expectations will be determined by domestic factors such as the rate of inflation, the budget deficit and views on government policy.

Little empirical work has been done on this subject apart from studies attempting to explain the term structure of interest rates. An earlier (unpublished) study by Richard Allan and myself produced equations of the form:

$$\begin{aligned} D = {} & \underset{(0.43)}{0.060} + \underset{(3.27^{**})}{0.346\,\Delta R2} + \underset{(2.85^{**})}{0.297\,\Delta R_{-1}} + \underset{(2.02^{**})}{0.017\,\Delta\% VM(12)} \\ & + \underset{(1.26)}{0.00082\,\Delta RS(12)} + \underset{(0.83)}{0.036 UR_{-1}} - \underset{(2.20^{*})}{0.106 UR_{-12}} - \underset{(1.86)}{0.269 S_8} \end{aligned}$$

$$R^2 = .379 \quad \text{D.W.} = 1.35 \quad \text{SE} = 0.37$$

R2 is the (rebateable) two-year bond rate, $\Delta\% VM(12)$ is the percentage increase in the volume of money over the twelve months up to the current month, $\Delta RS(12)$ is the increase in retail sales over the same period, *UR* is the unemployment rate and $S_8$ is the seasonal dummy variable for August. $R^2$ is the coefficient of determination, D.W. is the Durbin–Watson statistic and SE is the standard error of the regression. The figures under the coefficients are *t*-values and asterisks indicate the degree of the significance of the coefficients. One asterisk shows that it is significant at the 5 per cent level and two asterisks indicate that it is significant at the 1 per cent level. The equation was estimated from monthly data for the period January 1971 to December 1977. The dependent variable is a measure of the Capel Court expectations of movements in the government bond rate in the next month as indicated by their private monthly reports. It takes the value unity if an increase is expected and zero otherwise.[4]

The most convincing interpretation of this question is that it shows that those responsible for making the forecasts did so with reference to their view of the reaction function of the authorities. Thus, the authorities were expected to increase interest rates if the economy was expanding, i.e. if the money supply was growing, retail sales were increasing and unemployment low. There is considerable evidence that, prior to the period from which this equation was estimated and even during it, interest rates were determined by the authorities (see, for example, Dewald, 1973). The equation also indicates that expectations were formed extrapolatively; i.e. recent increases in interest rates were expected to be repeated in the coming month.

The equations in Table 17.2 are the result of experimentation with more recent expectations data. They have been estimated from quarterly data for 1975Q4–1982Q4. The expected value of the 90-day bank bill rate (*RE*90) was obtained from the relationship between the 90- and 180-day bill rates existing at each point in time; i.e. it was assumed that the term structure of interest rates on bank bills was determined entirely by expectations.[5] The value of *RE*90 was calculated at the end of each quarter. It could, of course, have been calculated at much shorter intervals, but most of the explanatory variables that were to be tested were available only on a quarterly basis.

**Table 17.2** *Equations explaining expectations of the 90-day bill rate, 1975Q4–1982Q4*

(a) $$RE90 = \underset{(0.67)}{0.006} + \underset{(12.61^{**})}{0.925R90} + \underset{(2.76^{**})}{0.880(DEF/PC)} + \underset{(1.62)}{0.008S_1}$$
$R^2 = .877$, D.W. = 1.71

(b) $$RE90 = \underset{(2.63^{**})}{0.024} + \underset{(8.12^{**})}{0.739R90} + \underset{(2.40^{*})}{0.257DEF_{-1}} + \underset{(2.08^{*})}{0.0972\,D^{*}USD}$$
$R^2 = .872$, D.W. = 1.70, SE 0.011

(c) $$RE90 = \underset{(2.69^{**})}{0.015} + \underset{(16.00^{**})}{0.830R90} + \underset{(2.38^{*})}{0.176DEF_{-1}} + \underset{(3.80^{**})}{0.0333PTN} - \underset{(3.16^{**})}{0.0113S_2}$$
$R^2 = .948$, D.W. = 1.86, SE = 0.007

(d) $$RE90_{-1} = \underset{(2.57^{**})}{0.037} + \underset{(6.09^{**})}{0.699R90} + \underset{(4.33^{**})}{0.627U_{-1}}$$
$R^2 = .548$, D.W. = 2.02, SE = 0.011

The equations show that these interest rate expectations can be well explained by two variables – the current value of the 90-day bill rate (*R*90) and some function of the Commonwealth budget deficit (*DEF*). For example, equation (a) includes the current budget deficit in constant prices (*PC* is the consumer price index). Some of the equations also include seasonal dummy variables ($S_i$ is the seasonal dummy variable for the *i*th calendar quarter). The coefficients of these variables are consistent with the information we have on the seasonal variation of interest rates. Interest rates are expected to increase in the June quarter and fall in the September quarter.

The variable *PTN* in equation (c) was included as a test of the usefulness of the expectations series. It is the proportion of Treasury notes in the portfolios of dealers in the official short-term money market. When interest rates are expected to increase, *PTN* will increase. It can, therefore, be regarded as a measure of the dealers' interest rate expectations.[6] The fact that it has a positive and highly significant coefficient in equation (c) provides some support for our interpretation of *RE*90. Equation (d) is a test of the rationality of the expectations. The coefficient of $U_{-1}$ is the estimated first-order autocorrelation coefficient. Since the slope coefficient is significantly below unity and the errors in the equation are highly autocorrelated, the hypothesis of rationality is rejected.

An initial experiment failed to detect any significant influence of overseas interest rates on *RE*90. The interest rate tested was the Federal Reserve discount rate (*USD*). However, the variable *D***USD*, where *D* is a dummy variable which takes the value unity from 1979Q1 on, is significant in equation (b). This suggests that overseas interest rates did not affect interest rate expectations until the end of the period. This is not surprising because, as was noted above, the integration of the Australian financial sector with the overseas monetary system appears to have been a fairly recent development and the recognition of it is certainly so.

The relationship between domestic and overseas interest rates is also affected by expectations about the exchange rate. However, attempts to find variables that might reflect such expectations (e.g. net monetary movements, Reserve Bank holdings of foreign exchange, etc.) were not successful.

An interesting aspect of this work is the variables that were tested but proved to be insignificant. I was unable to detect any sign of influence by lagged values of *R*90 on *RE*90. This indicates that expectations are basically static. The rates of change of the money supply in the previous quarter and over the preceding year were also insignificant when they were added to the equation. Also, there was no evidence that the rate of inflation (in the current quarter, the previous quarter and the preceding year) influenced interest rate expectations. Insignificant results were also obtained from the price expectations series discussed in Defris and Williams (1979) and from the change in this variable.

These results indicate that borrowers probably did not expect substantial changes in interest rates or that they would be influenced by high rates of inflation that prevailed throughout the period. This meant that borrowers would have seen indexed loans as likely to be substantially more expensive than fixed-interest loans, even ones of a short maturity. Fischer (1977) suggests that this argument requires borrowers to have had higher expectations of inflation than lenders and that it is impossible to verify or disprove this assertion. The earlier discussion indicates, however, that the anticipated rate of inflation does not appear to have been reflected in Australian interest rates and that market participants did not expect it to be.

This attempt to answer the question why private businesses did not issue indexed securities can be carried a little further by considering the implications of the model of a firm's supply of indexed bonds discussed in Fischer (1977). It suggests that the higher the correlation of a firm's profits with the price level, the more anxious it is likely to be to issue indexed paper. This conclusion is based on the assumption that there is a negative relationship between the market rate of return and the price level. The model also implies that indexed bonds become more attractive as the variance of inflation increases.

An earlier study by me (Valentine, 1980) of aggregate profits in Australia suggested that there is a positive relationship between profits and the price level.[7] It is true that Nevile (1975) discovered a negative impact of the rate of inflation on profits, but I could not detect this influence. It is also true, though, that Stammer and Valentine (1983) found a significant negative impact of inflation on share prices. This does not contradict the fact that there does appear to be a positive correlation between aggregate profits and the price level. It seems very likely, therefore, that there would have been some companies at least whose profits were highly correlated with the price level. It is possible, however, that this was not their perception at the time. It was inherent in the intellectual background to the 'inflation first' strategy that increases in the price level would lead to a worsening of economic conditions. In addition, some companies would have fears that their own prices might not keep up with the general price level. The uncertainty generated by this possibility would militate against the use of indexed bonds.

One type of business enterprise appears to have had profits that were positively correlated with the price level over most of the 1970s – financial institutions. Banks, for example, appear to have been able to increase the returns they received on their assets without being forced to pay equivalently higher rates on their liabilities (see Stammer and Valentine, 1983). It is likely, however, that the banks viewed this advantage as a transient one. More importantly, the profit criterion is not relevant for a financial institution. It is more important for it to maintain a high correlation between the returns on its assets and the costs of liabilities. In general, financial institutions have been unable to obtain assets that were indexed and, therefore, they had no incentive to issue indexed liabilities. One reason for this is that the government did not issue an indexed bond, and this point is taken up in the next section. Another reason is that interest rate ceilings would have prevented the charging of indexed rates on loans. On the whole, it seems less surprising that financial institutions did not issue indexed bonds than that non-financial companies did not issue them.

## OTHER IMPEDIMENTS

The issuing of a new form of financial instrument usually involves the innovator in some initial costs in order to obtain a clearance from the bureaucracy. For example, it is usually necessary to submit an application to the Corporate Affairs Commission. These costs are not negligible, but, as Fischer (1977) points out in the same context, they have not prevented the introduction of many other new instruments.

A more important obstacle may have been presented by the Loan Instruments Duty. This tax, which was represented as an anti-usury device, imposed a tax of $1\frac{1}{2}$ per cent of the face value of the loan per annum if the interest rate went above a nominated value.[8] In the case of a variable rate security, it appears that the tax was payable over the full term of the loan even if the interest rate exceeded the critical level for only a small proportion of that period. This was an obvious danger with an indexed loan and the possibility of it occurring added to the uncertainty involved in the issuing of indexed paper.

## III SHOULD THE GOVERNMENT HAVE ISSUED INDEXED BONDS?

In some ways the government was in a better position to issue indexed paper than private organizations. In this case, we mean the Commonwealth government. Most other government organizations were restricted by Loan Council control and there was apparently a prejudice against government authorities borrowing in a way that made their future nominal liabilities uncertain.

First, the Commonwealth government was not subject to Loan Instrument Duty. Secondly, it was in a position to increase its revenue by increasing taxes and would not therefore have been affected by the uncertainty attached to indexed loans. Indeed, in the absence of tax indexation, an increase in the inflation rate would have led to higher tax collections without any action on the part of the government. Against this, it must be remembered that, since the government seems chronically unable to restrict the number of people it employs, its costs would also go up with inflation.

In general, the government could have been expected to act in the same way as private borrowers to keep its financing cost down. If it did not expect interest rates to reflect inflation fully, it would prefer to issue nominal bonds (even ones with a short maturity) rather than indexed bonds. The argument that the government should have issued an indexed bond seems to come down, therefore, to the suggestion that this would have conferred a benefit on the community by allowing investors to avoid uncertainty about the real return on their savings. It is impossible to judge how important this benefit would have been, especially in the light of the earlier discussion, which suggests that the demand for indexed bonds might not have been particularly strong.

It might be worthwhile at this point to consider some of the objections that have been raised against the introduction by the government of indexed bonds.[9]

- Indexation represents an admission of the inability of the authorities to control inflation and institutionalizes an inflationary psychology.

- Protection of savings from the inroads of inflation would generate demands that other forms of income (e.g. business income) be similarly protected.
- The government would be faced with uncertainty about its future interest liabilities and, in any case, would have a higher interest bill.
- The introduction of an indexed bond would force private borrowers to offer similar instruments. Many of these would be unable to bear the risks involved and would be placed in difficulties. This is the case, for example, with financial institutions that hold long-term fixed interest securities.
- An indexed bond would represent unfair competition for private financial institutions, particularly as the government has the ability to raise taxes to meet any obligations it might incur.

These objections are not widely accepted and it is necessary to explain why this is so.[10]

First, Australian financial institutions have been less prone than those in the USA, say, to lend on a long-term fixed-interest basis. They would be in a better position, therefore, to deal with competition from indexed government securities. The situation would be eased by further deregulation of interest rates, which would allow financial institutions to adjust their loan rates more easily.

Secondly, the experience with the ASB suggests that there is a danger that the government might provide over-generous terms on an indexed security. If, however, the security is sold at tender, this risk is minimized. Once this danger is removed, private financial institutions should be able to compete with indexed government securities by offering indexed deposits that they can support by investing in indexed assets.

Thirdly, it is true that the government interest bill would probably increase, but this would simply correct the inequitable redistribution that is presently occurring between lenders and those who benefit from government spending. In addition, uncertainty about the government's future interest liability has already been created by the shortening of maturities discussed above.

Fourthly, it is possible that indexation of financial instruments would add to the demand for the indexation of other incomes. Nevertheless, these demands should be evaluated on the merits of the case. There are, in fact, good arguments for indexation of some incomes and of the taxation system. In the case of wages, this has already been partly achieved. As I have already noted, the evidence suggests that business income is not in fact eroded by inflation and there seems to be little reason for action in this area.

Fifthly, introduction of indexation would give the authorities an incentive to control inflation because this would reduce their interest costs. This incentive would be particularly strong if the taxation system was also indexed. Moreover, the present situation of non-indexation has generated a pressure group that benefits from inflation – particularly those who have borrowed heavily to invest in housing. In addition, a number of writers (e.g. Tobin, 1971; Steinherr, 1980) have suggested that the introduction of indexed securities would actually increase the effectiveness of monetary policy and make the control of inflation easier. For example, it is suggested that, because the real rate of interest would not then be influenced by the anticipated rate of inflation, the authorities would have better control over it.

## IV CONCLUSION

This survey of explanations of the non-existence of indexation in the Australian financial system has been extensive. It will be useful at this point to mention only those explanations that appear to have some validity. First, businesses appear not to have introduced indexed securities because their expectations about interest rates indicated that this would have increased their cost of financing. Financial institutions were unwilling to do so because they could not obtain indexed returns on their assets. In addition, the Loan Instrument Duty might have represented an important impediment for some potential issuers. Secondly, savers might not have demanded indexed bonds because they had adequate hedges against inflation in the form of wage income and investment in real estate. In addition, the taxation of nominal interest returns would have made indexed bonds a less attractive alternative. Thirdly, the government probably did not issue indexed bonds because this would have increased its interest payments and because there was not a particularly strong demand for them.

In spite of these explanations of the government's decision not to issue indexed paper, it nevertheless remains true that a bond of this type would have allowed many investors to avoid uncertainty about the real return on their savings and would have prevented an inequitable transfer of wealth from savers to users of government services. It can be argued, therefore, that an indexed government security should have been introduced. There is also an argument that the Australian Savings Bond should have been discontinued at the same time because it would probably have been more attractive to household investors than an indexed security. This argument is likely to have more weight at the present time because investors are no longer confident that real estate provides a satisfactory hedge against inflation. In addition, the government should avoid introducing any additional impediments to the private introduction of indexed securities similar, for example, to the Loan Instrument Duty and reconsider its approach to the taxation of nominal interest returns.

## NOTES

1 The difficulties involved in examining the effect of inflation on the savings ratio are discussed in Anstie, Gray and Pagan (1983).

2 Formula (1) is a simplication of the correct formula

$$r = \frac{1 + R}{1 + \pi - 1}$$

where the term $r.\Pi$ is ignored. This approximation will be used throughout.

3 There is some evidence that this is also the case in the United States. See Fischer (1975, p. 527).

4 It is well known that dependent variables of this type create estimation difficulties (see Goldberger, 1964, p. 248). In particular, the variance of the disturbance in the equation is not constant and the regression estimates are therefore inefficient although unbiased. More importantly, the standard errors of the estimates are not calculated correctly by the usual formulae.

5 The value of the 90-day bill rate expected to hold 90 days from the present was calculated from the formula

$$RE90 = \left[ \frac{(1 + (180/365)\ R180}{(1 + (90/365)\ R90)} \right]^{-1} \frac{365}{90},$$

where $R90$ and $R180$ are the current 90- and 180-day bill rates.

6 The use of this variable was suggested by M. Kearns.

7 It should be noted that the profit series used in this analysis is the gross operating surplus of companies, which includes interest rates (like the individual company data used by Fischer, 1977) but which is not net of tax payments (as are Fischer's data).

8 The tax was removed at the time the Financial Institutions Duty was introduced.

9 The first two of these arguments have been taken from a speech by the Deputy-Governor of the Reserve Bank of Australia, D.N. Sanders, given at the seminar on *Inflation and Financial Markets*, Melbourne University, June 1980. See also AAPBS (1983) and Australian Financial System (Review Group) (1984).

10 The following discussion draws on Steinherr (1980) and the address given by Professor A. D. Bain at the seminar mentioned in the previous footnote.

## BIBLIOGRAPHY

Anstie, R. K., Gray, M. R. and Pagan, A. R. (1983), 'Inflation and the consumption ratio', in A. R. Pagan and P. K. Trivedi (eds), *The Effects of Inflation: Theoretical Issues and Australian Evidence*, Australian National University, Centre for Economic Policy Research, Canberra.

Australian Association of Permanent Building Societies (AAPBS) (1983), *The Case Against Indexed Securities*, December.

Australian Financial System Inquiry (1981), *Final Report*, Canberra, Australian Government Publishing Service.

Australian Financial System (Review Group) (1984), *Report*, Canberra, Australian Government Publishing Service.

Carmichael, J. and Stebbing, P. W. (1983), 'Some macroeconomic implications of the interaction between inflation and taxation', in A. R. Pagan and P. K. Trivedi, (eds), *The Effects of Inflation: Theoretical Issues and Australian Evidence*, Australian National University, Centre for Economic Policy Research, Canberra, 101–136.

Crowley, P. T. and Vlastuin, C. (1981), 'Inflationary anticipations and nominal interest rates: the Australian case', paper presented to the Tenth Conference of Economists, Canberra, August.

Davies, P. H. (1982), 'Equity finance and the ownership of shares', *Commissioned Studies and Selected Papers*, Part 3, Australian Financial System Inquiry, Canberra, Australian Government Publishing Service.

Defris, L. V. and Williams, R. A. (1979), 'The formation of consumer inflationary expectations in Australia', *Economic Record*, 55(149), June, 136–148.

Dewald, W. G. (1973), 'The term structure of interest rates in Australia, 1957–66', *Economic Analysis and Policy*, 4(2), September, 1–17.

Fischer, S. (1975), 'The demand for index bonds', *Journal of Political Economy*, 83(3), June, 509–534.

Fischer, S. (1977), 'On the non-existence of privately issued index bonds in the United States capital market', in E. Lundberg (ed.), *Inflation Theory and Anti-Inflation Policy*, London, Macmillan, 502–518.

Goldberger, A. S. (1964), *Econometric Theory*, London, John Wiley.

Horne, J. (1981), 'Rational expectations and the Defris–Williams inflationary expectations series', *Economic Record*, 57(158), September, 261–268.

Nevile, J. W. (1975), 'Inflation, company profits and investment', *Australian Economic Review*, 32(4), 35–36.

Parkin, M. (1975), 'Inflation and the redistribution of wealth', in E. V. Morgan (ed.), *Indexation and Inflation, London, Financial Times.*

Poole, W. (1981), 'Australian monetary policy: an outsider's view', paper presented to the 51st ANZAAS Congress, Brisbane, May.

Saunders, A. and Tress, R. B. (1981), 'Inflation and stock market returns: some Australian evidence', *Economic Record*, 57(156), March, 58–66.

Stammer, D. W. and Valentine, T. J. (1983), 'Inflation and the financial system', in A. R. Pagan and P. K. Trivedi (eds), *The Effects of Inflation: Theoretical Issues and Australian Evidence*, Canberra, Australian National University, Centre for Economic Policy Research, 183–219.

Steinherr, A. (1980), 'Indexation of monetary assets and credit instruments', in M. Sarnat (ed.), *Inflation and Capital Markets*, Cambridge, Mass., Ballinger.

Tobin, J. (1971), 'An essay on the principles of debt management', in *Essays in Economics Vol. 1 Macroeconomics*, Chicago, Ill., Markham.

Valentine, T. J. (1980), 'The effect of wage levels on prices, profits, employment and capacity utilisation in Australia: an econometric analysis', *The Australian Economic Review*, 49(1), 13–22.

Volker, P. A. (1980), 'Expectations of inflation and short-term interest rates in Australia 1968(1)–1979(2)', D. J. Juttner (ed.), *Interest Rates*, Melbourne, Longman-Cheshire, 235–256.

Weiner, S. E. (1983), 'Why are so few financial assets indexed to inflation', *Economic Review* (Federal Reserve Bank of Kansas City), 68, May, 3–18.

# Acknowledgements

The conference of which this volume is the proceedings was financially supported by the following institutions:

Reserve Bank of Australia
M.L.C. Assurance Company Limited
Citicorp Australia Limited
Australia–Japan Research Centre, Australian National University
Goethe Institut
Federal Reserve Bank of New York
Bank for International Settlements
Organisation for Economic Co-operation and Development

The editors wish to thank Rebecca Bishop and Colleen Hodge for assistance in preparing the papers for publication in this book.

# List of Participants

Dr B. Aghevli, International Monetary Fund
Professor V. E. Argy, Macquarie University
Professor A. Budd, London Business School
Dr A. Braun, International Monetary Fund
Professor W. Buiter, London School of Economics and Political Science
Dr J. Carmichael, Reserve Bank of Australia
Dr C. Challen, University of Tasmania
Dr J. C. Chouraqui, Organisation for Economic Co-operation and Development
Dr P. B. Clark, United States' Federal Reserve System
Professor M. Corden, Australian National University
Mr J. Fahrer, Reserve Bank of Australia
Professor S. Fischer, Massachusetts Institute of Technology
Dr V. Fitzgerald, Prime Minister's Department, Australia
Professor R. G. Gregory, Australian National University
Professor F. Gruen, Australian National University
Dr V. Hall, University of Sydney
Professor K. Hamada, Tokyo University
Mr J. Hawkins, Reserve Bank of Australia
Professor J. Hewson, University of New South Wales
Dr J. Horne, University of Melbourne
Dr B. Hughes, Flinders University
Dr P. Jonson, Reserve Bank of Australia
Mr P. Ledingham, Reserve Bank of New Zealand
Dr M. Lewis, University of Adelaide
Dr W. D. McClam, Bank for International Settlements
Professor J. Nevile, University of New South Wales
Dr A. Pagan, Australian National University
Professor J. Perkins, University of Melbourne
Professor J. Pitchford, Australian National University
Professor M. Porter, Monash University
Dr R. E. Smith, Australian National University
Dr P. Trivedi, Australian National University
Dr T. Valentine, Macquarie University
Professor M. Willms, Kiel University

# Index

For Product Safety Concerns and Information please contact our EU representative GPSR@taylorandfrancis.com Taylor & Francis Verlag GmbH, Kaufingerstraße 24, 80331 München, Germany